D1486639

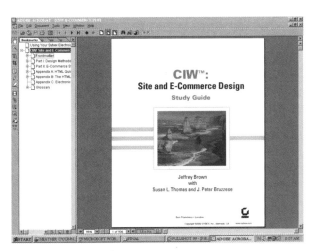

Search through the complete book in PDF!

- Access the entire *CIW: Site and E-Commerce Design Study Guide*, complete with figures and tables, in electronic format.

- Search the *CIW: Site and E-Commerce Design Study Guide* chapters to find information on any topic in seconds.

- Use Adobe Acrobat Reader (included on the CD-ROM) to view the electronic book.

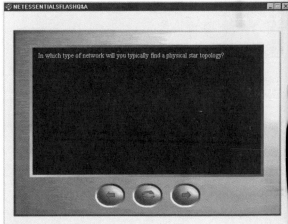

Use the Electronic Flashcards for PCs or Palm devices to jog your memory and prep last minute for the exam!

- Reinforce your understanding of key concepts with these hardcore flashcard-style questions.

Prepare for the Site and E-Commerce Designer Exams on the go with your handheld device!

- Download the Flashcards to your Palm device and go on the road. Now you can study for the CIW Site and E-Commerce Designer exams anytime, anywhere.

SYBEX

CIW: Site and E-Commerce Design Study Guide

1D0-420 & 1D0-425

OBJECTIVE GROUPS	CHAPTER NUMBER
Site Designer Exam	
Develop effective and usable corporate Web sites within a reasonable timeframe, including but not limited to: design concepts and goals, Web site vision statements, Web strategy and tactics, site metaphors, mindmapping, audience usability testing, navigation conventions, file structure hierarchy, download time.	2, 5
Use HTML to create related Web pages that can be deployed as a Web site.	9
Use advanced HTML formatting to enhance the usability of Web sites, including but not limited to: tables, frames, Cascading Style Sheets (CSS), metadata.	
Create and effectively use graphics in Web sites.	
Use client-side and server-side programming to enhance Web site functionality, including but not limited to: basic programming concepts, JavaScript, DHTML, XML, HTTP servers, ports, CGI, cookies.	
Identify ways to use Web-authoring software to develop Web sites quickly.	
Add downloadable Web content to a site, including but not limited to: executable files, plug-ins, multimedia, applets.	
Define database and identify major types of database management systems (DBMS).	
Identify important Internet standards, including but not limited to: Internet governing organizations, domain names, RFCs.	
Publish and maintain a production Web site.	

SYBEX

E-Commerce Designer Exam

Define e-commerce, and identify its current and potential effects on business operations and revenue generation.

Identify legal and governmental issues related to e-commerce, including but not limited to: jurisdiction, taxation, intellectual property.

Define the role of marketing in e-commerce site development, including but not limited to: market identification, pricing, promotion.

Define Web site usability and its significance, and identify ways it can be analyzed and improved.

Define the role of customer service in e-commerce operations.

Define standards and initiatives that support supplier transactions using e-commerce, including but not limited to: EDI, OBI, OTP.

Develop and host an e-commerce site using outsourcing and instant storefront services.

Configure Web server software for an e-commerce site.

Design an e-commerce site using Web development software.

Accept payments through an e-commerce site, including but not limited to: setup and processing of electronic payment services.

Identify various types of security available for e-commerce, including but not limited to: encryption, certificates, SET, SSL.

Analyze and improve the performance of an e-commerce site using a transactional system model.

Manage inventory and fulfillment for an e-commerce site.   7

SYBEX

CIW:
Site and E-Commerce Design

Study Guide

CIW™:
Site and E-Commerce Design
Study Guide

Jeffrey Brown
with
Susan L. Thomas and J. Peter Bruzzese

San Francisco • London

Associate Publisher: Neil Edde
Acquisitions and Developmental Editor: Heather O'Connor
Editor: Judy Flynn
Production Editor: Teresa L. Trego
Technical Editor: Warren Wyrostek, John Johnson
Graphic Illustrator: Tony Jonick, Rappid Rabbit
Electronic Publishing Specialist: Interactive Composition Corporation
Proofreaders: Laurie O'Connell, Nancy Riddiough, Emily Hsuan, Dave Nash, Amey Garber, Abigail Sawyer, Suzanne Stein
Indexer: Lynnzee Elze
CD Coordinator: Dan Mummert
CD Technician: Kevin Ly
Book Designer: Bill Gibson
Cover Designer: Archer Design
Cover Illustrator/Photographer: Jeremy Woodhouse, PhotoDisc

SYBEX

To Our Valued Readers:

The Certified Internet Webmaster (CIW) program from ProsoftTraining™ has established itself as one of the leading Internet certifications in the IT industry. Sybex has partnered with ProsoftTraining to produce Study Guides—like the one you hold in your hand—for the Associate, Master Administrator, and Master Designer tracks. Each Sybex book is based on official courseware and is exclusively endorsed by ProsoftTraining.

Just as ProsoftTraining is committed to establishing measurable standards for certifying IT professionals working with Internet technologies, Sybex is committed to providing those professionals with the skills and knowledge needed to meet those standards. It has long been Sybex's desire to help bridge the knowledge and skills gap that currently confronts the IT industry.

The authors and editors have worked hard to ensure that this CIW Study Guide is comprehensive, in-depth, and pedagogically sound. We're confident that this book will meet and exceed the demanding standards of the certification marketplace and help you, the CIW certification candidate, succeed in your endeavors.

Good luck in pursuit of your CIW certification!

Neil Edde
Associate Publisher—Certification
Sybex, Inc.

Acknowledgments

I'd like to thank all those who helped in this exciting effort. My wife, Kellie, who gave me love, support, and encouragement during all the hectic times. To Morea, who has always been a faithful companion and loves to play Frisbee. To everyone at ProsoftTraining who works so hard to make sure a quality product is produced. To Jud Slusser, who has provided a great place to work and develop CIW Site Designer and CIW E-Commerce Designer, along with project Sybex. Also, special thanks to Heather O'Connor at Sybex who took the lead on this project and made it happen.

—Jeffrey S. Brown

I would like to thank, first and foremost, my husband, Richard Watson, for all his guidance and support throughout this project. Without him, I would have never switched careers to web development and teaching it to others. I would like to thank my parents, Barbara and Dudley, for their unwavering faith in me and all I undertake. Kira and Sampson deserve my thanks for understanding about all the time I didn't spend with them. Finally, I would like to thank the staff at Sybex with whom I worked: Heather O'Connor, Judy Flynn, and Teresa Trego. I appreciate all of their help and input in creating a comprehensive, high-quality text for future website designers.

—Susan Thomas

For helping me to remain organized and scheduled for this project I'd like to thank my developmental editor Heather O'Connor. I'd also like to thank the team at Sybex—the editors and those in the art department—for all of their hard work. I'd like to thank Tim Duggan (my colleague and fellow CIW E-Commerce Design Master) for his assuring that the materials were always focused toward the exam. Finally, I'd like to thank New Horizons of Princeton, NJ, for encouraging me toward the CIW certifications as one of their Certified Instructors for the CIW program.

—J. Peter Bruzzese

Contents at a Glance

Contents

Table of Exercises

Introduction

The Prosoft CIW (Certified Internet Webmaster) certification affirms that you have the essential skills to create, run, and update a website. These skills are exactly what employers in today's economy are looking for, and you need to stay ahead of the competition in the current job market. CIW certification will prove to your current or future employer that you are serious about expanding your knowledge base. Obtaining CIW certification will also provide you with valuable skills—including basic networking, web page authoring, internetworking, maintaining security, and website design—and expose you to a variety of vendor products made for web design and implementation.

This book is meant to help you prepare for the Master CIW Designer certification, including the Site Designer Exam (1D0-420) and the E-Commerce Designer Exam (1D0-425). However, before beginning the exams on the Master CIW Designer track, you must first have obtained your CIW Associate Certificate by completing the CIW Foundations Exam (1D0-410).

The Certified Internet Webmaster Program

The CIW Internet skills certification program is aimed at professionals who design, develop, administer, secure, and support Internet- or intranet-related services. The CIW certification program offers industry-wide recognition of an individual's Internet and web knowledge and skills, and certification is frequently a factor in hiring and assignment decisions. It also provides tangible evidence of a person's competency as an Internet professional; holders of this certification can demonstrate to potential employers and clients that they have passed rigorous training and examination requirements that set them apart from noncertified competitors. All CIW certifications are endorsed by the International Webmasters Association (IWA) and the Association of Internet Professionals (AIP).

CIW Associate

The first step toward CIW certification is the CIW Foundations exam. A candidate for the CIW Associate certification and the Foundations exam has the basic hands-on skills and knowledge that an Internet professional is expected to understand and use. Foundations skills include basic knowledge of Internet technologies, network infrastructure, and web authoring using HTML.

The CIW Foundations program is designed for all professionals who use the Internet. The job expectations of a CIW Associate, or person who has completed the program and passed the Foundations exam, include the following:

- Understanding Internet, networking, and web page authoring basics
- Application of Foundations skills required for further specialization

There are a few prerequisites for becoming a CIW Associate. For instance, although you need not have Internet experience in order to start Foundations exam preparation, you should have an understanding of Microsoft Windows.

Table I.1 shows the CIW Foundations exam and the corresponding Sybex Study Guide that covers the CIW Associate certification.

TABLE I.1   The CIW Associate Exam and Corresponding Sybex Study Guide

Exam Name	Exam Number	Sybex Study Guide
Foundations	1D0-410	*CIW: Foundations Study Guide* (ISBN 0-7821-4081-5)

CIW accepts score reports from CIW Associate candidates who have passed the entry-level CompTIA i-Net+ exam (IKO-001) and will award Foundations certification to these individuals. For more information regarding the i-Net+ and other CompTIA exams, visit www.comptia.org.

After passing the Foundations exam, students become CIW Associates and can choose from four Master CIW certification tracks by choosing a path of interest and passing the required exams:

- Master CIW Designer
- Master CIW Administrator
- CIW Web Site Manager

- Master CIW Enterprise Developer
- CIW Security Analyst

Master CIW Designer

The Master Designer track is composed of two exams, each of which represents a specific aspect of the Internet job role:

- Site Designer
- E-Commerce Designer

Site Designer Exam   The CIW Site Designer applies human-factor principles to designing, implementing, and maintaining hypertext-based publishing sites. The Site Designer uses authoring and scripting languages, as well as digital media tools, plus provides content creation and website management.

E-Commerce Designer Exam   The CIW E-Commerce Designer is tested on e-commerce setup, human-factors principles regarding product selection and payment, and site security and administration.

Table I.2 shows the CIW Site Designer and E-Commerce Designer exams and the corresponding Sybex Study Guide for each of these steps toward the CIW Master Designer certification.

TABLE I.2   The Master Designer Exams and Corresponding Sybex Study Guides

Exam Name	Exam Number	Sybex Study Guide
Site Designer	1D0-420	*CIW: Site and E-Commerce Design* (ISBN 0-7821-4082-3)
E-Commerce Designer	1D0-425	*CIW: Site and E-Commerce Design* (ISBN 0-7821-4082-3)

Master CIW Administrator

The CIW Administrator is proficient in three areas of administration:

- Server
- Internetworking
- Security administration

After passing each test, you become a CIW Professional in that specific area.

Server Administrator Exam   The CIW Server Administrator manages and tunes corporate e-business infrastructure, including web, FTP, news, and mail servers for midsize to large businesses. Server administrators configure, manage, and deploy e-business solutions servers.

Internetworking Professional Exam   The Internetworking Professional defines network architecture, identifies infrastructure components, and monitors and analyzes network performance. The CIW Internetworking Professional is responsible for the design and management of enterprise TCP/IP networks.

Security Professional Exam   The CIW Security Professional implements policy, identifies security threats, and develops countermeasures using firewall systems and attack-recognition technologies. As a CIW Security Professional, you are responsible for managing the deployment of e-business transactions and payment security solutions.

The Exams in the Master Administrator track are listed in Table I.3.

TABLE I.3   The Master Administrator Exams and Corresponding Sybex Study Guides

Exam Name	Exam Number	Sybex Study Guide
Server Administrator	1D0-450	*CIW: Server Administrator Study Guide* (ISBN 0-7821-4085-8)
Internetworking Professional	1D0-460	*CIW: Internetworking Professional Study Guide* (ISBN 0-7821-4083-1)
Security Professional	1D0-470	*CIW: Security Professional Study Guide* (ISBN 0-7821-4084-X)

Other CIW Certifications

Prosoft also offers three additional certification series in website management, enterprise development, and security analysis.

Master CIW Web Site Manager   The Web Site Manager certification is composed of two Internet job role series exams (Site Designer 1D0-420 and Server Administrator 1D0-450) and two additional language exams (JavaScript 1D0-435 and Perl Fundamentals 1D0-437 from the CIW Web Languages series).

Master CIW Enterprise Developer   The Enterprise Developer certification is composed of three Internet job role series (Application Developer 1D0-430, Database Specialist 1D0-441, and Enterprise Specialist 1D0-442) and three additional language/theory series (Web Languages, Java Programming, and Object-Oriented Analysis).

CIW Security Analyst   The Security Analyst certification recognizes those who have already attained a networking certification and demonstrated (by passing the CIW Security Professional 1D0-470 exam) that they have the in-demand security skills to leverage their technical abilities against internal and external cyber threats.

For more information regarding all of Prosoft's certifications and exams, visit `www.ciwcertified.com`.

Special Features in This Book

What makes a Sybex Study Guide the book of choice for over 500,000 certification candidates across numerous technical fields? We take into account not only what you need to know to pass the exam, but what you need to know to apply what you've learned in the real world. Each book contains the following:

Parts   This book is split into 2 parts. Chapters 1–19 cover the Site Designer Exam (1D0-420) and Chapters 20–30 cover the E-Commerce Designer Exam (1D0-425). Look for "part openers" that separate one half of the book from the other.

Objective Information   Each chapter lists at the outset which CIW objective groups are going to be covered within.

Assessment Test   Directly following this introduction is an assessment test that you can take to help you determine how much you already know about site design methodologies and technologies as well as e-commerce strategies and practices. Each question is tied to a topic discussed in the book. Using the results of the assessment test, you can figure out the areas in which you need to focus your study. Of course, we do recommend that you read the entire book.

Exam Essentials   To review what you've learned, you'll find a list of exam essentials at the end of each chapter. The exam essentials briefly highlight the topics that need your particular attention as you prepare for the exam.

Key Terms and Glossary   Throughout each chapter, you will be introduced to important terms and concepts that you will need to know for the exam. These terms appear in italic within the chapters, and a list of the key terms appears just after the exam essentials. At the end of the book, a detailed glossary gives definitions for these terms, as well as other general terms you should know.

Review Questions, Complete with Detailed Explanations   Each chapter is followed by a set of review questions that test what you learned in the chapter. The questions are written with the exam in mind, meaning that they are designed to have the same look and feel of the questions you'll see on the exam.

Hands-On Exercises   Throughout the book, you'll find exercises designed to give you the important hands-on experience that is critical for your exam preparation. The exercises support the topics of the chapter, and they walk you through the steps necessary to perform a particular function.

Interactive CD   Every Sybex Study Guide comes with a CD complete with additional questions, flashcards for use with a palm device or PC, and a complete electronic version of this book. Details are in the following section.

What's on the CD?

Sybex's *CIW: Site and E-Commerce Design Study Guide* companion CD includes quite an array of training resources and offers numerous test simulations, bonus exams, and flashcards to help you study for the exam.

We have also included the complete contents of the study guide in electronic form. The CD's resources are described here:

The Sybex Ebook for the *CIW: Site and E-Commerce Study Guide*
Many people like the convenience of being able to carry their whole study guide on a CD. They also like being able to search the text via computer to find specific information quickly and easily. For these reasons, the entire contents of this study guide are supplied on the CD, in PDF format. We've also included Adobe Acrobat Reader, which provides the interface for the PDF contents as well as search capabilities.

The Sybex CIW Edge Tests   The Edge Tests are a collection of multiple-choice questions that will help you prepare for your exams. There are three sets of questions:

- Three bonus exams designed to simulate each live exam.

- All the review questions from the study guide, presented in an electronic test engine. You can review questions by chapter or by objective area, or you can take a random test.

- The assessment test

Sybex CIW Flashcards for PCs and Palm Devices   The "flashcard" style of question offers an effective way to quickly and efficiently test your understanding of the fundamental concepts covered in the exams of the Master Designer track. The Sybex CIW Flashcards set consists of 150 questions presented in a special engine developed specifically for this study guide series. We have also developed, in conjunction with Land-J Technologies, a version of the flashcard questions that you can take with you on your Palm OS PDA (including the Palm and Visor PDAs).

How to Use This Book

This book provides a solid foundation for the serious effort of preparing for the exam. To best benefit from this book, you may wish to use the following study method:

1. Take the assessment test to identify your weak areas.

2. Study each chapter carefully. Do your best to fully understand the information.

3. Study the exam essentials and key terms to make sure you are familiar with the areas you need to focus on.

4. Answer the review questions at the end of each chapter. If you prefer to answer the questions in a timed and graded format, install the Edge Tests from the book's CD and answer the chapter questions there instead of in the book.

5. Take note of the questions you did not understand, and study the corresponding sections of the book again.

6. Go back over the exam essentials and key terms.

7. Go through the study guide's other training resources, which are included on the book's CD. These include electronic flashcards, the electronic version of the chapter review questions (try taking them by objective), and the two bonus exams.

To learn all the material covered in this book, you will need to study regularly and with discipline. Try to set aside the same time every day to study, and select a comfortable and quiet place in which to do it. If you work hard, you will be surprised at how quickly you learn this material. Good luck!

Exam Registration

CIW certification exams are administered by Prometric, Inc. through Prometric Testing Centers and by Virtual University Enterprises (VUE) testing centers. You can reach Prometric at (800) 380-EXAM or VUE at (952) 995-8800 to schedule any CIW exam.

You may also register for your exams online at www.prometric.com or www.vue.com.

Exams cost $125 (U.S.) each and must be paid for in advance. Exams must be taken within one year of payment. Candidates can schedule exams up to six weeks in advance or as late as one working day prior to the date of the exam. To cancel or reschedule an exam, contact the center at least two working days prior to the scheduled exam date. Same-day registration is available in some locations, subject to space availability. Where same-day registration is available, registration must occur a minimum of two hours before test time.

When you schedule the exam, the testing center will provide you with instructions regarding appointment and cancellation procedures, ID requirements, and information about the testing center location. In addition, you will receive a registration and payment confirmation letter from Prometric or VUE.

Tips for Taking the CIW Site and E-Commerce Design Exams

Here are some general tips for achieving success on your certification exams:

- Arrive early at the exam center so that you can relax and review your study materials. During this final review, you can look over tables and lists of exam-related information.

- Read the questions carefully. Don't be tempted to jump to an early conclusion. Make sure you know *exactly* what the question is asking.

- For questions you're not sure about, use a process of elimination to get rid of the obviously incorrect answers first. This improves your odds of selecting the correct answer when you need to make an educated guess.

- Mark questions that you aren't sure of and return to them later. Quite often something in a later question will act as a reminder or give you a clue to the correct answer of the earlier one.

Contacts and Resources

Here are some handy websites to keep in mind for future reference:

Prosoft Training and CIW Exam Information	www.CIWcertified.com
Prometric	www.prometric.com
VUE Testing Services	www.vue.com
Sybex Computer Books	www.sybex.com

Assessment Test

1. What is the purpose of the Microsoft Management Console (MMC)?

   A. To delete the anonymous login account

   B. To allow anonymous logins

   C. To collect log files

   D. To simplify administering IIS

2. When analyzing the performance of a particular service, it is important to also analyze what?

   A. Client computers requesting the service

   B. Related services

   C. The operating system

   D. The Internet connection speed of the server

3. What is the Automated Clearing House (ACH)?

   A. An international payment-processing system

   B. A nationwide payment-processing system

   C. An international check-verification system

   D. A nationwide check-verification system

4. With a SET transaction, what is encrypted when an order is sent to a merchant that it cannot decrypt?

   A. The customer's credit card number

   B. The customer's shipping cost

   C. The merchant's bank account number

   D. The customer's bank account number

5. Allowing customers to check the status of their shipments with a confirmation number is what form of customer service?

A. Co-browsing

B. Horizontal marketing system

C. Order tracking

D. Asynchronous service

6. Which is an example of offline product promotion?

A. Banner ads

B. Referrer programs

C. Targeted E-mail

D. TV commercials

7. Which of the following best describes a shopping cart in e-commerce?

A. A catalog description of a product

B. A transaction system

C. An search engine

D. The component that helps users track items to buy

8. What do you call an outsourcing method you would use when you want to establish a shopping cart for your online catalog but you want another company to handle the transactions?

A. Contract transaction placement

B. A shopping cart

C. A purchase button

D. A search engine

9. Which of the following are the primary steps in preparing for online transactions? (Choose three.)

A. Prepare the server and the e-commerce site

B. Choose a web-hosting service

C. Setup an online merchant account

D. Install payment software

E. Select a form of digital cash

10. What is the purpose of a database?

   A. To structure queries, updates and inserts

   B. To track website usage patterns

   C. To support Internet and intranet sites

   D. To store information for retrieval

11. Which of the following is one of the main responsibilities held by a e-commerce website administrator?

   A. Monitoring performance of a site

   B. Changing background colors periodically

   C. Rewriting online catalog information

   D. Making sure taxes are being paid for every purchase

12. Kamila is the administrator of an e-commerce site. One of his main concerns is making the website understandable to the different locales it targets. After translating the information into national languages, what else should Kamila consider?

   A. Vertical marketing system

   B. Horizontal marketing system

   C. Telephony

   D. Localization

13. What is the least effective product/service awareness method an online marketer can use?

   A. Search engine placement

   B. Spam e-mail

   C. Banner ads

   D. Referrer sites

14. Which of the following combines a portal storefront with the infra-structure of an established e-commerce company?

A. iWon

B. Yahoo!

C. Amazon

D. MerchandiZer

15. What is symmetric encryption?

A. A type of encryption that requires both participants to have a single secret key

B. A type of encryption that requires each participant to have a public key and a private key

C. A type of encryption that is easy to compute in one direction but difficult to compute in the other direction

D. A message digest involving a digest or hash algorithm that produces a short unique message.

16. Tyra's company spends a large sum of money each month on telephone charges. To lower these costs, she decides to use a technology in which telephone calls that are normally routed via standard telecommunications means are instead sent over the Internet. What is this technology called?

A. Telephony

B. OTP

C. Teleconferencing

D. Procurement

17. Lisa owns a company that sells women's sports equipment and clothes. She decides to move her company online. In terms of promotion, what category would Lisa's site be?

A. Marketer site

B. Publisher site

C. Referrer site

D. Business site

18. When using e-commerce to make purchases, what is the main concern of most consumers?

    A. Privacy

    B. Speed of connection

    C. Product warrantee

    D. Price

19. What is the part of the database that contains a description of the data commonly called?

    A. Free source code

    B. A channel

    C. The default document

    D. The system catalog

20. What is the most important factor when considering web servers?

    A. Hard disk size

    B. CPU speed

    C. Amount of memory

    D. Motherboard bus speed

21. Which of the following is the best definition of an application service provider?

    A. A company that writes Active Server Pages applications.

    B. A company that hosts server-based Web applications and charges other companies a fee for their use.

    C. A company that installs and maintains applications on a local area network.

    D. A company that processes and files job applications.

22. What is the primary drawback to digital cash?

    A. The need for all participants in the transaction to use the same software package

    B. The lack of a need for back-end transaction processing

    C. The high cost involved in setting up and using digital cash packages

    D. The requirement for consumers to sacrifice anonymity by providing personal information

23. What type of certificate identifies a web server and the company running it?

    A. The certificate authority certificate

    B. The software publisher certificate

    C. The server certificate

    D. The personal certificate

24. What is a simple definition of Open Buying on the Internet (OBI)?

    A. An Internet e-commerce specification based on open technologies

    B. An open protocol that defines trading protocol options

    C. A business-to-business network focused on bringing buyers and sellers together

    D. The inter-organizational exchange of documents in standardized electronic form

25. The percentage of times an ad is viewed resulting in a user clicking the ad is called what?

    A. Ad clicks

    B. The CPC

    C. Clickthrough rate

    D. Page views

26. Julian owns a motorcycle shop and decides to buy new signs for his building. He orders the new signs from an online company. What form of e-commerce has Julian participated in?

 A. Business-to-consumer (B2C)

 B. Business-to-business (B2B)

 C. Business purchasing

 D. Consumer-to-business (C2B)

27. Greg has changed the default TCP port for HTTP connections to 8080. Now users complain that they cannot access the site. What is the proper way for users to enter the site?

 A. They need to use a username and password.

 B. They need an SSL connection.

 C. They need to type www.whatever.com:8080.

 D. They need to type www.8080.com

28. A queue of more than how many processes for a sustained period of time indicates that your CPU may need an upgrade?

 A. 1

 B. 0

 C. 3

 D. 2

29. Which fulfillment and order-processing step should an effective e-commerce package allow the online merchant to follow?

 A. Publishing customer information to the Web

 B. Building community by publishing customers' e-mail addresses

 C. Offering encryption for customer information

 D. Processing only credit-card payments immediately

30. What is a payment gateway?

    A. An online component that processes a credit-card transaction to validate the account number and begin the transfer of funds

    B. An electronic wallet that holds digital cash and a point-of-sale module

    C. A point-of-sale module that integrates with the website, the merchant's wallet, and the bank's financial network

    D. A credit-card company that accepts or denies online transaction payments based on available funds

31. Which one of the following is a hash algorithm?

    A. DES

    B. RC5

    C. CC5

    D. MD5

32. Brandon is setting up a website for his corporation. He is concerned about making sure the website is professional looking and his home page is not too cluttered with information. Which of the following of the seven ingredients to successful storefronts is Brandon considering?

    A. Generating demand

    B. Ordering

    C. Fulfillment

    D. Community

33. Joel is purchasing a new program to work with his Linux server. He pays for it and downloads the software off the Internet. Which type of goods has Joel purchased?

    A. Soft goods

    B. Hard goods

    C. Linux goods

    D. Software goods

34. Which of the following is defined as a science that can help anticipate the specific positive, negative, or neutral psychological impact of words, symbols, shapes, textures, colors, fonts, or scale on consumer target market groups?

   A. Demographics

   B. A survey

   C. Focus groups

   D. Psychographics

35. Randy is developing a website for his company called Blue Moose Design, which puts together skateboard parks for kids in the New Jersey area. What type of market is Randy in?

   A. A competitive one

   B. A global market

   C. A universal market

   D. A niche market

36. Which of the following would be considered a barrier to e-commerce growth?

   A. Around-the-clock service

   B. Rapid change

   C. Diversification of offerings

   D. Centralization

37. What law prevents an ISP from being held accountable for copyright infringement by its subscribers?

   A. The Lanham Act

   B. NET Act

   C. Online Commercial Liability Act

   D. Online Copyright Infringement Liability Limitation Act

38. For goods shipped across international borders, each state and country has its own set of taxes called _____ .

  A. Taxes

  B. Customs

  C. Tariffs

  D. Patents

39. Which of the following laws is intended to protect children from pornography and privacy violations?

  A. Online Child Protection Act.

  B. Children's Online Privacy Protection Act.

  C. Protection and Privacy Act.

  D. There is no such legislation currently available.

40. Tyra's company spends a large sum of money each month on telephone charges. To lower these costs, she decides to use a technology in which telephone calls that are normally routed via standard telecommunications means are instead sent over the Internet. What is this technology called?

  A. Telephony

  B. OTP

  C. Teleconferencing

  D. Procurement

41. What is a simple definition of Open Buying on the Internet (OBI)?

  A. An Internet e-commerce specification based on open technologies

  B. An open protocol that defines trading protocol options

  C. A business-to-business network focused on bringing buyers and sellers together

  D. The inter-organizational exchange of documents in standardized electronic form

42. Kamila is the administrator of an e-commerce site. One of his main concerns is making the website understandable to the different locales it targets. After translating the information into national languages, what else should Kamila consider?

A. Vertical marketing system

B. Horizontal marketing system

C. Telephony

D. Localization

43. Allowing customers to check the status of their shipments with a confirmation number is what form of customer service?

A. Co-browsing

B. Horizontal marketing system

C. Order tracking

D. Asynchronous service

44. Danielle is clicking through a website in a manner that reflects her personal decisions and likes. What is this type of navigation called?

A. A controlled-click pattern

B. Screen flow

C. A random-click pattern

D. Hyperlink placement test

45. What is the main difference between WYSIWYG editors and HTML text editors?

A. WYSIWYG editors require HTML knowledge; HTML text editors do not.

B. WYSIWYG editors do not require HTML knowledge; HTML text editors do.

C. You can use WYSIWYG editors to insert images directly into the HTML; you cannot use HTML text editors to insert images.

D. You cannot use WYSIWYG editors to insert images directly into the HTML; you can use HTML text editors to insert images.

46. Which type of database management system stores related information in a collection of tables and must be capable of growing significantly?

   A. Flat-file database management system

   B. Relational database management system

   C. Multidimensional database management system

   D. Hypertext database management system

47. Which of the following describes an applet?

   A. A full-sized program written only in Java

   B. A software program that runs only outside of a browser

   C. A mini-application

   D. A mini web page

48. How can tables be used to create page structure?

   A. Tables be created so only specified portions of the page move when the page is scrolled.

   B. Borderless tables can be used to create page structure by holding elements in place and allowing the user to see the structure of the table.

   C. Borderless tables can be used to create page structure by holding elements in place without allowing the user to see the structure of the table.

   D. Information in tables cannot be bookmarked, so tables should not be used to create page structure.

49. Website designers should use multimedia technology whenever possible when designing a website.

   A. True

   B. False

50. In what way do proprietary HTML extensions affect web development?

   A. Proprietary extensions do not affect web development.

   B. Proprietary extensions offer compelling advantages to users of the associated proprietary browsers.

   C. Proprietary extensions cost the developer a fee to use, which increases development expenses.

   D. Proprietary extensions are not supported by all browsers, so developers may have to revise a site to appeal to a wider audience.

51. What is the range of port numbers?

   A. 0 to 1023

   B. 1 to 1023

   C. 0 to 65535

   D. 1 to 65535

52. It is a good idea to use as many colors as possible in a website graphic.

   A. True

   B. False

53. What should website designers keep in mind when implementing frames in their websites?

   A. Frames should be used in all websites because of their tremendous advantages over tables.

   B. Frames can be used only if a WYSIWYG editor has been used to create web pages.

   C. Content of frames pages cannot be bookmarked and older versions of browsers do not support them.

   D. Frames should only be used for intranet or extranet applications.

54. What is the role of FTP in the website publishing process?

A. FTP allows website developers to transfer their websites to a web server over the Internet.

B. FTP allows website developers to edit their websites on a web server.

C. FTP allows website developers to create their websites on a web server.

D. FTP allows website developers to test their websites to a web server.

55. Usability tests indicate which of the following?

    A. Users want more innovation in website design.

    B. Users are upgrading their browsers more frequently than in recent years.

    C. Users do not upgrade their browsers when updates become available.

    D. Users do not have expectations for narrative flow and user options.

56. Which of the following is *not* one of the goals of XML?

    A. XML shall be straightforwardly usable over the Internet.

    B. XML shall be compatible with SGML.

    C. The design of XML shall be informal and loosely defined.

    D. XML documents shall be easy to create.

57. Tim is looking for an answer to his questions regarding a product he has purchased. Which two resources provide the answer?

    A. FAQ

    B. An outside website with support documentation

    C. A knowledge base

    D. Co-browsing

58. Creating new methods of navigation outside of the commonly understood ones on the World Wide Web today is a good idea because they create interest in your website.

    A. True

    B. False

59. JavaScript can be used to create what with the user?

   A. Cookies

   B. Interactivity

   C. Relationships

   D. Brand recognition

60. Design on the Web mirrors design in traditional forms of media (print, television, radio).

   A. True

   B. False

61. What is the name of the document that allows Internet users to provide input concerning emerging standards?

   A. RFC

   B. IRQ

   C. PFC

   D. FAQ

62. What is the purpose of style sheets?

   A. Style sheets designate the version of HTML used in the document.

   B. Style sheets allow website designers to make one change that affects multiple HTML elements.

   C. Style sheets generate style guides.

   D. None of the above.

63. The <META> tag is placed in which portion of the HTML page?

   A. <TITLE>

   B. <HEAD>

   C. <BODY>

   D. <STYLE>

64. What is the status of DHTML with the World Wide Web Consortium (W3C)?

    A. The W3C has not provided a Recommendation for DHTML.

    B. It was recently approved and is known as DHTML 1.

    C. It has been approved for over five years; the current recommendation is 3.

    D. It is approved for Recommendation 2 for Netscape browsers and version 1 for Microsoft browsers.

65. Markup specifically designed to affect the appearance of a document is commonly referred to as what type of markup?

    A. Structural

    B. Content

    C. Reference

    D. Procedural

66. What is the definition of Cascading Style Sheets?

    A. Multiple and overlapping style definitions that control the appearance of HTML elements

    B. One style definition that controls the appearance of HTML elements

    C. Multiple and overlapping style definitions that control the function of HTML elements

    D. One style definition that controls the function of HTML elements

67. What is Open Database Connectivity (ODBC)?

    A. A method for accessing related information in a collection of tables

    B. A method for accessing information in organized groups of records

    C. A method for accessing a database regardless of which DBMS or application program is used

    D. A method for accessing information in a single table

68. DHTML describes a set of technologies. Because these technologies are browser independent, how does DHTML work in Netscape and Microsoft browsers?

  A. Files render the same way in both browsers.

  B. At this time, DHTML only works in Netscape browsers.

  C. Files written specifically for Internet Explorer could crash the Navigator browser and vice versa.

  D. At this time, DHTML only works in Microsoft browsers.

69. What is a good layout example of screen flow?

  A. The employment ads in a newspaper.

  B. The comics in a newspaper.

  C. The front page of a newspaper.

  D. A website is not comparable to a standard newspaper.

70. What is the difference between Java and JavaScript?

  A. Both Java and JavaScript are programming languages but Java is object oriented and JavaScript is object based.

  B. Java is object based and JavaScript is object oriented.

  C. Java is a programming language and JavaScript is a scripting language.

  D. There is no difference between the two.

71. You can only use one <FRAMESET> tag on a page when creating a frames page.

  A. True

  B. False

72. True or False. Cookies can be read by sites that did not set them.

  A. True

  B. False

73. Which of the following elements is essential to website design because it distributes content and reduces clutter on a page?

   A. White space

   B. Hyperlinks

   C. Headings

   D. Sans-serif fonts

74. Which organization passes recommendations to the IAB about languages and technologies relating to the World Wide Web?

   A. IETF

   B. IRTF

   C. ICANN

   D. W3C

75. Which of the following best describes how navigation in website design is commonly referred to?

   A. Linear

   B. Hierarchical

   C. Conventional

   D. Browsing

76. Which option includes some of the more familiar types of multimedia technology?

   A. DHTML, XML, XHTML

   B. CSS, C++, Java

   C. Animated GIFs, Java applets, JavaScript, Macromedia Flash

   D. ASP, JSP, PHP

77. Which type of program offers built-in FTP capabilities in addition to other features?

    A. Third-party FTP programs

    B. WYSIWYG editors and HTML text editors

    C. Image editing programs

    D. ISP software programs

78. Which of the following is *not* a reason the ALT attribute of an image tag is useful?

    A. Users can read the image name or description while an image loads.

    B. Software can provide accessibility options for visually and hearing-impaired users.

    C. Users can determine the number of colors the image supports.

    D. Users who have disabled the image-viewing capability on their browsers can read the image name.

79. A major site implementation factor requires you to decide the initial state of the website. The initial state is typically Internet, intranet, or extranet. Which site implementation factor is defined by this choice?

    A. Scope of the project

    B. Skill resources available

    C. Technology you plan to use

    D. Time allotted for implementation

80. HTML evolved from which other markup languages?

    A. SGML and Java

    B. Java and C++

    C. GML and SGML

    D. XML and GML

81. What do WYSIWYG editors and HTML text editors offer website designers?

    A. A faster way to create websites than manual coding

    B. The ability to create and modify images

    C. The ability to create web-based animation

    D. A faster way to create server-side programming

82. Which method would you use to create tables whose content will adjust to the browser environment?

   A. Use percentages instead of pixels in HEIGHT and WIDTH attributes.

   B. Use pixels instead of percentages in HEIGHT and WIDTH attributes.

   C. Use points instead of pixels in HEIGHT and WIDTH attributes.

   D. Use pixels instead of points in HEIGHT and WIDTH attributes.

83. Which of the following best describes a program created with an object-oriented programming language?

   A. A program that can be created many times and reused (with some modification) once.

   B. A program that can be created once and reused (with some modification) any number of times.

   C. A program that can be created once and not reused.

   D. A program that can be created many times and reused any number of times.

84. If an HTTP server application provides administration through a browser interface, which port is used to connect to the administration interface?

   A. Port 80

   B. Port 443

   C. The default web administration port

   D. The port specified by the system administrator

85. Which of the three forms of e-service includes services such as chat, co-browsing, and telephony?

   A. Synchronous

   B. Asynchronous

   C. Self-service

   D. Isochronous

Answers to Assessment Test

1. **D.** The MMC was designed to simplify administration of Internet Information Server (IIS) as well as the other components needed to configure within a Windows 2000 server, including the Active Directory and all the administrative applications. For more information, see Chapter 27.

2. **C.** When you analyze the performance of a particular service, you must also analyze the operating system on which the service runs. Each operating system has a level of efficiency that should be maintained. You can use several different types of tools to monitor both your system and your surrounding network. For more information, see Chapter 30.

3. **B.** The Automated Clearing House (ACH) Network is a nationwide batch-oriented EFT system governed in the United States by the National Automated Clearing House Association (NACHA) operating rules. These rules provide for the inter-bank clearing of electronic payments for participating financial institutions. The American Clearing House Association, Federal Reserve, Electronic Payments Network, and Visa act as ACH Operators, or central clearing facilities through which financial institutions transmit or receive ACH entries. The electronic network transfers and clears funds between banking institutions for merchants and customers. For more information, see Chapter 28.

4. **A.** In a conventional credit-card transaction, a cardholder forwards details to the merchant, who then contacts its acquirer to obtain clearance for the payment. The acquirer can obtain this authorization from the institution that issued the card via a financial network operated by the card association. However, with a SET transaction the credit-card information is encrypted so that the merchant never sees this information. It is passed on to the payment gateway. For more information about SET transactions, see Chapter 29.

5. **C.** Allowing customers to check the status of their shipments with a confirmation number is a valuable form of customer service. Customers must be told the status of their shipments so they will know where their orders are and whether they were fulfilled. For more information on order tracking, see Chapter 25.

6. D. TV commercials are the only offline promotion method mentioned; the others are all used on the Internet. For more information, see Chapter 23.

7. D. A shopping cart tracks users' purchases until they are ready to buy. It keeps a full listing of what users would like to purchase and then gives them the ability to see the list, make revisions to it, choose a shipping method, and then proceed checkout. For more information, see Chapter 23.

8. C. *Purchase button* is a generic term for a button that users select to complete their purchase. After the user makes a purchase, a purchase button connects the transaction to an alternate server for processing. For more information, see Chapter 23.

9. A, C, D. The three steps in setting up online transactions are preparing the server and the site, setting up an online merchant account, and installing payment software. Choosing a web-hosting service is not an integral part of preparing for online transactions. Digital cash is only one payment option and is not part of the process. For more information, see Chapter 28.

10. D. A database is a formally arranged set of persistent information stored by a computer program. It is a collection of data organized to provide efficient management as well as easy access. For more information, see Chapter 27.

11. A. Monitoring site performance is one of the three main responsibilities of a site administrator. When a website is not performing well—taking an excessive amount of time to load or having other difficulties—it can cause a loss in potential customers. The other key tasks of an administrator are maintenance of the site and its contents and maintaining the security of the site. For more information, see Chapter 30.

12. D. When content is localized, more than just the national language is considered. Many details, such as geographic location and climate, cultural practices, currency, observed holidays, and gender distinctions or preferences, are also considered. In many countries certain words or phrases are used in one region but not in another even though the same language is spoken. Such a situation calls for localization of information. For more information about localization, see Chapter 25.

13. B.   Spam is considered the least effective; in fact, it is counterproductive. Consumers consider spam intrusive. For more information, see Chapter 23.

14. C.   Of the portal solutions listed here, only Amazon allows merchants to leverage the company's e-commerce infrastructure in an online instant storefront. iWon and Yahoo offer shopping as an ancillary business, and MerchandiZer is a mid-level offline instant storefront. For more information, see Chapter 26.

15. A.   Symmetric encryption is a type of encryption that requires both participants to have a single secret key. The other answers involve other methods of encryption and the definition of hashing. For more information, see Chapter 29.

16. A.   *Telephony* is the technology in which telephone calls that are normally routed via standard telecommunications means are instead sent over the Internet. The average mid-size company spends a high monthly sum on telecommunications, thus making telephony an attractive option. With high-bandwidth connections, voice degradation is unnoticeable. For more information on telephony, see Chapter 25.

17. A.   A marketer site's main source of revenue is selling products or services, which is what a site selling women's sports equipment and clothes does. For more information, see Chapter 23.

18. A.   Privacy is the most common concern among e-commerce consumers because they send sensitive information across the Internet during transactions. The other answers might be concerns, but they aren't the main concerns. For more information, see Chapter 20.

19. D.   The system catalog is the part of a database that describes the data in the database. Some databases use the term *data dictionary* (or *metadata*, which is data about data). For more information, see Chapter 27.

20. B.   Although CPU speed will have a great effect, the most important factor when considering web servers is the amount of RAM. Web pages will be requested from the server, and the more RAM the system has, the greater its capability to handle requests. For more information, see Chapter 30.

21. B.   An application service provider takes on the responsibility of maintaining the hardware and software infrastructure for an application suite. This allows other companies to outsource this function to the ASP. For more information, see Chapter 26.

22. A.   The need for both the buyer and seller to use the same software is the biggest deterrent to using digital cash. The other answers are actually selling points for using digital cash because doing so eliminates back-end transactions, there isn't a high cost involved, and consumers don't have to sacrifice anonymity. For more information on digital cash, see chapter 28.

23. C.   The server certificate is used on web servers to identify the web server and the company running it and to allow for encrypted SSL sessions between the server and browsers. Server certificates are also necessary for a server to participate in SET. The other certificates have other functions. For more information about certificates, see Chapter 29.

24. A.   Open Buying on the Internet is an Internet e-commerce specification based on the Internet. For more information on OBI, see Chapter 25.

25. C.   The clickthrough rate is the percentage of times an ad is viewed and then clicked. The CPC is the cost-per-click, an Internet marketing formula used to price ad banners. Advertisers will pay Internet publishers based on the number of clicks a specific ad banner receives. For more information, see Chapter 23.

26. B.   Julian has conducted business-to-business e-commerce. There are only two forms of e-commerce: business-to-business (B2B) and business-to-consumer (B2C). In this scenario, Julian is purchasing signs from an online business for his business. For more information, see Chapter 20.

27. C.   The default port for a site is 80. If you change the port number, your users will need to use the port number at the end of the Web address., as in www.*whatever*.com:8080. For more information, see Chapter 27.

28. D.   A queue of more than two processes for a sustained period of time indicates that your CPU may need an upgrade. This shows that your CPU is not fast enough to handle the demands placed upon it by both the operating system and the services running in conjunction with the operating system. For more information, see Chapter 30.

29. C.   An effective e-commerce package allows online merchants to offer security (such as encryption) for customer information. Because the majority of consumers consider privacy the most important factor of e-commerce, offering security becomes even more important. For more information, see Chapter 26.

30. A. A payment gateway is the connection between the online catalog and a merchant bank. For an electronic transfer to be completed, information must be transferred between merchant banks. Before this transfer can occur, the transaction must be introduced to the system via a payment gateway. For more information, see Chapter 28.

31. D. SHA and MD5 are hash functions. A good hash function has two properties. It is difficult to invert, and it is resistant to collisions. For more information on hash functions, see Chapter 29.

32. A. Generating demand involves pulling people to your site in some fashion (through banner ads or other methods) and then keeping them on your site. For more information, see Chapter 20.

33. A. Soft goods include electronically dispensable goods. Hard goods are those that have to be physically shipped. Linux and software goods might be somewhat reasonable conclusions, but only the terms *hard goods* and *soft goods* are used to refer to categories of goods sold on the Internet. For more information, see Chapter 22.

34. D. Psychographics is a science that can help anticipate the specific positive, negative, or neutral psychological impact of words, symbols, shapes, textures, colors, fonts, or even scale on consumer target market groups. The other options are good tools to help determine consumer likes and dislikes, but none is considered a science. For more information, see Chapter 22.

35. D. Randy is in a niche market, one in which only a small subsection of the population will be interested in his services. This doesn't mean he will not want a Web presence or that business will not come from other locations. The only other real market listed in the options is a global market, which would have a larger consumer base. For more information, see Chapter 22.

36. B. Rapid change is considered a barrier to e-commerce growth. The models that work today on the Internet may not perform well or may become obsolete in the future. The other options are considered drivers, which encourage growth. For more information, see Chapter 22.

37. D. The Online Copyright Infringement Liability Limitation Act excuses an online provider from liability for copyright infringement by its subscribers. For more information, see Chapter 21.

38. C. Tariffs are taxes placed on goods and products sent from state to state or country to country. For more information, see Chapter 21.

39. B. The Commission on Online Child Protection passed the Children's Online Privacy Protection Act, effective April 21, 2000. The privacy measures prevent websites from collecting information about children 13 and younger without a parent's consent. For more information, see Chapter 21.

40. A. *Telephony* is the technology in which telephone calls that are normally routed via standard telecommunications means are instead sent over the Internet. The average mid-size company spends a high monthly sum on telecommunications, thus making telephony an attractive option. With high-bandwidth connections, voice degradation is unnoticeable. For more information on telephony, see Chapter 25.

41. A. Open Buying on the Internet is an Internet e-commerce specification based on the Internet. For more information on OBI, see Chapter 25.

42. D. When content is localized, more than just the national language is considered. Many details, such as geographic location and climate, cultural practices, currency, observed holidays, and gender distinctions or preferences, are also considered. In many countries certain words or phrases are used in one region but not in another even though the same language is spoken. Such a situation calls for localization of information. For more information about localization, see Chapter 25

43. C. Allowing customers to check the status of their shipments with a confirmation number is a valuable form of customer service. Customers must be told the status of their shipments so they will know where their orders are and whether they were fulfilled. For more information on order tracking, see Chapter 25.

44. C. An examination of the server logs would indicate that Danielle is using a random-click pattern. Her navigation of the site is not restricted by a requirement that would control her clicks, in other words, by a controlled-click pattern. For more information about click patterns, see Chapter 24.

45. B. WYSIWYG editors do not require HTML knowledge, but HTML text editors do. WYSIWYG editors are ideal for those who have limited or no HTML knowledge; to use HTML text editors successfully, designers must have a certain level of proficiency in HTML. For more information, see Chapter 18.

46. B. A relational database management system (RDBMS) stores related information in a collection of tables. Because queries to a relational database can create new tables, a relational database requires the capability to grow significantly to handle the demands of new input. For more information, see Chapter 15.

47. C. Applets are small applications that adhere to a set of conventions based on the Java programming language. They require a Java-compatible browser in order to be viewed over the Internet. For more information, see Chapter 14.

48. C. Borderless tables can be used to create page structure by holding elements in place without allowing the user to see the structure of the table. Tables with no borders are frequently used for page layout, whereas tables with the border showing are commonly used for displaying data. For more information, see Chapter 7.

49. B. Website designers should resist the temptation to use the latest and most dazzling technology because the standard user on a dial-up connection with a standard browser cannot support it. This does not mean that you cannot use new technology, but you must be aware that you will exclude some of your audience. A balance between traditional website design and new technology is required so that the technology doesn't compromise the functionality of the site. For more information, see Chapter 4.

50. D. Some browsers simply ignore proprietary tags, which can have a significant effect on how your HTML documents are displayed. In addition, a browser can misinterpret proprietary extensions, which can also have an effect on your documents. For more information, see Chapter 6.

51. D. Port numbers range from 1 to 65535. Ports 1 through 1023 are reserved for use by certain privileged services and are referred to as well-known port numbers. For example, port 21 is reserved for FTP and port 110 is reserved for POP3. For more information, see Chapter 16.

52. B. Using multiple colors will increase the file size of the image, which will increase the time it takes for the web page to download. For more information, see Chapter 3.

53. C. Content of frames pages cannot be bookmarked; only the frameset page itself can be bookmarked in a browser. In addition, you cannot view frames through older versions of browsers. For more information, see Chapter 8.

54. A. FTP is an networking protocol used to transfer files between computers. It allows file transfer without corruption or alteration. Transferring files over the Internet requires an FTP client and a destination FTP server to receive the files. For more information, see Chapter 19.

55. C. The rate at which users upgrade their browsers has actually decreased as more users come online. Studies indicate that users took twice as long to upgrade their 3.*x* versions of browsers to the 4.*x* versions than they did to upgrade from 2.*x* versions to the 3.*x* versions. For more information, see Chapter 5.

56. C. The goals of XML are clearly defined by the W3C. One of them is that XML shall be formal and concise. The others range from XML shall be straightforwardly usable over the Internet to XML documents should be human-legible and reasonably clear. For more information, see Chapter 13.

57. A, C. A FAQ is an easy solution to set up for quick searches of standard product information. A knowledge base enlivens that FAQ documentation by making it searchable. Going outside the site is usually less effective. Co-browsing, although a good support forum, is not needed here. For more information, see Chapter 24.

58. B. Using familiar navigation elements will help users to efficiently and quickly move through your website. If you create new methods, users often must learn new techniques, increasing the likelihood that they will leave the site out of frustration. For more information, see Chapter 2.

59. B. Even with the improvements to HTML, there is little or no possibility of creating a page users can interact with if you use just HTML alone. To create interactive pages, you can use Common Gateway Interface (CGI) server-side scripts or JavaScript. JavaScript is easier to learn and allows you to create web pages that your users can interact with based on their keyboard and mouse inputs. For more information, see Chapter 11.

60. B. Companies have found that simply translating their existing media into web format is ineffective. Consequently, new forms of design that are uniquely suited to the Web have been developed to address the needs of the Web. For more information, see Chapter 1.

61. A. A Request for Comments (RFC) is a document used to collect information on Internet-related technologies and issues. Internet users can provide input concerning emerging standards. For more information, see Chapter 17.

62. B. Style sheets allow website designers to make one change that affects multiple HTML elements. They are valuable time-saving devices in website development because they allow the website designer to determine how an element will look throughout the whole website. For more information, see Chapter 10.

63. B. The <META> tag is placed in <HEAD> portion of the HTML page. It includes information such as a description of your website and the keywords used to categorize it. For more information, see Chapter 9.

64. A. It is unclear whether the W3C will eventually provide a Recommendation for DHTML, in part because of the disparity between current browsers. Unfortunately, the only documentation the W3C has produced to date is an outline of the capabilities a DHTML document should incorporate. Considering the advances in XML and XSL, it is believed that the W3C may not spend the time to mature DHTML. For more information, see Chapter 12.

65. D. Markup specifically designed to affect the appearance of a document is commonly called procedural markup because it tells the computer how to render the text. For more information, see Chapter 13.

66. A. Cascading Style Sheets are multiple and overlapping style definitions that control the appearance of HTML elements. They allow website designers to control the appearance of their websites from a central document or place in an HTML document. For more information, see Chapter 10.

67. C. ODBC is a standard method for accessing a database regardless of which DBMS or application program is used. Though this technology is language independent, both the DBMS and the application must be ODBC compliant. For more information, see Chapter 15.

68. C. DHTML is not yet standardized; therefore, Microsoft and Netscape implementations are different. Files written specifically for Internet Explorer could crash the Navigator browser and vice versa. For more information, see Chapter 12.

69. C. The front page layout of a newspaper is a good example of how screen flow should work in a website. For more information about screen flow, see Chapter 24.

70. C. Although the names are similar, Java and JavaScript are different languages. Java is a full-fledged object-oriented programming language developed by Sun Microsystems, Inc. Java can be used to create stand-alone applications and a special type of mini-application called a Java applet. JavaScript is an object-based scripting language. Although it uses some of Java's expression syntax and basic program flow controls, JavaScript stands alone and does not require Java. For more information, see Chapter 11.

71. B.   You can use more than one <FRAMESET> tag on a page, but you cannot combine ROWS and COLS (rows and columns) within the same <FRAMESET> tag. For more information, see Chapter 8.

72. B.   Cookies can only be read by the server that originally placed them on the user's system. Users should not be concerned that a cookie set by one server can be read by another, thereby exposing potentially confidential information to anyone other than those for whom it was originally intended. For more information, see Chapter 9.

73. A.   Most users prefer a page with even distribution and some blank space. White space is essential to website design because it distributes content and reduces clutter on a page. Each web page should contain approximately 50 percent less text than a printed version of the same information would contain. For more information, see Chapter 1.

74. D.   The W3C (World Wide Web Consortium) is responsible primarily for creating recommendations for languages and technologies such as HTML, XML, and Cascading Style Sheets. These recommendations are passed to the IETF, which creates standards based on the recommendations. For more information, see Chapter 17.

75. B.   Navigation on websites is commonly referred to as hierarchical because the home page provides the top layer of the hierarchy and all other pages take their appropriate place below it. For more information, see Chapter 2.

76. C.   Animated GIFs, Java applets, JavaScript, and Macromedia Flash are some of the most familiar and popular types of multimedia technology. For more information, see Chapter 4.

77. B.   WYSIWYG editors and HTML text editors offer built-in FTP tools. Third-party FTP tools offer only FTP capabilities. For more information, see Chapter 19.

78. C.   Users cannot determine the number of colors the image supports from the ALT attribute. The ALT attribute is used to provide alternative text in place of an image or when the mouse is placed over the image. For more information, see Chapter 3.

79.   A.   Determining the scope of the project requires you to decide the initial state of the website. If you do not anticipate a change in the site's scope, then less planning is required to address possible implementations of a larger scope. If, however, a change is likely, the initial scope must address how this changes will be accommodated in the website vision. For more information, see Chapter 5.

80.   C.   HTML has evolved from GML and SGML. The Generalized Markup Language (GML) was created by IBM in the late 1960s as a way to move formatted documents across different computer platforms. GML evolved into the Standard Generalized Markup Language (SGML) in 1986 and was ratified by the International Organization for Standardization (ISO). HTML is an application of SGML. For more information, see Chapter 6.

81.   A.   WYSIWYG editors and HTML text editors offer website designers a faster way to create websites than manual coding does because of all the features they offer, such as built-in support for web technologies. For more information, see Chapter 18.

82.   A.   If you use percentage values (%) for HEIGHT and WIDTH attributes, the table becomes dynamic and will change as content and the size of the browser window change. If you use pixel values for HEIGHT and WIDTH attributes, the table remains static and will not change as content changes and as browser window size changes. For more information, see Chapter 7.

83.   B.   An *object-oriented* program is a program that can be created once and reused (with some modification) any number of times. Java is an example of an object-oriented programming language, and Java applets are objects you plug into your web page. For more information, see Chapter 14.

84.   D.   An HTTP server application that provides administration through a browser interface uses the port specified by the system administrator. Port 80 is usually used for HTTP services and port 443 is for Secure Sockets Layer (SSL). For more information, see Chapter 16.

85.   A.   A synchronous e-service allows for human interaction between support and client. In an asynchronous service, there is a bit of time delay between the request for help and the response. Self-service forces a person to find their own solutions through the site-based help procedures. For more information on e-services, see Chapter 24.

Design Methodology and Technology

Chapter 1

Overview of Web Design Concepts

THE CIW EXAM OBJECTIVE GROUP COVERED IN THIS CHAPTER:

✓ Develop effective and usable corporate websites within a reasonable time frame, including but not limited to: design concepts and goals, web strategy.

Web design has grown from simply replicating printed material on a web page to using technology that exists strictly for web development. A website designer needs to understand the vast array of web design tools and technologies available to create effective, user-friendly websites. Throughout this book, we will explore using layout and navigation for effective website design, using optimized graphics and design elements to create pages that load quickly, the importance of understanding the business process in the web design life cycle, how programming on both the client and server side affect a web user's experience, the impact of standards created by Internet governing bodies on web design, the role web authoring software plays in website design, and how to publish and maintain a website.

Although many may think that a website's design is secondary to its content, this chapter will illustrate the important role that design plays in the users' experience. Common design principles—such as color, font choice, and effective placement of elements on the page—all factor into a user-friendly website. To fully appreciate and understand the vital role design plays, we'll explore the important aspects surrounding this area: web technology, how the web differs from traditional forms of media, design concepts, and the tools and technologies used to create a website.

Web Technology

The web technology that we now enjoy is the fastest growing means of communication that humankind has ever experienced. It empowers both the message sender and the message recipient—in other words, the publisher of content and the reader of that content. Many people now turn to the Web instead of using the newspaper or other traditional means to find information. Information on the Web is available to users worldwide and can be disseminated with speed, accuracy, and detail. Web addresses are now included in most businesses' radio, television, and print ads, offering customers immediate access to a more personalized and specific method of information retrieval that assists in learning and decision making.

It is the website designer's responsibility to convey the appropriate visual message to recipients; thus, the concepts of design are as important as the content itself. For long-time web users, the transformation of website design is clear. Early sites consisted of content that was lengthy and displayed in plain text. This trend evolved into developed design practices that rival ad media such as television and print in their complexity and sophistication.

To be competitive, everyone in the modern office environment will contribute to the development of the information infrastructure. Websites are becoming complex structures that can include information from all parts of an organization: human resources, sales and marketing, and inventory and distribution, for example. Those contributing to the content must understand what the effective forms of displaying information on the Web are because they differ from traditional forms of communication.

Tools and technologies abound to make website design easier, for both the novice and the experienced website designer. Designers must choose the tools that will give them the competitive edge for their organizations. In Chapter 18, "Applications and Tools," we will examine some of the more widely used tools for website design, such as Microsoft's FrontPage; Macromedia's Dreamweaver, Flash, and HomeSite; and Jasc's Paint Shop Pro. As you'll discover, each tool has its own unique features and benefits; based on those elements, you can choose which tool is best for the design you are trying to achieve.

The Nature of the Web

Most website designers approach development from a self-reflective point of view. They are interested in presenting information to a mass audience with the known metaphors of mass advertising. However, the Internet offers an alternative: the capability for one-to-one relationships. Users of websites respond better to information and product offerings that are tailored to their specific needs. You should understand that, by nature, the Internet is a medium that enables the user to decide what information to access and when to access it. This fact makes the Internet a *one-to-one medium* as opposed to a *broadcast medium*. Thus, the concepts and applications of mass media are not necessarily valid for the Internet.

The goal of mass media is to create in the viewer or reader interest that eventually will lead to a desired outcome. In essence, the act of reading a magazine or watching a television program is not inherently transactional. The only action required from readers or viewers is to read or watch. The information is broadcast to a passive audience. Thus, creating information for mass media requires a different strategy than creating information for the Internet.

By its nature, the Internet is transactional. The entire Internet experience, from accessing the Internet to browsing the Web, is predicated on user requests and server responses—in other words, *transactions*. Furthermore, by its nature, the Internet is nonlinear. The user constantly makes transactional decisions, first leading to the site, then staying within the site, then conducting e-commerce, and then deciding to return to the site in the future. However, users can switch to another site—and another business—anytime they choose.

Current Web Development Direction

Development for the Web has become more sophisticated in the past three years. Sophistication has increased in terms of significant multimedia advances; new types of data are now accessible via the Web. Data-driven content has become a main component of many web applications and projects. The advantage of data-driven content is that it reflects the most current information, numbers, and statistics because the data is drawn from a database at the time the user requests it.

After e-commerce, intranet development has been the second-largest growth area in web development. *Intranets* bring web-based networking in-house, supplying a network for use by employees or members of a specific organization. The result is a more efficient and productive work environment because employees have easy access to frequently used data and documents. Time-sensitive information can be accessed on an intranet in a more timely and efficient manner than it can be accessed via traditional forms of media. For outside vendors and business partners, extranets are rapidly emerging to fulfill data requirements outside the company and streamline the business process. *Extranets* are designed to provide access to selected external users to expedite the exchange of products, services, and key business information. For example, Company A supplies Company B with paper. If Company A has access to Company B's inventory status via an extranet, it will know when Company B needs another shipment. Company A can then initiate the shipment without a request from Company B.

Design Concepts

Web design concepts are always evolving. It is important to remember that the Web is not a static medium like print media. Therefore, the rules and concepts are in constant fluctuation. One of the most common misconceptions about website design is that a good site must dazzle the user with a multimedia experience and that the content of the site is of secondary importance. This assumption is false.

As a website designer, you want users to have a satisfying experience, but dazzling them is not your goal. The primary goal in website design is to give users what *they* want, not what *you* think they want. This goal can be achieved with a complex balance of well-planned design, quality content, and proper use of available media. Numerous studies confirm that the overuse of multimedia will discourage visitors because they either do not have the capabilities to support it or do not want to wait for lengthy downloads (the ideal download time for a web page is 10 seconds or less).

Ultimately, if you do not satisfy the web users' needs or desires, they will find other sites that will. Website designers who think only from their own perspective and not the users' will certainly find dissatisfied web visitors, clients, and customers.

Web Medium vs. Traditional Media

Website designers are becoming more aware of the differences between designing for the Web and designing for other media, especially print. In the early years of website design, many websites were simple HTML reproductions of printed brochures and other marketing tools. This approach resulted from companies attempting to post their information to the Web quickly. Further, the Web was new territory and did not have proven techniques or statistical data to validate its effectiveness.

Some companies learned early that posting "brochures" on the Web was not an effective use of the medium. They simply re-created their print campaigns on the Web, assuming that they would be just as successful in an electronic format as they had been in print. Print media is *linear* in nature: one line to the next, one page to the next. The Web is a *nonlinear* medium, allowing users to link (hyperlink) to different areas within the site or to websites outside of the site; a user decides where to go and does not have to follow the strict organization set forth in a book, for example. Therefore, the Web has different properties that are not exploited when used in traditional linear format. The most distinctive is the interaction that is possible between the user and a business through its website. Traditional print media cannot personalize the user's experience. By contrast, the web medium can optimize the possibilities of interactivity and personalization for the user, creating a direct connection between the business and the visitor. This is accomplished through the new technologies, such as Dynamic HTML (DHTML), Cascading Style Sheets (CSS), Extensible Markup Language (XML), JavaScript, and Java applets.

Tools and Technology

Several years back, there was much debate about whether or not to use specialized tools to help the web development process. Now, however, many of the HTML-editing tools and WYSIWYG (What You See Is What You Get) editors are in their third and fourth generations and have become very sophisticated applications. The debate is no longer whether designers should use these tools, but rather, which tools they should use.

Ideally, a combination of manual coding and WYSIWYG functionality is the best option from today's development perspective. It simply takes too much time to develop a dynamic site by only manually coding HTML. The need for constantly updated information and design on both a corporate website and an intranet or extranet site necessitates an alliance between the two methods of site design. Two WYSIWYG design tools stand out in the marketplace today: Macromedia Dreamweaver and Microsoft FrontPage. In Chapter 18, we will discuss the tools available for creating websites and consider the features that will optimize your HTML efficiency. We will discuss the design options in these types of programs, as well as the more important features for site management. These powerful site management features give programs such as these a competitive edge in the industry.

Generally, many tools are used in unison for website development; this book focuses on the collaborative application approach to website design. For more advanced topics, such as images and animation, we'll profile applications that assist in the development of web graphics and animation. Macromedia Flash is one of these products; Flash enables media-rich content to be delivered while also conserving bandwidth, which is a valuable commodity to the website designer. Flash is also profiled in Chapter 18.

New Technologies

Soon after you learn what tools are available for designing websites, you will need to evaluate them to determine whether they are capable of incorporating new technologies that allow you to build dynamic sites that create a more personalized experience for the user. For example, both Microsoft FrontPage and Macromedia Dreamweaver implement *Dynamic HTML (DHTML)* functions that will allow you to take advantage of this available technology.

We will discuss other recently developed technologies in this book as well, such as *Cascading Style Sheets (CSS)* and *Extensible Markup Language (XML)*, and we'll discuss the use of JavaScript and Java applets in your website design for further functionality. In addition, we will discuss the World Wide Web Consortium's advancement of the newest standards and the ways in which browser manufacturers contribute to development of new technologies.

Remember that, in this book, you will read about several tools you can use in the development of websites. The goal of this book is not to make you an expert user of any one tool, but to give you enough information about the key components of each tool that you can make educated decisions about which tool will best meet your needs.

Web Users and Site Design

How much of the text on a web page would you guess web users really read? All of it? Most of it? The truth is that users read almost none of it. Numerous surveys confirm that as many as 80 percent of web users merely scan web page content, looking for key words and phrases. Furthermore, the average person reads 25 percent more slowly from a computer monitor than from print.

So how does this fact affect web page layout? As a designer, you must create a page that allows users to quickly scan and find the information they seek. Remember that one of the misconceptions of current website design is that the web is just another form of print media. When a designer creates a page with the same content as a brochure or newsletter, the user will likely move on to another site.

When users arrive at your site, their first impressions are important. The website may be the only window to the world for your business. If it is unappealing to the customer, you will likely lose the customer to a competitor. So, if you know that users only scan your page, why try to force them to read a lot of content that may not interest them? Keep users satisfied, give them what they want, and they will come back. Users do not want to see cluttered pages with irrelevant content and images. Content is essential; however, the layout and delivery are just as important.

The web is self-centric: Users are interested in only what they want. People who work in the retail business will agree that customers are selfish because they know they pay the bills that keep a business's doors open. Users usually visit your site because they want specific information, whether for research or purchases. The easier you make their tasks, the more likely you are to earn their business. If you understand this, you will create web pages with layout features that will earn your users' business.

Consider a website such as www.cnn.com. Upon arrival, you are greeted with the lead headline, a picture from that story, a paragraph summarizing the story, and a link to the full story. You know the topic of the story immediately from the picture and summary, and you can find out more if you want. Otherwise, you can scan down the page to the next headline, determining the topic of just about every story on the CNN site in about a minute. You are only one click away from any full story. The CNN site provides easy scanning, and you are more likely to return later because you got what you wanted quickly.

Design Fundamentals

As a website designer, it is exciting to think about new technology and how to implement it into the latest designs. Generally, website designers are likely to have the most recent hardware, software, and plug-ins. However, as tempting as it may be to create the most dynamic and interactive site that new hardware and software can support, the vast majority of the web audience is not seeking high-end design. A good guideline to follow when designing for the masses is to design for the *lowest common denominator*. Consider the following:

- Most users have a 15-inch or smaller monitor.

- Many users utilize a 640×480 resolution setting.

- Most users have a 28.8Kbps modem connection.

- Most users have a version 4.*x* or earlier browser.

- Very few users will take the time to download plug-ins.

Exceptions to the rules always exist. Many users are upgrading to 56Kbps modems and are using 800×600 screen resolution settings. But observing the rules will guide you in creating websites that the majority of users can use or view.

Effective Web Page Layout

Consider how your favorite newspaper is laid out. The front page has the lead story, and it might also contain a column along one margin listing other feature stories in the paper. How does this affect your reading experience? The layout does not force you to read one story on the front page and then flip through all pages to find others that interest you. If you see a summary for a story that you want to investigate further, a page number, or a "link," directs you to the full story.

This layout style is often compared to an inverted pyramid, as depicted in Figure 1.1. This style offers the user first a list of story summaries, then links or references to the details. The Web is an ideal medium for this type of delivery.

FIGURE 1.1   Inverted pyramid style

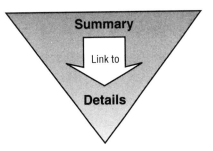

Using hyperlinks, you can send users to any number of elaborations on subjects, stories, news, products, or services. You can also provide links to archived or related information, which is something newspapers cannot provide because of lack of space, time, and resources. If users want further information, they can browse to it at their discretion. Otherwise, they can move on to other pursuits.

Web Page Layout Elements

Before you begin the website production process, consider the look and structure of your site. You must understand the elements that will make up the completed web page and how they interact with each other, from a visual as well as a technical standpoint. You should then carry the chosen elements throughout the website. These web page elements include layout, color, fonts, and images and other multimedia.

Page layout refers to the way in which the website designer presents information to users. The format should be logical and easy to understand. As they do in documents or reports, structured formats help categorize, simplify, and clarify information for distribution. As a website designer, you must develop a structure and adhere to it so the user's experience will be meaningful and productive.

Consider the following items when planning your web page layout:

Frameset   Allows multiple pages to be displayed simultaneously

Margin   Controls how close the content displays to the browser window edges

Border   Provides visual boundaries for HTML tables and frames

Color   Provides an overall sense of the organization of the site and enhances readability

Navigation   Controls the user's movement through the site

Rule   Divides the page content into related sections

White space   Reduces page element clutter and separates elements on the page

Table   Distributes and positions elements on a page and forms data into rows and columns

List   Organizes and emphasizes certain items of information

Paragraph   Groups text characters on a page

Heading level   Organizes content visually through text that is a different size and style than the text used for most of the content on a page

Image   Provides visual appeal, information, and navigation

Determining which of these elements your site will include helps focus the development process. If you do not address these items early in the development process, you might waste resources correcting problems that develop later.

Common Layout Format

Website designers use some common, basic elements on websites to perform certain important navigational functions. You can see these common features—page structure, buttons, text, and images—in action by browsing several sites. When users visit your site, they should know what to expect. This is not to say that they should know all about the content or products you offer, but rather that they should be able to figure out fairly easily how to use the site.

Site layout can be categorized by the way the navigational elements are placed. The type of layout that is chosen depends largely on the type and amount of content. For example, navigation elements are generally located on the left and top margins. The background for navigation elements often has a slightly different color or appearance than the rest of the page. Also, additional navigational features are frequently included at the bottom of the page. Black text on a white background is common, as are company logos in the upper-left corner of the display. Because they are used so often, these and other formatting techniques help to make navigation more intuitive for the user. Following are some samples of common layout types.

Figure 1.2 shows an example of the traditional left-margin layout. You can see the navigational elements in the left margin. Figure 1.3 shows the top-margin layout, in which navigational elements are placed along the top of the page.

Figure 1.4 shows the most commonly used layout, the distributed left- and top-margin layout. Figure 1.5 shows the less commonly used right-margin layout. And finally, Figure 1.6 shows an example of the distributed layout, which works well for sites with a great deal of content.

FIGURE 1.2 Left-margin layout (traditional)

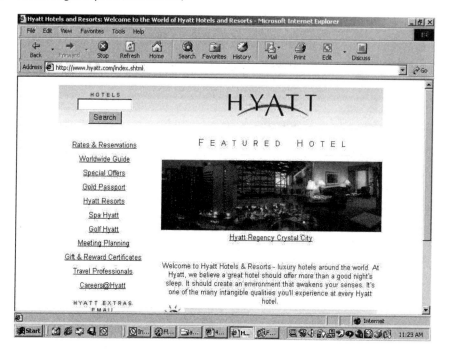

FIGURE 1.3 Top-margin layout

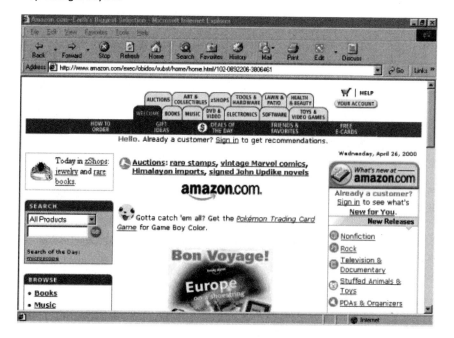

FIGURE 1.4 Distributed left- and top-margin layout

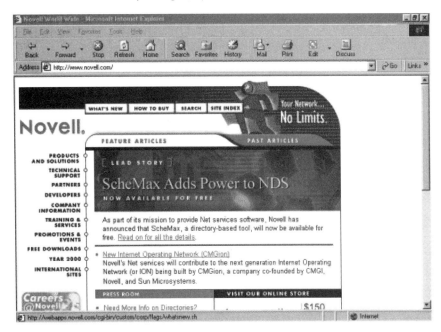

FIGURE 1.5 Right-margin layout

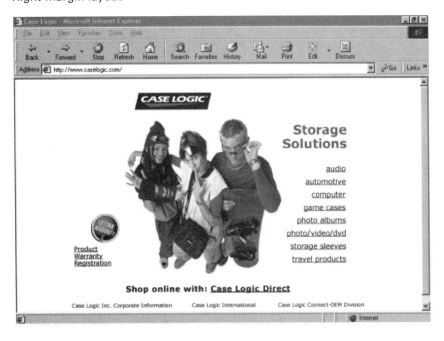

FIGURE 1.6 Distributed layout

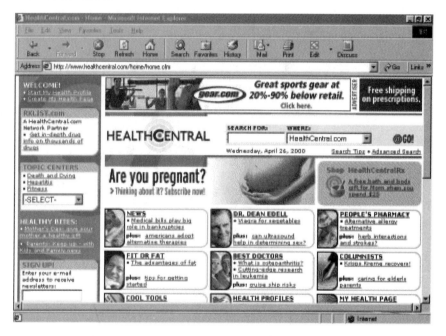

White Space

Recall your web browsing experiences at various sites you have visited. When a page initially loads into your browser, you are greeted either with content on every part of the page or with limited well-distributed content resulting in less clutter. What is your initial impression of both these scenarios? If you are like most users, you prefer the page with even distribution and some blank space, known in the development community as *white space*.

Remember that users do not appreciate useless clutter and masses of content on web pages. Users quickly scan pages, and the more content they must scan through, the more information they will miss. This does not mean that you cannot provide the user with a lot of information, just not all on one page. Each web page should contain approximately 50 percent less text than a printed version of the same information would contain.

A web page should be designed to offer information concisely. Provide users with the basics and then give them links to more depth and detail. Not every user wants every piece of information; let each user choose whether to go deeper with links. Also, do not divide a page just to make it shorter unless it is at a logical breaking point. Each page should be able to stand on its own.

Developers use tables and transparent GIF images to add white space to pages. After determining what users need to know, you can lay out the page using borderless HTML tables to position content and to provide content-free areas. In some cases, a table may be all that is required.

Page Layout with Transparent GIFs

A transparent image can be inserted into the page as a blank space placeholder. *Transparent GIFs* are images are used as placeholders in web pages. They are images of varying sizes that have a transparent background, so that the background of the web page appears through the image. They are invisible to the user. You can assign height and width attributes in the <IMG> tag to create the desired white space dimensions. For example, if you want to indent a paragraph, you can insert the following tag prior to the first letter of the new paragraph:

```
<IMG SRC="transparent.gif" HEIGHT="2" WIDTH="15">
```

This value will indent the paragraph 15 pixels from the left.

The same procedure can be used to increase the line space between paragraphs; simply place the following tag between them:

```
<IMG SRC="transparent.gif" HEIGHT="20" WIDTH="2">
```

This value places 20 pixels of space between the paragraphs.

Transparent GIFs can also be placed into table data cells to control column or row size if necessary. Keep in mind that the goal is to reduce clutter on the page, enabling users to easily scan the document and select links if they choose.

Page Layout with Tables

The website designer must understand the construction and use of tables in page layout. By default, everything in HTML aligns to the left. Developers use HTML tables to distribute content over the entire browser display. A table structure can be populated with content, and table borders can be set to zero so the user never sees the table.

Cascading Style Sheets (CSS) can be used in place of tables in some circumstances in HTML layout design. Unfortunately, not all browsers support all features of CSS. Until CSS become a standard in most browsers, using tables will remain the standard way to position text on a page. Later in this book, you will practice using tables for high-quality page layout. (CSS will be discussed in detail in Chapter 10.)

Page Layout with Frames

Frames can be used for page layout, although they also play a vital role in navigation. You should decide early in the design and planning process whether to use frames because they can dramatically affect layout and navigation. Frames affect other factors in the development and deployment of the site as well. They are discussed in detail in Chapter 8.

Page Layout Using Positioning

Layered or stacked elements are becoming more popular, and more browsers are supporting them. The main disparity with layering is that Netscape Navigator uses the <LAYER> tag whereas Microsoft Internet Explorer conforms to the W3C standard on CSS positioning of all elements. Therefore, two separate scripts must be used to ensure cross-platform compliance. Fortunately, some HTML editors automatically code both versions. In Chapter 10, we will examine the difference in detail.

Speed and Scrolling

Users demand speed. You can fulfill this demand by limiting the file size of the elements you use in the pages you design. Users feel impatient after about 1 second; after 10 seconds, you are likely to lose their attention. Therefore, the website designer must use images sparingly and choose file formats carefully. Optimizing graphics is an important component to quick downloads. We will discuss file formats in detail in Chapter 3, "Web Page Graphics."

Table 1.1 shows the maximum page size allowable to produce desired response times for various connection speeds.

T A B L E 1.1   Page Size and Response Time

Connection Speed	One-Second Response Time	Ten-Second Response Time
Modem (28.8Kbps)	2KB (kilobytes)	34KB
ISDN BRI (128Kbps)	8KB	150KB
T1 (1.544Mbps)	100KB	2MB (megabytes)

Page size is defined as the sum of the file sizes for all elements that make up a page, including the HTML file and all embedded objects (e.g., GIF and JPG image files).

In mid-1997, a study found that the average web page size was 44KB, more than five times too large for optimal response time for ISDN users. Thus, even when more users have mid-band connections, the Web will still be much too slow. Also note that 44KB is 30 percent larger than even the most generous size limit for modem users.

Design with Screen Resolution in Mind

It is still advisable to design for a screen resolution of 640×480 unless you know with certainty that your users will have a different resolution. By designing for 640×480 resolution, you ensure that users will not have to scroll left or right. To avoid horizontal scrolling, do not design pages wider than 600 pixels. Remember that users only scan; many do not scroll down, nor will they scroll to the right or left.

When you design for 640×480 resolution, the display is still effective at higher resolutions. Figures 1.7 through 1.9 show the same website displayed at three different resolutions. You can see that the page shown in Figure 1.7 requires no horizontal scrolling at the 640×480 resolution and that the site was designed for that resolution. Figure 1.10 shows the same site displayed on a WebTV viewer.

FIGURE 1.7   Site displayed at 640×480 resolution

FIGURE 1.8 Site displayed at 800×600 resolution

FIGURE 1.9 Site displayed at 1024×768 resolution

FIGURE 1.10   Site displayed on WebTV

Color and Web Design

The element of color plays a vital role in the perception and presentation of a website. A company's style, culture, and mood can be portrayed by the colors presented in the site and how they blend, coordinate, or contrast.

Color is perceived as a representation of the type of culture and industry in which a company participates. For example, a website with primarily hard, bright colors such as red, pink, yellow, and green may give the impression of a flashy, artistic type of industry and culture, such as a high-tech software design or graphic art firm. On the other hand, a site with more subdued colors such as white and soft blue or gray might be perceived as a more conservative or traditional organization, perhaps a bank or investment firm.

One of the issues you face in website development is how to address these perceptions when selecting a color scheme for a company website. Which colors are most complementary? How many colors should be present? Background design also plays a role, even after the color scheme has been chosen.

Should you use basic horizontal or vertical lines? Will you include other geometric objects, such as triangles or other polygons? These and other questions must be addressed to best represent the image a company wants to portray to the audience.

Because it's such an important element in the design of a website and can be affected by elements outside your control, there are certain aspects of working with color that you should understand:

- How color is displayed
- Color formats (RGB and hexadecimal code)
- Basic color combinations
- Browser-safe colors
- How to select color combinations
- Color transitions

Color Display

A computer monitor consists of thousands of pixels. A *pixel*, which stands for picture element, is the smallest element that can display on a screen. The screen uses pixels to display text or graphics; each pixel can display only one color at a time. When viewing an image, you see hundreds or thousands of pixels that each have a particular color and combine with the others to create the image you see.

Colors that create black when mixed together are called *subtractive colors*. In print media, all colors are a combination of cyan, magenta, yellow, and black; this color scheme is referred to as CMYK. All colors within the spectrum can be created by combining percentages of cyan, magenta, yellow, or black. Adding more of any of the these colors to the mix results in the movement of the color toward black. For example, 100% cyan, 100% yellow, 100% magenta, and 100% black results in black.

Colors that create white when mixed together are referred to as *additive colors*; this color scheme consists of red, green, and blue and is called RGB. The computer monitor displays additive colors. All colors within the spectrum can be created by combing percentages of red, green, and blue. Adding more of any of the RGB colors to the mix results in the movement of the color toward white. For example, 100% red, 100% green, and 100% blue results in white.

Color Formats

Colors are standardized in two numeric formats:

- Red, green and blue values (RGB)
- Hexadecimal code

To comply with strict HTML, a website designer should use hexadecimal values exclusively; however, for the purpose of this discussion, we will consider the use of both.

Both RGB and hexadecimal colors can produce any color in the visible spectrum when combined in various proportions. These color formats are each capable of displaying 16,777,216 colors (256 times 256 times 256). The number 256 is used in this equation because values of the colors range from 0 to 255, which equals 256.

RGB

RGB values are formatted in base-10 numbers ranging from 0 to 255. Base 10 refers to the use of the digits 0 through 9 in the decimal system; when the digit 1 is reached, the value increases from 0 to 1 (the next whole number), and so forth. Using the RGB scheme, the color white is stated as follows:

R=255

G=255

B=255

Thus, the RGB value for white is 255,255,255, which represents the maximum presence of red, green, and blue.

The RGB value for the color green is stated as follows:

R=0

G=255

B=0

Thus, the RGB value for green is 0,255,0, which represents no presence of red, maximum presence of green, and no presence of blue.

You can declare the RGB value for green in HTML code as follows:

```
<BODY BGCOLOR="0,255,0">
```

RGB color format is a 24-bit coloring scheme that forms 1 byte (8 bits) for each RGB value:

8 bits (red)+8 bits (green)+8 bits (blue)=24 bits

For a complete listing of RGB colors and their corresponding hexadecimal values, visit www.lynda.com/hexh.html. This listing is provided by Lynda Weinman of the Ojai Digital Arts Center.

Hexadecimal Code

Hexadecimal code values range from 00 to FF (0, 1, 2, 3, 4, 5, 6, 7, 8, 9, A, B, C, D, E, F). The hex code uses base-16 numbers. It is similar to the RGB color scheme in that the lowest value (00) represents no presence of a color and the highest value (FF) represents maximum presence of a color.

The color white is represented in hexadecimal code as follows:

Red=FF

Green=FF

Blue=FF

These values represent maximum presence of red, green, and blue.

The color green is represented in hexadecimal code as follows:

Red=00

Green=FF

Blue=00

These values represent no presence of red, maximum presence of green, and no presence of blue.

Thus, hex code assigns each color a two-character code for each red, green, and blue value, whereas the RGB scheme uses digits from 0 to 255 for each red, green, and blue value. Table 1.2 shows some examples.

When hex-code values are used in HTML, they are preceded by the # symbol, which is not required but is part of the HTML 4.0 specification. In the <BODY> tag, for example, the background color green is specified as follows:

```
<BODY BGCOLOR="#00FF00">
```

Netscape 4.x has difficulty with the quotation marks (" ") around the attribute value. Remove the quotation marks when using hex-code values in the header section's <STYLE> tag.

TABLE 1.2 RGB and Hexadecimal Code Value Examples

Color	RGB	Hex Code
RED	255,0,0	FF0000
GREEN	0,255,0	00FF00
BLUE	0,0,255	0000FF
WHITE	255,255,255	FFFFFF
BLACK	0,0,0	000000

Basic Color Combinations

To display color, a computer monitor uses three electron guns. Each gun is responsible for a single color: red, green, or blue. Various combinations of guns and intensities of electron streams form all the colors.

The simultaneous full-intensity firing of these guns produces white on the screen. Firing the red and green guns produces yellow. Firing the green and blue guns produces cyan. The combination of red and blue produces magenta. Figure 1.11 illustrates these color combinations and the relationships between them.

FIGURE 1.11 Basic color combinations

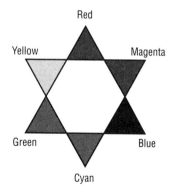

Several inconsistencies exist among monitor displays. These variables include monitor type and design, graphics cards, computer configurations, and even ambient room lighting.

Browser-Safe Colors

Although any of the RGB and hexadecimal code values can be used to specify colors, it is important to remember that both Netscape Navigator and Microsoft Internet Explorer guarantee only 216 colors. Each browser has a maximum of 256 colors it can display, and 40 of those colors are used by the operating system. This leaves 216 colors that can be guaranteed; all other colors will dither. *Dithering* is the process by which the browser approximates a color to the closest browser-safe color it supports. Table 1.3 lists the RGB and hexadecimal values that will render safely in multiple browsers. If values other than these are used, the browser will dither them to the nearest values it can determine.

TABLE 1.3   Browser-Safe Color Palette

RGB	Hex
0	00
51	33
102	66
153	99
204	CC
255	FF

Each of the RGB values in Table 1.3 corresponds to the matching hex-code value. For example, using a value of 51 in RGB is the same as using the value of 33 in hexadecimal code. In other words, an RGB value of 51,153,204 is the same as the hexadecimal value of #3399CC.

Using any combination of these values will result in a browser-safe color that will render consistently across platforms.

The intensity of each red, green, and blue combination determines the color to be displayed. Table 1.4 represents the intensity in percentages for each of the browser-safe color values, from least to greatest.

TABLE 1.4 Browser-Safe Color Intensities

Hex	Intensity in Percentage	RGB
00	0%	0
33	20%	51
66	40%	102
99	60%	153
CC	80%	204
FF	100%	255

A complete listing of browser-safe RGB and hex colors and their respective RGB and hexadecimal values can be found at www.lynda.com/hexh.html.

Color Combination Selection

Color combinations should complement each other, but more important, they should allow the user to easily discern and read any text that resides on the page. Some designers believe that black text on a white background is ideal. The reasoning is that this combination offers the highest contrast and readability and is most comfortable for users because it matches most of the text they read in other media. Usability studies show that this reasoning is accurate.

Most situations allow for the use of this black-text-on-white-background scheme, and it should be used whenever possible. Many sites have colors that represent the company, or branding colors, which will not always conform to the black-on-white scheme. Categorically, the only place that a site can venture away from black and white without compromising usability would be on the site's home page. Beyond the home page, content becomes more abundant, and the site should aim to make the user feel comfortable. Business or branding colors can be used in other page elements, such as images and borders, to give the desired look and feel.

Color Transitions

Color transitions are created when adjacently placed colors blend together or stand apart from each other. Color transitions are especially noticeable between text and background colors and can be used to help separate various parts of a web page. Transitions become more of an issue, however, when colors are introduced to the page in images. Although smooth color transitions are desirable in images, they require higher color support, which in turn requires longer download times.

Fonts and Web Design

The two fonts that have been used most often on the Web are Times New Roman (the PC equivalent of Times on the Macintosh) and Arial (the PC equivalent of Helvetica on the Macintosh). These fonts give a site a clear, attractive presence. If you have used the Web for some time, you probably don't even notice them because they are so commonly used.

However, technologies such as dynamic and embedded fonts are rapidly emerging to offer more choices. On occasion, you may see a site with a unique font that catches your eye simply because it is not widely used. Your reaction will be largely determined by how effectively the font has been used. Font usage can add interest to your web pages and can indicate to the user when transitions are made or emphasize portions of text or the page.

To use fonts effectively, you need to understand some basic things about typography, such as how serif and sans-serif fonts are used, how font size affects the presentation of your page, what a TrueType font is, how anti-aliasing affects the look of fonts, and how much type to put on the page.

One of the limitations of font usage is that the chosen font must be registered on the user's system to be rendered in the browser. If the user does not have the font, the browser will render its default font instead (typically Times New Roman on a PC and Times on a Mac). If you intend to use an obscure font, the source of the font should be made available to users so they can download it and install it on their systems. This way, you can ensure that the user has the browsing experience you intended.

Typography

Because fonts are a necessary component to any site, choose a font and color that make a visual statement along with the other elements of the page. Too much text can be overwhelming, distracting, or tedious. The font you choose and how it's laid out on the document send a clear message to users, even if they take only a quick glance. It usually signals a well-thought-out site that will be easy to view and navigate.

Serif Fonts

Serifs are the small decorative strokes added to the ends of a letter's main strokes, as shown in Figure 1.12. Times New Roman is an example of a *serif font*.

FIGURE 1.12   Letters with serifs

Serifs improve readability by leading the eye along the line of type. However, they are more difficult to read in small scale (smaller than 8 point) and very large sizes. Therefore, serif fonts are best suited for body text.

There are four types of serifs: Old Style, Transitional, Modern, and Slab Serif.

Sans-Serif Fonts

Sans-serif fonts do not have serifs, as shown in Figure 1.13. Arial is an example of a *sans-serif font*.

FIGURE 1.13 Sans-serif letters

The letters' appearance is reduced to the essential strokes. Sans-serif text must be read letter by letter. It is recommended that you use sans-serif fonts for small (smaller than 8 point) text such as footnotes and very large-scale text such as headlines. Generally, one serif font (used for body text) and one sans-serif font provide a good mixture on a web page.

Once you have selected a font for a certain element, it should be used consistently throughout the site. More than one font can be present in the site, but the same font should represent data or information of the same type. For example, all navigation text should look the same, and normal text within paragraphs should look the same. But text that needs to be differentiated from other text, such as numbers or facts, can be presented in a different font. Avoid using a lot of different fonts within a page, however, because it tends to make the page busy and difficult to read. Font colors should also be consistent so the user can easily determine what different text and colors represent.

Font Size

The default font size for most browsers is "size = 3" for the base font size. All other font sizes should be determined by the default size. For example, if you want to increase a font size to size = 5, you must code the font tag to read <FONT SIZE = "+2"> rather than <FONT SIZE = "5">. If the browser default is other than size = 3, the browser will still render the font with your original intended ratio.

One common problem involves the difference between how the Macintosh and the PC display fonts. Macs display fonts at 72 dots per inch (dpi), whereas PCs display fonts at 96dpi. This disparity results in the Macintosh displaying the font smaller than the PC does for any given size. If you are designing on a PC and the font looks small, remember that it will look even smaller when displayed on a Mac.

TrueType

Many fonts are known as TrueType, which means they can be rendered in any point-size value without degradation of letter quality. TrueType is a digital technology developed by Apple Computer and now used by both Apple and Microsoft operating systems. Times New Roman is a TrueType font, as is Arial. Some relatively new TrueType fonts appearing more frequently are Verdana and Georgia. These fonts render nicely and give the page a richer look.

Anti-Aliasing

The *anti-aliasing* process maintains rich-looking letters that do not have jagged edges. Often, graphics are used to represent letters, words, or sentences. The anti-aliasing process makes the text look smooth by blurring the lines between text and background. This removes the harsh, jagged edges of the letters, which is especially noticeable with large fonts. One drawback to anti-aliasing is that it adds more colors to the image, resulting in large file sizes and longer downloading. Figure 1.14 shows an example of normal text next to text that has had the anti-aliasing process applied.

FIGURE 1.14 Plain text next to anti-aliased text

Horizontal Line Length

To make reading easy, avoid long lines of text that span the entire browser window. It is difficult to read line after line, returning to the left margin each time, if the lines are long. It is advisable to keep the lines in your paragraphs no more than 10 to 12 words long for normal reading and browsing.

Other Considerations

To find the best font to fulfill your purpose and match your general concept, you need to recognize a font's scope for variation and its range of expression. For example, does the font choice allow for italic and bold variations? You must use all techniques and materials in the best ways. The following recommendations can help you avoid common mistakes, and you will develop a personal style over time:

- Always consider how an individual font fits into your web page and how the font relates to the whole design. Do not use different fonts simply for the sake of using multiple fonts on a web page. Make sure that your chosen font flows with the overall design of the page and the site as a whole. For example, you would not use Comic Sans MS (a light-hearted, childlike font) to convey important information (such as a warning message) to a user.

- No single font can serve all purposes at once.

- Design elements such as margins, line spacing, background color, and foreground color all help determine the end result. Even a relatively neutral typeface such as a sans serif can produce a rich variety in the look and feel of your website simply through different arrangements.

Netscape Fonts

For Netscape, the Bitstream TrueDoc software development kit (SDK) records character shapes used in a page and stores them in a compressed file called a portable font resource (PFR) file. You can reference this PFR file in an HTML page or style sheet document. When the page is viewed in a browser that supports TrueDoc, the browser reads the PFR and re-creates the characters. In essence, with TrueDoc the characters used in the original document accompany that document almost anywhere. For more information on TrueDoc, follow the Font Technology link at Bitstream's site (`www.bitstream.com`).

Microsoft Fonts

The Microsoft web-font initiative is called OpenType (`www.microsoft.com/typography`), and it is a joint effort between Microsoft and Adobe Systems. From a web perspective, OpenType works like TrueDoc in that it enables character shapes to travel with a document in a compressed form. However, OpenType is a broader initiative that merges the TrueType and PostScript Type 1 font formats into a single format. It is currently in the press release/technical background stage.

Microsoft Fonts vs. Netscape Fonts

Although TrueDoc and OpenType are competing technologies, they will be able to coexist—on the same computer as well as the same web page. You will be able to make any font you choose appear on your pages whether visitors have it installed in their systems or not.

This capability is possible if visitors are using browsers that support these technologies. As always, some users have older, less-capable browsers, and as a website developer, you must balance your desire for font fidelity against the need to reach the broadest audience. Therefore, you must work harder to create pages that look good regardless of the browser used to view them. Throughout this book, we will discuss how web pages can look different in the various versions of browsers as well as between the major browsers, Internet Explorer and Netscape.

Summary

In this chapter, you were introduced to the concepts of web technology and the use of design principles in creating an attractive and usable site. It's important to keep in mind the differences between designing for traditional media and designing for the web as well as the importance of understanding and addressing the users' needs. The web is a nonlinear, one-to-one medium as opposed to more traditional forms of media, which are linear and broadcast in nature.

There are tools available—such as Microsoft FrontPage and Macromedia Dreamweaver—to help you create dynamic, interactive websites that will address the needs of the user. And throughout this book you'll learn about new technologies such as DHTML, CSS, XML, JavaScript, and Java applets.

You need to understand the elements of web page design so you can use them to your advantage. Color plays a vital role in the perception and presentation of a website. Because it's such an important element in the design of a website, there are certain aspects of working with color that you should understand, such as how it's displayed and how to use RGB and hexadecimal values to specify color. Fonts are also an important element in page design. To use them effectively, you should understand some of the basic rules of typography. For example, serif fonts are best used in body text and sans-serif fonts are best for headlines. Finally, you can use white space, tables, and frames to position elements on a page.

Exam Essentials

Know the relationship between web technology and design concepts. Web design benefits from technology not found in traditional media, such as the ability to use hyperlinks to access topics of interest. On the Web, companies cannot use the same forms of information presentation, such as the brochure or catalog, in the manner they were originally designed. Because website users can follow hyperlinks to get to areas of interest, information must be presented in a manner that works with the nonlinear nature of the Web.

Understand the current direction and application of web technology and design. Web technology and design are moving in the direction of the user experience. The Web is interactive, which allows users to have a personalized experience, unlike the one they encounter with traditional forms of media. For the exam, you should understand how and why web technology and design are changing.

Know the differences between tools and technology. Tools such as Macromedia Dreamweaver and Flash and Microsoft FrontPage allow website designers to use new technologies, such as DHTML, CSS, JavaScript, and Java applets, with ease and effectiveness to create dynamic, interactive websites.

Know common page layout formats. There are several common page layout formats used on the Web: left-margin layout (the traditional layout format), top-margin layout, distributed left- and top-margin layout, right-margin layout, and distributed layout. Know what the advantages of using each one are.

Understand layout elements and their usage. There are numerous elements you can use on your pages to aid navigation and make the site easy for the reader to use. Identify certain page elements such as framesets, margins, borders, and so on, and know how you can use them to create effective pages.

Know how color can be used to convey a company's culture and industry. The element of color plays a vital role in the perception and presentation of a website. Color is perceived as a representation of the type of culture and industry in which a company participates. Know what types of messages certain color combinations can convey.

Be able to describe color in numeric formats.   Colors are standardized in two numeric formats: RBG and hexadecimal code. Both RGB and hexadecimal colors can produce any color in the visible spectrum when combined in various proportions.

Understand how to choose fonts for a website.   Font choice is an important element of website design. Commonly used fonts such as Times New Roman, Times, Arial, and Helvetica give a site a clear, attractive look and feel because most browsers use these fonts as their default font choice. Unique fonts are eye-catching but cannot be rendered in a user's browser as the default font if the browser does not have the font installed in its system.

Know the importance of white space on a web page.   White space is essential to website design because it distributes content and reduces clutter on a page. Your understanding of the use of white space will aid in the flow of your website and not distract visitors with cluttered pages.

Key Terms

Before you take the exam, be certain you are familiar with the following terms:

additive colors	lowest common denominator
anti-aliasing	nonlinear
broadcast medium	one-to-one medium
Cascading Style Sheets (CSS)	pixel
dithering	sans-serif font
Dynamic HTML (DHTML)	serif font
Extensible Markup Language (XML)	subtractive colors
extranets	transactions
intranets	transparent GIFs
linear	white space

Review Questions

1. Before website design practices evolved, early sites resembled HTML versions of what?

   A. Maps

   B. Newspapers

   C. Brochures

   D. Television ads

2. The Internet is which type of medium?

   A. Broadcast

   B. One-to-one

   C. Electronic print

   D. Broadband

3. Which of the following terms describe the nature of the Internet?

   A. Transactional

   B. Linear

   C. Passive

   D. Self-reflective

4. Advances in technology have provided sophisticated tools that website designers can use to create and manage websites. From today's development perspective, which is the best option for creating a dynamic site?

   A. Manual HTML coding

   B. WYSIWYG tool

   C. A combination of manual coding and WYSIWYG functionality

   D. One method or the other depending on the site, but not both

5. What does WYSIWYG stand for?

  A. What You See Is What You Get

  B. When You See It Where You Go

  C. Why You See It What You Get

  D. When You See Is While You Get

6. You are designing a website for a general public audience. Which of the following guidelines should you follow?

  A. Create a very dynamic site using high-end software.

  B. Use the newest multimedia and plug-ins available.

  C. Design for the lowest common denominator of hardware.

  D. Design for the most recent browsers but slower modems.

7. The most effective Web page layout scheme can best be compared to which of the following media types?

  A. A magazine

  B. A newspaper

  C. A television newscast

  D. A brochure

8. Which of the following basic elements of web page layout is used to control the user's movement through the site?

  A. Frameset

  B. Table

  C. Image

  D. Navigation

9. Which layout format is the most commonly used on the Web?

    A. Left-margin layout

    B. Top-margin layout

    C. Left- and top-margin layout

    D. Right-margin layout

10. Users perceive color on a website as a representation of a company's culture or industry. Which of the following color schemes would best convey a conservative law firm's style on its website?

    A. Several bright colors on a dark background

    B. Red and white text on a black background

    C. Pinks, yellows, and reds

    D. White, blues, and grays

11. Which of the following best describes the benefit a business gives the consumer by having a website available for use?

    A. Temporary access to assistance in learning and decision-making

    B. Immediate access to assistance in learning and decision-making

    C. Person-to-person assistance 24 hours a day

    D. Free service and support for all business problems

12. True or False. The concepts and applications of mass media are valid for the Internet.

    A. True

    B. False

13. After e-commerce, what has made up the second largest growth area in web development?

   A. Intranet

   B. Personal websites

   C. Information-only websites

   D. Chat sites

14. What use of the Internet is rapidly emerging to fulfill data requirements outside the company and streamline the business process for outside vendors and business partners?

   A. Outranets

   B. Intranets

   C. Extranets

   D. Exteriornets

15. True or False. The Internet is a static medium; therefore, rules and concepts are at a constant standstill.

   A. True

   B. False

16. What is the primary goal a website designer is looking to fulfill when creating any website?

   A. To dazzle the user with a multimedia experience

   B. To encourage buying with good design

   C. To have as much information as possible on the home page

   D. To give the user what they want, not what you think they want

17. The web medium can optimize the possibilities of _____ for users, creating a direct connection between the business and visitor?

    A. Interconnectivity

    B. Speed of connection

    C. Interactivity and personalization

    D. Multimedia

18. Why is manual coding HTML alone not the best choice for the development of websites?

    A. It is too time-consuming.

    B. It doesn't support enough features.

    C. HTML coding is out-of-date.

    D. HTML coding cannot be used for website development.

19. How much text of a web page does the majority of web users actually read?

    A. Eighty percent

    B. Most of the website's home page

    C. Close to none; most users only scan a web page

    D. Fifty percent

20. Which of the following best describes what page layout refers to?

    A. How much text is on each page

    B. How many pages make up the website

    C. How the tree structure of pages making up the website is designed

    D. How the website designer presents information to the users

Answers to Review Questions

1. C. Many companies duplicated their print advertising on the Web.

2. B. Users of websites respond better to information and product offerings that are tailored to their specific needs. By nature, the Internet is a medium that enables the user to decide what information to access and when to access it. This fact makes the Internet a one-to-one medium as opposed to a broadcast medium.

3. A. The entire Internet experience is based on user requests and server responses (transactions).

4. C. It takes too much time to create a dynamic site by only manually coding HTML. Using a WYSIWYG will allow you to make changes quickly and easily. A combination of manual coding of HTML and using a WYSIWYG tool will give the greatest control over a creating a dynamic site.

5. A. WYSIWYG stands for What You See Is What You Get. WYSIWYGs tools are tools that allow website designers to see what the page looks like as it is being designed. Designers do not need to know HTML to use a WYSIWYG program.

6. C. To ensure that the highest number of users can view your website using the hardware they commonly use, developers should design their sites for the lowest common denominator of hardware.

7. B. The most effective Web page layout scheme is compared to a newspaper; it is often called an inverted pyramid because summaries of stories are listed first.

8. D. Navigation is used to control the user's movement through the website. You should follow commonly used practices for navigation, such as placing navigation elements on the left and top margins of the page and using a different color background for them.

9. C. The left- and top-margin layout, also referred to as a distributed layout, is the most commonly used layout in website design. Navigation elements commonly are placed at the top and left side of a Web page with additional navigation elements at the bottom.

10. **D.** Color is perceived as a representation of the type of culture and industry in which a company participates. White, blues, and grays convey a more conservative culture or industry than would pinks, yellows, or reds, for example.

11. **B.** By having a website available to customers, a business is providing them with immediate access to assistance in learning and decision-making. Web addresses are now included in most businesses' radio, television, and print ads. This assistance is not limited by a time frame, but it is also not a person-to-person experience, so options A and C are incorrect. Having a website does not provide free service and support to all business problems either.

12. **B.** The concepts and applications of mass media are not necessarily valid for the Internet. The Internet is a medium that enables the user to decide what information to access and when to access it. Mass media is mostly passive. Its goal is to create in the viewer or reader interest that eventually will lead to a desired transaction.

13. **A.** After e-commerce, the intranet has been the second-largest growth area in web development. As data-driven content becomes more common, companies and industries are more often putting their in-house business processes on the Web for their employees to access. The result is a more efficient and productive work environment because employees have easy access to frequently used data and documents.

14. **C.** For outside vendors and business partners, extranets are rapidly emerging to fulfill data requirements outside the company and streamline the business process. Extranets give partner companies access to business information that can be used to first see a need and then supply needed parts or materials without a request from the other company.

15. **B.** The Internet is not a static medium like print media. Therefore, the rules and concepts are in constant fluctuation.

16. D. The primary goal in website design is to give users what they want, not what you think they want. This goal can be achieved with a complex balance of well-planned design, quality content, and proper use of available media. As a website designer, you want users to have a satisfying experience, but dazzling them is not your goal. Cramming lots of information on the home page is a bad idea and may turn users away from your site. Not all sites are merchant sites that will be looking to sell products.

17. C. The web medium can optimize the possibilities of interactivity and personalization for the user, creating a direct connection between the business and the visitor. This is accomplished through the new technologies, such as Dynamic HTML (DHTML), Cascading Style Sheets (CSS), Extensible Markup Language (XML), JavaScript, and Java applets.

18. A. It simply takes too much time to develop a dynamic site by only manually coding HTML. A combination of manual coding and WYSIWYG functionality is the best option from today's development perspective. The need for constantly updated information and design on both a corporate website and an intranet or extranet site necessitates an alliance between the two methods of site design.

19. C. The majority of users read almost none of the text on a web page. Numerous surveys confirm that as many as 80 percent of web users merely scan web page content, looking for key words and phrases. As a designer, you must create a page that allows users to quickly scan and find the information they seek.

20. D. Page layout refers to the way in which the website designer presents information to users. The format should be logical and easy to understand. As a website designer, you must develop a structure and adhere to it so the user's experience will be meaningful and productive.

Chapter 2

Navigation Concepts

THE CIW EXAM OBJECTIVE GROUP COVERED IN THIS CHAPTER:

✓ Develop effective and usable corporate websites within a reasonable time frame, including but not limited to: navigation conventions and file structure hierarchy.

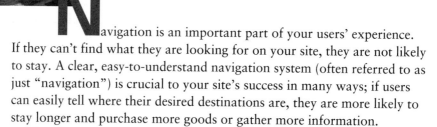

avigation is an important part of your users' experience. If they can't find what they are looking for on your site, they are not likely to stay. A clear, easy-to-understand navigation system (often referred to as just "navigation") is crucial to your site's success in many ways; if users can easily tell where their desired destinations are, they are more likely to stay longer and purchase more goods or gather more information.

This chapter explores the crucial elements of effective navigation: the browsers' role in navigation, navigation hierarchy, the different types of navigation, how your site structure factors into navigation, and familiar navigation conventions.

Why Is Navigation Critical?

Designing the navigation system of a website is often left to chance. When creating a website, you generally start with one page; then you create links as you add other pages. However, if you do not give some thought as to how users will navigate your pages, the result will be confusion and frustration. Navigation is not simply moving from one location to another; it is moving from one point to another with a purpose or goal in mind. Without planning on your part, the user will often end up aimlessly browsing instead of successfully navigating your site.

When you drive your car, you navigate to your destination: the store or work, for example. The first time you made the journey, you weren't sure how to get to your destination. The second time, it was much easier because you were familiar with the roads and signs along the way. Now you probably make the trip without even thinking about where to turn or which freeway to use. You are comfortable because you do not feel confused and you know where you are at all times.

Now, think about traveling in a new city. How do you feel? The uncertainty of where you are and how you will navigate to your destination resurfaces. Contributing to the confusion are different types of road signs, streetlights, and freeway structures. You feel out of your element because what you see is new. New users have this same feeling when visiting your website. They are "tourists" and do not know where to go when they arrive at the home page.

As a website designer, it is your duty to provide clear navigation so users can simply enjoy the ride. Once they become familiar with the site, users will recognize where they are going and how to get there. The learning curve doesn't need to take days, weeks, or hundreds of visits, though; if your site is well designed, your users should understand your navigation system after only a few clicks.

Browsers and Navigation

Most web browser architectures are developed with the following layers of functionality:

Internet access layer   Includes the protocols for communicating with remote websites, ranging from HTTP to various encryption types such as Secure Sockets Layer (SSL).

Navigation layer   Keeps track of where users have been on the Web and helps them go where they want to go. This layer can include a history list, which includes the sites they have visited.

Presentation layer   Displays the page the user has requested through the browser window.

Each browser has unique components that help the user navigate, but all browsers have some common user features:

- Toolbar Back button
- Toolbar Forward button
- URL address field
- URL drop-down menu
- History list
- Bookmarks or Favorites
- Status bar

A common practice is to rely on only these elements for site navigation. Some designers create dead-end pages, requiring users to click the Back button and return to the previous page to continue browsing. The user should never be forced to use the Back button in response to being trapped. Other designers change the default link colors, further confusing users, making it harder for them to tell where they have been. Although elements such as changing link colors are designed to assist the user, they should be a secondary element of navigation.

Primary and Secondary Navigation

Navigation elements are commonly classified as either primary or secondary in nature. *Primary navigation elements* are accessible from most locations within the site. *Secondary navigation elements* allow the user to navigate within a specific location. For example, many sites have a page that offers information about the company. The primary navigation element may be an About Us link. Once the user arrives on the About Us page, there will be other links (secondary navigation elements) they can use to navigate within the About Us page. For example, there may be links to investor information, corporate locations, press releases, and so forth. These links are secondary navigation elements because they are relevant to the About Us page but not to other pages of the site and therefore will not be found in other areas of the site.

Navigation Hierarchy

The most dynamic aspect of the Web is that any page on any site is only one click away. This feature removes the limitations you must follow in a linear world. Most activities you normally engage in—reading, working, driving—follow a linear model. You start at the beginning, move through the task, and reach the end. This mindset contributes to many website design practices that limit the Web's usefulness.

Your place of work uses a hierarchy or organizational chart to visually define the dynamics of the organization. Your home may have an organizational structure as well: the parents are at the top and the children are layered below. This concept clearly describes how a family or business operates. A website is no different. At the top is the home page or site entrance; below are the other pages, which are referred to as *child pages*. The site does not follow a linear model; it branches out and grows to various depths, depending on how much content each branch supports. This structure is known as the information architecture of the site.

The hierarchy of the site should be immediately apparent to users regardless of where they are in your site. Positional awareness, navigation depth, icons, controls, and elements inside and outside the browser give the user an indication of where they have been and where they can go in your website. These elements all assist the user in navigating through your website successfully. In the following sections, we'll look at each in more depth.

Positional Awareness

For users to understand your site, they need to understand its organizational chart or architecture. Users should never wonder where they are within the site. At all times, there should be indicators that users can reference for positional awareness. *Positional awareness* includes understanding where any parent, peer, or child pages are relative to the current location. Many techniques can be used to provide the user with this important information, including the following:

Headings   Current page headings provide an effective means for users to determine where they are within the site. A limitation of using only headings for positional awareness is that they provide only the current location, not the relative location of parent, peer, or child pages.

Colors   Some sites use colors to indicate position by applying different color values to different content. One limitation of using colors is that the users must first understand the color scheme and then associate it as they move through the site. Another drawback is the ineffectiveness of this strategy for visually impaired users.

Images   Images provide useful indicators of positional awareness. For example, on Amazon's site, there is a file folder structure at the top of the page that is used for navigation. You can always tell which page you're on because the tab for the page is highlighted. This scheme provides better positional awareness because many peer and parent pages are visible from any given location.

Bread crumbs   Symbols such as arrows or lines that indicate the navigational path that the user took to arrive at the current location are called *bread crumbs*. They are helpful as the user moves through multiple pages on many levels of the site.

Site map   A *site map* is a graphical representation of a website's hierarchy. The site map exists in a separate HTML document in which each page of your site can be represented by a simple text or graphical description. Users can then follow links from the site map to the desired page. The disadvantage is that users must leave their current location to visit the site map.

Navigation Depth, Icons, and Controls

Once they find your website, users should not have to click more than three times to find the information they seek, depending on your website's purpose. This is referred to as the *three-click rule* for managing user access to linked files. This guideline is especially important for informational or research-oriented websites.

A clear sense of direction is very important to the user. Unclear navigational paths will confuse users and discourage them from returning to the site. You should also consider whether any particular multimedia elements will provide the navigational framework for the site or merely supplement it. For example, using a Macromedia Flash navigation bar on your site will present navigational problems for users who cannot support Flash. Navigation toolbars should be simple, easily understood, and intuitive. The following image shows one example.

Icons are very popular and most people are familiar with them. Although there are two types of icons—labeled and unlabeled—they should be labeled; users should not have to guess where the icon link will take them. The following image shows examples of labeled icons.

Other common navigation elements include (but are not limited to):

- Buttons
- Image maps and hot spots
- Rollover mouse events
- Arrows
- Navigation bars and menus
- Drop-down select menus

Beyond the Browser

Browsers provide limited navigational support. Therefore, you should design your website with an extensive navigation system to help users overcome the limitations of their software. Consider some of the following elements when planning your navigation system:

Site identifiers Include a site identifier on every page to let users know where they are. A corporate logo is often placed in the upper-left corner of the screen for this purpose (upper-right corner for sites in languages that read right to left).

Landmark page access Make it easy to get to landmark pages. Every page should be linked to the home page (typically by hyperlinking the logo) and the search page.

Browser history Do not use <META> tags or scripts to prevent access to the history list of the browser. Some sites use the <META> tag to automatically refresh pages in an effort to prevent users from going back to previously visited pages. This strategy is considered poor design.

Information architecture Emphasize the structure of your site—its information architecture. Make every page show structural elements, and include links to the overview page or main pages at least one level up in the structure from the current page. Such links should not have generic names such as "Go Up One Level" but should be specific and name the level to which they point.

Link colors Do not change the default link colors if possible. Links to unvisited pages should be some shade of blue; links to previously visited pages should be some shade of magenta. Using the default colors helps users know which pages they have already seen. Users can form a mental picture of the site when they can relate its structure to their personal navigation history.

Site map   Include a site map that shows the most important levels of your information structure and how different parts of the site relate to each other and to the site's structure.

Site Structure

Websites are structured in a hierarchical format. The format provides the information a browser needs to find a given web page using a *Uniform Resource Locator (URL)*, which is a text string that supplies an Internet or intranet address and the protocol by which that site can be accessed: `http://www.usatoday.com`, for example.

Site structure describes how a website is stored on the web server. You can think of files residing on the server just as they do on your PC. The primary drive is normally C: followed by directories, as in `C:\Program Files`, `C:\Windows`, `C:\My Documents`, and so forth. Each directory is further divided into subdirectories. This arrangement creates a file hierarchy that helps you manage your system.

When a user enters `http://www.company.com` in the browser address field, they access the web root directory. This path can be compared to the root of your C: drive. Beyond that, the structure is determined by how the files were named and uploaded to the server.

The web server also stores files and images in directories that you designate. It is recommended that you organize files on the server into directories and subdirectories to maintain order and manageability. Imagine all the files on your PC residing in one directory; this structure would be very difficult to manage.

Figure 2.1 shows a sample site directory structure. When expanded, the directory structure might resemble Figure 2.2.

Notice that each folder resides under the root and each has a subdirectory into which images can be placed. It is good practice to keep files of similar types in their own directories for better organization. This structure could be further expanded. For example, subdirectories of `Marketing` might include New Products, Sale Products, or Discontinued Products. The point is that however you choose to organize your site architecture, use a method that is meaningful and easy for others to understand.

FIGURE 2.1 Sample company website directory structure

FIGURE 2.2 Expanded directory structure

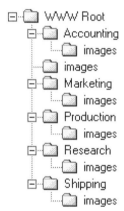

URLs

URLs can be used to determine location and depth. For example, a user who is unsure where they are in the site hierarchy could look at the URL in the browser window to help visualize their location. Consider how the following URL can indicate a user's current location:

http://www.companyname.com/marketing/newproducts/pricing

This URL indicates that the user is in the pricing portion of the new products area of the marketing section of the companyname.com website. This technique only works if the directories were given meaningful names. Once again, it is important to name files on the web server descriptively to aid in navigation and organization.

Filenames

Filenames play an important part in web page addressing. Together, filenames and URLs help give web users a better understanding of a website's structure. Filenames can be as helpful as directory names. If the name of the HTML file confirms to the user which page they are viewing, it helps in the process of navigation and awareness. For example, the following URL and filename (`Quarter2.htm`) tell the user exactly which page is being viewed:

`http://www.companyname.com/financials/`**`Quarter2.htm`**

As with directories, give your HTML files meaningful names.

Familiar Navigation Conventions

The type of site navigation you choose need not be unique to your site. In fact, it is advantageous for it to be similar to other sites. Many common elements used throughout the World Wide Web have become familiar to users and therefore have predefined meanings.

Some of these elements are labeled to give users a clear idea of what they lead to. For example, when users see a button or link labeled Home Page, they know that link will take them back to the first page of the site. Do not use a clever label such as Entry Point for a link to the home page; Entry Point may mean different things to different people. Remember that visitors are "tourists" and you should try to make them feel as if they are still in their own neighborhood.

In addition, corporate logos and branding images should be linked to the home page. Users have come to expect this link. A Search (or Find) link, which links users to a page through which they can conduct a site search, is another common element. Links or buttons that are labeled FAQ (or Frequently Asked Questions), Downloads, News, Site Map, About Us, Contact Us, and Help are all common as well. Do not try to be unique; it is wise to use familiar labels because users expect them.

Guided Navigation

Another popular technique for helping users through a convoluted process is to guide them. Provide a link to the next step, and continue by establishing links that keep users on track. These links should supply the necessary information, as well as an alternate course clearly marked to allow the user to exit. For example, to make an online purchase, the user should be led to pages with shipping information, then payment information, then receipt information. If you use a graphical interface, it must be intuitive. The audience must be able to navigate easily through the site and recognize which elements are clickable.

The Federal Express site (`www.fedex.com`) offers a good example of user-friendly navigation and technological adeptness. It is well organized, functional, and attractive, as shown in Figure 2.3.

FIGURE 2.3   A well-designed site

Navigation Action Plan

Creating a navigation system can be difficult because it is subjective. Designers have different opinions about which strategies work best. This observation is extremely important from a usability perspective. If the site's navigation does not function as it should, you may risk losing customers.

When navigation works well, users flow smoothly from action to action, from page to page. Navigation must be tested; this process takes careful planning.

Consider the following points in your site design:

- Determine goals and needs.

- Learn from navigation that works.

- Go deeper than the home page.

- Provide quick links.

- Expect all users to have different backgrounds.

Determine Goals and Needs

Navigation design is about predicting your site users' actions and building a site to support them. To do this, you must understand your audience's goals and needs.

To determine your users' goals and needs, you must interview the people who will use the site. If your site will be on a company intranet, spend time talking with employees about their daily activities. For a commercial site, talk to potential customers and discuss their preferences. Try to learn what their goals are by listening to their comments. Real solutions must be uncovered, not constructed; talking to your audience and using their input is the fastest way to accomplish this.

Learn from Navigation That Works

Much can be learned from studying sites that are easy to navigate. Consider the elements common to successful navigation, regardless of the approaches used. Those sites that share certain qualities display good navigation planning. Generally, good navigation includes several characteristics:

- Offers easy-to-learn elements
- Remains consistent
- Provides feedback
- Appears in context
- Offers alternatives
- Provides clear visual messages
- Offers clear and understandable labels
- Remains appropriate to the site's purpose
- Supports user goals and behaviors

All these qualities are important, but the concept of providing feedback probably has the biggest impact on users. People should be able to tell where they are and, if possible, where they have been. Users should also be able to easily determine linked or clickable material. They need to know whether they successfully made a purchase, conducted a search, or completed some other task. You can meet these fundamental navigation needs by providing feedback.

Go Deeper than the Home Page

Even on sites with truly poor navigational design, it is usually possible to move from the home page to an interior page without incident. However, planning your home page is only a small fraction of your job as a navigation designer. The deeper you can plan your site's structure and navigation, the more successful your site's navigation will be. The more detailed you are in the early planning phases, the fewer unpleasant surprises your users will encounter.

Most navigation problems have nothing to do with moving from the home page to another page. Problems tend to involve being stranded inside a site. Typically, this happens because great attention has been paid to navigation design, but only in one direction or on the top level.

In navigation design, the details count. Plan out as far as you can, down to the deepest level you can predict. The worst problems usually do not occur on a site's top level.

Provide Quick Links

Once you consider the structure of the site as a whole, spend some time thinking about shortcuts through the structure. Shortcuts provide quick links and easy access to small pieces of content. Some common shortcuts include search features, site maps, and tables of contents.

The goal of shortcuts is to help users find information easily and rapidly. Design your shortcuts with this goal in mind. Many examples of search screens are unusable because they offer a confusing array of options: site maps that take too long to load or tables of contents that require endless scrolling. Shortcuts should by nature be streamlined, brief, fast, and clear. They should also be convenient and close at hand.

Expect All Users to Have Different Backgrounds

An example of how personal preferences affect your approach to navigation can be found in searching and browsing behaviors. Some people like to search for the exact information they need, and they refuse to browse unless forced. Others prefer to browse through information to find what they need. Children, for example, generally respond better to browsing than searching when it comes to finding information.

Navigation design is complex, but it is key to helping your users accomplish their goals. Remember that a navigation system that supports users is vital to the success of your website. For more tips on navigation and design, visit Alertbox at `www.useit.com/alertbox/`.

Summary

Structured navigation is critical to website design. Without a defined system in place that assists users in getting from one page to another in your site, users are browsing aimlessly. Website hierarchy helps users identify where they are in your site. The hierarchy reflects the structure of the site on a web server. Navigational elements such as headings, colors, images, bread crumbs and site maps provide positional awareness to users so that they always know where they are in your website.

The browser also assists in navigation through components such as the toolbar, Back and Forward buttons, the URL address field and drop-down menu, the browser history list, Bookmarks or Favorites, and the status bar. In addition to the navigation you include, these elements help the user successfully navigate through your site. Creating an action plan for the navigation of your website that includes determining the goals and needs of the user, learning from navigation that works, going deeper than the home page, providing quick links, and expecting users to have different backgrounds will help you create a navigation system that assists users in successfully maneuvering around your website.

Exam Essentials

Know why navigation is critical.   Navigation does not simply mean moving from one location to another. It is moving from one point to another with a purpose or goal in mind. Without planning, you will not promote true site navigation, but rather aimless browsing.

Understand how browsers control navigation.   Each browser has unique components that help the user navigate, but all browsers have some common user features. Be familiar with common browser components—the toolbar Back and Forward buttons, the URL address field and drop-down menu, the browser history list, Bookmarks or Favorites, and the status bar—that help users navigate your site.

Understand website hierarchy.   At the top of the hierarchy of a website is the home page or site entrance; below are the other pages, which are referred to as child pages. Websites do not follow a linear model; they branch out and grow to various depths, depending on how much content each branch supports. This structure is known as the information architecture of the site.

Know familiar conventions.   Be sure you understand common navigation elements that users are familiar with and know how to use them to make your site easy to navigate. Using familiar navigation elements will help users efficiently and quickly move through your website. For example, users are familiar with labels such as Home Page, Search or Find, FAQ or Frequently Asked Questions, Downloads, News, Site Map, About Us, Contact Us, and Help.

Be able to apply a navigation action plan. A plan of action will help you to keep the important aspects of your navigation system in mind as you design your site. It will assist you in creating an easy-to-use and effective navigation scheme for your website. When navigation works well, users flow smoothly from action to action and from page to page.

Key Terms

Before you take the exam, be certain you are familiar with the following terms:

bread crumbs	secondary navigation elements
child pages	site map
positional awareness	three-click rule
primary navigation elements	Uniform Resource Locator (URL)

Review Questions

1. What is navigation?

    A. The same as browsing.

    B. Not a critical factor in website design.

    C. Movement from one location to another.

    D. Movement among locations with a purpose or goal in mind.

2. Which of the following is an example of a primary navigation element?

    A. A Back button on a browser

    B. A link to the home page

    C. Links within the About Us page

    D. Colored hyperlinks

3. What is the term for understanding where in the navigational hierarchy any parent, peer, or child page is relative to the current location?

    A. Positional awareness

    B. Organizational chart

    C. Navigational depth

    D. Site structure

4. As a website designer, why should you use familiar navigational conventions in a site?

    A. Because it is advantageous for your site navigation to be different from other sites

    B. Because the familiar conventions are required by the W3C

    C. So you do not waste development time by inventing unique site navigation

    D. Because common elements have predefined meanings and their familiarity makes users comfortable

5. A good navigation action plan includes taking several steps to ensure that users can navigate your site easily. One step involves studying other sites that are easy to navigate. Which of the following is a common characteristic of good navigation?

   A. Each page should be designed differently so users can identify the page topic by its unique design.

   B. Few alternatives should be offered so that users go where you want them to go.

   C. Feedback should be provided so users can see where they are and where they've been and whether they've completed a task.

   D. Visual messages should be artful and abstract so users can guess their meaning and approach the site as a game.

6. Which of the following is *not* a characteristic of good navigation?

   A. Remains consistent

   B. Offers alternative

   C. Supports user goals and behaviors

   D. Provides unique images

7. Which part of the URL `http://www.mysite.com/technical/courses/winter_classes.htm` is the filename?

   A. `www.mysite.com`

   B. `technical`

   C. `courses`

   D. `winter_classes.htm`

8. Susan is navigating a website and comes across symbols such as arrows or lines within the navigational path. What is the term commonly used to refer to these symbols?

   A. Site maps

   B. Bread crumbs

   C. Headings

   D. Images

9. Predicting your audience's actions is crucial to designing a site that meets their goals and needs. What is the best way to do so?

   A. Look at other sites and model yours after sites similar to yours.

   B. Ask friends and relatives what they like best in a site.

   C. Talk to your audience.

   D. Let the marketing department guide you based on what worked best in traditional media campaigns.

10. What is the cause of most navigation problems on a site?

   A. Being stranded inside the site

   B. Moving from the home page to another page within the site

   C. Moving from the shopping cart to the main site

   D. Finding shortcuts

11. Which of the following is a layer used in the architecture of most web browsers?

   A. Home page layer

   B. Start layer

   C. Presentation layer

   D. Site layer

12. True or False. A website designer should place dead-end pages in a website in order to keep the user involved in navigation.

   A. True

   B. False

13. What two terms are commonly used to classify the nature of navigation elements?

   A. Passive and strong

   B. Browser and site

   C. Distinct and faded

   D. Primary and secondary

14. Sarah is designing her website for her business. She plans to have an entrance page, which will then lead to her home page. From there she will create several child pages, which will branch off the home page. What is this website architecture known as?

    A. Information architecture

    B. Child architecture

    C. Page structure

    D. Branch structure

15. What is one common technique used to provide a user with positional awareness?

    A. Page count

    B. Hit count

    C. Headings

    D. A site search engine

16. It is important to design your website with an extensive navigation system to help users overcome the limitations of their software. What is one element that can be used to accomplish this task?

    A. Using generic names for links to main pages

    B. Using site identifiers

    C. Changing the color of hyperlinks

    D. Using <META> tags prevent use of the Back button

17. What determines the site structure of a website?

    A. How it is stored on the web server

    B. In what order the pages were created

    C. What browser the visitor is using

    D. The hardware in use by the host

18. What is a simple way in which to learn how to design a website with easy navigation for the user?

   A. Reading many books on website design

   B. Additional schooling

   C. Studying other sites

   D. Trial and error

19. What is the goal of having shortcuts through the structure of a website?

   A. Keep users at your site

   B. Provide positional awareness

   C. Add a familiar look to a website

   D. Help users find information easily and rapidly

20. What effect should the three-click rule have on the design of website navigation?

   A. It should take a user only three clicks to reach what they are looking for on your website.

   B. It should take the users only three clicks to enter your website.

   C. It should take the user only three clicks to make a purchase on your website.

   D. It should take the user only three clicks to reach a site map.

21. What effect does deeper planning of your website's structure and navigation have overall?

   A. Navigation will be less successful.

   B. Navigation will be more successful.

   C. Users will more often be stranded.

   D. Users will browse your site longer.

Answers to Review Questions

1. D.   Navigation is movement among locations with a purpose or goal in mind. Without planning, you will not promote true site navigation, but rather aimless browsing.

2. B.   Primary navigation elements are accessible from most locations within the site. There is generally a link to the home page on all pages within a well-designed site.

3. A.   Users should never wonder where they are within the site. At all times, there should be indicators that users can reference to give them positional awareness, which is understanding where a parent, peer, or child page is to the current location.

4. D.   The goal of navigation is for users to easily and effectively move through your website. Implementing common elements that are familiar to users allows them to easily locate areas of interest rather than hunt for them.

5. C.   People should know where they are within a site and, if possible, where they have been. They need to know whether they successfully made a purchase, conducted a search, or completed some other task. You can meet these fundamental navigation needs by providing feedback.

6. D.   Good navigation should provide clear visual images that the user does not have to interpret.

7. D.   The filename in the URL is `winter_classes`. You can tell this is the filename because it has a three-letter extension and because it appears at the end of the URL. It appears after `/technical/courses/`, which are subdirectories.

8. B.   Symbols such as arrows or lines within a navigational structure are commonly referred to as bread crumbs. They indicate the navigational path the user took to arrive at the current location.

9. C.   Real solutions must be uncovered, not constructed; talking to your audience and using their input is the fastest way to accomplish this goal.

10. A. Most navigation problems involve being stranded inside the site, not moving from the home page to another page. This commonly happens when great attention has been paid to navigation design from the top level or from one direction.

11. C. The presentation layer is one of the three commonly used layers in web browser architecture. It includes the browser window, which displays the page that the user requested. The remaining two are Internet access and navigation layers.

12. B. Some designers create dead-end pages, requiring users to click on the Back button and return to the previous page to continue browsing. The user should never be forced to use the Back button in response to being trapped.

13. D. Navigation elements are commonly classified as either primary or secondary in nature. Primary navigation elements are accessible from most locations within the site. Secondary navigation elements allow the user to navigate within a specific location.

14. A. This structure is known as the information architecture of the site. The site does not follow a linear model; it branches out and grows to various depths, depending on how much content each branch supports.

15. C. Current page headings provide an effective means for users to determine where they are within the site. A limitation of using only headings for positional awareness is that they provide only the current location, not the relative location of parent, peer, or child pages. Some other examples of commonly used techniques are colors, images, bread crumbs, and site maps.

16. B. Include a site identifier on every page to let users know where they are. A corporate logo is often placed in the upper-left corner of the screen for this purpose. A website designer can also use links to main pages, but you would not want to use generic names for these links. Changing the color of hyperlinks may confuse visitors. Using <META> tags to prevent the use of the Back button or prevent users from viewing history lists is considered poor design.

17. A. Site structure is determined by how a website is stored on the web server. You can think of files residing on the server just as they do on your PC. The primary drive is normally C:, followed by directories, as in `C:\Program Files`, `C:\Windows`, `C:\My Documents`, and so forth. Each directory is further divided into subdirectories. When a user enters `http://www.company.com` in the browser address field, they access the web root directory. This path can be compared to the root of your C: drive. Beyond that, the structure is determined by how the files were named and uploaded to the server.

18. C. Much can be learned from studying sites that are easy to navigate. By using techniques shared by good sites, a new website designer can establish a familiar feel for visitors and simplified navigation.

19. D. The goal of shortcuts is to help users find information easily and rapidly. You should design your shortcuts with this goal in mind. Shortcuts provide quick links and easy access to small pieces of content. Some common shortcuts include search features, site maps, and tables of contents.

20. A. Once they find your website, users should not have to click more than three times to find the information they seek, depending on your website's purpose. This is referred to as the three-click rule for managing user access to linked files. This guideline is especially important for informational or research-oriented websites.

21. B. The deeper you can plan your site's structure and navigation, the more successful your site's navigation will be. The more detailed you are in the early planning phases, the fewer unpleasant surprises your users will encounter. Problems tend to involve being stranded inside a site. Typically, this happens because great attention has been paid to navigation design, but only in one direction or on the top level.

Chapter

3

Web Graphics

THE CIW EXAM OBJECTIVE GROUP COVERED IN THIS CHAPTER:

✓ Create and effectively use graphics in websites.

Images play an important role in website design; they add to a website visual interest that's difficult to achieve with just plain text. You can use images to illustrate important points, reinforce name recognition and branding, and help users navigate through the site.

This chapter will guide you through the most important points of website image design: digital imaging concepts, bitmap vs. vector graphics, graphic applications, image file formats, and image creation and optimization.

Website Images

Images are essential in website design. Users have come to expect a visually pleasing experience that can only be achieved with the use of images. Images can also be used for navigation in the form of image maps and graphical buttons that link to other pages or resources. On a corporate site, the organization's logo and trademarks are crucial for name recognition and branding.

Good web graphics must be aesthetically pleasing and essential to the site. The most important characteristic, though, is that they are small in file size. File size directly affects download time and is a key consideration for the website developer. Download speed is a vital ingredient in the success of any web page. Developers must consider bandwidth requirements for the images used on a page. Although users expect to see images, they become frustrated when waiting for pages to download. A graphic-intensive page can create poor reviews if the content is overwhelmed by a lengthy download time due to image misuse.

If a site will be used as an intranet application over a network, then many hurdles are removed, such as connection speed outside of the network. At the same time, remember that an intranet application serves a different purpose than an Internet application. A site on the Internet is for public use and presents the organization to the outside world. Accessing it should not be a frustrating experience. An intranet is meant to provide quick and easy access to information and resources, usually for employees of company. If an intranet application is too graphical and flashy, it can reduce worker productivity. You can think of an intranet as function oriented and the Internet as presentation oriented.

Graphics illustrate content, provide backdrops for other activities, and offer a means for navigating a website. In the following sections, we'll discuss the concepts that are important to web graphic artists and what you need to know to use graphics effectively on your site.

Digital Imaging Concepts

Digital images are those produced for an electronic format such as the Internet. All digital images have certain attributes that can drastically affect quality and file size. Among the most important are pixels, color depth, image resolution, and palettes. All of these elements work together to produce an image that is appropriate to add to a web page.

Pixels

As discussed in Chapter 1, "Overview of Web Design Concepts," a computer monitor consists of thousands of picture elements called pixels. The *pixel* is the smallest unit displayed by a computer monitor. Each pixel can display only one color at a time. Pixels in a grid form the building blocks for graphics and other images a computer can display. The more pixels that are used to create an image, the larger the file size. For example, a color photograph with 100 colors will have more pixels than a photo with 50 colors.

Color Depth

Pixels provide some amount of color information. This information, measured in bits, determines how many colors each pixel can display. For example, pixels with 4 bits of grayscale information can display up to 16 shades of gray, 8 bits of color information per pixel produces up to 256 bits of color information, and so forth. Higher bit values (also called *bit depths*) result in more intense or realistic colors. As the color depth increases, however, so does the file size.

Table 3.1 illustrates the varying levels of bit depths and the number of colors supported at each level.

TABLE 3.1 Bit Depths

Bit Depth	Colors Supported
32	16.7 million plus an 8-bit grayscale mask
24	16.7 million
16	65.5 thousand
15	32.8 thousand
8	256

Image Resolution

A user's monitor resolution determines how precisely on-screen images will be displayed. Screen resolution depends on the number of pixels present in a monitor's screen area, which is represented by the monitor's height and width. Higher screen resolutions display sharper, clearer images. The standard screen resolution used as the lowest common denominator is 640×480 (screen width × screen height), or 72 dots per inch (dpi). Dots per inch are the number of pixels per inch on a screen. For a mass audience, you should develop your web elements with this setting.

Screen resolutions range from 640×480 to 1280×1024. Here are the screen resolutions most commonly available on monitors currently on the market:

- 640×480
- 800×600
- 1024×768
- 1152×864
- 1280×960
- 1280×1024

Palettes

Although an 8-bit color display can show millions of colors, it can display only 256 colors at one time. The system maintains these 256 colors in a system palette.

When you create an 8-bit image using vector or paint programs, the program builds a palette based on the colors used in the image. The system palette then adjusts slightly to convey the correct colors when the image is displayed. When you display several images, either in sequence or simultaneously, you might experience a disconcerting flash of colors known as *palette flash* or palette shift.

Palette flash occurs when a significant discrepancy exists between the image bit depth or palette and the system bit depth or palette. To overcome this limitation, the browser automatically applies a technique called dithering to the image.

Dithering

Dithering is the approximation or reconciliation of colors between an image palette and the system palette. Colors on the image palette are replaced to match the colors on the system palette. If the system cannot find a color to match, it will use whatever color it thinks is appropriate, which could lead to some unusual color combinations!

Unfortunately, dithering can alter the image's appearance in ways you might not want. You should use colors from the web-safe color palette for your graphics to ensure that they will not dither.

Web-Safe Color Palette

The web-safe color palette is made up of the 216 colors that are supported by an 8-bit monitor. Remember that both Netscape Navigator and Microsoft Internet Explorer guarantee only 216 colors. Each browser has a maximum of 256 colors it can display, and 40 of those colors are used by the operating system. This leaves 216 colors that can be guaranteed; all other colors will dither. If you choose your colors from the web-safe color palette, you will be sure that, regardless of the bit depth of the monitor, the colors you selected for your graphics, background, and text will be the same each time your website is viewed. Here are some links; the first link is to a site from which you can download a plug-in you can use to create browser-safe custom colors and the second is to a web-safe color palette:

```
http://webdesign.about.com/library/weekly/aa032698.htm
http://html.about.com/library/bl_colors.htm.
```

Bitmap vs. Vector Graphics

Web graphics can be categorized into two file types: bitmap and vector. Each type has its advantages and disadvantages and each is suited for certain types of images. Let's look at the two in more depth.

Bitmap

The most common graphic type is *bitmap*. Each color that appears in bitmap graphics is represented by a unique value. Both JPEG and GIF formats are bitmaps. If you increase the dimensions of an image, the associated file size will be larger. When viewed with magnification, a bitmap resembles a series of little squares, each of which has a color value that contributes to the overall shape. Bitmaps have a very rough appearance when viewed closely but form images when viewed from a distance, similar to Impressionist pointillism or the currently popular photo mosaics. One drawback of bitmaps, however, is that the original files are large. A bitmap's appearance is greatly affected by screen resolution. Figure 3.1 shows a bitmap image as it looks when magnified.

FIGURE 3.1   Magnified view of bitmap image

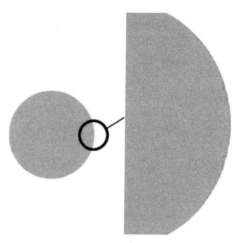

For a bitmap to render its shape, the browser and the available RAM work in unison to load the graphic. The information for each pixel is stored and then rendered in the browser to create the image. Larger bitmap images result in larger file sizes because more pixels must be told which values to display. Bitmaps are best suited for photos, drop-shadow effects, and soft, glowing, or blurry edges.

Vector

Vector graphics are quite different from bitmap graphics in their rendering process. *Vector* graphics store the information about the image in mathematical instructions that are interpreted to display the image.

For example, to create a circle as a vector image, the program used to display the image needs to know only the center coordinates, radius, and color values. With this information, mathematical instructions are used to render the graphic. To increase the size of the circle, only the information values need to change; therefore, increasing the size of a vector graphic does not increase its file size. Figure 3.2 shows a sample graphic and how the graphic uses lines to interpret and render the shape.

FIGURE 3.2   Vector image using mathematical interpretation

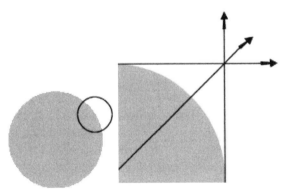

Another advantage to vector graphics is that they are capable of scaling to the output device being used. Vector graphics have this capability because they're not dependent on the resolution of the monitor. Vector graphics are best suited for line art, shapes, and illustrations.

Graphic Applications

You can create digital images with a variety of graphics programs. Recent upgrades to basic image-editing software make it easier to create, retouch, and export web-ready image files.

These programs can be divided into two general groups: vector-based drawing programs and paint-type programs.

Vector-Based Drawing Programs

Vector-based drawing programs such as Adobe Illustrator map shapes that you create onto an invisible grid. Image information is stored as a set of mathematical instructions. As previously discussed, vector graphics are resolution independent, meaning that computer monitor settings do not affect their size or appearance. Vector files are also smaller than similar paint-type image files. Vector graphics are commonly used in high-end three-dimensional and Virtual Reality Modeling Language (VRML) environments.

Currently, vector graphics cannot deliver truly photo-realistic detail, and they display somewhat more slowly on screens. They also require a browser plug-in or helper application for viewing on the Web. However, vector graphics work very well for industrial, manufacturing, scientific, and educational purposes.

You will be introduced to applications that support vector graphics, like Flash 5, in Chapter 18, "Applications and Tools."

Paint Programs

Paint-type programs create bitmaps from scanned photos and video frame captures, or they can be used to create original artwork. Bitmap files can represent highly detailed images. As previously discussed, a bitmap is an arrangement of small dots, and each dot corresponds to a pixel on the screen. Bitmaps can be edited pixel by pixel if necessary.

If you want to develop your own graphics, the following applications are commonly used in the industry:

- Adobe Photoshop
- Microsoft Image Composer
- Jasc Paint Shop Pro

You will be introduced to some basic functions of a paint application in Chapter 18.

Image File Formats

Graphic images come in numerous file formats: bitmap (BMP), Tagged Image File Format (TIFF), Windows metafile (WMF), Graphics Interchange Format (GIF), and Joint Photographic Experts Group (JPEG).

Only GIF and JPEG are natively supported by browsers; other file formats can be viewed with the aid of a plug-in. *Native support* means that the browser does not require any special software or plug-in to display the image. When creating web graphics, designers must choose between GIF and JPEG based on the type of images they desire. Table 3.2 lists various image file formats and their filename extensions.

TABLE 3.2   Image File Formats

Filename Extension	File Format	Origin
`.jpg, .jpeg`	Joint Photographic Experts Group (JPEG)	Joint Photographic Experts Group
`.gif`	Graphics Interchange Format (GIF)	CompuServe
`.tif`	Tagged Image File Format (TIFF)	Aldus Corporation
`.bmp`	Bitmap (BMP)	Microsoft Corporation
`.wpg`	WordPerfect Graphic	WordPerfect Corporation (Novell)
`.png`	Portable Network Graphics	The PNG Development Group is overseeing organization for PNG. For more information visit www.libpng.org/pub/png.
`.wmf`	Windows Meta File	Microsoft

Graphics Interchange Format (GIF)

GIF is a platform-independent file format that is limited to a display of 256 colors. Originally developed by CompuServe for its online service, GIF has been adopted by most developers because of its small file size. *Graphic interlacing* (the progressive rendering of images) is unique to GIFs and is a preferred method for displaying large graphic files.

GIF is considered a *lossless* format; this means that as the image is compressed, no information is lost. Consequently, a GIF file may not compress as much as a JPEG file of the same size. The amount of compression cannot be determined by the designer for a GIF file, though it can for a JPEG file.

Animated GIF (GIF 89a)

The 89a version of GIF allows storage and playback of a sequence of still images to create the illusion of animation. GIF files can provide many full animation and video effects without the need for plug-ins.

Regular GIF files contain only one static image; the animated GIF functions much like a cartoon flip book. Animated GIF files consist of sequential frames that reload from a browser's cache and replay in an infinite or predetermined loop to simulate motion. One advantage that animated GIFs have over other image animation is that they do not depend on interaction from the client or the server. This is referred to as *client-pull* and *server-push*; both require a file to be downloaded sequentially with numerous exchanges between the user's computer and the server.

Transparent GIF

An advantage that a GIF image has over a JPEG image is that the designer can designate a color of the GIF image to be transparent. This feature removes the constraints of square or rectangular graphics. For example, the designer can create a circular logo in a square image by making the background color of the square transparent. Thus the image appears to be circular when, in fact, it is square with information to make the background appear transparent.

Joint Photographic Experts Group (JPEG)

Graphics in the JPEG format are capable of much greater color depth than GIFs, but they usually require more time to download. JPEG files can contain up to 24 bits of color information (16.7 million colors) and work well for powerful corporate graphics and photographs. You must remember, however, that the lowest common denominator recommendation is 8-bit color (256 colors).

JPEG files are compressed automatically. They are decompressed when they arrive at the web page. Compression effects vary: the greater the compression, the greater the level of degradation in the final image. JPEG is considered a *lossy* format type; this means that as the compression of the image is increased, colors are dropped from the image color palette, resulting in image degradation. For example, a 100KB JPEG file can be compressed to perhaps 10KB. However, this amount of compression may diminish the image quality to the point where the image is unusable.

One drawback to this format is that the designer has no control over how the 24 bits are mapped into the 256-color palette used by a client's display. Also, considerable differences exist between the way Netscape Navigator and Microsoft Internet Explorer display images. Further, the display results of PCs and Macintoshes also differ. Designers should test their images in both browsers and multiple operating systems before deciding which format best serves their purposes.

JPEG 2000

A new JPEG format aims to enhance the compression feature of standard JPEGs. As discussed, the current JPEG format is lossy, which results in information about the image being discarded upon compression. This effectively creates "holes" in the image, which are filled, creating a speckled effect. With JPEG 2000, the compression will include a new wavelet technology that will store the information differently, reducing the amount of speckling that occurs when the JPEG is decompressed.

Portable Network Graphics (PNG)

The PNG file format is emerging as the new format for web graphics. PNG brings together the best features of the GIF and JPEG formats into one format. PNG files are lossless and support transparency as GIFs do, yet they also support compression and high bit depth as JPEGs do. In addition, PNG bit depth can be adjusted, whereas GIFs and JPEGs must be 8-bit and 24-bit depth, respectively. Compression is enhanced in PNGs by using compression filters that can support up to 48-bit color.

Browser support for the PNG format is currently not complete. Netscape Navigator 4.7 and Microsoft Internet Explorer 5 have varying levels of support for PNG. Although the World Wide Web Consortium (W3C) recommended PNG in 1996, it is not advisable to rely on PNG as a fully supported format for the Web.

Scalable Vector Graphics (SVG)

Scalable Vector Graphics (SVG) format is currently in a working draft phase in the W3C. (As this book was being written, the W3C was nearing its final phase of Working Draft 8.) SVG uses Extensible Markup Language (XML) to describe certain shapes. As with other vector graphics, SVG is best suited for line art and shapes.

The use of XML allows the graphic to become an object in the HTML page, giving it access to the full XML document object model. This means that filters, masks, scripting, and mouse events can be tied to SVG files.

XML will be discussed in more detail in Chapter 13. Figure 3.3 shows a brief sample of well-formed SVG syntax.

FIGURE 3.3   SVG image file syntax

```
<?xml version="1.0" standalone="no"?>
<SVG WIDTH="5in" HEIGHT="4in"
 XMLNS = 'http://www.w3.org/2000/svg-2000-stylable'>
  <DESC><!-- put image description here -->
  </DESC>
  <G><!-- place graphic here -->
  </G>
</SVG>
```

SVG is still in its working draft phase; it is not yet a Recommendation. Links to software that supports SVG can be found at the following URL:

`http://graphicssoft.about.com/msubsvgauth.htm`

Creating Images

Creating web-quality images requires the knowledge and use of a graphics application. This aspect of website design can be the most difficult to master. Depending on the size of your organization, a graphic artist might design all the images. If you are not artistically inclined, many resources on the Web offer images for free use. High-quality graphics are not free typically. As an alternative, you can subscribe to websites that offer tens of thousands of graphics. Subscriptions can range from a nominal monthly fee to more substantial annual fees.

Be sure that any graphics you use on your website are copyright free. Website text must also be your company's original creation or licensed for you to use. Always check the legal statements on any website whose material you want to borrow. Copyright infringement is illegal and punishable by fine and imprisonment.

The ALT attribute

The ALT attribute provides alternative text in place of an image on an HTML page. The syntax for using the ALT attribute is as follows:

```
<IMG SRC="filename.gif"
    ALT="This is a link to the search page">
```

The ALT attribute is useful for several situations:

- Users who have disabled the image-viewing capability on their browsers can read the image name or link destination.

- Users can read the image name or description while an image loads.

- Software can provide accessibility options for visually and hearing-impaired users.

- Netscape Navigator version 4.*x* (and later) or Microsoft Internet Explorer version 3.*x* (and later) can provide tool tips that pop up when the cursor is placed over the image.

Image Optimization

For the website designer, the benefits of the GIF, JPEG, or PNG formats are not realized if optimization is not considered. As you learned earlier, each image format has special benefits that make it unique. As a website designer, you must learn which format to use for any particular graphic, but you must also make sure your images are optimized. The basic procedure of optimization is determining the smallest color palette possible and choosing a file format that results in the desired quality.

Following are some guidelines you can use to help optimize your web graphics:

- Use colors from the web-safe color palette. This prevents dithering.

- Use the least number of colors possible. Colors add to the file size of the image.

- Use solid colors whenever possible. Color blends and fades also add file size and can go outside of the web-safe color range.

- Avoid anti-aliasing when possible. Anti-aliasing adds more colors to the image, resulting in large file sizes and longer downloading times.

- Use optimization utilities. To ensure that your images are as efficient as possible, use one of the utilities outlined in the next section.

A misconception regarding the *use* of GIFs and JPGs is that one of these formats is better than the other. Consistently using GIFs or JPGs does not ensure that you are optimizing your images on a page. Ultimately, you need to know which graphic format will work best in a particular web page. This is something that may come with time and experience, but the more you experiment, the more your artistic eye will be able to guide you in providing the best images for your particular page situation.

Optimization Sources

Many sources are now available to help the website designer optimize graphics. The most commonly used optimization tools are included in graphics applications such as Photoshop, Fireworks, ImageReady, and others. There are also online and desktop versions of stand-alone optimizers available.

Online image optimizers typically require an annual subscription fee, which varies depending on the number of pages or graphics you want to optimize. Some other services are free. The website designer simply enters a URL for the images. The online program visits the site to download and optimize the images. The designer is then granted access to the optimized images. The following services provide online image optimization:

- GIFBot from NetMechanic.com (`www.netmechanic.com/accelerate.htm`)

- OptiView (`www.optiview.com`)

The desktop image optimizers perform the same task, except the images being optimized don't need to be made available on the Web for the service to access them. The following services provide desktop image optimization:

- SmartSaver Pro from Ulead Systems (`www.ulead.com/ssp/runme.htm`)

- GIF Cruncher from Spinwave.com (`www.spinwave.com`)

By optimizing all the images on a page (and a site), you can dramatically reduce download time, providing users with a faster browsing experience.

Image Slicing and Splicing

Another technique that is used to help shorten download time of large images (such as image maps) is a process called slicing. *Slicing* involves dividing images into several smaller images. With the use of HTML tables, the image can be reconstructed or spliced back together in the browser window. Slicing doesn't change the file size of the image, but the image appears to load faster because the user sees portions of it (the smaller image sections) before the entire image has downloaded. Chapter 18 includes a list of programs that support image slicing.

Summary

Web graphics are important because they help make your web pages more visually appealing to the user. They should be aesthetically pleasing, essential to the site, and small in file size.

GIF and JPEG are the formats most commonly used in website design because they are supported by both Microsoft Internet Explorer and Netscape Navigator.

Between vector graphics and bitmap graphics, bitmap graphics are the most common; both JPEG and GIF are bitmap graphics. Bitmap graphics are made up of colors represented by individual values, whereas vector graphics are based on mathematical instructions. Bitmap graphics can be very large in file size; vector graphics are smaller. Vector graphics require the use of a plug-in viewer to be seen.

Website designers use tools and techniques to create and optimize images. Creating images by using solid colors from the web-safe color palette, incorporating the least number of colors possible, and avoiding anti-aliasing when possible will help you to create optimized images for your web pages. You can further ensure that you have the most functional and compact image file for placement in your website by using online and desktop versions of optimization utilities.

Exam Essentials

Know the function of graphics in your website. Users have come to expect a visually pleasing experience that can only be achieved with the use of images. Images can also be used for navigation in the form of image maps and graphical buttons that link to other pages or resources. On corporate sites, logos and trademarks are crucial for name recognition and branding.

Be able to define color depth and resolution. Pixels provide some amount of color information. This information, measured in bits, determines how many colors each pixel can display. Higher bit values (also called bit depths) result in more intense or realistic colors. A user's monitor resolution destermines how precisely on-screen images will be displayed. Screen resolution depends on the number of pixels present in on the screen, as represented in height and width.

Understand image tool functions. Image tools, such as Adobe Photoshop, Microsoft Image Composer, and Jasc Paint Shop Pro, can assist you in creating, retouching, and editing web-ready image files.

Be able to choose graphic file formats. Graphic images come in numerous file formats: bitmap (BMP), Tagged Image File Format (TIFF), Windows metafile (WMF), Graphics Interchange Format (GIF), and Joint

Photographic Experts Group (JPEG). Only GIF and JPEG are natively supported by browsers. GIF is a platform-independent file format that is limited to a display of 256 colors. GIF 89a supports transparency and animation. Graphics in the JPEG format are capable of much greater color depth than GIFs are but usually require more time to download. JPEG files can contain up to 24 bits of color information (16.7 million colors).

Key Terms

Before you take the exam, be certain you are familiar with the following terms:

bit depths	native support
bitmap	palette flash
client-pull	pixel
dithering	server-push
graphic interlacing	slicing
lossless	vector
lossy	

Review Questions

1. What is the most crucial element of a website image?

   A. It has many colors.

   B. It downloads quickly.

   C. It is animated.

   D. It appears throughout the website.

2. You have created an image for your website. When users view it on an 8-bit monitor, the colors are not those that you originally chose. What could be the problem?

   A. The resolution has been changed from 640×480 to 1024×768.

   B. The image was not optimized.

   C. The colors are dithering because you used colors outside of the web-safe color palette.

   D. You have used a JPEG instead of GIF image.

3. What are the two different file types for web graphics?

   A. Bitmap and vector

   B. GIF and JPEG

   C. Optimized and nonoptimized

   D. Drawing and paint

4. Which option describes how bitmap images can be edited?

   A. Region by region

   B. Vector by vector

   C. Pixel by pixel

   D. Point by point

5. Which option describes JPEG images?

   A. Lossless

   B. Animated

   C. Interlaced

   D. Lossy

6. Images are essential in website design because users expect a visually pleasing experience. What should good web graphics be?

   A. Aesthetically pleasing, regardless of file size

   B. Either functional or aesthetically pleasing

   C. Small in file size, regardless of aesthetics

   D. Aesthetically pleasing, essential to the site, and small in file size

7. Screen resolution is dependent upon which of the following?

   A. The number of pixels present in a monitor's screen area

   B. The file sizes of graphics on a page viewed in the monitor

   C. The bandwidth available to download the pages viewed on-screen

   D. The bit value (or color depth) provided by each pixel

8. Which of the following accurately describes a difference between bitmap and vector graphics?

   A. A bitmap graphic can be increased in scale without increasing file size, whereas a vector graphic cannot.

   B. Vector graphics are best suited for photos and drop-shadow effects, whereas bitmaps are best suited for line art and illustrations.

   C. Bitmaps use individual values for each color displayed, whereas vector graphics use mathematical calculations.

   D. Vector graphics are dependent on resolution, whereas bitmaps are not.

9. You are creating a graphic image for your Web Design Professionals site. Most of your users are Internet professionals with high-speed connections. Therefore, download time is not an issue, but you want to achieve the greatest color depth possible. Which image file format should you use?

    A. TIFF

    B. JPEG

    C. GIF

    D. GIF 89a

10. Which image file format supports transparency, compression, and high bit depth but is not yet widely supported by browsers?

    A. JPEG

    B. PNG

    C. GIF

    D. BMP

11. Besides creating a visually pleasing experience for the user, images can also be used for what essential part of the site?

    A. Feedback

    B. Navigation

    C. Pictures of the designer

    D. A search engine

12. What's the downside to designing an intranet application that is too graphical and flashy?

    A. It creates a visually pleasing experience.

    B. It becomes function oriented.

    C. It reduces worker productivity.

    D. It causes longer download time.

13. What is the smallest element that a display device can use to render text or graphics?

    A. Dot

    B. Graphic unit

    C. Mark

    D. Pixel

14. Eight bits of color information per pixel provides up to how many bits of color information total?

    A. 256

    B. 16

    C. 16.7 million

    D. 65.5 thousand

15. What are the only two image file formats natively supported by browsers?

    A. Bitmap and TIFF

    B. TIFF and JPEG

    C. GIF and JPEG

    D. PNG and GIF

16. What benefit of the GIF file format has caused most website developers to adopt it?

    A. GIF is lossy.

    B. Its file size is small.

    C. It yields the greatest color depth.

    D. It provides sound.

17. Which version of GIF allows storage and playback of a sequence of still images to create the illusion of animation?

A. GIF 89a

B. GIF 2

C. Internet GIF

D. Transparent GIF

18. How many colors make up the web-safe color palette that is supported by an 8-bit monitor?

A. 256

B. 16

C. 216

D. 16 million

19. Graphics in JPEG file format are capable of greater color depth than GIFs, but what is a drawback of using JPEG images?

A. JPEG images are lossless.

B. JPEG images are smaller in file size.

C. JPEG images do not require a plug-in.

D. JPEG images require more time to download.

20. What is one of the drawbacks of using bitmap graphics?

A. The range of colors within a bitmap image is limited, allowing for only black and white.

B. The original files are too large for many Internet users' bandwidth conditions.

C. Bitmaps are smooth in appearance when viewed closely but rough from a distance.

D. Bitmaps are not suited well for pictures, which are commonly used on web pages.

Answers to Review Questions

1. B. How quickly images will download is a critical factor in website design. Users usually do not want to wait for images to download.

2. C. The colors are dithering because you used colors outside of the web-safe color palette. If you choose your colors from the web-safe color palette, you will be sure that the colors you selected for your graphics, background, and text will be the same each time your website is viewed regardless of the bit depth of the monitor.

3. A. There are two types of web graphics: bitmap and vector. There are advantages to using both, and each is suitable for certain types of images.

4. C. Bitmap images can be edited pixel by pixel because the image is an arrangement of small dots.

5. D. JPEG images are considered to be lossy because, as the compression of the image is increased, colors are dropped from the image color palette, resulting in image degradation.

6. D. Good web graphics must be aesthetically pleasing, essential to the site, and small in file size. Large image files can cause the web page to download slowly, frustrating users.

7. A. Screen resolution is the number of pixels present in a monitor's screen area. The lowest screen resolution is 640×480, which represents the width and height of the screen area.

8. C. Bitmaps use individual values for each color displayed, whereas vector graphics use mathematical calculations. The larger the dimensions of a bitmap image, the larger the associated file size will be. Vector graphics store the information about the image in mathematical instructions that are then interpreted and displayed. The file size will remain the same regardless of how large or small the image is.

9. B. JPEGs support 16.7 million colors, whereas GIF and GIF 89a support 256. TIFF files have to be viewed through a plug-in viewer.

10. B. Browser support for the PNG format is currently not complete. It is a new format and browsers have been slow to adopt it as a standard image format.

11. B. Images can also be used for navigation, an essential part of a website. You can use image maps and graphical buttons that link to other pages or resources.

12. C. An intranet is meant to provide quick and easy access to information and resources, usually for employees of a company. If an intranet application is too graphical and flashy, it can reduce worker productivity. Option B is incorrect because an intranet should be function oriented, whereas the Internet is presentation oriented. Answer D is incorrect as well; connection speed outside of the network isn't a factor in designing an intranet page.

13. D. A pixel is a picture element, the smallest element that a display device can use to render text or graphics. Pixels in a grid form the building blocks for graphics and other images a computer can display.

14. A. Eight bits of color information per pixel produces up to 256 bits of color information. This information determines how many colors each pixel can display. Although an 8-bit color display can show millions of colors, it can display only 256 colors at one time. Higher bit values (also called bit depths) result in more intense or realistic colors.

15. C. Only GIF and JPEG are natively supported by browsers; you need to use a plug-in to view other file formats. Native support means that the browser does not require any special software or plug-in to display the image.

16. B. GIF has been adopted by most developers because of its small file size. Graphic interlacing (the progressive rendering of images) is unique to GIFs and is a preferred method for displaying large graphic files. GIF is a lossless format rather than a lossy format. JPEG yields the most color depth. GIF is an image file format, so it would not be used for sound.

17. A. The 89a version of GIF allows storage and playback of a sequence of still images to create the illusion of animation. GIF files can provide many full animation and video effects without the need for plug-ins. Regular GIF files contain only one static image; the animated GIF functions much like a cartoon flip book.

18. C. The web-safe color palette is made up of the 216 colors that are supported by an 8-bit monitor. Both Netscape Navigator and Microsoft Internet Explorer guarantee only 216 colors; each has a maximum of 256 colors it can display, and 40 of those colors are used by the operating system. This leaves 216 colors that can be guaranteed; all other colors will dither.

19. D. Although graphics in the JPEG format are capable of much greater color depth than GIFs, they usually require more time to download. JPEG files can contain up to 24 bits of color information (16.7 million colors) and work well for powerful corporate graphics and photographs. The lowest common denominator recommendation is 8-bit (256) color.

20. B. Although bitmaps are used in many other document processing solutions, they tend to be too large for the general populace. GIFs and JPEGs are better for web pages as a result. Option A is incorrect because BMPs certainly allow for color. Option C is incorrect because just the opposite is the case; they are rough up close and smooth from a distance. Option D is incorrect because BMPs are fine for pictures; they just have a larger file size that proves ineffective for web pages.

Chapter 4

Multimedia and the Web

**THE CIW EXAM OBJECTIVE GROUP COVERED
IN THIS CHAPTER:**

✓ Add downloadable web content to a site, including but not
limited to: executable files, plug-ins, multimedia, and applets.

If your screen is to be filled with visuals of all kinds, how will users distinguish hot spots from the rest of the screen? Visual design can entice users to stay and interact. How will you now use multimedia and Internet technology to help add value to your website? There are many choices on the market now: Java applets, JavaScript, and Macromedia Flash, for example. How do you decide which is best for your website and what is the right mix of traditional design and multimedia technology?

In this chapter, we'll discuss how multimedia can enhance your site or detract from it; what technology is currently available on the market for incorporation into your website; how animation, audio, and video affect your site and its performance; the goal of your site and how multimedia can add to that goal; and the role user interaction plays in a website.

Multimedia and Websites

Planning is the key to successful creation of a multimedia website. Although multimedia has existed for some time, applying it on the Web is not an exact science. Multimedia on the Web is made possible with various tools and technologies that are not always compatible. In this chapter, you will learn how to effectively plan a multimedia website.

Multimedia is gaining popularity on the Web because advances in Internet technology now allow developers to mix different media objects in web pages. Multimedia such as animation, audio, and video can supplement bland text or two-dimensional graphics as well as complement the visual design, tone, and message of a website.

However, multimedia technologies also present great challenges to website developers. Predicting how, or if, they will react and display on various platforms and in different browsers requires planning, patience, and lots of trial and error. Further, the appeal of using complex technologies can sometimes overshadow the goals of a site; complex technologies can even discourage or exclude some audience members from using your site.

Current Multimedia Capabilities

The current capabilities of multimedia on the Web are astounding. For a website designer, it is tempting to utilize these tools and technologies. In the future, new technology will be adopted at a much more rapid pace. However, today's designers are limited by two major factors that inhibit rapid multimedia technology adoption: bandwidth and the capability of browsers to support such technology. To enjoy the full effect of many new technologies, a high-bandwidth connection is usually required, as well as browser *plug-in* support or other third-party applications.

Therefore, website designers should resist the temptation to use the latest and most dazzling technology, because the standard user on a dial-up connection with a standard browser cannot support it. This does not mean that you cannot use new technology, but you must be aware that you will exclude some of your audience. A balance between traditional website design and new technology is required so that the technology doesn't compromise the functionality of the site. If your defined audience is a particular segment that will be able to support the technology and you are not concerned about other users, then use any technology that enhances the site. Most of the decisions regarding the use of multimedia are made during the planning and storyboarding phases of site design, which we will discuss in Chapter 5, "The Web Development Process."

Time Factor

The Web has created a new paradigm by allowing users to change their minds and choose new sources with no consequence. For example, when a person subscribes to a magazine or purchases a book, they become a captive audience. The person has a vested interest in the magazine or book (the cost) and is therefore more likely to spend time reading it rather than throw it away without reading it and purchase a different one. By contrast, the Web requires no vested interest on the part of the visitor. Users are therefore more likely to change their minds and visit different sites without fully exploring your site.

However, web users do make an investment: their time. It is difficult to assign a value to the time spent by the average web user, but from a design point of view, the user's time is valuable. Mere seconds can determine whether you keep or lose visitors. The correct choice of multimedia will help conserve your visitors' time and maintain their attention, increasing the chances of longer visits and potential business.

Animation and the Web

Animation is an important component that distinguishes the Web from other media (except television). There are different levels of animation, ranging from simple animated GIF images to 3D renderings and virtual environments. The most common types of basic animation are animated GIFs, rollovers, and Macromedia Flash files. Animation gives the user a sense of movement and engagement. Sometimes it is used to attract attention and other times to illustrate a concept. However it's used, meaningful design and implementation allows the benefits of animation to enhance the presence of the site rather than distract from it.

Animated GIFs

As previously discussed, an *animated GIF* is a compilation of still images that is set into motion at a designated sequence, speed, and repetition. Many banner ads are animated GIFs. Often, animated GIFs rotate a logo with a slogan or tag line. An animated GIF can be very effective for displaying additional information in the same area of the screen. It can also attract the user's attention, and it adds motion to a page that would otherwise be static.

Rollovers

Rollovers are buttons, images, or other designated areas of the web page that trigger actions when an event such as the user passing the mouse cursor over them occurs. Rollovers are commonly used as navigation elements. They engage the reader by creating interaction with user events, and they can also indicate that the object is a hyperlink. This practice deviates from the basic default hypertext link that is blue and underlined, but it has become an acceptable alternative. Using this type of navigation element means that users will not have the benefit of a color indicator for a visited hyperlink. However, with effective use of other navigational aides and indicators, the user should notice little difference.

Macromedia Flash Files

Macromedia Flash is gaining widespread acceptance in website design. Flash introduced a new form of animation that was previously not possible: It offers media-rich content while conserving bandwidth. Flash has allowed website designers to create visually appealing, animated sites that offer an alternative to the sites that are normally static. We will discuss Flash in more depth in Chapter 18, "Applications and Tools."

Animation to Avoid

One type of animation that has proved to annoy users is scrolling text, whether it's used in Java applets, marquees, or the browser status bar. Critical information should not scroll because the user will probably pay little attention to it. Often, scrolling text is difficult to read, so rather than take the time to concentrate on the passing words, users skip scrolling text altogether. Additionally, not all forms of scrolling text are supported in all browsers. For example, Navigator does not support the <MARQUEE> tag, whereas Internet Explorer does. The result in Navigator is static, unformatted text, which can look out of place on a formatted page.

Audio and the Web

Audio differs from other web content in that it does not rely on the display for the user to experience the media. The constraints of monitor size, operating system, and color bit depth do not apply. Audio can now be delivered in two distinct ways. The user can download an entire audio file and then begin the playback process, or the audio file can be delivered in *streaming* format. The playback quality of any sound recording is dependent on the process and formats used to create the digital file and the quality of the output devices (such as speakers and sound cards) on the users' systems.

Downloaded Audio

The first appearance of audio on the Web was downloadable files. A file could be *embedded* into an HTML page and *downloaded* with other files, such as images. Once the audio file was downloaded, the playback began. As you can imagine, the larger the audio file, the more time was required to download it. In contrast to images, audio files require much more memory to store and play. Thus, sound files take significantly longer to download compared to their relatively short playback length. This trade-off is usually not acceptable to the user and becomes an annoyance.

Embedded audio differs from other audio formats in that it does not give the user the option to download (or more important, to not download). Unless it is an integral and necessary component to the site, do not embed audio; instead, allow the user to choose whether to download and listen. Currently, the only acceptable form of embedded audio used on the Web is the Macromedia Flash file. Flash files have the capability to specifically control audio playback and timing. In addition, Flash applies compression to audio files, and that immensely reduces file size and streams them to the user, which decreases download time.

Table 4.1 lists common audio file types and their corresponding filename extensions.

TABLE 4.1 Audio File Types

Filename Extension	File Type
.aiff	Macintosh native format
.au	Unix native format
.mid	MIDI format; produces small file size by creating music algorithms
.mov	QuickTime format; supports both audio and video
.wav	Windows native format
.swf	Shockwave/Flash format

Streaming Audio

Streaming audio differs from downloaded audio files in that the user does not wait to hear the file. As soon as the connection is made to the streaming audio server, a small buffer is created and the audio file begins to play.

Consider a 10MB sound file. Downloading it over a dial-up connection would be prohibitive. In streaming format, the file would play while it is downloading, decreasing delivery wait time to the user. Livecasts demonstrate the benefit of streaming technology. Listening to a one-hour livecast that is streamed to the user can be compared to listening to a radio. As the livecast happens, it is streamed down and then becomes history.

RealNetworks is a leader in the streaming audio arena. Their RealOne player, which replaced RealPlayer, has the capability to play streaming audio and video live through connections as slow as 28.8Kbps with acceptable monophonic quality.

Video and the Web

Video for the Web is another evolving technology that will become as common as static images in the coming years. Currently, the video available to users via dial-up connections is considered low quality. A visit to any major news site offers examples of the type of video files that are currently available and played back using *RealNetworks RealOne, Windows Media Player*, and other less-common applications. This type of video is typically low resolution, pixilated, slow in frame rate, and small in dimension. Nonetheless, it is generally viewable and understandable. Playing back video on the Web should never be mandatory for anyone outside of a network such as a LAN or an intranet. You should provide links along with file types and sizes to give users the option to proceed. For video longer than a few minutes, you should offer the option to stream the audio to help conserve bandwidth and download time.

Video is like audio in that it can be either downloaded and then played or streamed down to the user using a streaming server and player application. Options for video use increase with high-bandwidth connections. Video conferencing, webcasts, and web cameras use the Internet as a transport vehicle.

Internet TV

Internet TV has not yet evolved into a solid, universally accepted means of connecting people to the Internet, but most experts believe it will. In fact, Microsoft acquired this technology, called MSN TV (formerly WebTV) as part of its strategy to increase Internet usefulness to the consumer.

The controlling device is similar to a cable box and connected to the Internet through a high-speed line. To use MSN TV, users need only a phone line to connect their televisions to the Internet. Once connected, users can perform almost all the same functions that a computer-using Internet surfer can. They can visit a site, see all the latest graphics, experiment with interactivity, survey available products, and buy directly from the site—much as they would online or through a home shopping club. Companies such as Sony and Philips Magnavox have incorporated this technology in conjunction with MSN TV Networks (www.msntv.com).

The possibilities for Internet TV are impressive. Imagine the increased number of potential customers your site might reach. Bandwidth and slow-connection constraints on multimedia content are not as restrictive with Internet TV as they are with a 28.8Kbps modem.

Goals of a Multimedia Site

Multimedia provides so much content depth and so many ways to present information that your intent can be unclear. Early in multimedia development, web professionals were so excited by its tools that they forgot the greater importance of content.

It is important to clarify the goals of your multimedia website before you create the first page or an animation sequence. Ask yourself these questions before you get started:

- What is your message and who is your audience?

- How will the setting or interface look?

- Which multimedia elements fit into the interface and complement your message?

- What types of tools and expertise do you need to create the multimedia elements and author the website?

In other words, what do you want users to do when they visit your site? Do you want them to browse? Do you want them to explore? Buy? Research? Sign up for your update list? Consider these sample outcome statements:

- Users will be encouraged to fill out a survey or sign a guest book before leaving or upon entering the site. This data will be collected and incorporated into the company mailing list(s) or followed up by sales associates.

- Users will purchase or request purchasing information on the products listed by responding via e-mail, calling a toll-free number, or submitting an interactive form.

- Users will subscribe to our newsletter.

All websites should have an outcome, and once you have identified what that outcome will be, it will be easier to design with that goal in mind.

Multimedia Site Design Basics

Multimedia website designers must present elements on-screen so the user's expectations are met. Coordinating expectation and function is not an easy task; it must be planned in advance by the development team. Issues to be addressed include the following:

- What is the navigational structure of the website?

- What is your target audience's viewing capability?

- With what speed are Internet users connecting?

- Which operating systems are they using?

- Will a text-only or low-resolution graphics mirror site be provided? How will users access it?

- Are necessary plug-ins readily and easily available? Where on the page will you place the link to a plug-in? Will you provide a plug-in on your site or will the user click to go to another website? How will the user return to your site?

Scene and Setting

Multimedia website design is more than just random placement of text, graphics, and multimedia. It focuses on providing the proper mental model to which users can relate and interact. As the content of a site changes, your style and function remain the same, especially if you expect return visitors. Choosing a theme for the site in the very beginning will help you keep its focus even as content changes down the road. Most people do not want to have to relearn your content arrangement each time they visit. Much can be said in favor of consistency.

User Interaction

Web professionals can deliver content through a number of acceptable models. The most successful model seems to be the spiral concept and its three elements: interest, activity, and resolution. Each element is encountered in succession until the user's experience is completed or the website's navigable channels have been explored. A "How To" website might attract the user with its intriguing original graphics (interest), provide menu options (activity), and lead the user to the desired goal (resolution).

Remember that the more focused the user's experience with your website content is, the more enjoyment they will have and the greater the likelihood that they will return. For example, you may have lost track of time while "surfing" the Web. Users surfing top-quality websites are frequently unaware that time is passing and are in a state of complete engagement during this heightened level of experience. This state of mind on your prospective customer's part is likely to have a desirable outcome on their purchasing behavior. Consequently, one of the web professional's objectives is to create a user experience that elevates the potential customer into the heightened state. Psychological research has concluded that people achieve this state under the following conditions:

- When they concentrate
- When they are challenged
- When they become mesmerized
- When they lose self-consciousness
- When they lose sense of time

Thus, to help your user achieve this frame of mind, you must provide a website that supports these conditions. An effective example is the Disney site (`www.disney.com`), which takes the user into an immediate state of heightened interest. The graphics and content cause intrigue sufficient enough to encourage the user to start exploring, or interacting. The user is quickly transported to a heightened interactivity phase. The web graphics become more sophisticated, and the options for sound and video inspire more intrigue. With each click of a navigation button, the user is rewarded with additional content. (You may not be able to experience the interactivity of this site in some browsers until you download Flash 5.) This content model is important for any area of business—training, human resources, and sales and marketing, for example.

A more business-related website might use less excitement and more conservative media for rapid content dissemination and delivery, such as well-written text to generate excitement and interest about the product or service. An exciting, nonstandard image can intrigue users and draw them to your online business presence.

Selecting Multimedia Elements

The most daunting task for the multimedia web page designer is to manage screen space and select the most effective format for the media elements. The number of file formats from which to choose has grown exponentially for both of the dominant browsers (Netscape Navigator and Microsoft Internet Explorer), as has the number of plug-ins available for use with each. Designers must perform careful research to discover the most widely used plug-ins for their audiences.

Website designers also must plan their sites for users who do not have the necessary plug-ins. Rather than accepting a limited audience, you can provide links or instructions to help users find and install the plug-ins your site requires. Microsoft has addressed this potential problem by automating installation of the most common plug-ins as soon as the browser reads a file that needs one. Netscape provides a link from its Help menu to download pages for plug-ins.

As you think about which file format to use, consider the many technical aspects of each multimedia element. For example, ask yourself if JavaScript is important to the website or if you want to add it merely because you can.

Similarly, there are good reasons to use a Java applet or to place an ActiveX object in the browser status bar.

A good website designer will create content and graphical design to satisfy user expectations about the interface. Rollovers, or mouseover effects, can provide interaction and feedback. Designers need to consider that some software applications, such as Macromedia Director and Flash, have offered cross-platform availability for some time but others have not.

The model presented in Figure 4.1 is useful for determining which multimedia formats to use. Note that you can achieve the same results with various file formats.

FIGURE 4.1   Relationship between file size and media format

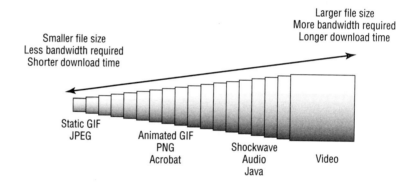

The best website designers have some programming knowledge and understand how to implement some multimedia elements. Nondesigning programmers should learn the rudiments of design or consult a design professional for assistance. Web professionals must consider their site's purpose, the tools they have, and the resources they know best. They must also try to determine what percentage of the intended audience has Java-enabled browsers or the willingness to download a plug-in.

Multimedia Authoring

Each multimedia application can be an exciting new tool that helps you construct robust multimedia elements and, ultimately, your website. Because each application has its own characteristics, each must be carefully selected to maximize the viewing potential.

The size of your design team will determine how many roles you must play yourself and how many other professionals, such as graphic artists, you must involve. In the design phase, you must understand the strengths and weaknesses of the new multimedia opportunities. Many corporations are rethinking their overall information strategies. Content areas must be transmitted successfully to the consumer. The web professional must address all these issues, including electronic-commerce strategy and the interoperability between different operating systems and hardware platforms. Given the considerable time and money required to learn the new technologies, website design must be given proper attention and not treated as a minor "additional duty" for someone who is already overloaded.

Designing, implementing, and maintaining a website that can deliver content with advanced multimedia capabilities and state-of-the-art interactivity is easier than it was in the past. New applications are constantly introduced to put bigger and better multimedia on the Web. In the current developmental stage, there is no agreed-upon multimedia standard to which each Internet application developer can work. The challenge in building multimedia-rich websites is deciding which methods, resources, and tools are necessary for successful deployment. With the growth in consumer interest and online buying activity, your question becomes this: How can my company best use its knowledge of web interactive programs and multimedia content to successfully reach customers before the competition does? This business question differs from the traditional only in its emphasis on web technology.

Like a magazine rack, a web page gives its author only a few seconds to convince the reader that the information inside is of interest. The page's look and feel is an important tool in this effort. Graphics play an important part in your users' experience. For this reason, showy graphics are important at this level of website development, and the first page of your site must display exact pathways for the user to gather information. This navigability should also help users in an intuitive way.

Java vs. Plug-In

A website designer must also think in terms of choosing between, for example, a plug-in architecture that requires the user to perform a one-time download or a Java applet, which currently requires the user to download the Java files for every playback. For many, this design selection is critical.

Since Java was released, a serious debate has ensued over whether plug-ins or Java applets are superior. Many prefer the wisdom of sending both content and the necessary engine to drive it across the bandwidth rather than just sending the content itself. Many also feel that a few security problems remain with Java. The possibility of crashing the user's computer is now remote, but it's still a possibility. Others say that many of the virtues attributed to Java come not from the language but from the environment in which it runs. The converse is also true: many of its drawbacks come from the environment as well. However, the website designer has little control over the user's environment.

Visualize and Understand the User

First, create a mental picture of your website user. If you really know who your users are, you should have a good sense of the hardware, software, and browsers they use. How big are their monitors: 15 inches or 21 inches? What kind of graphics accelerator cards do they have? Which type of memory do they have and how much? As you know, a video card's primary duty is to hold onto a picture to allow the monitor to display it, so the more RAM your users' video cards have, the larger graphics they can handle in terms of both numbers of colors and pixels. A single 640×480 256-color graphic demands more than 300KB of memory. For your users to see your image in true color demands at least 2MB. So for whom do you design your website? The user with the best and most equipment? The least equipment? Or somewhere in between?

Although improvements are continually being made, digital video through the Internet can be jerky, pixilated, and very small, sometimes playing at less than one-eighth the screen size. How much video do you need on your website? Three-dimensional acceleration and graphics cards have become popular. Intel MMX technology from a few years ago embeds multimedia acceleration into a single chip, eliminating video and graphic accelerator cards altogether. If approximately half of your website depends on well-chosen multimedia, most of your users will be happy, well-informed prospective customers with this technology.

Performance

You can create smaller, more compressed graphics, animation, video, and audio with applications specifically designed for online usage. These applications allow you to apply a number of graphic optimization processes to still image and movie files. The end result of simple compression is smaller files with little or no loss of quality.

Another option is to store multimedia files locally and keep the logic (or code) on the Internet or an intranet. Some multimedia-authoring programs, such as Asymetrix Multimedia ToolBook and Macromedia Authorware and Director, allow you to call multimedia files from a local source (such as a network or CD-ROM).

Copyright Infringement

Although users can view and retrieve source code for just about anything on the Web, inappropriate use of other people's work is illegal. As the Web develops and programs are invented to track site visitors, anonymity will decrease. Remember that it is illegal under copyright law to use any published Internet material (text, art, music, code, etc.) without permission from its creator or owner. To avoid legal penalties, all website designers should opt for a conservative interpretation of intellectual property issues.

Summary

There are many new advances in multimedia technology that a website designer can use in website development. The challenge lies in how much technology to incorporate into your website while recognizing the potential limitations users have in supporting multimedia technology in their browsers.

Animation, audio, and video also can be included in your site to add interest and to add to the content. Levels of animation can vary, depending on the technology used to create it. Animation gives the user a sense of movement and engagement. Sometimes it is used to attract attention and other times to illustrate a concept. Audio differs from other web content in that it does not rely on the display for the user to experience the media. The constraints of monitor size, operating system, and color bit depth do not apply. Video for the Web is another evolving technology that will become as common as static images in the coming years. Currently, the video available to users via dial-up connections is considered low quality.

Basic website design principles must be kept in mind when including multimedia in your website. Multimedia website designers must present elements on-screen so the user's expectations are met. Coordinating expectation and function is not an easy task; it must be planned in advance by the development team.

You should now be able to choose which technologies make the most sense for your business. Combining multimedia technology with traditional website design is a challenge for the website designer because of bandwidth and browser support issues.

Exam Essentials

Understand multimedia web-enabling technologies.   Animated GIFs, rollovers, Macromedia Flash, and audio and video technology are all multimedia technology that can be incorporated into websites.

Be able to apply multimedia design principles.   Multimedia website designers must present elements on-screen so the user's expectations are met. You need to take into consideration such issues as the navigational structure of the website, your target audience's viewing capability, and whether the necessary plug-ins are readily and easily available.

Be able to choose the best multimedia for your site.   The most daunting task for the multimedia web page designer is to manage screen space and select the most effective format for the media elements. Designers must perform careful research to discover the most widely used plug-ins for their audiences. Website designers also must plan their sites for users who do not have the necessary plug-ins. Rather than accepting a limited audience, you can provide links or instructions to help users find and install the plug-ins your site requires.

Key Terms

Before you take the exam, be certain you are familiar with the following terms:

animated GIF	RealNetworks RealOne
downloaded	rollovers
embedded	streaming
Internet TV	streaming audio
plug-in	Windows Media Player

Review Questions

1. What is *not* a factor a website designer should consider when choosing multimedia for a website?

   A. Website designer's technological capabilities

   B. Browser support for multimedia technology

   C. Goal of the website

   D. Available multimedia technology

2. Website designers are advised to avoid which type of animation multimedia?

   A. Animated GIFs

   B. Macromedia Flash

   C. JavaScript

   D. Scrolling text

3. What two major factors inhibit rapid technology adoption and limit today's website designers' use of multimedia?

   A. Designer qualifications and software availability

   B. Internet information delivery and user system RAM

   C. Bandwidth and browser support

   D. Technology training and browser upgrades

4. Which of the following multimedia technology types is commonly delivered in GIFs, rollovers, and Flash files?

   A. Audio

   B. Video

   C. Animation

   D. Streaming capability

5. In what two distinct ways can audio files be delivered?

   A. With or without video

   B. Through browser or plug-in

   C. Digital or analog

   D. Downloaded or streaming

6. Multimedia design principles require the website designer to create a user experience that elevates the potential customer to a heightened state. One of the most successful models for achieving this user state is the spiral concept. The spiral concept includes which group of elements?

   A. Interest, activity, and resolution

   B. Audio, video, and animation

   C. DHTML, JavaScript, and Flash

   D. Graphics, marketing, and product information

7. You are designing a website for your online sporting goods business. You want to include several Flash animations to demonstrate products. Which of the following should you consider including when you plan your site design?

   A. Few image files, because the Flash files will require a great deal of bandwidth

   B. A built-in Flash player so users need not download one

   C. A link that users can follow to download the Flash plug-in

   D. A link that users can follow to download an updated browser version

8. Which of the following conditions are present when a user is in a state of complete engagement with your website?

   A. Concentration, loss of self-consciousness, and loss of sense of time

   B. Video, audio, and animation

   C. Browser support, plug-in support, and technology support

   D. Goal of the site, design of the site, and size of the site

9. You are considering including video in your website. Which of the following should you take into consideration when designing your site?

    A. You should make the video an integral part of your website.

    B. You should include a built-in player so users can see the video through their browsers.

    C. You should state the file size and provide a link to download the video.

    D. You should include video of all lengths to provide the user with variety.

10. Which of the following has the potential to grow into a universally accepted means of delivering web-based content?

    A. Plug-ins

    B. Macromedia Flash

    C. Java applets

    D. Internet TV

11. What is the key to successful creation of a multimedia site?

    A. Planning

    B. Bandwidth

    C. Browser ability

    D. Cost

12. Which of the following is a compilation of still images that is set into motion at a designated sequence, speed, and repetition?

    A. Flash

    B. DHTML

    C. Animated GIF

    D. JavaScript

13. Which of the following companies creates the Flash software?

    A. Microsoft

    B. Macromedia

    C. Macintosh

    D. MyFlash.com

14. What is another term for downloaded audio?

    A. Streamed

    B. Linked

    C. Hyperlinked

    D. Embedded

15. Which of the following filename extensions is used for the QuickTime format?

    A. `.au`

    B. `.mov`

    C. `.mid`

    D. `.aiff`

16. Which of the following companies is the leader in the streaming audio arena?

    A. Macromedia

    B. Microsoft

    C. StreamMachine

    D. RealNetworks

17. In trying to create a mental picture of your website users for your multimedia design, which of the following would not apply?

    A. Sound card

    B. Video graphics card

    C. Monitor size

    D. Memory

18. Joel has decided to create his own website. He likes the pictures that he sees on the Sybex site. He decides to "borrow" these images for his own. What violation has Joel just committed?

   A. Trademark

   B. Customs

   C. Copyright

   D. Tariff

19. One way to allow for files to download easier on a user's system is to do what with the file?

   A. Delete unimportant content

   B. Compress it

   C. Encrypt it

   D. Remove it

20. Which of the following HTML tags is used for a form of scrolling text?

   A. <META>

   B. <MARQUEE>

   C. <SCROLL>

   D. <BANNER>

Answers to Review Questions

1. **A.** Designers often have more advanced technology available to them than the average user does. Browser support of multimedia technology is of utmost concern.

2. **D.** Scrolling text should be avoided because the user will probably pay little attention to it. Additionally, some types of scrolling text are not supported equally in browsers such as Netscape Navigator and Microsoft Internet Explorer.

3. **C.** Bandwidth and browser support limit today's website designers' use of multimedia. To enjoy the full effect of many new technologies, a high-bandwidth connection is usually required, as well as browser plug-in support or other third-party applications.

4. **C.** Animation is the multimedia technology commonly delivered in GIFs, rollovers, and Flash files. Animation allows for a sense of movement and engagement on the part of the user.

5. **D.** The user can download the entire audio file and then begin the playback process, or the audio file can be delivered in streaming format.

6. **A.** The most successful model seems to be the spiral concept and its three elements: interest, activity, and resolution. Each element is encountered in succession until the user's experience is completed or the website's navigable channels have been explored. A "How To" website might attract the user with its intriguing original graphics (interest), provide menu options (activity), and lead the user to the desired goal (resolution).

7. **C.** Website designers also must plan their sites for users who do not have the necessary plug-ins. Rather than accepting a limited audience, you can provide links or instructions to help users find and install the plug-ins your site requires.

8. **A.** Psychological research has concluded that people achieve this state when they concentrate, are challenged, become mesmerized, lose self-consciousness, and lose sense of time. To help your user achieve this frame of mind, you must provide a website that supports these conditions.

9. C. Playing back video on the Web should never be mandatory for anyone outside of a network such as a LAN or an intranet. You should provide links along with file types and sizes to give users the option to proceed.

10. D. Internet TV has not yet evolved into a solid, universally accepted means of connecting people to the Internet, but most experts believe it will.

11. A. Although multimedia has existed for some time, applying it on the Web is not an exact science. Multimedia on the Web is made possible with various tools and technologies that are not always compatible. Planning is the only way to ensure that the process of creating your website will be smooth.

12. C. Animated GIFs can be very effective for displaying additional information in the same area of the screen. Often, they are used to rotate a log with a slogan or tag line. They can also attract the user's attention and add motion to a page that would otherwise be static.

13. B. Macromedia is the company that has developed some of the more well-known animation software for website design, such as Flash, Directory, and Fireworks. It also creates web page creation software called Dreamweaver.

14. D. An audio file could be embedded into an HTML page and downloaded with other files, such as images. Once the audio file is downloaded, it can begin to play. The larger the file, the longer the download takes. Streaming is the other method offered for sending audio over the Web.

15. B. The QuickTime format supporting both audio and video is `.mov`. The Unix native format is `.au`, and `.mid` is the MIDI format. The Macintosh native format is `.aiff`.

16. D. RealNetworks has created some really great tools for sending and receiving streamed audio. RealOne (formerly RealPlayer) has the capability to play streaming audio and video live through connections as slow as 28.8Kbps.

17. A. A sound card is not that important in your multimedia design. If you really know who your users are, you should have a good sense of the hardware, software, and browsers they use. How big are their monitors, and what kind of graphics accelerator cards do they have? Which type of memory do they have and how much? A video card's primary duty is to hold onto a picture to allow the monitor to display it, so the more RAM your users' video cards have, the larger graphics they can handle in terms of the number of both colors and pixels. A single 640×480 256-color graphic demands more than 300KB of memory. For your users to see your image in true color, their computers must have at least 2MB.

18. C. Inappropriate use of other people's work is illegal. As the Web develops and programs are invented to track site visitors, anonymity will decrease. Remember that it is illegal under copyright law to use any published Internet material (text, art, music, code, etc.) without permission from its creator or owner. To avoid legal penalties, you should opt for a conservative interpretation of intellectual property issues.

19. B. You can create smaller, more compressed graphics, animation, video, and audio with applications specifically designed for online usage. These applications allow you to apply a number of graphic optimization processes to still image and movie files. The end result of simple compression is smaller files with little or no loss of quality. You might not be able to remove a file or delete unimportant content within it, and encrypting the file will only make it a longer download for your users.

20. B. Only the <MARQUEE> tag can provide for scrolling text. The <META> tag allows for search engines to place your site correctly within their database for queries. The tags in options C and D are fictitious and therefore incorrect.

Chapter 5

The Website Development Process

THE CIW EXAM OBJECTIVE GROUP COVERED IN THIS CHAPTER:

✓ Develop effective and usable corporate websites within a reasonable time frame, including but not limited to: website vision statements, web strategy and tactics, site metaphors, mindmapping, audience usability testing, and download time.

Developing a website is a complex and involved project that requires a variety of tools and technologies as well as a team that includes members with expertise in various areas. Creating a site that serves only the goals of the designer doesn't meet the overriding purpose of a website: to attract and retain visitors. If website developers ignore the principles of the website development process, the importance of web usability, and the factors of site implementation, their websites will not meet their goals.

In this chapter, we will explore how website design teams contribute to the development of a website, what the phases of the website development process are, and how to define the website project goals. You'll learn about the role the business process plays in website development, how to define a vision and then create a strategy and tactics to support it, how metaphors and the mindmapping process assist in development, and the importance of audience usability and web usability testing. In addition, we'll discuss how to determine site implementation factors and characteristics and how to calculate web page download times.

Website Design Teams

The preparation of a website requires a multitude of skills rarely found in a single individual. When the website designer assumes the role of project manager, the first task is to understand the skills required for building and maintaining the site. Next, you need to take inventory of the available skills within your organization.

The role of the website designer requires more than the production and maintenance of a website. Websites are complex entities with technological and human resources that must be managed. As with any complex system, the website designer's goal is not to become an expert in all the components of the system but rather to be a creative manager of the resources that are available to build and maintain your website. Web professionals each have different skill sets geared toward different areas of website development. Generally, a website development team contains the skill disciplines illustrated in Figure 5.1.

FIGURE 5.1   Skills contributing to website design teams

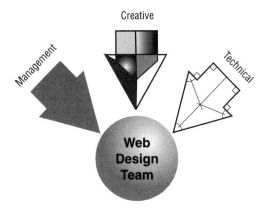

Although website development projects vary, expertise in the areas of project management, graphic design, information technology and architecture, marketing, and writing and editing should be represented in any well-rounded website design team. Each professional brings a different skill set to the task. It would be ideal for an individual to possess all the engineering, programming, editorial, design, and organizational skills required to develop a website, but the reality is that such individuals are extremely rare. Website design is an exercise in bringing the right people and technologies together to achieve the desired vision. Because we deal with finite resources and limited skill sets in the real world, website development is more an art than a science. It is an art that requires you to make the best product with the resources available.

The concept of teams in the workplace is not new. However, only recently have teams been used to develop web projects. In early website development, one person was often responsible for the development of an entire project, usually because of the lack of knowledge about web technology. In addition to the limited knowledge pool, there was an uncertainty and a lack of commitment from management to allocate resources to website development.

This is no longer the case. Management has seen the need for web-enabling technologies. Design teams are now organized and used for website projects and development.

The team approach to website development is critical if the application is to have a well-rounded design. To a certain degree, having creative input from many disciplines is undeniably beneficial. Gathering this type of input is good practice, and it is expected if the website project is to follow the same development cycle other business projects follow.

Bottom-Up Approach for Website Development

It is tempting to approach the design process from the top down: define and design the look and feel of the site and then conform user interaction to that particular design. However, there is a development process that involves creating scenarios, and it is centered on identifying desired system behaviors in response to user behaviors. Thus, the site design process is reversed. The look, feel, and functionality of a website emerge as the various user scenarios are developed from the user's point of view—a *bottom-up approach*.

You can establish a set of desired user behaviors for a website. Each desired behavior brings possible scenarios to be considered. Scenarios greatly facilitate the process of developing a website. First they provide you with a clear image of the project scope; then they serve as a tool during site development to keep the project on track, budget, and schedule.

Website Development Phases

There is a common misconception in website development that you can just sit down and start creating a website. Creating websites has been made much simpler because you can use a WYSIWYG (What You See Is What You Get) editor to assist in developing your site. Although the tool has helped hundreds of thousands of website designers, it has also given them a false sense of security when it comes to planning the site. It is easy to use the WYSIWYG editor to make changes as you design (including reassigning hyperlinks and referencing directory structures). However, a website can become a huge mess very quickly if you subscribe to this method of website design. If you don't have a master plan for the site before you start, changes will quickly become necessary and may conflict with tasks that must be preformed later in the process. The website development process is, therefore, very important in creating a comprehensive site that addresses your users needs.

The website development process consists of five distinct phases:

Conceptualization   The process of developing the vision and strategy for the website. The site vision will encapsulate the overall objectives of the site. This vision is similar to a company mission statement that gives an overview of the company's purpose, creation, and existence.

Design visualization   The process of preparing the transactional, navigational, and hierarchical construction of content. Mindmaps, storyboards, and flowcharts are used in this phase.

Analysis   The process of testing concepts for achieving the site vision. Analysis allows you to determine whether modifications must be made to the design prior to the next phase.

Production   The process of executing the designed plan. This phase includes the creation of all content and the usability testing of the site.

Evolution   The process of refining and updating the site design. This phase is ongoing in website development.

Each phase has an integral component needed for the next phase. For example, if you skip over or rush through the design visualization phase, your site's navigation may suffer from lack of attention. Additionally, the analysis phase will suffer because your navigation concept has not been fully developed and is subject to significant changes. These phases can also be considered milestones for the entire process. Of these, only evolution will have an ongoing life cycle.

Defining and Meeting the Web Project Goals

Defining the goals of a project is crucial to ensuring that everyone's expectations are understood and met. Most web projects have a project manager (PM) who takes a proactive role in the overall organization of the development team. In many cases, the project manager is not a technical guru but has a necessary understanding of the scope of the website development process. As such, the PM oversees project leaders (PLs), each of whom possesses the technical knowledge for the project phase that they oversee. For example, a project will commonly have a technical PL, a creative PL, and a content management PL, and they each act as the expert in their particular area for the team. PLs collaborate with the PM for guidance and clarification as it relates to the project as a whole. This team generally performs the following steps to successfully define and meet the project's goals:

Step 1: Project analysis   Analysis must be performed to identify the strengths and weaknesses of the project, including the strengths and weaknesses of the team members. This step helps establish the hierarchy of the team. Sometimes the team must consult an outside source to assist in some areas of the project where weaknesses or lack of experience exist. The strengths and weaknesses of the project can include the viability of the product or service as it lends itself to the Web. For example, could purchasing or shipping constraints cause difficulty for the project? Will the project have limited funding that could strand it short of completion? Is the time frame realistic for the project's scope? The project team should consider such questions at this time.

Step 2: Client expectations and evaluation   Client expectations must be clearly understood. Clients often have unrealistic expectations of the completed project's capabilities. How will the client evaluate the progress of the project, and how will discrepancies be mediated and resolved?

Step 3: Sign-off stages   Milestones and sign-off stages for the project must be established to evaluate its direction toward the site's goals. For example, is market trend still heading in the same direction, or has a new technology been discovered that can substitute for previously defined technology? It is important to anticipate changes that can occur during the project and consider how best to integrate them. The client should be involved in the sign-off stages.

Step 4: Project transition   You must establish how or at what point the project will be turned over to the client. This step includes defining the responsibilities and duties of the project team and the client. The transition may be difficult if you assume that the client will be ready and able at any time to accept the web project and associated maintenance.

Understanding the Business Process

The role of the website designer is becoming more complex. In the past, website designers could suffice with the skills to create a web presence for the client organization. Today, just having a web presence is not enough. The Internet is no longer a repository of electronic brochures; it's a collection of increasingly sophisticated technologies that offer the ability to develop lucrative Internet-based businesses.

The concepts for these successful electronic businesses are varied. Generally, they can be placed into two categories: sites that deliver products intrinsically dependent on the Internet (such as interactive games or tools for searching the Internet) and sites that deliver existing products and services to a global market on the Internet. What successful websites that have proven success have in common is that they have fulfilled an unmet need for the individual user.

Bookselling is an excellent example. Bookstores in major metropolitan areas are exciting, large, and comprehensive. However, they cannot each carry five million titles, and they are accessible only to people near the major metropolitan areas. Amazon.com responded to the need to overcome these limitations. Anyone with access to the Web has access to the millions of book titles at www.amazon.com. How does one start such a business? It begins with a vision. In this case, the vision was to sell books on the Internet without maintaining an inventory.

Jeff Bezos, founder and CEO of Amazon.com, realized that publishers are always faced with a difficult dilemma: They must invest heavily in the production of a book. In turn, they sell the book to a retail store at wholesale price. If the retailer is conscientious, it will pay the publisher 30 days later. Amazon.com approached publishers and told them that each book it sells on the Internet will be paid for before it is shipped from the publisher. In return, Amazon.com wanted the capability to "drop-ship" books directly from the publisher to the reader.

Because of its success, Amazon.com's model has changed somewhat. The company now has huge inventories of many books, which results in a quicker turnaround for high-volume items. More than 70 percent of Amazon.com's business is with repeat customers.

Defining a Vision

The vision statement is the fundamental framework that defines the scope and intent of a website. The statement should be concise enough that everyone involved in the development process can focus on fulfilling the intended vision. The *vision statement* should include a value and a measurable goal.

The following can be considered a good vision statement:

> We will become the world's preeminent Internet book retailer, selling $1 million in books per day by the turn of the century.

Inherent in this statement is a value ("preeminent Internet book retailer") and a measurable goal ("$1 million per day by the turn of the century").

From Vision to Strategy

In the preceding section, you saw a vision statement strong enough to address the first driving question of the development process: Does our proposed strategy support the vision for the website? For example, the goal of electronic commerce—indeed, of any business—is to make money, and to achieve this goal, businesses and websites need to attract and keep customers. To accomplish this, you can use the unique features of the Internet to your advantage.

As stated earlier, individual needs can be addressed on the Internet. It is more similar to the local grocery store than to the media of television or publishing. You enter a grocery store when you please. Once inside, you decide whether to just browse or to shop, and you choose how you move around the store. Thus the web strategy is not to build the best-looking or most useful website. The web strategy is to build a site to attract and retain users. The details of implementing a web strategy make the task complex.

A tactic is a method used to implement your strategy. For example, if you want to gather personal information from your users, you need a tactic. A widely used tactic is to offer something in exchange for that information. A business might offer a screensavers, software, tickets, or books in return for the requested information. Another common tactic rewards the first-time buyer. If you place an order now, you will receive an additional discount or bonus.

The net effect is that you now have the customer's information. The next time the customer visits your site, you can use this data to complete their purchase or transaction much more quickly.

The Metaphor

A *metaphor* describes one object or experience by using another to suggest a likeness. The most common metaphors used by websites are brochures, prospectuses, and catalogs—all tools of the print medium. Some sites use the familiar metaphor of television. As often pointed out, the Internet offers different opportunities for user interaction. The site visitor is more like a visitor to a store or an art gallery who is interested in the total experience of the visit and not just purchasing a product or looking at a work of art. Even when it is appropriate to use an instrument of the print medium as the metaphor, it should be done intentionally, using the best principles from that medium.

Metaphor Guidelines

Metaphors can be valuable to website design. Consider the following guidelines when developing a metaphor for your site:

- Consider whether a metaphor is needed to express the desired idea.
- Select a metaphor that is familiar to the chosen audience.
- Use the familiar to explain the unfamiliar.
- Keep metaphors light and effective.
- Be sure that the comparison shares characteristics with your theme.
- Use the metaphor consistently in the design.
- Do not overuse the metaphor.
- Do not use a metaphor that may have a negative connotation.
- Choose a metaphor that is easy to remember.
- Do not mix metaphors.

The Mindmapping Process

Imagine creating an entire website or report page by page and writing down all your ideas. If you were to write your thoughts on a piece of paper, describing each page and its content, you would have a list. This list might be incomplete, however, because the linear process stifles your thinking and limits your ideas. In the end, could you correlate all these thoughts easily, and would they flow together?

Now consider mindmapping. *Mindmapping* is a process that allows you to structure ideas on paper in the order your brain follows rather than the linear order normally used when forming ideas. Instead of beginning in the upper-left corner of the paper and proceeding down line by line, place your subject in the middle of the page and circle it. From there, draw branches, which are ideas about your topic. If any topics are related in a more definitive way, create another branch off the current idea branch. Within minutes, you will see your mindmap develop into a dynamic sketch. You might find that a standard sheet of paper is not enough to contain all your thoughts. Use more paper, create more branches, and keep the ideas flowing.

Mindmapping is a process of moving ideas from thought to paper. Do not think about whether your ideas are good or bad: just write them down and move on to the next thought. After you complete your mindmapping process, you can go back and refine or eliminate ideas. Some techniques for mindmapping include using a large chalkboard or white board. You can also use different colors in the process, or thick markers and thin markers—whatever you can find to help stimulate the process.

The Importance of Audience Usability

Some of the most valuable information website developers can have is knowledge of their audience. Along with navigation, knowing your audience is crucial to the success of a site. For example, if you are creating a site for an older audience yet you choose to implement cutting-edge multimedia technology, perhaps you do not know your audience.

To know your audience, you must gather demographic information about its members: age, education, income, and location. In addition, you need to determine the technology they can support with their current computer systems; to do so, you need data such as speed, connections, browser versions, and available plug-ins. Once you know these factors, you can tailor your content to maximize user support.

Usability Elements

The *usability* of a site can be divided into a few distinctive elements that are essential to quality design. These elements are in no particular order; each is of equal importance because it is the combination of these elements that determines usability. Removing even one element will diminish usability.

The elements of usability are as follows:

Quality content   The quality of the content offered by a site is ultimately the value that the site provides.

Easy navigation   Users must be able to navigate the site intuitively with little effort on their part. Otherwise, they will become frustrated and likely go elsewhere.

Information architecture   Quality content is of little use if it is not organized in a way that the average user can effectively navigate. This means that a site's information must be organized in a logical structure.

Search capability   All users are familiar with conducting searches, so providing search engine capability will enhance content identification and retrieval.

These usability elements can be addressed, implemented, and improved even as web and browser technology are in the process of change and improvement.

Software Technology

Usability tests conducted during recent years have shown an increasing reluctance among users to accept innovations in website design. The prevailing attitude favors designs similar to those already common on the Web.

The Web is establishing expectations for narrative flow and user options, and users want pages to stay within these expectations. The Web constitutes a single interwoven user experience rather than a set of separate publications accessed one at a time like traditional books and newspapers. The Web as a whole is the foundation of the user interface, and individual sites are mere particles in the Web universe.

The solution is to advance website design in modest increments, with new sites following conventions while pushing a few innovative ideas. Some of these new ideas will emerge as conventions by their own merits.

The rate at which users upgrade their browsers has actually decreased as more users come online. Studies indicate that it took twice as long for users to upgrade their 3.x versions of browsers to the 4.x versions than it did for them to upgrade from 2.x versions to the 3.x versions. Following are some factors involved in the slower browser migration:

- The user base has grown beyond technically adept users who are interested in the Internet for its own sake. Most current users care about content, not technology or software. Therefore, they are not as motivated to upgrade.

- Many new users do not know how to upgrade their browsers, so they continue to use whichever version they have. Early Internet users were more skilled; many users today are less skilled in their abilities to download, install, and configure software.

- Recent browser upgrades have been less compelling than previous ones in terms of added features or improved usability. The earliest browsers were primitive. The relative improvements from one release to the next were thus fairly significant, offering past users increased benefits for upgrading.

- The download size (in megabytes) of upgrades has grown faster than available bandwidth, thus upgrading requires more time or more costly connection services.

Usability Testing

The only way to achieve maximum site usability is to conduct a usability test. The developer cannot validly indicate that their site design will be functional for the audience. The developer has an intimate knowledge and understanding of the intentions of the site from their production efforts. However, this closeness gives the developer a biased perspective of the site's actual usefulness. They can navigate and find information only because of the close relationship to the project. A site's effectiveness should be tested with users who have little or no exposure to the site and, if possible, the Internet. Conducting a usability test provides the developer with an objective view of the site.

Before the Test

The first step in testing usability is to develop the site to a point very close to the finished product. If the project is not yet at this stage, a usability test cannot provide an accurate evaluation.

Who Should Test for Usability?

The test pool can range from as few as five or six users to as many as you can accommodate. Testing the site with other design team members is inconclusive. Further, the test subjects should include actual target audience members. For example, you should not use children to test an online stock-trading site, nor should you limit yourself to professional stockbrokers. A good cross-section should include some professionals as well as those who know little about trading or have never traded online.

This type of pool provides valuable input from professionals, and non-traders can gauge how effectively your site accommodates entry-level users (and such a site could also provide a stream of new online traders to build the business). Whoever the users, be sure you clearly understand their backgrounds so that their evaluations can be put into perspective.

An exception to the diverse-background rule exists if the site is for internal corporate use as an intranet. In this case, the project team is very likely a part of the audience. However, you should still include other members of the organization, particularly those who are removed from the development process. This more objective group will give the most accurate representation of successful site usability.

Usability Tasks

During the test, participants should be asked to perform actual tasks. If the testing is choreographed with no real-world circumstances, you are unlikely to discover potential problems. Provide a list of tasks and operations to each participant, with no indication of how to perform them. The site itself should tell users all they need to know. As a developer, you may find it difficult to watch test participants stumble through tasks or get frustrated, but you must not interfere in the process. In fact, if you feel observation is necessary, use a video or a one-way mirror. This method precludes any contamination of the testing. Participants should also be asked to note elements they like as well as those they do not. This feedback will make the site more effective.

Results

Be sure to interview the participants upon the completion of the test. You can often help them recall observations they forgot or did not have time to write down. You can include questions such as the following:

- What was your first impression when you saw the site?
- What type of company image did the site portray?
- Do you understand the site structure?
- Can you recall the site's major elements?

Written data should be compiled and analyzed from an objective viewpoint. How many users had the same experience? Were any problems consistently noted? These trends are the real indicators of usability. Be sure to take a closer look at these problems individually to see how you as the developer can increase user awareness and usability.

Some insufficiencies will probably surface during the testing. As a designer, you may find it difficult to take criticism for a site that you put much effort into producing, but you must consider feedback constructively and address the issues. The sting of critique from a few participants will be short-lived compared to a website catastrophe that could occur if you go online with a faulty site and receive widespread criticism for a foolish mistake.

Determining Site Implementation Factors

As you prepare to construct your website, you should be aware of several factors that will affect implementation. These include the scope of the project, the skill resources available, the technology you plan to use, and the time allotted for implementation.

Scope

To determine the scope of the project, you must determine whether the site will be on the Internet, on an intranet, or on an extranet. This does not limit your site to its initial state, but it does give you the ability to prepare for the site's evolution. If you do not anticipate a change in the site's scope, then less planning is required to address possible implementations of a larger scope. If, however, a change is likely, the initial scope must address how this change will be accommodated in the website vision.

The scope of the site will typically fall under one of the following definitions:

Internet   The site is intended for public use and will supply information to random users.

Intranet   The site is intended for internal use and will supply information to known users.

Extranet   The site is intended for known external users and will supply specific information required by those users.

Skills

The skill resources you require will vary depending on which aspect of the web application is being developed. Most tasks involved in the project fall into one of two general categories:

Development and construction   The skills required to design and build the site range from programming HTML to administering systems and databases. The majority of these tasks will be complete when the site is published and running.

Maintenance   The skills required to maintain the site after construction is complete are more limited. Maintenance might require only HTML programming to provide and update content. Depending on the complexity of the site, you may also require the skills of system and database administrators on a limited basis.

Technology

You will be tempted to use cutting-edge technology simply because it is available. However, it is prudent to determine whether a particular technology enhances the usability of the site.

As noted in previous chapters, website designers should use the lowest common denominator, which is based upon the intended audience. To maximize the number of users who can view the site as intended, it is important to keep abreast of user-technology demographics.

Time

Time is often the most valuable resource, and it is easy to underestimate. Its importance must not be overlooked or understated. Deadline and maintenance issues impact time during and after the development of a website:

Deadlines   During the construction of the site, various deadlines must be met. To help relieve stress and keep the morale of the project team high, employ proper time-management techniques and time-frame estimates to ensure that the deadlines are realistic and achievable.

Maintenance   After construction, the ongoing upkeep of the site can also be time-consuming. Budgeting time for maintenance is important if the site is to contain the most recent and accurate information. Even though the site is "live," the work is not complete.

Website Characteristics

Every website contains elements of appearance and functionality that serve its purpose. These characteristics vary depending on whether the site is used for informational purposes only or for e-commerce. Table 5.1 describes these characteristics and their significance to informational and e-commerce sites.

TABLE 5.1   Website Characteristics

Characteristic	Description	Informational Website	E-Commerce Website
Web presence	The basic element of any website. Web presence is the impression created by the overall look and feel of the site.	Gives the user an intrinsic impression of the organization.	Important, but insufficient to accomplish e-commerce goals.
Web interactivity	The element that keeps users who are just browsing engaged in the site.	Optional.	Required. Without interactivity, no e-business can occur. Listing an 800 number for purchases is ineffective.

TABLE 5.1   Website Characteristics *(continued)*

Characteristic	Description	Informational Website	E-Commerce Website
Navigation	The logic of movement a user experiences in navigating through the site and completing transactions.	Important.	Crucial.
Personalization	A customized interface for each user.	Marginally useful.	Extremely useful.
Permission marketing	Marketing in which users give permission to market to them. The marketer generally offers something of perceived value in exchange for personal information.	Not applicable.	Good strategy for successful e-commerce.
Participating in and/or forging a web community	Groups in which members share similar interests and engage with each other.	Can increase user participation.	Can significantly increase e-commerce objectives.
Advertising	Method for promoting the website and opening the site to outside advertisers.	Not applicable.	As with any business, can solely determine success.
Database integration	Method for integrating complex database structures for information storage and access.	Optional.	Required.
Web data analysis	Method for gaining intelligence on the performance of a website.	Optional.	Good strategy for continual improvement of e-commerce.

Calculating Download Times

When constructing a website, another important aspect to consider is the amount of time it takes users to download information. Users become frustrated if they must wait to see parts of the site, and they may move on to another site rather than be patient.

To calculate *download time*, follow these steps:

1. Check the size of the HTML file and any associated images, files, or programs. For example, you may have a page that consists of 11 files, for a total of 84 kilobytes (KB).

2. Determine the speed of your network connection. The following list includes some of the more common connection speeds:

   - 14.4Kbps (slow modem speed)

   - 28.8Kbps (typical modem speed)

   - 33.6Kbps (typical modem speed)

   - 56Kbps (typical modem speed)

   - 1.544Mbps (full T1, enterprise-grade network line)

   For this example, we will use 56 kilobits per second (Kbps).

3. The connection speed and the file size must be converted to a common unit of measure for division: either bytes or bits. Remember that 1 byte equals 8 bits. The connection speed is already defined in bits: 56 kilobits = 56,000 bits. To convert the file size to bits, you should first convert it to bytes (84 kilobytes = 84,000 bytes). Then convert the bytes to bits by multiplying 84,000 by 8 (1 byte = 8 bits), which results in 672,000 bits.

4. Divide the file size (672,000 bits) by the connection speed (56,000 bits per second). The bits cancel out, and the result is 12 seconds. This is the amount of time it will theoretically take to download the web page.

Remember that the figure derived from these four steps represents a theoretical measurement. It does not account for certain factors, such as the fact that 56Kbps modems rarely operate above 50Kbps. Nor does it account for network overhead, noisy phone lines, or network congestion. Therefore, the best way to determine how quickly users can download your HTML pages is to test them in a real-world setting. For example, test your website by accessing it through a dial-up (telephone) connection. That method will give you a much more reliable estimate.

Some reference books refer to bits per second as "characters per second," although these terms are not technically equivalent.

Summary

Although website development projects vary, expertise in the areas of project management, graphic design, information technology and architecture, marketing, and writing and editing should be represented in any well-rounded website design team.

One of the first steps in developing a website is to develop a concept for your website. To form the concept, you should focus on creating a vision for your web-based business and thinking of strategies and tactics to fulfill your vision.

Metaphors can play an important role in the look, feel, and overall understanding of a site. The site visitor is more like a visitor to a store or an art gallery, they are interested in the total experience of the visit and not just purchasing a product or looking at a work of art. Even when it is appropriate to use an instrument of the print medium as the metaphor, it should be done intentionally, using the best principles from that medium.

Mindmapping is a process of moving ideas from thought to paper, and it is another tool that can be very helpful in designing a website. You can also conduct usability testing. To do so, you must gather a groups of diverse individuals who represent a good cross-section of experienced and inexperienced Internet users and people who are familiar with the topic matter as well as novices.

Every website contains elements of appearance and functionality that serve its purpose. They vary depending on whether the site is used for informational purposes only or for e-commerce.

Exam Essentials

Understand the collaborative nature of website development.   It's critical to use a team approach to website development if the application is to have a well-rounded design. Having creative input from many disciplines can be beneficial. Gathering this type of input is good practice, and it is expected if the project is to follow the same development cycle as other business projects. You should know the specific areas of expertise and the responsibilities each encompasses.

Know the importance of design goals. Defining the goals of a project is crucial to ensure that everyone's expectations are understood and met. You should know the specific design goals and their purposes.

Understand a website vision statement. The vision statement is the fundamental framework that defines the scope and intent of a website. The statement should be concise enough that everyone involved in the development process can focus on fulfilling the intended vision. The vision statement should include a value and a measurable goal.

Be able to develop a web strategy and the tactics to support it. A web strategy is used to support the vision of your site. If your vision is to be the largest online retailer in your segment, then your strategy would be to attract and retain users to generate business. A tactic is a method used to implement your strategy.

Know the site metaphor concept. A metaphor describes one object or experience by using another to suggest a likeness. Brochure, prospectus, and catalog metaphors are commonly used on websites. Some sites use the familiar metaphor of television.

Understand the mindmapping process. Mindmapping is a process that allows you to structure ideas on paper in the order your brain follows rather than the linear order normally used when forming ideas. Mindmapping is a process of moving ideas from thought to paper, not judging whether ideas are good or bad, just writing them down and moving on to the next thought.

Know the importance of audience usability. Some of the most valuable information a website developer can have is knowledge of their audience. Along with navigation, knowing your audience is crucial to the success of a site.

Be able to conduct a usability test. You should try to get users who have little or no exposure to the site and, if possible, to the Internet to text the site's effectiveness. Find user who have all levels of experience with the topic matter. Testers should be asked to perform specific tasks with no instructions. They can then provide feedback regarding their experiences. You can use the feedback to improve the usability of the site.

Understand site implementation factors. Critical factors that affect site implementation include the scope of the project, the skills that will be required to develop the site, determining the technology to be included and the time required to meet the deadlines associated with the development of the site, and the required maintenance after completion.

Know site characteristics and their significance. Web presence, web interactivity, navigation, personalization, permission marketing, participating in and/or forging a web community, advertising, database integration, and web data analysis are characteristics of website appearance and functionality. You should know each characteristics and their importance.

Be able to calculate download time. To calculate download time, convert both the file size of the page (including all image files) and the connection speed into the same unit of measure (bits) and then divide the file size by the connection speed.

Key Terms

Before you take the exam, be certain you are familiar with the following terms:

bottom-up approach	mindmapping
download time	usability
metaphor	vision statement

Review Questions

1. Why is it critical to approach website development as a collaborative effort?

   A. Because there is uncertainty and lack of resource commitment from management.

   B. Because there is a short supply of knowledge about web technology.

   C. Because a team approach provides the web project with a well-rounded design.

   D. Because development is faster, even though one person can handle the development of an entire web project.

2. A website development team takes several steps throughout the project to establish goals and ensure that the goals are met. Which of the following is a step taken to establish site design goals and/or ensure that they are met?

   A. Analyze the project to identify its strengths and weaknesses as well as the strengths and weaknesses of team members.

   B. Consult an outside source who can oversee the team, ensuring that all team members are equal.

   C. Specify the intended project result to the client to ensure that the client does not expect something else.

   D. Establish a final sign-off point to occur only when the project is completed in its entirety.

3. Which of the following describes a good web project vision statement?

   A. A statement that specifies financial and technological requirements

   B. A document that identifies the responsibilities of team members

   C. A concise statement that includes a value and a measurable goal

   D. A legal contract that includes client expectations and deadlines

4. Skill resources required for a web project generally fall into two categories. Which of the following options lists these two categories?

   A. Lowest common denominator and highest common denominator

   B. Development/construction and maintenance

   C. Deadlines and maintenance

   D. Technology and time

5. In website design, what is a metaphor?

   A. A visual suggestion of similarity to another thing or idea

   B. A comparison of dissimilar things using the words *like* or *as*

   C. A literal comparison of ideas described in the text of the site

   D. A strict formula for effective layout of images on a home page

6. Which option best describes the process of mindmapping?

   A. Quickly develop a site map to place on your site.

   B. Structure ideas on paper in an order your brain follows.

   C. Quickly develop a plan to mastermind a web project.

   D. Structure ideas on paper in a linear order.

7. The document mindmapping produces is most similar to what?

   A. A list

   B. A report

   C. A storyboard

   D. A dynamic sketch

8. Which of the following site characteristics describes the impression created by the overall look and feel of the site?

   A. Personalization

   B. Web interactivity

   C. Web presence

   D. Navigation

9. An important usability factor in designing for the Web is knowledge of your audience. Designers can study demographics to determine the audience's hardware and software capabilities. How can they use this information?

   A. To tailor content to maximize user support

   B. To persuade users to upgrade their browsers

   C. To create a site that users can test for usability

   D. To implement intuitive navigational elements

10. The usability of a website can be divided into four distinct elements. Which usability element is ultimately the value that the site provides?

    A. Search capability

    B. Information architecture

    C. Easy navigation

    D. Quality content

11. Which of the following is not one of the initial scopes to a website design?

    A. Internet

    B. Intranet

    C. Extranet

    D. Virtual private network

12. Which of the following is a good goal for the project manager of a website?

    A. To posses all the skills needed to create the entire website

    B. To understand the skills needed and pool together those skills in your company

    C. To find someone else who will manage the project

    D. To create the desired vision

13. The look and feel and functionality of a website should be developed from the users' point of view. What term defines this approach?

   A. Bottom up

   B. Top down

   C. Side to side

   D. Vertical engineering

14. A project manager (PM) will commonly appoint which of the following types of project leaders (PLs)?

   A. Technical, creative, design

   B. Technical, creative, content

   C. Hardware, practical, creative

   D. Technical, design, content

15. Which of the following usability elements involves the organization of content in such a way that it is structured in a logical format?

   A. Quality content

   B. Easy navigation

   C. Information architecture

   D. Search capability

16. A project will have two distinct skill sets required, one of which is development and construction. Which of the following defines this form of skill set?

   A. The skills required to manage the site after construction is complete

   B. The ability to communicate verbally the site's focus

   C. The ability to manage the website development team

   D. The skills required to build the site, including programming HTML and administering systems and databases

17. Which of the following modem speeds would be considered slow by modern standards?

A. 14.4Kbps

B. 56Kbps

C. DSL speed

D. T1

18. In web usability testing, which of the following statements is accurate?

A. You should limit the number of users to five or six people.

B. You should not use members of the design team.

C. There should not be a time limit on the testing process.

D. Simulations are better than real-world tasks.

19. Which of the following defines *navigation*?

A. The overall look and feel of the site

B. The element that keeps users who are just browsing engaged in the site

C. The logic of movement a user experiences

D. A customized interface for each user

20. Which of the following website characteristics is required for e-commerce website development?

A. Web data analysis

B. Database integration

C. Permission marketing

D. Web presence

Answers to Review Questions

1. C.   The team approach to website development is critical if the application is to have a well-rounded design. It's beneficial to have creative input from many disciplines. It is good practice to gather this type of input, and it is expected if the web project is to follow the same development cycle other business projects follow.

2. A.   Analysis must be performed to identify the strengths and weaknesses of the project, including the strengths and weaknesses of the team members. This step helps establish the hierarchy of the team. It also helps to determine whether the team must consult an outside source to assist in some areas of the project where weaknesses or lack of experience exist.

3. C.   The vision statement is the fundamental framework that defines the scope and intent of a website. The statement should be concise enough that everyone involved understands the intended vision. The vision statement should include a value and a measurable goal.

4. B.   The skills required to design and build a site fall into the development and construction categories. They range from HTML programming to system and database administrators. The majority of the tasks associated with development and construction will be complete when the site is published and running, but the maintenance category includes skills required to maintain the site after construction is complete.

5. A.   A metaphor describes one object or experience by using another to suggest a likeness. The most common metaphors used by websites are tools of the print medium—brochures, prospectuses, and catalogs—and the metaphor of television.

6. B.   Mindmapping is a process that allows you to structure ideas on paper in the order your brain follows rather than the linear order normally used when forming ideas.

7. D.   When creating a mindmap, you place your subject in the middle of the page and circle it; then you draw branches for the ideas about your topic. If any topics are related in a more definitive way, you create another branch off the current idea branch. This way, your mindmap develops into a dynamic sketch.

8. C.   Web presence is the basic element of any website. It is the impression created by the overall look and feel of the site.

9. A. To know the audience, you must know the demographics: age, education, income, and location. You also need to determine the technology these users can support with their current computer systems; to do so, you need data such as speed, connections, browser versions, and available plug-ins. Once you know these factors, you can tailor your content to maximize user support.

10. D. Users will evaluate your website on the quality of the content that you provide. Without quality content, users will not be compelled to stay on the site.

11. D. A virtual private network may assist in formulating an extranet, but this would not be considered one of the scope definitions. The initial state gives you the ability to prepare for the site's evolution. If you do not anticipate a change in the site's scope, then less planning is required to address possible implementation of a larger scope. The other options are initial state possibilities.

12. B. The goal of project manager is to understand the skills required and then take inventory of the available skills within your organization. The goal is not to become an expert in all the components of the system but to be a creative manager of the resources that enable the website. The vision is a team project.

13. A. You can establish a set of desired user behaviors for a website. Each desired behavior brings possible scenarios to be considered. In putting together these scenarios, you reverse the process. Rather than approaching the design process from the top down, defining and designing the look and feel of the site and then conforming user interaction to that design, you work on design first and then create the look and feel of the site.

14. B. A project will commonly have a technical PL, a creative PL, and a content management PL, and they each act as the expert in their particular area for the team. PLs collaborate with the PM for guidance and clarification as it relates to the project as a whole.

15. C. Information architecture means that a site's information must be organized in a logical structure. The other responses have their own separate meanings. Quality content is ultimately the value that the site provides. Easy navigation means users will be able to navigate the site intuitively with little effort on their part. Search capability would involve providing a search engine, which will enhance content identification and retrieval.

16. D. The skills required for designing and building the site range from programming HTML to administering systems and databases. The majority of these tasks will be complete when the site is published and running. These abilities are all part of the development and construction skill set. Communication and management abilities are not necessary (although they do prove helpful). To manage a site after construction, you need maintenance skills, and these are not as intensive.

17. A. Okay, easy question right? That depends; many would include 56Kbps in the list of slow modem speeds because of the overwhelming move to either cable modem or DSL line speeds. It's helpful to remember that this technology is still not available in all areas and that 56Kbps is considered a typical modem speed, as opposed to slow.

18. B. Testing the site with other design team members is inconclusive. Further, the test subjects should include actual target audience members. For example, you should not use teenagers to test an online stock-trading site, nor should you limit yourself to professional stockbrokers. You don't have to limit the number of people used; it really amounts to how many you can accommodate. A deadline is a good idea for testing, and it is certainly good for testers to use a real-world scenario to test a site.

19. C. Navigation is the logic of movement a user experiences in navigating through the site and completing transactions. The other definitions relate to web presence, web interactivity, and personalization.

20. B. Successful e-commerce sites almost universally integrate complex database structures for information storage and access. The other options all have necessary functions and will certainly assist in the formation of an e-commerce site's success, but without a database, there is no way to keep track of who purchases what, the inventory remaining, all of the data about customers, or even all the data about merchandise for the online catalog (if there happens to be one). A database is most definitely a requirement for e-commerce.

Chapter
6

HTML Standards and Compliance

THE CIW EXAM OBJECTIVE GROUP COVERED IN THIS CHAPTER:

✓ Identify important Internet standards, including but not limited to: HTML recommendations.

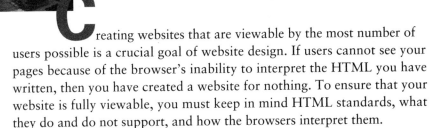

reating websites that are viewable by the most number of users possible is a crucial goal of website design. If users cannot see your pages because of the browser's inability to interpret the HTML you have written, then you have created a website for nothing. To ensure that your website is fully viewable, you must keep in mind HTML standards, what they do and do not support, and how the browsers interpret them.

In this chapter, we will explore the development of HTML, how browsers support HTML, the standards surrounding and who controls HTML, the role tags play in HTML and what happens when they are no longer part of a current standard, and the role accessibility plays in website design.

What Is HTML?

*H*TML stands for Hypertext Markup Language. It was developed by Tim Berners-Lee of the Massachusetts Institute of Technology invented HTML with colleagues from CERN (the European Particle Physics Laboratory) as a means of distributing nonlinear text, called *hypertext*, to multiple points across the Internet. One document links to another through pointers called hyperlinks. *Hyperlinks* are embedded instructions within one text file that call another file when they are accessed, usually by a click of a mouse. The global set of linked documents across the existing Internet framework grew into what is now known as the World Wide Web.

Hypertext was first conceived by Ted Nelson in 1965. The first widely commercialized hypertext product was HyperCard, conceived by Bill Atkinson and introduced by Apple Computer in 1987. It incorporated many hypertext and hypermedia concepts, but it was a proprietary system that worked only on Macintosh computers. *Hypermedia* is an extension of hypertext. It includes images, video, audio, animation, and other multimedia data types, which can be incorporated into HTML documents. The Web can be accurately described as a hypermedia system.

In contrast, HTML is a cross-platform language that works on Windows, Macintosh, and Unix platforms. In addition, HTML and the Web are client/server systems; HyperCard works only on a stand-alone Macintosh computer. A markup language is very different from a programming language. Program files and data files exist separately in traditional applications. When a markup language is used, the instructions and the data reside in the same file. In addition, HTML does not provide data structures or internal logic as do procedural programming languages such as C and Pascal.

HTML has evolved from other markup languages. IBM created the Generalized Markup Language (GML) in the late 1960s as a way to move formatted documents across different computer platforms. GML evolved into the Standard Generalized Markup Language (SGML) in 1986 and was ratified by the International Organization for Standardization (ISO). Although SGML is a powerful markup language, it is also very complex and difficult to learn.

HTML is an application of SGML. Although it has fewer language elements than SGML, it is easier to use and has become the standard method of encoding information for web documents. As with GML, HTML facilitates data exchange through a common document format across different types of computer systems and networks on the Web.

Whereas SGML is used specifically to define context as opposed to appearance, HTML has evolved into both a contextual and a formatting language. By applying a heading style to text using HTML, for example, you are not only marking that text contextually as an important line that begins a new section, you are also applying the visual formatting elements of boldface and a larger font size. HTML files are plain-text files that have been "marked up" with special language elements called tags, which are embedded in the text. *Tags* are pieces of text that are enclosed in angle brackets and provide instructions to programs designed to interpret HTML. For example, you might want to change the color of some text in your file. You can do this by embedding opening and closing tags around the text you want colored. That section of HTML would appear like this: `<FONT COLOR="red">Welcome to my website!</FONT>`. "Welcome to my website!" would appear in red text. If you want an image to appear in your document, you can use a tag to specify the source and placement of the image.

HTML interpreters are programs such as Netscape Navigator and Microsoft Internet Explorer that process HTML pages and render them to the user as text pages formatted in accordance with the embedded instructions. These two programs are also called web browsers; we will discuss them in more detail later in this chapter.

HTML interpreters are not limited to browsers, however. Many programs that have come on the market since 1996 include HTML reading and exporting capabilities as built-in features. Netscape Communicator, for example, now allows you to send and receive HTML messages, and you can post fully formatted HTML messages to news and discussion groups. HTML files are very small and extremely portable, making this format an ideal choice when exchanging documents across any kind of network.

Web Browser HTML Support

Web browsers are programs designed specifically to render hypermedia documents from the Internet. They allow HTML pages, sound files, images, video, and other media to be viewed across the Internet or enterprise intranet by the user.

Figures 6.1 and 6.2 show the same page rendered by two different browsers. Because this page was created using standard HTML code, the page's appearance will not change even though the browser interface is different.

Although standard HTML should render the same results across browsers, each browser manufacturer supports additional code that others may or may not support. Using the nonstandard, proprietary code will likely cause the page to be rendered differently across browsers, as demonstrated by Figures 6.3 and 6.4.

Good HTML coding practice involves ensuring that content is rendered correctly regardless of which browser is used. Microsoft and Netscape, for example, each supports its own extensive proprietary HTML extensions. If you are coding an HTML page for your company's intranet and all employees use the same browser, you can comfortably use proprietary language extensions and technology. But if you are preparing a site for public use, it is best to code the page using the most widely supported standards.

FIGURE 6.1   CIWCertified.com web page displayed in Netscape Navigator 6

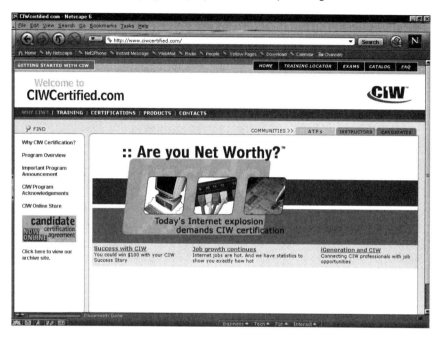

FIGURE 6.2   CIWCertified.com web page displayed in Microsoft Internet Explorer 5

FIGURE 6.3   Web page displayed in Netscape Navigator 4

FIGURE 6.4   The page shown in Figure 6.3, this time displayed in Microsoft Internet Explorer

The HTML Standard

The HTML standard defines the individual elements that make up the language. These elements are the instructions, or tags, that indicate how HTML documents should be displayed in a browser. This standard ensures that hypertext is displayed consistently in different browsers and on computer platforms. Standardization limits the proprietary software specifications that do not operate with other vendors' products.

Currently, the HTML standard includes four versions: 1.0, 2.0, 3.2, and 4.0. There is one subversion as well, 4.01. Additionally, individual browser vendors have developed their own HTML extensions. Remember as you design your web pages to consider the users for whom you are designing.

Some organizations recognize the existence of six versions of HTML: 1.0, 2.0, 3.0, 3.2, 4.0, and 4.01. Version 3.0 was never ratified by the W3C and 4.01 is a subversion of the HTML 4.0 Recommendation. Technically, there are only four versions of HTML.

Who Controls HTML?

The *World Wide Web Consortium (W3C)* is an international industry consortium founded in 1994 to develop common standards for the World Wide Web. It controls the evolution of HTML. When the W3C has fully endorsed a technology, it publishes a Recommendation to the Internet community. When a proposed standard is being evaluated, it is in a state of constant flux. Be sure the HTML you support conforms to the latest Recommendation from the W3C. Do not write to specifications indicated in working drafts; technologies addressed in working drafts are undergoing discussion and consideration and are probably not yet supported by the major vendors. Recommendations from the W3C become the standards to which vendors pledge full support.

HTML 1.0 and 2.0

The HTML 1.0 standard is essentially the first version of HTML used for graphical browsers. It was equivalent to the first HTML specification (version 0), with added support for images. Version 0 was used as a prototype to test the Web with the first generation of character-based browsers, such as Lynx from CERN.

HTML 2.0 includes all the capabilities of version 1.0 plus support for user input fields, which is necessary for forms. In practice, browser developers such as Microsoft and Netscape have moved well beyond the HTML 2.0 standard.

HTML 3.0 and 3.2

HTML 3.0 was never ratified. As more browser-specific tags were introduced, it became obvious that a new standard was needed. For this reason, version 3.0 was abandoned for version 3.2.

HTML 3.2 added widely deployed features such as tables, applets, and text flow around images while providing full backward compatibility with the existing standard HTML 2.0. The major enhancements included support for the following elements:

- Tables

- Figures

- Frames

- Mathematical equations

- Improved tags

HTML 4.0

HTML 4.0 is the W3C standard for the latest version of HTML. The new Recommendation provides support for elements that were not included in HTML 3.2. The major areas of change are as follows:

- Style sheets

- Internationalization features (e.g., reading from right to left)

- Accessibility features (e.g., disability issues)

- Enhanced tables and forms

- Scripting and multimedia

HTML version 4.0 is specified in three variants:

HTML 4.0 Transitional   Most people creating web pages for public access will want to use HTML 4.0 Transitional. This version takes advantage of HTML 4.0 features including *Cascading Style Sheets (CSS)*, but it does not rely on them, which benefits those viewing pages with older browsers. HTML 4.0 dropped some common attributes and tags that style sheets now handle. This variation of the standard allows you to use some of those elements.

HTML 4.0 Strict   The HTML 4.0 Strict Recommendation should be used if you want to rid your document of structural markup, leaving it free of any tags associated with layout. You can use this version with Cascading Style Sheets to produce the font, color, and layout effects you want.

HTML 4.0 Frameset   The HTML 4.0 Frameset Recommendation is appropriate when you want to use frames to partition the browser window into two or more adjacent windows.

HTML 4.01

HTML 4.01 is the latest subversion from the W3C regarding HTML. It was approved in 1999 and includes a few minor modifications to the standard to fix errors found in HTML 4.0, and it calls for support of XHTML. HTML 4.01 encourages website designers to consider the following when writing HTML:

Separate structure and presentation.   Style sheets have assisted designers in separating the structure of their web pages from the presentation by taking the presentational elements out of the HTML and placing them in a style sheet. A reduction in cost in serving a wide range of platforms can be realized through separating presentational aspects from the structure of a document. Additionally, it facilitates document revisions because the structures are clearly separated.

Consider universal accessibility to the Web.   HTML 4.01 urges website developers to consider how documents are rendered on a variety of platforms (speech-based readers, for example) in order to make the World Wide Web accessible everyone, notably those with disabilities. Additionally, designers should consider the wide variety of platforms (computer configurations, software use) across the world used to view web pages. Web pages should include information about the native language of the document, the direction of the text, how the document is encoded, and other issues related to internationalization.

Help user agents with incremental rendering.   This area deals specifically with tables and how they are rendered in a browser. User agents are speech-based readers and braille readers, for example. These user agents have a difficult time interpreting the information in tables correctly unless the table is laid out to meet the specifications of the user agent (all content running left to right instead of top to bottom, for example).

XHTML

A new Recommendation has emerged from the W3C called Extensible Hypertext Markup Language (XHTML). XHTML is a combination of Extensible Markup Language (XML) 1.0 and HTML 4.01.

XHTML will allow XHTML-compliant documents to be used, viewed, and validated by both HTML and XML processors. Therefore, developers can begin using some of the features of XML with the confidence that backward-compatibility issues with HTML as well as future issues with XML will be addressed.

In Chapter 13, "Extensible Markup Language (XML)," you will be introduced to XML and its future in the arena of web applications.

Deprecated Tags

Deprecated tags and attributes are those that have been replaced by other HTML elements. Deprecated tags are still included in the HTML draft or Recommendation but are clearly marked as deprecated. Deprecated tags might become obsolete. The draft strongly urges you to not use deprecated tags. Tags are deprecated each time a new Recommendation becomes a standard. The HTML 4.01 Recommendation deprecated many text-formatting tags because style sheets will handle most text-formatting options.

The following HTML 4.01 tags are deprecated:

- <ISINDEX>

- <APPLET>

- <CENTER>

- <FONT>

- <BASEFONT>

- <STRIKE>

- <U>

- <DIR>

- <MENU>

You can still use deprecated tags; most browsers continue to support them. If you use deprecated tags, you will be using the HTML 4.01 Transitional Recommendation. One of the difficulties of deprecated tags, however, is that some browsers may not support the new tag that replaces the deprecated one.

For example, <APPLET> has been deprecated in favor of <OBJECT>. However, Netscape Navigator versions as late as 4.7 do not support the <OBJECT> tag, so it is still necessary to use the <APPLET> tag even a year after the W3C has deprecated it. As of this writing, Netscape Navigator version 6 still does not support the <OBJECT> tag.

Extensions to HTML

Browsers such as Internet Explorer and Navigator have moved ahead to include features that are not part of the current HTML 4.01 standard. These proprietary features are called *extensions* because they "extend" the existing HTML standard, and they may or may not be included in the next HTML standard. Two common extensions to the HTML standard are <BLINK> (supported by Navigator) and <MARQUEE> (supported by Internet Explorer). If you develop your website with proprietary extensions, you might be forced to revise your site to comply with the proposed standard and appeal to a wider audience.

Some browsers simply ignore proprietary tags, which can have a significant effect on how your HTML documents are displayed by the browser; proprietary extensions can be misinterpreted by a browser, which can have a destructive effect on your documents. HTML authors should be aware of these effects and test web documents in several browsers.

Web Page Accessibility

Web pages should be accessible to all people, including those with disabilities. To assist in this mission, the W3C has created the *Web Accessibility Initiative (WAI)*. According to the WAI, the Web's full potential can only be realized by "promoting a high degree of usability for people with disabilities." The WAI works with worldwide organizations in five main areas: technology, guidelines, tools, education and outreach, and research and development.

WAI aims to ensure that core technologies used on the Web—such as HTML, CSS, XML, and the Document Object Model (DOM)—are equally accessible to users with physical, visual, hearing, and cognitive disabilities. For example, a person with a visual disability may be unable to view a multimedia presentation on the Web. One way to solve this problem is to include text equivalents of the presentation in the code. The multimedia player, such as RealNetworks RealPlayer or Microsoft Windows Media Player, could then access the text equivalent and present it to the user in braille or as speech.

The WAI works with various W3C working groups to ensure that the standards for various W3C technologies include accessibility options. For example, the HTML standard supports improved navigation, extended descriptions of complex graphics, and multimedia captions. It also supports device-independent user interface descriptions that allow users to interact with web pages using a mouse, keyboard, or voice input.

You can visit the following websites to learn more about web page accessibility for the disabled:

- Web Accessibility Initiative (WAI) at www.w3.org/WAI/

- Curriculum for Web Content Accessibility Guidelines 1.0 at www.w3.org/WAI/wcag-curric/

Conformance

The WAI Web Content Accessibility Guidelines 1.0 specification divides conformance requirements into a hierarchy with three levels. Note that in accordance with accessibility guidelines, conformance level names are spelled out in text so they may be understood when rendered to speech. The conformance levels are defined as follows.

Conformance Level "A"   All Priority 1 checkpoints are satisfied.

Conformance Level "Double-A"   All Priority 1 and 2 checkpoints are satisfied.

Conformance Level "Triple-A"   All Priority 1, 2, and 3 checkpoints are satisfied.

Each level of conformance encompasses a specific set of checkpoints, each with an assigned priority level. The WAI defines the three priority levels of checkpoints as follows.

Priority 1   A web content developer *must* satisfy this checkpoint to provide accessibility for all users. If a Priority 1 checkpoint is not satisfied, then one or more groups of users will be unable to access information in the web document. This checkpoint is a basic requirement for some groups to access web documents.

Priority 2   A web content developer *should* satisfy this checkpoint. If a Priority 2 checkpoint is not satisfied, then one or more groups of users will have difficulty accessing information in the web document. This checkpoint removes significant barriers to accessing web documents.

Priority 3   A web content developer *may* address this checkpoint. If a Priority 3 checkpoint is not satisfied, then one or more groups will have some difficulty accessing information in the document. This checkpoint improves access to web documents.

All checkpoints are organized under 14 specific guidelines. The guidelines are developed with consideration for groups of users with specified disabilities or needs. The WAI defines the 14 guidelines as follows.

1. Provide equivalent alternatives to auditory and visual content.
2. Do not rely on color alone.
3. Use markup and style sheets properly.
4. Clarify natural language usage.
5. Create tables that transform gracefully.
6. Ensure that pages featuring new technologies transform gracefully.
7. Ensure user control of time-sensitive content changes.
8. Ensure direct accessibility of embedded user interfaces.
9. Design for device-independence.
10. Use interim solutions.
11. Use W3C technologies and guidelines.
12. Provide context and orientation information.
13. Provide clear navigation mechanisms.
14. Ensure that documents are clear and simple.

Although different situations should be considered when designing web documents, each accessible design choice generally benefits several disability groups and the web community as a whole. For more detailed information, you can read the WAI specification at `www.w3.org/TR/WAI-WEBCONTENT/`.

Summary

HTML provides the absolute basis for web content behind nearly every website viewed. HTML was created by Tim Berners-Lee of the Massachusetts Institute of Technology with colleagues from CERN (the European Particle Physics Laboratory). From its creation to its current state, it has been the cornerstone of website development. Continuous developments have been made in HTML, starting with version 1.0 and continuing through version 4.0 and revision 4.01 along with the newest Recommendation, XHTML.

Companies who make web browsers have created their own extensions outside of the HTML Recommendations. Although these extensions can add content and exciting elements to a web page, proprietary extensions can be misinterpreted by a browser, which can ultimately have a destructive effect on documents. Being aware of the limitations of proprietary extensions is an important responsibility of a website designer and should always be taken into account when creating sites.

Finally, the Web Accessibility Initiative (WAI) plays a great role in website design. This initiative aims to make web content accessible to all people, including those with disabilities. Although the rules involved in the WAI may seem daunting at first glance, they are actually very logical and provide common sense regulations for making websites more accessible to every user, ultimately increasing a website's reach across many audiences.

Exam Essentials

Know the origins of HTML. Tim Berners-Lee of the Massachusetts Institute of Technology invented HTML with colleagues from CERN (the European Particle Physics Laboratory) as a means of distributing non-linear text, called hypertext, to multiple points across the Internet.

Know the HTML standard. The HTML standard defines the individual elements that make up the language. These elements are the instructions, or tags, that indicate how HTML documents should be displayed in a browser. This standard ensures that hypertext is displayed consistently in different browsers and on different computer platforms. Standardization limits the proprietary software specifications that do not operate with other vendors' products.

Understand the differences between various HTML versions.   The HTML 1.0 standard is essentially the first version of HTML used for graphical browsers. HTML 2.0 includes all the capabilities of version 1.0 plus support for user input fields, which is necessary for forms. HTML 3.0 was never ratified; instead, it evolved directly into HTML 3.2. HTML 3.2 added widely deployed features such as tables, applets, and text flow around images while providing full backward compatibility with the existing standard HTML 2.0. HTML 4.0 is the W3C standard for the latest version of HTML. You should know the modifications and enhancements that have evolved over time in HTML.

Understand how proprietary extensions affect website development. Browsers such as Internet Explorer and Navigator have moved ahead to include features that are not part of the current HTML 4.01 standard. These proprietary features are called extensions because they "extend" the existing HTML standard, and they may or may not be included in the next HTML standard. Some browsers simply ignore proprietary tags, which can have a significant effect on how your HTML documents are displayed by the browser. Also, proprietary extensions can be misinterpreted by a browser, which can have a destructive effect on your documents. HTML authors should be aware of these effects and test web documents in several browsers.

Key Terms

Before you take the exam, be certain you are familiar with the following terms:

Cascading Style Sheets (CSS)	hypermedia
deprecated tags	hypertext
extensions	tags
HTML	Web Accessibility Initiative (WAI)
hyperlinks	World Wide Web Consortium (W3C)

Review Questions

1. What does the abbreviation HTML stand for?

   A. Hypertext Markup Language

   B. Hypotext Markup Language

   C. Hypermedia Markup Language

   D. Hypertest Markup Language

2. What is the term for the specialized pieces of code used by HTML to instruct HTML interpreters how to display text?

   A. Code

   B. Hypertext

   C. Tags

   D. Extensions

3. Who controls HTML?

   A. ICANN

   B. World Wide Web Consortium

   C. InterNIC

   D. World Wide Web Committee

4. What is a deprecated tag?

   A. Deprecated tags are those that have been replaced by browsers in favor of their own extensions.

   B. Deprecated tags are those that have not been replaced by other HTML elements.

   C. Deprecated tags are those that have been replaced by other WAI elements.

   D. Deprecated tags are those that have been replaced by other HTML elements.

5. Which of the following best describes the origins of HTML?

   A. HTML was developed by university students at MIT so they could e-mail each other.

   B. HTML was generated by web servers when they were connected in a network; it was then modified for human use.

   C. HTML was invented by Tim Berners-Lee to distribute nonlinear text to multiple points across the Internet.

   D. HTML was created during the invention of the hypercard, a cross-platform product that is no longer in use.

6. WAI aims to ensure that core technologies used on the Web—such as HTML, CSS, XML, and DOM—are equally accessible to users with physical, visual, hearing, and cognitive disabilities. What does Conformance Level "A" ensure?

   A. All Priority 1 checkpoints are satisfied.

   B. All Priority 1 and 2 checkpoints are satisfied.

   C. All Priority 1, 2, and 3 checkpoints are satisfied.

   D. None of the checkpoints has been satisfied.

7. What defines the individual elements that make up the HTML language, ensuring that hypertext is displayed consistently in different browsers and on different computer platforms?

   A. Proprietary HTML extensions

   B. The HTML standard

   C. MIT and Tim Berners-Lee

   D. The HTTP protocol

8. HTML 3.2 introduced enhancements that included support for which new features?

   A. Frames and tables

   B. Background images and colors

   C. User input fields and forms

   D. Support for style sheets

9. The latest W3C standard version of HTML is HTML 4.0. This version of HTML is specified in three variants. Which variant should be used by most developers creating pages for public access?

    A. HTML 4.0 Transitional

    B. HTML 4.0 Strict

    C. HTML 4.0 Frameset

    D. HTML 4.0 Standard

10. Which version of HTML was never ratified?

    A. 1.0

    B. 2.0

    C. 3.0

    D. 4.0

11. What do procedural programming languages such as C and Pascal provide that HTML does not?

    A. Data structure or internal logic

    B. Ability to work on multiple platforms

    C. Instructions and data in the same file

    D. Extreme portability

12. Which of the following is an example of an HTML interpreter?

    A. Notepad

    B. Gnotepad+

    C. Microsoft Internet Explorer

    D. Web developer

13. Which version of HTML 4.0 would a website designer use if they were looking to rid documents of structural markup?

    A. HTML 4.0 Transitional

    B. HTML 4.0 Frameset

    C. HTML 4.0 Basic

    D. HTML 4.0 Strict

14. Extensible Hypertext Markup Language (XHTML) is a combination of what two languages?

    A. XML 1.0 and HTML 4.01

    B. XML 1.0 and HTML 3.2

    C. GML and SGML

    D. XML 3.0 and HTML 1.0

15. Which of the following options is an example of an HTML 4.01 deprecated tag?

    A. <SELECT>

    B. <FONT>

    C. <TITLE>

    D. <BODY>

16. According to the WAI, a website developer must satisfy the Priority 1 checkpoint. What is the Recommendation for addressing a Priority 3 checkpoint?

    A. Must

    B. Should

    C. May

    D. Within a year

17. Which of the following is one of the 14 specific guidelines under which the WAI defines and organizes all checkpoints?

    A. Rely on specific devices.

    B. Do not rely on color alone.

    C. Do not use deprecated tags.

    D. Do not use dead-end pages.

18. Which HTML version was the first version of HTML used for graphical browsers?

    A. HTML 1.0

    B. HTML 2.0

    C. HTML

    D. HTML 3.2

19. What is one problem with deprecated tags?

    A. You can still use them.

    B. A website with deprecated tags will not display at all.

    C. They take on new meanings.

    D. Some browsers may not support the new tags that replaced them.

20. When is the HTML 4.0 Frameset Recommendation appropriate for use?

    A. When you want to use frames to partition the browser window

    B. When you want to place different color frames throughout your website

    C. When naming different child pages.

    D. When registering your site with directories.

Answers to Review Questions

1. A.   HTML stands for Hypertext Markup Language. It was developed as a means of distributing hypertext to multiple points across the Internet.

2. C.   Tags are pieces of text enclosed in angle brackets that provide instructions to programs designed to interpret HTML.

3. B.   The World Wide Web Consortium (W3C) is an international industry consortium founded in 1994 to develop common standards for the World Wide Web. It controls the evolution of HTML.

4. D.   Deprecated tags are those that have been replaced by other HTML elements. Deprecated tags are still included in the HTML draft or Recommendation but are clearly marked as deprecated.

5. C.   Tim Berners-Lee of the Massachusetts Institute of Technology invented HTML with colleagues from CERN (the European Particle Physics Laboratory) as a means of distributing nonlinear text, called hypertext, to multiple points across the Internet.

6. A.   All Priority 1 checkpoints are satisfied. Priority 1 checkpoints are the basic requirements for some groups to access web documents. This checkpoint must be satisfied in order to provide accessibility for all users.

7. B.   The HTML standard defines the individual elements that make up the language. The elements are the instructions that indicate how HTML documents should be displayed in a browser. The standard ensures that hypertext is displayed consistently in different browsers and on different computer platforms.

8. A.   HTML 3.2 added widely deployed features such as frames, tables, applets, and text flow around images while providing full backward compatibility with the existing standard HTML 2.0.

9. A.   Most people creating web pages for public access will want to use HTML 4.0 Transitional. This variant of HTML 4.0 is used to take full advantage of the Recommendation while allowing users to view the pages with older browsers.

10. C.   HTML 3.0 was never ratified; instead, it evolved directly into HTML 3.2.

11. A. HTML does not provide data structures or internal logic as procedural programming languages such as C and Pascal do. A markup language is very different from a programming language. Program files and data files exist separately in traditional applications. In a markup language, the instructions and the data reside in the same file.

12. C. HTML interpreters are programs such as Netscape Navigator and Microsoft Internet Explorer that process HTML pages and render them to the user as text pages formatted in accordance with the embedded instructions. These two programs are also called web browsers. HTML interpreters are not limited to browsers, however. Many programs that have come on the market since 1996 include HTML reading and exporting capabilities as built-in features.

13. D. The HTML 4.0 Strict Recommendation should be used if you want to rid your document of structural markup, leaving it free of any tags associated with layout. You can use this version with Cascading Style Sheets to produce the font, color, and layout effects you want.

14. A. Extensible Hypertext Markup Language (XHTML) is a combination of Extensible Markup Language (XML) 1.0 and HTML 4.01. XHTML-compliant documents can be used, viewed, and validated by both HTML and XML processors. Therefore, developers can begin using some of the features of XML with the confidence that backward-compatibility issues with HTML, as well as future issues with XML, will be addressed.

15. B. Deprecated tags and attributes are those that have been replaced by other HTML elements. Deprecated tags are still included in the HTML draft or Recommendation but are clearly marked as deprecated. HTML 4.01 deprecated tags include <ISINDEX>, <APPLET>, <CENTER>, <FONT>, <BASEFONT>, <STRIKE>, <U>, <DIR>, and <MENU>.

16. C. A website content developer may address this checkpoint. If a Priority 3 checkpoint is not satisfied, then one or more groups will have some difficulty accessing information in the document.

17. B. All checkpoints are organized under 14 specific guidelines. The guidelines are developed with consideration for groups of users with specified disabilities or needs. The WAI defines the 14 guidelines as follows: (1) Provide equivalent alternatives to auditory and visual content; (2) Do not rely on color alone; (3) Use markup and style sheets properly; (4) Clarify natural language usage; (5) Create tables that transform gracefully; (6) Ensure that pages featuring new technologies transform gracefully; (7) Ensure user control of time-sensitive content changes; (8) Ensure direct accessibility of embedded user interfaces; (9) Design for device-independence; (10) Use interim solutions; (11) Use W3C technologies and guidelines; (12) Provide context and orientation information; (13) Provide clear navigation mechanisms; (14) Ensure that documents are clear and simple.

18. A. The HTML 1.0 standard is essentially the first version of HTML used for graphical browsers. It was equivalent to the first HTML specification (version 0), with added support for images.

19. D. One of the difficulties of deprecated tags is that some browsers may not support the new tag that replaces the deprecated one. You can still use deprecated tags; most browsers continue to support them. If you use deprecated tags, you will be using the HTML 4.01 Transitional Recommendation.

20. A. The HTML 4.0 Frameset Recommendation is appropriate when you want to use frames to partition the browser window into two or more adjacent windows. HTML 4.0 is the W3C standard for the latest version of HTML. HTML version 4.0 is specified in three variants: HTML 4.0 Transitional, HTML 4.0 Strict, and HTML 4.0 Frameset.

Chapter

7

HTML Tables and Web Page Structure

THE CIW EXAM OBJECTIVE GROUPS COVERED IN THIS CHAPTER:

- ✓ Use advanced HTML formatting to enhance the usability of websites, including but not limited to: tables.

So far in this book, we have discussed the important elements of website development and design. Now we will explore the techniques that will allow you to create those elements. Tables are the building blocks of web page design, and they play a critical role in effective web page layout. They play a critical role because they allow designers to have complete control over how and where elements are displayed on the page. Designers can overcome variables such as monitor resolution and size by using tables to place elements. Tables allow for a more visually appealing web page layout because of the interesting structures that can be created through the structure of the table. Take time to look at the source code of web pages on the Internet and you will discover just how widely they are used!

In this chapter, we will discuss creating page structures with tables; diagramming tables; how attributes of the <TABLE>, <TR>, and <TD> tags affect how a table looks and acts; how to create simple and complex tables; and how to use a borderless table for page structure.

Creating Page Structure with HTML Tables

Using tables, website designers can create interesting and complex page structures as well as display data in tabular form. Without tables, alignment is based on ALIGN attributes and can change depending on monitor resolution and size. Tables allow a designer to have complete control over where elements are placed and how they appear in the browser window. In this chapter, you will learn how to create complex tables to develop interesting page structures, thereby allowing you to have more freedom in your design as well as more control over it.

Consider Figure 7.1. This page is divided into three areas: a navigation area on the left, a header on top, and a content area in the lower-right portion of the window. This layout is advantageous from a design standpoint because it gives the designer more control over the placement of elements on the web page and provides for a design that is more visually appealing than traditional vertical and horizontal alignment allows. You can format this design in two ways: you can use a borderless table as discussed in this chapter, or you can use frames, which we will discuss in the next chapter.

FIGURE 7.1   Page structure with table

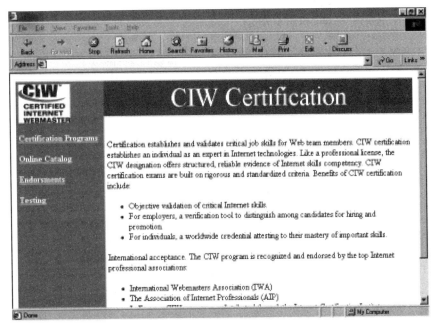

There is one great advantage to using tables instead of using frames: the user can easily bookmark the page or add it to the Favorites folder, whereas a frameset page cannot be bookmarked. (We will discuss why frameset pages cannot be bookmarked or added to the Favorites folder in Chapter 8, "HTML Frames.") The disadvantage is that when the viewer scrolls vertically or horizontally, all of the content on the page scrolls together, as you can see in Figure 7.2. The navigation elements on the left are accessible only when the viewer is looking at the top of the page. With frames, on the other hand, you can create an environment where different portions of the page can scroll independently from each other.

Within the standards of HTML 3.2, table structure is the only way (other than basic alignment) to create page divisions and add interesting structures to the page, such as in Figure 7.3. In this layout, the table is used to separate text and graphical elements, which provides a more complex page structure. In the exercises in this chapter, you'll use tables to re-create this page.

FIGURE 7.2 Text scrolls in table structure

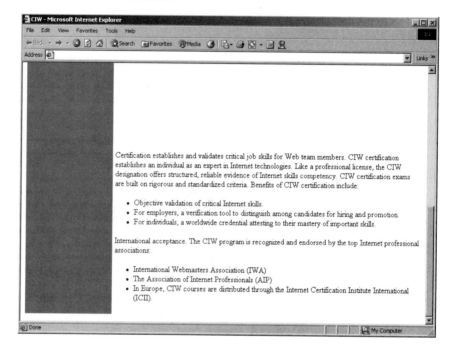

FIGURE 7.3 Tables add page division and structure

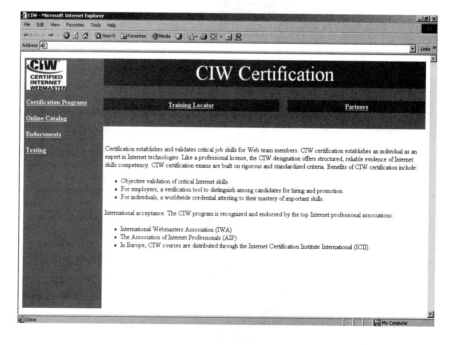

Body Tag

The <BODY> tag marks the beginning and end of the body section in an HTML document. It is where the majority of your HTML content goes. The <BODY> tag can be modified to move the top and left margins of your page to the edge of the browser window. By default, an 8-pixel border exists between the content and the edge of the browser window. By using the following attributes—there is one set for Navigator and another for Internet Explorer—in the <BODY> tag, you can remove the margin completely. The attributes for Navigator are as follows:

```
MARGINHEIGHT="0" MARGINWIDTH="0"
```

For Internet Explorer, use these attributes:

```
TOPMARGIN="0" LEFTMARGIN="0"
```

Following is an example of the <BODY> tag used for this purpose:

```
<BODY MARGINHEIGHT="0" MARGINWIDTH="0"
     LEFTMARGIN="0" TOPMARGIN="0">
```

Table Tag

The <TABLE> tag is the first required tag in constructing your table. A table is contained within the opening and closing <TABLE> tags. This tag can be modified to allow your table to occupy the entire space of the browser window, depending on which attributes you use. If you use percentage values (%) for HEIGHT and WIDTH attributes, the table becomes *dynamic* and will change as content and the size of the browser window change. If you use pixel values for HEIGHT and WIDTH attributes, the table remains *static* and will not change as content changes and as browser window size changes. To ensure consistent display across different browsers, do not mix and match pixels and percentages; use one or the other.

You can adjust the BORDER, HEIGHT, WIDTH, CELLPADDING, and CELLSPACING attributes to control how your table displays in the browser window. The BORDER attribute controls how large the border of the table will be and is usually represented in a fixed pixel value. HEIGHT and WIDTH control how much of the browser window your table will cover. HEIGHT and WIDTH attributes can also be used in individual cells within your table. CELLPADDING controls the amount of space *within* the cell, and CELLSPACING controls the amount of space *between* cells. All of these attributes will have an impact on how your table looks and acts and the space it takes up.

The BGCOLOR attribute specifies the color to be used in your table and overrides any color information specified in your web page's <BODY> tag.

The BACKGROUND attribute can be used with the <TABLE>, <TR>, or <TD> tags but is only supported in Internet Explorer.

Table Row Tag

The <TR> tag is the second tag that is required when constructing a table. It is used to define the rows of a table. Modification of the <TR> tag will allow you to create uniform attributes—such as ALIGN, VALIGN, or BGCOLOR—for all cells in a row. The ALIGN attribute is used to align text to the left, center, or right of the cell, and the VALIGN attribute is used control the vertical alignment of cells (top, middle, or bottom). The BGCOLOR attribute specifies the color to be used in a row and overrides any color specified in the <TABLE> tag.

Table Data Tag

The last essential tag in your table is the <TD> tag. It defines a cell within a row. The <TD> tag has a counterpart in table creation: The <TH> tag is used to define a cell whose purpose is to act as a table heading. The <TH> tag is not a required tag in an HTML table, but it can be used as an alternative to the <TD> tag when formatting is desired. The table header tag has built-in formatting and alignment features; data in a <TH> cell automatically will be bold and will align to the center of the cell. Both tags can be modified by changing the BGCOLOR, HEIGHT, WIDTH, and ALIGN attributes. Narrow cells can be used to create visual separations between rows and cells. COLSPAN and ROWSPAN attributes are also used in the <TD> or <TH> tags to change the amount of space cells occupy. COLSPAN specifies the number of columns a cell should span, and ROWSPAN specifies the number of rows a cell should span. Using the COLSPAN and ROWSPAN attributes allows you to have one cell span multiple columns or rows.

Diagramming an HTML Table

As you've seen, tables can be used for both simple and complex page layouts. The easiest way to create a table to use as a structure for a web page is to first diagram the table. Consider the page structure shown in Figure 7.1. The three-cell table has two rows, and Cell 1 spans two rows. It can be diagrammed as shown in Figure 7.4.

FIGURE 7.4   Page structure diagram

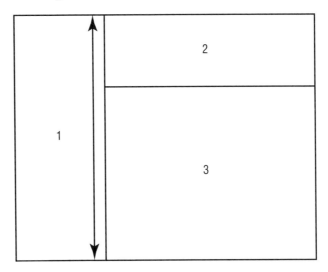

The table for the more complex page structure (shown in Figure 7.3) can be diagrammed as shown in Figure 7.5. This example has eight cells. Cells 3, 5, and 7 are used for border separation. Cells 2, 3, 7, and 8 each spans across columns to remain as single cells. In Exercise 7.1, you'll create a simple table structure.

FIGURE 7.5   Complex page structure diagram

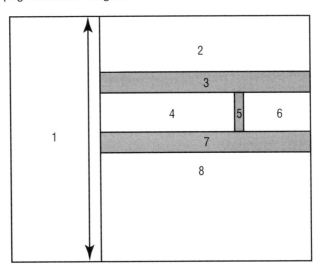

The files used in the exercises in this chapter as well as examples of the completed pages are located in the Chapter 7 `Exercises` and `Complete` folders on the CD-ROM that accompanies this book.

EXERCISE 7.1

Creating a Simple HTML Table

Follow these steps to create a simple table structure:

1. Type the following HTML in a Notepad document:

```
<HTML>
<HEAD>
<TITLE>Basic Table</TITLE>
</HEAD>
<BODY>
<TABLE BORDER="2">
<TR>
        <TD ROWSPAN="2">Cell 1</TD>        <TD>Cell 2</TD>
</TR>
<TR>
        <TD>Cell 3</TD>
</TR>
</TABLE>
</BODY>
</HTML>
```

2. Save the document as `basictable.htm`.

3. Preview `basictable.htm` in your browser. Your results should resemble the following diagram.

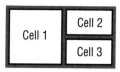

Now that you've created a simple table, you'll add additional ROWSPAN and COLSPAN attributes to create a more complex table in Exercise 7.2.

EXERCISE 7.2

Creating a Complex HTML Table

In this exercise, you will build your skills by creating a more complex table. To do so, follow these steps:

1. Diagram the table as shown in the following graphic.

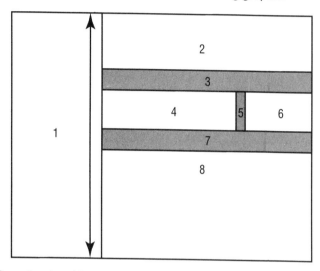

2. Open basictable.htm in Notepad.

3. Choose File ➤ Save As. Save the file to your hard drive and name it complextable.htm.

4. Modify the HTML by typing in the text that appears in bold:

```
<HTML>
<HEAD>
      <TITLE>Complex Table</TITLE>
</HEAD>
<BODY>
<TABLE BORDER="2">
<TR>
      <TD ROWSPAN="5">Cell 1</TD>
      <TD COLSPAN="3">Cell 2</TD>
</TR>
<TR>
      <TD COLSPAN="3">Cell 3</TD>
</TR>
```

EXERCISE 7.2 *(continued)*

```
<TR>
      <TD>Cell 4</TD>
      <TD>Cell 5</TD>
      <TD>Cell 6</TD>
</TR>
<TR>
      <TD COLSPAN="3">Cell 7</TD>
</TR>
<TR>
      <TD COLSPAN="3">Cell 8</TD>
</TR>
</TABLE>
</BODY>
</HTML>
```

5. After saving your changes, open complextable.htm in your browser. It should resemble the following diagram.

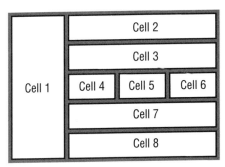

It's important to keep in mind that if you use percentage values (%) for HEIGHT and WIDTH attributes, the table becomes dynamic and will change as content and the size of the browser window change.

Borderless Web Page Structure

Y ou have created the basic table structures; in Exercises 7.3 and 7.4, you will transform them into page structures. Page structures are created by adding attributes to the HTML table, table row, and table data tags. When you change the value in the BORDER attribute to "0", the border on your table will disappear. Tables with no borders are frequently used for page layout, whereas tables with the border showing are commonly used for displaying data.

EXERCISE 7.3

Creating a Simple Web Page Structure

To transform your basic table into a page structure, follow these steps:

1. Open basictable.htm in Notepad.

2. Modify the HTML by adding the text that appears in bold:

```
<HTML>
<HEAD>

<TITLE>Page Structure</TITLE>

</HEAD>

<BODY>

<TABLE WIDTH="100%" HEIGHT="100%"
CELLSPACING="0" CELLPADDING="2" BORDER="0">

<TR>

<TD ROWSPAN="2" WIDTH="20%"
BGCOLOR="yellow" ALIGN="center"
VALIGN="middle">Cell 1</TD>
<TD HEIGHT="20%" BGCOLOR="lightblue"
ALIGN="center" VALIGN="middle">Cell 2</TD>

</TR>

<TR>
<TD HEIGHT="80%" BGCOLOR="beige"
ALIGN="center" VALIGN="middle">Cell 3</TD>

</TR>

</TABLE>

</BODY>
</HTML>
```

EXERCISE 7.3 *(continued)*

3. Save this HTML as `basicstruct.htm` on your hard drive.

4. Open `basicstruct.htm` in your browser and compare your results to the following page structure.

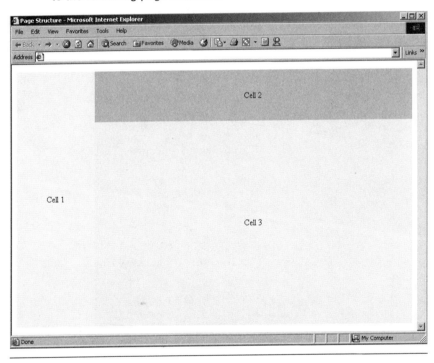

EXERCISE 7.4

Creating a Complex Web Page Structure

In this exercise, you will build your skills by creating the page structure for the complex table you created in Exercise 7.2, shown in the following diagram.

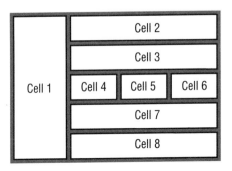

1. Open `complextable.htm` and modify the HTML by adding the text that appears in bold:

```
<HTML>
<TITLE>Complex Table</TITLE>
<BODY BGCOLOR="#FFFFFF">
<TABLE WIDTH=100% HEIGHT="100%"
CELLPADDING="5" CELLSPACING="0" BORDER="0">
  <TR>
    <TD ROWSPAN="5" WIDTH="20%" BGCOLOR="#669999">
    Cell 1
    </TD>
    <TD COLSPAN="3" HEIGHT="20%" BGCOLOR="#336699">
    Cell 2
    </TD>
  </TR>
  <TR>
    <TD COLSPAN="3" BGCOLOR="#669999" HEIGHT="3%">
    Cell 3
    </TD>
  </TR>
  <TR>
    <TD BGCOLOR="#336699" HEIGHT="2%">Cell 4</TD>
    <TD BGCOLOR="#669999" HEIGHT="2%" WIDTH="2%">5</TD>
    <TD BGCOLOR="#336699" HEIGHT="2%">Cell 6</TD>
  </TR>
  <TR>
    <TD COLSPAN="3" BGCOLOR="#669999" HEIGHT="3%">
    Cell 7
    </TD>
  </TR>
  <TR>
    <TD COLSPAN="3" BGCOLOR="#FFFFFF" HEIGHT="70%">
    Cell 8
    </TD>
  </TR>
</TABLE>
</BODY>
</HTML>
```

2. Save the changes and then view the `complextable.htm` file in the browser. The table should be borderless and occupy the entire area. Compare your results with the following page structure.

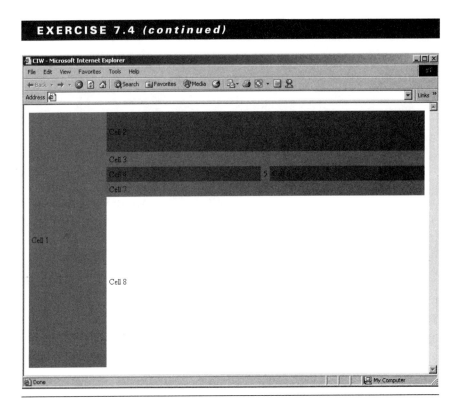

You have created simple and complex tables as well as borderless tables to use for page structure. You can now incorporate them into your web page designs.

Summary

Website designers can use tables to create interesting and complex page structures as well as display data in tabular form. Without tables, alignment is based on ALIGN attributes and can change depending on monitor resolution and size. Using tables, a designer has complete control over where elements are placed and how they appear in the browser window. By using the various attributes that coordinate with the essential table tags (<TABLE>, <TR>, and <TD> or <TH>), you can create page structures that are visually appealing and functional.

Exam Essentials

Be able to use tables for page structure.   Website designers can use tables to create interesting and complex page structures and to display data in tabular form. Alignment is usually based in ALIGN attributes and can change depending on monitor resolution and size, but by using tables, a designer can completely control the placement of elements and how they appear in the browser window.

Be able to construct a simple page structure using tables.   Using the <TABLE>, <TR>, and <TD> tags, you can create a simple table that can either display data (with borders turned on) or act as the foundation for a page (with borders turned off).

Know how to construct a complex page structure using tables.   Using the attributes that belong to the essential table tags, you can create complex tables. The BORDER attribute controls how large the border of the table will be and is usually represented in a fixed pixel value. HEIGHT and WIDTH control how much of the browser window your table will cover. HEIGHT and WIDTH attributes can also be used in individual cells within your table. CELLPADDING controls the amount of space *within* the cell, and CELLSPACING controls the amount of space *between* cells. All of these attributes will have an impact on your table and the space it takes up. The BGCOLOR attribute specifies the color to be used in your table and overrides any color information specified in the <BODY> tag of your web page.

Key Terms

Before you take the exam, be certain you are familiar with the following terms:

<TABLE>	dynamic
<TD>	static
<TR>	

Review Questions

1. When specifying HEIGHT and WIDTH attributes in the tags that make up a table, what unit of measure should you use to express the values if you want the table to be dynamic?

   A. Points

   B. Pixels

   C. Percentages

   D. Parameters

2. How do you make your table transparent or invisible on the page you are structuring?

   A. Use percentages to express HEIGHT and WIDTH values.

   B. Do not use the BORDER attribute.

   C. Set the <TABLE> tag to "0".

   D. Set the BORDER attribute to "0".

3. What are the three main HTML tags used to create tables for page structure?

   A. <TITLE>, <TR>, <TD>

   B. <TABLE>, <TT>, <TD>

   C. <TABLE>, <TR>, <TEXTAREA>

   D. <TABLE>, <TR>, <TD>

4. What advantage do tables offer over frames when used for page layout?

   A. With tables, you can create a more dynamic page layout than you can with frames.

   B. Tables allow page areas to scroll independently of each other, whereas frames do not.

   C. A page that was created with a table for layout can be bookmarked, whereas a frames page cannot.

   D. Tables can always be created more quickly than frames.

5. How is page structure created from a basic HTML table?

   A. By making any table borderless (invisible borders)

   B. By simply placing page content within the table cells

   C. By adding attributes to the table, table row, and table data tags

   D. By creating the table on top of the content in an existing page

6. Which option best describes a simple page structure?

   A. It can only be created with HTML tables.

   B. It can be created with a table that divides the page into a navigation area, a header, and a content area.

   C. It is not recommended because it is unclear and does not provide transparent navigation.

   D. It requires the use of a WYSIWYG HTML editor.

7. Which of the following is not an essential table tag?

   A. <TABLE>

   B. <TD>

   C. <TR>

   D. <TT>

8. What does the ROWSPAN attribute control?

   A. ROWSPAN specifies the number of rows a cell should span.

   B. ROWSPAN specifies the number of columns a cell should span.

   C. ROWSPAN specifies the number of cells a row should span.

   D. ROWSPAN specifies the number of cells a column should span.

9. What will adding the BGCOLOR attribute to your <TR> or <TD> tag do?

   A. The BGCOLOR attribute specifies the background image to be used in a row or cell.

   B. The BGCOLOR attribute specifies the color to be used in a row or cell.

   C. The BGCOLOR attribute specifies the color to be used in the entire table.

   D. The BGCOLOR attribute specifies the background image to be used in the entire table.

10. How do tables differ from frames?

A. The content of a page created with a table scrolls all at once, whereas the content in a frames page can remain static or dynamic, depending on how the frame is created.

B. The content of a page created with frames scrolls all at once, whereas the content in a tables page can remain static or dynamic, depending on how the table is created.

C. The content of a page created with a table cannot scroll, whereas the content in a frames page can scroll.

D. The content of a page created with a table can scroll, whereas the content in a frames page cannot scroll.

11. Tim is a website designer. He has decided to use dynamic table attributes by using percentages for height and width. What will this accomplish for the web page Tim is creating?

A. It will allow his tables to retain their original size.

B. It will allow tables to expand to the screen size of the user's system.

C. It will allow tables to change slightly to accommodate the browser.

D. It will make European users see the site properly.

12. Which of the following tags is essential and required for any web page content to exist?

A. <TABLE>

B. <TH>

C. <ALIGN>

D. <BODY>

13. By default, what exists between the content of your web page and the edge of the browser window?

A. An 8-pixel border

B. A 3-percent border

C. A blank frame

D. A blank table border

14. Which of the following is an advantage of frames over tables?

   A. With the use of frames, the user can easily bookmark the page.

   B. Frames can create an environment in which different portions of the page can scroll independently of each other.

   C. Frames are easier to work with.

   D. Frames are supported by all browsers, as opposed to tables, over which there have been browser conflicts.

15. Which of the following attributes controls the amount of space within a cell?

   A. HEIGHT

   B. WIDTH

   C. CELLPADDING

   D. CELLSPACING

16. Which of the following is a <BODY> tag attribute used for Navigator but not for Internet Explorer?

   A. TOPMARGINHEIGHT

   B. MARGINWIDTH

   C. TOPMARGIN

   D. LEFTMARGIN

17. Which of the following tags is used to define a cell whose purpose is to act as a table heading?

   A. <TD>

   B. <HT>

   C. <TH>

   D. <HEADER>

18. You have a web page that includes a table with borders. What is the most likely purpose of your table?

    A. To display borders

    B. For page layout

    C. To display data

    D. To structure graphics

19. Which of the following attributes controls the amount of space between the cells?

    A. HEIGHT

    B. WIDTH

    C. CELLPADDING

    D. CELLSPACING

20. Consider the following HTML: <TD COLSPAN="3">Cell 3</TD>. What does the COLSPAN attribute indicate?

    A. The background color of the cell

    B. The color of the border lines.

    C. The number of columns to span

    D. The column width

Answers to Review Questions

1. C. If you use percentage values (%) for HEIGHT and WIDTH attributes, the table becomes dynamic and will change as content and the size of the browser window change.

2. D. Tables can be used to create the structure of a page without the user knowing they are part of the page. The border then becomes invisible or transparent. To achieve this effect, set the BORDER attribute of the table to "0".

3. D. <TABLE>, <TR>, <TD> are the three main HTML tags used to create tables for page structure. The <TABLE> tag is used to denote where the beginning and end of a table is in your HTML document. The <TR> tag is used to create the rows that make up the table, and the <TD> tag is used to place the contents of the table in specific cells.

4. C. A page that uses a table for layout can be bookmarked, whereas a frames page cannot. Creating a more dynamic page layout and allowing page areas to scroll independently of each other are actually advantages of using frames. How quickly you create your page depends on how complex it is, regardless of whether you use tables or frames.

5. A. Page structure is created by adding attributes to the HTML table, table row, and table data tags. By changing the value in the BORDER attribute to "0" (making the borders invisible), you can make the border on your table disappear. Tables with no borders are frequently used for page layout, whereas tables with the border showing are commonly used for displaying data.

6. B. Simple page structures can be created through the use of tables by creating a table that divides the page into a navigation area, a header, and a content area. By creating tables for these elements, the website designer ensures that they remain exactly where they want them to be on the page regardless of the browser window size.

7. D. <TT> is not an essential table tag. <TT> creates typewriter text. The essential table tags are <TABLE>, <TR>, and <TD>.

8. A. ROWSPAN specifies the amount of rows a cell should span. The ROWSPAN attribute allows website designers to create tables that have a complex structure by combining rows.

9. B. The `BGCOLOR` attribute specifies the color to be used in a row or cell. It overrides any color information specified at the <TABLE> tag or page level.

10. A. When you create a page using tables, the content of a page scrolls all at once, which can be an advantage, depending on the content of the page and the look you are trying to create. On the other hand, the content in a frames page can remain static or dynamic, depending on how the frame is created. This allows content to stay in one place while other content on the page moves. There are advantages and disadvantages to using both tables and frames in web page design. You have to decide which technique works best for your content and the design of your website.

11. B. If you use percentage values (%) for `HEIGHT` and `WIDTH` attributes, the table becomes dynamic and will change as content changes and as the size of the browser window changes. Option A is incorrect because, for tables to retain their original size, you would want them to be static, which would require you to use pixels, not percentages.

12. D. The <BODY> tag marks the beginning and end of the body section in an HTML document. It is where the majority of your HTML content goes. The other tags mentioned are important tags, but they do not hold the status of being required for a page's content.

13. A. By default, an 8-pixel border exists between the content and the edge of the browser window. By using the following attributes in the <BODY> tag, the margin can be completely removed:

```
<BODY MARGINHEIGHT="0" MARGINWIDTH="0"
      LEFTMARGIN="0" TOPMARGIN="0">
```

14. B. Frames can create an environment in which different portions of the page can scroll independently from each other. If you wanted to create a page that could be bookmarked, you would use tables. Frames are not easier to work with according to most designers. There are no browser conflicts over the use of tables, but over the years, it has been a struggle to have frames supported by both IE and Navigator simultaneously.

15. C. `CELLPADDING` controls the amount of space *within* the cell. `HEIGHT` and `WIDTH` control how much of the browser window your table will cover. `HEIGHT` and `WIDTH` attributes can also be used in individual cells within your table. `CELLSPACING` controls the amount of space *between* cells.

16. B.   The <BODY> tag requires two sets of attributes: one set for Navigator and another for Internet Explorer. The attributes for Navigator are as follows: MARGINHEIGHT="0" MARGINWIDTH="0". Internet Explorer requires the following attributes: TOPMARGIN="0" LEFTMARGIN="0".

17. C.   The <TH> tag is used to define a cell whose purpose is to act as a table heading. The table header tag has built-in formatting and alignment features; data in a <TH> cell will automatically be bold and align to the center of the cell. The <TD> tag defines a cell within a row. The other two tags mentioned here are fictitious.

18. C.   Tables allow website designers to create interesting and complex page structures as well as display data in tabular form. Tables with no borders are frequently used for page layout, whereas tables with the border showing are commonly used for displaying data.

19. D.   CELLSPACING controls the amount of space *between* cells. HEIGHT and WIDTH control how much of the browser window your table will cover. HEIGHT and WIDTH attributes can also be used in individual cells within your table. CELLPADDING controls the amount of space *within* the cell.

20. C.   COLSPAN specifies the number of columns a cell should span and ROWSPAN specifies the number of rows a cell should span. Using the COLSPAN and ROWSPAN attributes allows you to have one cell span multiple columns or rows.

Chapter 8

HTML Frames

THE CIW EXAM OBJECTIVE GROUPS COVERED IN THIS CHAPTER:

- ✓ Use advanced HTML formatting to enhance the usability of websites, including but not limited to: frames.

- ✓ Use HTML to create related web pages that can be deployed as a website.

Frames offer another way to create interesting and useful page structures. Implementing frames in your web pages allows you to create areas of the page that move independently from one another. They also allow you to have important content remain on the page regardless of where the user scrolls or which hyperlinks they click on. Creating framesets is not difficult, but getting them to work correctly can be a challenge!

In this chapter, we will explore frames and framesets, where <FRAME> and <FRAMESET> tags are placed in an HTML page, and how to create framesets using both rows and columns. In addition, we'll show you how to target hyperlinks to the correct frame, how to create nested framesets, and how the associated attributes affect how a frame looks and acts. Finally, we will discuss what to do if a browser does not support frames.

HTML Frames and Framesets

When designing your website, you may want to create a page structure in which certain information is visible and persistent while other information changes. This structure is used to create static navigation elements in a window alongside content elements that can scroll. You can produce this functionality by creating separate panes called *frames* in the browser window. Frames allow you to have separate scrollable regions in which pages can be displayed. Each frame contains its own URL. As noted in Chapter 7, the content of frames cannot be bookmarked or made a Favorite in the browser; only the frameset itself can be designated this way.

In the exercises in this chapter, you will develop frames from existing HTML files, combining them in structures called *framesets*, which are a web pages that define a set of frames in which other web pages are displayed.

Using Frames

Frames are an extension of the HTML 3.2 standard introduced by the Netscape release of the Navigator 2 browser, and expanded by the Microsoft Internet Explorer 3 browser. Frames were submitted to the Internet Engineering Task Force (IETF) and the W3C for consideration as an HTML standard and are now part of the HTML 4 Recommendation.

Elements that users should always see, such as navigation links, copyright notices, and title graphics, can be placed in a static individual frame. As users navigate the site, the static frame's contents will remain fixed, even though the contents of the adjoining frames may change.

The advantage of using frames is that static and dynamic information can be combined. Figure 8.1 shows a web page with a table of contents on the left. The table of contents frame contains a set of links, each of which accesses a URL when clicked and displays the corresponding page in the adjoining frame. The web page thus contains two separate files loaded into two frames. Figure 8.2 shows the same page after clicking on the Certification Programs link.

FIGURE 8.1   Web page using frames

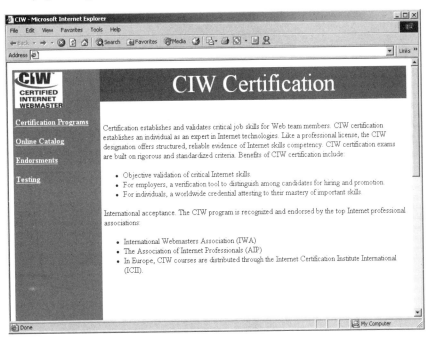

FIGURE 8.2 Frames after clicking on Certification Programs link

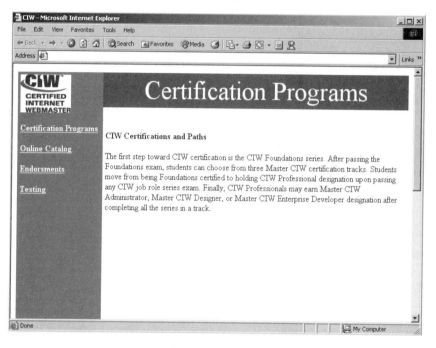

The HTML <FRAMESET> Tag

The <FRAMESET> tag is a container tag that allows you to define regions in your browser window and assign separate files to each region. It requires an attribute of either COLS or ROWS to designate the number and size of columns or rows in a browser window.

You can specify the COLS and ROWS attributes in two ways: by percentages or by pixels. For example, the following tag indicates two frames:

```
<FRAMESET COLS="35%,65%">
```

One column occupies 35 percent of the available screen width, and the other column occupies the remaining 65 percent. When frame sizes are expressed in percentages, it's referred to as *relative sizing*. Though these windows can be resized, the proportion of the page division remains constant. This feature can cause problems, however, because the user might choose to browse in a small window, in which case your intended design could be greatly altered.

Expressing the size of frames in pixels is called *absolute sizing* because the size of each frame remains constant regardless of browser window size. In addition, you can use a wildcard character for the second row. For example, by specifying the following, you use the first 150 pixels available for the top frame and the remaining space for the bottom frame:

```
<FRAMESET ROWS="150,*">
```

In the HTML document for the page shown in Figure 8.3, the <FRAMESET> tag is defined using the wildcard character and the ROWS attribute as follows:

```
<FRAMESET ROWS="100,*">
```

The first row is 100 pixels high, and the second row uses the remaining space in the browser window. You can tell that this is a frameset page with a row at the top because the scroll bar on the right side of the browser window does not go all the way to the top.

FIGURE 8.3 Frameset page with a row at the top

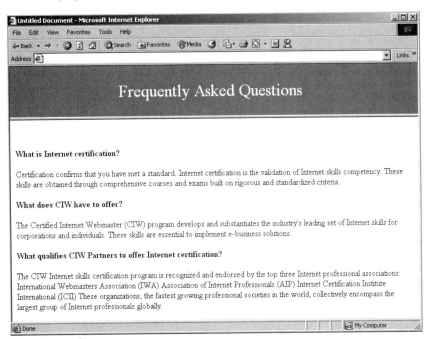

The HTML <FRAME> Tag

The <FRAME> tag defines the content that will appear in each frame. It is enclosed within the <FRAMESET> tag. The SRC attribute specifies which file will appear in the frame.

In the following example, the frame source for the top frame is the file named `top.htm`, and the frame source for the lower frame is named `bottom.htm`. The frameset defines two rows and opens the frames with the files specified in the <FRAME> tag. The frame source can be a local document or a URL pointing to a website. In this example, the frame sources are local documents:

```
<FRAMESET ROWS="100,*">
    <FRAME SRC="top.htm">
    <FRAME SRC="bottom.htm">
</FRAMESET>
```

Placement of <FRAMESET> Tags

The <FRAMESET> tag will create frames only if it is placed correctly into the HTML document. The following example demonstrates proper structure for creating frames. This HTML source code was used to create the frames in Figure 8.1:

```
<HTML>
<HEAD>
<TITLE>Simple Frameset</TITLE>
</HEAD>
<FRAMESET COLS="30%,70%">
    <FRAME SRC="nav.htm">
    <FRAME SRC="main.htm">
</FRAMESET>
</HTML>
```

Following are two key points to observe:

- The opening <FRAMESET> tag must follow the closing <HEAD> tag and must precede the opening <BODY> tag. If you do not plan to use alternate text for browsers incapable of rendering frames, you do not need the <BODY> tag at all.

- The <FRAMESET> tag must contain either the ROWS attribute or the COLS attribute. You cannot specify both ROWS and COLS in the same <FRAMESET> tag. For example, you cannot write a frameset like this:

```
<FRAMESET COLS="30%,70%" ROWS="100,*">
```

Exercises 8.1 and 8.2 will introduce you to frame creation. Exercise 8.1 deals with row creation and Exercise 8.2 addresses columns. Rows and columns are the two methods of defining regions in a frameset. Remember that frames have structure, content, links, and targets. Structure and content are distinctly named entities. These exercises demonstrate a good process for designing frames.

The files used in the exercises in this chapter as well as examples of the completed pages are located in the Chapter 8 Exercises and Complete folders on the CD-ROM that accompanies this book. Save the files to your hard disk in a folder named Exercise Files before starting these exercises. Make sure you save files you create during these exercises to the folder in which the exercise files are located! Otherwise, your links will not work correctly.

EXERCISE 8.1

Creating a Rows Frameset in HTML

In this exercise, you will create a frameset with the contents of a.htm in the top frame and the contents of b.htm in the bottom frame. The frame structure is illustrated in the following diagram.

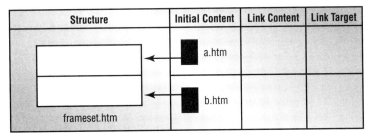

To create the frameset, follow these steps:

1. Type the following HTML into a Notepad document:

```
<HTML>
<FRAMESET ROWS="50%,50%">
```

EXERCISE 8.1 *(continued)*

```
<FRAME SRC="a.htm">
<FRAME SRC="b.htm">
</FRAMESET>
</HTML>
```

2. Save the document as `frameset.htm`.

3. Open `frameset.htm` in your browser and analyze your results.

EXERCISE 8.2

Creating Columns Frameset in HTML

In this exercise, you will build your skills by creating another frameset, this one with columns instead of rows:

1. Open `frameset.htm` in Notepad.

2. Modify the HTML as follows (changes are noted in bold):

```
<FRAMESET COLS="25%,75%">
<FRAME SRC="a.htm">
<FRAME SRC="b.htm">
</FRAMESET>
```

3. Save the file as `frameset2.htm` and then open it in the browser. It should resemble the structure shown in the following graphic.

| This is page A | This is page B |

If you are using Netscape Navigator, you may need to hold the Shift key on the keyboard while clicking on the Reload button in the browser. This action will clear the browser cache and load the new frameset.

Creating a Navigation Frame

The main purpose of a navigation frameset is to create independent windows in which a constant navigation frame is maintained, with navigational links that bring the desired content into an adjacent frame. In Exercise 8.3, you will create a navigation frame by adding hyperlinks to one of the frames created in Exercise 8.2.

EXERCISE 8.3

Hyperlinking Frame Content in HTML

In this exercise, you will add hyperlinks to your frameset structure. The following graphic shows the frameset structure you will create.

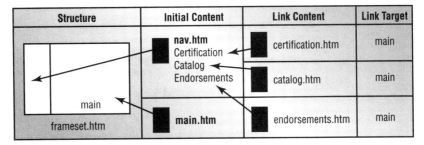

Structure	Initial Content	Link Content	Link Target
	nav.htm Certification Catalog Endorsements	certification.htm	main
		catalog.htm	main
main frameset.htm	**main.htm**	endorsements.htm	main

To add hyperlinks to the frameset, follow these steps:

1. Open frameset2.htm in Notepad.

2. Modify the two frame source attributes as shown to call different files:

```
<FRAME SRC="nav.htm">
<FRAME SRC="main.htm">
```

3. Save frameset2.htm and open it in your browser.

4. Click on the Certification Programs hyperlink. What happens? Did your hyperlink work as intended? The file the hyperlink points to should have opened in the same frame as the navigation bar, which is not the desired effect.

5. Click on the Back button, and then click on the Online Catalog hyperlink. It is targeted to the wrong frame as well. To solve this problem, you need to specify the target of the hyperlink. You'll do that in Exercise 8.4.

Targeting Hyperlinks in HTML

When you create hyperlinks, you can designate internal links without specific file addresses by using the <A NAME="anyName"> tag. Once you create a name to which you can anchor your link, you can create the <A HREF="#anyName"> tag and attribute combination. Exercise 8.4 will illustrate this point; you'll name the frame in the frameset and then create a target to it in the HTML document that will appear in the frame when the corresponding link in the navigation frame is clicked.

The NAME attribute can also be used to target hyperlinks from the navigation division of your frame to the main area of your browser window. When you name a frame, files are loaded into the frame when the frame is requested by name. Remember that target names are case sensitive; they will not work unless the name and target are the same.

EXERCISE 8.4

Creating Targeted Hyperlinks in HTML

In this exercise, you will structure your frameset so that you can click on the hyperlink in the navigation area and bring the selected content into the adjoining area:

1. Open frameset2.htm in Notepad.

2. Modify your HTML as shown in bold:

   ```
   <FRAME SRC="nav.htm" NAME="nav">
   <FRAME SRC="main.htm" NAME="main">
   ```

3. Save and close frameset2.htm.

4. Open nav.htm. Add the attribute and its value (shown in bold) to your HTML:

   ```
   <A HREF="certification.htm" TARGET="main">
   ```

5. Save and close nav.htm.

6. Open frameset2.htm in your browser.

7. Click on the Certification Programs hyperlink. The page your hyperlink points to should open in the main (or right) frame. The frame was modified so that the certification.htm page opens in the correct frame.

EXERCISE 8.4 *(continued)*

8. Click on the Back button and then click on the Online Catalog hyperlink. The page the hyperlink points to still opens in the nav frame, not in the main frame. This hyperlink does not target correctly because you did not change the target information on the `nav.htm` page as you did the `certification.htm` page. You will learn how to target all pages at once in Exercise 8.5.

Specifying a Base Target

From Exercise 8.4, you can see it would be helpful to avoid manually entering targets for every link on the page. By specifying a base target, you can automatically set a default target for all links.

A special empty tag called the <BASE> tag allows you to specify both the URL for a document and a default target frame for all the links in a frameset.

For example, if you want all the links in the table of contents frame to target the main frame, you can include the following source code in the <HEAD> tag section:

`<BASE HREF="`*URL*`" TARGET="main">`

The optional HREF attribute can be used to indicate the full URL in case the page on which this tag resides is read out of context. For example, if users download this page to their systems, how will they know where it came from? If you have indicated a base URL, users will be able to find your site again.

As mentioned earlier, the TARGET attribute specifies a default target for all hyperlinks on the page. However, you can still link to targets other than the base. If the TARGET attribute is specified in the anchor tag (e.g., <A HREF>), that target will be used. Only when no target is present will the base target be used, if it's present. In Exercise 8.5, you will practice targeting all the links in a document at once to the same frame.

EXERCISE 8.5

Targeting Links from a <BASE> Tag in HTML

In this exercise, you will reduce the amount of HTML by using the base target. You will no longer have to repeat the `TARGET="main"` value for each hyperlink.

EXERCISE 8.5 *(continued)*

To use a base target, follow these steps:

1. Open nav.htm in Notepad.

2. Within the <HEAD> tags under the <TITLE> line, enter the HTML that appears in bold:

```
<HEAD>
<TITLE>Navigation</TITLE>
<BASE TARGET="main">
</HEAD>
```

3. Save and close nav.htm.

4. Open frameset2.htm in your browser.

5. Click on the hyperlinks. They should all target to the main frame now.

Frame Relationships

You can target frames in two ways: by name or by relationship. You have already seen that the target name is defined in the <FRAME> tag. The frame relationship, however, is less tangible. It targets based on the location, or relationship, to the frame. Figure 8.4 shows the relationship of files and frame names used in Exercise 8.5.

FIGURE 8.4 Hierarchy of files and frame names

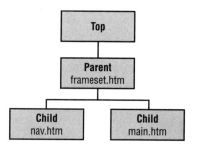

In the example in Figure 8.5, the target is set to display the linked page in the adjacent frame. Therefore, when you click on the CIW logo, the CIW home page is displayed in a frame next to your navigation window. Figure 8.5 displays this result when viewed in a browser.

FIGURE 8.5 Simple frameset

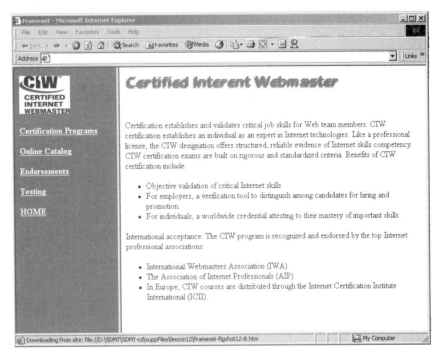

You have already created a target from one frame to another. However, in the case of the CIW link, it would be preferable to allow the CIW home page to be displayed in its own window. You have three targeting options: target a parent page, target a top page, or target a new browser session. If you target a parent page, you will open the page the hyperlink targets in the frame that contains the current frameset, thereby replacing the frameset with the new page. If you target a top page, you'll get the same result you would get if you targeted a parent page. If you use a nested frameset (one frameset inside of another) and you target the parent page, the hyperlinks in the inner frameset will be targeted to the outer frameset. If you target a new browser session, the page your hyperlink points to will open in a brand-new browser window, leaving your frameset in an open browser window. In Exercise 8.6, you'll see how frame relationships work by targeting a hyperlink to the uppermost frame in the frameset.

EXERCISE 8.6

Targeting Links to the Top Frame in HTML

In this exercise, you will retarget the CIW link to the top frame of your site:

1. Open nav.htm in your editor.

EXERCISE 8.6 (continued)

2. Modify the link for the CIW logo as shown in bold:

```
<A HREF="http://www.ciwcertified.com" TARGET="_top">
<IMG SRC="ciw-logo.gif" BORDER=0></A>
```

3. Save the changes.

4. Open `frameset2.htm` in your browser. What happens when you click on the hyperlink?

5. Change "`_top`" to "`_blank`" in your HTML of the `nav.htm` page. What happens when you click on the hyperlink? The page should open in a new browser window.

The following image shows the completed structure for your frameset.

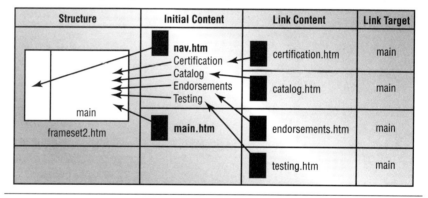

Structure	Initial Content	Link Content	Link Target
	nav.htm Certification Catalog Endorsements Testing	certification.htm	main
main		catalog.htm	main
frameset2.htm	**main.htm**	endorsements.htm	main
		testing.htm	main

Combining rows and columns allows for more creativity in your design. However, it does reduce the amount of space available to display your pages in the main frame. Consider the frameset shown in the following diagram.

This is A	This is B
	This is C

Hyperlinks that are clicked on in frame A will appear as pages in frame C of this frameset. Frame C has been reduced by frame B, which is where a banner or advertising usually goes on a page. You will learn how to combine rows and columns to create a nested frameset in Exercise 8.7.

EXERCISE 8.7

Combining Rows and Columns in Nested Framesets

In this exercise, you will combine columns and rows to add a banner to your frameset. The following diagram shows the frameset structure you will create.

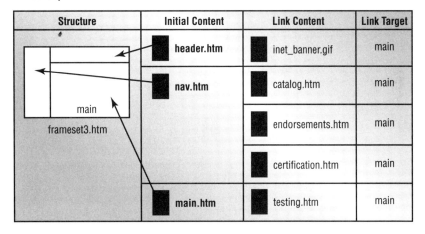

Structure	Initial Content	Link Content	Link Target
	header.htm	inet_banner.gif	main
	nav.htm	catalog.htm	main
main		endorsements.htm	main
frameset3.htm		certification.htm	main
	main.htm	testing.htm	main

To combine columns and rows in your frameset, follow these steps:

1. Open `frameset2.htm` in your editor.

2. Modify the existing HTML as shown in bold:

```
<FRAMESET COLS="25%,75%">
    <FRAME SRC="nav.htm" NAME="nav">
<FRAMESET ROWS="30%,70%">
    <FRAME SRC="header.htm">
    <FRAME SRC="main.htm" NAME="main">
</FRAMESET></FRAMESET>
```

3. Save the file as `frameset3.htm` and open it in your browser.

4. Click on any hyperlink. It should target to the lower frame on the right.

Adding a Frame to a Frame in HTML

The frameset shown in the following diagram resembles the frameset in Exercise 8.7.

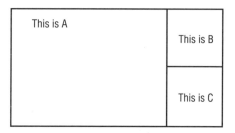

However, this frameset is different. It combines two framesets: one divided into two columns, and the other into two rows. The first frameset is two columns: column A has no content in it and column B holds the frameset containing the two rows, rows B and C. The following diagram illustrates this frameset as a three-dimensional model.

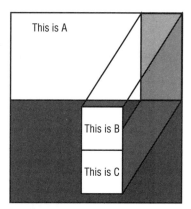

This combined structure allows you to target the second frame structure into the adjoining panel and other linked content from the banner area into the bottom panel. Thus, in the example from Exercise 8.7, the Certification, Catalog, Endorsements, and Testing pages could be designed as framesets, each with a top banner area and a bottom content area. For each of the sections, you could create subject-appropriate links that will bring content into the top and bottom panes.

The easiest way to build these complex frame structures is to build them one at a time, as demonstrated in Exercise 8.8.

EXERCISE 8.8

Combining Frames in HTML

In this exercise, you will build your skills by combining frames:

1. In Notepad, create a new frameset with the following criteria:

- Two rows.
- Top row is 25 percent of screen.
- Bottom row occupies the remainder of the window.
- Initial content for the frames should be certheader.htm and certmain.htm.
- Name of the lower section should be bottom.
- Name of the top section should be top.

Your HTML should resemble the following:

```
<HTML>
<HEAD>
<TITLE>Sub-Frameset</TITLE>
</HEAD>
<FRAMESET ROWS="25%,*">
    <FRAME SRC="certheader.htm" NAME="top">
    <FRAME SRC="certmain.htm" NAME="bottom">
</FRAMESET>
</HTML>
```

2. Save this file as subframeset.htm and close it.

3. Open frameset3.htm in your editor. Change the frameset HTML to the following, leaving only one frameset:

```
<FRAMESET COLS="25%,75%">
<FRAME SRC="nav.htm">
<FRAME SRC="main.htm" name="main">
</FRAMESET>
```

4. Save the file as frameset4.htm and close it.

EXERCISE 8.8 (continued)

5. Open nav.htm and change the link for Certification Programs page as shown in bold:

   ```
   <STRONG>
   <A HREF="subframeset.htm">Certification Programs</A>
   <P>
   ```

6. Save the changes.

7. Open frameset4.htm in your browser.

8. Click on the hyperlink. Notice how the subframeset loads into the right-hand frame.

HTML Frameset Attributes

To realize the full potential of a frameset, it is often desirable to create borderless frames and "freeze" the navigation and header frames to a set size without scrolling capabilities. To accomplish this, you'll modify the BORDER, FRAMEBORDER, FRAMESPACING, and SCROLLING attributes in Exercise 8.9. The BORDER attribute changes the amount of space between the frames, as specified in pixels. A value of "0" in the BORDER attribute makes the frame disappear. The FRAMEBORDER attribute controls the sculpted borders of the frames. Setting the value of this attribute to "0" in conjunction with the BORDER attribute will make all your frames disappear. FRAMESPACING is used only in Internet Explorer and it controls the amount of space between frames. The SCROLLING attribute controls whether scroll bars are visible to the user when the frames are displayed. A value of "yes" designates that the scroll bars will always appear, "no" eliminates the scroll bars altogether, and "auto" indicates that the scroll bars will appear only if needed (if the contents do not fit within the frame).

EXERCISE 8.9

Adding Attributes to the Frameset

In this exercise, you will add attributes to various elements of the frameset.

EXERCISE 8.9 *(continued)*

1. Open `frameset2.htm` and add the attributes indicated in bold:

```
<HTML>
<HEAD>
<TITLE>Frameset</TITLE>
</HEAD>
<FRAMESET COLS="20%,*" FRAMEBORDER="0"
BORDER="0" FRAMESPACING="0">
<FRAME SRC="nav.htm" SCROLLING="no"
FRAMEBORDER="0" NORESIZE>
<FRAME NAME="main" SRC="main.htm"
SCROLLING="auto" FRAMEBORDER="0">
</FRAMESET>
</HTML>
```

2. Save the file as `frameset5.htm` and open it in your browser to review your results. You should notice that the frame border has disappeared, organizing the pages without wasting space on the frame border.

If the frame is not working properly, try changing the value of the SCROLLING attribute from "auto" to "no". Then save the changes and click on the link to the online catalog. You will notice that no scroll bars appear, preventing you from scrolling down to see the rest of the catalog. Remember to use caution when setting the SCROLLING value to "no".

The HTML <NOFRAMES> Tag

Browsers that do not support frames are still in use, though they are certainly the minority. Nonetheless, you should still inform users of these browsers that they cannot view your frames-based web pages. The <NOFRAMES> tag, which you'll add in Exercise 8.10, makes this possible. After completing this exercise, you will be able to test your page only if you can locate a browser that does not support frames.

When you use the <NOFRAMES> tag, it is placed after the <BODY> tag in your HTML document. You only have to use the <BODY> tag on a frameset document when you are including the <NOFRAMES> tag.

EXERCISE 8.10

Adding the <NOFRAMES> Tag (Optional)

In this exercise, you will add the <NOFRAMES> tag to the bottom of your frameset:

1. Open the file `frameset5.htm`. Add the HTML shown in bold:

```
<HTML>
<HEAD>
<TITLE>Frameset</TITLE>
</HEAD>
<FRAMESET COLS="150,*" FRAMEBORDER="0"
BORDER="0" FRAMESPACING="0">
<FRAME NAME="Navigation" SRC="nav.htm"
SCROLLING="no" FRAMEBORDER="0" NORESIZE>
<FRAME NAME="main" SRC="main.htm"
SCROLLING="auto" FRAMEBORDER="0">
</FRAMESET>
<NOFRAMES><BODY>
If you had a frames-capable browser,
you would see my brilliant creation.
</BODY>
</NOFRAMES>
</HTML>
```

2. Save the file as `noframes.htm`. When you view this page in a browser that does not support frames, you will see the sentence you added in the body portion of the page. You can modify the sentence to say whatever you want. You could also put a hyperlink to a non-frames site so users could see your website without frames.

Summary

Frames allow you to create areas that move independently from one another in web page structures. There are various types of frames: simple frames, nested frames, and combined frames. Each type requires that the source of the frame be designated as well as whether the page should be divided into rows or columns. You can combine rows and columns on the same page, but you must use a different <FRAMESET> tag for each type. Frames, however, are not without their disadvantages. For instance, you cannot bookmark content in specific frames, and there is little technical support for frames in older versions of browsers.

You can target to adjacent frames, as well as to the top, parent, and new windows. Using the "_top" and "_parent" values to target allows you to control where the page will display once the hyperlink is clicked. The "_top" and "_parent" values both display the page the hyperlink points to in the same frame, and the same browser window, as the original frameset, and "_blank" opens the page in a new browser window.

The attributes that modify the frame style include BORDER, FRAMEBORDER, FRAMESPACING, and SCROLLING. Each attribute affects how the frame acts and looks in regard to borders and scrolling. Finally, you can use the <NOFRAMES> tag to let users of older browsers know that they are viewing a no-frames version of a site for which frames have been used.

Exam Essentials

Understand the uses of frames.   Frames allow you to create a page structure in which certain information is visible and persistent while other information changes. You can use this type of structure to create static navigation elements in a window alongside content elements that can scroll. You can produce functionality such as this by creating separate panes called frames in the browser window. Frames allow the user to have some elements remain on the page while other elements change. Each frame in a frameset has its own pages that are targeted to it and appear in their assigned location.

Be able to build a simple frameset in columns and rows.   The <FRAMESET> tag is a container tag that allows you to define regions in your browser window and assign separate files to each region. It requires an attribute of either COLS or ROWS to designate the number and size of columns or rows in a browser window. You can specify the COLS and ROWS attributes in two ways: by percentages or by pixels. You should be able to resize windows and know the issues involved with resizing.

Be able to build nested framesets. A nested frameset is one frameset that is inside of another. A nested frameset allows you to combine rows and columns to create a unique page layout in which more than two areas of the page can be designated to be static or dynamic. Using a nested frameset, however, reduces the amount of space in which your pages can display.

Understand frameset hyperlinks and be able to manipulate frameset attributes. When you create hyperlinks, you can designate internal links without specific file addresses by using the <A NAME="anyName"> tag. Once you create a name to which you can anchor your link, you can create the <A HREF="#anyName"> tag and attribute combination. The NAME attribute can also be used to target hyperlinks from the navigation division of your frame to the main area of your browser window. When you name a frame, the files can be loaded when the frame is requested by name. Alternatively, you can automatically set a default target for all links by specifying a base target. A special empty tag called the <BASE> tag allows you to specify both the URL for a document and a default target frame for all the links in that file.

Key Terms

Before you take the exam, be certain you are familiar with the following terms:

frames   framesets

Review Questions

1. What is the advantage of using frames instead of tables?

   A. Frames offer a more static page layout than tables do.

   B. With frames, page areas can scroll independently of each other, which is not the case with tables.

   C. A page for which a table was used for layout can be bookmarked, whereas a frames page cannot.

   D. Tables can always be created more quickly than frames.

2. What is the difference between a frame and a frameset?

   A. A frameset holds the directions for how many rows or columns will be used, whereas a frame contains information about what its source will be.

   B. A frame holds the directions for how many rows or columns will be used, whereas the frameset contains information about what its source will be.

   C. A frameset and a frame are the same thing.

   D. The dimensions for a frameset can only be expressed in percentages, whereas the dimensions for a frame can be expressed in pixels or percentages.

3. Which of the following units would you use if you want to use relative sizing for frames?

   A. Points

   B. Pixels

   C. Picas

   D. Percentages

4. What is the purpose of frames?

   A. Frames provide templates that allow you to quickly create tables for page structure.

   B. Frames establish the basic site structure and hierarchy of all files used in a website.

   C. Frames provide a selection of predesigned graphical borders you can use to embellish pages or sections of pages.

   D. Frames create page structure in which some elements are static while other information changes.

5. Which of the following best describes a simple frameset?

   A. The <FRAME> tag with the COLS or ROWS attribute

   B. The <FRAMESET> tag with the COLS or ROWS attribute

   C. The <FRAME> tag with the COLS and ROWS attributes

   D. The <FRAMES> tag with the COLS and ROWS attributes

6. In a frames page, what can you create by using the <BASE> tag?

   A. A base frame, which specifies default frame dimensions for all frames in a site

   B. A base frameset, which is a default frameset consisting of a navigation frame, a header frame, and a content frame

   C. A base target, which sets a default target window for all links on a page

   D. A base link reference, which is a default URL that is used for all links unless otherwise specified

7. In what two ways can you target frames?

   A. By name or by relationship

   B. By name or by number

   C. By link or by anchor

   D. By URL or by filename

8. How do you create a frameset that combines columns and rows?

A. Use both the COLS and ROWS attributes in the same <FRAMESET> tag.

B. Within the same <FRAMESET> tag, use the COLS attribute for one <FRAME> tag and the ROWS attribute for the other.

C. Use the COLS attribute in one <FRAMESET> tag and the ROWS attribute in another <FRAMESET> tag.

D. Within the same <FRAME> tag, use the COLS attribute for one <FRAMESET> tag and the ROWS attribute for the other.

9. If you are using the <NOFRAMES> tag, which tag must also be present on your HTML page that is not necessary if you are using just the <FRAMESET> tag?

A. <HEAD>

B. <TITLE>

C. <HTML>

D. <BODY>

10. What does the "auto" value of the SCROLLING attribute control?

A. Scroll bars will appear only if needed.

B. Scroll bars will not appear.

C. Scroll bars will appear all the time.

D. None of the above.

11. With which version of HTML were frames first made a W3C Recommendation?

A. HTML 3.2

B. HTML 3.0

C. HTML 4.0

D. HTML 1.0

12. What is a benefit of specifying COLS and ROWS attributes by pixels instead of by percentages?

    A. The size of each frame remains constant regardless of the size of the browser window.

    B. The proportion of the page division remains constant.

    C. This accomplishes relative sizing.

    D. There is no benefit.

13. Which attribute of the <FRAME> tag specifies what file will appear in the frame?

    A. FRAMEFILE

    B. FILE

    C. INFO

    D. SRC

14. Where must the <FRAMESET> tag be placed in an HTML document in order for it to create frames?

    A. Following the closing <HEAD> tag

    B. Following the closing <BODY> tag

    C. Within <FRAME> tags

    D. Enclosing the <TITLE> tag

15. What is the main purpose of a navigation frameset?

    A. To combine all frames into one window

    B. To create a constant navigation frame

    C. To create separate rows and columns

    D. To specify files to be placed inside of frames

16. You can designate internal inks without specific file addresses by using what tag?

   A. `<INTERNAL= "filename">`

   B. `<A NAME = "anyName">`

   C. `<FILENAME>`

   D. `<LINK>`

17. If you target a new browser session, what window will the page the link points to open in?

   A. New browser window

   B. Current window

   C. Two separate windows

   D. The current window will be used by both the page the link points to and the current page.

18. Which type of frames would you use to realize the full potential of a frameset?

   A. Scrolling frames

   B. Bordered frames

   C. Borderless frames

   D. Small frames

19. The amount of space that the BORDER attribute changes between frames is specificd by _____.

   A. Vertical lines

   B. Percentages

   C. Pixels

   D. Color

20. What is the result of using a value of `"0"` in the BORDER attribute?

   A. The frame will remain the same size no matter the browser's window size.

   B. All borders will be white no matter what the background color is.

   C. Borders will be specified by percentages.

   D. Borders will disappear.

Answers to Review Questions

1. B. With frames, page areas can scroll independently of each other. In addition, you can have important content remain on the page regardless of where the user scrolls or which hyperlinks they click on.

2. A. A frameset holds the directions for how many rows or columns will be used, whereas the frame contains information about what the source of the frame will be. In the following example, the first line divides the frameset into two columns, where the first one is 30% of the browser window and the second one is 70%. The second line indicates that the source of the first frame is `nav.htm` and the source of the second one is `main.htm`.

```
<FRAMESET COLS="30%,70%">
     <FRAME SRC="nav.htm">
     <FRAME SRC="main.htm">
```

3. D. When frame sizes are expressed in percentages it's referred to as relative sizing. The windows can be resized, but the proportion of the page division remains constant.

4. D. Frames create page structure in which some elements do not change while other information changes. They also allow you to have important content remain on the page regardless of where the user scrolls or which hyperlinks they click on.

5. B. The <FRAMESET> tag with the `COLS` or `ROWS` attribute will create a page with either columns or rows. One column or row, which creates a frame, can be used for navigation and the other for content.

6. C. In a frames page, you can create a base target, which sets a default target window for all links on a page, by using the <BASE> tag. This saves time when creating a frameset because individual hyperlinks do not have to be targeted.

7. A. You can target frames in two ways: by name or by relationship. The target name is defined in the <FRAME> tag by the `NAME` attribute. The frame relationship, however, is less tangible. It targets based on the location, or relationship, to the frame. Relationship values are `"_top"`, `"_parent"`, or `"_blank"`.

8. C. To create a frameset that combines columns and rows, use the COLS attribute in one <FRAMESET> tag and the ROWS attribute in another <FRAMESET> tag. COLS and ROWS cannot be combined in one <FRAMESET> tag.

9. D. The <BODY> tag is required if you want to display a message informing the user that frames have been used on the page but they cannot see them.

10. A. The "auto" value of the SCROLLING attribute indicates that the scroll bars will appear only if needed (if the contents do not fit within the frame).

11. C. Frames were submitted to the Internet Engineering Task Force (IETF) and the W3C for consideration as an HTML standard and are now part of the HTML 4.0 Recommendation. Frames are an extension of the HTML 3.2 standard.

12. A. The benefit of expressing the size of frames in pixels, which is called absolute sizing, is that the size of each frame remains constant regardless of the size of browser window. Expressing frame size in percentages is referred to as relative sizing. When you use relative sizing, the windows can be resized but the proportion of the page division remains constant.

13. D. The SRC attribute specifies which file will appear in the frame. For example, <FRAME SRC="bottom.htm"> would specify that the bottom.htm file will be in the frame.

14. A. The <FRAMESET> tag will create frames only if it is placed correctly into the HTML document. The opening <FRAMESET> tag must follow the closing <HEAD> tag and must precede the opening <BODY> tag. If you do not plan to use alternate text for browsers incapable of rendering frames, you do not need the <BODY> tag at all.

15. B. The main purpose of a navigation frameset is to create independent windows in which a constant navigation frame is maintained, with navigational links that bring the desired content into an adjacent frame.

16. B. When you create hyperlinks, you can designate internal links without specific file addresses by using the <A NAME="anyName"> tag.

17. A. If you target a new browser session, the page your hyperlink points to will open in a brand-new browser window, leaving your original page in its open browser window. If you target a parent page, the page your hyperlink points to will open in the frame that contains the current frameset, thereby replacing the frameset with the new page.

18. C. To realize the full potential of a frameset, it is often desirable to create borderless frames and "freeze" the navigation and header frames to a set size without scrolling capabilities.

19. C. You use pixels to specify the amount of space between frames that the BORDER attribute changes.

20. D. A value of "0" in the BORDER attribute makes the frame disappear. The FRAMEBORDER attribute controls the sculpted borders of the frames. Setting the value of this attribute to "0" in conjunction with the BORDER attribute will make all your frames disappear.

Chapter

9

Metadata, Cookies, and the Web

THE CIW EXAM OBJECTIVE GROUPS COVERED IN THIS CHAPTER:

✓ Use advanced HTML formatting to enhance the usability of websites, including but not limited to: metadata.

✓ Use client-side and server-side programming to enhance website functionality, including but not limited to: cookies.

✓ Use HTML to create related web pages that can be deployed as a website.

Helping users find your website and then creating a personalized experience once they establish contact with you will help you increase the visibility of your website as well as increase the chances of users returning again. It will be relatively easy to create personalized experiences for visitors to your website once you take full advantage of using metadata and cookies, two HTML features that help in describing the content of your web pages.

In this chapter, we will explore metadata and <META> tags, the different forms of <META> tags and their uses, and how <META> tags arc used by search engines and directories to find your web pages. We'll also discuss cookies: how they work, the myths and truths surrounding them, and how to enable and disable them.

Metadata and <META> Tags

*M*etadata can be defined as data about data; it is data that embraces and describes a larger body of data. The <META> tag describes the content of a web page and has several uses and forms. <META> tags were developed to address specific information about a web page that does not affect its appearance. Meta information consists of general information about the document or page content that should be available, but not necessarily displayed, for the user. The <META> tag is one of the elements found in the <HEAD> portion of an HTML document. Here are some examples of the type of information that could be included:

- Expiration date

- Author name

- Keywords to be used by some search engines
- A description attribute to specify a synopsis of the page in some search engines

The <META> tag requires the CONTENT attribute and either the NAME or HTTP-EQUIV attribute. The syntax for the <META> tag with the NAME attribute is as follows:

```
<META NAME="nameValue" CONTENT="contentValue">
```

Here is the syntax when it's used with the HTTP-EQUIV attribute:

```
<META HTTP-EQUIV="nameValue" CONTENT="contentValue">
```

The HTTP-EQUIV and NAME attributes define the general information you are creating or changing in the document, and the CONTENT attribute defines the value of the general information. We will explore the differences between the HTTP-EQUIV and NAME attributes in the following sections.

HTTP-EQUIV Attribute

<META HTTP-EQUIV> tags are part of HTTP headers. To understand how headers play a part in the meta process, you must understand the process that occurs when you use a web browser to request a document from a web server. When you request information using your browser, the web server receives your request via Hypertext Transfer Protocol (HTTP), the standard web protocol. When the web server finds the page you requested, it generates an HTTP response. The initial data in that response is called the HTTP header block. This header gives the web browser information useful for displaying the page. Figure 9.1 illustrates this data flow.

FIGURE 9.1   Flow of information from Web server to user's computer

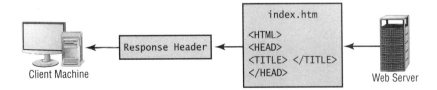

<META HTTP-EQUIV> tags can be used to control the actions of web browsers and further refine the information provided by the actual default headers. If you use the <META HTTP-EQUIV> tag, you force your web server to add or change content in the response header, as shown in Figure 9.2.

FIGURE 9.2 Adding content to response header

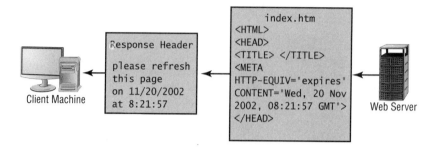

In this example, the `"expires"` value tells the web browser not to use the page from the cache after November 20, 2002. Other values of the HTTP-EQUIV attribute that control the browser's functions include `"pragma"`, `"refresh"`, `"set-cookie"`, and `"window-target"`. Table 9.1 describes these values.

TABLE 9.1 Values of <META> Tag HTTP-EQUIV and CONTENT Attributes

HTTP-EQUIV Attribute Value	CONTENT Attribute Value	Description
`"expires"`	`"Wed, 20 Nov 2002 08:00:00 GMT"`	Defines a date when the file will be considered expired in cache and a new page request will be generated
`"pragma"`	`"No-cache"`, `"no-store"`, `"public"`, `"private"`	Controls the page cache to the browser folder
`"refresh"`	`"seconds; URL=http:// newpage.com"`	Loads the page after the specified number of seconds and then takes the user to the specified URL
`"set-cookie"`	`"cookievalue=xxx; expires=Wednesday, 20-Nov-02 8:00:00 GMT"`	Creates a cookie to collect information
`"window-target"`	`"Name of frame in which to open"`	Changes the default location where hyperlinks open

The values in Table 9.1 are known to affect the browser. You can define other HTTP-EQUIV values to add to the header information, though they will not affect the browser in any way. A better method for delivering this information is provided by the NAME attribute.

NAME Attribute

<META> tags with a NAME attribute are used for information types that do not correspond to HTTP headers. The distinction can be unclear because some browsers interpret values such as "keywords" whether they are declared as either NAME or HTTP-EQUIV. If you use the NAME attribute, the information specified in the <META> tag will not be added to the HTTP header but will remain in your HTML document, as you can see in Figure 9.3.

FIGURE 9.3 Response header with NAME attribute

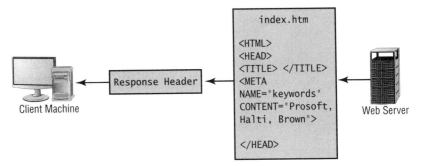

Using <META> Tags

Some servers use the CONTENT and HTTP-EQUIV values to define the HTTP response header name-value pairs. When the browser requests a page, a request header is generated. The server then responds with a response header, providing identifying information about the requested document.

For example, suppose the following information resides on a web page:

```
<META HTTP-EQUIV="expires"
CONTENT="Mon, 18 Feb 2002 00:00:00 GMT">
<META HTTP-EQUIV="keywords" CONTENT="HTML,Instruction">
<META HTTP-EQUIV="reply-to"
CONTENT="info@company.com (Help Center)">
```

The server will include this information in the response header when the document is requested, as follows:

```
Expires: Mon, 18 Feb 2002 00:00:00 GMT
Keywords: HTML,Instruction
Reply-to: info@company.com (Help Center)
```

The "keywords" value is usually specified using the NAME attribute instead of HTTP-EQUIV. The "expires" value helps refresh the cache. For example, you would want a weekly newsletter to expire weekly so when the next HTTP request arrives, the updated page will appear rather than the old one cached on the user's computer. The "reply-to" return e-mail address value can be referenced by some search engines when compiling sets of links and is worth including.

Many HTML-generating programs (e.g., the Netscape Navigator Composer editor or Microsoft FrontPage) add the following <META> tag information:

```
<META NAME="generator" CONTENT="Some program">
```

For example, when you create a page using Netscape Navigator Gold 3, the following information will be added to your document's header:

```
<META NAME="generator"
CONTENT="Mozilla (Win98; I) [Netscape]">
```

Another common use of the <META> tag is to add author information:

```
<META NAME="author" CONTENT="Author's Name">
```

If the author was Greta Marsh, the tag would read as follows:

```
<META NAME="author" CONTENT="Greta Marsh">
```

<META> Tags and Search Engines

Statistics show that only about one in every four websites uses keyword and description <META> tags. However, if you use these tags, you can give your site an advantage over sites that don't use them. <META> tags enable most visitors to find your site initially if they use the same words to search for your site that you have used in the "keywords" and "description" values. If your site isn't placed properly (that is, registered with various search engines), it is highly unlikely that users will find it unless you use some other form of promotion, such as banner ads or unfavorable methods like spam e-mail.

Unfortunately, not all search engines use metadata, and the ones that do often have different criteria for how it is used. This variable makes ensuring proper placement with various search engines a daunting task for the website designer. Contrary to popular myth, there are no search engine secrets that guarantee you a top listing. However, website designers can take some action to improve placement for their websites. Services and applications exist to make search engine placement more manageable.

Before we discuss these services and applications, consider the most commonly used <META> tags and their attributes.

Keywords

Some search engines will search for values specified by the CONTENT attribute on pages that use the <META> tag NAME attribute value of `"keywords"`, as shown in the following example:

```
<META NAME="keywords"
CONTENT="keyword1, keyword2, keyword3">
```

Keywords can contribute significantly to your site's ranking by search engines and directories if search engines use them to help rank sites. Keyword values are usually separated by commas and should reflect the content of your site. Also, do not use keywords excessively; several occurrences of the same word can cause the tag to be ignored. The maximum number of characters a keyword is allowed to have is 1,000; however, it is believed that anything over 255 characters is ignored. Regardless of the search engines or directories to which you will submit, consider the following guidelines:

- Choose keywords that are relevant to your site and do not use misleading words.

- If possible, choose a domain name that includes your keywords.

- When possible, use keywords when naming your HTML files (for example, `cellular1.htm`, `cellular2.htm`, and so forth).

- Include combination keywords, such as *cellular phones* in addition to *cellular* and *phones*. Studies indicate that as many as 60 percent of all searches use two or more words.

- Test your chosen keywords on some popular search engines to see what results are returned. Then visit those sites and look at the text and source code to see other keywords that were used.

- Check to see if the keywords you have selected are among commonly misspelled words. Commonly misspelled words can be used in the <META> tags to help users find your site, but do not misspell words on your pages.

- Avoid using keywords that search engines do not index, such as *to*, *the*, *and*, *or*, *of*, and so forth.

- Use both singular and plural spellings and other variations of keywords (for example, *phones*, *phone*, and *telephone*).

- Use abbreviations (if appropriate) as well as both uppercase and lower-case spellings.

- Use the HTML <TITLE> tag to include a brief 7-to-12-word description of your site, using as many as 3 of your keywords. Many search engines use the title as the site description, so make it appealing. You should not let the length of your title exceed 70 characters, nor should you use all uppercase letters. Avoid using your company name (unless it is highly recognizable) because this wastes space that could be used for keywords.

- Create a logical descriptive summary paragraph using as many keywords as possible. Place it in the first section of the body of the document, within the first 200 characters. Remember that users will read it, so it must make sense. Also, include the keywords in other areas of the document, including the last sentence.

- Use the ALT attribute of the <IMG> tag to include keywords.

- Avoid using graphics exclusively on your home page. Search engines read text, not graphics.

- Do not try to mask a field of repeated keywords with background color.

- Do not place a banner ad at the top of your home page. Using the ALT attribute and hyperlink this way describes keywords other than your own.

Description

When the <META> tag NAME attribute specifies the "description" value, the CONTENT attribute value will appear as a short site description in some search engine results. The syntax for this use of the <META> tag is as follows:

```
<META NAME="description"
CONTENT="This site provides recipes.">
```

Keep this description brief: no more than 25 words (maximum allowance is 150 characters). Make sure that you put the relevant words in the first part of the sentence so your description sentence has meaning when it appears as part of the search engine results. Not all search engines recognize this tag.

Robots

Certain pages should not be indexed by search engines, such as personal pages you do not want the general public to view or intranet/extranet sites. When this is the case, the following <META> tag syntax can be used to tell search engines not to index the page:

```
<META NAME="robots" CONTENT="noindex">
```

Other CONTENT values for "robots" include the following:

"nofollow"   Prevents the crawler from following the links on the page and indexing the linked pages.

"noimageclick"   Prevents links on other sites from pointing directly to images. Instead, only links to the page will be allowed.

"noimageindex"   Prevents the images on the page from being indexed, but the text on the page can still be indexed.

Search Engines vs. Directories

The term *search engine* is used loosely in the web community to include both *search engines* and *directories*. The distinction between the two is that a search engine uses an automated process to discover new web pages. The program that handles this search, sometimes called a *robot* or a *spider*, crawls around the Web following hyperlinks and indexing the content that it finds. This means that eventually a search engine will find your page, assuming that a link to your site exists somewhere on the Web. However, it is impossible to determine how long it will take. For this reason, it is important to submit your site to the search engines. Submitting your site speeds the process and increases your chances for higher placement in search results, thus giving the website designer some control over placement.

A directory differs from a search engine in that it will only find sites based on manual submissions. Thus, if you do not manually submit your site to the directory, the directory will never know of or index your site, therefore never listing your site in search results. Some directories, such as Yahoo! and Magellan, send personnel to visit the site to determine the content and its relevance to the submitted topic. After the review, the website designer may receive an e-mail message asking for additional information so a site description can be created before the site is placed in the directory.

The advantage to this type of directory is that search results are more likely to contain quality content matches to any given query. However, increasing the chances for a higher placement in search results is usually not within the control of the website designer.

Relevance

Search results are ranked according to relevance to the given search criteria. Among searches and search engines, relevance varies. However, a few common characteristics exist:

Titles   A search engine will first scan the HTML <TITLE> tag to look for words that match the query.

Beginning content   A search engine will then look for the query word(s) near the top of the document, assuming that relevant content is mentioned immediately.

Frequency   A search engine will look for frequency of the query word(s), assuming that the more times a word appears, the more likely the document is a good match to the search query.

Now that you understand some of the key components to indexing, consider a few variables. Each search engine indexes sites to different levels and at different frequencies and then uses some proprietary steps to create relevance. For example, some search engines weigh factors such as the number of other sites that link to a given site, which may indicate the site's popularity. Lycos and Northern Light do not consider <META> tags, but other search engines do. Some search engines penalize the overuse of words by refusing to index a site. Some search engines do not catalog common words such as *the*, *and*, *web*, or *of* in an effort to conserve storage space. These are some reasons that different search engines yield different results for the same search.

In addition to search engine placement and advertising, another effective way to help drive visitors to your site is to develop a list of websites that you can benefit or complement and then ask their owners to provide a link to your site and offer them one in return.

<META> Tags and Delayed File Change

To change a web page after a specified delay without user interaction, you can use the HTTP-EQUIV="refresh" attribute and value. For example, your company logo could appear for five seconds and then automatically change to the main menu. The syntax is as follows:

```
<META HTTP-EQUIV="refresh"
CONTENT="seconds;URL=http://anywhere.com">
```

Consider the following example: Users are on the home page of your site and you want them to automatically go to the CIW Certified home page after a three-second delay. The following code demonstrates the <META> tag that will do this:

```
<META HTTP-EQUIV="refresh"
CONTENT="3;URL=http://www.ciwcertified.com">
```

This effect can be used to change URLs without user interaction. For example, you may want to direct where the user goes next from a page without relying on them to click on a link. Do not set the seconds to "0"; this setting prohibits the user from using the browser's Back button. Browsing back to a page that immediately sends the user forward is frustrating for the user.

Understanding Cookies

Cookies are small text files that have a variety of uses. The term *cookie* was chosen at random and has no special meaning. Cookies are sent from a server to the user's browser in the HTTP response header. The browser accepts the response from the page assigning the cookie and then accepts (or gives the user the chance to accept or reject) the cookie. Once the cookie has been accepted, the browser program stores the cookie information in a file on the user's system.

When the HTTP request is generated, any cookies on the user's system with a path and domain name matching the current HTTP request will be passed along in the request header. The server can then test for and evaluate the contents of the incoming cookies. Currently, a server can pass no more than 20 cookies to a user's computer, and a user can store no more than 300 cookies total.

A cookie in a request header appears to the server as follows:

```
Cookie: name=value; name2=value2; etc.
```

The server does not see any information other than the name=value pairs. Only URLs matching the path and domain values in the cookie file can be read again and evaluated by the server.

Cookies store name-value pairs as text strings. Cookies can expire as soon as the user exits their browser, or they can be set to expire on some future date. For this reason, cookies are formally known as *persistent client state HTTP cookies*. They persist until they expire or are deleted by the user.

A cookie header appears to your browser as follows:

```
Set-Cookie: name=value; expires=date;
path=path; domain=domain; secure
```

Each cookie header contains a set of parameters. Not all these parameters must be assigned to use cookies, nor must they be assigned in the following formats. The cookie header parameters include the following:

name=value   The name=value pair is the only information required to generate a cookie. All other cookie attributes are optional.

expires=date   The expires=date pair determines when the cookie will expire. If this attribute is not present, the cookie will expire at the end of the browser session. This attribute can also be used to overwrite and expire cookies that currently have future expiration dates by reassigning them an expiration date in the past.

The date is formatted as follows (GMT stands for Greenwich mean time):

```
weekday, DD-Mon-YY HH:MM:SS GMT
```

Here is an example: Wed, 20-Nov-2002 08:21:57 GMT.

path=path; domain=domain   The path and domain pairs contain the path portion and domain name of the URL that issued the cookie. When an HTTP request header is formed, the path and domain pairs are checked;

if they match the page being requested, any cookies pertaining to that URL are passed back to the server for evaluation.

secure   If this parameter is present, the cookie is sent only when a secure protocol such as Secure Sockets Layer (SSL) is present.

State Maintenance with Cookies

One of the most common uses of cookies is to store information about a user to maintain state between the client and the server. State information is information about a communication between a user and a server. For example, suppose you have set up a personal page at Yahoo! or CNN so that when you visit the site, you get the information you want, such as news about a particular area or quotes on specific stocks. Cookies are used to tell the server which information you want. Or suppose you are playing an adventure game and decide to log off. A cookie can be created and set in your system to tell the site where you left the game; when you return, you can resume at the point you left. In both examples, state is maintained between the client and the server so the server knows who you are and can respond accordingly.

Online purchases can also be conducted using cookies. As the customer adds products to their shopping cart, cookies can be created by the server to list the items chosen. When the customer checks out, the cookie can be evaluated, resulting in the total purchase price.

Cookie Myths and Truths

Cookies have received some criticism because most people do not see them or know what information they are passing. Some of these concerns have some validity but others do not.

The following facts about cookies dispel some common myths:

- Cookies cannot read files from your hard drive.

- Cookies cannot contain viruses.

- Once set, cookies are sent from your system (one way) to the server. The server does not access your computer to read the cookies. After a server sends you a cookie, it has no knowledge that you have the cookie until you request another page from that server.

- Cookies can respond only to the server that sent them. In other words, a cookie sent from Yahoo! cannot respond to AltaVista.

- Cookies cannot gather your passwords and distribute them.

- Cookies are stored in one unique place as text files only and are not executable. The Netscape browser stores cookies in the `Program\User Profile` folder in a file named `cookies.txt`. Microsoft Internet Explorer stores cookies in `Windows\Cookies`.

Cookies can be used for multiple purposes:

- They can keep track of the sites you have browsed.

- They can store personal information. However, they store only information that you provided to the server that wrote the cookie. An example is personal information that you submitted to a site in a web-based form.

- They are not encrypted. However, a server can encode a cookie so that it is unreadable except to that server. Secure cookies are encrypted only because all data transmissions across a secure connection are encrypted.

- They can be used to target you for marketing and banner advertisements.

Enabling and Disabling Cookies

Any user can choose which cookies to accept by adjusting the settings in the browser. In Exercise 9.1, you'll learn how to enable warnings of inbound cookies in Netscape Navigator. In Exercise 9.2, you'll enable warnings in Microsoft Internet Explorer. If you have both browsers installed, you can complete both exercises.

EXERCISE 9.1

Modifying Cookie Settings in Netscape Navigator

To enable or disable notices of incoming cookies in Netscape Navigator, follow these steps.

1. Choose Edit ➤ Preferences.

EXERCISE 9.1 *(continued)*

2. Click on Advanced in the Category list to access the cookies options.

3. Click on the appropriate radio button or check box in the cookies section to enable or disable cookie warnings, as shown in the following graphic.

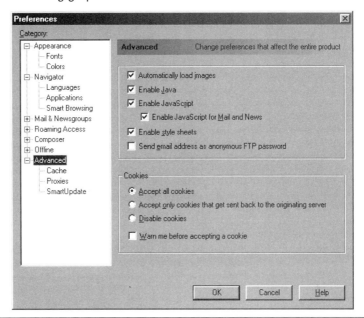

EXERCISE 9.2

Modifying Cookie Settings in Microsoft Internet Explorer

To enable or disable cookie warnings in Microsoft Internet Explorer, follow these steps:

1. Choose Tools ➢ View ➢ Internet Options.

2. Click on the Security tab, shown in the following graphic.

EXERCISE 9.2 (continued)

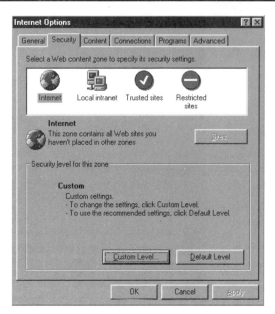

3. Click on the Internet icon to select it and then click on the Custom Level button.

4. Scroll down to the Cookies section, shown in the following graphic.

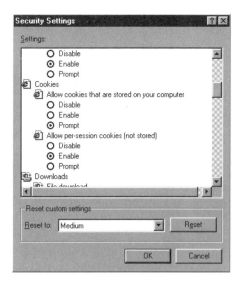

EXERCISE 9.2 *(continued)*

5. Select the appropriate option to disable or prompt for cookies. Then click on OK.

If you enable Allow Cookies That Are Stored on Your Computer, you will allow Internet Explorer to accept cookies on your computer without notifying you. If you disable Allow Cookies That are Stored on Your Computer, you will not allow Internet Explorer to accept cookies on your computer at all. If you select Prompt as the choice for Allow Cookies That Are Stored on Your Computer, you will allow Internet Explorer to accept cookies on your computer after notifying you that a cookie will be created. The Allow Per-Session Cookies section enables, disables, or prompts for cookies in the same way "Allow Cookies That Are Stored on Your Computer" does but deals with temporary cookies (only used during the current browsing session).

Deleting Cookie Files

You can delete cookie files from your system manually. If you delete them, any level of personalization you have created with websites will have to be reestablished. Cookie files are stored differently, depending on which browser you use.

Navigator stores cookies in the `cookies.txt` file, which is located in the `User Profile` folder. This file lists all the cookies downloaded by the browser. Selecting and deleting the contents of this file will remove the cookies from your system.

The `cookies.txt` file contains a statement that reads as follows: "This is a generated file! Do not edit." Disregard this statement. Deleting the contents of this file will not damage any other files on your system.

Internet Explorer stores cookies under a subfolder of `Windows` called `Cookies`. Internet Explorer stores each cookie as its own individual text file rather than concatenating them to one file as Navigator does. Deleting files from the `Cookies` folder will eliminate the cookies from your system. Each time you delete a cookie, you will be prompted to confirm whether you want to delete that file. Click on Yes.

Summary

Assisting users in finding your site is a crucial part of website development. If users cannot locate your site, they will never see it. There are some tools you can use to help users successfully locate your site. By applying metadata to your HTML documents, you can make them more descriptive and accessible to search engines and directories. Metadata is expressed in an HTML document through the use of <META> tags, which are placed in the <HEAD> portion of the document. <META> tags include information about a document, such as the expiration date of the web page, the author's name, keywords to be used by some search engines, and a description to specify a synopsis of the page in some search engines.

Some search engines and directories use keywords to rank sites. If your site isn't placed properly (that is, registered with various search engines), it is highly unlikely that users will find your site unless you use some other form of promotion. Unfortunately, not all search engines use metadata, and the ones that do often have different criteria for how it is used. Because of this variable, ensuring proper placement with various search engines can sometimes be a daunting task for the website designer. Contrary to popular myth, no search engine secrets exist to guarantee you a top listing.

Cookies are small text files that primarily are used to create a personalized experience for the user. Cookies are sent from a server to the user's browser and the browser accepts the response from the page assigning the cookie. Users have the opportunity to accept or reject a cookie, depending on how they have configured their browser. You can delete cookie files from your system manually. If you delete them, though, any level of personalization you have created with websites will have to be reestablished. Once the cookie has been accepted, the browser program stores the cookie information in a file on the user's system. Cookie files are stored differently depending on which browser you use.

Exam Essentials

Know how to add metadata to an HTML document.   Meta information, which is general information about a document or page, is not displayed to the user but is available through the source code. It includes information such as expiration date of the web page, author name, keywords to be used by some search engines, and a description to specify a synopsis of the page in some search engines.

Be able to use the <META> tag and know its attributes.   <META> tags are located in the head portion of a web page and contain information about a web page that does not affect its appearance. One use of the <META> tag is to describe the content of a web page. The two types of <META> tag attributes are NAME and HTTP-EQUIV. Two of the most common NAME values are "keywords" and "description". Common HTTP-EQUIV values are "pragma", "refresh", and "expires".

Understand search engine placement.   Some search engines will search for values specified by the CONTENT attribute on pages that use the <META> tag NAME attribute value of "keywords". If a search engine or directory uses keywords in its ranking system, including them in your site can contribute significantly to your placement in the search results. There are guidelines you should follow when developing the keywords for your website: They are usually separated by commas and reflect the content of your site; they should not be used excessively; and the maximum allowance for keywords is 1,000 characters, but realistically, they should be kept to 255 characters.

Understand cookies and how they can be used to enhance a website. Cookies are used to create a personalized experience for the web user. They are small text files that are sent from a server to the user's browser in the HTTP response header. The browser accepts the response from the page assigning the cookie and then accepts (or gives the user the chance to accept or reject) the cookie. Browsers store cookies in text files on the user's system once they have been accepted.

Know how to enable your browser to warn you before accepting cookies. Any user can choose which cookies to accept by adjusting the settings in the browser. You can adjust the settings so your system will automatically accept cookies, you will be warned before a cookie is accepted, or cookies are rejected altogether.

Know how to delete cookies from your system. You can delete cookie files from your system manually. If you delete them, any level of personalization you have created with websites will have to be reestablished. Cookie files are stored differently depending on which browser you use.

Key Terms

Before you take the exam, be certain you are familiar with the following terms:

cookies	metadata
directories	search engines

Review Questions

1. Which of the following best defines *metadata*?

   A. Internet or web data

   B. A computer language used to create or interpret data

   C. The <META> tag

   D. Data about data

2. Meta information generally consists of what?

   A. Information about the document or content that should be available but not necessarily displayed to the user

   B. Statistics, dimensions, and other technical documentation about the website

   C. Information about the document that will affect only the page's appearance

   D. Information that is reserved for other web page authors who may be maintaining or updating the site later

3. Which one of the following types of meta information can you specify using the <META> tag NAME attribute?

   A. Web page expiration date

   B. Time delay before page refreshes

   C. Web page author

   D. Cookie data

4. Which of the following <META> tag attributes can you use to control the way in which the page is cached to the browser?

   A. `HTTP-EQUIV="pragma"`

   B. `NAME="cache"`

   C. `HTTP-EQUIV="cache"`

   D. `CONTENT="pragma"`

5. You have created a pop music website and you want to specify key-words that a search engine can use to match your site to a search query. Which of the following demonstrates the correct syntax for a <META> tag that will perform this function?

   A. <META="name" KEYWORDS="rock, reggae, rap">

   B. <META KEYWORDS="rock, reggae, rap">

   C. <META NAME="keywords" CONTENT="rock, reggae, rap">

   D. <META CONTENT="keywords" DESCRIPTION="rock, reggae, rap">

6. Which of the following best defines a cookie?

   A. A small text file that is sent from a client to a server and lists the contents of the client system's hard drive

   B. A small text file sent from a server to a browser to store information on the user's system

   C. A small text file that passes data or viruses from a server to a client system via the browser

   D. A small text file that gathers passwords from a server and distributes them to client systems

7. For what reason are cookies commonly thought to pose a security threat?

   A. Users place cookies on other user's systems to obtain information.

   B. Cookies often spread bugs and viruses on the Web.

   C. Cookies are capable of reading files on your hard drive.

   D. Most users do not see cookies or know what data they pass.

8. For which purpose can a cookie be used to enhance the user's experience at a website?

   A. Maintain state with the web server

   B. Pass information from one server to another

   C. Deliver executable files

   D. Contact other sites visited by the client

9. If you use Internet Explorer or Navigator, you can configure the browser to do which of the following?

   A. Send cookies to the websites you visit

   B. Warn you before accepting cookies

   C. Delete cookies from the websites you visit

   D. Delete cookies automatically before closing the browser

10. You want to manually delete all the cookies stored on your system. Under what circumstances would all the stored cookies be placed in one text file called `cookies.txt`?

    A. If you stored more than 300 cookies before deleting them

    B. If you were warned about cookies and accepted them anyway

    C. If you use the Netscape Navigator browser

    D. If you use the Microsoft Internet Explorer browser

11. What is the initial data in an HTTP response called?

    A. HTTP response

    B. HTTP data

    C. HTTP header block

    D. HTTP content

12. Which of the following `HTTP-EQUIV` values for <META> tags loads the page after the specified number of seconds and then takes the user to the specified URL?

    A. `"expires"`

    B. `"pragma"`

    C. `"refresh"`

    D. `"set-cookie"`

13. Which of the following <META> tag attributes can be used to name the frame to open?

    A. HTTP-EQUIV= "REFRESH"

    B. HTTP-EQUIV= "WINDOW-TARGET"

    C. FRAME= "Any frame"

    D. HTTP= "Frame"

14. The KEYWORDS value is usually specified using what attribute?

    A. HTTP-EQUIV

    B. NAME

    C. KEY

    D. HEAD

15. What advantage can <META> tags give your site?

    A. <META>tags help users find your site.

    B. <META>tags create banner ads for your site.

    C. <META>tags describe your site to directories.

    D. <META>tags delete cookies at each visit.

16. Which of the following is a guideline to use to achieve higher ranking on a search engine for a website?

    A. Avoid using keywords that search engines do not index.

    B. Use only the plural form of keywords.

    C. Do not have a domain name that includes your keywords.

    D. Do not use abbreviations.

17. Which of the following should you use with the <TITLE> tag to make sure search engines list your site?

    A. Your company name

    B. All uppercase letters

    C. A description that is over 70 words long

    D. A 7- to 12-word description of your site with as many as 3 keywords

18. What type of sites should not be indexed on search engines?

    A. Personal or intranet sites

    B. Small businesses

    C. Large businesses

    D. Information-only sites

19. What is the proper syntax to use when you do not want a search engine to index your site?

    A. `<META NAME="ROBOTS" CONTENT="NOFOLLOW">`

    B. `<META NAME="ROBOTS" CONTENT="NOIMAGECLICK">`

    C. `<META NAME="ROBOTS" CONTENT="NOINDEX">`

    D. `<META NAME="KEYWORDS" TITLE="NOFOLLOW">`

20. What is one key difference between search engines and directories?

    A. Search engines will not automatically find your site, whereas directories will.

    B. Search engines will automatically find your site, but directories will not.

    C. Directories use an automation process, including the use of a spider.

    D. Directories use an automation process, including the use of a robot.

Answers to Review Questions

1. D. *Metadata* can be defined as data about data; it is data that embraces and describes a larger body of data. The <META> tag describes the content of a web page.

2. A. Meta information consists of general information about the document or page content that should be available, but not necessarily displayed, for the user. Meta information, as expressed by <META> tags in HTML documents, was developed to address specific information about a web page that does not affect its appearance.

3. C. The web page author is one of the types of information you can specify using the NAME attribute of the <META> tag. The web page expiration date, the time delay before the page refreshes, and cookie data are types of information you can specify using the HTTP-EQUIV attribute.

4. A. HTTP-EQUIV="pragma" will control the way in which a page is cached in the browser. Caching is the process of storing information on the user's computer so it can be accessed more quickly.

5. C. This is the correct syntax for specifying keywords that a search engine can use to match your site to a search query about pop music:

   <META NAME="keywords" CONTENT="rock, reggae, rap">

   The "keywords" value is used to list the words that users will most likely use to search for your site. The maximum number of characters you can use in a "keywords" value is 1,000.

6. B. Cookies are small text files that are sent from a server to the user's browser in the HTTP response header. A user can choose to accept or reject a cookie. Cookies are stored on the user's system in a plain-text file once they are accepted by the browser.

7. C. Cookies commonly are thought to pose a security threat because some people mistakenly think they are capable of reading files on your hard drive. Cookies cannot read files on your hard drive. Once set, cookies are sent from your system (one way) to the server. The server does not access your computer to read the cookies. After a server sends you a cookie, it has no knowledge that you have the cookie until you request another page from that server.

8. A.   A cookie can be used to enhance the user's experience at a website by maintaining state with the web server. This creates a personalized experience on that website for the user.

9. B.   If you use Internet Explorer or Navigator, you can configure the browser to warn you before accepting cookies. You also have the option to accept all cookies without warning or choose to be prompted before accepting cookies.

10. C.   Navigator stores cookies in the `cookies.txt` file, which is located in the `User Profile` folder. This file lists all the cookies downloaded by the browser. Selecting and deleting the contents of this file will remove the cookies from your system.

11. C.   When the web server finds the page you requested, it generates an HTTP response. The initial data in that response is called the HTTP header block. This header gives the web browser information that is useful for displaying the page.

12. C.   The `"refresh"` attribute will load the page after the specified number of seconds and then take the user to the specified URL. Option A is incorrect because `"expires"` defines a date when the file will be considered expired in cache and a new page request will be generated. Option B is incorrect because `"pragma"` controls the page cache to the browser folder. Option D is incorrect because `"set-cookie"` creates a cookie to collect information.

13. B.   `HTTP-EQUIV= "WINDOW-TARGET"` will specify for the browser which frame to open. Other values of the `HTTP-EQUIV` attribute that control the browser's functions include `"PRAGMA"`, `"REFRESH"`, `"SET-COOKIE"`, and `"EXPIRES"`.

14. B.   The `"KEYWORDS"` value is usually specified using the `NAME` attribute instead of `HTTP-EQUIV`.

15. A.   <META>tags can give your site an advantage by enabling most visitors to find your site initially. Search engines use web crawlers that search, in most cases, for the <META> tags looking for key words to place the site under.

16. A.   Keywords can contribute significantly to your site's ranking by search engines and directories if search engines use them to help rank sites. You can increase your chances of a higher ranking if you avoid using words that search engines do not index, such as *the*, *to*, *and*, *or*, *of*, and so forth.

17. D.   Use the HTML <TITLE> tag to include a brief 7- to-12-word description of your site, using as many as 3 of your keywords. The length of your title should not exceed 70 characters, nor should you use all uppercase letters. Avoid using your company name because it takes up space you could use for keywords.

18. A.   Sites such as personal pages, which you do want the general public to view, or sites meant for an intranet and extranet should not be indexed by search engines.

19. C.   When a site should not be indexed by a search engine, the proper <META> tag syntax to use is <META NAME="ROBOTS" CONTENT="NOINDEX">. "NOFOLLOW" prevents a search engine's crawler from following the links on the page and indexing the linked pages. Answer B is incorrect because "NOIMAGECLICK" prevents links on other sites from pointing directly to images. Instead, only links to the page will be allowed.

20. B.   The distinction between how a directory and a search engine work is that a search engine uses an automated process to discover new web pages. The program that handles this search , sometimes called a robot or a spider, crawls around the Web following hyperlinks and indexing the content that it finds. A directory differs from a search engine in that it will only find sites based on manual submissions.

Chapter
10

Cascading Style Sheets

THE CIW EXAM OBJECTIVE GROUPS COVERED IN THIS CHAPTER:

✓ Use advanced HTML formatting to enhance the usability of websites, including but not limited to: Cascading Style Sheets (CSS).

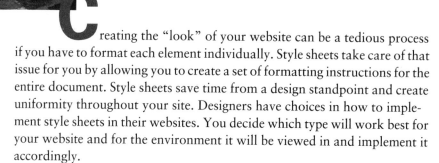

reating the "look" of your website can be a tedious process if you have to format each element individually. Style sheets take care of that issue for you by allowing you to create a set of formatting instructions for the entire document. Style sheets save time from a design standpoint and create uniformity throughout your site. Designers have choices in how to implement style sheets in their websites. You decide which type will work best for your website and for the environment it will be viewed in and implement it accordingly.

In this chapter, we will discuss style sheets and Cascading Style Sheets (CSS) and their role in website design. We'll cover the four methods of creating Cascading Style Sheets, the elements of the CSS1 and CSS2 Recommendations, and the role style inheritance plays in style sheets.

Style Sheets

A style is a set of formatting instructions placed in the HEAD portion of an HTML document. Many webmasters are already using styles in their web pages because of their usefulness. Styles allow you to make one change that affects multiple HTML elements. Style changes can be made to occur periodically or throughout a document. For example, the heading tags <H> represent various styles: Heading level 1 is bold, Times New Roman, and 24 point by default; heading level 4 is bold, Times New Roman, and 12 point. You can change these default attributes. You can also control margins, line spacing, and placement of design elements as well as specify colors, fonts, and point sizes.

The W3C Recommendation for HTML 3.2 includes typographical control elements called *style sheets*, which enable you to create web pages with the layout sophistication of many desktop publishing programs. A style sheet defines style instructions for an HTML document, though the term is often used to refer to an external style-controlling file. Style sheets solve several design problems. Imagine that your web page has 12 different level-2 headings that you want to appear in red. Normally, you would need to wrap a pair of <FONT> tags (<FONT COLOR="red"> and </FONT>) around each of the 12 headings. What if you wanted to try blue headings? You would have to do a considerable amount of recoding. With style sheets, however, you could add just a few lines of code and change the colors of all the headings with a single word.

 A style sheet can be a powerful tool for website authors. Think about the time saved by changing an HTML tag in one place instead of having to change many individual tags throughout the HTML document. Attaching external style sheets can be even more useful because this method allows you to change the look of an entire website by changing a single file. Keep in mind that not all browsers support style sheets. How would you design your web page to accommodate different browsers? As always, keep your target audience in mind.

Style sheets have enhanced website design since the HTML 3.2 designation as a web standard. They have solved a number of HTML design limitations, including proprietary HTML extensions, text-to-image conversion to retain fonts, page layout using tables, and images controlling white space. These workarounds are still used by those who do not know how to employ style sheets in their website design environment.

Cascading Style Sheets

*C*ascading Style Sheets (CSS) refers to the use of multiple style definitions in a single document. A style sheet file can link to every document in a website, thus controlling the overall look and feel of the site. However, within any of the linked documents, a style header block can override the linked style sheet. Within the same file, a spanned style (one in which the <SPAN> tag is used to control style information in small sections of an HTML document) can also override the style information embedded in the header block, along with any style information from the linked style sheet. The term *cascading* refers to inheritance, or the hierarchical relationship between linked, imported, embedded, and inline styles.

Microsoft Internet Explorer 3 (and later) is compliant with the Cascading Style Sheets (CSS) 1 specification. Netscape Communicator 4 (and later) partially supports the W3C Recommendation for style sheets. The W3C published a new Recommendation in 1998 called CSS2, which addresses version 4 browsers. The entire W3C CSS1 style sheet specification can be found at the following URL:

`www.w3.org/TR/REC-CSS1.`

As is the case with all aspects of website design, consider your audience and the browser versions they might be using in your decision about implementing CSS1 or CSS2. The W3C provides a CSS1 test suite that can be used to test your browser's compliance with CSS1. Visit the following URL:

`www.w3.org/Style/CSS/Test/.`

Defining and Using Styles

The HTML 3.2 Recommendation for Cascading Style Sheets specifies the four ways to apply style variations. The first two methods (linking from an HTML file and importing style information) refer to external style sheets (text files that use the `.css` filename extension and contain nothing but style definitions), which allow you to use styles across multiple web pages. The third method (embedding style information) defines styles for a single page. The fourth method (using an inline style) makes quick, temporary style changes to existing HTML text, such as spanning a background color or an image behind words.

Linking to Style Sheets from an HTML File

When you use a *linked style*, a single style sheet controls multiple web pages. However, each page must be linked to the style sheet by a plain-text file with the `.css` extension. To link a website file back to the style sheet, use the following syntax:

```
<LINK REL=STYLESHEET TYPE="text/css"
   HREF="http://www.domain.com/styles.css">
```

Style sheet files should include only style information. HTML tags should not be included in your plain-text style file.

The terms *style sheet* and *cascading style sheets* are often used to refer to linked or imported style information.

Importing Style Information

Another method for accessing an external style file involves using *imported styles*. This method allows you to keep all your style information in the same place in your HTML document, within the <STYLE> tag, while also loading external files as style commands. To use this method, apply the @import command, which has the following syntax:

```
<STYLE TYPE="text/css">
        @import url(http://www.domain.com/styles.css);
        H1 { color: blue }
</STYLE>
```

Note that in this method, a semicolon is needed at the end of the import statement to separate it from any following style information. This method is only supported by Internet Explorer and will not function in Netscape Navigator.

Embedding Style Information

Using an *embedded style* is perhaps the simplest method for using styles. This method defines styles for a single page. It uses the <STYLE> tag to place information in the head portion of an HTML document. Style information is contained within comment tags so older browsers do not display them as text, and it is placed in curly brackets after the element you want to change. The components are separated by a semicolon. The syntax for embedding a block of style information in a single document is as follows:

```
<HTML>
<HEAD>
<STYLE>
<!--
H1  {color: blue;font-family: "Arial";font-size: 20pt}
-->
</STYLE>
</HEAD>
```

Using an Inline Style

Inline styles are added to existing HTML tags or used in conjunction with the approved HTML 4 <SPAN> tag. The <SPAN> tag is a container tag that affects everything on the page between it and the closing </SPAN> tag. For example, the following syntax would place a yellow highlight behind the words *World Enterprises*:

```
<SPAN STYLE="background: yellow">World Enterprises</SPAN>
```

You can use style attributes to add inline style definitions to existing HTML tags. The following examples demonstrate this technique:

```
<H1 STYLE="color: blue;font-size:30pt">Join the Club!</H1>
<P STYLE="background: black;
color: white;text-indent:.25in">
It was a dark and stormy night.</P>
<UL STYLE="font-family: Verdana">
<LI>Events
<LI>Meetings
</UL>
```

The advantage of using inline styles is that you can designate a set of attributes with a single tag. This method should be used only for occasional style changes. If you plan to use the same inline style more than once, you should consider defining it as a style element in an embedded style header block so you do not waste time repeating inline instructions.

Changeable Style Elements

Table 10.1 contains a partial list of some of the style attributes that can be changed with style variation methods. These style attributes are part of the CSS1 specification. A colon and the appropriate value follow each of these attributes. Multiple attribute/value pairs can be separated with a semicolon. All should be enclosed within curly braces {}.

TABLE 10.1   Changeable Style Elements

Attribute	Sample Value	Description	Example
color	Any HTML color name or hexadecimal value	Sets font color.	`color: red`
background	Any HTML color name or hexadecimal value; also accepts images	Displays a background color or background image. You can use any image types your browser recognizes. Both Navigator and Internet Explorer recognize GIF and JPG file types; Internet Explorer recognizes the BMP format also.	`background: yellow` `background:` `url(filename.gif)` *Note: When using a file for background, the* `url` *attribute must be followed with the filename in parentheses.*
font	Bold, 10 point, Verdana	Sets the three important attributes of a font: the weight (bold, normal, or light), the size (in points), and the font name. Not all attributes must be specified.	`font: 38pt "Times New Roman"` `font: light 18pt "Arial"`
font-family	Times, Palatino, and so forth	Specifies type. If multiple fonts are given, the browser uses the first in the list found on the end user's site.	`font-family: Garamond` `font-family: Arial, "Sans Serif"`
font-size	12 point, 1 inch, .5 centimeters, 200 pixels	Sets text character size.	`font-size: 48pt` `font-size: .25in`
font-style	Italic (defaults to normal)	Specifies italic type.	`font-style: italic`
font-weight	Bold, normal, light	Specifies weight, or "thickness."	`font-weight: bold`
text-decoration	Underline or not	Adds or removes underline.	`text-decoration: underline` `text-decoration: none`

TABLE 10.1 Changeable Style Elements *(continued)*

Attribute	Sample Value	Description	Example
line-height	150 percent, 75 pixels, 1.08 inches	Specifies leading (amount of vertical space) between lines.	line-height: 90% line-height: 1.5in
text-indent	.25 inch, three em spaces (3em), 24 point, 50 pixels, 3 centimeters	Specifies first-line indent for paragraphs. Affects first line only; the rest of the paragraph will wrap to the left margin setting.	text-indent: .25in
margin-left	.25 inch, 3 em spaces, 24 point, 50 pixels, 3 centimeters	Sets left margin for given element. Can be set to a positive or negative number.	margin-left: 1in margin-left: -4em
margin-top	.25 inch, 3 em spaces, 24 point, 50 pixels, 3 centimeters	Sets top margin for given element. Can be set to a positive or negative number.	margin-top: 48pt margin-top: -1.5in
text-align	Center, left, right	Specifies horizontal alignment of any given text element.	text-align: center

Style Inheritance

One of the most important benefits of style sheets is that a few simple statements can dramatically alter the appearance of large amounts of text. This benefit occurs because styles allow for inheritance. *Inheritance* is the principle of passing on style definitions from parent elements to other elements. For example, to set a default text style, you can define a style specification for the BODY element:

```
BODY {color: navy; font-family: Arial}
```

All text elements in HTML inherit the characteristics of the <BODY> font. If the preceding HTML source code was in the style file or style header block, all the other text heading levels, table text, or other elements would inherit the Arial font and the navy color (except links, which have their own overriding color definitions).

Style Guides

A *style guide* is a standards document or manual that establishes a set of conventions or rules for performing common tasks. For example, style guides are often used by technical writers for general information, ranging from editorial style to specific guidelines for font sizes and types. Website designers frequently use style guides because they provide general design guidelines for creating effective web pages.

Consider creating a style guide for your organization. It will standardize your company's look and define a common format for your website. The style guide is also useful for integrating documents from many departments or individuals.

You may want to include some of the following topics in a style guide:

- Default body text styles

- Default background images or colors

- Rules for heading levels

- Preferred methods for emphasizing text (e.g., italic or bold)

- Guidelines for use of images and logos (e.g., size, format, and scaling)

- Templates for standard pages (e.g., press releases)

- Guidelines for using navigation links and image maps

Changes from CSS1 to CSS2

We have delved briefly into the world of style sheets using mainly the CSS1 Recommendation. However, it is important to understand the functionality presented by the CSS2 Recommendation. In Table 10.2, notice the expanded functionality of CSS2 and consider the problems these new features will solve in the online world. Currently, CSS2 has limited browser support.

You can learn more about the problems each browser has with supporting cascading style sheets by visiting the following site:

`www.richinstyle.com/bugs/`.

T A B L E   1 0 . 2   CSS2 Features

CSS2 Function	Definition
Media types	You can determine a document's appearance based on whether it will be presented on screen, in print, with a speech synthesizer, or using a braille device. Font type can be subtly changed to optimize it for reading in a specific environment (e.g., sans serif for on-screen reading, serif fonts for print media).
Paged media	CSS2 determines the display of paged media (such as transparencies) using a page box with finite width and height. This feature provides areas that act as page breaks between information for transfer to print media.
Aural style sheets	The use of voice synthesizers for hearing-impaired users can now be optimized using aural style sheets. CSS properties also allow authors to vary the quality of synthesized speech (voice type, frequency, inflection, and so forth).
Bidirectional text	Support for bidirectional text is imperative for international organizations with informational display requirements in other languages. For example, sometimes Arabic and Hebrew scripts cause documents to render with mixed directionality. The CSS2 properties define an algorithm that ensures proper bidirectional rendering.
Font support	In CSS1, all fonts were assumed to be supported on the client side. In other words, the font had to be loaded on the user's system for the page to render correctly. By contrast, CSS2 allows for improved client-side font matching, enables font synthesis and progressive rendering, and enables fonts to be downloaded from the Web.
Relative and absolute positioning	The need for the browser-proprietary <LAYER> tag is eliminated with CSS2, which provides a z-axis that allows elements to be stacked on a page and displayed accordingly. Absolute positioning with style sheets allows you to form pages that resemble frames.

Absolute Positioning with CSS

According to Nick Heinle in his article "Absolute Positioning with CSS" (`www.webreview.com/1997/06_27/webauthors/06_27_97_2.shtml`), Netscape and Microsoft finally agree that absolute positioning should be performed by CSS and not with proprietary tags such as the Netscape <LAYER> tag. The browser companies are now working together with the W3C to provide users with technology that's universal to the next-generation browsers. Both absolute and relative positioning with style sheets will allow for dramatically improved site design functionality and will improve the overall aesthetic quality of third-generation sites.

W2CSS

Created by Lewis Gartenberg, W2CSS is a Microsoft Word translator macro program existing as shareware (it can be downloaded from `www.geocities.com/w2css/`). It takes a Microsoft Word document as input and produces an HTML file. How does this program differ from the Save As HTML function in Microsoft Word 97 and 2000? Every element in HTML, such as lists, headings, and paragraphs, is tagged with a CSS class. The classes are created by reading the style definitions within the Word document and translating them into the equivalent CSS definitions.

Summary

Style sheets can be used to apply styles to all HTML elements in a document. Styles allow you to make one change that affects multiple HTML elements. You can make style changes occur periodically or throughout a document. Style sheets were introduced in the W3C Recommendation for HTML 3.2. They enable you to create web pages with the layout sophistication of many desktop publishing programs. A style sheet defines style instructions for an HTML document, though the term is often used to refer to an external style-controlling file. Style sheets solve several design problems, such as absolute and relative positioning and bidirectional text support.

There are four ways to create style sheets: linking, importing, embedding, and using an inline style. When you use a linked style, a single style sheet controls multiple web pages. Each page must be linked to the style sheet by a plain-text file with the `.css` extension. You can also access an external style file by using the @import method; however, this method will not function in Netscape Navigator. Using an embedded style is perhaps the simplest method for using styles. This method defines styles for a single page. Inline styles are added to existing HTML tags or used in conjunction with the approved HTML 4 <SPAN> tag. The advantage of using inline styles is that you can designate a set of attributes with a single tag. This method should be used only for occasional style changes.

Exam Essentials

Know four ways to apply style variations with CSS.   There are four ways to create style sheets: linking, importing, embedding, and using an inline style. A single style sheet controls multiple web pages in a linked style. This method uses the .css extension to link a plain text file to the style sheet. The @import method uses the <STYLE> tag to include style information in the head portion of the HTML document. The disadvantage of this method is that the @import command will not function in Netscape Navigator. The embedded style method defines styles for a single page and is perhaps the easiest method to use. The inline style method is used in conjunction with the approved HTML 4 <SPAN> tag or applied directly to a tag in HTML document and is used for occasional style changes because it must be applied to individual elements instead of an entire document or section of a document. Its advantage lies in that it gives you the ability to designate a set of attributes with a single tag.

Key Terms

Before you take the exam, be certain you are familiar with the following terms:

Cascading Style Sheets (CSS)	inline styles
embedded style	linked style
imported style	style guide
inheritance	style sheets

Review Questions

1. The HTML 3.2 Recommendation for Cascading Style Sheets specifies four ways to apply style variations. Which of these four techniques can be used to define styles in a block for a single page?

   A. Linked

   B. Imported

   C. Embedded

   D. Inline

2. Which of the four techniques for applying style sheets can be used to define styles in existing HTML or in conjunction with the HTML 4 <SPAN> tag?

   A. Linked

   B. Imported

   C. Embedded

   D. Inline

3. Which of the four techniques for applying style sheets allows you to create an external style sheet that can be used across multiple pages and functions in both the Navigator and Internet Explorer browsers?

   A. Linked

   B. Imported

   C. Embedded

   D. Inline

4. What must you do to embed a style into a web page?

   A. Create a separate text file that specifies the style instructions.

   B. Add the <STYLE> tag specifying the style instructions.

   C. Add the <EMBED> tag with an attribute specifying the style instructions.

   D. Add the <SPAN> tag with a STYLE attribute specifying the style instructions.

5. Which of the following is the correct syntax to link your web page to an external style sheet named `style.css`?

   A. `<LINK REL="stylesheet" TYPE="text/css" HREF="style.css">`

   B. `<A HREF="style.css" TYPE="text/css">`

   C. `<SPAN TYPE="text/css" LINK="style.css">`

   D. `<STYLE REL="stylesheet" TYPE="text/css" HREF="style.css">`

6. Where can you locate the most reliable Cascading Style Sheet support resources?

   A. Visit the World Wide Web Consortium at `www.w3.org`.

   B. Using a search engine, search for "CSS resources".

   C. Consult any style guide.

   D. Browse other sites to see the effectiveness of various style choices.

7. Which of the following is not a feature of CSS2?

   A. Bidirectional text

   B. Font support

   C. Layers

   D. Aural style sheets

8. Why is support for bidirectional text important?

   A. So text can scroll across the browser screen

   B. So support exists for languages that do not read like English (left to right)

   C. So you can use animated text in programs like Flash

   D. So fonts are supported on the client side

9. What is the principle of style inheritance?

  A. Passing style definitions from parent elements to other elements

  B. Passing style definitions from other elements to parent elements

  C. Passing style definitions from child elements to other elements

  D. Passing style definitions from other elements to child elements

10. Style sheets have been a part of HTML designations since which Recommendation?

  A. 2.0

  B. 3.2

  C. 4.0

  D. 4.01

11. A style is a set of formatting instructions placed in which part of an HTML document?

  A. BODY

  B. TABLE

  C. HEAD

  D. FOOTER

12. Which of the following HTML design limitations does style sheets not address?

  A. Proprietary HTML extensions

  B. Security

  C. Page layout using tables

  D. Text-to-image conversion to retain fonts

13. What is a standards document that establishes a set of conventions or rules for performing common tasks called?

  A. Style standards

  B. Style guide

  C. Style technical specs

  D. Style limits

14. Which of the following topics would you *not* include in a style guide?

    A. Default body text styles

    B. Default background images or colors

    C. Preferred methods for e-commerce transactions

    D. Templates for standard pages

15. Which tag is a container tag for using inline styles?

    A. <INLINE>

    B. <SPAN>

    C. <SPANSTYLE>

    D. <STYLESPAN>

16. What method is used to access an external style file?

    A. <IMPORT>

    B. `@insert`

    C. <INSERT>

    D. `@import`

17. Which option best describes what style sheet files should include?

    A. Style information

    B. HTML tags

    C. Hyperlinks

    D. Security

18. The `@import` command will not function in which of the following applications?

    A. Internet Explorer

    B. Netscape Navigator

    C. CSS

    D. HTML

19. Which of the following is a Microsoft Word translator macro program that produces an HTML file?

    A. CSS

    B. MACROWEB

    C. W2CSS

    D. Flash

20. Which proprietary tag has Netscape been using in place of absolute positioning through CSS?

    A. <AS>

    B. <ABSOLUTE>

    C. <LAYER>

    D. <APOS>

Answers to Review Questions

1. C. An embedded style controls a block of style information in a single document. It is the easiest of the style sheet methods to use. It uses the <STYLE> tag to embed style information in the head portion of an HTML document.

2. D. Inline styles are added to existing HTML tags or used in conjunction with the approved HTML 4 <SPAN> tag. Using this method allows a website designer to control style elements in a portion of an HTML document.

3. A. With a linked style, a single style sheets controls multiple web pages. This method of applying style sheets is supported by both Internet Explorer and Netscape Navigator browsers. For this method to work properly, each page must be linked to the style sheet by a plain-text file with the .css extension.

4. B. To embed a style into a web page, you must add the <STYLE> tag specifying the style instructions. The <STYLE> tag is placed in the head section of an HTML document, and style information is enclosed in a comment tag so older browsers will not display the information as text.

5. A. To link a website file back to the style sheet, use the following syntax:
   `<LINK REL="stylesheet" TYPE="text/css" HREF="style.css">`
   This is known as a linked style. With a linked style, a single style sheet controls multiple web pages. Each page must be linked to the style sheet by a plain-text file with the .css extension.

6. A. The World Wide Web Consortium (W3C) creates the Recommendations for CSS as well as HTML and other web elements.

7. C. CSS2 eliminates the need for layers with the introduction of relative and absolute positioning.

8. B. Support for bidirectional text is important for international organizations with informational display requirements for languages that use non-English characters, like Hebrew or Japanese, which are read from right to left or top to bottom.

9. A. The principle of style inheritance is passing style definitions from parent elements to other elements. This allows website designers to define the style once—for example, in the body portion of the HTML document—and have the rest of the document pick up the style designations.

10. B. Explanation: Style sheets have been a part of HTML designations since the 3.2 Recommendation. The HTML 3.2 Recommendation added typographical control elements called style sheets. Style sheets allow website designers to have control over the appearance individual HTML elements.

11. C. A style is a set of formatting instructions placed in the HEAD portion of an HTML document. Many webmasters are already using styles in their web pages because of their usefulness.

12. B. Security is not included in HTML design limitations. Style sheets have enhanced website design since the HTML 3.2 designation as a web standard. They have solved a number of HTML design limitations, including proprietary HTML extensions, text-to-image conversion to retain fonts, page layout using tables, and images controlling white space. These workarounds are still used by those who do not know how to employ style sheets in their website design environment.

13. B. A standards document or manual that establishes a set of conventions or rules for performing common tasks is called a style guide. Technical writers often use them for general information, ranging from editorial style to specific guidelines for font sizes and types. Website designers also frequently use style guides because they provide general design guidelines for creating effective web pages.

14. C. E-commerce transactions have nothing to do with a style guide. The topic is a bit too technology specific. Some topics you may want to include in a style guide are default body text styles, default background images or colors, rules for heading levels, preferred methods for emphasizing text, guidelines for use of images and logos, templates for standard pages, and guidelines for using navigation links and image maps.

15. B.   Inline styles are added to existing HTML tags or used in conjunction with the approved HTML 4.0 <SPAN> tag. The <SPAN> tag is a container tag that affects everything on the page between it and the closing </SPAN> tag.

16. D.   Use the `@import` method to access an external style file.

17. A.   Style sheet files should include only style information. HTML tags should not be included in your plain-text style file.

18. B.   The `@import` command will not function in Netscape Navigator.

19. C.   W2CSS is a Microsoft Word translator macro program. Every element in HTML is tagged with a CSS class. W2CSS reads the style definitions within the Word document and translates them into the equivalent CSS definitions to create the classes.

20. C.   Netscape has been using the <LAYER> tag instead of CSS for absolute positioning, but Netscape and Microsoft now agree that absolute positioning should be performed by CSS and not with proprietary tags and are working together with the W3C to provide users with technology universal to the next-generation browsers. Both absolute and relative positioning with style sheets will allow for dramatically improved site design functionality and will improve the overall aesthetic quality of third-generation sites.

Chapter

11

JavaScript Fundamentals

THE CIW EXAM OBJECTIVE GROUP COVERED IN THIS CHAPTER:

✓ Use client-side and server-side programming to enhance website functionality, including but not limited to: JavaScript.

Creating interactivity between the user and the server used to be virtually impossible because HTML was the only tool available. With the advent of Common Gateway Interface (CGI) scripts and JavaScript, website designers can now create interactive environments on their web pages where users can, for example, input data and respond to questions. CGI scripts are difficult to write because knowledge of a programming language like C, C++, Perl, or Java is required. JavaScript, on the other hand, is comparatively easy to learn. JavaScript relies on the same principles that programming languages do: objects, properties, and methods. We will discuss these concepts in detail throughout this chapter.

In addition, we will explore the difference between programming and scripting languages; the definition, characteristics, and strengths of JavaScript; and how JavaScript compares to other languages. We'll also explain how it is placed into an HTML document and how it is used to communicate with the user as well as its functions and how it can be used for browser detection and image preloading.

Why Script?

When the World Wide Web first became popular, HTML was the only language used to create web pages. HTML is not a programming language but a markup language, and it's still quite limited in what it can do. HTML positions text and graphics on a web page but offers relatively limited potential for interactivity with the user.

Most computer users are now accustomed to *graphical user interfaces (GUIs)*, which are interfaces that provide graphical navigation with menus and screen icons, whether they use Windows, Macintosh, Unix, or some combination thereof. Users click on buttons to execute command sequences, enter values into text boxes, and choose options from menu lists. This increase in user abilities and expectations has resulted in the continuous improvement of HTML and the advent of powerful scripting languages such as JavaScript.

Even with the improvements to HTML, there is little or no possibility of creating a page with which users can interact if you use just HTML alone. That can be achieved through the use of Common Gateway Interface (CGI) server-side scripts or JavaScript. It's easier to learn JavaScript than it is to learn how to create CGI scripts, and with JavaScript, you can create web pages that your users can interact with based on keyboard and mouse input. For example, you can use JavaScript to check for errors in a field in which users type their names. Or you can write a script for a mouse event that makes help files visible at the point on your page where the user needs them.

JavaScript is a runtime interpreted language. Therefore, some of the script-processing burden can be passed from the server to the client machine. Allowing the client to do the work frees the server to perform other, more important functions and services.

JavaScript and Common Programming Concepts

Before we discuss JavaScript in particular, you should understand some key concepts. Some of these concepts are simple, and others are more advanced. Do not be concerned if some concepts do not make sense right away. You will acquire a better understanding of these concepts as you apply them.

Scripting languages are subsets of larger languages. They provide less functionality than full programming languages but are often easier to learn. Your investment in learning a scripting language is valuable if you are interested in programming languages because you will gain basic conceptual awareness of programming practices. Many concepts are handled similarly between languages.

Objects, Properties, and Methods

Serious programmers tend to code in C++, Visual Basic, or Java. These are powerful, high-level programming languages that provide rich functionality to the program developer. These languages are also *object oriented*. In programming, *objects* encapsulate predetermined attributes and behavior. An object is a programming function that models the characteristics of abstract or real objects; they are often grouped with similar objects into classes.

Developers tend to call attributes and behaviors by two other terms: properties and methods. *Properties* represent various attributes of the object, such as height, color, font size, and age, for example. *Methods* are the actions an object can be made to perform, such as a calculation, on-screen movement, or the writing of text.

Think of a pen as an object. It has definite, discernable properties, such as length, ink color, point style, and so forth. Two pens may be similar yet have different values for these same properties. All pens have a color, for example, but not all pens have the *same* color.

A pen has methods as well. It can write, spin, flip, and have its cap removed or replaced. A developer creating a virtual pen object would want to simulate natural attributes and behaviors so that, for example, if the user tried to write with the pen, he might receive an error telling him he must first remove the cap.

Now consider a sentence, which is a string of words. To a programmer, that sentence might be an object, which has minimum properties of color, font style, and character length. In addition, it might have a method by which it could be converted to all uppercase or all lowercase letters.

You already use and change objects, properties, and methods, although you may not have thought of them in these terms. Each time you load a web page, you access the `window` and `document` objects. When you specify a background color for your page, you specify a property for that `document` object. When you click on the Back and Forward buttons on your browser to change pages, you access the history method associated with the `window` object, allowing you to navigate among previously loaded pages.

Later in this chapter, we will explore how to work with some of the basic objects, properties, and methods available for scripting purposes.

What Is JavaScript?

JavaScript is a relatively easy language to learn. Originally created by Netscape as a way to control the browser and add interactivity to web pages, it is now widely used throughout the World Wide Web to create such effects as rollovers, pop-up boxes, and user prompts. Before you start writing in JavaScript, you should understand three basic things about this language:

- JavaScript is a scripting language.

- JavaScript is an object-based language.

- JavaScript is an event-driven language.

JavaScript Is a Scripting Language

A scripting language is a simple programming language designed to enable computer users to write useful programs easily. JavaScript was designed as an extension to HTML to allow designers to manipulate web page elements simply and easily.

If you have ever written a macro in Microsoft Excel or used WordBasic to perform some task in a Microsoft Word document, you have already used a scripting language. Smaller and less powerful than full programming languages, scripting languages provide easy-to-access functionality.

JavaScript is a scripting language. Its syntax is similar to that of C or Pascal. When you use JavaScript, it's part of the text within your HTML document. When your browser retrieves a scripted page, it executes the JavaScript programs and performs the appropriate operations.

JavaScript Is Object Based, Not Object Oriented

Object oriented is a term commonly used in relation to programming languages. An object-oriented program is handled as a collection of individual objects that perform different functions and not as a sequence of statements that performs a specific task. These objects are usually related in a hierarchical fashion; new objects and subclasses of objects inherit the properties and methods of the objects above them in the hierarchy. JavaScript is not considered object oriented because it does not allow for object inheritance and subclassing. JavaScript is, however, an *object-based* language in that, for functionality, it depends on a collection of built-in objects. With JavaScript, you can also create your own objects.

JavaScript Is Event-Driven

The World Wide Web is based upon an *event-driven model*. For example, when you click on an element on a web page, an event occurs. The other common programming model is the procedural model. In the *procedural model*, the user is expected to interact with the program in a fairly sequential manner. On a web page, by contrast, the user is in control and can click or not click, move the mouse or not move the mouse, or change the URL at will. Because of the unpredictability of a user's actions, you can create programming modules (called subroutines or functions) that are independent of each other and do not require a sequential set of operations.

Events trigger functions. Event triggers can be as simple as the user clicking on a button, moving the mouse over a hyperlink, or entering text into a field. Scripting can be tied to any of these events. You will learn to use JavaScript to tell the browser what to do when the event that you designate as the trigger for the script occurs.

JavaScript vs. Other Languages

JavaScript was developed by Netscape. It is not a full programming language like Java. JavaScript must reside within HTML documents to run properly. It allows users to add interactivity to web pages without using server-based applications such as CGI programs.

Java and JavaScript

Although the names are similar, Java and JavaScript are different languages. Java is a full-fledged object-oriented programming language developed by Sun Microsystems, Inc. Java can be used to create stand-alone applications and a special type of miniapplication called a Java applet. Applets are written in Java, compiled, then referenced via the <APPLET> tag in a web page when the HTML 3.2 standard is used. (The HTML 4 standard uses the <OBJECT> tag to reference applets in a web page.) Applets can provide a great variety of added functionality to websites. We will discuss applets in more detail in Chapter 14.

JavaScript is an object-based scripting language. Although it uses some of Java's expression syntax and basic program flow controls, JavaScript stands alone and does not require Java. Table 11.1 compares the features of JavaScript and Java.

TABLE 11.1 Comparison of JavaScript and Java

JavaScript	Java
Interpreted (not compiled) by client.	Compiled on server before execution on client.
Object based. Code uses built-in, extensible objects, but no classes or inheritance.	Object oriented. Applets consist of object classes with inheritance.
Variable data types need not be declared (loose typing).	Variable types must be declared (strong typing).

(continued)

TABLE 11.1 Comparison of JavaScript and Java *(continued)*

JavaScript	Java
Dynamic binding. Object references checked at runtime.	Static binding. Object references must exist at compile time.
Secure. Cannot write to hard disk.	Secure. Cannot write to hard disk.
Code integrated with and embedded in HTML.	Code located on server and not seen by user.

JavaScript and LiveWire

LiveWire is the Netscape server add-on software package. The LiveWire technology includes new server-side programming objects, which can work with and manipulate relational databases such as Informix, Oracle, and Sybase. LiveWire also provides a WYSIWYG editor and browser and a graphical website manager. JavaScript can be used on either the server side or the client side to work with LiveWire. However, server-side JavaScript will function only if LiveWire is installed. Currently, JavaScript does not support direct database access without LiveWire.

JavaScript vs. VBScript

VBScript, a scripting language developed by Microsoft, is a subset of the Visual Basic programming language. VBScript is considerably easier to learn than its parent language because it is an interpreted language, not a compiled language.

Both JavaScript and VBScript extend browser capabilities. JavaScript was the first scripting language developed for web page design, and VBScript is the Microsoft response. The VBScript visual approach might be easier to understand initially, but Netscape Navigator is still one of the most widely used browsers and it does not support VBScript. JavaScript works relatively smoothly with both Internet Explorer and Navigator. VBScript is more powerful in its functionality, but Internet Explorer is the only browser that will interpret it.

In terms of implementing JavaScript or VBScript, each language has somewhat different requirements. If most of your audience has Netscape Navigator 2.1 or later, they will have JavaScript support.

JavaScript vs. JScript

The Microsoft implementation of the Netscape JavaScript language is called JScript. It was created after VBScript and was designed to be able to run in Navigator, unlike VBScript, which only runs in Internet Explorer. Several minor differences exist between these two implementations of essentially the same language. However, these differences can cause problems. If you decide to learn JScript, be sure to test your code's execution in the Navigator browser.

JavaScript, JScript, and ECMA Script

The many scripting language choices have created a bit of a battle between developers. In an effort to standardize, Netscape and Microsoft are moving toward the European Computer Manufacturers Association (ECMA) version of scripting language called ECMA Script.

ECMA Script development began in 1996, and the first edition was adopted by the ECMA General Assembly of June 1997. In the coming years, browser manufacturers and developers will move steadily toward ECMA. At this time, however, JScript is fully compliant with the ECMA Script standard.

Embedding JavaScript into HTML

JavaScript resides within HTML documents. It is usually placed into an HTML document with the <SCRIPT> tag. You can add script to the HEAD or BODY element (or both) of an HTML document. You can also embed scripting instructions directly into certain HTML tags. This technique is called inline scripting.

The basic structure of an HTML file with JavaScript is as follows (JavaScript is indicated in bold):

```
<HTML>
<HEAD>
<TITLE>Page Title Here</TITLE>
<SCRIPT LANGUAGE="JavaScript">
<!--
JavaScript code goes here
```

```
// -->
</SCRIPT>
</HEAD>
<BODY>
Page text here
<SCRIPT LANGUAGE="JavaScript">
<!--
JavaScript goes here too
// -->
</SCRIPT>
Page text here too
</BODY>
</HTML>
```

The language attribute in the <SCRIPT> tag tells the browser which type of script it is about to read. If you do not add the language attribute, the default scripting language in both Microsoft Internet Explorer and Netscape Navigator is JavaScript. However, to ensure that the browser interprets the script as JavaScript, it is recommended that you always add the language attribute. By doing so, you give the browser an explicit instruction rather than implying one. This attribute will also support a designated version of the language. For example, consider the following attribute:

```
LANGUAGE="JavaScript1.1"
```

This attribute tells the browser to ignore code that is not part of the 1.1 standard.

Notice that the comment tag <!-- is used to comment out, or hide, text in the script. You can add this tag in case a user visiting your page has an old browser that is incapable of interpreting JavaScript. As more people upgrade their browsers, using the comment tag in this fashion will become unnecessary.

Notice too that the closing comment tag line has a special addition. The // characters at the beginning of this line demonstrate the JavaScript method of commenting out an item. JavaScript does not expect to see the -- characters of the closing comment tag and considers it a decrement operator; therefore, it must be commented out. Failure to include these characters will result in an error message when the page is loaded and will prevent the script from executing properly.

Dot Notation

Dot notation is used to associate an object's name with its properties or methods. The syntax for dot notation is as follows:

```
objectName.objectProperty
objectName.objectProperty = value
objectName.objectMethod()
objectName.objectMethod(argument1,argument2,...)
parentObjectName.objectName.objectProperty
parentObjectName.objectName.objectMethod
```

For example, a statement to close a window uses dot notation to associate the close() method to the window object named myWindow, as follows:

```
onClick="myWindow.close()"
```

Some objects are themselves properties of a higher object. Dot notation is also used to depict this hierarchy. Figure 11.1 shows how the object hierarchy works, using a web page as an example.

FIGURE 11.1 Hierarchy of objects (http://www.htmlgoodies.com/primers/jsp./hgjsp_8.html), © 2002 INT Media Group, Incorporated, All Rights Reserved

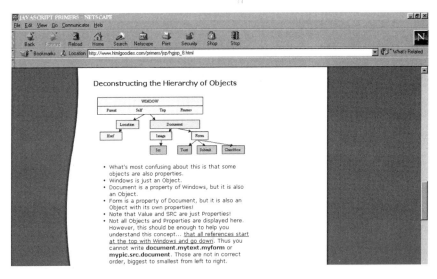

Window is the top object in the hierarchy; it designates the browser window. Parent, Self, Top, and Frames are all locations to which the document in the window can be targeted. Document indicates the page on which the information is located and, in this example, is a property of window. Underneath document are image and form, which are properties of document. Src, Text,

Submit, and Checkbox are properties of image and form, respectively. URL.location displays the location of the page. If you wanted to write the hierarchy of the checkbox, it would be written as window.document.form .checkbox. The value of the checkbox ("on" or "off") has not been noted in this example.

Strengths of JavaScript

JavaScript provides several benefits to the web programmer, including a short development cycle, a mild learning curve, and platform independence. These benefits mean that JavaScript can be easily and quickly used to extend HTML pages on the Web. JavaScript is well suited for small, simple programs. It also handles repetitive tasks well. For larger programs, Java is the better choice.

Quick Development

Because JavaScript does not need time-consuming compilation, scripts can be developed in a relatively short period of time. This advantage is enhanced by the fact that most of the interface features, such as forms, frames, and other graphical user interface (GUI) elements, are handled by the browser and HTML code. JavaScript programmers need not need worry about creating or handling these elements in their applications.

Easy to Learn

JavaScript does not include the complex syntax and rules associated with Java. Even if you know no other programming language, it will not be difficult for you to learn JavaScript. It also makes troubleshooting easy. You can write, test, and change the program without having to recompile the script.

Platform Independence

The World Wide Web is by nature platform independent. Because JavaScript programs are designed to run inside HTML documents, they are not tied to any specific hardware platform or operating system. The same program can be run on any platform using Netscape Navigator 2 or later or Microsoft Internet Explorer 3 or later.

Using JavaScript to Communicate with the User

In many programs, you will see message windows from time to time alerting you to changing conditions, choices to make, warnings, and other notices.

As a web page developer, you can quickly and easily script user messages that will pop up when the page loads or upon some other event, such as a mouse click. In the examples in the following sections, the primary event—the page loading into the window—is used to launch the scripts. We will examine three ways of communicating with the user: a text message that displays in a pop-up window, a request for information that displays in a pop-up window, and a text message that displays in the browser window.

Giving the User a Message: The *alert()* Method

The `alert()` method is a simple JavaScript method that allows you to communicate with the user. It is a method of the `window` object, part of the JavaScript language. We will discuss the `window` object in more detail later when we look at the `open()` method.

To call the `alert()` method, all you need is a simple line of code called a *statement* that will be executed in a script or program in a script block somewhere in your document. If you have no other statement in your script, the message will pop up every time the page is loaded. If your script has other statements, the message window will pop up when it is called in the code sequence.

The syntax for the `alert()` method is as follows:

```
alert("message")
```

Here is an example of using the `alert()` method to greet the user. This example uses a script with a single statement (the JavaScript is shown in bold):

```
<HTML>
<HEAD>
<TITLE>Alert</TITLE>
```

```
<SCRIPT>
<!--
alert("Good Morning!")
// -->
</SCRIPT>
</HEAD>
<BODY>
<H1>Welcome to my page!</H1>
<HR>
</BODY>
</HTML>
```

Figure 11.2 shows what the alert message looks like when it's displayed in a browser window. Figure 11.3 shows the message that is displayed when you click on OK.

FIGURE 11.2 Alert message

FIGURE 11.3 HTML displayed following JavaScript statement

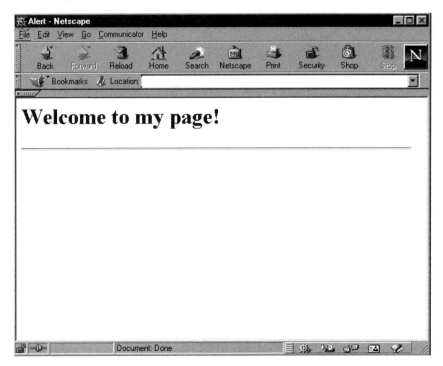

Alert messages can be used to display whatever you want: copyright information, notices of website changes, current date and time information, or a quote of the day. In time, you will discover the usefulness of these messages when you need to debug your own script. Alert messages can be added before and after problem areas so you can see the script running as you debug it, thereby helping you narrow down where the problem area is.

Getting Data from the User: The *prompt()* Method

Sooner or later, you will want to ask the user a question and be able to capture their answer. This process requires a different method. The prompt() method requests user input through a text field within a dialog box. Whatever the user types into the text box is returned as the result of prompt(). The result can then be used as an argument to another method. The basic syntax for using prompt() is as follows:

```
prompt("Message to user", "default response text")
```

Concatenation

Concatenation is the process of linking two or more units of information, such as strings or files, to form one unit. It is used frequently in JavaScript to combine text strings, especially in conjunction with prompt() and alert(). For example, you might want to personalize the alert message used in the preceding example. To do this, you can concatenate the "Good Morning" message with the result of a prompt screen in which the user enters their name.

Concatenation is used in the following example. The user is prompted for and enters their name, which is then tied to the string "Good Morning," using the + character. The user then sees a message saying "Good Morning, *name*." In this example, the JavaScript prompt() method is used to elicit user information (the JavaScript appears in bold):

```
<HTML>
<HEAD>
<TITLE>Prompt</TITLE>

<SCRIPT>
<!--
alert("Good Morning, "
+ prompt("We would like to get to know you,
please supply us with your name","") )
// -->
</SCRIPT>

</HEAD>
<BODY>
<H1>Welcome to my page!</H1>
<HR>
</BODY>
</HTML>
```

Figure 11.4 illustrates what the dialog box looks like when it's displayed in the browser. Figure 11.5 shows the message that is displayed after the user enters their name and clicks on OK. When the user clicks on OK in this box, the page shown in Figure 11.6 is displayed.

FIGURE 11.4 User prompt dialog box

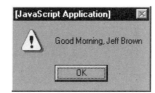

FIGURE 11.5 Alert message box

FIGURE 11.6 Web page displayed following JavaScript statement

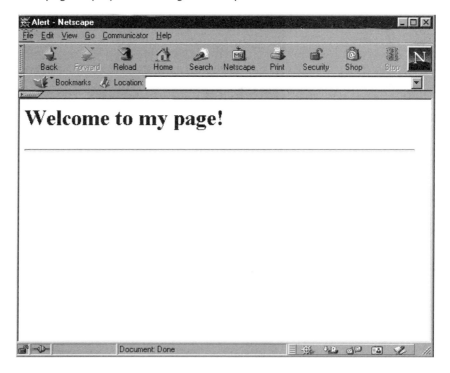

In the preceding example, `prompt()` is processed first and then replaced in the expression by whatever the user entered. Now examine the `prompt()` method a bit closer. Suppose the prompt portion reads as follows:

```
prompt("What is your name?","")
```

Notice the two sets of quotation marks within the parentheses. The first set of quotation marks encloses the text that will appear above the text field on the prompt message. The second set of quotation marks can be used for default text or (as in the last example) to indicate an empty text string.

Opening Additional Windows: The *open()* Method

JavaScript gives you the ability to open new windows at will and populate them with existing information, information created on the fly (dynamically), or no information at all. The `open()` method is part of the `window` object. You can open a new window by using the `open()` method; the syntax is as follows:

```
open("URL","WindowName","Feature List")
```

For example, to open a new browser window showing the HotBot search page, you can use the following statement:

```
open("http://www.hotbot.com","SearchWindow",
"toolbar=1,location=1,menubar=1,scrollbars=1,
status=1,resizable=1")
```

The feature list in this method consists of a series of attributes that you specify as either displayed or not. The accepted values for each of these attributes are 1 (or yes) if the attribute is to be displayed and 0 (or no) if it is not. Table 11.2 lists possible window attributes.

TABLE 11.2 Window Attributes Accessible with the open() Method

Name	Description
toolbar	Creates the standard toolbar.
location	Creates the location entry field.
directories	Creates the standard directory buttons.

(continued)

TABLE 11.2 Window Attributes Accessible with the open() Method *(continued)*

Name	Description
status	Creates the status bar.
menubar	Creates the menu at the top of the window.
scrollbars	Creates scroll bars when a document grows beyond the current window.
resizable	Enables window resizing by the user.
width	Specifies the window width in pixels.
height	Specifies the window height in pixels.
top	Specifies the top *y* coordinate on-screen where the window will open in Internet Explorer 4 and Navigator 4 only.
left	Specifies the left *x* coordinate on-screen where the window will open in Internet Explorer 4 and Navigator 4 only.

You cannot add a space to *WindowName*. In the preceding example, "SearchWindow" is valid, but "Search Window" would return an error. In addition, you cannot add spaces around the = character in the window feature list options. For example, "toolbar = 1" will not cause the toolbar to display, but "toolbar=1" will.

This example demonstrates using the JavaScript open() method to launch a new browser window (the JavaScript appears in bold):

```
<HTML>
<HEAD>
<TITLE>New Window</TITLE>
</HEAD>
```

```
<BODY>
<FORM>
<INPUT TYPE="button" VALUE="Open a HotBot Search Window"
onClick="newWindow=open('http://www.hotbot.com',
'HotBotWin',
'toolbar=0,location=1,menubar=1,
scrollbars=1,resizable=1')">
</FORM>
</BODY>
</HTML>
```

Figure 11.7 shows the message that is displayed in the browser window.

FIGURE 11.7 Message displayed in browser window

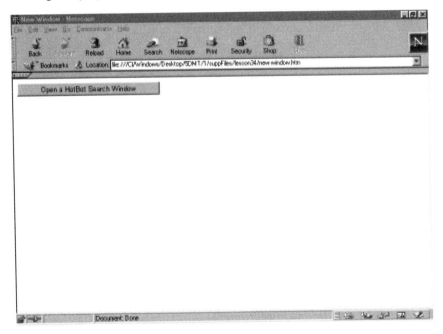

In this example, a specific URL was targeted and used to fill the new window that opened. The onClick event was used to trigger the open() method from an inline script. Because we did not specify a size, the new window's size will match the existing window's size exactly.

JavaScript Functions

JavaScript uses functions to call multiple commands. Commands such as `alert()` and `prompt()` will all execute at the time of page loading, which is also known as the *load event*. At times, the developer may want to restrain the execution of commands for a specific event other than load. To accomplish this, the commands must be placed in a function that will be called based on the required event.

Think of a function as a container that allows you to give a common name to a series of commands so that they can be executed as a single unit.

Functions can be defined, if necessary, to describe the type of commands they encompass, as shown in the following sample code:

```
function myFunctionName() {
        one or more commands;
}
```

The commands are enclosed within curly braces { }, which group them to the function name declared prior to the opening curly brace. The `function` keyword must be typed in lowercase as shown. You can use both upper- and lowercase letters for the name you give the function, but JavaScript is case sensitive, so you must call it exactly as it has been declared.

Using JavaScript for Browser Detection

Website designers commonly target specific browsers that can support certain design features and then write code to take advantage of that browser's added functionality. Therefore, if you determine which browser is being used to visit your page, you can use JavaScript to design certain elements for the page. Similarly, by determining which plug-ins a browser supports, you can include content that the plug-in supports.

JavaScript can be used to detect browser type. Browsers that do not support JavaScript can be provided with alternative HTML code. However, it is unlikely that current users have browsers that do not support JavaScript.

The *navigator* Object

The `navigator` object is part of the JavaScript Object Model. It allows access to information specific to the browser. Within the `navigator` object are several properties that can be tested. Table 11.3 lists some of the properties of the navigator object.

TABLE 11.3   Properties of the navigator Object

Property/Method	Description
appCodeName	Code name of browser
appName	Official browser name
appVersion	Version of browser (e.g., 3.x, 4.x, 5.x)
plugins	Plug-in installed in browser
userAgent	User agent header

This example shows how some of the navigator object properties are used (the JavaScript appears in bold):

```
<HTML>
<HEAD>
<TITLE>Browser Detection</TITLE>
<SCRIPT>
<!--
function yourBrowser() {
document.details.Name.value=navigator.appName;
document.details.Version.value=navigator.appVersion;
document.details.Code.value=navigator.appCodeName;
document.details.Agent.value=navigator.userAgent;
}
// -->
</SCRIPT>
<BODY bgcolor="#FFFFFF">
<DIV ALIGN="center">
<TABLE BORDER>
<FORM NAME="details">
<TR><TD> Browser Name: </TD>
<TD> <INPUT TYPE="text" NAME="Name" Size="50"></TD>
</TR>
<TR><TD> Browser Version: </TD>
```

```
<TD> <INPUT TYPE="text" NAME="Version" Size="50"></TD>
</TR>
<TR><TD> Browser Code Name: </TD>
<TD> <INPUT TYPE="text" NAME="Code" Size="50"></TD>
</TR>
<TR><TD> User-Agent: </TD>
<TD> <INPUT TYPE="text" NAME="Agent" Size="50"></TD>
</TR>
<TR><TD>
<INPUT TYPE=BUTTON VALUE="Test Your Browser"
    ONCLICK="yourBrowser()"></TD>
</TR>
</FORM>
</TABLE>
</DIV>
</BODY>
</HTML>
```

When viewed in a browser, your screen should resemble Figure 11.8 if you use Internet Explorer.

FIGURE 11.8 Identifying navigator object properties

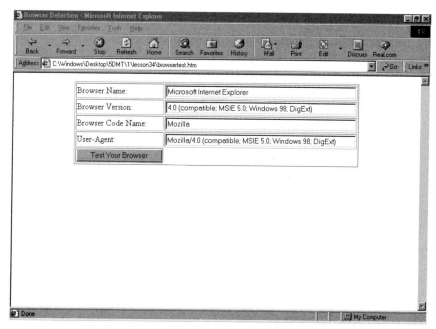

Sniffers and Redirections

A *sniffer* is a piece of code that determines status. In this case, we refer to a sniffer as a piece of code that determines which browser is in use and then takes a specific action depending on the browser type. The following example illustrates a sniffer code that will direct the user based on the browser in use (the JavaScript appears in bold):

```
<HTML>
<HEAD>
<TITLE>Browser Redirect</TITLE>
<SCRIPT>
<!--
function checkBrowser() {
     var name=navigator.appName;

     if (name.indexOf('Netscape') != -1) {
         document.location.href="netscape.htm"

     } else {
     if (name.indexOf('Microsoft') != -1) {
         document.location.href="microsoft.htm"
          }
     }
}
//-->
</SCRIPT>
</HEAD>
<BODY BGCOLOR="#FFFFFF">
<P>When you click this button, your browser version will
be determined and you will be sent to a page telling what
type of browser you have.</P>
<FORM METHOD="post" ACTION="">
  <DIV ALIGN="center">
    <INPUT TYPE="button" NAME="Button"
VALUE="Test your browser"
ONCLICK="checkBrowser()">
  </DIV>
</FORM>
</BODY>
</HTML>
```

Figures 11.9 and 11.10 show the results when you click on the Test Your Browser button. You will receive a message based on which type of browser you are using.

FIGURE 11.9 JavaScript message to Netscape Navigator users

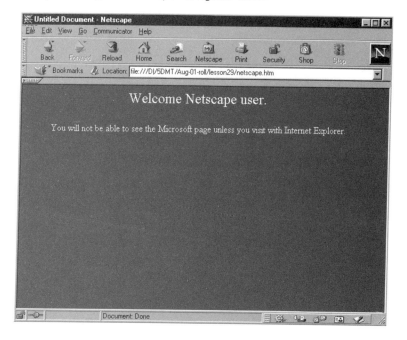

FIGURE 11.10 JavaScript message to Microsoft Internet Explorer users

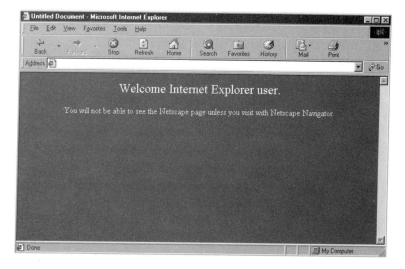

Image Preloading

Website designers commonly use rollover elements on their pages. A rollover occurs when a user moves the mouse cursor over an image and the image changes. A minimum of two images are involved in a rollover. The first image is the one that the user sees when the page initially loads. The second image is seen when the user moves the mouse cursor over the first image and it changes.

The problem that website designers face is that when the mouse event (mouseover) occurs, the browser must replace the current image with the second image. Unless the second image is preloaded into the cache, a lag time exists and the image will not change until the browser downloads the second image from the server. To prevent this lapse from occurring, the images must be preloaded into the cache. Preloading makes a significant difference when pages are viewed over a slow Internet connection. The image object accomplishes this task by defining the location of the required images.

The next example shows eight instances of the image object used to preload all the images into the browser's cache. Before the preloading begins, a simple condition is tested to see whether the browser understands the image object. If it does, the preloading begins; otherwise, nothing happens (the JavaScript appears in bold):

```
<HTML>
<HEAD>
<TITLE>IMAGE PRELOADER</TITLE>
<SCRIPT>
<!--
if (document.images) {
    one = new Image
        one.src = "1.gif"
    two = new Image
        two.src = "2.gif"
    three = new Image
        three.src = "3.gif"
    four = new Image
        four.src = "4.gif"
    oneOver = new Image
        oneOver.src = "1over.gif"
    twoOver = new Image
        twoOver.src = "2over.gif"
```

```
            threeOver = new Image
                threeOver.src = "3over.gif"
            fourOver = new Image
                fourOver.src = "4over.gif"
    }
    //-->
    </SCRIPT>
    </HEAD>
    <BODY BGCOLOR="#FFFFFF">
    <A HREF="../lesson12/certification.htm"
    onMouseOver="document.cert.src=oneOver.src"
    onMouseOut="document.cert.src=one.src">
    <IMG src="1.gif" NAME="cert" BORDER="0"></A>
    <BR>
    <A HREF="="../lesson12/catalog.htm"
    onMouseOver="document.cat.src=twoOver.src"
    onMouseOut="document.cat.src=two.src">
    <IMG src="2.gif" NAME="cat" BORDER="0"></A>
    <BR>
    <A HREF="="../lesson12/endorsements.htm"
    onMouseOver="document.end.src=threeOver.src"
    onMouseOut="document.end.src=three.src">
    <IMG src="3.gif" NAME="end" BORDER="0"></A>
    <BR>
    <A HREF="="../lesson12/testing.htm"
    onMouseOver="document.test.src=fourOver.src"
    onMouseOut="document.test.src=four.src">
    <IMG src="4.gif" NAME="test" BORDER="0"></A>
    <BR>
    </BODY>
    </HTML>
```

You can use this example as a template for the next time you include roll-overs in your web pages to speed the loading process.

Summary

In programming, objects are functions that provide a way to define how abstract or real objects look and their behavior. They are often grouped with similar object into classes and have attributes and behaviors. Developers often use the terms *properties* and *methods* instead of *attributes* and *behaviors*. Properties represent various attributes of an object, such as height, color, font size, age, and so forth. Methods are the actions an object can be made to perform, such as a calculation, on-screen movement, or the writing of text. JavaScript allows you to create web pages your users can interact with based on their keyboard and mouse inputs.

JavaScript stands alone and does not require Java (which is a full-fledged object-oriented programming language that can be used to create stand-alone applications and Java applets). JavaScript resembles Java in that it uses some of its expression syntax and basic program flow controls. It provides several benefits to the web programmer, including a short development cycle, a mild learning curve, and platform independence. These benefits mean that JavaScript can be easily and quickly used to create interactivity between the user and HTML pages on the Web. The Microsoft implementation of the Netscape JavaScript language is called JScript, which was developed after VBScript, also a Microsoft creation. JScript runs in Netscape, whereas VBScript only runs in Internet Explorer. Several minor differences exist between these two implementations of essentially the same language, so you should test your JScript in Navigator to ensure it works correctly.

We discussed three JavaScript methods in this chapter: `alert()`, `prompt()`, and `open()`. These three methods all are part of the `window` object. The `alert()` method is a simple JavaScript method that allows you to communicate with the user. The `prompt()` method requests user input through a text field within a dialog box. Whatever the user types into the text box is returned as the result of `prompt()`. This result can then be used as an argument to another method. You can open a new window by using the `open()` method. JavaScript objects and properties follow a hierarchy, which describes where they are in relation to each other. The highest-level object in the hierarchy is `window`. Dot notation is used to depict the hierarchy of objects and the association of their properties and methods.

If you determine which browser is being use to visit your page, you can use JavaScript to design certain elements for the page. Similarly, by determining which plug-ins a browser supports, you can include appropriate content. You can also use image preloading to preload images used in rollovers. A lag time exists between when the first image of a rollover is displayed and when the second image appears. The image will not change until the browser downloads the second image from the server. To prevent this lapse from occurring, the images must be preloaded into the cache. Preloading makes a significant difference when pages are viewed over a slow Internet connection.

Exam Essentials

Know basic programming concepts, including objects, properties, and methods.   C++, Visual Basic, and Java are powerful, high-level programming languages that provide rich functionality to the program developer. These languages are also object oriented. In programming, objects encapsulate predetermined attributes and behavior. An object is a programming function that models the characteristics of abstract or real objects using classes. They are often grouped with similar objects into classes. Attributes and behaviors are also called properties and methods. Properties represent various attributes of the object, such as height, color, font size, age, and so forth. Methods are the actions an object can be made to perform, such as a calculation, on-screen movement, or the writing of text.

Understand how JavaScript differs from HTML, Java, and Java applets. JavaScript is an object-based scripting language. Scripting languages provide less functionality than full programming languages but are often easier to learn. A scripting language is a simple programming language designed to enable computer users to write useful programs easily. Your understanding of these languages and their differences is essential to your knowledge of how each functions within a website.

Know dot notation.   Dot notation is used to associate an object's name with its properties or methods. Some objects are themselves properties of a higher object. Dot notation is also used to depict this hierarchy. At the top of the hierarchy is window, which depicts the browser window. All of its associated properties and methods are below it in the hierarchy structure.

Know JavaScript functions.   JavaScript uses functions to call multiple commands. At times, the developer may want to restrain the execution of commands for a specific event other than load. To accomplish this, the commands must be placed in a function that will be called based on the required event. Think of a function as a container that allows you to give a common name to a series of commands so that they can be executed as a single unit. Functions can be defined, if necessary, to describe the type of commands they encompass.

Key Terms

Before you take the exam, be certain you are familiar with the following terms:

concatenation	objects
event-driven model	procedural model
graphical user interfaces (GUIs)	properties
load event	rollovers
methods	sniffer
object-based	statement
object oriented	

Review Questions

1. Which of the following best describes scripting languages?

   A. Subsets of full programming languages

   B. Metalanguages used to create other languages

   C. Markup languages used to position text and graphics

   D. Programming languages used for dialog-based functions

2. In programming, which of the following items is often grouped into classes with similar items?

   A. Code

   B. Script

   C. Object

   D. Method

3. In programming, developers tend to call attributes and behaviors by what two other terms?

   A. Characteristics and actions

   B. Properties and methods

   C. Elements and values

   D. Events and actions

4. Which of the following accurately describes a difference between Java and JavaScript?

   A. JavaScript is object oriented, whereas Java is object based.

   B. JavaScript is interpreted by the client, whereas Java is precompiled on the server.

   C. JavaScript is a programming language, whereas Java is a scripting language.

   D. JavaScript can be used to create applets, whereas Java is used to create applications.

5. Which tag is used to embed JavaScript into an HTML document?

A. The HTML <LANGUAGE> tag

B. The HTML <JAVASCRIPT> tag

C. The JavaScript <SCRIPT> tag

D. The HTML <SCRIPT> tag

6. In programming, which of the following terms refers to the syntax used to associate an object's name with its properties or methods?

A. JavaScript

B. Comment out

C. Dot notation

D. Coding

7. Which of the following is used to provide a simple communication to the user?

A. The open() method

B. The alert() method

C. The prompt() method

D. Concatenation

8. What does the abbreviation GUI stand for?

A. Graphical user interface

B. Graphical user interaction

C. Graphic user interface

D. Graphical utility interface

9. What are the characteristics of an object, such as width or color, called in programming?

A. Functions

B. Methods

C. Properties

D. Values

10. What term is used to refer to programming languages that support object inheritance and handle functions as a collection of objects performing different tasks?

    A. Function oriented

    B. Function based

    C. Object based

    D. Object oriented

11. Writing CGI scripts is comparatively more difficult than writing scripts with JavaScript because it requires knowledge of _____ .

    A. Framesets

    B. HTML 3.2

    C. Programming language

    D. Cascading style sheets

12. JavaScript was written as an extension to which language?

    A. Java

    B. HTML

    C. C

    D. C++

13. Which of the following best describes JavaScript?

    A. Object oriented

    B. Object based

    C. Extension of Java

    D. A full programming language

14. The World Wide Web is based on what type of model?

   A. Event-driven

   B. Object-oriented

   C. Object-driven

   D. Procedural

15. Using Java, programmers can write special types of mini-applications called _____ .

   A. Stand-alone applications

   B. JavaScripts

   C. Web pages

   D. Java applets

16. What is needed for sever-side JavaScript to function?

   A. LiveWire

   B. Java

   C. Sunbreeze

   D. Pearl

17. To standardize scripting languages, Microsoft and Netscape are moving toward what script?

   A. JavaScript

   B. VBScript

   C. ECMA Script

   D. M-N Script

18. Which tag is used to hide text or a script within an HTML document?

   A. <HIDE>

   B. <!--"content"//-- >

   C. <INVISIBLE>

   D. <HIDETEXT>

19. What benefits does JavaScript provide to the web programmer?

    A. Short development cycle

    B. Platform dependence

    C. Powerful programming language

    D. Suitability for complex programs

20. What is the word used to describe the linking of two or more units of information, such as strings or files, to form one unit?

    A. LinkScript

    B. Alert message

    C. Unit string

    D. Concatenation

Answers to Review Questions

1. A. Scripting languages are subsets of larger languages. They provide less functionality than full programming languages but are often easier to learn. A scripting language is a simple programming language designed to enable computer users to write useful programs easily.

2. C. Objects are often grouped with similar objects into classes. An object in programming uses attributes and behaviors of real or abstract objects.

3. B. Developers tend to call attributes and behaviors by two other terms: *properties* and *methods*. Properties represent various attributes of the object, such as height, color, font size, age, and so forth. Methods are the actions an object can be made to perform, such as a calculation, on-screen movement, or the writing of text.

4. B. JavaScript takes the burden off the server by doing the processing on the client side. Java, on the other hand, has to be compiled on the server before being sent to the client, thereby placing a heavier load on the server.

5. D. JavaScript resides within HTML documents. It is usually placed into an HTML document with the <SCRIPT> tag.

6. C. Dot notation is used to associate an object's name with its properties or methods. The dot notation syntax must be followed in order for the association, and your JavaScript, to function correctly.

7. B. The `alert()` method is a simple JavaScript method that allows you to communicate with the user. This method uses boxes that appear in the browser window to give users messages or greet them when they enter the site.

8. A. GUI stands for graphical user interface. Programs that use GUIs utilize buttons and icons to help users navigate through the program.

9. C. Properties represent various attributes of the object, such as height, color, font size, age, and so forth. Methods describe the actions an object can take. Functions allow you to give a common name to a series of commands so that they can be executed as a single unit. Values identify specific information about an attribute.

10. D.   *Object oriented* is a term commonly used in relation to programming languages. An object-oriented program is handled as a collection of individual objects that perform different functions and not as a sequence of statements that performs a specific task. These objects are usually related in a hierarchical fashion, in which new objects and subclasses of objects inherit the properties and methods of the objects above them in the hierarchy. JavaScript is not considered object oriented because it does not allow for object inheritance and subclassing.

11. C.   CGI scripts are difficult to write because knowledge of a programming language like C, C++, Perl, or Java is required. JavaScript, on the other hand, is comparatively easy to learn.

12. B.   JavaScript was designed as an extension to HTML to allow designers to manipulate web page elements simply and easily.

13. B.   JavaScript is not considered object oriented because it does not allow for object inheritance and subclassing. JavaScript is, however, an *object-based* language in that for functionality it depends on a collection of built-in objects. With JavaScript, you can also create your own objects.

14. A.   The World Wide Web is based on an *event-driven model*. For example, when you click on an element on a web page, an event occurs.

15. D.   Java can be used to create a special type of mini-application called a Java applet. Applets are self-contained in that all of their structure is part of a single program that doesn't change, nor is it edited from within a web browser. The entire applet downloads off the web page and runs.

16. A.   Server-side JavaScript will only function if LiveWire is installed. Currently, JavaScript does not support direct database access without LiveWire.

17. C.   In an effort to standardize, Netscape and Microsoft are moving toward the European Computer Manufacturers Association (ECMA) version of scripting language called ECMA Script.

18. B.   The comment tag <!--"content"//-- > is used to "comment out" or hide text in the script. Comments are important to website developers because, although they're not visible to the public, they can help to leave instructions or ideas or even reminders about the script that is put into the page at the point.

19. A. JavaScript provides several benefits to the web programmer, including a short development cycle, a mild learning curve, and platform independence. Because of these benefits, JavaScript can be easily and quickly used to extend HTML pages on the Web.

20. D. *Concatenation* is linking two or more units of information, such as strings or files, to form one unit. It is used frequently in JavaScript to combine text strings, especially in conjunction with `prompt()` and `alert()`.

Chapter

12

Dynamic HTML

THE CIW EXAM OBJECTIVE GROUP COVERED IN THIS CHAPTER:

✓ Use client-side and server-side programming to enhance website functionality, including but not limited to: Dynamic HTML (DHTML).

ynamic HTML (DHTML) offers website developers a method for creating interactive pages using three technologies: the Document Object Model (DOM), Cascading Style Sheets (CSS), and scripting. It provides an alternative to using Java applets, animated GIFs, and ActiveX controls to provide dynamic pages for web users. Although DHTML is not a recommendation of the World Wide Consortium (W3C), both Microsoft and Netscape have implemented it in their browsers. This has led to problems for designers, however, because tags that are used in Microsoft browsers could potentially crash Netscape browsers and vice versa. You can write code that will work in both simultaneously, but this code does not cover all situations in which DHTML could be implemented. Therefore, you are limited in what DHTML can do for you if you choose to use code that works in both browsers simultaneously.

In this chapter, we will explore DHTML, the technologies it relies upon, and its limitations. We'll also discuss the roles of the DOM, CSS, and scripting languages in DHTML and how DHTML is implemented specifically in Microsoft and Netscape browsers.

Dynamic HTML

ynamic HTML (DHTML) extends beyond the HTML 4 standard. DHTML is not a single technology; it is a set of interrelated technologies that allows the website author to create pages that are more interactive than pages created with just HTML. DHTML foundations are within HTML, yet DHTML allows HTML elements to be manipulated through the use of a scripting language. DHTML is made possible through the use of script (written in JavaScript or VBScript, for example), the Document Object Model (DOM), and two specifications that work together: HTML 4.0.1 and CSS1. HTML 4.0.1 represents the most powerful development to date in the evolution of HTML. Coupled with the CSS1 standard and linked by script, Dynamic HTML can be used in some cases to replace functions currently performed by Java applets, ActiveX controls, or animated GIFs. DHTML can be described as HTML with a scripting language's capability to interact with the tags.

DHTML extends HTML by adding new methods for formatting text and HTML page elements as well as new scripting event handlers that can trigger script with a wider variety of mouse and keyboard events. For example, text on a loaded page could previously be manipulated only with a Java applet, an ActiveX control, or animated GIF files. With DHTML, any HTML element (including plain paragraphs) can be made to change after the page has loaded. The entire page is considered "active" and awaits user input, which can be controlled by script. HTML elements constitute programmable objects on a web page. HTML objects can be referenced by script through the use of the ID property. The various attributes provided by HTML 4.0.1 and the CSS1 specification constitute programmable properties.

In addition, DHTML could offer an alternative to some server-side technologies such as *Active Server Pages (ASPs)*. ASPs is a technology developed by Microsoft that uses the server to run scripts and then passes the output back to the browser. It provides dynamic content to the browser rather than the typical static HTML, but it doesn't need to access the server each time it receives browser input (such as information a user has entered into a form). The possibilities are exciting. The more you know about HTML, styles, and scripting, the more attractive and functional the pages you create will be.

It is important to note that DHTML is an extremely time-sensitive subject matter. As this book is being written, all information is current, but the technology used to create DHTML can change at any time.

DHTML Limitations

Currently, DHTML browser support is increasing; however, its partial support presents some disadvantages. Enormous differences exist in the way

DHTML performs in Netscape and Microsoft browsers. Netscape has added a new tag for DHTML, and Microsoft has added new attributes for existing tags. In fact, both Netscape and Microsoft have their own implementations of DHTML, and neither works correctly with the other's browser.

It is unclear whether the W3C will eventually provide a recommendation for DHTML, in part because of the disparity between the current browsers. Unfortunately, the only documentation the W3C has produced to date is an outline of the capabilities a DHTML document should incorporate. Considering the advances in XML and XSL, which can offer many DHTML features and more, it is believed that the W3C may not spend the time to mature DHTML.

Document Object Model

The *Document Object Model (DOM)* is a key component in DHTML. Originally considered mainly in terms of browsers, the DOM is manipulated by script and often used with forms. It was developed by Netscape as a specification or instance hierarchy of JavaScript objects. This concept was introduced in 1995 with Netscape Navigator 2. Figure 12.1 illustrates the Document Object Model.

The Document Object Model provides a structured syntax that can uniquely identify many objects within the browser and the displayed document. It is important to note that the DOM has no relevance until an HTML document is loaded by the browser. The browser provides the context for viewing the document, while the document provides the HTML code and programming elements that are required to access the DOM.

Web designers can use the DOM to extend HTML documents and forms with interactive features based on client-side scripting. They can also use the DOM to access browser features, such as the history list, from within HTML documents and scripts, all in a predictable and convenient manner.

Currently, the W3C's goal for the Document Object Model is to provide a standard programming interface that is compatible with various applications and environments yet works within existing HTML, style sheets, and scripting languages. The solution for DHTML's incompatibility across browsers will be an expanded DOM. Netscape, Microsoft, and the W3C are striving for a DOM that will provide access to all elements, their attributes, and content through the use of a scripting language such as JavaScript.

FIGURE 12.1 Document Object Model

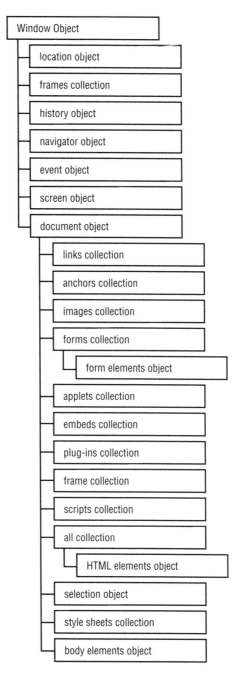

Be sure to visit www.w3.org occasionally for updates about the W3C Recommendation for a Document Object Model standard.

CSS and DHTML

HTML enables you to create the layout and structure of your document, but you can't use it to define the appearance of the page. HTML 4.0.1 supports the W3C Recommendation for Cascading Style Sheets (CSS1), which includes typographical control elements known as style sheets. Style sheets enable you to create web pages with the layout sophistication of desktop publishing programs such as Microsoft Word, Adobe PageMaker, and QuarkXPress. CSS allows you to define tag properties to create your own text effects, as well as control absolute positioning of elements on a page. We discussed style sheets in Chapter 10, so we will not go into depth here, but you should keep in mind that CSS is a part of DHTML.

Scripting Languages and DHTML

HTML and style sheets enable you to control page structure, but scripting allows you to interact with tags and styles. Scripting lets you design a response or function to a user event, such as a mouse move. You can use VBScript or JavaScript to interact with the DHTML Document Object Model.

DHTML Events

An *event* in an HTML document is anything that occurs during the life of the HTML page in the browser. The event can be as simple as loading or unloading, which occur when a file is opened or closed in the browser, respectively. Another example of an event is moving your mouse over an object on a web page (text, a graphic, or any object in the DOM). Other events include mouse clicks, mouse movements, form input, form submission, and even changing focus from one form element to the next.

Each event that is defined in the DOM is linked to a specific event attribute, or keyword that identifies the event. When the browser loads the HTML document into RAM, the browser parses, recognizes and catalogs any event attributes that are included or mapped in the document. Thus, the browser is building a map of the event attributes that the web document wants the browser to monitor.

When the browser detects a mapped browser event, the browser's scripting engine then executes the event handler that is linked to that specific event attribute. The event handler is usually a short piece of client-side script that defines specific actions the browser's scripting engine will take when the browser detects that specific event.

Table 12.1 outlines the objects and event handlers supported in both Netscape Navigator 4.0*x* and Microsoft Internet Explorer 4.0*x*.

TABLE 12.1   Objects and Event Handlers Supported in Both Browsers

Event Attributes	Object(s)	Description of the Event
onAbort	Image	User aborts loading the page.
onBlur	Password, Text, Select, Window	User leaves the object.
onChange	Text	User changes the object.
onClick	Area, Button, Checkbox, Link, Radio, Reset, Submit	User clicks on the object.
onError	Window	Script encounters an error.
onFocus	Password, Text, Textarea, Window	User makes an object active.
onKeydown	Password, Text, Textarea	User presses a key.
onKeypress	Password, Text, Textarea	User presses or holds down a key.
onKeyup	Password, Text, Textarea	User releases a key.

(continued)

TABLE 12.1 Objects and Event Handlers Supported in Both Browsers *(continued)*

Event Attributes	Object(s)	Description of the Event
onLoad	Window	Object loaded in window.
onMousedown	Button, Checkbox, Link, Radio, Reset, Submit	User presses a mouse button.
onMouseout	Area, Link	Cursor moves off an object.
onMouseover	Area, Link	Cursor moves over an object.
onMouseup	Button, Checkbox, Link, Radio, Reset, Submit	User releases a mouse button.
onReset	Form	User resets a form.
onResize	Window	User or script resizes a window or frame.
onSelect	Password, Text, Textarea	User selects the contents of an object.
onSubmit	Form	User submits a form.
onUnload	Window	User leaves the window.

DHTML Implementation

Because DHTML is not yet standardized, we will focus on the Microsoft and Netscape implementations separately. Then we will look at code that will perform in both browsers. Note that the files specific to Internet Explorer could crash the Navigator browser and vice versa.

Microsoft Implementation

The Microsoft implementation of DHTML uses a combination of the <SPAN> tag, CSS, and scripting. The CSS and scripting information is placed in the head portion of the HTML document. The <SPAN> tag contains additional CSS information. The <SPAN> tag is a container tag used with style information applied to a span of text. You can find the most current information about the Microsoft DHTML implementation at the following URL:

```
http://msdn.microsoft.com/library/default.asp?url
   =/workshop/entry.asp
```

In Listing 12.1, DHTML positioning is used to lay out text in a document. The text is made up of elements of a table of contents that will drop down when clicked on in Internet Explorer. The page shows the words *Certification*, *Training*, and *Job Roles* when it is first displayed in the browser window. When clicked on, each word displays a table of contents below it. The DHTML portion is highlighted.

The code in Listing 12.1 can only be used with Microsoft Internet Explorer 4.*x*. It will not work in Netscape Navigator and could potentially crash it. Do not attempt to use it with Netscape Navigator.

Listing 12.1: Using DHTML with Microsoft Internet Explorer

```
<HTML>
<HEAD>
<TITLE>Table of Contents</TITLE>
<STYLE>
.headings   {font: bold 24pt; cursor: hand}
.subheadings {padding-left: 12}
</STYLE>
<SCRIPT LANGUAGE="JavaScript">
<!--
//
function displaySubs(subNum){
//display the section if hidden; hide it if displayed
  if (subNum.style.display=="none")
  {subNum.style.display=""}
```

```
        else{subNum.style.display="none"}
    }
    //-->
    </SCRIPT>
    </HEAD>
    <BODY BGCOLOR=#FFFFFF>
    <SPAN CLASS="headings" onclick="displaySubs(sub1)"
    STYLE="color: green">Certfication</SPAN><BR>
       <DIV CLASS="subheadings" ID="sub1"
    STYLE="display: none; color: blue">
         CIW<BR>
         Foundations<BR>
         Designer<BR>
       </DIV>
    <SPAN CLASS="headings" onclick="displaySubs(sub2)"
    STYLE="color: brown">Training</SPAN><BR>
       <DIV CLASS="subheadings" ID="sub2"
    STYLE="display: none; color: blue">
         Internet<BR>
         Intranet<BR>
         E-commerce<BR>
       </DIV>
    <SPAN CLASS="headings" onclick="displaySubs(sub3)"
    STYLE="color: red">Job Roles</SPAN><BR>
       <DIV CLASS="subheadings" ID="sub3"
    STYLE="display: none; color: blue">
         Designer<BR>
         Developer<BR>
         Administrator<BR>
       </DIV>
    </BODY>
    </HTML>
```

Figure 12.2 demonstrates what you will see in the browser window once the user clicks on an item.

FIGURE 12.2 Drop-down table of contents made with DHTML

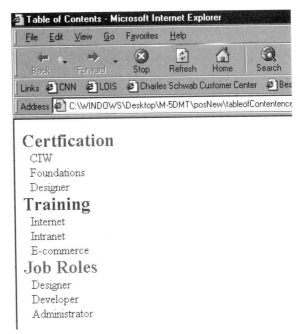

Netscape Implementation

One of the main differences in the Netscape implementation is the use of the <LAYER> tag. Layers can be used to show, hide, or move blocks of HTML, and they can be manipulated based upon events activated by the user. You can think of layers as being similar to cards, which can be moved, shuffled, displayed, and hidden.

You can find the most current information about the Netscape DHTML implementation at the following URLs:

`http://developer.netscape.com/tech/dynhtml/index.html`

`http://developer.netscape.com/docs/manuals/communicator /dynhtml/index.htm`

In Listing 12.2, you will see how the <LAYER> tag can be used in a document. It illustrates the layer effect in Netscape Navigator. The DHTML is highlighted.

The code in Listing 12.2 is specific to Netscape Communicator and the Navigator 4.*x* browser. This example will not work in Microsoft Internet Explorer and could potentially crash it. Do not attempt to use this example with Microsoft Internet Explorer.

Listing 12.2: Using DHTML with Netscape Navigator

```
<HTML>
<HEAD>
<TITLE>Layer Exercise</TITLE>
</HEAD>
<BODY BGCOLOR="#FFFFFF">
<LAYER ID="layer1" TOP="20pt" LEFT="5pt"
BGCOLOR="#669999" WIDTH="200">
<P>
 <H1>Layer 1</H1>
 <P>This is the bottom layer<BR></P>
 <P>Netscape uses layers<BR> to position</P>
 <P>Each of these overlap</P>
</LAYER>
<LAYER ID="layer2" TOP="60" LEFT="150"
BGCOLOR="#FF0000" WIDTH="200" HEIGHT="50">
 Layer 2 - This is the middle layer
</LAYER>
<LAYER ID="layer3" TOP="90" LEFT="180"
BGCOLOR="#336699" WIDTH="120" HEIGHT="250">
 <H1>Layer 3</H1>
This is the layer on top<BR>
<IMG SRC="ciw-logo.gif" ALIGN="right">
</LAYER>
</BODY>
</HTML>
```

Figure 12.3 demonstrates what you will see in the browser window.

FIGURE 12.3 Layers displayed in Netscape Navigator

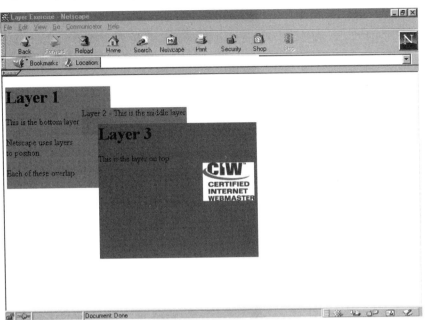

Cross-Browser DHTML

The Dynamic HTML code in the previous examples is browser-specific. The code will execute properly only in the specific brand and version of the web browser application. DHTML code that uses Netscape-specific DOM objects will fail in a Microsoft browser, because the Microsoft browser does not map or monitor the Netscape objects. Likewise, DHTML code that references Microsoft-specific DOM objects will fail in a Netscape browser. Of course, DHTML that is written with VBScript or JScript will fail in Netscape browsers, as Netscape supports its own version of client-side JavaScript.

When you begin to work with DHTML, you will probably not be hand-coding your work, as with the code in Listing 12.3. Many of the high-end HTML editors, such as Dreamweaver and FrontPage, have DHTML capabilities. The advantage to using those tools is that they create a dual set of code that allows the DHTML to work in either browser.

Keep in mind that, although we refer to this as cross-browser DHTML, it still has some browser-specific code, which you will see indicated by the comments. The DHTML is highlighted.

Listing 12.3: Creating Cross-Browser DHTML

```
<HTML>
<HEAD>
<SCRIPT LANGUAGE="JavaScript">
<!--
    //Determine whether the browser supports
     layers = Netscape
     browsObj = (document.layers) ?
     'document' : 'document.all';
   //If the browser does not support layers
       styleVal = (document.layers) ? '' : '.style';

    //Function that determines visibility and changes
   accordingly
     function showBox(action,textLink){
     if (document.layers || document.all) {
     domStyle = eval(browsObj +
       '.' + textLink + styleVal);

    //Determine visibility of the pop-up box
 state = domStyle.visibility;

    //If it is visible, it is changed to hidden
    //If it is hidden, it is changed to visible
    if (state == "visible" || state == "show"){
    domStyle.visibility = "hidden";
    }else {
        //Instructions for Navigator to position box
   coordinates
        if (document.layers) {
        topCoord = eval(action.pageY + 5);
        leftCoord = eval(action.pageX - 100);
        }
        //Instructions for IE to
```

```
            position box coordinates
            if (document.all) {
            topCoord = eval(event.y + 5);
            leftCoord = eval(event.x - 100);
            }
            //Applies the coordinates
             determined by conditions
            domStyle.top = topCoord;
            domStyle.left = leftCoord;
            domStyle.visibility = "visible";
            }
        }
}
// -->
</SCRIPT>
<STYLE>
        <!--
            #box1 {
                position: absolute;
                z-index: 10;
                top: 0px;
                left: 10px;
                visibility: hidden }

            .boxtext {
                color: #336699;
                background-color: #CCCCCC;
                padding: 5px;
                border: solid 5pt #669999;
                width: 250px;
                layer-background-color:#FFFFFF; }
    -->
</STYLE>
</HEAD>
```

```
<BODY BGCOLOR="#FFFFFF">
<TABLE WIDTH="100%">
<TR ALIGN="center">
     <TD>
     Using Dynamic HTML can provide a
much more interactive feel to a web document.
<BR> Mouse over the CIW logo to see the popup.
     </TD>
</TR>
<TR ALIGN="center">
     <TD>
     <A HREF="http://www.ciwcertified.com"
onMouseover="if (document.layers || document.all)
{
{showBox(event,'box1') }"
     onMouseout="if (document.layers || document.all)
   {showBox(event,'box1') }">
     <img src="ciw-logo.gif" BORDER="0"></A>.
     </TD>
</TR>
</TABLE>
<SPAN ID="box1" CLASS="boxtext">
Learn more about CIW and the
CIW Certification Tracks</SPAN>
</BODY>
</HTML>
```

Figure 12.4 demonstrates what the code in Listing 12.3 will look like in an Internet Explorer browser window; the code will function the same in both browsers.

FIGURE 12.4 Cross-browser DHTML code

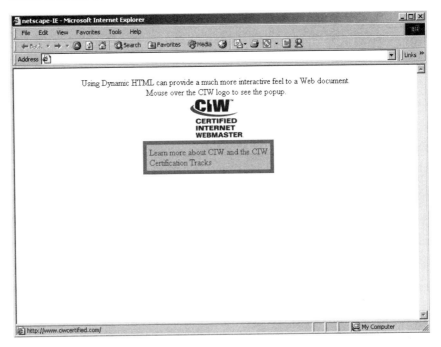

Summary

DHTML consists of Cascading Style Sheets, HTML, the Document Object Model, and scripting. Developing real-world applications involves a combination of these four technologies to make web pages more dynamic. Dynamic HTML, when used with the CSS1 Recommendation and linked with script, can be used in some cases to replace functions currently performed by Java applets, ActiveX controls, or animated GIFs. CSS1, DOM, HTML, and scripting extend HTML by adding new methods for formatting elements as well as supporting many event attributes that can trigger script with a wider variety of mouse and keyboard events.

The Document Object Model has a special relationship with DHTML. The Document Object Model allows programmers to describe a page's structure, what tags are on a page, and how they are presented. DOM is the

DHTML interface that accesses and manipulates HTML and XML documents and provides them with logical structure by creating objects that have associated properties that describe them; methods, or things the properties can do; and event handlers that allow the methods to occur.

Cross-browser implementation of DHTML is difficult currently. In fact, both Netscape and Microsoft have their own implementations of DHTML, and neither works correctly with the other's browser. The Microsoft implementation of DHTML uses a combination of the <SPAN> tag, CSS, and script. One of the main differences in the Netscape implementation is the use of the <LAYER> tag. Layers can be used to show, hide, or move blocks of HTML, and they can be manipulated based upon events activated by the user. Layers can be moved, shuffled, displayed, and hidden, depending on the effect you choose to create.

There are cross-browser codes that will function the same in both Internet browsers. Many of the high-end HTML editors, such as Dreamweaver and FrontPage, have DHTML capabilities, and the advantage to using them is that they create a dual set of code that allows the DHTML to work in either browser.

Exam Essentials

Understand Dynamic HTML and know the technologies it includes. DHTML allows the website author to create interactive pages. It is a set of interrelated technologies: scripts written in JavaScript or VBScript, the Document Object Model (DOM), HTML 4.0.1, and CSS1.

Understand the Document Object Model and its relationship to DHTML. The Document Object Model (DOM) is a key component in DHTML. Originally considered mainly in terms of browsers, the DOM is manipulated by script and often used with forms. It was developed by Netscape as a specification or instance hierarchy of JavaScript objects. The Document Object Model enables programmers to create document structure, navigate it, and add or change content.

Know browser-specific code for use with Microsoft Internet Explorer and Netscape Navigator. One limitation of DHTML is its lack of cross-browser compatibility. There are significant differences in the way DHTML performs in Netscape and Microsoft browsers. Netscape and

Microsoft each has its own implementation of DHTML; Netscape's implementation doesn't work correctly in Microsoft's browser and vice versa. You should know the code and tags used for each browser. Cross-browser code exists that allows website developers to use one set of code for both browsers for limited DHTML events but developers lose the strength of DHTML when this method is used.

Key Terms

Before you take the exam, be certain you are familiar with the following terms:

Active Server Pages (ASPs)	Dynamic HTML (DHTML)
Document Object Model (DOM)	event

Review Questions

1. What is currently the major limitation of DHTML?

   A. It has not been fully developed by the W3C.

   B. It relies heavily on technology that has not been approved by the W3C.

   C. Enormous differences exist in the way DHTML performs in Netscape and Microsoft browsers.

   D. Internet Explorer will render DHTML; Netscape will not.

2. What role does the DOM play in DHTML?

   A. The DOM has been phased out of DHTML.

   B. The DOM is the DHTML interface that accesses and manipulates HTML and XML documents.

   C. The DOM is the HTML interface that accesses and manipulates DHTML documents.

   D. The DOM is the XML interface that accesses and manipulates HTML and DHTML documents.

3. What is a DHTML event?

   A. The execution of the DOM in the browser

   B. The implementation of a CSS in an HTML page

   C. An animated GIF, JavaScript, or a Java applet

   D. Anything that occurs during the life of the HTML page in the browser

4. Which of the following best describes DHTML?

   A. HTML with built-in animation capabilities

   B. HTML with the capability for dynamic functionality

   C. HTML with an applet's capability to interact with the server

   D. HTML for developers who prefer to write their code manually

5. DHTML combines HTML 4 with which group of other technologies?

  A. Animated GIFs, the Document Object Model, and JavaScript

  B. JavaScript, Active Server Pages, and applets

  C. Document Object Model, Cascading Style Sheets, and a scripting language

  D. VBScript, metadata, and Cascading Style Sheets

6. Which of the following best defines the Document Object Model?

  A. The standard layout and format for object-based documents

  B. The list of tag elements and attributes available to DHTML

  C. The hierarchy of DHTML commands and scripts

  D. The hierarchy developers use to structure and manipulate content

7. The Netscape implementation of DHTML uses which tag to show, hide, or move blocks of HTML?

  A. <LAYER>

  B. <SPAN>

  C. <BLOCK>

  D. <DIV>

8. What type of technology could DHTML offer an alternative to?

  A. ASP

  B. CSS

  C. DOM

  D. XML

9. What is the name of the mechanism that responds to an event?

  A. Event handler

  B. Event manager

  C. Event controller

  D. Event developer

10. Coupled with CSS1 and linked by script, what can DHTML be used to replace?

    A. Functions currently performed by ASPs, JSPs, or PHPs

    B. Functions currently performed by JavaScript or VBScript

    C. Functions currently performed by Flash, Shockwave, or Photoshop

    D. Functions currently performed by Java applets, ActiveX controls, or animated GIFs

11. What concept was introduced with Netscape Navigator 2 in 1995?

    A. DHTML

    B. DOM

    C. HTML

    D. XML

12. What goal does the W3C have for the Document Object Model (DOM)?

    A. Provide a standard programming interface.

    B. Enable programmers to create document structure.

    C. Replace DHTML.

    D. Replace HTML.

13. What does scripting allow a programmer to do that HTML and style sheets do not?

    A. Control page structure.

    B. Interact with tags.

    C. Change font color.

    D. Use animated GIFs.

14. Which of the following is an event handler supported by both Netscape and Microsoft browsers?

   A. onFocus

   B. onAlign

   C. onReload

   D. onDoubleclick

15. What is one way to create DHTML pages that will work with both Netscape and Microsoft browsers?

   A. Use DOM along with DHTML.

   B. Do nothing; DHTML will always work with both browsers.

   C. Use a high-end HTML editor.

   D. Use XML along with DHTML.

16. What does DHTML add to HTML?

   A. Methods for formatting text

   B. Methods for running images

   C. The ability to use scroll down boxes

   D. The ability to change background color

17. What two products may cause the W3C to not allow DHTML time to mature?

   A. HTML 4.0 and XML

   B. DOM and HTML

   C. JavaScript and Java

   D. XML and XSL

18. HTML 4 supports what W3C Recommendation, which includes typographical control elements?

    A. XML

    B. CSS1

    C. DHTML

    D. DOM

19. Which of the following is an event handler in an HTML document?

    A. Quickload

    B. Halfload

    C. Site Split

    D. onLoad

20. Even when using a high-end HTML editor to create cross-browser DHTML code, it still contains _____ .

    A. XML code

    B. <LAYER> tag

    C. Browser-specific code

    D. Deprecated tags

Answers to Review Questions

1. C.   Code does exist for a limited number of DHTML events that will work in both browsers, but the range of this code is limited. In order for all DHTML events to function correctly in both Internet Explorer and Navigator, separate code must be written for each browser.

2. B.   The Document Object Model (DOM) is a key component in DHTML. It allows programmers to use objects and their associated event handlers to create events in HTML pages. It is the DHTML interface that accesses and manipulates HTML and XML documents. It also provides logical structure to these documents.

3. D.   An event in an HTML document is anything that occurs during the life of the HTML page in the browser. Events are controlled by event handlers, which perform the designated event when called upon. An example of an event is onLoad, which occurs when the HTML document is loaded in the browser window from the server.

4. B.   DHTML is a set of technologies that allows the website author to create pages that are more interactive than pages created with just HTML.

5. C.   DHTML combines HTML 4.0.1 with the Document Object Model (DOM), Cascading Style Sheets (CSS1), and a scripting language (such as JavaScript or VBScript). It allows website designers to add interactivity and interest to their websites through a combination of technologies.

6. D.   The Document Object Model describes the flow of a document. It gives programmers the ability to create document structure or add or change content. It is an essential component of DHTML.

7. A.   Netscape uses the <LAYER> tag to implement DHTML. Layers can be used to show, hide, or move blocks of HTML, and they can be manipulated based upon events activated by the user.

8. A.   DHTML could offer an alternative to some server-side technologies such as Active Server Pages (ASPs). It provides dynamic rather than the typical static HTML content to the browser, but it doesn't need to access the server each time it receives browser input.

9. A. An event handler is executed when the browser detects an event that has been mapped by the appropriate event attribute within the document.

10. D. Coupled with the CSS1 standard and linked by script, Dynamic HTML can be used in some cases to replace functions currently performed by Java applets, ActiveX controls, or animated GIFs. DHTML brings to HTML the interactivity possible with scripting languages.

11. B. The Document Object Model (DOM) was introduced in 1995 with Netscape Navigator 2. It was developed by Netscape as a specification or instance hierarchy of JavaScript objects.

12. A. The W3C's goal for the DOM is to provide a standard programming interface that is compatible with various applications and environments yet works within existing HTML, style sheets, and scripting languages.

13. B. Scripting allows you to interact with tags and styles. It lets you design a response or function for a user event, such as a mouse move. You can use VBScript or JavaScript to interact with the DHTML Document Object Model.

14. A. The `onFocus` event handler is supported by both Netscape and Microsoft browsers. The objects associated with the `onFocus` event handler are `Password`, `Text`, `Textarea`, `Window`.

15. C. Many of the high-end HTML editors, such as Dreamweaver and FrontPage, have DHTML capabilities. The advantage to using those tools is that they create a dual set of code that allows DHTML to work in either browser.

16. A. DHTML standards extend HTML by adding new methods for formatting text and HTML page elements as well as new scripting event handlers that can trigger script with a wider variety of mouse and keyboard events.

17. D. The advances in XML and XSL can offer many DHTML features and more, so the W3C may not spend the time to mature DHTML.

18. B. HTML 4 supports the W3C Recommendation for Cascading Style Sheets (CSS1), which includes typographical control elements known as style sheets. With style sheets, you can create web pages with the layout sophistication of desktop publishing programs such as Microsoft Word, Adobe PageMaker, and QuarkXPress.

19. D.   An *event* in an HTML document is anything that occurs during the life of the HTML page in the browser. The event can be as simple as a file opening or closing in the browser. The associated event handler, in this case onLoad, detects when the event occurs and then performs a defined action as a result.

20. C.   Although high-end HTML editors can create cross-browser DHTML, it still contains some browser-specific code.

Chapter 13

Extensible Markup Language (XML)

THE CIW EXAM OBJECTIVE GROUP COVERED IN THIS CHAPTER:

✓ Use client-side and server-side programming to enhance website functionality, including but not limited to: Extensible Markup Language (XML).

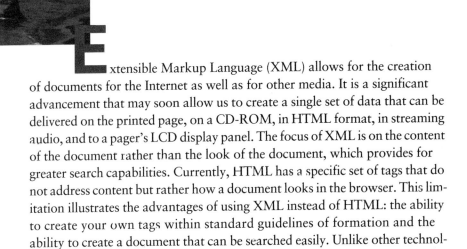

Extensible Markup Language (XML) allows for the creation of documents for the Internet as well as for other media. It is a significant advancement that may soon allow us to create a single set of data that can be delivered on the printed page, on a CD-ROM, in HTML format, in streaming audio, and to a pager's LCD display panel. The focus of XML is on the content of the document rather than the look of the document, which provides for greater search capabilities. Currently, HTML has a specific set of tags that do not address content but rather how a document looks in the browser. This limitation illustrates the advantages of using XML instead of HTML: the ability to create your own tags within standard guidelines of formation and the ability to create a document that can be searched easily. Unlike other technologies we have discussed thus far in this book, XML is natively supported in the most current versions of both Microsoft's and Netscape's browsers.

In this chapter, we will explore XML and its relationship to SGML and HTML. We'll discuss HTML's limitations and how it compares to and works with XML. We'll examine the goals of XML as well as the rules for well-formed XML, and we'll look at XHTML, the newest recommendation from the W3C.

What Is XML?

XML stands for *Extensible Markup Language*. This new language enables users to create documents that contain information about content that is more specific than ever before, adding a certain level of "intelligence." Consider the following statement:

> The Web itself is becoming a kind of cyborg intelligence: human and machine, harnessed together to generate and manipulate information. If automatability is to be a human right, then machine assistance must eliminate the drudge work involved in exchanging and manipulating knowledge....

This quotation is from the paper "The Evolution of Web Documents: The Ascent of XML" (`www.cs.caltech.edu/~adam/papers/xml/ascent-of-xml.html`; *World Wide Web Journal, Special Issue on XML*, Volume 2, Number 4, Fall 1997), in which authors Dan Connolly, Rohit Khare, and Adam Rifkin illuminate the potential of XML as a markup language that describes content in meaningful terms. XML was created to function transparently, providing machines with document information that will facilitate decision making at the machine level.

XML is derived from the Standard Generalized Markup Language (SGML). SGML is called a metalanguage, which is a language for creating other languages. To understand XML, you should first have a basic understanding of what a markup language is, what a metalanguage is, how SGML spawned XML, and how XML differs from HTML.

What Markup Languages Do

Markup languages are designed to tell computers how to process data. The term *markup* derives from early print publishers, who would "mark up" text by hand to indicate to the printer which font size to use where and in which weight, what form of alignment to use, and so forth. In other words, the earliest markup languages were dedicated to passing formatting instructions.

Markup instructions are generally referred to as *tags*, and the process of marking up a document is sometimes called *tagging*. Early word processing programs required the user to perform manual tagging. Today, most tagging in programs happens transparently and usually takes place using a proprietary system. The different methods for tagging text made it difficult for people to exchange data with each other. With the advent of the Internet, it became more valuable and more imperative for authors to be able to exchange documents in a format that was easy to use yet powerful and aesthetically acceptable.

Markup specifically designed to affect the appearance of a document is commonly called *procedural* markup because it tells the computer how to render the text. However, organizations that process huge numbers of documents, such as government and bureaucratic entities, quickly found that it was more important to know what the data represented rather than how it looked. Markup was then created to describe the content of the page. This type of markup is called *descriptive* or *logical* markup. The following is

HTML procedural markup for tagging the word *Summary* to appear in bold print:

```
<B>Summary</B>
```

In logical or descriptive markup, it makes more sense to designate the word *Summary* as a section header. The following is HTML logical markup for tagging the word *Summary* as a subheading:

```
<H4>Summary</H4>
```

SGML: A Short History

In the late 1960s, as computers were starting to be widely used in certain arenas, a group called the Graphic Communications Association (GCA) created a layout language called GenCode. GenCode was designed to provide a standard language for specifying formatting information so that printed documents would look the same regardless of the hardware used.

In 1969, Charles Goldfarb led a group of people at IBM who built upon the GenCode idea and created what became known as the General Markup Language (GML). Whereas GenCode was primarily a procedural markup language, GML aimed to define not only the appearance but to some degree the structure of the data.

Nearly 10 years after GML emerged, the American National Standards Institute (ANSI) established a working committee to build upon GML and create a broader standard. Goldfarb was asked to join this effort and has since become known as the "Father of SGML," which was the end product of ANSI efforts. The first draft of SGML was made public in 1980; the final version of the standard emerged in 1986.

Since that time, the language has been enhanced as needed. For example, in 1988 a version of SGML that was designed specifically for military applications (MIL-M-28001) was created. Other additions to the language have been incorporated over the years, and now some people feel that SGML suffers from complexity bloat.

XML: A Subset of SGML, Not HTML

Many people think XML is an addition of tags to HTML. This assumption is incorrect. The following was noted in the second annual XML conference held in 1998 in Seattle, Washington:

- HTML is display.

- XML is content.

- XML is not HTML.

Unlike HTML, XML is not an application of SGML; it's a subset of SGML. XML is SGML made simpler and more accessible; it is sometimes referred to as "SGML Lite." As such, XML qualifies as a metalanguage and can be used to write other languages. XML offers users the ability to define their own set of markup tags—to write their own version of HTML, so to speak.

HTML Goals

In 1989, Tim Berners-Lee wanted to find a language that would allow people from all over the world to create documents that could be read by a universal client, a product more commonly called the web browser. From that idea, HTML was born.

Berners-Lee thought that SGML provided the most promising model, but he knew that the difficulty of mastering the language would hamper the development and sharing of information. He created a very simple, efficient language for marking up text. HTML is based on SGML. HTML is not extensible. There is a finite set of HTML elements, which are entered into pages as tags.

HTML was originally created to define structure, not formatting. The original specification had a limited set of markup elements that designated text as a header, a paragraph, a list item, and other simple units. In its earliest form, HTML provided an incredibly simple and effective way for people to generate clear, readable documents.

Remember that the Internet was originally made popular by academics who wanted to share research across great distances. You can understand why the first version of HTML was mostly focused on creating clear, simple pages rather than flashy, interactive home pages for movie studios and other corporations. The following code represents a simple page marked up with HTML 1 tags:

```
<TITLE>Body Surfing</TITLE>
<H1>Body Surfing</H1>
This document is designed to teach you
how to enjoy the ride of your life.<P>
You will find many good tips and tricks here.
Read, and then go out and try this on your own!
<H2>Finding the Wave</H2>
The following are the key elements to look for in a wave:
<UL>
<LI>Height
<LI>Speed
<LI>Shape
</UL>
```

Notice that the markup is straightforward. A title for the document is identified by opening and closing <TITLE> tags. The main heading is marked as a heading level 1 by the <H1> tag. The <H2> tag marks the beginning of a subheading. Plain text is not marked up, but when a paragraph break is needed, the <P> tag is used to start a new paragraph. The <UL> tag begins an unordered or bulleted list, and <LI> indicates a list item.

This original language focused on the structure of the data and presented a simple set of tags to represent very simply structured documents. HTML made it possible for anyone to easily create web pages. The sheer amount of data that was suddenly available in a short time quickly made the Web an integral part of society, blossoming beyond even the most optimistic projections in terms of widespread acceptance and popularity.

HTML Extensions and False Structure

With the commercialization of the Internet, the number of web page creators grew exponentially, and not all users cared about Berners-Lee's original vision for HTML. Raised in the WYSIWYG environment of the current word processor generation, users wanted the ability to make type bold, change the font size or face, and add color. Netscape, producer of the first widely successful browser, responded to users who were frustrated with HTML's limitations by creating extensions to the language. As these extensions became widely used, they were ultimately folded into later versions of the language. The following code demonstrates a page that contains both structural markup and procedural markup. Both indicate formatting characteristics. The tags that do not define structure appear in bold:

```
<TITLE>Body Surfing</TITLE>
<CENTER><FONT FACE="Arial" COLOR="#0000FF" SIZE="6">
Body Surfing
</CENTER></FONT>
This document is designed to teach one
how to enjoy <B>the ride of your life.</B><P>
You will find many good tips and tricks here.
Read, and then go out and <I>try this on your own!</I>
<FONT FACE="Arial" COLOR="#0000FF" SIZE="5">
Finding the Wave
</FONT>
The following are the key elements to look for in a wave:
<UL>
<LI>Height
<LI>Speed
<LI>Shape
</UL>
```

You can see that, although this document may be more visually attractive, it is losing structure. In essence, the <FONT> tags have been used to simulate structure. Visually, the headings are clearly defined; to a machine, it is all just text.

If a computer program is written to search headings for keywords, in the code example in the preceding section it would have found the heading "Finding the Wave" rather easily. But in the second example, nothing indicates that "Finding the Wave" is a heading; a computer would know only that it is to be displayed differently. The text's relative role in the document could not be determined. In essence, the document became less "intelligent," offering less useful information to a machine.

Although users enjoyed the ability to choose from a wide variety of font options and colors, most were unaware that Pandora's box had been opened. Netscape added nonstandard formatting elements to HTML. Microsoft followed, adding its own propriety language extensions. Soon, page developers found themselves frustrated. The tantalizing extensions were not part of any standard and were usually recognized only in the browser made by the company that created the extension. It takes a long time for a new markup element to be proposed, discussed, and accepted into a new version of HTML; Netscape and Microsoft opted to present first and propose later.

Separating Format from Structure in HTML

The WYSIWYG wave made Tim Berners-Lee's vision of well-structured documents readable with a universal client more remote. In an effort to regain the original vision, a proposal was made and accepted by the W3C for separating formatting elements from HTML. The first version of this effort came to fruition in the Cascading Style Sheets, Level 1 Recommendation (CSS1). As discussed earlier in this book, CSS2 is now the Recommendation that supersedes and extends CSS1.

CSS states that all formatting should be defined in a separate document called a style sheet, in a STYLE section within an HTML page, or as values for a STYLE attribute within tags. In other words, the use of tags such as <CENTER> and <FONT> is now discouraged by the W3C, and these elements are said to be *deprecated* in favor of style sheets. Web authors are strongly discouraged from using deprecated elements when creating code for their web pages.

HTML Limitations

Although HTML will be used for a long time because of its simplicity in allowing the presentation of complex pages, continued devotion to it causes other problems that may not be immediately apparent, such as increased Internet traffic and search engine excesses.

You have probably noticed that the Web slows down at certain times of the day. Traffic increases, and with all the page requests hitting servers, delays are to be expected. Given the current state of HTML, much data is processed on the server. If you want to view a data report and then view the same data sorted in a different order, you probably have to query the server twice. This action creates a load on the server, increases traffic across telephone lines, and adds to the congestion on the Internet. One of the goals of those who are developing new specifications for the Internet is finding new ways of shifting processing to the client's computer and away from the server. Dynamic HTML offers potential for reducing some of this load, but without intelligently coded data, its potential is still limited.

Anyone who has tried to search for a document on the Internet has inevitably entered a search word or phrase that returned literally thousands of matches, called *hits*. Too much data is almost as useless as no data, because by the time you read through all the Internet documents returned from your search, you probably could have found the information you needed by some other means.

HTML has devolved from its original intent of defining structure. But even defining structure is not enough. To fully exploit the potential of evolving technologies, we must define not only the document structure, but the actual content as well.

The great advantage of using more specific structure and defining content will come from the ability to make searches across data that are much more refined. For example, if you want to search for information relating to the box office performance of the 1997 film *Titanic*, you might not want to be deluged with articles about the ship *Titanic*, the numerous books about its fatal voyage, or pages with sales promotions touting "titanic" discounts.

With the advent of XML, search engines will be able to perform searches that are more directly targeted, enhancing the precision of the results.

Consider the value of being able to define content by comparing the following code examples. In this example, a search engine cannot determine whether the word *Titanic* refers to a ship, a play, a film, or an adjective:

```
The best picture award in 1998
went to the film <I>Titanic</I>.
```

The next markup example is more useful:

```
The best picture award in 1998
went to the film <FILM>Titanic</FILM>.
```

Now you know that this reference to *Titanic* is a reference to a film by that name. The following example takes XML a step further:

```
The
<ACADEMY-AWARD-CATEGORY>best picture
</ACADEMY-AWARD-CATEGORY> award in
<YEAR>1998</YEAR> went to the film
<TITLE MEDIA="Film">Titanic</TITLE>.
```

This example makes the most "intelligent" document because the markup is explicit as to the document's contents. Suppose you were to ask an intelligent search engine the question, Which film won the Academy Award for best picture in the year 1998? This document would have a high degree of precision in matching your search query.

XML Goals

Imagine that while driving through unknown territory, you could ask your onboard car computer for directions to the nearest gas station. For that to be possible, markup must be more specific in terms of the actual content contained within documents. XML was created expressly to provide a manner of defining both structure and content.

XML was created by the XML Working Group and the XML Special Interest Group at the W3C under chairman Jon Bosak of Sun Microsystems. The W3C Recommendation for XML 1.0 was published in February 1998.

The XML Recommendation delineates the 10 goals that XML creators aimed to achieve (`www.w3.org/TR/2000/REC-xml-20001006`):

1. XML shall be straightforwardly usable over the Internet.

2. XML shall support a wide variety of applications.

3. XML shall be compatible with SGML.

4. It shall be easy to write programs which process XML documents.

5. The number of optional features in XML is to be kept to the absolute minimum, ideally zero.

6. XML documents should be human-legible and reasonably clear.

7. The XML design should be prepared quickly.

8. The design of XML shall be formal and concise.

9. XML documents shall be easy to create.

10. Terseness in XML markup is of minimal importance.

In HTML, the user is presented with a defined set of HTML tags to use in the creation of pages. The advantage is that the tags will work and the user needs to learn just a small amount of information about how the tags work in order to be able to publish web pages. HTML browsers are so tolerant of sloppy code that even a poorly constructed page will render in a readable, sometimes even pleasing form in the browser. Browsers will not, however, interpret tags they do not recognize, thereby limiting website developers to using predefined tags.

XML, on the other hand, offers far more freedom. Web page developers can now create tags and name them anything at all. The following is an example of XML markup:

```
<greeting>Hello, World!</greeting>
```

"Hello, World!" becomes not just two words and some punctuation but an exclamation or greeting. Because XML is not a language but a metalanguage, it has no predefined tags to use.

There is, however, a price for this ability to create your own tags. In HTML, a user can often omit the ending </P> tag because the browser can usually infer from other tags where the next block of data begins. But with XML, the browser has no way of knowing when the greeting ends without the closing </greeting> tag. For this reason, the requirements for XML are stricter than those for HTML. This strictness may frustrate page developers, but it will be worthwhile. The more specifically the markup relates to the content, the more powerfully that content can be used.

What Is an XML Document?

Consider exactly what constitutes an XML document, according to the W3C's Recommendation for XML 1.0 (www.w3.org/TR/1998/REC-xml-19980210#sec-well-formed):

> A data object is an XML document if it is well-formed, as defined in this specification. A well-formed XML document may in addition be valid if it meets certain further constraints.

From this quote, you see that the minimum requirement for a document to be considered an XML document is that it be well-formed. In addition, a well-formed XML document can also be valid.

HTML rendering programs are very tolerant with developers. If you forget to close a tag, the closing tag is usually inferred. If you use the wrong tag, the browser disregards it and renders the document no matter how poorly constructed it is. For that reason, HTML is great for the lazy developer. Less-than-thorough effort can still produce attractive pages.

XML, on the other hand, is far stricter. Any single error will prevent your page from rendering. XML is not for those who dislike detail or want to construct pages haphazardly. XML requires attention and discipline.

How difficult will it be to meet the stringent requirements of XML? Surprisingly, there is little to learn, and if you adhere to a small and simple set of rules, you should have few problems creating usable, well-formed XML pages.

Rules for Well-Formed XML

Well-formed tags in documents are essential in XML. Documents that are not well-formed will not load in the browser, according to the XML Recommendation. The W3C instructs us that "violations of well-formedness constraints are fatal errors." Therefore, the page will not appear in the browser at all unless this minimum requirement is met.

Five basic rules will help you construct well-formed XML documents. You should commit these rules to memory:

- Tags must be explicit; they cannot be implied. All opening tags must have corresponding closing tags. All closing tags must have corresponding opening tags.

- Empty tags require a forward slash (/) character before the closing angle bracket.

- All attribute values must be enclosed in single or double quotation marks.

- Tags must be properly nested.

- Tags are case sensitive and must match each other in every implementation.

We will examine each of these rules in detail.

Explicit Tags

In HTML, you became familiar with the fact that you could use the following syntax to create a bulleted list:

```
<UL>
<LI>Bullet list item one
<LI>Bullet list item two
<LI>Bullet list item three
</UL>
```

Note that the <UL> and </UL> tags denote the beginning and ending of an unordered list. The <LI> tag denotes the beginning of the current list item, but it can be implied that it denotes the end of the preceding list item in its second and third appearance. In other words, the end of the element has been implied. If you were to code this way in an XML document, however, the browser would be instructed not to render this page because it is not well-formed.

In XML, tags will never be implied and must always be made explicit. In other words, if the preceding example were to be included in an XML document, it would have to be written like this:

```
<UL>
<LI>Bullet list item one</LI>
<LI>Bullet list item two</LI>
<LI>Bullet list item three</LI>
</UL>
```

In the second instance of this list, you see that each list item is enclosed between opening and closing tags, meeting one criterion for a well-formed XML document.

Empty Tags

Tags that contain the relevant information within the tag boundaries but enclose no text are called empty tags. Examples of empty tags in HTML are <BR> and <IMG>, neither of which requires a closing tag because the tag itself carries all the relevant information. The <BR> tag instructs the rendering program to display a line break at that point. The <IMG> tag is used to include an image in the text, and the name of the image file is specified as a value of the required SRC attribute within the tag.

HTML is a language with a set number of recognized tags. It is important to bear in mind that XML is not a language and has no recognized tags. Rather, XML is a metalanguage that allows you to create a language of your own for your pages. For this reason, XML cannot be expected to recognize that <BR> and <IMG> are empty tags. To indicate to XML that a tag is actually empty, you must include the forward slash character (/) at the end of the tag. If you had <BR> and <IMG> tags in your XML document, you would code them as follows:

```
<BR/>
<IMG SRC="image.gif"/>
```

According to the W3C's guidelines, failure to do this will prevent your XML document from being well-formed and prevent it from rendering.

Attribute Values

In HTML, either of the following would be considered correct:

```
<TD WIDTH=25%>
<TD WIDTH="25%">
```

XML, however, requires that all attribute values be enclosed in quotation marks. In other words, of these two examples, only the second would be valid for XML (and then only presuming that the closing </TD> tag was also present).

Proper Nesting

In XML documents, tags must follow the strictest nesting rules. A tag cannot close once a new tag has opened after it; the new tag must close first. Layers of code must nest one within the other. In XML, you must simply close tags from the inside out, as in this example:

```
<name>Samson<surname>Lane</surname></name>
```

Case Sensitivity

In XML, case specificity is required. Consider the following tags:

```
<P>The quick brown fox jumped over the lazy dog.</p>
```

These tags would result in a fatal error in an XML document. The </p> tag cannot be used to close the <P> tag because it is written in a different case. All tags must match in case to be considered part of a matching set.

Simple Well-Formed XML

The following text demonstrates complete, well-formed XML (it is not a large sample, but it is error free):

```
<greeting>Hello, World!</greeting>
```

For reasons of forward compatibility, one additional element is requested, but not required, at the start of XML documents: the XML declaration that specifies to which version of XML the document conforms. The following example begins with an XML declaration providing version information:

```
<?xml version="1.0"?>
<greeting>Hello, World!</greeting>
```

Although the opening <?xml?> declaration statement is considered optional, it is highly recommended for forward compatibility. As the language evolves, it will be helpful to future browsers to know which version of the XML specification was used to create the document. If used, this declaration must be all lowercase.

HTML Transition to XML

As you can imagine, most HTML documents do not currently meet the simple but strict requirements they need to meet to be XML documents. However, a properly coded HTML document could become a well-formed XML document without much work. You can correct a poorly formed HTML document so that it meets the well-formedness requirements of XML with some attention to detail.

Consider a simple letter. Attorneys, among other business professionals, need to be able to track all correspondence. Some law offices have developed complex, coded directory structures for storing letters for retrieval. Others store letters in databases. Some perform full-text searches of the data by looking for names until they find the needed document. Many other variations exist. Now suppose attorneys start creating letters as XML documents. They could search using more specific criteria to find what they need more quickly, reducing the amount of time required to serve one client and freeing up time to pursue additional revenue.

Examine the basic business letter in Figure 13.1. What do you see in terms of structure?

FIGURE 13.1 Specifically structured document

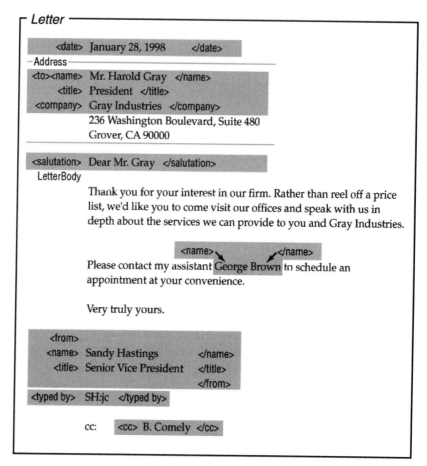

Following is the XML code for the version of the letter shown in Figure 13.1. This sample demonstrates how XML tags are used to indicate the content of the document rather than how the document should look (the XML tags are shown in bold):

```
<?xml version="1.0"?>
<Letter>
<date>January 28, 1998</date>
```

```
<Address>
<name>Mr. Harold Gray</name>
<title>President</title>
<company>Gray Industries</company>
236 Washington Boulevard, Suite 480
Grover, CA 90000
</Address>
<salutation>Dear Mr. Gray:</salutation>
    <LetterBody>
Thank you for your interest in our firm.
Rather than reel off a price list,
we'd like you to come visit our offices
and speak with us in depth about the
services we can provide to you and
Gray Industries.
Please contact my assistant
<name>George Brown</name>
to schedule an appointment
at your convenience.
Very truly yours,
    </LetterBody>
<from>
<name>Sandy Hastings</name>
<title>Senior Vice President</title>
</from>
<typed-by>SH:jc</typed-by>
cc: <cc>B. Comely</cc>
</Letter>
```

Remember that XML is case specific. You can choose to use any capitalization scheme you desire, but you must adhere to your choice strictly. This example uses a combination of cases, which makes it difficult to remember whether to capitalize certain tag names. This method is not recommended. Some people prefer all lowercase; others prefer to use all uppercase.

As you can imagine, XML is not appropriate for every task. As in carpentry, users are encouraged to use the most appropriate tool to complete the job at hand. If this letter is never going to be searched for, referenced, or read again, there is no point in making it an XML document. But if this document will be kept and viewed in the future, then thought should be given to structuring the information for maximum usability in the future.

You may be tempted to start using XML for your web pages. One concern you need to be aware of is the support browsers offer for this technology. Both Microsoft Internet Explorer 5 and Navigator 6 natively support XML pages. Older versions of both browsers offer limited support of XML.

Uses of XML beyond the Web

A substantial benefit of using XML is the ability to define a language that allows different types of presentation. Using XML, you may soon be able to create a single set of data that can be delivered on the printed page, on a CD-ROM, in HTML format, in streaming audio, and to a pager's LCD display panel. The format could be controlled by settings in the style sheet, but no recoding of XML pages need necessarily take place. Imagine the power of outputting any document you create to any of these formats without additional modification.

Will XML Replace HTML?

Will XML replace HTML? The short answer is no, but over time, the answer may well be yes. HTML presents severe limitations to page authors. It will continue to be the appropriate language for documents not intended for future use. But XML will better serve the purposes of those looking to retrieve and reuse data that needs to be maintained over time.

XML will redefine the way HTML is coded. In the short run, XML will be used in conjunction with HTML. As browsers develop and style technologies progress, XML may be used without HTML. But HTML and XML are separate and different, and one technology is not necessarily better or worse than the other. Both are tools that have appropriate and inappropriate uses. The more you know about each, the better equipped you are to choose the best tools to meet your enterprise's needs.

For more information about XML visit the W3C site at the following URL:

```
http://www.w3.org/XML/
```

What Is XHTML?

XHTML is the latest Recommendation from the W3C. XHTML combines HTML and XML to create a transition from HTML to XML while still providing current browsers with backward compatibility.

This means that the XHTML developer who adheres to the requirements of XML well-formedness can use HTML tags and XML tags within the same document and have it be valid. The following sample code demonstrates a valid and well-formed XHTML document:

```
<?xml version="1.0" encoding="UTF-8"?>
<!DOCTYPE html
     PUBLIC "-//W3C//DTD XHTML 1.0 Strict//EN"
     "DTD/xhtml1-strict.dtd">
<HTML XMLNS="http://www.w3.org/1999/xhtml"
XML:LANG="en" lang="en">
  <HEAD>
    <TITLE>CIW Certification</TITLE>
  </HEAD>
  <BODY>
    <P>Learn more:
<A HREF="http://www.ciwcertified.com">
CIW certified.com</A></P>
  </BODY>
</HTML>
```

XHTML is also designed to make web documents accessible and interoperable across platforms, partly because of the strictness of XML.

For more information about XHTML, visit the W3C site at the following URL:

```
http://www.w3.org/TR/xhtml1/
```

Summary

XML, Extensible Markup Language, is an emerging markup language that organizes information intelligently. Website designers can now add a certain level of "intelligence" to their web documents because of the ability to define the content as well as the structure of a document. XML is derived from the Standard Generalized Markup Language (SGML), which is a metalanguage. XML is SGML made simpler and more accessible; it is sometimes referred to as "SGML Lite." As such, XML qualifies as a metalanguage and can be used to write other languages.

Unlike HTML, XML is not an application of but a subset of SGML. HTML was originally created to define structure, not formatting. The original HTML specification had a limited set of tags with which developers could work. As long as tags were used as they were defined in the specification, developers could be rather sloppy in the writing of HTML and still have their pages render in HTML browsers. XML, on the other hand, was created to provide developers with a way to define content and structure. Developers can create their own tags as long as they follow the rules of well-formed XML set forth by the W3C.

XHTML is the latest recommendation from the W3C. The strength of XHTML lies in the combination of HTML and XML; as long as the developer follows the rules of XML, they can use XML and HTML tags within the same document and have it render correctly in the browser. XHTML is a transition from HTML toward XML and is designed to make web documents accessible and interoperable across platforms. It provides current browsers with backward compatibility.

Exam Essentials

Know the history of XML. XML stands for Extensible Markup Language. XML is a new language governed by the W3C that allows website designers to provide more specific information about the content of the document. You should know from which language XML is derived and understand its function in writing other languages.

Understand the differences between HTML and XML. XML is a subset of SGML, not an application of it. HTML was originally created to define structure, not formatting. HTML is limited to predefined tags that must be used according to the specification if they are to render correctly in the browser. XML offers users the ability to define their own set of markup tags, thereby giving them the freedom to define the content of their web documents.

Understand why HTML alone is not sufficient.   The original intent of HTML was to define the structure of a document. But defining structure is not enough. To fully exploit the potential of evolving technologies, not only the document structure must be defined, but also the actual content. The ability to use more refined searches that incorporate the content as well as the specific structure of the document is a great advantage of evolving technologies such as XML.

Know the elements of a well-formed XML document.   You should know the five basic rules that help construct well-formed XML documents. Know how explicit tags, empty tags, attribute values, nesting, and case sensitivity fit into the equation.

Know how XML functions in website design.   XML allows companies that need to store documents to create a system where these documents are easily retrievable and searchable. By creating and defining tags that have meaning to the organization or profession, companies can use XML to define the content rather than presentation of a document.

Understand the W3C's XHTML Recommendation.   XHTML is a combination of HTML and XML and is the latest Recommendation from the W3C. XHTML provides current browsers with backward compatibility. This means that the XHTML developer who adheres to the requirements of XML well-formedness can use HTML tags and XML tags within the same document and have it be valid. Using the strictness of XML, XHTML allows web documents to be accessible and interoperable across platforms.

Key Terms

Before you take the exam, be certain you are familiar with the following terms:

Extensible Markup Language (XML)   XHTML

Review Questions

1. What does XML stand for?

   A. Extra Markup Language

   B. Extensible Markup Language

   C. Extensible Marked-Up Language

   D. Extendible Markup Language

2. What is a metalanguage?

   A. A language that is a subset of another language

   B. A language within a language

   C. A language that has strict rules

   D. A language for creating other languages

3. What are two limitations of HTML that may not be immediately apparent?

   A. Lack of well-formedness and inconsistency in usage of closing tags

   B. Reliance on structure markup and lack of backward compatibility

   C. Increased Internet traffic and search engine excesses

   D. Lack of interaction with a server and set number of tags

4. Which of the following is a substantial benefit of using XML?

   A. The ability to use tags that the website developer makes up

   B. The ability to define a language that allows different types of presentation

   C. The ability to combine XML with HTML to create XHTML

   D. The ability to use a metalanguage to create the foundation of XML

5. XML is derived from which of the following languages?

  A. HTML

  B. XHTML

  C. GML

  D. SGML

6. Which of the following accurately describes a difference between XML and HTML?

  A. XML is display, whereas HTML is content.

  B. XML is a subset of HTML.

  C. XML is a metalanguage, whereas HTML is not.

  D. XML applies procedural markup, whereas HTML applies descriptive markup.

7. Which of the following best describes why HTML is not sufficient for processing documents online?

  A. HTML tags are often used to fake document structure.

  B. HTML does not render pages to look like the developer intended them to look.

  C. HTML tags do not make pages more visually attractive.

  D. HTML tags provide only logical markup instructions.

8. Which of the following is a required element of a well-formed XML document?

  A. Tags must be implicit.

  B. Empty tags require a forward slash before the opening wicket.

  C. Attribute values must be enclosed in parentheses.

  D. Tags are case sensitive and must match.

9. Which of the following currently offers native support for XML?

    A. The XML plug-in

    B. Netscape Navigator 5

    C. Microsoft Internet Explorer 5

    D. HTML 4

10. What does XHTML allow the developer who adheres to the requirements of XML well-formedness to do?

    A. Use HTML tags and XML tags within the same document

    B. Automatically convert HTML documents to XML documents

    C. Use a specified set of XML tags that are similar to HTML tags

    D. Use HTML tags to give meaning to data and make documents "intelligent."

11. What is the process of marking up a document sometimes called?

    A. Tagging

    B. Formatting

    C. Editing

    D. Marking

12. Which of the following layout languages was created in the late 1960s as one of the original foundations for markup languages?

    A. GML

    B. SGML

    C. GenCode

    D. GCH

13. Who is considered to be the "Father of SGML"?

    A. Alan Greenspan

    B. Jeff Goldblum

    C. Timothy Duggan

    D. Charles Goldfarb

14. Why is HTML not considered extensible?

    A. It doesn't provide for formatting text.

    B. There is a finite set of HTML elements.

    C. It provides only data tags.

    D. It requires strict coding schemes.

15. What problems were caused by both Microsoft and Netscape in terms of HTML's development?

    A. Both rejected HTML for their browsers.

    B. They tried to take complete ownership of the language.

    C. They each created proprietary formatting elements.

    D. They presented all ideas for standardization and waited for approval before implementing these ideas within their browsers.

16. Which of the following options would classify one distinction between XML and HTML for website developers?

    A. HTML is more strict than XML.

    B. XML is more strict than HTML.

    C. XML is impossible to learn if you already know HTML.

    D. HTML has a defined set of rules, whereas XML has no rules.

17. In XML, how do you indicate that a tag is empty?

    A. With a closing empty set of brackets <>.

    B. With a forward slash /.

    C. With a backward slash \.

    D. As with HTML, it's unnecessary.

18. In the following example, which XML rule is not being followed?

```
<UL>
<L1>First Bullet Item
<L2>Second Bullet Item
</UL>
```

A. Explicit tags

B. Empty tags

C. Attribute value

D. Proper nesting

19. In <NAME>John<name>, which of the following XML rules is not being followed?

A. Explicit tags

B. Empty tags

C. Case sensitivity

D. Proper nesting

20. Where can you look to find more information about XML?

A. www.xml.com

B. www.w3.org/XML/

C. www.microsoft.com

D. www.netscape.com

Answers to Review Questions

1. B.   XML stands for Extensible Markup Language. XML allows website developers to create and define their own tags. It defines the content of a document rather than how the document should look.

2. D.   A metalanguage is a language for creating other languages. SGML is a metalanguage.

3. C.   Increased Internet traffic and search engine excesses are two limitations of HTML that may not be immediately apparent. Much of the processing of an HTML document occurs on the server, and increased traffic on the Internet can cause an HTML page to load slowly. Additionally, searching for information on the Internet can be difficult because of the inability to clearly distinguish how a word is used.

4. B.   XML can be used with different types of media, such as the printed page, a CD-ROM, or a pager's LCD display. This allows website developer's to use a language that allows for different types of presentation, unlike HTML, which is only used for web-based documents.

5. D.   XML is derived from Standardized Markup Language (SGML). XML is a subset of SGML and can be used to write other languages. It is often referred to as "SGML Lite."

6. C.   XML is a metalanguage, whereas HTML is not. XML is not an application but a subset of SGML, whereas HTML is based on SGML. As such, XML qualifies as a metalanguage and can be used to write other languages.

7. A.   HTML is not sufficient for processing documents online because HTML tags are often used to fake document structure. Netscape, producer of the first widely successful browser, responded to users who were frustrated with HTML's limitations by creating extensions to the language. As these extensions became widely used, they were ultimately folded into later versions of the language. Now, website developers can use HTML to create pages that contain both structural markup and procedural markup and have both indicate formatting characteristics.

8. D. A well-formed XML document must use tags that are case sensitive and matching. Additionally, tags must be explicit; they cannot be implied. All opening tags must have corresponding closing tags. All closing tags must have corresponding opening tags. Empty tags require a forward slash (/) character before the closing angle bracket. All attribute values must be enclosed in single or double quotation marks. Tags must be properly nested.

9. C. Microsoft Internet Explorer 5 offers native support for XML. Netscape Navigator 6 also natively supports XML pages.

10. A. XHTML uses a combination of HTML tags and the well-formedness of XML in order to make web documents accessible and interoperable across platforms. A website developer who adheres to XHTML can use HTML tags and XML tags within the same document and have it be a valid document.

11. A. Markup instructions are generally referred to as tags, and the process of marking up a document is sometimes called tagging. Early word processing programs required the user to perform manual tagging. Today, most tagging in programs happens transparently and usually takes place using a proprietary system.

12. C. In the late 1960s, computers were starting to be widely used in certain arenas. A group called the Graphic Communications Association (GCA) created a layout language called GenCode. It was designed to provide a standard language for specifying formatting information so that printed documents would look the same regardless of the hardware used.

13. D. Nearly 10 years after GML emerged, the American National Standards Institute (ANSI) established a working committee to build upon GML and create a broader standard. Goldfarb was asked to join this effort and the end product was SGML. Goldfarb has since become known as the "Father of SGML."

14. B. There is a finite set of HTML elements, which are entered into pages as tags. HTML was originally created to define structure, not formatting, but formatting and graphic elements have been incorporated since its first inception. HTML is not really strict and is often called the "lazy programmers'" language.

15. C. Netscape added nonstandard formatting elements to HTML. Microsoft then added its own propriety language extensions. Because the extensions were not part of any standard and were usually recognized only in the browser made by the company that created the extension, page developers became frustrated. It takes a long time for a new markup element to be proposed, discussed, and accepted into a new version of HTML; Netscape and Microsoft presented first and proposed later.

16. B. HTML is great for the lazy developer. You can produce attractive pages with less-than-thorough effort. XML is far stricter though. Any single error will prevent your page from rendering. XML is not for those who dislike detail or want to construct pages haphazardly; it requires attention and discipline.

17. B. Empty tags require a forward slash (/) character before the closing angle bracket. This is one of the rules for XML, although it is unnecessary in HTML.

18. A. Note that the <UL> and </UL> tags denote the beginning and ending of an unordered list. The <LI> tag denotes the beginning of the current list item, but it also can be inferred to denote the end of the previous list item in its second and third appearance. In other words, the end of the element has been inferred. If you were to code this way in an XML document, however, the browser would be instructed not to render this page because it is not well-formed.

19. C. In XML, case sensitivity is required. These tags would result in a fatal error in an XML document. The <name> tag cannot be used to close the <NAME> tag because it is written in a different case. All tags must match in case to be considered part of a matching set.

20. B. For more information about XML, visit the W3C site at `www.w3.org/XML/`.

Chapter

14

Java Applets

THE CIW EXAM OBJECTIVE GROUP COVERED IN THIS CHAPTER:

✓ Add downloadable web content to a site, including but not limited to: Java applets.

We have discussed a number of different methods for adding interest and interactivity to your websites: DHTML, JavaScript, and plug-in technology. Java applets can also be used to create dynamic websites. They have extended the HTML page beyond its static nature and allowed website developers to add interactivity and creativity to their websites. For example, you can use them for interactive applications such as customizing a new vehicle, tracking stock quotes in real time, taking a virtual tour of the human body from the inside out, and simulating a mission to Mars. Java applets incorporate server-side and client-side technologies to perform a range of tasks, from simple animation to complex virtual tours.

In this chapter, we will explore the role Java plays in creating your applets and what applets can and cannot do. We'll also show you how to embed an applet into an HTML page and how to use Java applets for animation. Finally, we'll tell you about resources you can use to incorporate Java applets into your web pages.

Why Use Java and Applets?

Java and Java applets are creating exciting commercial web environments for developers and users. You can already see improved interactivity and services and access to more types of vital information via systems that are simpler to use. The website creator can expect lower development and deployment costs by using Java, which means distribution requires less time and effort. When you use Java and Java applets, you can offer more multimedia on your intranet and on the Internet without the traditional limits of desktop computing, such as CGI dependency and proprietary software platforms. Java allows web professionals to extend their companies' business-computing investments by extending the use of existing PCs, servers, host systems, and software. Java applets make sense for businesses, especially those that are serious about maximizing the benefits of their Web presence. In addition, opportunities for the enterprising web professional are mushrooming. Java's capabilities have already enabled new and unexpected web applications that translate into global business opportunities, such as virtual tours of facilities or products.

Introduction to Java

Java is a programming language derived from C++. It provides an exciting model for communicating in a secure environment on the Internet and the Web. Business applications created using this cross-platform model can be distributed on the Internet and run entirely on the client side. Java also provides a way to quickly develop applications with minimal disruption or downtime.

An *object-oriented* program can be created once and reused (with some modification) any number of times. In object-oriented programming, you can concentrate exclusively on the method for making the program function. Java is an object-oriented programming language, and the Java applet is an object you plug into your web page.

Strengths of Java

Java provides a welcome, necessary, and timely solution to the limitations of authoring HTML-only documents. Once the Java object (applet) has been created, Java tracks it for you. Java mini-applications (hence the name *applets*) are ideally suited to the Internet because they can run on a variety of operating systems, hardware platforms, and web browsers. The same applet can be executed on different systems without being recompiled.

Because Java applets are platform neutral, all that is required to run them is a Java-enabled web browser. Programs written in Java can function in any computer environment, but Java applets will work only in web-based applications. To this extent, when you're developing a web page, the only use for Java on a client machine is the applet.

To promote its use as a cross-platform Internet programming language, Sun freely licenses Java. Currently, Sun has released version 2, which is the next generation of Java and runs faster than its previous version. This advance will further increase Java's acceptance as a suitable alternative to other languages.

Demystifying Applets

The Java programming language was designed specifically to address software application development for the Internet. Java supports Internet programming in the form of platform-independent applets. Applets can create animation: classic, cartoon-style, actual program-generated lines such as flowing sine waves or simple static images moving across the screen.

Java applications are stand-alone programs when they're not used on the Internet. *Applets* are small applications, but they do not run outside of a browser; they adhere to a set of conventions that enables them to run within a Java-compatible browser. Applets are embedded in HTML pages for web viewing.

Applets Are Platform-Independent

Java enables applet construction on any computer with the Java 2 Software Development Kit (SDK) installed, and it can be used to create stand-alone applications. These two important features allow Java applications and applets to be run on many systems, including portable computers.

Applets Are Fast

Java applets are much faster than CGI scripts because they are downloaded to the client when called upon instead of running off the server, as CGI scripts do. Java applications are slower, however, than those written in traditional programming languages such as C because of the compiler used to process it, but this performance gap is closing. Sun released a compiler called HotSpot to address this speed issue.

Applets Are Multithreaded

Many operating systems—such as Windows Me, Windows 2000, and Unix—support multitasking. Java supports multitasking as well, also referred to as multithreading. *Multithreading* allows more than one thread of execution; each thread is a separate process within a document. One thread might handle user interaction while another carries out a computation. Thus, Java does not make the user wait for one program to finish an operation before starting the next operation.

Multithreaded behavior interacts with the multitasking capability of the platform on which the applet is running. Stand-alone Java runtime environments and applets have excellent real-time behavior, meaning they work quickly and efficiently. An example of this multithreaded behavior is a joystick functioning quickly and efficiently so that the game player sees the effect of moving the joystick as soon as it is moved.

However, when a multithreaded application runs on top of a multitasking operating system such as Windows, the operating system limits its real-time responsiveness. The technology can sometimes surpass the capability of the user's operating system. Now, however, most systems being sold can easily handle the increased demand.

Applets Run on the Client Side

Many server-side tasks can be sent to a Java-enabled web browser that is running an applet, shifting the processing from the server exclusively to client as well. Some functions that were subject to server-side dependence can now be performed entirely on the client side; form validation and the calculations for image maps are two examples. Applets require very little space and operate efficiently on the client side.

Embedding a Java Applet

You need two pieces of information to insert applets into your web pages. First, you must know the Java applet class file that will perform the function. A *class file* is a complied applet program. Applets may have more than one class file associated with them, depending on what the applet is designed to do. You must also know the parameters that the class file needs to run. The parameters of the class file allow you to customize the applet. Parameters are placed in the HTML page by using the <PARAM> tag while the class file resides on the server. The class file is the Java programming and the parameters will be the HTML element. Without each of these, the other is useless.

According to the HTML 4.0 Recommendation, the proper way to embed an applet is to use the <OBJECT> tag. The <OBJECT> replaced the deprecated <APPLET> tag from previous recommendations of HTML. It offers a generic way to include objects, such as images and applets, into a web page.

Netscape initiated support of the <OBJECT> tag with the release of its 6.*x* browsers. However, the older versions (4.*x* and below) do not support the

<OBJECT> tag; therefore, to remain platform-independent, your code must use the <OBJECT> tag as well as the older and deprecated <APPLET> tag.

Using the <OBJECT> Tag

The <OBJECT> tag provides the browser with information to load and render data types that are not natively supported in the browser. The <OBJECT> tag contains the information the browser needs to determine which external program must be loaded to view the content included with the web page. <OBJECT> tags can be nested so that alternate content can be loaded if the browser does not support your first chosen plug-in or content aid. The <OBJECT> tag has an extensive list of attributes that attempt to handle every possible data type you may encounter. Additionally, the <PARAM> tag can be used to denote content-specific parameters that may be required by an object at runtime.

The following example shows you how to use the <OBJECT> tag to embed an object in an HTML page. The object, when displayed in the browser, will fade text in and out between the display of designated URLs:

```
<OBJECT CODETYPE="application/java"
CLASSID="java:Fade.class" WIDTH="300" HEIGHT="50">
    <PARAM NAME="bgcolor" VALUE="0000ff">
    <PARAM NAME="txtcolor" VALUE="ff0000">
    <PARAM NAME="changefactor" VALUE="5">
    <PARAM NAME="text1" VALUE="Welcome to CIW.">
    <PARAM NAME="url1"
VALUE="http://www.ciwcertified.com">
    <PARAM NAME="font1" VALUE="Helvetica,PLAIN,14">
    <PARAM NAME="text2" VALUE="maintained by Kevin">
    <PARAM NAME="url2"
VALUE="http://www.voicenet.com/~beccaris">
    <PARAM NAME="font2" VALUE="TimesRoman,ITALIC,18">
    <PARAM NAME="text3" VALUE="Come back soon!">
    <PARAM NAME="url3"
VALUE="http://www.ciwcertified.com">
    <PARAM NAME="font3" VALUE="Courier,BOLD,18">
</OBJECT>
```

Using the <APPLET> Tag

The <APPLET> tag identifies the name of the class file to load and run. Like the <IMG> tag, which uses attributes to pull the image into your page, applets use the CODE attribute to reference the location of your Java applet file. Java applet files are always class files (with the .class extension). The class file is the compressed Java code that runs the applet function. Two other attributes required by the <APPLET> tag are HEIGHT and WIDTH. These attributes tell the browser how much space the applet needs to display.

The parameters of the applet are passed to the class using the <PARAM> tag. All <PARAM> tags are placed between the opening and closing <APPLET> tags. For each parameter of the applet, another <PARAM> tag is required. The NAME and VALUE attributes are used with each <PARAM> tag. The NAME attribute holds the name of the attribute (e.g., text color). The VALUE attribute supplies the desired effect. Following is an example of how the same code used in the preceding example would be written using the <APPLET> tag:

```
<APPLET CODE="Fade.class" WIDTH="300" HEIGHT="50">
    <PARAM NAME="bgcolor" VALUE="0000ff">
    <PARAM NAME="txtcolor" VALUE="ff0000">
    <PARAM NAME="changefactor" VALUE="5">
    <PARAM NAME="text1" VALUE="Welcome to CIW.">
    <PARAM NAME="url1"
VALUE="http://www.ciwcertified.com">
    <PARAM NAME="font1" VALUE="Helvetica,PLAIN,14">
    <PARAM NAME="text2" VALUE="maintained by Kevin">
    <PARAM NAME="url2"
VALUE="http://www.voicenet.com/~beccaris">
    <PARAM NAME="font2" VALUE="TimesRoman,ITALIC,18">
    <PARAM NAME="text3" VALUE="Come back soon!">
    <PARAM NAME="url3"
VALUE="http://www.ciwcertified.com">
    <PARAM NAME="font3" VALUE="Courier,BOLD,18">
</APPLET>
```

How the Applet Works

Regardless of whether you use the <OBJECT> tag or the <APPLET> tag to embed a Java applet into your web page, the single class file is transferred to the browser upon request by the user. The browser validates the class file according to its internal rules and reviews the parameters. If it is validated, the class file is initialized and the applet plays. One of the limitations of Java applets is that the whole applet file must be downloaded before it can begin execution. Currently, Java applets have no streaming technologies. In addition, they do not have caching capability, which means that the user must download the applet again upon each subsequent visit to the site.

Testing the Applet in a Browser

When testing applets, you should always reload the page. Some browsers merely restart applets without actually reloading them to receive any changes. If you do not completely reload your applet after making changes, you will not be able to see your changes. This problem is more widespread with older browsers; newer browsers are improving on this limitation. Also remember that applets are supposed to be saved on a web server and may not function properly if they are saved in an incorrect folder. The applet name that is used in the CODE and CLASSID attributes is case sensitive, so be sure that you type the name exactly as it is in the name of the class file.

Java Applets and Animation

Many forms of animation can be executed with Java. All types of animation create movement on the screen by drawing successive frames at a relatively high speed (usually about 10 to 20 frames per second). To update the screen many times per second, you must create a new Java thread that contains an animation loop. The animation loop keeps track of the current frame and requests periodic screen updates. Both Listing 14.1 and 14.2 use the <APPLET> method of embedding an applet in an HTML page. In Listing 14.1, you will see a typical applet embedded into a web page. The bold text shows the reference to the class file as well as the parameters for the class file for this applet. Figure 14.1 illustrates how the applet would look in a browser.

Listing 14.1: Embedding a Java Applet into a Web Page

```
<HTML>
<HEAD>
<TITLE>Java Applet</TITLE>
</HEAD>
```

```
<BODY>
<DIV ALIGN="center">
<H2>Java Applets</H2>
<APPLET CODE="RainbowText.class" WIDTH="400" HEIGHT="70">
<PARAM NAME="text" VALUE="CIW Site Designer">
<PARAM NAME="fontname" VALUE="TimesRoman">
<PARAM NAME="fontsize" VALUE="48">
<PARAM NAME="fontstyle" VALUE="BI">
<PARAM NAME="bgcolor" VALUE="880000">
<PARAM NAME="sleeptime" VALUE="100">
</APPLET>
</DIV>
</BODY>
</HTML>
```

FIGURE 14.1 Rainbow text Java applet

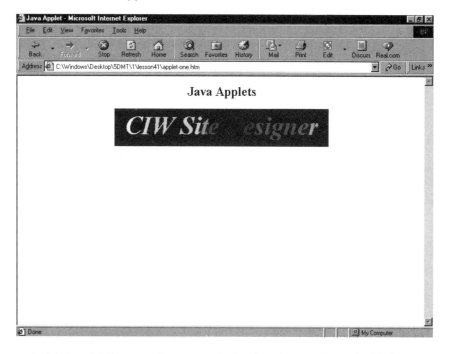

In Listing 14.2, you will see a typical animation applet embedded into a web page. The bold text shows the reference to the class file as well as the parameters for the class file for this applet. Figure 14.2 illustrates how the animated applet would look in a browser.

Listing 14.2: Embedding an Animation Applet into a Web Page

```
<HTML>
<HEAD>
<TITLE>Lake Java Applet</TITLE>
</HEAD>
<BODY>
<DIV ALIGN="center">
<H2>Java Applets</H2>
<APPLET CODE="Lake.class" WIDTH="240" HEIGHT="270">
<PARAM NAME="image" VALUE="sunset.jpg">
</APPLET>
</DIV>
</BODY>
</HTML>
```

FIGURE 14.2 Lake animation applet

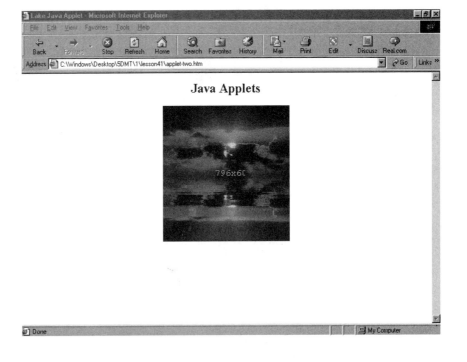

Java Applet Authoring Tools

Java applet tools make it possible for more developers to create Java applets such as animations and web forms and add them to web pages. Some tools are more difficult to use and are geared more toward experienced website design professionals. Applet utilities are beneficial because the website developer can use them to do the following:

- Develop faster

- Create web animations without programming

- Assign motion and hyperlinks to objects

- Create events for user interaction

Once you know how much interactivity you want on your web page, you will need to develop the applets. In addition to resources to help you create applets, you can use applet resources such as the following to help you add applets to your web pages:

- `http://javaboutique.internet.com`

- `www.java.sun.com`

- `http://softwaredev.earthweb.com/java`

These websites offer numerous applets and their corresponding code. If you decide to download Java applets from the Web, you should consider several points. First, many applets are free, which means you can use them without worrying about copyright laws or license fees. However, some applets require you to pay a fee. Additionally, you cannot typically change the name of a class file you download. The Java code makes reference to the class file by name; if you change the name, the code cannot find the class file. You will also need the parameters associated with the applet you download. You cannot create new parameters; the only parameters to which you have access are the ones the developer created before compiling the Java code.

Summary

Java allows website designers to go beyond the limitations of HTML. Java can also be used to create stand-alone programs not necessarily meant for the Internet. Programs written in Java can function in any computer environment, but Java applets will work only in web-based applications. The value of Java to the website developer lies in the Java applet, which is a platform-independent small application that runs in an HTML browser. To this extent, when you're developing a web page, the only use for Java on a client machine is the applet. Applets are embedded in HTML pages for web viewing. They can create animation ranging from simple movement to complex virtual tours.

Java applets are much faster than traditional CGI scripts written in programming languages such as Perl. Java supports multitasking as well, also referred to as multithreading. Multithreading allows more than part of an operation to occur at a time. One thread of the operation might handle user interaction while another carries out a computation. Thus, Java does not make the user wait for one program to finish an operation before starting the next operation.

Java applets allow the website designer to incorporate interactivity into web pages, creating a dynamic web environment for the user. Traditional, static pages can now be made dynamic with the inclusion of platform-independent Java applets.

Exam Essentials

Understand Java and its strengths.   Using Java, the website creator can expect lower development and deployment costs, which means distribution requires less time and effort. Java provides a welcome, necessary, and timely solution to the limitations of authoring HTML-only documents. The Java programming language was designed specifically to address software application development for the Internet. Java supports Internet programming in the form of platform-independent applets. You should understand how and why Java applets are tracked, how Java applications function outside of the Internet, and how Java programming can function in any computer environment.

Understand Java applets and how they function.   Applets (small applications) do not run outside of an HTML browser, but they require a Java-compatible browser in order to be viewed. They are embedded in HTML files, with a reference to a class file that resides on the server. Applets can be used for dynamic events ranging from animation to virtual tours. You should know why Java applets are suited to the Internet and what the requirements are for running them.

Know how Java applets create animation.   Java applets create animation through the use of a Java thread that contains an animation loop. This loop must update the screen many times per second (usually 10 to 20 times) in order to create the animation. Movement is created in all types of animation by drawing successive frames at a relatively high speed.

Key Terms

Before you take the exam, be certain you are familiar with the following terms:

applets	multithreading
class file	object-oriented

Review Questions

1. Which of the following is *not* a strength of Java programs?

   A. They can run on a variety of operating systems and hardware platforms and in a variety of web browsers.

   B. Java provides a welcome, necessary, and timely solution to the limitations of authoring HTML-only documents.

   C. Java can be used for software and Internet programs.

   D. They run entirely on the server side.

2. Which of the following is *not* a characteristic of an applet?

   A. Platform-dependent

   B. Multithreaded

   C. Fast

   D. Runs on client side

3. Which HTML tags are used to embed an applet in a web page?

   A. <OBJECT>, <EMBED>

   B. <APPLET>, <EMBED>

   C. <OBJECT>, <APPLET>

   D. <EMBED>, <IMG>

4. What is one of the disadvantages of using applets?

   A. They are large files.

   B. The whole applet file must be downloaded before it can begin execution.

   C. Applets are not supported by all versions of browsers.

   D. They run on the client side.

5. What is required to run a Java applet?

   A. A Java-enabled web browser

   B. A Java applet–enabled web browser

   C. A Java-enabled client computer

   D. A Java applet–enabled client computer

6. Which of the following best describes Java?

   A. A platform-dependent Internet programming language

   B. A mini-application that executes in the browser of any system

   C. A stand-alone software application not meant for the Internet

   D. An object-oriented cross-platform programming language

7. Which of the following best describes a Java applet?

   A. A small Java application that runs outside of a browser

   B. A stand-alone program that can run in various environments

   C. A platform-neutral mini-application that runs on the server side

   D. A platform-neutral mini-application that runs on the client side

8. What two pieces of information must you know in order to insert an applet into a web page using the <APPLET> tag?

   A. The applet name and the parameters

   B. The class file location and parameters

   C. The applet name and the filename extension

   D. The CODE attribute and the name of the class file

9. When creating animation in Java, which element of the new thread keeps track of the current frame and requests periodic screen updates?

   A. The animation loop

   B. The applet

   C. The <PARAM> tag

   D. The class file

10. Which of the following allows developers who are not experienced with Java to create animation and applets?

    A. Java-enabled browsers

    B. Java 2 Software Development Kit (SDK)

    C. Applet development utilities

    D. The <APPLET> tag

11. From what programming language is Java derived?

    A. C++

    B. Visual Basic

    C. Cobal

    D. XML

12. What does *object-oriented* mean?

    A. It means embedding an applet within an object.

    B. It means that a program can be created once and reused (with some modification) any number of times.

    C. It means that a program can perform simple animation and virtual tours.

    D. It means the program is placed in its own box for distribution.

13. Who is responsible for Java's development?

    A. Microsoft

    B. Netscape

    C. Sun

    D. It's open sourced to the public for development.

14. What does the term *multithreading* mean?

   A. Multithreading allows more than one thread of execution; each thread is a separate process within a document.

   B. Multithreading allows for more than one user to execute an application at the same time.

   C. Multithreading is the same as multiprocessing in that more than one processor is needed to run multithreaded applications.

   D. Multithreading is an older form of program execution.

15. If a Java applet were running through a Netscape 4.*x* version browser, which tag would be more important in the coding?

   A. <IMG>

   B. <OBJECT>

   C. <APPLET>

   D. <NETSCAPE>

16. Which tag is used with the <OBJECT> tag to denote content-specific parameters that may be required by an object at runtime?

   A. <APPLET>

   B. <PARAM>

   C. <IMG>

   D. <CODE>

17. Which attribute does the applet use to reference the location of your Java applet file?

   A. APPLET

   B. PARAM

   C. IMG

   D. CODE

18. What do Java applets currently *not* possess? (Choose all that apply.)

   A. Streaming capability

   B. Caching capability

   C. Dynamic abilities

   D. Multimedia capabilities

19. If you use a free Java applet, what portions of the applet cannot be changed? (Choose all that apply.)

   A. The name of the class file you download

   B. Your web page to accommodate for the applet

   C. The parameters

   D. The name of your home page

20. True or False. Java applets can be used on-site for such things as customizing a new vehicle, tracking real-time quotes of stocks, taking a virtual tour of the human body from the inside out, and simulating a mission to Mars.

   A. True

   B. False

Answers to Review Questions

1. **D.** Java programs run on both the client and server side, making Java a strong solution for writing programs for both software and the Internet.

2. **A.** Applets are platform neutral, allowing them to run in different browsers and on different operating systems.

3. **C.** <OBJECT> and <APPLET> are used to embed an applet in a web page. <APPLET> has been deprecated in favor of <OBJECT> but is still used to accommodate older versions of Netscape browsers, which do not support <OBJECT>.

4. **B.** Although applets run more quickly than CGI scripts, one of the limitations of a Java applet is the requirement that the whole file be downloaded before it can begin running. Java applets have no streaming or caching capabilities, which means the applet must be downloaded every time the user wants to view it.

5. **A.** Because Java applets are platform neutral, all that is required to run them is a Java-enabled web browser.

6. **D.** Java is an object-oriented cross-platform programming language. Java is used to create Java applets, which allow website designers to create dynamic, interactive web pages.

7. **D.** A Java applet is a platform-neutral mini-application that runs on the client side. It runs faster than a CGI script because it runs on the client rather than the server. Applets can be used to create dynamic objects on a web page, such as virtual tours.

8. **B.** You must know the location of the Java applet class file that will perform the function. You must also know the parameters that the class file needs to run. The class file is the Java programming and the parameters will be the HTML element. Without each of these, the other is useless.

9. **A.** The animation loop keeps track of the current frame and requests periodic screen updates. To update the screen many times per second (usually between 10 and 20), you must create a new Java thread that contains an animation loop.

10. **B.** The Java 2 SDK is a stand-alone program that assists both experienced and inexperienced Java programmers in creating animation and Java applets for their websites.

11. A.   Java is a programming language derived from C++. It provides a model for communicating in a secure environment on the Internet and the Web. Java also provides a way to quickly develop applications with minimal disruption or downtime.

12. B.   *Object-oriented* means that a program can be created once and reused (with some modification) any number of times. In object-oriented programming, you can concentrate exclusively on the method for making the program function. Java is an object-oriented programming language, and the Java applet is an object you plug into your web page.

13. C.   Sun Microsystems is responsible for the development of Java. Currently, Sun has released version 2. This advance will further increase Java's acceptance as a suitable alternative to other languages.

14. A.   Multithreading allows more than one thread of execution, and each thread is a separate process within a document. One thread might handle user interaction while another carries out a computation. Thus, Java does not make the user wait for one program to finish an operation before starting the next operation.

15. C.   Netscape initiated support of the <OBJECT> tag with the release of its 6.*x* version browsers. However, the older versions (4.*x* and below) do not support the <OBJECT> tag. Therefore, to remain platform independent, your code must use the <OBJECT> tag as well as the older and deprecated <APPLET> tag.

16. B.   The <PARAM> tag can be used to denote content-specific parameters that may be required by an object at runtime.

17. D.   Applets use the CODE attribute to reference the location of your Java applet file. Java applet files are always class files (with the .class extension). The class file is the compressed Java code that runs the applet function. Two other attributes required by the <APPLET> tag are HEIGHT and WIDTH. These attributes tell the browser how much space the applet needs to display.

18. A, B.   Currently, Java applets have no streaming technologies. In addition, they do not have caching capability, which means that the user must download the applet again upon each subsequent visit to the site.

19. A, C.   You cannot typically change the name of a class file you down-load. The Java code makes reference to the class file by name; if you change the name, the code cannot find the class file. You will also need the parameters associated with the applet you download. You cannot create new parameters; the only parameters to which you have access are the ones the developer created before compiling the Java code.

20. A.   Java applets have extended the HTML page beyond its static nature and allowed website developers to add interactivity and cre-ativity to their websites. Java applets incorporate server-side and client-side technologies to perform a range of tasks, from simple animation to complex virtual tours.

Chapter 15

Databases

THE CIW EXAM OBJECTIVE GROUP COVERED IN THIS CHAPTER:

✓ Define databases and identify major types of database management systems (DBMSs).

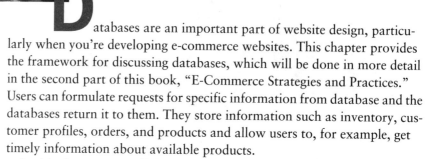

Databases are an important part of website design, particularly when you're developing e-commerce websites. This chapter provides the framework for discussing databases, which will be done in more detail in the second part of this book, "E-Commerce Strategies and Practices." Users can formulate requests for specific information from database and the databases return it to them. They store information such as inventory, customer profiles, orders, and products and allow users to, for example, get timely information about available products.

In this chapter, we will discuss the anatomy of a database, database queries, and database management systems. We'll also discuss tools, products, and programs for creating, accessing, and maintaining databases.

Website Design and Databases

It is important to understand database terminology and structure when connecting databases to websites. You will supply and use information stored on the database, and you will interface with those creating and administering the database.

Databases provide information storage. The information can be retrieved, in whole or in part, by a program designed to accept requests from users. A database can be housed in a single location, such as a PC or mainframe. It can also be constructed from multiple files and housed at different locations on the enterprise; this structure is known as a *distributed database*.

Traditional databases store and organize information in fields, records, files, and tables. This strategy is useful for analyzing information from different points of reference. It also provides a powerful numerical analysis tool.

Hypertext databases store information as objects. The hypertext database format is useful for storing different types of information, such as text, images, and multimedia (video or sound files). All data within this type of database is treated as objects; the data type is irrelevant. Any object within the database can be linked to any other object.

Once you understand how databases function and interact with information, you will understand the potential power a database can add to website design. We'll start by examining how a database is structured.

Database Anatomy

The *schema* is the structure of a database system and often depicts the structure graphically. The schema defines tables and fields and the relationships between them. All database information is contained in tables. A table is a repository of information divided into columns and rows, as shown in Figure 15.1.

FIGURE 15.1 Database table consisting of fields and records

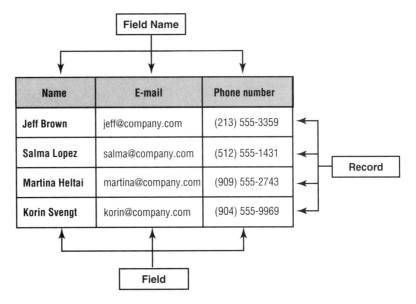

The table consists of *fields* (columns) and *records* (rows). A record includes a complete set of information, such as the name, e-mail address, and phone

number for one person. A set of records is referred to as a file. The table also has field names by which information can be sorted and retrieved, as it would when a list of all phone numbers in the table is output, for example.

Database Queries

The information shown in the table example can be accessed using a *query*. Queries can be thought of as questions from the user to the database table. The database returns a value in the form of a reply to the query; the value is taken from information stored in the database. For example, you could query a database that contained a list of phone numbers for an individual phone number (555-1234) or a range of phone numbers (all numbers beginning with 555). There are three general types of queries:

Menu query   The user is offered a list of options from which to choose.

Query by example   The user states which fields and values are to be used in the query.

Query in which query language is used   A specialized language called Structured Query Language (SQL) is used to retrieve or manipulate information in the database.

Structured Query Language (SQL)

SQL was developed by IBM in 1974 and originally called Structured English Query Language (SEQUEL). Oracle Corporation released the first commercial SQL application in 1979. Currently, Microsoft and Sybase both offer a database management system product called SQL (pronounced "sequel") Server. SQL has become the semistandard language for accessing information from a database.

Other sophisticated query languages, called fourth-generation languages (4GLs), also exist. These languages more closely resemble verbal language than the previous three generations of computer language. The first three generations are as follows:

First generation   Machine language

Second generation   Assembly language

Third generation   High-level programming language (e.g., Java, C++)

Database Management System

Database queries require a *database management system (DBMS)*. A DBMS is an application that allows users to manipulate information in the database. Database management systems follow an accepted format, which began with a DBMS called Vulcan. In 1981, Vulcan was marketed as dBASE II. Borland Corporation produced subsequent versions called dBASE III, dBASE III+, and dBASE IV.

These types of systems vary widely and include the following:

Flat-file   Stores information in a single table consisting of multiple rows and columns.

Relational database management system (RDBMS)   Stores related information in a collection of tables. The data in each field can be related to any field of any table, and a field can be related to many fields or many fields can be related to a single field. New information can form a new table, in which each field can in turn be related one-to-one, one-to-many, or many-to-one. Because queries to a relational database can create new tables, a relational database must be able to grow significantly to handle the demands of new input.

Multidimensional   Uses common field values and stores information in organized groups of records. This type of DBMS is usually generated from an RDBMS.

DBMS Technologies

A DBMS includes the following technologies or support for access, storage, and output of information.

Open Database Connectivity (ODBC)   A standard method for accessing a database regardless of which DBMS or application program is used. Developed by Microsoft, ODBC inserts a database driver as a middle layer between the DBMS and the application to translate requests and commands. Though this technology is language independent, both the DBMS and the application must be ODBC compliant.

Computer Output to Laser Disk (COLD)   Used for storage of information on CD-ROMs.

Binary Large Object (BLOB)   Used for storage of binary data in a single entry. Primarily used for multimedia objects (images, sound, and video).

Virtual Sequential Access Method (VSAM)   Used on IBM mainframes.

Indexed Sequential Access Method (ISAM)   Used for management of information storage and access on a hard drive (also known as indexing).

Online Analytical Processing (OLAP)   Used to analyze information and for data organization.

Report Program Generator (RPG)   Used for generating reports or other output. A programming language developed by IBM in the 1960s.

ActiveX Data Objects (ADO)   Used to access different information types, such as spreadsheets, web pages, and other documents. ADO is one of the main components of Universal Data Access (UDA), a specification developed by Microsoft to access data regardless of its structure.

Java Database Connectivity (JDBC)   Executes SQL statements via Java programming to communicate with any SQL-compliant database. Developed by JavaSoft, a subsidiary of Sun Microsystems.

Database Tools, Products, and Programs

The following list includes some common products used to store and manipulate database information:

Oracle   Top-of-the-line database, large and very powerful. For more information, visit www.oracle.com.

DB2   Family of products developed by IBM that can grow from a single-user to a multiuser database system. For more information, visit www.ibm.com.

Microsoft SQL Server   The high-end database application from Microsoft. For more information, visit www.microsoft.com.

dB2K and dQuery/Web   The latest versions of dBASE, the original DBMS. For more information, visit www.dbase.com.

BDE/SQL Links   The Borland Database Engine allows easy access to local and remote data on any format or platform. It is bundled with SQL Links, a program for integrating client- and server-side database functions. For more information, visit www.borland.com.

Paradox   A desktop database originally produced by Borland. The latest version is Corel Paradox 10. For more information, visit `www.corel.com`.

FileMaker Pro   A database geared toward simple Internet connectivity. Produced by FileMaker, Inc. (previously Claris). For more information, visit `www.claris.com`.

Lotus Domino   A web development tool and line of server-side software used for creating web applications, server-side scripting, database applications, and communication integration. For more information, visit `www.lotus.com`.

Microsoft Visual FoxPro   A web development tool used with Microsoft Internet Information Server (IIS) to build database applications. For more information, visit `www.microsoft.com`.

Microsoft Visual InterDev   A web development tool for programmers to build database applications. Interfaces with FrontPage (for nonprogrammers) to allow teams of people to work together at different skill levels.

Common Gateway Interface   First-generation database/web page integration language. There are many sites on the Internet that offer free CGI scripts for use in websites.

Active Server Pages (ASPs)   From Microsoft, the next generation of database/web page integration languages. Also the programming model for IIS. For more information, visit `www.microsoft.com`.

Allaire ColdFusion   Used to link databases to the Web. For more information, visit `www.macromedia.com`.

Macromedia Dreamweaver UltraDev   Creates databases and data-driven content. For more information, visit `www.macromedia.com`.

Pervasive.SQL 2000i   DBMS available for the Workstation, Workgroup, Windows NT/2000 Server, Linux Server, and NetWare Server platforms. For more information, visit `www.pervasive.com`.

DB-HTML Converter PRO   Generates HTML documents from database information. For more information, visit `www.primasoft.com`.

PowerBuilder   Used for creating web (client-side and server-side) applications. For more information, visit `www.sybase.com`.

SQL Anywhere Studio   Integrates and synchronizes database information. Can be used from laptops, handheld computer, pagers, and smart phones. For more information, visit www.sybase.com.

Summary

Databases provide a method of storing and retrieving information. There are different types of databases (distributed, traditional, and hypertext) and each has its own characteristics and method of storing and retrieving data.

Through queries, users can solicit particular pieces of information from the database. A DBMS (database management system) is required in order to query a database. There are three main categories: flat-file, relational, and multidimensional. Flat-file DBMSs store information on a single table, and relational DBMSs store related information in a collection of tables. Multidimensional DBMSs take their information from relational DBMSs.

There are many tools, programs, and products available to help the web developer and database designer create, access, and maintain databases. These tools range from very large and powerful tools like Oracle to more simple applications such as FileMaker Pro.

Exam Essentials

Understand the function of databases.   Databases provide a means of storing information. Information in a database can be retrieved through the use of a query, which is essentially a question from the user. Databases can be stored in a single location (one PC or mainframe) or at different locations (across a network).

Know the anatomy of a database.   A database is made up of schema, tables, fields, records and files. The schema defines tables and fields and the relationships between them. All database information is contained in tables, which are repositories of information divided into columns and rows. The table consists of fields (columns) and records (rows). A record includes a complete set of information, such as the name, e-mail address, and phone number for one person. A set of records is referred to as a file.

Understand general query types.   There are three general query types: menu query, query by example, and queries in which a query language is used. The menu query option offers the user a list of options from which to choose. The query by example allows the user to state which fields and values are to be used in the query. A specialized language called Structured Query Language (SQL) is used in some queries to retrieve or manipulate information in the database.

Understand database management systems.   A database management system (DBMS) is an application that allows users to manipulate database information. Three of the most common types of DBMSs are flat-file, relational database management system (RBDMS), and multidimensional. You should know these three common database management system types and understand their functions.

Key Terms

Before you take the exam, be certain you are familiar with the following terms:

database management system (DBMS)	query
distributed database	record
field	schema
hypertext databases	traditional databases

Review Questions

1. What does DBMS stand for?

   A. Database Management Schema

   B. Database Management System

   C. Distributed Management System

   D. Database Manager System

2. A database that is constructed from multiple files and housed at different locations on the enterprise is known as which of the following?

   A. Intranet database

   B. Hypertext database

   C. Distributed database

   D. Administration database

3. In a database table, columns and rows are known as _____?

   A. Queries and data

   B. Records and files

   C. Folders and files

   D. Fields and records

4. Which of the following is not a DBMS technology?

   A. Flat-file

   B. Open database management system.

   C. Relational database management system

   D. Multidimensional

5. Which of the following best describes a database management system?

   A. A single or distributed computer system in which a database is stored and managed

   B. A distributed computer system in which multiple databases are stored and managed

   C. An application that allows users to create databases and add information to them

   D. An application that allows users to manipulate database information

6. Which of the following is the term used to refer to the structure of a database system?

   A. Repository

   B. Schema

   C. Record

   D. File

7. Which type of query offers the user a list of options from which to choose?

   A. Menu query

   B. Option query

   C. Query by example

   D. Query language

8. What is a query?

   A. An answer from the user to the database table

   B. An answer from the database manager to the web user

   C. A question from the database manager to the web user

   D. A question from the user to the database table

9. What does a query return?

    A. Value

    B. Record

    C. File

    D. Field

10. What is the second generation of computer language?

    A. High-level programming

    B. Verbal

    C. Machine

    D. Assembly

11. Which type of database provides a powerful numerical analysis tools and is useful for analyzing information from different points of reference?

    A. Database management system

    B. Traditional database

    C. Distributed database

    D. Hierarchical database

12. What term is used to describe a repository for information divided into columns and rows?

    A. Table

    B. Database

    C. Field

    D. Record

13. Which of the following is not a general type of query?

    A. Menu query

    B. Query by example

    C. Relational query

    D. Query using query language

14. Which of the following DBMS is characterized by a collection of tables?

    A. Multidimensional database management system

    B. Hierarchical database management system

    C. Distributed database management system

    D. Relational database management system

15. Which of the following DBMS technologies is used on IBM mainframes?

    A. ISAM

    B. VSAM

    C. OLAP

    D. BLOB

16. Which of the following executes SQL statements via Java programming to communicate with any SQL-compliant database?

    A. JDBC

    B. JBDC

    C. RDBMS

    D. DBMS

17. Which of the following is not a database program?

    A. Oracle

    B. Paradox

    C. Dreamweaver

    D. Lotus Domino

18. Which of the following DBMS technologies is used for the storage of information on CD-ROMs?

    A. CLOB

    B. CSLD

    C. COLD

    D. COOL

19. Which of the following has become the semistandard language for accessing information from a database?

   A. SQL

   B. DBMS

   C. ODBC

   D. JDBC

20. Which type of database stores different types of information as objects?

   A. OLE database

   B. Relational database

   C. Hierarchical database

   D. Hypertext database

Answers to Review Questions

1. **B.** DBMS stands for Database Management System, which is an application that allows users to manipulate database information. Three of the most common types of DBMS are flat-file, relational database management system (RBDMS), and multidimensional.

2. **C.** A distributed database is constructed from multiple files and housed at different locations over the enterprise (network). It is referred to as a distributed database because parts of the database are spread throughout the enterprise system.

3. **D.** Columns ands rows are referred to as fields and records in a database table. A set of information about a customer, such as name, address, and phone number, is referred to as a record. The headings for that information in the database table (Name, Address, Phone Number) are called fields.

4. **B.** Three of the most common types of DBMSs are flat-file, relational database management system (RBDMS), and multidimensional. Open database management system is not a DBMS technology.

5. **D.** A database management system is an application that allows users to manipulate (store, access, and modify) database information. The three most common types of DBMS are flat-file, relational, and multidimensional.

6. **B.** The structure of a database system is referred to as the schema. The schema often depicts the structure of a database graphically, defining tables and fields and the relationships between them.

7. **A.** A menu query offers the user a list of options from which to choose. Other types of queries are query by example and a query using a query language (a query language is a specialized language used to retrieve or manipulate information in a database).

8. **D.** A query is a question from a user to a database. When a user submits a query to a database, the database returns a value, which is derived from information stored in the database.

9. **A.** A query returns a value. This value can be one piece of information, such as an individual phone number, or a range of information, such as all phone numbers starting with the same prefix.

10. D. The second generation of computer language is assembly language. The first is machine, the third is high-level programming, and the fourth is verbal.

11. B. *Traditional databases* provide a powerful means of analyzing numerical data as well as information from different points of reference because they store and organize information in fields, records, and files. This method of storage allows users to analyze data from many different points because of its flexibility.

12. A. A table is a repository for information divided into columns and rows. All database information is contained in tables.

13. C. The three general types of queries are menu query, query by example, and a query using query language. The menu query is characterized by the user being offered a list of options from which to choose. In a query by example, the user states which fields and values are to be used in the query. Query language, a specialized language called Structured Query Language (SQL), is used to retrieve or manipulate information in the database.

14. D. The relational database management system (RDBMS) stores related information in a collection of tables. The data in each field can be related to other fields in other tables. A relational database must be able to grow significantly to handle the demands of new input from queries, which can create new tables.

15. B. VSAM (Virtual Sequential Access Method) is used on IBM mainframes. ISAM (Indexed Sequential Access Method) is used for management of information storage and access on a hard drive. OLAP (Online Analytical Processing) is used to analyze information and for data organization. BLOB (Binary Large Object) is used for storage of binary data in a single entry. It is primarily used for multimedia objects.

16. A. Java Database Connectivity (JDBC) executes SQL statements through Java programming to communicate with any SQL-compliant database. JDBC was developed by JavaSoft, a subsidiary of Sun Microsystems.

17. C. Macromedia's Dreamweaver is a website development and management tool that does not include database access and management. Its Dreamweaver UltraDev does offer database features. Oracle, Paradox, and Lotus Domino are all database programs.

18. C. COLD (Computer Output to Laser Disk) is used for storage of information on CD-ROMs.

19. A. SQL has become the semistandard language for accessing information from a database. SQL was developed by IBM in 1974. Oracle Corporation released the first commercial SQL application in 1979.

20. D. *Hypertext databases* store information as objects. This format is useful for storing information such as text, images, and multimedia (video or sound files). All data within a hypertext database is treated as objects; the data type is irrelevant. Any object within this database can be linked to any other object.

Chapter
16

HTTP Servers

THE CIW EXAM OBJECTIVE GROUP COVERED IN THIS CHAPTER:

✓ Use client-side and server-side programming to enhance website functionality, including but not limited to: HTTP servers.

Where does a web page reside? What happens when a web user requests a web page? A web server stores files in directories, listens for requests for those files, and then responds with the specific file. A web server is required not only for providing a web page when a user requests it but also for the dynamic technologies we discussed in previous chapters. These technologies (Java and Java applets, CGI, ASPs, JSPs, and SSJS) require server-side support in order to function. There are a number of different servers on the market that will satisfy these requirements.

In this chapter, we will explore the definition of a web server, the role ports play in servers, how remote administration of a server can occur through a browser, and some of the more popular web servers.

What Is an HTTP Server?

A *Hypertext Transfer Protocol (HTTP) server* is commonly known as a web server. It serves HTML documents over the Internet, intranets, extranets, local area networks (LANs), and wide area networks (WANs). The HTTP server uses software that listens on TCP port 80 for an HTTP request and then responds with a file from a specific directory configured by the server administrator. Any client computer with a web browser installed, regardless of operating system, can connect to the server by using the http:// addressing protocol. Simply put, a web server stores documents that it presents to a browser when requested.

Some of the more popular HTTP servers include Microsoft Personal Web Server, Apache (a freeware HTTP server application that runs on Unix, Windows NT, and Novell NetWare 6), Netscape Enterprise Server (which can be purchased from Netscape Communications and runs on Unix,

Windows, and Novell NetWare 6), and Microsoft Internet Information Server (IIS). Microsoft IIS is included with Windows 2000.

Ports

A *port* is a logical connection point. Clients access servers using a consensual specified port, depending on the service. Port numbers range from 1 to 65535. Ports 1 through 1023 are reserved for use by certain privileged services and are known as well-known port numbers. Ports 1024 through 65535 are known as registered port numbers and are not controlled by the IANA. Table 16.1 lists some of the well-known port numbers.

TABLE 16.1   Selected Well-Known Port Numbers

Protocol	Port Number
FTP	21
Telnet	23
SMTP	25
HTTP	80
POP3	110
NNTP	119
SSL	443

As noted in Table 16.1, port 80 is the default port that HTTP servers use for web page retrieval. It is implied by URLs that do not specify a port. For example, `http://www.ciwcertified.com` implies `http://www.ciwcertified.com:80`. Webmasters often use a port other than 80 when they want to "hide" certain content; most users cannot connect to hidden content because they do not know the port number used. The webmaster and development team can then access it by specifying the port number (for example, 8181) at the end of the URL entered (`http://www.server.com:8181`).

Another web server default port is 443, which is used for Secure Sockets Layer (SSL) connections. Developed by Netscape Communications, SSL is a protocol that provides data security layered between Transmission Control Protocol/Internet Protocol (TCP/IP) and application protocols (such as HTTP, Telnet, NNTP, or FTP). SSL provides data encryption, server authentication, message integrity, and optional client authentication for a TCP/IP connection. SSL is an open, nonproprietary protocol. Additional information can be found at the Netscape website.

Basic HTTP Server Administration

Ports are also used for remote web server administration by using a port number higher than 1023. Many HTTP server applications provide administration through a browser interface. This type of connection uses a specified port number. A web system's administrator can specify one of these ports for administration and then reference it when entering the URL. For example, if a company uses port 8974 for administration, the administrator would enter `http://www.companyname.com:8974` to access the administration interface. This address would return the default document for web server administration after the client has successfully supplied a username and password.

The browser interface serves as a useful tool for system administration. It empowers the administrator to remotely administer the web server from almost any computer with a current browser on almost any operating system anywhere in the world. For example, this technology permits administration of a Unix server running Netscape SuiteSpot 3.5 from a Macintosh computer running Netscape Communicator.

Server administration can also be performed by applications that run on the server; editing and manipulation of the server configuration can be performed by a basic text editor such as Vi (a Unix text editor). Some, but not all, HTTP server applications offer a local application such as Microsoft Management Console (MMC), shown in Figure 16.1, for server administration. When a local application is the only server administration tool installed, it can help prevent unauthorized administrative changes from the Internet.

FIGURE 16.1 Microsoft IIS 4 MMC server administration

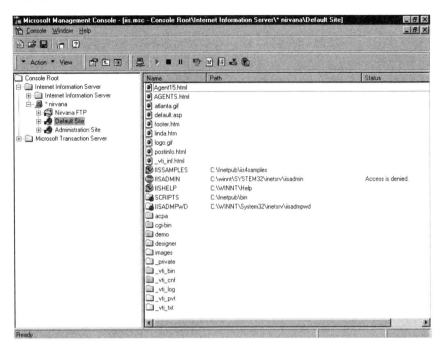

Microsoft Personal Web Server 4

Microsoft has introduced a product that allows a standard PC running Windows 98 to function as a basic web server. The Personal Web Server installs files that enable other PCs on the network to use the HTTP addressing protocol to view its HTML documents through a browser.

Apache

Despite its less-than-user-friendly administration, Apache is probably the most widely used HTTP server because it runs on Unix, Windows, and Novell NetWare 6 and it is free. It is the most widely used, and because it is released as "open source" and with no fee for use, there have been a lot of modifications and modules made for it. You can download the source code and compile it for your machine, or you can download binary versions for many operating systems (like Windows, Solaris, Linux, OS/2, FreeBSD, and many more). There are many different add-ons for Apache, as well. The drawback to Apache is that you may not be able to get support as easily as you can for other commercial servers. However, there are many pay-for-support options now available.

Netscape Enterprise Server

Netscape Enterprise Server is most often the server of choice for corporations that are using Unix web server machines. Netscape offers some of the best of both Apache and IIS in that it is a supported web server with strong backing by a well-known company. It also has a lot of support with add-in components and applications programming interfaces (APIs) to give it more options. This server provides good support and flexibility on Unix and on Novell NetWare 5 and 6 platforms.

Microsoft Internet Information Server (IIS)

The Internet Information Server (IIS) is Microsoft's addition to the web server arena. Windows 2000 Server now comes standard with IIS; however, it will not run on Windows Me. If you are running on an NT system, this might be the best solution for you to implement. It interfaces cleanly with the NT operating system, and it is backed by the support and power of Microsoft. The biggest drawback to this web server is that NT itself is very expensive. It is not meant for running the web services of small businesses, and unless you have all your data in an Access database and plan to run a solely web-based business, it is much more than a beginning website development team needs. However, its connections to Active Server Pages (ASPs) and the ease with which you can connect to Access databases make it ideal for web businesses. Microsoft IIS also allows administration through a browser interface.

Server-Side Technologies

Technological advances have allowed the server to play a more proactive role in distributing dynamic content (as opposed to static HTML content) to users. This capability increases the power of the web server beyond previous standards. Technologies such as Common Gateway Interface (CGI), server-side includes, Active Server Pages (ASPs), and Server-Side JavaScript (SSJS) perform functions on the web server based on client input and then return relevant HTML content. These technologies help eliminate some client-incompatibility issues (e.g., Netscape does not support VBScript). However, dynamic content comes at a price: it slows the server down, especially on high-traffic sites whose servers interpret hundreds, even thousands, of scripts simultaneously.

Many WYSIWYG HTML editors use the HTTP server to help you build dynamic websites without knowledge of programming languages (such as Perl, JavaScript, or VBScript). Examples of such applications include Microsoft FrontPage, NetObjects Fusion, and Allaire ColdFusion. With FrontPage, a designer can build a website that accepts data from an HTML form, writes the data to a variety of file formats, and then sends the data to a specified recipient via e-mail or writes it to a database dynamically. Before such applications were available, these tasks would have required you to write a custom script and configure the server to use Perl (or another language interpreter) to interpret the submission and format the output data. With applications such as FrontPage and its extensions on the HTTP server, you can perform these functions with a few clicks of a mouse button.

Common Gateway Interface (CGI)

Common Gateway Interface (CGI) is not a language; it is a simple protocol that can be used to communicate between HTML forms and an application. CGI permits Macintosh, PC, and Unix computers to post data to or retrieve data from an HTTP server through a web browser. This technology is very powerful but requires some programming knowledge to be used effectively. A number of languages can be used to write CGIs, including Perl, C, or shell scripting.

Files used for CGI commonly use the `.cgi` or `.pl` filename extension and typically reside in a `cgi-bin` or `scripts` directory that permits execute privileges.

One of the most common uses of CGI is the guest book. CGI is not implemented when a browser opens a guest book page from a web server; it is initiated upon submission of the page. The HTML form page specifies within it a path to the directory containing the CGI and the CGI file itself. Upon receipt of the data, the server launches its interpreter and performs the function specified. Once completed, the server returns data to the browser, confirming that the submission was successful. Although returning a confirmation page to the browser is not required, it prevents confusion for the submitter of the data, who might otherwise submit the data more than once.

CGI can also be used to extract data from a database or file on the web server. For example, if a browser requests an option from a selection list, the server can retrieve content that meets that request. This feature eliminates the editing of HTML pages each time new content is added. By modifying the content within the file to which the CGI refers, you have performed the same function. CGI simply requires a directory within the HTTP server with execute permissions enabled and a language interpreter.

JavaServer Pages (JSPs) and Active Server Pages (ASPs)

JavaServer Pages (JSPs) and Active Server Pages (ASPs) are technologies that enable data and applications to be run on the server before information is sent to the client.

JSPs and ASPs code is executed by the server at the time a client requests a page. The server then processes the code and sends the results to the client. In addition, the server removes all the coding instructions it just processed so that the client browser receives only HTML. Thus, the technology is not reliant on browser type, yet it allows real-time data to be sent.

For example, suppose a user wants to obtain their company's latest sales projections. They click a link that will return this information. The sales projection page has either JSPs or ASPs code that instructs the server to go to the database and retrieve the requested information. The information is then written to the file dynamically and sent to the user.

JSPs can run on multiple platforms (as long as Java code processing is enabled). By contrast, ASPs will run effectively only on Microsoft IIS or the new Windows 2000 Server, although it can be ported to other platforms.

This technology is very powerful and is becoming quite popular on the Web because it helps alleviate some incompatibility issues between script and browser. Because the script is run on the server, it makes no difference which browser (or even version) is making the request.

CGI vs. JSPs and ASPs

The main difference between CGI and the new technologies of JSPs and ASPs is in how the processes are executed on the server. CGI must start a new process for each request or client; this type of processing is known as out-of-process. The more processes that are requested, the busier the server becomes. The load can become overwhelming on a server that encounters a high volume of requests and cause the server to slow and even crash.

By contrast, JSPs and ASPs are multithreading processes, which means they utilize the same instance of a process to run operations at the same time, thus reducing the load on the server and allowing more requests to be processed.

Summary

An HTTP server, or web server, consists of software that stores and presents documents to web browsers. The web server listens on a specific port for a request for a web page and then responds with the appropriate file. Some ports are reserved for specific purposes, and others can be used for purposes such as the remote administration of a web server through a browser.

Server-side technologies, including CGI, JSPs, and ASPs, provide dynamic content to web pages. These technologies reside on the server and present content to the web user based on input from the client. They allow website developers to go beyond static pages and create content that is interactive and dynamic.

Exam Essentials

Know the function of an HTTP server.   Simply put, a web server (also known as an HTTP server) stores documents that it presents to a browser when requested. These documents can be served over the Internet, intranets, extranets, local area networks (LANs), and wide area networks (WANs). A client computer, regardless of the operating system, connects to the HTTP server through a web browser using the Hypertext Transfer Protocol (HTTP). The web server listens on the well-known port number 80 for an HTTP request and then responds with a file from a specific directory set up by the server administrator.

Know the use of ports for web servers and server administration.   A port is a logical connection point that allow clients to access servers. Port numbers range from 1 to 65535. Clients and servers use well-known port numbers (ports 1 through 1023) to access certain privileged services, such as FTP, Telnet, SMTP, HTTP, POP3, and SSL. You should also know how ports are used for remote web server administration.

Understand the server-side technologies used to create dynamic content for web pages. Technologies such as Common Gateway Interface (CGI), server-side includes, Active Server Pages (ASPs), and Server-Side JavaScript (SSJS) perform functions on the web server based on client input and then return relevant HTML content. These technologies help eliminate some client-incompatibility issues (e.g., Netscape does not support VBScript). You should also understand the drawbacks of using dynamic content.

Key Terms

Before you take the exam, be certain you are familiar with the following terms:

Hypertext Transfer Protocol (HTTP) server

port

Review Questions

1. What is an HTTP server more commonly known as?

   A. Website server

   B. Web application server

   C. Web page server

   D. Web server

2. Which of the following options is not a network over which an HTTP server can serve HTML documents?

   A. LAN

   B. NAN

   C. WAN

   D. Internet

3. What is the default port for HTTP servers?

   A. 23

   B. 23

   C. 80

   D. 110

4. For what purpose is port 443 used?

   A. NNTP

   B. SSL

   C. SMTP

   D. POP3

5. What is the purpose of an HTTP server?

   A. It stores protocols that are called by various web functions when needed.

   B. It is the default port used by the World Wide Web.

   C. It stores documents that it presents to a browser when requested.

   D. It is a logical connection point to the Web that is reserved for use by privileged services.

6. Which ports are reserved for use by certain privileged services?

   A. Ports 1 through 65535

   B. The default ports

   C. Any port specified in the URL

   D. Ports 1 through 1023

7. Which of the following is an out-of-process server-side technology that can be used to communicate between HTML forms and an application?

   A. Active Server Pages (ASPs)

   B. Common Gateway Interface (CGI)

   C. JavaServer Pages (JSPs)

   D. Secure Sockets Layer (SSL)

8. Which of the following accurately describes the difference between Active Server Pages (ASPs) and JavaServer Pages (JSPs)?

   A. JSPs must start a new process for each request or client.

   B. ASPs can run on multiple platforms.

   C. JSPs can run on multiple platforms.

   D. ASPs must start a new process for each request or client.

9. What is the purpose of a browser interface in web server administration?

 A. It allows web users to input information into forms when server-side technology is used on a web page.

 B. It allows web users to change information input into forms when server-side technology is used on a web page.

 C. It empowers the administrator to remotely administer the web server from almost any computer with a current browser on almost any operating system anywhere in the world.

 D. It empowers the administrator to administer the web server using a current browser on almost any operating system on the same server.

10. Which of the following is a freeware HTTP server application that runs on Unix and Windows 2000?

 A. Apache

 B. Enterprise Server

 C. Internet Information Server

 D. Personal Web Server 4

11. What is the reserved port number for SMTP?

 A. 21

 B. 23

 C. 25

 D. 119

12. Which port does www.ciwcertified.com:7979 run on?

 A. Default port

 B. Port 80

 C. www.ciwcertified.com

 D. Port 7979

13. Which Microsoft server product runs on Windows 98 and functions as a basic web server?

    A. Personal Web Server

    B. SuiteSpot

    C. IIS

    D. Apache

14. Which web server is considered to be the most commonly used?

    A. IIS

    B. Apache

    C. SuiteSpot

    D. Enterprise

15. Which is the most commonly used server for corporations using Unix web server machines?

    A. Personal Web Server

    B. IIS

    C. Apache

    D. Netscape Enterprise Server

16. Microsoft's Internet Information Server comes standard with which operating system? (Choose all that apply.)

    A. Windows 2000 Server

    B. Windows 2000 Professional

    C. Windows 98

    D. Windows Me

17. What does JSPs stand for?

   A. Joint Server Pages

   B. Joint Server Package

   C. Java Server Package

   D. JavaServer Pages

18. What is the main difference between CGI technology and technologies like ASPs and JSPs?

   A. CGI utilizes multithreading processing, whereas JSPs and ASPs use out-of-process processes.

   B. CGI utilizes out-of-process processing, whereas JSPs and ASPs use multithreading processes.

   C. CGI can run on multiple platforms, whereas JSPs and ASPs are limited to a single platform.

   D. CGI runs on a single platform, whereas JSPs and ASPs can run on multiple platforms.

19. What type of privileges must the directory in which CGI files reside permit?

   A. Read

   B. Write

   C. Execute

   D. Delete

20. What is the default port number for POP3?

   A. 21

   B. 25

   C. 110

   D. 119

Answers to Review Questions

1. D. An HTTP server is referred to more commonly as a web server. A web server stores HTML documents and serves them to a browser when requested.

2. B. An HTTP server serves HTML documents over the Internet, intranets, extranets, local area networks (LANs), and wide area networks (WANs). There is no such thing as a NAN.

3. C. The default port for HTTP servers is 80.

4. B. Port 443 is used for SSL (Secure Sockets Layer).

5. C. An HTTP server uses software that listens on a well-known port number (port 80) for a request from a browser. It stores the documents that make up a website and presents them to the browser when requested.

6. D. Ports 1 through 1023 are reserved for use by services such as HTTP, Telnet, SMTP, NNTP, and SSL.

7. B. CGI can be used to communicate between HTML forms and an application, but it must start a new process for each request or client, which is known as out-of-process processing. The server becomes busier as more processes are requested.

8. C. Although ASPs can run on other platforms, it performs best on Microsoft IIS or the new Windows 2000 Server. JSPs, on the other hand, can run on multiple platforms as long as Java code processing is enabled.

9. C. Using the browser interface, the administrator can remotely administer the web server from almost any computer with a current browser on almost any operating system anywhere in the world. You could, for example, administer a Unix server running Apache from a Windows computer running Internet Explorer.

10. A. Apache is a freeware HTTP server application that runs on Unix and Windows NT. Enterprise Server is a Netscape product. Internet Information Server and Personal Web Server are Microsoft products.

11. C. SMTP (Simple Mail Transfer Protocol) runs on port 25.

12. D. The website address `www.ciwcertified.com:7979` runs on port 7979. Port 7979 is an unreserved port, designated by the server administrator. To reach the site, the user would have to know what port the site is running on and include it in the website address.

13. A. Microsoft has introduced a product that allows a standard PC running Windows 98 to function as a basic web server. The Personal Web Server allows individual computers to act as a web server by installing files that enable other PCs on the network to view web pages through a browser.

14. B. Apache runs on Unix, Windows, and Novell operating systems and it's free, so even though it's more difficult to administer than other web servers, it's probably the most widely used. In addition, because it is released as "open source" and there is no fee to use it, it has had a lot of modifications and modules made for it.

15. D. Netscape's Enterprise Server is most often the server of choice for corporations that are using Unix web server machines. This server provides good support and flexibility on a Unix platform.

16. A, B. Internet Information Server (IIS) comes standard with Windows 2000 Server and interfaces easily with the Windows NT operating system. It will not run on Windows Me.

17. D. JSPs stands for JavaServer Pages. JavaServer Pages is a technology that enables data and applications to be run on the server before information is sent to the client.

18. B. CGI must start a new process for each request or client; this type of processing is known as out-of-process processing. By contrast, JSPs and ASPs are multithreading processes, which means they utilize the same instance of a process to run operations simultaneously, thus reducing the load on the server and allowing more requests to be processed.

19. C. Files used for CGI must reside in a directory that permits execute privileges, typically a `cgi-bin` or `scripts` directory. The filename extension is usually `.cgi` or `.pl`.

20. C. The default port number for POP3 (Post Office Protocol 3) is 110.

Chapter

17

Standards Organizations

THE CIW EXAM OBJECTIVE GROUP COVERED IN THIS CHAPTER:

✓ Identify important Internet standards, including but not limited to: Internet governing organizations, RFCs.

The organizations that govern the growth and development of the Internet and the World Wide Web play a vital role in identifying and addressing the issues surrounding these two entities. Each organization has specific tasks for which it is responsible, all contributing to the growth of the Internet and seeing it reach its greatest potential.

In this chapter, we will discuss the Internet governing bodies and the role they play in the growth and development of the Internet. We'll also discuss Requests for Comments (RFCs).

Internet Governing Bodies

Many organizations facilitate the growth of the Internet, including the Internet Society (ISOC), the Internet Architecture Board (IAB), the Internet Engineering Task Force (IETF), the Internet Research Task Force (IRTF), the World Wide Web Consortium (W3C), and the Internet Corporation for Assigned Names and Numbers (ICANN). Each organization handles different aspects of the Internet. Table 17.1 summarizes the main responsibilities of each of the organizations discussed in this chapter.

TABLE 17.1 Standards Organizations and Their Main Responsibilities

Governing Body	Abbreviation	Main Responsibility
Internet Society	ISOC	Heads groups responsible for Internet infrastructure standards.
Internet Architecture Board	IAB	Provides leadership for technical management and direction of Internet; defines rules and standards for Internet operation.

TABLE   17.1   Standards Organizations and Their Main Responsibilities *(continued)*

Governing Body	Abbreviation	Main Responsibility
Internet Research Task Force	IRTF	Researches and develops new technologies, Internet protocols, and the future of the Internet (long-term issues). Consists of small research groups.
Internet Engineering Task Force	IETF	Addresses short-term technical Internet issues; makes recommendations to the IAB for standards approval.
World Wide Web Consortium	W3C	Creates recommendations for languages and technologies for the World Wide Web.
Internet Corporation for Assigned Names and Numbers	ICANN	Allocates IP addresses, assigns protocol parameters, manages domain name systems and root servers. Oversees the accreditation of domain name registrars.

As you can see from Table 17.1, each organization performs an important function in the development of the Internet and the World Wide Web. In the following sections, we'll look at these organizations in more detail.

Internet Society (ISOC)

The *Internet Society (ISOC)* is a professional membership society with more than 150 organizational members and 6,000 individual members in more than 100 countries. It provides leadership in addressing issues that confront the future of the Internet and heads the groups responsible for Internet infrastructure standards, including the Internet Engineering Task Force (IETF) and the Internet Architecture Board (IAB). You can visit the Internet Society's main page at `www.isoc.org`.

Internet Architecture Board (IAB)

The *Internet Architecture Board (IAB)* was created in 1983 and was originally called the Internet Activities Board. Today, the IAB is a technical advisory group that conducts research and makes recommendations to the Internet Society. The IAB is responsible for appointing a chairperson to the IETF. The IAB also provides leadership for the technical management and direction of the Internet and defines rules and standards for Internet operation.

The IAB consists of 13 members, 6 of which are nominated for 2-year terms. The board of trustees must approve IAB membership. One of the main reasons for creating the Internet Society was to provide a legal umbrella for the IAB. Its 13 members attend IAB meetings along with representatives from the RFC Editor, the Internet Engineering Steering Group (IESG), and the Internet Research Task Force (IRTF). You can visit the IAB's main page at www.iab.org.

Internet Research Task Force (IRTF)

The *Internet Research Task Force (IRTF)* is concerned with the evolution of the Internet and long-term issues surrounding it. The IRTF consists of small research groups that research and develop new technologies. It is also concerned with Internet protocols and the future of the Internet.

A chairperson is appointed by the IAB to direct the IRTF. The chairperson appoints members to the IRTF research groups and assigns projects. Research group members are usually individuals, not organizations. The research groups are deemed stable and long term, thus all members and chairpersons must be approved by the IAB. You can visit the IRTF's main page at www.irtf.org.

Internet Engineering Task Force (IETF)

The *Internet Engineering Task Force (IETF)* is concerned with short-term technical Internet issues and makes recommendations to the IAB for standards approval. One IETF task is the standardization of Internet languages such as HTML, JavaScript, and XML. The IETF is also concerned with transporting and routing data over the Internet. It relies heavily on W3C recommendations.

The IETF consists of network designers, operators, vendors, and researchers who are interested in improving the Internet. Anyone can become a member of the IETF. As with the IRTF, work is performed by work groups and managed by area directors (ADs). Much work is conducted via e-mail; members meet three times a year. It is easier to join the IETF than other Internet organizations. You can find the IETF's main page at `www.ietf.org`.

World Wide Web Consortium (W3C)

The *World Wide Web Consortium (W3C)* is located at the Massachusetts Institute of Technology Laboratory for Computer Science. It was founded in 1994 to lead the World Wide Web to its full potential. Note that the W3C is focused on the World Wide Web, not the Internet. The W3C deals mostly with creating recommendations for languages and technologies such as HTML, XML, and Cascading Style Sheets (CSS). It passes these recommendations to the IETF, which creates standards based on the recommendations.

The W3C is led by Director Tim Berners-Lee (creator of the World Wide Web). The W3C is funded by member organizations and is vendor neutral, working with the global community to produce specifications and reference software made freely available throughout the world. The W3C is governed by the Internet Society. You can find the W3C's main page at `www.w3.org`.

Internet Corporation for Assigned Names and Numbers (ICANN)

The *Internet Corporation for Assigned Names and Numbers (ICANN)* is a nonprofit private-sector corporation that was formed in October 1998 to assume responsibility for IP address space allocation, protocol parameter assignment, domain name system management, and root server system management. These functions previously were performed under U.S. government contract by the Internet Assigned Numbers Authority (IANA) and other entities. You can visit the ICANN main page at www.icann.org.

The ICANN does not register domain names but rather oversees the accreditation of domain name registrars. The Shared Registration System established with ICANN's creation allows an unlimited number of registrars to compete for domain name registration business. You can visit the following URL for a list of the companies that are accredited by ICANN to assign IP addresses:

www.icann.org/registrars/accredited-list.html

Requests for Comments (RFCs)

The IAB is responsible for editorial management and publication of the RFC document series. *Requests for Comments (RFCs)* are created to collect information on all types of Internet-related issues, and they give Internet users the opportunity to provide input concerning emerging standards. RFCs are referenced by ID numbers and cover most topics relating to Internet standards and organizations. Currently, more than 2,200 RFCs exist.

Once feedback has been collected for an RFC, the feedback is reviewed and the RFC is considered for standardization. If members of the IAB vote to make the RFC a standard, the standard is declared but the RFC remains an RFC and people can still provide input about it. The declared standard has the same number associated with it as the original RFC. The first few lines in an RFC declare its current state. If modifications to a standard are required, a new RFC is issued to address the problem. Multiple RFCs can define one standard.

To research an RFC, go to the following URL and use the RFC search engine to find the RFC you are seeking:

www.rfc-editor.org/rfcsearch.html

Some RFCs that may interest you are RFC 1855 (Netiquette Guidelines), RFC 1942 (What Is the Internet Anyway?) and RFC 1983 (Internet Users' Glossary).

Summary

The ISOC, IAB, IETF, IRTF, W3C, and ICANN are organizations that govern the development of the Internet and the World Wide Web, and each performs a vital role in their continuing development. The organizations' responsibilities range from providing leadership to all the other groups to overseeing the assignment of domain names and IP addresses. They deal with both short- and long-term technical Internet issues.

The Internet evolves through Requests for Comments (RFCs) by allowing Internet users to provide input concerning emerging standards.

Exam Essentials

Know the Internet governing organizations and their roles.   The Internet Society (ISOC) heads the groups responsible for Internet infrastructure standards. The Internet Architecture Board (IAB) provides leadership for the technical management and direction of the Internet's growth. It also defines rules and standards for Internet operation. The Internet Research Task Force (IRTF) comprises small research groups that research and develop new technologies. It deals with long-term issues such as Internet protocols and the future of the Internet. The Internet Engineering Task Force (IETF) is responsible for short-term technical Internet issues and it makes recommendations to the IAB for standards approval. The World Wide Web Consortium (W3C) deals with creating recommendations for languages and technologies for the World Wide Web. The Internet Corporation for Assigned Names and Numbers (ICANN) handles IP address allocation, protocol parameter assignment, domain name system management, and root server management as well as overseeing the accreditation of domain name registrars.

Know the importance of Requests for Comments (RFCs).   RFCs are used to collect input from Internet users on all types of Internet-related issues. RFCs are considered for standardization once feedback has been collected and reviewed. There can be multiple RFCs for one standard.

Key Terms

Before you take the exam, be certain you are familiar with the following terms:

Internet Architecture Board (IAB)

Internet Corporation for Assigned Names and Numbers (ICANN)

Internet Engineering Task Force (IETF)

Internet Research Task Force (IRTF)

Internet Society (ISOC)

Requests for Comments (RFCs)

World Wide Web Consortium (W3C)

Review Questions

1. Which organization oversees the groups responsible for Internet infrastructure standards?

    A. IRTF

    B. IETF

    C. ISOC

    D. IAB

2. Which organization's website can you visit if you want to find an accredited registrar in order to obtain a domain name for your website?

    A. ISOC

    B. ICANN

    C. IETF

    D. W3C

3. Which Web address should you visit if you want to research an RFC?

    A. `www.isoc.org/rfcsearch.html`

    B. `www.icann.org/rfcsearch.html`

    C. `www.rfc-editor.org/rfcsearch.html`

    D. `www.iana.org/rfcsearch.html`

4. Which of the following is a technical advisory group that conducts research and makes recommendations to the Internet Society?

    A. World Wide Web Consortium (W3C)

    B. Internet Research Task Force (IRTF)

    C. Internet Engineering Steering Group (IESG)

    D. Internet Architecture Board (IAB)

5. What is the role of the Internet Society in relation to the other major Internet governing organizations?

    A. The Internet Society heads the other groups responsible for Internet infrastructure standards.

    B. The Internet Society submits proposals to the other groups.

    C. The Internet Society formed the other groups.

    D. The Internet Society does research for the other groups.

6. Tim Berners-Lee is the director of which group?

    A. ISOC

    B. W3C

    C. IAB

    D. ICANN

7. What is the role of the ICANN?

    A. To manage RFCs

    B. To register Internet domain names

    C. To oversee accredited domain name registrars

    D. To make recommendations to the Internet Society

8. A Request for Comments (RFC) is a document used to collect information on Internet-related technologies and issues. Which of the following accurately describes an aspect of RFCs?

    A. Only W3C and IAB members can contribute input to RFCs.

    B. An RFC being considered for standardization is called a proposal.

    C. When a standard is declared, the RFC remains an RFC with the same number.

    D. After a standard is declared, people can no longer provide input about the RFC.

9. What was one of the organizations in charge of IP address allocation and domain name registration prior to the ICANN assuming responsibility in 1998?

    A. IANA

    B. IETF

    C. IRTF

    D. W3C

10. Which organization is responsible for long-term technical issues surrounding the Internet?

    A. ISOC

    B. IAB

    C. IETF

    D. IRTF

11. What year was the IAB created?

    A. 1981

    B. 1983

    C. 1985

    D. 1987

12. The IAB consists of how many members?

    A. 25

    B. 20

    C. 15

    D. 13

13. Which of the following best describes the members of IRTF research groups?

  A. Individuals

  B. Corporations

  C. Individuals and corporations

  D. Other ISOC members

14. Which Internet organization relies heavily on W3C recommendations?

  A. IAB

  B. IRTF

  C. IETF

  D. ISOC

15. Who can be a member of the IETF?

  A. Other ISOC members

  B. Corporations

  C. Appointed members

  D. Anyone

16. Which organization governs the W3C?

  A. IRTF

  B. IETF

  C. ISOC

  D. IAB

17. How many registrars can compete for domain name registration business?

  A. 1

  B. 100

  C. 1 million

  D. Unlimited

18. Which organization is responsible for editorial management and publication of the RFC document series?

A. IAB

B. IRTF

C. W3C

D. ICANN

19. What is the name of the system that allows an unlimited number of registrars to compete for domain name registration business?

A. Shared Registration System

B. IP Address Registration System

C. Domain Name Registration System

D. Shared Registration Database System

20. Which RFC deals with netiquette guidelines?

A. RFC 1983

B. RFC 1987

C. RFC 1855

D. RFC 1942

Answers to Review Questions

1. C. The ISOC is responsible for overseeing the groups responsible for Internet infrastructure standards, such as the IAB and the IETF. The IAB is responsible for technical management and direction of Internet and the IETF addresses short-term technical Internet issues.

2. B. Although the ICANN does not register domain names itself, you can visit its site to view the list of accredited registrars. The ICANN oversees the accreditation of domain name registrars.

3. C. You can use the RFC search engine at `www.rfc-editor.org /rfcsearch.html` to research an RFC.

4. D. The IAB conducts research and makes recommendations to the Internet Society. In addition, it provides leadership for the technical management and direction of the Internet and defines rules and standards for Internet operation.

5. A. The Internet Society provides leadership in addressing issues involving the Internet and its future. It also heads the groups responsible for Internet infrastructure standards.

6. B. The W3C is led by Director Tim Berners-Lee, who was the creator of the World Wide Web. The W3C was founded in 1994 and primarily deals with creating recommendations for languages and technologies such as HTML, XML, and Cascading Style Sheets (CSS).

7. C. The ICANN oversees the accreditation of domain name registrars. It is a nonprofit private-sector corporation formed in October 1998 to assume responsibility for allocating IP address space, assigning protocol parameters, and managing domain name and root server systems.

8. C. When an RFC becomes a standard, the standard is declared but the RFC remains an RFC. The declared standard and the original RFC are identified by the same number.

9. A. IP address space allocation, protocol parameter assignment, domain name system management, and root server system management were performed under U.S. government contract by the Internet Assigned Numbers Authority (IANA) and other entities.

10. D. The IRTF is concerned with the evolution of the Internet and long-term issues surrounding it. The IETF is concerned with short-term technical Internet issues.

11. B.   The IAB was created in 1983; it was originally called the Internet Activities Board. It is a technical advisory group that conducts research and makes recommendations to the Internet Society.

12. D.   The IAB consists of 13 members; 6 members are nominated for and serve 2-year terms. All members attend IAB meetings with representatives from the RFC Editor, the Internet Engineering Steering Group (IESG) and the Internet Research Task Force (IRTF).

13. A.   Research group members are usually individuals, not organizations. The research groups are regarded as stable and long term, so all members and chairpersons must be approved by the IAB.

14. C.   The IETF deals with the standardization of Internet languages such as HTML, JavaScript, and XML, so it must rely heavily on W3C recommendations.

15. D.   Anyone can become a member of the IETF. It is easier to join the IETF than other Internet organizations. The work of the IETF is performed by work groups and managed by area directors (ADs). A lot is accomplished via e-mail; members meet only three times a year.

16. C.   The ISOC (Internet Society) governs the W3C. Although the ISOC is primarily concerned with the Internet, the W3C deals with the World Wide Web, not the Internet.

17. D.   The Shared Registration System established with ICANN's creation allows an unlimited number of registrars to compete for domain name registration business. The ICANN does not register domain names; it oversees the accreditation of domain name registrars.

18. A.   The IAB is responsible for editorial management and publication of the Request for Comments (RFC) document series. There are currently more than 2,200 RFCs.

19. A.   The Shared Registration System allows an unlimited number of registrars to compete for domain name registration business. You can access the list of accredited registrars at www.icann.org/registrars /accredited-list.html.

20. C.   RFC 1855 addresses netiquette guidelines. You can find this and other RFCs that may interest you by using the RFC search engine at www.rfc-editor.org/rfcsearch.html.

Chapter

18

Applications and Tools

THE CIW EXAM OBJECTIVE GROUP COVERED IN THIS CHAPTER:

✓ Identify ways to use web authoring software to develop websites quickly.

In today's rapid web development environments, developers commonly use production tools to minimize manual processes and maximize development time. These tools enable even those with minimal HTML experience to develop effective websites in a collaborative environment.

In this chapter, we'll discuss how applications and tools are commonly used in web project development. The tools profiled in this chapter were selected to represent the capabilities that are currently available in products that have proven successful in the marketplace. The tools are widely used by individuals and businesses alike and are therefore most useful for demonstrating the concepts of site production and management.

Using Applications and Tools to Assist in Web Design

The ideal combination for a website developer is to use HTML and web authoring software to create dynamic websites. Writing HTML manually is time consuming, and simply using web authoring software can be very limiting. Using both together will allow you to extend the web authoring software when necessary as well as take advantage of the speed and efficiency with which web authoring programs use new technology such as DHTML, JavaScript, and Java applets to create web pages.

There are many web authoring tools and applications on the market today. Each one has its own unique features as well as advantages and disadvantages. In the following sections, we will explore the major categories of web authoring applications and tools: WYSIWYGs, text editors, image editing programs, and web-based animation.

WYSIWYGs

*W*YSIWYG *(What You See Is What You Get) editors* allow the website developer to visually lay out a web page without knowing HTML. As noted earlier, a combination of HTML and a web authoring program is ideal, but WYSIWYGs allow the beginning website developer to start designing web pages without having mastered HTML. These applications require little technical knowledge of website design and the coding that creates web pages.

With today's sophisticated web projects, website management has become as important as design. WYSIWYG programs incorporate three distinct functions within the application to assist in the overall development process:

Site management   Through the use of the various views, preferences, file sharing, and reporting capabilities, management of large web applications is easily integrated.

Page layout and design   Designing web pages is simplified because WYSIWYG editors allow the developer to see how the page looks as it is being designed. Additionally, the developer can choose tables or CSS positioning for page layout as well as use HTML code preservation, advanced DHTML, and multimedia and scripting technologies.

Data connection   Generating content with dynamic data has become an integral part of large web applications. By using the data connection features, it's possible for nonprogrammers to create, add, retrieve, and delete data.

Here are some of the advantages associated with WYSIWYG applications:

Time-saving   WYSIWYGs can dramatically reduce the time required to manage and develop a website. Time is saved by using the WYSIWYG interface for HTML design, and if you use other products with a similar GUI interfaces, such a Microsoft Word and Microsoft FrontPage, the learning curve can be reduced.

Easy to use   You do not need to know HTML to use a WYSIWYG application. They are usually easy-to-learn programs that rely on pull-down menus and mouse usage. You don't have to learn new technology either; using step-by-step instructions provided by the programs, you can create dynamic effects with technologies such as DHTML, JavaScript, or Java applets.

Design oriented   WYSIWYG programs allow website designers to concentrate on the look of the page rather than the technology behind it. Instead of looking at a screen full of HTML, WYSIWYG users can see what the page looks like as it is designed.

Speed   Creating technology like DHTML, JavaScript, and Java applets is much faster in a WYSIWYG program than coding manually or using a text editor because the website designer does not need to learn and then remember the different languages, procedures, and rules for each. HTML effects, such as tables and frames, can be created easily in a WYSIWYG program. Depending on their complexity, it can take considerable time to create these effects manually.

No HTML required   WYSIWYG programs allow novice website designers to create attractive and dynamic pages without learning any HTML. This means that beginning website designers can start creating websites sooner than they could if they had to learn HTML.

Here are some of the disadvantages of WYSIWYG programs:

Lack of control   Changing the HTML in a WYSIWYG program can be challenging. You have to rely on the program to generate the HTML for you and modifying it may not be as easy as going into the code view and writing your own HTML. Many programs require that you use options menus to locate and edit HTML.

Nonconforming HTML   Each WYSIWYG program has its own way of creating HTML. This may create problems for those who try to edit the website through the HTML rather than the design view. For example, some WYSIWYGs put ending tags on all HTML tags and others do not.

Possible lack of features   Some WYSIWYG programs offer server extensions that allow you to create effects that require server-side support, and others offer them as an add-on to the program or not at all. If the features aren't included, the website developer must use other programs to make the site complete. For example, to use all the power and benefits that FrontPage 2000 offers, a developed site must be hosted on a web server that offers FrontPage support using the FrontPage server extensions. The server extensions are available for most Windows and Unix servers at no charge from Microsoft.com.

Job specific   You must learn a WYSIWYG program to use it effectively. If you are using a WYSIWYG in an employment setting and you change jobs, you may be required to learn another program.

Professional website design opportunities   Professional website designers do not rely on a WYSIWYG program alone. They can manually code HTML and all the facets of the other technologies they use. By doing so, they are not reliant on the program and can work in many different environments. If you only know a WYSIWYG program, you are limited to that program and its features and to employment opportunities that include that program.

Examples of WYSIWYGs

The following list includes some common WYSIWYG applications:

Macromedia Dreamweaver   Available for both Mac and Windows. Dreamweaver is a great choice for everyone from the novice to the professional. It is a powerful program that can be customized and extended. For more information, go to `www.macromedia.com/software/dreamweaver`.

Microsoft FrontPage   Available for Windows. FrontPage is ideal for those familiar with other Microsoft products, such as Office Suite. It offers templates and wizards to make the design process simpler, and it comes with server extensions. For more information, go to `www.microsoft.com/frontpage`.

Adobe GoLive   Available for both Mac and Windows. Those familiar with Adobe products will like the similar interface and the ability to integrate other Adobe products. This is a great choice for more experienced designers. For more information, go to `www.adobe.com/golive`.

NetObjects Fusion   Available for Windows. This is a powerful program originally designed for small-business owners. NetObjects Fusion offers a wide variety of design styles and produces cross-browser HTML. For more information, go to `www.netobjects.com/products/html/nfmx.html`.

Namo WebEditor   Available for Windows. This is a good choice for beginning to intermediate website designers. Included with WebEditor is a database wizard for creating database-driven pages. For more information, go to `www.namo.com`.

452 Chapter 18 · Applications and Tools

HotDog PageWiz Available for Windows. Sausage Software produces a simple tool for the novice website designer. It comes with templates to assist in design. For more information, go to `www.sausagetools.com/pagewiz/overview.html`.

HTML Text Editors

HTML text editors differ from WYSIWYG programs in that you need to know HTML in order to use them. *HTML text editors* assist website developers in writing HTML with the use of tag completion tools and validators. Validators are tools that check your HTML and flag such things as missing opening or closing tags and lack of adherence to the HTML recommendation designated for the document.

Here are some of the advantages of HTML text editors:

Full control of HTML HTML text editors allow the website designer to have full control over the HTML used in their websites. With this type of editor, designers can easily modify or change the HTML in pages that were designed in WYSIWYGs.

Professional web design opportunities Employers often seek website designers who know HTML and can use different programs in conjunction with one another. To use HTML text editors, designers must know HTML, which increases their employment opportunities.

Speed Using an HTML text editor to create websites is faster than manually coding a site. Designers can manually code in addition to using an HTML editor to create sites.

Support for other languages Many HTML text editors come with support for other languages and technologies, such as JavaScript, Personal Home Pages (PHP), ASPs, Perl, Java, and Cascading Style Sheets (CSS). Designers can use one tool instead of many to design dynamic websites.

There are some disadvantages to using HTML text editors:

Page layout and design Some HTML text editors do not have a design view that allows website designers to view their pages as they are being created as WYSIWYG editors do. Designers must save their pages and view them directly in the browser, which can slow the design process.

Knowledge of HTML   Designers must know HTML to effectively use an HTML text editor. With a WYSIWYG editor, no HTML knowledge is required, but designers must learn HTML prior to creating sites with HTML text editors.

Examples of HTML Text Editors

Some common HTML text editing applications include the following:

HomeSite   For Windows. HomeSite is an advanced HTML editor used to create complex web pages in seconds. It can also create JavaScript pop-up windows, dynamic expandable outlines, and page transitions. For more information, go to `www.macromedia.com/software/homesite`.

FlexSite   For Windows. This is a shareware program produced by Lincoln Beach Software. It has the same type of interface as HomeSite. For more information, go to `www.lincolnbeach.com`.

BBEdit   For the Mac. This is also a shareware program and it is produced by Bare Bones Software. For more information, go to `www.barebones.com`.

HotDog Professional   Available for Windows. Sausage Software produces a more advanced tool for the experienced website designer. It comes with templates to assist in design. For more information, go to `www.sausagetools.com/professional/overview.html`.

Image Editing Programs

An essential part of any website designer's toolbox is an *image editing program*, ideally one suited for creating and editing web graphics. Designers can use image editing programs to perform such tasks as modifying photographs, creating buttons and banners, optimizing images, and creating special effects with images and text.

Image editing programs come in differing levels of complexity and with various features, such as slicing, HTML conversion, and compression. The major image editing programs on the market today produce web-quality images in both vector and bitmap graphic types.

Images are inserted in HTML files through the use of the <IMG> tag. For example, to insert the image `logo.gif` into a web page, you would use the following HTML:

```
<IMG SRC="logo.gif">
```

Examples of Image Editing Programs

Here are some common image editing applications:

Macromedia Fireworks   For Windows and Mac. Produces vector and bitmap graphics. For more information, go to `www.macromedia.com /software/fireworks`.

Adobe Photoshop   For Windows and Mac. A very popular graphics tool to produce web-quality images. For more information, go to `www.adobe.com/products/photoshop/main.html`.

Adobe Illustrator   For Windows and Mac. A powerful tool for novices and professionals alike. For more information, go to `www.adobe.com /products/illustrator/main.html`.

Jasc Paint Shop Pro   Originally a shareware program, Paint Shop Pro does not have many system requirements and is easy to use. For more information, go to `www.jasc.com/products/psp`.

Corel Graphics Suite   For Windows and Mac. This suite has drawing tools, image editing features, and vector animation software designed specifically for Mac OS/2 as well as Windows environments. For more information, go to `www.corel.com`.

Xara X   For Windows. A vector-based drawing tool that allows designers to create web-quality images and animation. For more information, go to `www.xara.com`.

Web-Based Animation

In addition to HTML in its various versions, web-based animation is one of the most influential media to enhance the Web and Web-browsing experience. *Web-based animation* is used for high-end multimedia websites and presentations. It adds interactivity to your site while conserving bandwidth. The drawback of web-based animation at this time is its dependence on plug-ins to function in the browser.

Web-based animation combines three elements that define its functionality:

Vector Graphics   Web-based animation programs use vector graphics rather than bitmapped graphics such as GIF, JPG, or PNG. As you learned in Chapter 3, vector graphics perform more efficiently on the Web because they are based on mathematical computations rather than the pixel-by-pixel information used by bitmaps.

Streaming Capability   In addition to using vector graphics, web-based animation programs offer another important feature that increases their Web compatibility: streaming capability. Streaming allows multimedia content to begin playing as soon as it reaches its destination—in this case, the client browser. For example, suppose a web-based animation file (also known as a movie) has a total size of 100KB. Using a standard 28.8Kbps modem, a user must wait approximately 28 seconds for the entire file to download before the movie can begin to play. With streaming capability, the movie begins as soon as the initial information about the file reaches the browser. Therefore, the user can begin watching the movie while the rest of the data continues to download.

Timeline   Web-based animation programs use the combination of vector graphics and streaming capability to deliver animation that is created using a timeline. The timeline can be thought of as a series of movie frames. As you develop more frames (or longer timelines), the movie begins to take action. Each movie is a timeline consisting of a series of frames. Each frame contains vector graphics that are opened at a designated sequence and speed, creating the animation.

The timeline enables you to specify the speed at which the movie is played. You can also specify the time the movie starts or stops playing, such as when the user moves their mouse. The motion of the movie is controlled by the timeline, which is divided into frames. Each frame has its designated moment in the movie, and the movie's action in that frame depends on the action you have assigned to it. You need not assign content to every frame.

Web-Based Animation and the Browsers

Currently, web-based animation is not natively supported in browsers. Therefore, for a user to play these movies, their browser needs a plug-in

(Flash/Shockwave or QuickTime). Because web-based animation does not rely on the browser, it is a cross-platform technology, which is another advantage. The 4.*x* versions of both Navigator and Internet Explorer include the Flash plug-in installed by default. AOL and MSN TV (formerly WebTV) also provide some web-based animation support in their browsers.

How Web-Based Animation Works with HTML

When you create a web-based animated movie, you initially create a working file. That file format can then be converted and compressed into a SWF (pronounced "swiff") or QuickTime file, which is then inserted into the HTML code using the <OBJECT> tag (for Internet Explorer) or the <EMBED> tag (for Navigator) to display in the browser. When the browser encounters the SWF file, the Flash plug-in is used to display the movie in the browser. Thus, the only HTML code on which web-based animation relies is the <OBJECT> and <EMBED> tags.

Some sites are created entirely with web-based animation, and others use it to provide simple animation such as navigation menus and rollover effects. Therefore, although web-based animation does not rely on HTML, the two technologies can coexist and complement each other.

Totally Web-Based Animation?

Whether or not to create a site entirely with web-based animation is a question commonly asked by website designers. As with many questions about the Web, the answer depends on many factors.

Although simple in terms of using its graphical interface for development, creating web-based animated movies can still be time-consuming. You must also consider how often your content will need updating, which is a task that is becoming more common in companies but still requires an advanced user. Therefore, if the site you are developing will require frequent content updates, or if inexperienced web-based animation developers will perform updates, it is not advisable to develop a site using this technology entirely.

Common uses for web-based animation generally serve the purpose of adding of rich multimedia design to websites. For example, splash pages provide a quick movie introduction lasting from 10 to 30 seconds before refreshing automatically to the home page. When using the splash page technique, always provide a link for users to bypass the introduction. Return visitors may not want to see the splash again.

Examples of Web-Based Animation Programs

This list includes some common web-based animation applications:

Macromedia Flash   For Windows and Mac. A powerful vector-based animation tool. It is designed to function independently or integrated with Macromedia's other web design tools. For more information, go to www.macromedia.com/software/flash.

Adobe LiveMotion   For Windows and Mac. LiveMotion is Adobe's answer to Flash. It has many of the same features as Flash and can produce files in both the SWF format and the QuickTime format. For more information, go to www.adobe.com/products/livemotion.

Summary

Website designers have a variety of tools and applications available to them to create dynamic sites. Each designer needs to pick the application that will match their abilities as a website developer. Some applications require that other tools are used in conjunction with them, and others are powerful packages that are virtually all-inclusive.

There are two type of website design applications: WYSIWYGs and HTML text editors. WYSIWYG editors do not require knowledge of HTML, whereas HTML text editors do. Each has its advantages and disadvantages, which designers must take into consideration when choosing which ones to use.

Because they can be used to create images for websites, image editing programs are an essential component of a website designer's toolbox. These programs range in complexity and the level of features supported.

You can use animation programs to create vector-based animation for the Web. With these programs, you can add interactive, dynamic content to websites. However, animated content created by these programs must be viewed through a plug-in, which can limit the number of users that can see it.

Exam Essentials

Know the different types of web authoring programs available. WYSIWYG editors allow website designers to create websites without knowledge of HTML. They have interfaces that show the designer what the site looks like as it is being designed. To successfully use HTML text editors, on the other hand, the website designer must know HTML. Image editing programs give the website designer the ability to produce web-quality images in both vector and bitmap graphic types. Animation programs assist designers in creating vector-based animation, which can add interactivity to a website. You should know the different types of web authoring programs and the advantages and disadvantages of using them.

Key Terms

Before you take the exam, be certain you are familiar with the following terms:

HTML text editors

image editing program

web-based animation

WYSIWYG (What You See Is What You Get) editors

Review Questions

1. What does WYSIWYG stand for?

   A. What You Save Is What You Get

   B. What You See Is What You Gain

   C. Where You See Is What You Get

   D. What You See Is What You Get

2. Which of the following is not one of the main functions of WYSIWYG editors?

   A. Page layout and design

   B. Database integration

   C. Site management

   D. Data connection

3. Which of the following is a disadvantage of WYSIWYG editors?

   A. Possible lack of features

   B. Speed

   C. Ease of use

   D. Design orientation

4. Which of the following is not an example of a WYSIWYG editor?

   A. Dreamweaver

   B. FrontPage

   C. HomeSite

   D. NetObjects Fusion

5. What level of website designer is the WYSIWYG geared toward?

   A. Beginner

   B. Intermediate

   C. Advanced

   D. Manual coder

6. How do HTML text editors differ from WYSIWYG editors?

   A. HTML text editors do not require HTML knowledge, whereas WYSIWYG editors do.

   B. HTML text editors require programming language knowledge, but WYSIWYG editors do not.

   C. HTML text editors require HTML knowledge, and WYSIWYG editors do not.

   D. HTML text editors do not require programming language knowledge, but WYSIWYG editors do.

7. Which of the following is not an advantage of an HTML text editor?

   A. Speed

   B. HTML control

   C. Professional web design

   D. HTML knowledge

8. Why is "professional web design opportunities" an advantage of HTML text editing programs and a disadvantage of WYSIWYG programs?

   A. Knowing HTML, as is required by HTML text editing programs, gives website designers more employment opportunities because they are not limited to any particular program.

   B. Knowing HTML, as is required by WYSIWYG programs, gives website designers more employment opportunities because they are not limited to any particular program.

   C. Knowing HTML, as is required by HTML text editing programs, gives website designers more employment opportunities because they are limited to a particular program.

   D. Knowing HTML, as is required by WYSIWYG editing programs, gives website designers more employment opportunities because they are limited to a particular program.

9. Which of the following is not an example of an HTML text editor?

   A. HomeSite

   B. BBEdit

   C. HotDog PageWiz

   D. HotDog Professional

10. Why are image editing programs an important part of a website designer's toolbox?

   A. They are essential to creating clear, readable text for websites.

   B. They allow designers to write their own HTML.

   C. They allow designers to create dynamic sites through the use of animation.

   D. They allow designers to create images suitable for use in websites.

11. Which of the following is an example of an image editing program?

   A. Flash

   B. NetObjects Fusion

   C. LiveMotion

   D. Fireworks

12. Which of the following is an image editing program made by Jasc?

   A. Photoshop

   B. Paint Shop Pro

   C. Illustrator

   D. Graphics Suite

13. What is the name of the element that is an individual unit in an animated movie?

   A. Frame

   B. Fragment

   C. Layer

   D. Cell

14. Which of the following best describes the timeline of a web-based animated movie?

    A. The area in which you place objects used in a movie

    B. A series of movie frames used to control the movie and how it plays

    C. A canvas used to control and position objects on the stage

    D. A tool used to draw, color, move, or resize objects on the stage

15. Which of the following describes the relationship between web-based animated movie files and HTML?

    A. Web-based animated movie files and HTML are competing technologies.

    B. Web-based animated movie files are supported by all browsers, whereas HTML is not.

    C. Web-based animated movie files create compact files, whereas HTML does not.

    D. Web-based animated movie files can be embedded into HTML.

16. The motion of a web-based animated movie is controlled by
    _____ .

    A. The frames, which combine to form the stage

    B. The layers, which combine to form a timeline

    C. The timeline, which is divided into frames

    D. The stage, which is divided into layers

17. What is the main limitation of web-based animation?

    A. It requires different tags for Internet Explorer and Netscape Navigator in order to be embedded in HTML.

    B. It relies on a plug-in to be viewed in a browser.

    C. It produces large files that take a long time to download.

    D. It uses vector-based graphics.

18. What is one of the main drawbacks to creating a website using only web-based animation?

   A. Web-based animation programs are expensive.

   B. It is difficult to learn web-based animation programs.

   C. Updating the content requires an advanced user.

   D. Web-based animation websites are very expensive to develop.

19. What are two of the most common web-based animation programs?

   A. Flash and LiveMotion

   B. Flash and NetObjects Fusion

   C. LiveMotion and Fireworks

   D. LiveMotion and Freehand

20. Which tag is used to insert an image into a web page?

   A. <OBJECT>

   B. <EMBED>

   C. <IMG>

   D. <INSERT>

Answers to Review Questions

1. D.   WYSIWYG stands for What You See Is What You Get. WYSIWYG editors allow website designers to easily create websites without knowing HTML or other web technologies.

2. B.   Database management is not one of the main functions of WYSIWYG editors. WYSIWYG editors perform page layout, site management, and data connection.

3. A.   Lack of features is a disadvantage of WYSIWYG editors. Some support server-side functions but others do not, for example. You sometimes need to use other programs to supplement WYSIWYG editors with limited features.

4. C.   HomeSite is a text editor, not a WYSIWYG editor. Text editors require HTML knowledge and WYSIWYG editors do not.

5. A.   The WYSIWYG editor is geared toward the beginning website designer because HTML knowledge is not required to use it effectively.

6. C.   HTML text editors require HTML knowledge, and WYSIWYG editors do not. HTML text editors are designed so those who have existing HTML knowledge can efficiently create websites using HTML.

7. D.   HTML text editors require HTML knowledge. This excludes those who do not know HTML from using these types of programs.

8. A.   Knowing HTML gives website designers more employment opportunities because they are not limited to any particular program. WYSIWYG applications do not require HTML knowledge, and they limit designers to specific programs and employers who support those programs.

9. C.   HotDog PageWiz is an example of a WYSIWYG editor.

10. D.   Image editing programs allow designers to create images for their websites; for example, they can use the programs to modify photographs, and create buttons and banners and special effects with text and images.

11. D.   Fireworks is an example of an image editing program. It is produced by Macromedia, and you can use it to create vector and bitmap images for the Web.

12. B. Jasc produces Paint Shop Pro, an image editing program that is easy to use and has low system requirements.

13. A. A frame is the individual unit in an animated movie. The animation is produced by playing the frames in the movie.

14. B. The timeline can best be described as a series of movie frames used to control the movie and how it plays. Content is placed in the individual frames of the timeline and the sequence of the frames playing produces the movie.

15. D. Web-based animated movie files can be embedded into HTML using the <OBJECT> (for Internet Explorer) or <EMBED> (for Navigator) tags. When the browser encounters the animated movie file, the Flash plug-in is used to display the movie in the browser.

16. C. The motion of a web-based animated movie is controlled by the timeline, which is divided into frames. The timeline can be thought of as a series of movie frames. As you develop more frames (or longer timelines), the movie begins to take action.

17. B. The main limitation of web-based animation is its reliance on a plug-in to be viewed in a browser. If the browser doesn't have a Flash/ Shockwave or QuickTime plug-in, web-based animation cannot be viewed.

18. C. Updating content with HTML is becoming more common in the workplace, but updating the content of a web-based animation site requires an advanced user. Because of the advanced skills required, it is not advisable to use this technology for an entire website if an inexperienced user will be responsible for making frequent updates or changes to the site.

19. A. Flash and LiveMotion are two of the most common web-based animation programs. Both use streaming technology, a timeline, and vector graphics to create web-based animated movies.

20. C. The <IMG> tag is used to insert an image in a web page. <OBJECT> and <EMBED> are used to add content such as multimedia to a page. <INSERT> is not a valid HTML tag.

Chapter

19

Website Publishing

Until you publish your website to a web server for viewing over the Internet, you don't have a finished product. Chapter 18, "Applications and Tools," addressed the WYSIWYG and HTML text editing programs used for creating websites. Those applications can also be used to publish your website to a web server. If you manually code, you can use a third-party FTP program to transfer your website to the server.

In this chapter, we will discuss what is involved in website publishing, the different options available for publishing, and issues to consider when evaluating your hosting options.

Publishing Your Website

The final step in website development is publishing your site to the Internet. You can publish your site in several ways depending on the tools used to create it. You can either transfer your files to a web server using an FTP client (WS_FTP Pro is the one we'll discuss in this chapter) or use a WYSIWYG editor or an HTML text editing application.

File Transfer Protocol (FTP), a networking protocol used to transfer files between computers, allows file transfer without corruption or alteration. It can be used over the Internet or outside of it, such as on an intranet. Transferring files over the Internet requires an FTP client on the user's computer and a destination FTP server to receive the files. FTP can also be used to transfer files to an HTTP (web) server, provided that server is also running FTP. Before you can transfer your website files, however, you must decide where your site will be hosted.

Website Hosting

To make your website available to users on the World Wide Web, you need a web server to "host" your site. The server must have a dedicated (24 hours per day, 7 days per week) connection to the Internet so that any time your users want to obtain information from you, they can. You can host your own web server in-house, or you can have an Internet service provider (ISP) host your site.

When it is time to publish your website, you generally need three pieces of information: the IP address or URL of the computer to which you want to copy your site, a username, and a password (the username and password are needed to access and publish your content to that server).

The IP address or URL usually refers to a web server that will make your content available to users. The web server to which you choose to publish might use the URL of a corporate website or intranet site. The address can also refer to a backup server in case your web server crashes. It is highly recommended that you keep a backup copy of all your website files; do not rely on your web server for the backup copy.

Your username and password to access the web server are of critical importance and should be kept secure. The only people able to transfer content to your servers via FTP are those who have the passwords. Usernames and passwords ensure that only authorized persons, rather than any skilled Internet user, can publish or change content on your site.

Advantages and Disadvantages of Hosting

Deciding how to host your website for public access can be difficult. You must choose where to host the information and analyze the cost, speed, and reliability of that decision:

Cost   The cost of hosting your website can be the largest expense associated with site development. You will incur charges from an ISP that hosts your site, or you will pay costs associated with hosting and maintaining your own server in-house.

One disadvantage of hosting your website internally is the startup cost of purchasing a server and a dedicated connection to the Internet. These can be very costly. If you host your site internally, you might also need to hire personnel to continuously maintain the servers and network connectivity for your company. If you contract an ISP to host your site, it will provide all equipment, service, and maintenance for a fee. However, you will lose some control and options that you would have if you maintained your own servers.

Speed   You must also consider how your server will be connected to the Internet. Internet connection is usually referred to as *bandwidth*, which is the amount of data that can be transmitted in a fixed amount of time. The more bandwidth you have available, the faster users can access your website. However, as the bandwidth increases, so does the price.

A disadvantage of hosting internally is that you must pay all costs associated with establishing the best Internet connection possible and keeping that connection in service. If your website is hosted externally, you generally have higher bandwidth available to you without the setup costs.

Reliability   The reliability of the web server is another important issue. Where your website is hosted (internally or externally) is not a factor in your web server's reliability; you must count on the resources available to you to keep the server functioning properly.

If your website is hosted externally, you will share a server with many different companies, which can affect the reliability of your site. If something happens to another site and the server has to be taken offline to repair the problem, your site will be affected. If you host your website internally, your site is the only site on your server and you cannot be compromised by sites outside of your control. Consider this question seriously: If the server fails in the middle of the night, who is going to restore it?

Comparing Web Publishing Tools

One advantage of using web publishing software (WYSIWYG editors or HTML text editing programs) to perform publishing activities is that the FTP tool is already built into the software. You need not obtain, install, and learn another piece of software to publish your site.

If you are using some other authoring tool or hand-coding your Web pages, you need only an FTP client for publishing. WS_FTP Pro is downloadable for a free trial period and provides a reliable FTP publishing program.

FrontPage publishes the entire website at one time, which means that you can publish multiple files and folders simultaneously. This process ensures that no files are overlooked. However, you cannot copy one file at a time. If you want to publish only one file, WS_FTP Pro and Dreamweaver both allow you to select the file(s) you want to upload. Another advantage of WS_FTP Pro and Dreamweaver is that you can see both the local and remote servers at the same time. FrontPage allows you to see only one or the other.

Consider your page design method and tools and the software available to you. Fitting these pieces together will help you decide which web publishing method is best for you and your project.

Web Publishing with FTP

Using FTP is the generic method of publishing a website. Many tools are available for this purpose. We will examine how to transfer files with the WS_FTP Pro application.

WS_FTP Pro

WS_FTP Pro is shareware, and it has some features that make transferring files over the Internet simple. The graphical interface was designed with the beginning FTP user in mind, but it includes more complex features for advanced users as well.

Figure 19.1 shows the WS_FTP Pro version 7.04 dialog box. The screen's left window lists all the files and directories on the local machine; the right window lists all the files and directories on the remote machine to which you are connecting. Both areas are scrollable and function in a manner similar to Windows Explorer in the Microsoft Windows environment.

The graphical interface provides buttons for the most common functions. You will notice two sets of these buttons in the WS_FTP Pro dialog box. The button set on the left controls your local machine settings, and the button set on the right controls the remote machine settings.

FIGURE 19.1 WS_FTP Pro dialog box

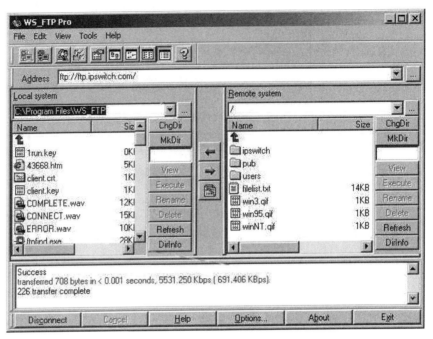

You click on the buttons to perform common operations, such as deleting and renaming files. You can use the arrows in the middle to transfer files from the local machine to the remote machine (and vice versa). WS_FTP Pro also supports the drag-and-drop method for moving files, and it bundles utilities that allow your client to perform common Unix networking functions, such as Ping, Whois, traceroute, and nslookup.

Though WS_FTP Pro is a basic program, it keeps track of your FTP priorities. When you open your profiles, you see only the information you need to connect to a server. All other information, such as default port numbers and file mask settings, remains in the background.

WS_FTP Pro provides advanced support for handling frequently visited FTP sites, time-outs, port numbers, and passive file transfers. WS_FTP Pro also enables remote-to-remote transfers and has command-line support for automating file maintenance operations. It retains profiles of previously accessed servers.

WS_FTP Pro allows you to specify ASCII, binary, or auto-detect as your default transfer mode as well as a different transfer mode for any file extension. You can also configure WS_FTP Pro to automatically convert file extensions on the local or remote machine to ensure that all filenames are uniform (e.g., every `.htm` filename extension becomes `.html`).

WS_FTP Pro is shareware provided by Ipswitch, Inc. Go to `www.ipswitch .com/Products/file-transfer.html` to download a trial version of the software for an evaluation period or to purchase a full copy. A free version of the software, WS_FTP LE, can be downloaded and used for an unrestricted period of time, but it has limited features.

Publishing Your Site with WS_FTP Pro

When you publish with WS_FTP Pro, you will enter in the Session Properties dialog box all the information you need to connect to your web server. If you tend to copy files to the same location repeatedly, you might want to set up a profile. A profile will save all relevant information from a given FTP session and recall it for you.

Once you have connected to the web server of your choice, select the files you want to transfer. As mentioned earlier, the arrows between the left and right panes on the interface allow you to move files between the local and remote machines. For example, if you select the arrow pointing toward the remote machine, you will copy selected files from your local machine to the remote machine. You can perform this transfer function in either direction.

It is recommended that you copy files in binary format instead of ASCII. ASCII format saves information as 7 bits of code and adds a 0 to the leftmost side; binary format saves information as 8 bits of code. Bits are the 1s and 0s that make up the information in your file or program at the lowest levels. The basic operating system was designed with binary naming in mind, so copying files in binary format increases the chance of proper processing.

Web Publishing with Web Publishing Software

As discussed in Chapter 18, many WYSIWYG editors and HTML text editing programs have built-in publishing capabilities designed to simplify the task of publishing your websites. These programs allow you to save your web pages and sites on the local system and then transfer your files to a fully functional web server via FTP or HTTP. One disadvantage of relying on these types of programs for your website publishing is availability. If you need to transfer your site's files and you're not at a computer that has the particular program you need, you will be unable to transfer them without the use of a third-party program like WS_FTP Pro.

Your website consists of several components: web pages, images, text, and hyperlinks, to mention a few. As you build your site in a WYSIWYG editor, many folders are created to store the different site elements. For example, in FrontPage a site is referred to as a Web, and FrontPage creates a Web folder for each new Web. The Publish Web command accesses the Web folder and copies the entire structure to a web server of your choice. Once you move your Web with FrontPage, your website will mirror the structure you created on your own machine. In Dreamweaver, you use the Site Definition dialog boxes to transfer your website (which is referred to as a root folder). In HomeSite, you use the Deployment Wizard to transfer your website.

Summary

After you have finished creating your website, the final step is to publish it to a web server. Publishing your website to a web server requires an FTP program. You can use a third-party FTP program like WS_FTP Pro or the publishing feature of a WYSIWYG editor or HTML text editing program. You can host your website at a web hosting service, such as an ISP, or you can use your own web server. When considering your options for hosting, you should keep cost, speed, and reliability in mind. Support of the web server is also a crucial factor in making this decision.

Exam Essentials

Compare in-house website hosting to hosting with an Internet service provider. In-house website hosting gives you more control over the website and does not expose you to reliability issues that web servers hosting multiple sites may encounter. However, hosting a website in-house can be very expensive because of server hardware and software and high-speed Internet connection requirements. Hosting with an ISP does not require the resource dedication that the in-house solution does, but reliability can come into question when you are sharing a server with other websites.

Compare publishing a website with an FTP program to publishing with WYSIWYG editors or HTML text editing applications. Both solutions require making an FTP connection between the client computer and the web server. Using an FTP program allows you to transfer your website if you manually code it or if you are in a location that does not have a WYSIWYG editor or HTML text editing program available. Publishing a website through a WYSIWYG editor or HTML text editing program allows you to create your website and publish it within one environment.

Key Terms

Before you take the exam, be certain you are familiar with the following terms:

bandwidth   File Transfer Protocol (FTP)

Review Questions

1. What does two things are required to transfer files over a network (including the Internet)?

   A. An FTP client and a password

   B. An FTP client and an FTP server

   C. A username and a password

   D. An FTP client and an ISP

2. What is the purpose of FTP?

   A. FTP is an Internet procedure used to transfer files between computers.

   B. FTP is a networking protocol used to transfer files between computers.

   C. FTP is a networking protocol used to track database transactions.

   D. FTP is an Internet protocol used to transfer applications between computers.

3. What does ISP stand for?

   A. Internet service provider

   B. Internet server provider

   C. Information service provider

   D. Internet service procedure

4. What two options exist for website hosting?

   A. Using an FTP program or using a website hosting service

   B. Using an ISP or a website hosting service

   C. Using an FTP program or a WYSIWYG program

   D. Hosting the website yourself or using a website hosting service

5. What three factors must be considered when deciding how to host your website?

   A. Speed, method of FTP, and cost

   B. Space, reliability, and capabilities of server administrator

   C. Speed, reliability, and cost

   D. Server type, reliability, and cost

6. How can you make your website available to users on the World Wide Web?

   A. Transfer files using FTP to a web server with FTP access.

   B. Create the site on an HTTP server.

   C. Host the site on a web server with a dedicated Internet connection.

   D. Transfer files to an FTP server with a dedicated Internet connection.

7. What three pieces of information do you need to publish your website?

   A. The address of the server and a username and password to access the server

   B. The username and password of the server and permission to publish to it

   C. The website name, the filenames, and the FTP site to which you can connect to transfer the files

   D. The name and address of the Internet service provider that will host the site and the cost of the service

8. Which of the following factors is a disadvantage of contracting an ISP to host your website?

   A. You lose some control over the site.

   B. Your site is the only site on the server.

   C. You generally have less bandwidth available to you.

   D. You must pay startup costs for server, connection, and personnel.

9. Which of the following applications is strictly an FTP program?

    A. Paint Shop Pro

    B. WS_FTP Pro

    C. FrontPage 2000

    D. Dreamweaver 4

10. Binary format saves information as _____ bits of code?

    A. 7

    B. 8

    C. 9

    D. 10

11. What is one disadvantage of hosting your site internally?

    A. Server space

    B. Startup cost

    C. ISP charges

    D. FTP program

12. What is the definition of bandwidth?

    A. The bit speed that can be transmitted in a fixed amount of time

    B. Amount of data that can be stored in a fixed amount of time

    C. Amount of data that can be transmitted in a given session

    D. Amount of data that can be transmitted in a fixed amount of time

13. What is one advantage of using a WYSIWYG editor or HTML text editing program to perform publishing activities?

    A. The FTP tool is already built into the software.

    B. The FTP function is generally faster in a WYSIWYG editor or HTML text editing program.

    C. FTP tools in WYSIWYG editors and HTML text editing programs can access HTTP servers and third-party FTP programs cannot.

    D. The FTP function is generally more reliable in a WYSIWYG editor or HTML text editing program.

14. Where should a backup copy of your website files be stored?

    A. Externally, at your web hosting service.

    B. Externally, at your ISP.

    C. Internally, where you have access to it.

    D. There is no need for a backup copy as long as you have a full version on the web server.

15. Which of the following programs is free?

    A. WS_FTP LE

    B. WS_FTP Pro

    C. WS_FTP Lite

    D. WS_FTP SE

16. Which of the following programs does not allow you to copy one file at a time?

    A. FrontPage

    B. Dreamweaver

    C. WS_FTP Pro

    D. WS_FTP LE

17. WS_FTP Pro and Dreamweaver allow you to _____ .

    A. Upload files remotely

    B. See both the local and remote servers at the same time

    C. Upload files locally

    D. See only the local or the remote server but not both at the same time

18. What is one disadvantage of using a WYSIWYG editor or HTML text editing program for transferring your website to a web server?

    A. Availability

    B. Reliability

    C. Speed

    D. Cost

19. Which company produces WS_FTP Pro?

    A. Macromedia

    B. Microsoft

    C. RealPlayer

    D. Ipswitch

20. What does the left window of the WS_FTP Pro window list?

    A. All the websites on the remote machine

    B. All the websites on the local machine

    C. All the files and directories on the local machine

    D. All the files and directories on the remote machine

Answers to Review Questions

1. B. You need an FTP client and an FTP server to transfer files across a network. The FTP client must have FTP software running on it and the user must have a username and password to access the FTP server.

2. B. FTP is a networking protocol used to transfer files between computers. It can be used over the Internet or outside of it. It allows file transfer without corruption or alteration. To transfer files, the user needs an FTP client to send the files and a destination FTP server to receive the files.

3. A. ISP stands for Internet service provider. An ISP provides web hosting and Internet connection services.

4. D. The two options available for website hosting are hosting the site yourself on an in-house web server or using a website hosting service, such as an ISP. Each method has advantages and disadvantages.

5. C. First, you must consider speed, or how fast users can access your site. Reliability, the resources available to you to keep your website running consistently, is also an important consideration. Finally, you must consider the cost; compare the investment you need to make in all the hardware and software you would need to host your site internally versus the monthly fee you would need to pay to have a website hosting service host your site.

6. A. To make your website available to users on the World Wide Web, you must use FTP to transfer files to a web server with FTP access. FTP is a networking protocol that is used to transfer files between computers and allows file transfer without corruption or alteration.

7. A. You need the address of the server and a username and password to access the server. The IP address or URL usually refers to a web server that will make your content available to users. Your username and password to access the web server are of critical importance and should be kept secure. Usernames and passwords ensure that only authorized persons can publish or change content on your site.

8. A. One potential disadvantage of contracting an ISP to host your website is the loss of some control over the site. You may lose the ability to do maintenance on the site when you choose, and if the site goes down, you have to wait for the ISP's personnel to correct the problem.

9. B. WS_FTP Pro is a site publishing program that does not have site creation capabilities. It is strictly an FTP application. FrontPage 2000 and Dreamweaver 4 are site creation and publishing programs. Paint Shop Pro is an image editing program.

10. B. Binary format saves information as 8 bits of code, whereas ASCII format saves information as 7 bits of code and adds a 0 to the leftmost side. Bits are the 1s and 0s that make up the information in your file or program at the lowest levels. Because the basic operating system was designed with binary naming in mind, copying files in binary format increases the chance that files will be properly processed.

11. B. The startup cost of purchasing a server and a dedicated connection to the Internet can be very costly. Hiring personnel to continuously maintain the servers and network connectivity for your company can add to the cost.

12. D. Bandwidth is the amount of data that can be transmitted in a fixed amount of time. The more bandwidth you have available, the faster users can access your website. Internet connection is also referred to as bandwidth.

13. A. One advantage of using a WYSIWYG editor or HTML text editing application to perform publishing activities is that the FTP tool is already built into the software. You need not obtain, install, and learn another piece of software to publish your site.

14. C. It is highly recommended that you keep a backup copy of all your website files; do not rely on your web server for the backup copy.

15. A. WS_FTP LE is a free program with limited features. WS_FTP Pro is available for a trial period and can be purchased after that period expires.

16. A. FrontPage publishes the entire website at one time, which means that you can publish multiple files and folders simultaneously. This process ensures that no files are overlooked. However, you cannot copy one file at a time. If you want to publish only one file, WS_FTP Pro and Dreamweaver both allow you to select the file(s) you want to upload.

17. B. WS_FTP Pro and Dreamweaver allow you to see both the local and remote servers at the same time. FrontPage allows you to see only one or the other.

18. A. One disadvantage of relying on a WYSIWYG editor or HTML text editing program for your website publishing is its availability. If you need to transfer your site's files and you're are not at a computer that has the WYSIWYG editor or HTML text editing program you need, you will be unable to transfer them because you may not know how to use an FTP program like WS_FTP Pro.

19. D. Ipswitch produces WS_FTP Pro. It can be downloaded from the Internet for a free trial period or for purchase.

20. C. The left window of the WS_FTP Pro screen lists all the files and directories on the local machine; the right window lists all the files and directories on the remote machine.

E-Commerce Strategies and Practices

Chapter

20

Electronic Commerce Foundations

THE CIW EXAM OBJECTIVE GROUP COVERED IN THIS CHAPTER:

✓ Define e-commerce, and identify its current and potential effects on business operations and revenue generation.

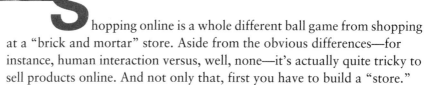

Shopping online is a whole different ball game from shopping at a "brick and mortar" store. Aside from the obvious differences—for instance, human interaction versus, well, none—it's actually quite tricky to sell products online. And not only that, first you have to build a "store."

As an e-commerce design engineer, you have the heavy responsibility of assisting others in creating a functional, inviting, and secure environment for customers. Every business will hold different needs that you must evaluate to produce the best design. And much like a traditional store, you want customers to return again and again. How can you accomplish all of that?

Well, you need to start somewhere, so in this chapter, we'll introduce e-commerce by discussing the fundamental background for understanding the Web commerce model, and we'll explore the advantages of deploying a Web commerce infrastructure. As you progress through each of the remaining chapters, you will gain greater knowledge of the aspects of e-commerce that together complete the picture: legal issues, security concerns, and possible software enhancements.

Impetus for Web Commerce

Some experts believe the ability to engage in Web commerce will soon be a requirement for most businesses. According to recent research by the Yankee Group (`www.yankeegroup.com`), the business-to-business Web commerce marketplace is expected to reach $6.3 trillion in 2005 and the business-to-consumer Web commerce market is expected to reach $250 billion in the same year, despite a recession that began in early 2001. These figures indicate that Web commerce is becoming a permanent part of business' efforts.

The following statistics also support this assertion:

- The global online population in February 2002 was 445.9 million Web users (eMarketer, per Cyberatlas.com).

- As of February 2002, there were 31,847,892 registered domain names worldwide (Netnames International, Ltd. per NetBenefit).

- In 2001, there were an estimated 603 million PCs in use worldwide (Computer Industry Almanac).

- In 2005, there will be an estimated 729 million Wireless Access Protocol (WAP)—capable mobile devices in use worldwide. Mobile devices are such things as wireless phones and personal digital assistants, or PDAs (Intermarket Group).

- In the United States and Canada, there are 181.2 million online users (Various Sources/NUA Internet Surveys).

- Email advertising revenue is estimated to reach $1.26 billion in 2002, up from $948 million in 2001 (GartnerG2/NUA Internet Surveys). In March 2002, 54% of shoppers aged 35 to 54 shopped more online than they did during the same period in 2001 (WSL Strategic Research/NUA Internet Surveys).

- In March 2001, eMarketer reported that worldwide e-business will reach nearly $2.4 trillion by 2004 (eMarketer/NUA Internet Surveys).

- The total worldwide value of goods and services purchased by businesses online will increase from $282 billion in 2000 to $4.3 trillion by 2005 (IDC/NUA Internet Surveys).

Note that as the Internet continues to expand, statistics continue to change.

Business owners, aware of the increasing number of potential customers using the Web, are responding by making their products and services available to online users with web technology.

Companies are using the Internet as a novel way to reach out to consumers and to conduct *intercompany commerce*, which is business conducted between two different companies. CyberAtlas predicts that the U.S. online B2B trading will reach $823.4 billion by December 2002.

Electronic Commerce

Everyone remembers this definition from second grade social studies class: commerce is the exchange of goods and services. Historically, commerce has been accomplished when the buying party exchanges a fee with the selling party for the goods purchased or services rendered. Barter systems notwithstanding, the fee so far has been paper money and checks, bank drafts, credit cards, or other representations of paper money.

Electronic commerce (or e-commerce) can be defined on two levels. The first definition is somewhat broad: e-commerce is commerce conducted via any electronic medium, such as TV, fax, or the Internet. The first two media have been in use for long enough that issues such as data management and security are well understood. The third medium has changed the equation somewhat, because it ties commerce, data management, and security capabilities together.

A second, more-specific definition is more suitable to Internet users: electronic commerce is an integration of communication transport, data management, and security capabilities that allows organizations to exchange information about the sale of goods and services.

Communication transport services support the transfer of information between the buyer and the seller. Unlike in traditional transactions, the communications aspects go beyond sharing the same spoken language.

Data management services define the exchange format of the information. These services help establish a common digital language between applications to successfully complete electronic transactions.

Security mechanisms authenticate the source of information and guarantee its integrity and privacy. Security mechanisms are of paramount importance here because, unlike with traditional transactions, completing electronic transaction does not require physical proximity between the buyer and seller.

Electronic Commerce vs. Traditional Commerce

The preceding section touched upon some aspects of how electronic commerce differs from traditional commerce. Let us quantify these differences more concretely.

One difference between e-commerce and traditional commerce lies in how information is exchanged and processed. Traditionally, information was exchanged via person-to-person contact or through telephone or postal systems. In electronic commerce, information is carried through a networked computer system.

In traditional commerce, participants act upon the information that accompanies a typical business transaction; for example, merchandise is reviewed up close (even physically trying on an item or looking through a book), a salesperson often assists, and payment methods are handled face-to-face. In electronic commerce, physical presence is limited and almost the entire transaction processing is automated. Electronic commerce pulls together a variety of business support services, including e-mail, online directories, ordering and logistical support systems, settlement support systems, inventory control systems, and management information and statistical reporting systems.

In traditional commerce, the physical proximity between the participating business entities allows *non-repudiation*. Non-repudiation prevents a person from refusing to acknowledge a debt or contract. Traditional commerce also allows authentication to be verified with a request for a standard identification item such as a driver's license or a passport.

The electronic commerce infrastructure does not lend itself well to the traditional model: non-repudiation and authentication must be provided digitally. Digital signatures and encryption frameworks have been developed to address these security issues.

So, on the one hand, although traditional commerce allows for that up-close and personal feeling, for visual proof of identity and, by extension, responsibility, it does fall short in the one area that allows e-commerce to shine: customers can shop anywhere at any time without being physically present at a particular place or time. With e-commerce, you take your business to the global scale without all the effort of placing physical stores around the globe. In fact, one of the most unpredictable things about e-commerce involves your inventory because, as soon as you put yourself out on the Web, if your product is a seller, your customer base could potentially go through the roof.

Advantages/Disadvantages of Electronic Commerce

Electronic commerce has the potential to markedly increase the speed, accuracy, and efficiency of business and personal transactions. Establishing a Web storefront can be as simple as allowing an Internet service provider (ISP) to host your electronic storefront for a low cost and setting up an effective e-commerce page. Some ISPs charge very low fees for web hosting services, and this book (as well as several do-it-yourself software packages that we will discuss later in this chapter in the section "Instant Storefront") can help you establish your e-commerce page in record time, at very little cost to you. Compare the costs of setting up an e-commerce site to the costs associated with leasing and upkeep of a prime real estate parcel; then consider the broader reach of a Web storefront.

Here are some of the benefits of electronic commerce:

- Instant worldwide availability. The store is always open, 24/7 365 days a year, and is accessible to a global audience.

- A streamlined buyer-to-seller relationship resulting from simplified communication and direct interaction.

- Reduced paperwork, allowing a better focus on customer needs.

- Reduced errors and time and overhead costs in information processing because redundant data entry requirements are eliminated.

- Reduced time to complete business transactions, specifically from delivery to payment.

- Easier entry into new markets, especially geographically remote ones. For instance, customers in Australia, North America (and anywhere else with Internet capabilities) can access a website selling Persian rugs.

- New business opportunities as entrepreneurs design innovative ways to use the Internet for commerce.

- Improved market analysis. The large base of Internet users can be surveyed for an analysis of the marketability of a new product or service idea.

- Wider access to assistance and advice from experts and peers.

- Improved product analysis, because businesses can collect, collate, and make available their product information over the Internet.

- The ability to streamline and automate purchasing. Companies allow customers to generate and send purchase orders online, thereby minimizing the costs associated with handling sales orders.

So far we have discussed the benefits that electronic commerce offers business owners and customers. It also has some disadvantages. One important disadvantage is increased vulnerability to fraud. The public network allows anyone to offer products or services for sale with anonymity, increasing the potential for misrepresentation.

The following list includes some other potential problem areas:

Intellectual property   Protecting intellectual property becomes a problem when it's so easy to duplicate information and create illegal copies of copyright-protected material.

Confidentiality   Adding to the risk of sending financial information over the network are the mechanisms used to pay for goods and services online and the introduction of new products and services. Confidential transmission of data, authentication of the parties involved, and assurance of the integrity of the order data and payment instructions are all components of the new electronic business model.

Taxation   Assume a user living in Illinois buys something from a website in California. Is the purchase taxed? If so, does the buyer pay Illinois or California sales taxes?

Customs   The Internet spans international boundaries. Can users buy a product outlawed in one country from a website in another country if the product is legal in the country hosting the website? What are the laws and how will they be governed?

Regulations   Government bodies and regulators may enforce restrictions that invade privacy or hinder security. What are the rules?

Credit card fraud   The U.S. Electronic Funds Transfer Act stipulates a limited liability of $50 to the cardholder in case of fraud. In electronic commerce, what are the legal protections against unauthorized or fraudulent transactions?

Security   Authentication, non-repudiation, accountability, and physical delivery are all handled somewhat differently under the various electronic commerce packages now in use. When will a consistent baseline be available?

Trust   If a Web-based business is easy to set up, it is just as easy to tear down. In traditional transactions, the buyer and seller assess each other before completing the transaction. How does a new Web business assure customers that it will be there when they need service or support?

Availability 24 hours a day, 7 days a week   If constant worldwide availability is an advantage, it is also a risk. What happens to business opportunities that might be lost through service disruption?

If you consider the advantages and weigh them against the disadvantages, it's pretty obvious that e-commerce is a necessary means to move forward into the future of purchasing. For that to be possible, the disadvantages need to be addressed. Various organizations and government groups have begun to address the issues and will continue to do so.

Types of Electronic Commerce

Broadly speaking, the two models of electronic commerce are business-to-business and business-to-consumer. Just as in conventional commerce, business-to-business e-commerce connotes an exchange of goods or services from one business to another, and in business-to-consumer e-commerce, businesses sell goods or services to consumers. Online, the situations can be a little different than they are in brick-and-mortar storefronts.

Business-to-Business

In the business-to-business model, also referred to as the B2B model, e-commerce is conducted between two separate businesses. For example, consider a Fortune 500 company that wants to allow its employees to buy items such as office supplies online. It can set up an open purchase order with an office supplier and allow employees to access the supplier's Internet site to make purchases.

One characteristic of this model is multiple high-volume and low-price margins (such as 100 consumers buying a stack of notepads at $1.25 each) for each transaction. However, business-to-business e-commerce is not characterized only by high-volume purchases. Most studies indicate that, on average, the business-to-business transaction value is also three to four times higher than the average business-to-consumer transaction value.

Business-to-Consumer

In the business-to-consumer (or B2C) model, commerce is conducted between a consumer, such as a home user on a PC, and a business. For example, to buy books or music CDs on the Internet, the consumer accesses the business's Internet site and purchases the items.

Often this model is characterized by low volume and high prices, but as websites begin to increase their customer base, as B2C sites often do, the model can also be characterized by high volume and lower-than-retail pricing margins (100 consumers buying a CD or book at a discount). Most consumers shop on the Web because of some form of discount or advantage that they cannot achieve at a traditional store location. In Exercise 20.1, you'll examine the difference between a B2B website and a B2C website.

EXERCISE 20.1

Examining the Difference between B2B and B2C Websites

In this portion of the exercise, you will view the website of a company currently using the business-to-business model:

1. Open your browser.

2. In your browser's Address field, enter `http://www.works.com`.

3. View and examine the Works.com website. It is set up for businesses to automate their purchasing process by using the Internet.

In the next portion of the exercise, you will view the website of a company using the business-to-consumer model. As you probably know, thousands of sites use this model. In this exercise, you will look at Barnes & Noble at `www.bn.com`:

4. In your browser's Address field, enter `http://www.bn.com`.

5. View the Barnes & Noble website. It is set up for consumers to search for and order books, music, videos, and software online and have them delivered.

6. Click on the DVD & Video link up at the top of the page.

7. Enter **Top Gun** in the search box at the top of the page and then click on the Search button. The search results return information about the movie, including cast members' names, the price, the savings, other formats in which the movie can be purchased, and a review.

If you are familiar with business-to-consumer buying on the Web, then the process will seem familiar. In general, most B2C websites offer the same purchasing process, which has developed into an expected and understood format for the consumer. The next step the consumer takes is to add the product to his or her online *shopping cart*, continue shopping if desired, then proceed to the purchase phase. Some sites offer returning customers easier purchasing by storing information gathered from past shopping sessions; such information may include shipping addresses and credit card information.

E-Commerce Solutions

Having looked at some electronic businesses, we will now examine different solutions for implementing one. The implementation of an e-commerce storefront can be as complicated or as simple as you would like. We will briefly touch on the possible solutions now, but they will be discussed in greater detail in Chapter 26, "Electronic Commerce Site Creation Packages—Outsourcing." The choices for an e-commerce site can be categorized as follows:

- An *in-house* solution

- An *instant storefront*

In-House Solution

With the in-house option, a Web business must buy or develop and integrate an electronic commerce software package, a service platform, redundant Internet connections, secure payment processing network connections, and round-the-clock maintenance. Generally speaking, this approach is reserved for large businesses that have the staff and financial resources to support this effort.

The advantages of such a solution are obvious: complete control of the hardware and software infrastructure and an easier integration into existing back-end enterprise systems. The disadvantages are mainly monetary: implementing and maintaining an in-house elaborate electronic commerce system can cost more than $250,000. This cost effectively puts such systems beyond the range of most small businesses.

Instant Storefront

The alternative to an in-house solution is to use a software package from a vendor that can provide the desired features at a lower cost. Typically, these packages require very little technical knowledge. The more advanced ones allow for customization and also provide the necessary technology so the business can focus on selling goods and services.

The two categories of instant storefront packages are online and offline.

Online Storefront Solution

With an *online storefront* solution, the entire electronic commerce package is on the service provider's infrastructure. The business accesses it with a web browser. The advantage of an online storefront business is that it can be managed from anywhere that has an Internet connection. The business is freed from constant upgrades and other logistical issues associated with maintaining an Internet infrastructure. The disadvantage is that control of the software package is with the ISP and maintenance can be time-consuming, depending on the speed of the Internet connection.

Offline Storefront Solution

An *offline storefront* solution typically requires installing software on the business's computing infrastructure. The owner builds and maintains the online business inside the application. When the site is ready, it is then uploaded to the hosting web server to be accessed by the public. Any changes are made offline using the software and uploaded when ready. Advantages of an offline package include a modicum of control (the business owns the software) and speed (changes to the store can be made quickly and without an Internet connection, if necessary). The disadvantages include lack of software portability and installation and upgrade problems.

Small business owners do not usually have the time or energy to worry about technology. Technology should be an enabler, not a disabling force. Often, the quickest, best, and easiest way for a small business to establish a Web presence is to use an online, ready-to-use package.

In Exercise 20.2, you will examine a company that offers website hosting through an online storefront.

EXERCISE 20.2

Viewing an Instant Storefront Option

To view a site that offers website hosting, follow these steps:

1. Open your browser.

2. In the Address field, enter `www.verio.com`.

3. View the Verio website. Select the Products & Services link at the top of the page.

4. From here, you can select the Hosting link at the top to view the different packages available. Notice the different types of hosting: Web, E-commerce, and Application.

Components of a Web Storefront

Turning a business into a Web-based enterprise can be deceptively simple, or if the business's goals and expectations are not well defined, the task can also be unduly severe. The Web provides all the facets needed to turn a business into an organization that's enabled for electronic commerce. However, the final test is to ensure that these facets work well together.

To this end, we will discuss the various aspects of ensuring that a traditional business can successfully make the transition into a Web-enabled commercial concern.

Turning a business into a Web storefront is not a cure-all for business success but simply an additional way to sell products and services, particularly for new businesses. If a business is well established and has excellent name recognition, changing it to a completely Web-based concern may be a mistake. For example, consider a well-established retail store such as Macy's. If Macy's decided to move completely to the Web, it would alienate customers who actually want to shop in a physical store; after all, walking the aisles of a department store is an important part of shopping for many customers. In this example, Macy's should use the Web as a supplement to its advertising and selling infrastructure to drive people to its retail outlets and not as the only way it does business.

A newer business has more leeway in using the Web. Because it does not have the less tangible assets of name recognition and customer loyalty, it can exercise considerable freedom in how it uses the Web to conduct its business. It can truly become a virtual business by carrying no inventory and possessing no real estate.

Before we go too far, we'll consider for a moment some of the hardware/software needs of a Web storefront.

Hardware and Software Needs

This section provides a checklist of the hardware and software used in establishing a Web storefront. This list is not exhaustive, but it should be used as a starting point for planning a site enabled for electronic commerce.

To implement a storefront (in-house or instant), a business needs to consider having the following (this is more of an overall list of hardware needs than a discussion of specifications or vendor types):

Some form of Internet connection There are several suitable kinds: a *T1* (or fractional T1) connection, which is a high-speed (1.5Mbps) connection to the Internet using dial-up leased lines; a *digital subscriber line (DSL)*, which is a high-speed data and Internet connection that utilizes standard copper phone lines and is capable of speeds up to 1.5Mbps; an *Integrated Services Digital Network (ISDN)*, a high-speed data connection using standard copper phone lines and capable of speeds up to 128Kbps; or perhaps a *T3*, which is a high-speed digital carrier capable of 44.74Mbps and usually used by major ISPs and other large organizations. (Note that dial-up ISP account is usually not a viable or reliable option for any type of web server.)

Server hardware If the electronic commerce software is maintained in-house, powerful systems (Sun workstations or Windows NT/2000 servers) are needed to run the required servers and supporting software.

End-user computers Essentially, users will need systems of their own in order to access electronic commerce sites.

There are software needs too. Here is a list of a few:

- A solid and dependable web server software package. Web server software from Apache (`www.apache.org`), Netscape, or Microsoft will suffice. Web server software support of Secure Sockets Layer (SSL) is essential, and servers from all three companies mentioned support SSL.

- Certificates to authenticate the web servers and encrypt traffic. Certificates can be obtained from certifying authorities such as VeriSign.

- Network operating system (Unix, Linux, Windows, etc.).

- Payment infrastructure. VeriSign has the required servers and clients to implement the payment infrastructure, which includes a payment gateway. Other vendors, such as DigiCash, Microsoft, and Netscape, also provide certain components to support the payment infrastructure.

- A database and database management system. Databases are critical for storing customer and product information and catalogs.

Seven Components of Success

The statistics make it clear: electronic commerce is here to stay. How does one guarantee the success of a Web storefront? There are seven essential ingredients for success:

- Generating demand
- Ordering
- Fulfillment
- Processing payments
- Service and support
- Security
- Community

Generating Demand

For the storefront to be most effective, two situations must occur:

- Traffic must be attracted to the storefront.
- Lookers must be converted into buyers.

How successful online advertising will be in attracting traffic to a Web storefront and converting lookers into buyers depends on the vehicle used for online advertising. Unlike traditional forms of advertising, such as direct mail and telemarketing, Internet-based advertising is constantly changing. No single form of Internet advertising has proven more effective than others. In other words, despite the impressive numbers, the best method has not yet been established.

Advertisers in general so far have focused on *banner ads* (clickable advertisements found on frequently visited websites) and *targeted e-mail* (bulk e-mail sent to target consumers—the electronic equivalent of targeted junk mail).

Portal sites such as Yahoo! and America Online sell impressions, banner ads that are randomly displayed throughout their websites. Companies pay for the impressions based on the cost per thousand (CPM) impressions.

Targeted e-mail advertising is more cost effective, although it's more intrusive than banner ads. Targeted e-mail lists are constructed when consumers subscribe to services or submit online registration forms. Demographic data is collected, collated, analyzed, and compiled into various e-mail lists. Merchants can then purchase these lists based on their needs.

Ordering

Once the consumer has been attracted to a website, the next challenge is to persuade them to order. The biggest challenge is making sure that the ordering process is easy to use. Designing a Web storefront requires discipline in more than software engineering; the designer must understand visual design and human psychology.

When developing the ordering infrastructure, remember the following guidelines:

- *Be consistent.* This cannot be overstated. Consistency is the key to a good website. That includes making sure all the pages have a consistent look and feel, maintaining a navigation bar on each page, using consistent background and foreground colors, and using the same font size and logos.

- *Eliminate redundant information.* If the consumer provided their name upon entering the site, do not ask for it again on a form.

- *Make ordering easy.* Use techniques such as shopping carts and *cookies*. Make sure the consumer does not have to calculate any total manually. For instance, if the customer orders 63 CDs at $12.98 each, display the total amount of $817.74 plus taxes and shipping/handling.

A cookie, contrary to popular belief, is not the huge security risk that everyone thinks it is. Cookies are made up of information sent between a server and a client to help maintain, state, and track user activities. Cookies can reside only in memory or may be placed on a hard drive in the form of a text file. For more information check out www.cookiecentral.com.

- *Accept many substitutes.* Ensure that a wide variety of payment mechanisms are available: credit card, check, debit/ATM card, or COD.

- *Include a bailout mechanism.* Always include a phone number the consumer can call with questions. If a navigation bar is being maintained, the phone number should appear there so the consumer doesn't need to return to the main page to find the number and then navigate back to the problem page to recall the question.

Fulfillment

When the consumer clicks on the Order Now button, generate an order number (or any similar tracking number) and present it so they know the shipment is in progress. Ensure that the consumer's expectations of timely and undamaged delivery are met. Some electronic commerce software packages aid in this process by generating shipping labels and packing slips.

Most customers visiting your storefront will have e-mail addresses. As part of the ordering process, you should request the customer's e-mail address. Upon completion of the order, send the customer a confirmation and tracking number via e-mail, along with a phone number to call in case of problems.

For example, an electronic storefront that sells books can leverage its distributors' efficient shipping capabilities by having them drop-ship the products. By sending a UPS tracking number to customers via e-mail, the company directs users to the UPS website so they can track their merchandise during delivery.

Processing Payments

This is unarguably the most enjoyable step for the electronic merchant. At this juncture, they verify and transfer funds from the consumer's credit card or checking account to the merchant's bank. Approval must be quick so the merchant can expedite shipment of the order and still be sure of getting paid.

There are three models for payment in electronic commerce:

- The cash model

- The check model

- The credit model

The Cash Model

The cash model, or e-cash, is the easiest to understand but the hardest to implement on the Web. E-cash is analogous to the minting of electronic money or tokens. In electronic cash schemes, buyers and sellers trade electronic value tokens, which are issued or backed by some third party, usually an established bank.

The buyer (consumer) buys the digital equivalent of money from an established bank and deposits it in a digital wallet, which is stored on the PC. When they make a purchase from a website that accepts e-cash, the ordering software automatically deducts the correct amount from the consumer's digital wallet. The advantage is that during a transaction, funds are transferred immediately and no back-end processing is required.

One vendor providing e-cash is eCash Technologies (`www.ecashtechnologies.com`).

The Check Model

Using this model, a consumer presents a digital version of a check to a Web storefront. The digitized check is encrypted using the appropriate technologies (we will discuss security Chapter 29). The Web storefront verifies the check through its financial institution, which in turn consults the consumer's financial institution to ensure that funds are available. The biggest disadvantage of this model, at least for the storefront, is that the funds are not transferred immediately. One of the leading vendors in this area is iTransact, Inc. at `www.itransact.com`.

The Credit Model

The credit model works well on the Web, partly because existing credit card processing already uses much of the network infrastructure needed for electronic commerce. For instance, when presented with a credit card, a merchant in a traditional transaction scans the card through a reader and in turn authorizes the transaction through its financial institution. This authorization may be performed over the existing phone network using modems.

On the Web, once a consumer enters the credit card number on a web order form, the Internet could be used to deliver that information to an authorization server. From there on, the transaction proceeds similarly in both the traditional commerce and electronic commerce scenarios: assuming that authorization succeeded and enough funds are available in the consumer's account, a capture transfers the funds from the consumer's bank to the merchant's account.

Service and Support

At this stage, it is imperative to satisfy the consumer's support needs, such as presales inquiries, order tracking, and post-sales support. As mentioned earlier, the business's web page must be designed to allow the consumer to easily contact the merchant via an online form, e-mail address, or phone number.

A number of software packages cater to the specific needs encountered during service and support:

Automatic callback Many sites have a link that, when clicked on, sends an e-mail (or phone) message to a Web business's automatic call distribution center. This feature enables the business's staff to call the consumer back immediately, assuming the consumer has a second phone line (or with the push toward voice-over IP, a single line suffices).

Click-to-dial On many sites you can click on a link that initiates a phone call to a Web storefront's operator (again, assuming that the consumer has two phone lines or is using voice-over IP). The operator can assist the consumer as they browse the website.

Co-browsing Once a consumer has been assigned an operator through automatic callback or click-to-dial, the operator can assist the consumer by sharing the web page being viewed, a concept called *co-browsing*. Some software will show the same web page to both the operator and the consumer; a change of location by either party is reflected on both ends. Hipbone offers a co-browsing solution technology, which is used by Oracle Corporation. Hipbone allows Oracle's sales and service representatives to visually interact with customers or prospects over the Web during a normal telephone call.

Security

Security is a major concern for a consumer during an electronic transaction. Will the credit card number be stolen? Will someone find the consumer's home address? Although all these are valid questions, consumers should know that Web transactions are as secure, if not more so, than traditional transactions in which consumers routinely give their credit cards to waiters in restaurants or their credit card numbers to vendors over the phone. What is to prevent a waiter or a phone vendor from retaining the credit card number for future fraudulent charges?

Consumers can be made to feel more secure about transmitting personal information over the Internet when certificates are used to authenticate both parties in a transaction and when the transaction is encrypted. VeriSign (www.verisign.com) is a leading certificate vendor. With a VeriSign certificate to authenticate the parties and *Secure Sockets Layer (SSL)* to encrypt the traffic, Web transactions can be made very secure. SSL utilizes an encryption protocol to protect data that is transmitted between a client browser and a server. In Exercise 20.3 you will view the VeriSign website.

Besides these measures, educating the consumer is always helpful. An educated consumer can better discern what measures are being taken and how to detect them to ensure information security and privacy.

EXERCISE 20.3

Viewing a Site Secured with SSL

To see how a site secured with SSL looks to the user, follow these steps:

1. Open your browser.

2. In the Address field, enter www.verisign.com.

3. On the VeriSign website, click on the Repository link on the bottom of the page.

4. Click on the Search for and Check the Status of a Digital ID link.

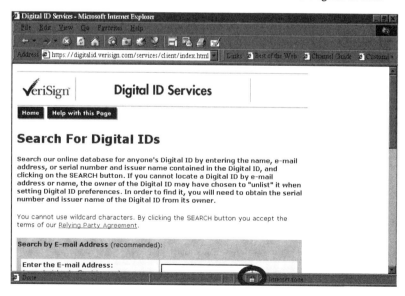

EXERCISE 20.3 *(continued)*

5. You should see a message indicating that you are connecting to a secure server, as shown in the following screen shots. One is for Microsoft Internet Explorer and the other is for Netscape Navigator.

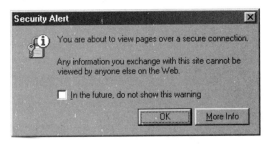

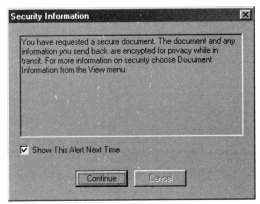

6. You are now on a secure connection. Look for the lock icon at the bottom of your browser. If you double-click on it, a window pops up indicating that SSL is being used and showing the certificate information.

7. From here, you can find a user's digital certificate. For example, enter **bill gates** in the Search by Name field to see matching certificates.

Community

Customer loyalty is something all Web businesses hope to obtain. To the extent possible, a Web storefront, through its services, sales, and support, must create a "stickiness" with the consumer to build loyalty and encourage repeat business.

You can use some powerful tools to achieve this result, such as sending special offers and new item announcements to consumers via e-mail, crediting frequent flier miles for dollars spent, and other such promotions. Amazon.com generates 58 percent of its sales from repeat customers as a result of its developed community.

The Virtual Enterprise

The Web connects islands of information, and the people seeking that information, from within corporate intranets and across the Internet. Sharing information without regard to physical location has prompted new forms of virtual business and social endeavors.

A virtual enterprise is a temporary partnership of independent companies or individuals, such as suppliers of goods and services and those suppliers' customers. Modern telephony and networking communications technologies link these parties so that they can profit from the rapidly changing business ventures and opportunities.

In a virtual enterprise, parties generally share costs, skills, and knowledge pertinent to a specific venture or goal. Each partner contributes skills according to specialty and can disseminate regional information and/or products to a larger, possibly global audience.

This enterprise is called "virtual" because it is composed of core partners but does not have a central office or a hierarchical structure. Through electronic communication, team members can work together in real time, regardless of geographic location. Partnerships are often temporary, informal, and focused upon special opportunities. Upon completion of a venture, a virtual enterprise typically dissolves.

Specific technologies that enable a virtual enterprise include the requisite web, application, and database servers and telephony services (help desks and teleconferencing services).

A *virtual private network (VPN)* is an encrypted data stream that exists between two computers. A VPN can exist between a standard client host and a server, between a client and a firewall, or between two firewalls.

A VPN allows two parties to use encryption to freely communicate across public networks, such as the Internet. Although connectivity mediums such as leased lines and Frame Relay allow virtual enterprises to exist, the Internet is quickly becoming the medium of choice. The Internet provides a common medium for setting up such enterprises, which allows for a standard collaboration of infrastructure. This infrastructure may include any necessary software (web and other Internet servers, databases, reporting software, accounting software) and the requisite hardware (servers, LAN cables, phone connections).

Site Implementation

When a new site is implemented, the development usually occurs in phases. This structure allows the site to progress step-by-step until it achieves all its goals. It is especially common when a site is being converted or upgraded to allow functional e-commerce transactions. This approach is called a phased approach or implementation.

Phased Approach

A gradual approach is generally advisable, especially for an established business with a reputation to uphold and customers to keep. A new business with few customers can afford to take a bigger risk in moving to electronic commerce. However, as a general rule, the following steps embody a phased approach to the Web storefront:

1. Information-only website
2. Limited transactions
3. Full transactions
4. Legacy system integration

Information-Only Website

This phase is the digital equivalent of testing to see if an online presence is appropriate for your business. An information-only website is the least intrusive and fastest way to establish a Web presence. In this stage, the business does not necessarily sell goods or services; it merely establishes an online presence to attract potential customers.

In the earlier days of the Web, many businesses started by using this stage. Fortune 500 companies such as Coca-Cola, IBM, and AT&T and newer companies such as Netscape Communications established a Web presence by setting up information-only websites.

Limited Transactions

Once an information-only website has been established, the next phase is a limited-transaction website. At this point, the intent is not to provide a fully developed Web storefront but to provide a rather limited form of sales using the Internet as a transaction medium.

This step is characterized by very limited Web-based customer support. The emphasis is more on offering limited goods and services with two goals: getting the customer accustomed to Web transactions and solving any problems in the merchant's ordering and delivery processes. Payment may be done through traditional means such as sending a check or giving a credit card number over the phone because the merchant may not be able or willing to deploy a fully integrated Internet security infrastructure.

Full Transactions

The next step after limited transactions is full transactions. At this stage, items such as security infrastructure become necessities. The merchant now offers a complete digital purchase option. Other offerings at this stage include complete services: product support and registration, a full catalog, and searching and querying capabilities.

Legacy System Integration

Overlapping the full transaction transition is legacy system integration. If a merchant already has computerized inventory control and billing systems, they are integrated into the Web storefront. Back-end databases are linked to the Web using browser-based front-end GUI applications. Once you have established a transition path, you can continue building the ingredients for a successful electronic storefront.

E-Commerce Guidelines

Established companies take a slightly bigger risk in moving to a Web storefront; they risk losing customers if they move too fast or choose the digital medium exclusively over more traditional ones. Smaller companies can afford to adopt the new medium quickly because the risks are smaller. Simply publishing a website does not constitute electronic commerce; the costs are high, but so are the advantages.

Overall, the following guidelines will provide a good path as your company moves toward a Web storefront:

- *Know your customer and use the information you have.* Notice how companies such as Amazon.com and Nabisco have used this information to their advantage.

- *Know whether you want to outsource or use in-house experts.* For maximum control, the latter route is preferable; the disadvantage is its expense, and it may not be suitable for smaller companies. Outsourcing electronic commerce infrastructure to entities such as iCat is an attractive solution for small businesses.

- *Evolve.* With standards being defined and key software (such as browsers) changing rapidly, evolution and adaptability are the keys to a successful electronic commerce site.

- *Be flexible.* Flexibility involves customer needs as well as technological needs. Businesses need to be flexible enough to accommodate varying customer needs including reverse credit, support, and ensured satisfaction.

- *Create a business framework.* This guideline encompasses defining business processes and building relationships with customers and vendors.

- *Anticipate hurdles.* Some hurdles, such as expansion, will be anticipated. Others will not.

Summary

As it applies to Internet users, electronic commerce is an integration of communication transport, data management, and security capabilities that allows organizations to exchange information about the sale of goods and services. There are, of course, advantages and disadvantages associated with moving toward electronic commerce, but there are also statistics that suggest that electronic commerce is a growing area in which businesses should establish a presence.

There are seven components that make up a successful Web storefront and you were able to see how these components are used to benefit a business.

This included a review of the proper implementation of the three standard modes of currency exchange (namely, cash, check, and credit) and of the two types of e-commerce (B2B and B2C). It's also important to keep in mind that a gradual, or phased, approach is the best approach to take. There are generally four phases: information-only website, limited transactions, full transactions, and legacy system integration.

Understanding the foundation of e-commerce design is essential to your being able to grasp the coming chapters. Later on you'll learn the need for security design, the need for solutions (even instant storefronts) to be tailored toward specific businesses, and the need for legal issues to be known in advance (as the next chapter, "Law and the Internet" clearly discusses).

Exam Essentials

Define electronic commerce (e-commerce). Electronic commerce is an integration of communication transport, data management, and security capabilities that allows organizations to exchange information about the sale of goods and services.

Know and understand the seven ingredients of a successful storefront. The seven ingredients of a successful storefront are generating demand, ordering, fulfillment, processing payments, service and support, security, and community.

Be able to determine whether an online or offline instant storefront or an in-house solution is best suited for a company. Different companies have different needs and capabilities in e-commerce design. At times, a company may even want a solution that is out of reach. Know the differences between an in-house solution and an instant storefront so you can help in the decision-making process to prevent additional expense and aggravation.

Understand the phased approach and why it is a key element to slow implementations. The phased approach is the approach a company should use to tackle its e-commerce plan. It allows for a smoother transition for companies to enter the e-commerce world by allowing them to gradually display their products, sell the products, and finally, tie the site in with legacy applications.

Know the difference between the B2B approach and the B2C approach. B2B is business-to-business e-commerce purchasing, and B2C is business-to-consumer e-commerce purchasing. These terms are used in the design world to quickly present a scenario. In a brick-and-mortar solution, it's obvious at times that you cater to consumers or businesses, but in design, the approach should be defined at the outset.

Key Terms

Before you take the exam, be certain you are familiar with the following terms:

banner ads	offline storefront
co-browsing	online storefront
cookies	Secure Sockets Layer (SSL)
digital subscriber line (DSL)	shopping cart
in-house	T1
instant storefront	T3
Integrated Services Digital Network (ISDN)	targeted e-mail
inter-company commerce	virtual private network (VPN)
non-repudiation	

Review Questions

1. Anthony has a mid-sized company that handles all control locally over inventory through SQL servers. He would like to initiate a Web presence but requires one that he can control internally. Which of the following would you recommend?

   A. In-house

   B. Offline storefront

   C. Online storefront

   D. Instant storefront

2. Sharon is looking into an e-commerce solution that will provide her with the fastest payment method. She owns a company that makes ceramic coffee mugs and hand-paints little characters on them, and she's eager but patient in her need to get her e-commerce site up and running. Which of the following would give Sharon what she wants?

   A. The traditional method

   B. The cash model

   C. The credit model

   D. The check model

3. Which of the following is an example of traditional commerce?

   A. Bob purchases a book from Amazon.com.

   B. Tim purchases supplies through a corporate account tied into a VPN store from a supplier.

   C. Danielle purchases a computer from the local Comp USA.

   D. Quinn pays a fee to purchase wallpaper for his computer background screen.

4. Jenny is having problems ordering some new winter sweaters from an online catalog. She isn't sure what she is looking for. The site she is ordering from has the option of co-browsing if requested. How would this help Jenny in her purchase?

    A. Co-browsing would allow Jenny to complete the transaction by using an e-mail message to directly request the item and give her credit card information.

    B. Co-browsing would allow a company contact to help Jenny navigate through the catalog and complete the purchase by seeing the same pages Jenny is seeing.

    C. Co-browsing would prove that Jenny is who she says she is.

    D. Co-browsing would protect the data between Jenny's browser and the server by encryption.

5. Wayne is looking to implement an e-commerce solution but hasn't quite decided on a transaction method. For now, he would prefer to use the current methods of transaction, which include over-the-phone credit card exchanges and/or check payments. Which of the following would be the phase that Wayne is currently implementing?

    A. Information-only website

    B. Limited transactions

    C. Full transactions

    D. Legacy system integration

6. Jaclyn buys a movie through her favorite online store. Which form of e-commerce has she participated in?

    A. Business-to-business (B2B)

    B. Personal purchasing

    C. Consumer-to-business (C2B)

    D. Business-to-consumer (B2C)

7. Which of the following is an advantage of e-commerce solutions over traditional ones?

    A. Additional security

    B. Fewer concerns about copyrights issues

    C. Global presence

    D. More difficult entry into new markets

8. Which of the following would be a poor recommendation for a business that requires a Web storefront that will receive about 10,000 transactions per day?

   A. Dial-up Internet connection

   B. T1 Internet connection

   C. T3 Internet connection

   D. DSL connection

9. What is a popular method for generating site traffic?

   A. Spamming

   B. Banner ads

   C. Word of mouth

   D. Newspaper ads

10. Winston has visited a website and explored several pages worth of information on science, particularly atomic science. He concludes his visit with a book purchase that required him to enter certain form information. Upon his next visit to the site, even before he fills out anything or logs in, the site magically welcomes Winston and presents material on atomic science. Which of the following options best explains why this happened?

    A. Secret web crawling probes are used by the site.

    B. The site scans Winston's private hard drive records and learns his likes and dislikes.

    C. On the first visit, Winston filled out a form that is linked to his account with the site.

    D. A cookie was created on the first visit that has now been used by the site to assist Winston.

11. Veronica is an e-commerce specialist who has been hired to design and implement an e-commerce site for a medium-size corporation. She tries to explain the benefit of certain features she is adding to the website to the company's owner. What would be the best explanation of a cookie and the function it accomplishes?

    A. Cookies are files that are sent from the client's computer to a web server and that provide information about software on the client's computer.

    B. Cookies are files that are sent from a web server to a client computer and that are subsequently used by the server for information such as what operating system is on the client computer.

    C. Cookies are dangerous text files that can transmit viruses over the Internet.

    D. Cookies are files that temporarily store information about a website so that the next time it is requested, it can be loaded faster.

12. Amanda is developing her e-commerce site. Which of the following should she do before creating the site or writing the text for her home page?

    A. Create an online catalog

    B. Set goals for her site

    C. Create a site map

    D. Advertise

13. Your boss wants to know the advantages of e-commerce along with the disadvantages. Which of the following would be one of the downsides you might mention?

    A. E-commerce allows easier transition into new markets.

    B. Security is a large concern in the marketing plan.

    C. E-commerce reaches a greater number of consumers.

    D. It is harder to advertise for e-commerce businesses than for traditional companies.

14. Peter needs to establish a connection for his web server to the Internet. This connection will provide Internet access for his mid-size company. He wants to have a reliable high-speed connection. What solution should Peter select?

A. T1

B. T3

C. ISDN

D. Dial-up

15. Which of the following are benefits of e-commerce? (Choose all that apply.)

A. Improved market analysis

B. Protection of intellectual property

C. The ability to streamline and automate purchasing

D. Vulnerability to fraud

16. Joe is implementing a phased approach to move his company to an online presence. What is the first step in the procedure?

A. Limited transaction

B. Full transaction

C. Information-only

D. Legacy system integration

17. Which of the following is a simple definition of e-commerce?

A. Commerce conducted between two or more corporations

B. Commerce conducted via any electronic medium

C. Commerce conducted personally between a consumer and merchant

D. International commerce

18. David works for a small office supply store. He is in charge of managing the inventory and discovers the need for certain items that he is missing. He orders these products from the company's primary supplier through a special extranet that has been established by the supplier. What type of e-commerce is taking place?

    A. Business-to-business (B2B)

    B. Business-to-consumer (B2C)

    C. Supply and demand (SND)

    D. Buyer-to-seller (B2S)

19. Which of the following companies would most likely be best suited to using an online instant storefront?

    A. A large corporation

    B. A local deli

    C. A mid-sized company

    D. A small mail order startup

20. Of the following, which is one of the seven components of success for an e-commerce website?

    A. Fulfillment

    B. Banner Ads

    C. Lowest pricing

    D. Purchasing

Answers to Review Questions

1. **A.** With this company, the staff seems relatively competent. That and the need for internal control should encourage you to choose the in-house solution as being the best.

2. **B.** The cash model would give Sharon the fastest payment method. It is the hardest to establish because of the need to use the same digital cash method as your consumers, but the transaction is immediate. The traditional method is still valid but will not provide the "e-commerce" side to the required solution.

3. **C.** Only the local purchase, for which people present themselves in person, can be considered a traditional purchase. The other options are obviously e-commerce transactions.

4. **B.** The customer can initiate co-browsing with the storefront's internal staff by requesting a call-back or using click-to-dial and then asking for assistance. This is a great feature that adds new meaning to the expression "Can I help you?" because now the operator can literally walk you through the store to items you want and then help you check out.

5. **B.** Wayne is going beyond the simple information-only phase and moving into the limited transaction stage by allowing for some form of transaction, although it's a traditional method.

6. **D.** There are only two types of e-commerce: B2B and B2C. Jaclyn is obviously not engaged in some form of business-to-business transaction unless the question specifically mentions that it's a work-oriented film that was somehow corporate related.

7. **C.** E-commerce opens up a global presence with remarkable availability. Security and copyright issues plague e-commerce concerns but the positives exceed the negatives. E-commerce actually allows for an easier entry into new markets. In addition, it streamlines the buyer-seller relationship and reduces paper work, which allows for a more focused approach to the customers needs.

8. **A.** A dial-up connection would be so slow that 10,000 transactions would take forever to process and this could cost the company business. With that many transaction going through, it would be better for the company to go with the fastest affordable connection.

9. B. Banner ads are clickable advertisements that can be placed on high-traffic sites, allowing visitors to reach your site with the click of a button. Spamming is a terrible, usually worthless, approach to getting people to your site.

10. D. A cookie can work even prior to logon. The original visit allowed the server to create a cookie and send it to the client's browser. On the next visit to the site, the client's browser presents the cookie and, in effect, says, "Hi, my name is Winston. Here is where I've been before on your site." This allows the site to configure itself for Winston's supposed needs.

11. B. Cookies are small text files sent initially by the server to the client computer and stored there on the hard drive. At later visits to the website, the cookie is used for information such as the operating system being used by the client computer. The other answers are either incorrect or add to the myth of the danger of cookies.

12. B. Before writing text or creating a look for her website, Amanda should set goals to determine such things as audience, budget, and how long she'll take to develop the site. She should also decide where to physically host the site and who should run it as well as review competitors' sites.

13. B. One disadvantage to e-commerce is that it complicates marketing plans. There are more decisions and choices to be made involving an e-commerce website. Rapid change also presents a difficulty for e-commerce. Easier transitions into new markets and a greater number of consumers are benefits to e-commerce. Advertising for e-commerce businesses is not harder; there are many avenues to use.

14. A. Peter should use a T1 line for his company's Internet connection. It provides a bandwidth of 1.5Mbps, a speed capable of supporting a mid-sized company. ISDN is a high-speed data connection that uses standard copper phone lines and is capable of speeds up to 128Kbps. T3 is a high-speed digital carrier that is capable of 44.74Mbps and is usually used by major ISPs and other large organizations; it would not be reasonable for a simple web server. A dial-up connection is usually not a viable or reliable option for any type of web server.

15. A, C. Improved market analysis is most definitely a key benefit to e-commerce. The large base of Internet users can be surveyed for an analysis of the marketability of a new product or service idea. In addition, the ability to streamline and automate purchasing is a benefit; because customers can generate and send purchase orders online, the costs associated with handling sales orders are minimized.

16. C. An information-only website is the first phase. It is the digital equivalent of testing to see if an online presence is appropriate for your business. The other options are all legitimate approaches in the phased procedure but not the first step for implementation.

17. B. The proper definition of e-commerce is commerce conducted via any electronic medium. Mediums might include the television, fax, or (more commonly) the Internet. The Internet has changed the scene of e-commerce because it ties commerce, data management, and security capabilities together.

18. A. Business-to-business commerce is conducted between two separate businesses. One characteristic of this model is multiple high-volume and low-price margins for each transaction. B2C is the other model of transaction (although not applicable in this case). The other options are fictitious models of e-commerce.

19. D. An instant online storefront would be the best option for a smaller company because it would be priced low enough for a startup and it would get the company started. A local deli is a small enough company but would really never need a Web presence. The other options would appear to have the revenue to generate a more specialized website solution.

20. A. The seven true components for success of e-commerce are generating demand, ordering, fulfillment, processing payments, service and support, security, and community.

Chapter

21

Law and the Internet

✓ Identify legal and governmental issues related to e-commerce, including but not limited to: jurisdiction, taxation, intellectual property.

Five centuries ago, the invention of the printing press changed the world. The printing press helped make knowledge more widely available by providing a way to produce multiple copies of books quickly. Today, the Internet is causing a more modern version of the same revolution. If information is power, no medium offers this power to more people.

The Internet is supplementing (and in some cases replacing) such societal hallmarks as libraries and town halls. Online services such as America Online and AT&T WorldNet are becoming popular sources of entertainment and information. Web addresses and e-mail addresses are used as status symbols. Magazines, books, and music are published and disseminated electronically.

As great as these advances are for society, they do present some disadvantages. Besides creating societies with artificial classes, the Internet is, ironically, affecting the companies that do the most to advance it: software companies. These companies claim to be losing money because of the Internet. Many software products are becoming commodities because they can be easily duplicated, thereby depressing prices. The boundaries associated with copyright and intellectual property are vague and can be crossed with hazy justifications.

Internet-related law is an emerging discipline; it constantly changes and incorporates elements of several legal issues, including copyright and trademark laws as well as international tariffs and import/export rules. This chapter is designed to introduce you to the basic legal concepts.

We'll discuss many of the complex issues surrounding law on the Internet: approaches, challenges, technologies, intellectual property, protection, security, and the law.

Your knowledge of legal concepts in e-commerce design scenarios should not be thought of as a substitute for sound legal counsel in establishing and maintaining an e-commerce business.

Electronic Publishing

Electronic publishing (EP) is distributing information through the use of computers rather than traditional print mechanisms. The term *EP* as used in this chapter does not refer to just material that would otherwise be printed. It also encompasses other fields that benefit from digital technology: music, movies, and video games.

Electronic publishing is becoming more popular because of the savings it offers over paper publishing. A CD-ROM holding more than 150,000 pages of information can be produced for only $2.50. Compare this amount to $1,300, which is the cost of producing the same information using traditional print methods. Electronic publishing is also making it easier for publishers to reach specific markets, allowing them to address particular target groups within those markets. Instead of using a broadcast advertising medium such as television, publishers can choose narrowcasting by advertising on a specific website that is routinely accessed by certain people.

One drawback of electronic publishing is that as more documents and more media such as music, movies, and games are being placed on the Internet, intellectual property rights may be at risk of being violated. Computer-based theft is rising, as are the lawsuits against companies for violating patents and copyrights. Intellectual property is closely guarded in today's digital age and has become a somewhat controversial topic in the age of electronic publishing. Consider the following examples:

Example 1: Images from Websites   A little girl named Sedona loves Barbie dolls. For her birthday, her father visits `www.mattel.com` looking for the perfect gift. After downloading images of a custom Barbie for Sedona, he saves a GIF image of Barbie on his computer to show his wife. His wife then sends the image to a friend who is also considering a Barbie for her daughter. Can she legally send that image to another person? Is the friend who unwittingly accepts this image of Barbie participating in a copyright violation? If so, who can be considered liable: Sedona's parents, the recipient friend, the Internet Service Provider who provided the medium for the information dissemination?

Example 2: Newsgroups and Message Boards   A subscriber uploads a game that belongs to him to a newsgroup, presumably for friends to use. Another subscriber downloads the game and finds it so fascinating that they immediately sends it to a dozen friends. Is this distribution an intellectual property violation? Did the first subscriber have the right to distribute the game without consulting the author? Is the newsgroup or message board liable for posting a private game to the rest of the world?

Example 3: Artistic Representations Users of a bulletin board digitize songs from an album (or clips from a movie) and places them on the bulletin board's website. Are users who (unwittingly or not) download the songs and save them on their computers violating copyright laws? Is the bulletin board itself in violation?

Example 4: Defamatory Information An Internet Service Provider hosts a web page on behalf of a subscriber. This page has a defamatory quality to it that offends other subscribers and users of the ISP. Is the ISP responsible for the content of the defamatory page? Or is it simply a conduit and not obligated to analyze the information it disseminates?

The questions presented in the examples also apply to universities and corporations. Is a university or corporation liable if one of its members creates a page that offends others? These are some issues that lead many corporations, universities, and ISPs to have strict monitoring and usage policies.

Intellectual Property Issues

The preceding examples demonstrate that *intellectual property* (which includes items such as written materials, musical compositions, and trademarks that are protected by copyright, trademark, or patent law) has become a controversial topic in the age of electronic publishing. As more things are published through electronic media, issues such as copyright, trademark, and patent infringement often arise. The speed with which technical advancements has occurred has exceeded the legal system's capacity to stay current. The U.S. legal system, obviously, was not developed with the digital age in mind. Increasingly, the union of digital technology and older laws has made interpretation necessary.

Rapid computer transmission, electronic reproduction, and text and image manipulation are destined to change how the ownership of information is treated under the law. The concept of the ownership of an idea or information, which has a long history of legal protection, is much easier to challenge because of how technology is used today.

Two Branches of Intellectual Property

There are two types of intellectual property: industrial property and copy righted material. Consider the differences between the two.

Industrial property includes inventions, trademarks, and industrial designs:

Inventions   An invention is a novel idea that permits in practice the solution of a specific problem in the field of technology. The protection is to prevent unauthorized persons from using, producing, or profiting from the invention without consent.

Trademarks and service marks   A mark is a sign, or a combination of signs, capable of distinguishing the goods or services of one undertaking from those of other undertakings. It may consist of distinctive words, letters, numbers, drawings, or pictures and can also include containers or packages.

Industrial designs   To be covered for industrial property protection, industrial designs must be original or novel and must be registered by a recognized governmental office, often the same office that registers patents. Essentially, such protection prevents any third party from using the design without consent of the rightful owner.

Copyright covers literary, musical, artistic, photographic, and audiovisual works. Copyright protection generally means that certain uses of the work are lawful only with the authorization of the copyright owner. Copyrighted material is usually described as "literary and artistic works"; that is, original creations in literature and arts. The works may consist of words, symbols, music, pictures, three-dimensional objects, or combinations thereof (as in the case of an opera or a motion picture). Copyright laws protect the following items:

Literary works   Novels, short stories, poems, computer programs and other written works

Musical works   Songs, choruses, operas, musicals

Artistic works   Drawings, paintings, etchings

Photographic works   Portraits, landscapes and photos of news events

Audiovisual works   Television broadcasting, film dramas, and documentaries

Software   Computer programs

Copyright protection is limited in time. Many countries have adopted, as a general rule, a term of protection that starts when the work is created and ends 50 years later.

International Protection

Copyright laws generally cover copyright issues only in the country in which the laws originate. However, many countries have agreed to treaties designed to provide reciprocal protection in the international arena. Because computers quicken the pace of copying, transmitting, and disseminating information, and because it is difficult to assert ownership of something so easily transferable, the entire idea of ownership of intellectual property is challenged. The following list enumerates some significant intellectual property issues:

- Copyright, trademark, and patent law:
    - What constitutes transmission of an electronic document?
    - How should patents be granted for algorithms and techniques?
    - How should domain names be allocated?
- Lawsuits
- Future litigation
- New laws

Some have characterized intellectual property law as obsolete and suited only to protecting tangible goods. To varying degrees, information is intangible, so how can it be protected? Recent legislation has sought to modify existing laws to cover online media and other intangible goods. As these laws are written and applied, considerable ambiguity is expected in defining intellectual property infringements. Once the laws are established and understood uniformly, protection will be more easily granted to, and guarded by, the rightful owners.

Areas of Liability

Areas of liability within electronic publishing can be divided into the following categories, all of which affect the Internet and EP:

- Copyright, trademark, and patent issues

- Privacy and confidentiality issues

- Jurisdictional issues

We will look at each of these categories in some detail. But first, in Exercise 21.1, you can get a bit of a background by examining some legal aspects of electronic commerce on the Web.

EXERCISE 21.1

Examining Electronic Commerce Law

To access some sites that provide additional information regarding legal issues in the electronic commerce environment, follow these steps:

1. Open your browser.

2. In the Address field, enter **www.yahoo.com**.

3. The Yahoo! home page appears. Select the Computers & Internet link.

4. Select the Internet link.

5. Select the Law@ link. From here you'll note the various websites that relate to Internet law, and you can choose more-specific topics that interest you.

Copyright, Trademark, and Patent Laws

Copyright, trademark, and patent laws address the issue of ownership of intellectual property.

Article 1, Section 8 of the United States Constitution gives authors exclusive rights to their own works for a limited time. Congress later enacted the Copyright Act of 1976, which protects "original works of authorship," including "literary works." The term *literary works*, under modern definition, now includes computer software. Section 103 of the Copyright Act protects compilations, which are defined in Section 101 as works "formed by the collection and assembling of preexisting materials or of data that are selected, coordinated, or arranged in such a way that the resulting work as a whole constitutes an original work of authorship."

To promote creative expression, copyright protection prevents anyone but the rightful owner from copying, distributing, displaying, and making derivative works from a copyrighted work. (Authors may transfer their copyrights to others, such as publishing companies, if they want to.) Copyright law does not protect others from independently creating the same idea or concept. A copyright usually lasts for the life of the author plus 50 years. Works protected include literary works (including computer programs); musical works; pantomimes and choreographic works; pictorial, graphic, and sculptural works; motion pictures and other audiovisual works; sound recordings; and architectural works. Although registering a copyright is not mandatory, it is advisable because legal owners of copyrights can more easily prove authorship and can seek legal remedies more easily if they hold registered copyrights.

The basic elements of a work are expression and originality. For copyright purposes, the work is considered original if it was independently created and not copied from others. Further, originality does not require novelty; that is, a work will not be denied copyright protection merely because it is similar to a work previously produced by someone else. Copyright protection does not extend to an idea or fact.

Many Internet users wonder, "What can copyright mean when millions of people are accessing the Internet and downloading any information they can find on any subject they desire?" Some of the following issues might arise in Internet-related situations:

- The author of a message posted to a newsgroup is entitled to copyright protection. Although reposting the message is common, it will generally constitute a copyright violation unless the author has relinquished rights to the message or has given permission for it to be circulated. However, many newsgroups require such permission as a condition of membership.

- Digitized images are also often transmitted and distributed on the Internet. The original creators of the digital image are protected by copyright law, assuming the original material was not in the public domain already. Beyond the initial creators, any individuals copying or scanning the image are duplicating someone else's work in violation of copyright law.

- A copyright violation may occur when software is copied and transmitted over the Internet.

- Authors of e-mail messages also own the copyrights to their work in most circumstances. Third parties cannot use the e-mail message without the owner's consent.

Copyright law is still very vague with respect to certain portions of the Internet. For instance, is the store-and-forward function of a mail transfer agent (or a router) owned by an ISP a form of copyright infringement?

The courts are attempting to settle these issues. Three precedent-setting cases have been decided in the digital arena.

Sega Enterprises Ltd. v. MAPHIA

The courts decided in favor of Sega Enterprises, which brought suit against MAPHIA, an electronic bulletin board service (BBS). Sega Enterprises claimed that MAPHIA copied a Sega game to its BBS and made the game available for user downloads. The courts found that MAPHIA sometimes charged the users a direct fee for downloading privileges or bartered for the privilege of downloading the Sega Enterprises game. Because Sega Enterprises's game was protected by copyright, MAPHIA violated Sega Enterprises's copyright by obtaining unauthorized copies of the game and placing them on the BBS's storage medium.

The Recording Industry Association of America v. Napster Inc.

Napster Inc. was sued in 2000 by the Recording Industry Association of America (RIAA) for allowing the free distribution of musicians' copyright-protected material through the use of file-swapping software. Using the Napster software, users could search for and download almost any song title in the MP3 format, allowing unlimited use and redistribution on computers, CD players, and MP3 players. The RIAA claimed that Napster was promoting copyright infringement by allowing users to freely distribute and use the material without paying royalties. Napster claimed it was only providing the service and that end users ultimately decided whether or not to use, download, or distribute music, for which Napster received no fees or royalties.

In June 2001, the U.S. Court of Appeals for the Ninth Circuit upheld a lower court's findings that Napster was in copyright violation and must remove all titles requested by the RIAA from user access.

In an effort to continue doing business as a legitimate provider, Napster is attempting to enter into agreements with some recording labels to offer the same service for a monthly subscription fee. The fees will be used to pay royalties to artists and record labels. Napster is planning on a relaunch of their services when all of the legal issues are resolved.

Feist Publications, Inc. v. Rural Telephone Service Company

In 1991 the U.S. Supreme Court heard the case of *Feist Publications, Inc. v. Rural Telephone Service Company*. In that case, Feist and Rural Telephone both published telephone directories that competed for advertising space. The Feist telephone directory covered 15 counties, one of which included the Rural Telephone service area. Rural refused to license its telephone directory information to Feist; therefore, Feist copied the Rural Telephone directory information. The Court sided with Feist and held that copyright protection afforded to databases (which was how Rural presented its directory information to the court) was thin, extending only to the author's selection and arrangement of the data. The Court also held that listing the names and numbers of all subscribers in a telephone service area in alphabetical order does not satisfy the minimum "original work of authorship" requirement for copyright protection.

As a consequence of the *Feist* decision, businesses that create and maintain databases currently have very limited protection under United States copyright laws. That protection now covers only the original selection, coordination, and arrangement of data but not the data itself. Furthermore, the selection, coordination, and arrangement are protected only to the extent that they satisfy the creativity requirement of being an "original work of authorship."

Information Infrastructure Task Force (IITF)

President Clinton formed the Information Infrastructure Task Force (IITF) in 1993. The IITF established the Working Group on Intellectual Property Rights to examine the intellectual property implications of electronic publishing. In July 1994, the group published the Green Paper, a preliminary draft report on intellectual property rights. The Working Group has recognized the need to review current copyright laws in light of the fact that copying and disseminating information are easy with electronic media. The organization has been relatively inactive since 1997. The IITF can be visited at `http://iitf.doc.gov`.

Trademarks in the United States

Trademark law is another area of interest in electronic publishing. Under common law and the *U.S. Lanham Act*, a trademark is "any word, name, symbol, or device or any combination thereof adopted and used by a manufacturer or merchant to identify his goods and distinguish them from those manufactured or sold by others." The Lanham Act is a 1964 law that was an important early step toward U.S. trademark legislation.

Nearly everyone is familiar with the golden arches of McDonald's and the wave design on a Coca-Cola bottle. Each of these identifying symbols is a form of property owned by the company that uses it. Besides symbols, a brand name or a company name is also one of the most common trademarks—Campbell's Chicken Noodle Soup, Heinz Tomato Ketchup, or IBM Personal Computers.

Trademarks originate from the rule that no one has the right to sell products that belong to another person or company. The law recognizes trademarks as property and grants to the trademark holder an exclusive right to use an individual mark. One way to lose the right to a trademark is by abandoning its use or by failing to renew registration. Loss of trademark right can also occur when it is transformed or when a term degenerates into a household term, as has happened with such well-known former trademark names as aspirin, cellophane, dry ice, shredded wheat, and thermos.

A direct contribution of electronic publishing to trademark law concerns domain names. A *domain name* is a company's logical address or source identifier on the Internet. The holder of a domain name may be entitled to protection from the U.S. Patent and Trademark Office (PTO) if the domain name also functions as a trademark or service mark. The Lanham Act defines a service mark as one "used in the sale or advertising of service to identify the services of one person and distinguish them from the services of another." The PTO may deny federal registration of a domain name if the mark is likely to be confused with a previously registered trademark or service mark. The test for confusion is based on the likelihood that an average consumer in a similar marketplace would confuse the source of the product or service given similarities in sound, appearance, meaning, or connotation of the two marks.

The Internet agency that assigns domain names does so on a first-come, first-served basis without examining whether the proposed name would violate anyone else's proprietary rights. The problem with the first-to-file approach is that the domain name may also function as a trademark or service mark, potentially subjecting the new user to infringement proceedings under the Lanham Act. If a domain name is challenged by another individual or organization as an infringement under trademark or service mark law, InterNIC (the authority on assigning domain names) will place the domain name "on hold" to make the domain name unusable by anyone until the matter is resolved.

Several domain name infringement suits have been brought to the courts in the United States, as discussed in the next sections.

Porsche Cars North America, Inc. v. Porsch.com

In January 1999, the Porsche automobile company brought a trademark infringement suit against the owners of 130 domain names for allegedly infringing or diluting the Porsche trademark. Porsche's attorneys argued that many domain name registrants use fictitious names, addresses, and other false information in registering domain names to insulate themselves from service of process. Porsche has since lost the suit and is now buying all the domain names from their owners.

Intermatic, Inc. v. Toeppen

Intermatic, Inc. sued Dennis Toeppen to cease and desist using the domain name `intermatic.com`. The court ruled in 1996 that Toeppen, "by registering `intermatic.com` as a domain name and attempting to sell or license the name to the owner of the famous Intermatic trademark, diluted that mark under the law, since traditional trademark law applies even though the Internet is a new medium of communication...."

Kaplan v. Princeton Review

Stanley Kaplan, the owner of various standardized testing preparation courses, sued competitor Princeton Review over Princeton's use of the domain name kaplan.com. Kaplan alleged that such "bait-and-switch" tactics appropriated the goodwill and recognition associated with Kaplan's trademark, service mark, and trade name. The dispute eventually led to an out-of-court settlement and a change of domain name by Princeton Review.

Patents in the United States

Patent law is another area of interest in electronic publishing. A *patent*, in law, is a document issued by a government conferring some special right or privilege. In the United States, the term is restricted to patents for inventions granted under federal statute. The specific attributes of novelty for which a patent is sought are called claims; thus, a patent can have several claims. The patent gives the inventor the exclusive right to use a certain process or to make, use, or sell a specific product or device for a specified time.

Once a patent is granted, issues of infringement, scope, or other questions related to the grant are within the jurisdiction of the U.S. district courts. Infringement consists of knowingly and wrongfully making, using, or selling someone else's patented invention. In general, a patent protects against infringement only within the jurisdiction of the government by which it is issued; therefore, inventors should secure a patent in all countries in which they want protection. Patent laws have been enacted in most countries; the most important applicable international treaty is the International Convention for the Protection of Industrial Property.

An important issue in EP-related patent law involves software and the exact determination of what should and should not be patented. Generally, software patents do not cover the entire program; instead, they cover algorithms and techniques. A problem may arise when the algorithms and techniques mentioned in a patent application may have been formulated and used independently by other programmers when the application was filed.

Some argue that the patent system opposes the nature of software development. Present computer programs contain thousands of algorithms and techniques; each could be patented, and some are. For example, Apple Computer was sued because its HyperCard program was alleged to violate U.S. Patent number 4,736,308. In simplified terms, that patent protects a product that entails scrolling through a database displaying selected parts of each line of text. Separately, scrolling and display functions are ubiquitous parts of graphical programming; they are everywhere in graphical programming, but the particular combination was the subject of the infringement action. Apple itself has sued Microsoft for allegedly infringing on the look and feel of what it claims is its invention of graphical rendering of information on a computer display.

Diamond v. Diehr

The judicial basis for software patent eligibility is found in the 1981 case of *Diamond vs. Diehr*, in which the court said, "a patent could be granted for an industrial process that was controlled by certain computer algorithms." Consequently, the U.S. PTO has used this case as a precedent for allowing patents on algorithms and techniques. The PTO's stance on patents for algorithms and techniques has increased the granting of software patents in the United States.

Privacy and Confidentiality

Discussing privacy and confidentiality appears to be paradoxical when information about anyone can often be obtained with a few keystrokes. This section discusses some ways in which some loss of privacy and confidentiality is the trade-off required for more advanced technology.

Easy Access to Public Information

Several easily accessible websites (for example, `www.switchboard.com` and `www.411.com`) provide directory listings so visitors can search for any publicly listed information (name, address, phone number). Some argue that finding such information does not hurt the subscriber because it is public. However, the point is not that the information can be found but that it can be so *readily* and *easily* found. Before the Internet was widely used, finding public information took time and effort because physical access to a telephone directory was needed. This requirement no longer exists. A browser and a connection to the Internet are all you need.

Another area in which privacy and confidentiality impose on public information is court documents. Many courts have discovered that they can scan legal documents pertaining to divorces, trials, felonies, and misdemeanors and store them digitally. Besides being easy to retrieve and having low maintenance costs, such documents can be easily indexed and searched. The disadvantage is that anyone with a browser can access these documents from anywhere in the world. Again, the crux of the matter is not that the information can be accessed, it's how easily it can be found. The chances of this information being used for malicious purposes rise as it becomes available to more people.

Back in early 1999, the chief executive officer (CEO) of Sun Microsystems said, "You have zero privacy anyway! Get over it." That wasn't very comforting to folks, especially back then, but was it true? Partially. Perhaps more appropriately his comments should have been, "You have zero privacy anyway, unless you do your best to protect yourself." You don't have to leave yourself wide open on the matter of privacy. Although you can't completely eliminate the ability for people to potentially invade your privacy, you can minimize it to a more reasonable level. In Exercise 21.2, you'll search the Internet to see just how well known you are.

EXERCISE 21.2

Examining Privacy on the Internet

How well known are you on the Internet? To find out, follow these steps:

1. Open your browser.

2. In the Address field, enter `www.yahoo.com`.

3. The Yahoo! home page appears. Click on the People Search link.

4. Enter your first and last names in the space provided in the Telephone Search section. To narrow the search, you can enter a city and state. If your telephone number is listed in the search results, your name will be a hyperlink. Try clicking on it to see what other information is listed about you.

5. Try searching for some information on someone else by entering their first and last names in the Telephone Search area.

You can also use a number of other free sites, including Switchboard.com and Bigfoot.com, to locate information on individuals. For more specific information, several fee-based sites exist, such as LexisNexis, located at `www.lexis.com`.

EXERCISE 21.2 *(continued)*

If you have time, go to www.directhit.com and enter **Internet privacy law** in the Search For box. Navigate through some of the links looking for current and relevant information.

Pending or Current United States Legislation

As mentioned earlier, the legal reach of any copyright or patent extends only as far as the government that recognizes it. In an effort to set forth guidelines to determine the direction of electronic publishing, certain pieces of legislation have been introduced to help enforce and protect intellectual property.

Online Copyright Infringement Liability Limitation Act

The *Online Copyright Infringement Liability Limitation Act* amends U.S. copyright law to exempt an online provider, such as an ISP, from liability for direct infringement based on the intermediate storage and transmission of material over the provider's network. This protection is valid if someone else (such as a subscriber) initiated the transmission, if the storage and transmission are automatic, and if the provider does not retain a copy for longer than is necessary to perform the transmission. The Act also protects the provider from financial liability if it did not know that the material was in violation of copyright laws and did not receive a direct financial benefit as a result of the transmission.

The provider is exempt from claims based on the provider's removing or disabling online access to the material when it learns that an infringement may have occurred whether or not such material is in fact an infringement.

No Electronic Theft (NET) Act

The *No Electronic Theft (NET) Act* amends U.S. copyright law so that "financial gain" includes the receipt of anything of value, including other copyrighted works.

The act establishes penalties for willfully infringing on someone else's copyright-protected material. By making a clearer definition of what "financial gain" is considered to be, the NET Act is ensuring less confusion on the subject. For example, you can't trade copyrighted materials for other copyrighted materials. These would constitute "value" according to the NET Act.

The penalties for these violations are pretty strong, including heavy fines, prison time, and even "victim impact" penalties because, obviously, the one bringing charges may feel that a person caused some form of financial damage in violating the NET Act.

The Digital Millennium Copyright Act (DMCA)

The *Digital Millennium Copyright Act (DMCA)* was created to allow U.S. copyright laws to conform to World Intellectual Property Organization (WIPO) treaties for international copyright standards. The act has four main parts:

Anti-Circumvention Provision   Makes it illegal to manufacture, import, distribute, or provide products designed to circumvent encryption, scrambling, or other technologies used to prevent piracy.

Protect Copyright Management Information (CMI)   Outlaws knowingly falsifying data that identifies works, copyright owners, key facts, and payment royalties.

Service Provider Liability   Defines situations in which a service provider may be immune from damages.

Webcasting   Provides for the licensing of sound recordings for webcasters and other digital audio services.

Marketing and Databases

Marketers can track almost anything you buy: Do you travel often? Airlines send you frequent flier deals. Do you own a PC? Circulars from PC warehouses will appear in your mailbox. Are you a member of a music club? You will receive offers to join video clubs, book clubs, and other music clubs. Every vendor is vying for your business, and technology enables merchants to track, index, and analyze your purchases. Isn't that great? Well … may be not.

Given the enormous appetite of marketers and the equally enormous databases that hold consumer information, privacy is rapidly disappearing. As soon as you fill out a product registration card, the vendor has learned some information about you and can then use that information digitally. Firms that analyze purchase data sometimes sell it. Most consumers would probably excuse the data analysis if it were used only for targeted advertising. It could be reasonably assumed that someone who recently bought a Bose audio system would have an interest in the latest Harmon Kardon digital receiver. But customers will probably perceive a misuse of data if they are suddenly bombarded with sales pitches from BMW or Columbia House as a result of their Bose purchases. However, this is the way targeted advertising works in some cases. Unrelated items are somehow correlated together, leaving the consumer with a mailbox full of "junk," either paper or digital.

Misuse of Sensitive Information

In the spring of 1997, the U.S. Social Security Administration (SSA) decided to allow citizens to access their retirement projections on the Web. The user had only to enter their social security number and birth date. However, the SSA soon discovered that malicious individuals who had access to both pieces of information could get other people's projections. Many such individuals were caught accessing others' accounts. The SSA promptly closed the site.

As a service to Social Security participants, the SSA site was a good idea. However, the information that was required to access the site was not difficult enough for imposters to figure out. Anyone with someone else's social security number and date of birth could masquerade as that person. How did malicious individuals get the social security numbers? From several possible sources: access to IRS documents, registration information, and even underground websites that trade in pirated social security numbers.

A new law intended to protect children from pornography and privacy violations on the Internet were part of a recent $500 billion U.S. spending bill. The Commission on Online Child Protection passed the *Children's Online Privacy Protection Act (COPPA)*, effective April 21, 2000. The privacy measures prevent websites from collecting information about children 13 and younger without a parent's verifiable permission. The law also requires website operators to block access by anyone 17 or younger to materials deemed "harmful to minors" by requiring all users to provide a credit card or personal ID number. For more information about the Children's Online Privacy Protection Act, go to www.coppa.org.

Jurisdiction

Jurisdictional issues are another legal area for electronic publishing. Some estimates contend that U.S.-based corporations are losing $60 billion annually because of intellectual property infringement. As a result, the U.S. government is trying to achieve a global standard for intellectual property law.

As computer crime proliferates, computer thieves disperse around the globe. To cause harm to a computer, the perpetrator need not be physically near the target. On the Internet, criminals can attack U.S. targets from outside the country. International borders often thwart the task of catching these thieves. Laws are territorial; they can be applied only within the jurisdiction of the body that issued them.

The HTTP/URL mechanism can be used on the Web to link computers from many countries with no regard for national or international boundaries. The same advancements in telecommunications have allowed information to be shared worldwide. This sharing creates a problem because of different intellectual property laws. For example, users in the United States can access from other sovereign countries information that, if obtained in the United States, would violate intellectual property rights. These foreign sites often provide the same information at a lower price, so the U.S. user would naturally be attracted to them. Jurisdictional issues are difficult to resolve among the various states and more difficult across international borders.

In some celebrated cases about crackers breaking into commercial and government computers, the crackers were operating from Europe. U.S. authorities could monitor their activities but could not apprehend them because their jurisdiction did not extend into the European countries. Finally, the crackers were apprehended in their home countries (with help from U.S. authorities) and stood trial on the grounds of conducting unwarranted and malicious espionage on foreign soil.

Although the terms *hackers* and *crackers* are used interchangeably, they really hold their own position in the world of security. *Hackers* are interested in obtaining knowledge. They use their knowledge of computers to obtain information without doing damage. *Crackers* go further and use their knowledge to do damage or perform illegal acts. Crackers are maliciously seeking to do harm.

Internet jurisdictional issues raise interesting problems. For example, gambling in most U.S. states is illegal unless conducted on Native American–owned lands or on a riverboat. Yet dozens of online gambling sites are available. Are these legal? Congress is considering two bills that would outlaw online gambling in the United States. In traditional commerce (even over the phone), both parties have some contact (physical or verbal) before a transaction is completed. Most electronic commerce scenarios do not offer this contact. If anything is wrong with the goods or services exchanged over the Internet, either of the parties can be sued.

The U.S. Constitution requires that for one state's court to have jurisdiction over a nonresident party, that party must have had "minimum contacts" with the court's state. An important element of "minimum contacts" is that the nonresident "purposely established" contacts and "created continuing relationships and obligations with the citizens of another state." How do these jurisdictional issues work on the Internet, where the participating parties may never come in physical contact? Interestingly, the courts have held that physical presence is not a prerequisite for jurisdiction. That is, under particular circumstances, Internet presence alone can be sufficient to grant jurisdiction over a nonresident.

Several cases have established jurisdictional precedent:

- In *State of Minnesota v. Granite Gate Resorts*, the state attorney general in Minnesota, where gambling is illegal, successfully sued Granite Gate Resorts, a sports betting service contracting out of Nevada.

- In Connecticut courts, a Connecticut company successfully sued a Massachusetts company for using an Internet domain name that it claimed infringed on its trademark.

However, the cost of conducting electronic commerce should not include lawsuits. Here are some methods for protecting a site against suits from other states:

- Do not advertise that products are available nationwide if some jurisdictions could be expected to consider them illegal. In *State of Minnesota v. Granite Gate Resorts*, if the online betting page had carried a disclaimer stating "Not valid in Minnesota," and the company had attempted to exclude Minnesota residents, the state's cause for action would have been diminished.

- Keep "interactivity" to a minimum. Some courts have found that when a site includes a toll-free telephone number, which presumably encourages contact (or interactivity) from out of state, jurisdictional precedence applies.

Jurisdictional restrictions do not protect patents. Under international laws, a patent must be secured in every country in which the patent holder intends to do business. To promote invention and protect intellectual property, 116 countries have organized an administration called the World Intellectual Property Organization (WIPO). WIPO attempts to promote technology sharing among member countries, especially the lesser-developed ones. It also administers two treaties, the Berne Treaty and the Paris Convention, both of which are multinational agreements governing the management of intellectual property.

In Exercise 21.3, you can explore the various issues involved in designing an e-commerce site for business products sold overseas. There are several things you need to consider before you can consider yourself Internet-ready. If you need to make the scenario more realistic to you, consider using a real company, like Sybex, for your design needs.

EXERCISE 21.3

E-Commerce Design Issues for an Overseas Business Site

Imagine that the company wishes to expand its e-commerce presence internationally. You will visit Web translation sites, begin considering import restrictions, and explore currency conversion options:

1. Start with an outline of your needs. The company hiring you would like to sell its products in France, the United Kingdom, Germany, and Italy. If this project goes forward, the website will need to be translated into French, German, and Italian. You will also need to determine how you will accept payment from overseas customers, and how the company will handle customs and import restrictions.

2. Visit www.welocalize.com and select the appropriate language or visit http://babelfish.altavista.com to access translation features. Do these companies provide translation services in your target languages? Decide which company offers the best value and why.

3. Because the company has previously sold products only in the United States, it has offered standard shipping times and prices. Determine how you will adjust these times and prices for European customers.

4. You need to learn about import restrictions into your new target countries. Visit www.hg.org/intergd.html for general information about exporting products.

5. What payment options do you plan to offer international customers? Must they pay in U.S. dollars, or will you accept foreign currencies? Check out the free currency conversion service Yahoo! offers at http://quote.yahoo.com/m3.

Internet Taxation

The U.S. Constitution currently prevents states from taxing transactions beyond their borders. The Supreme Court has ruled that states cannot require out-of-state companies to collect sales taxes unless Congress passes a law allowing them to do so.

In 1998, the Commerce Committee of the U.S. House of Representatives passed, and the president signed, the *Internet Tax Freedom Act (ITFA)* that imposed a three-year moratorium (suspension) on new Internet taxation. As part of the act, Congress established the Advisory Commission on Electronic Commerce to address the issues related to Internet taxation. The congressionally appointed members of the Commission include the following:

- Three representatives from the federal government: the secretary of commerce, the secretary of the treasury, and U.S. trade representatives (or their delegates).

- Eight representatives from state and local governments (including at least one representative from a state or local government that does not impose a sales tax and one from a state that does not impose an income tax).

- Eight representatives of the electronic commerce industry (including small business), telecommunications carriers, local retail businesses, and consumer groups.

The Advisory Commission conducted a thorough study of federal, state, local, and international taxation and tariff treatment of transactions using the Internet and Internet access and other comparable intrastate, interstate, or international sales activities. The Commission was assigned to produce an important policy initiative.

The ITFA initially placed a three-year moratorium, which was due to expire October 2001, on various taxes on Internet access and e-commerce so the Commission would have time to review the issues before making recommendations.

Due to events beyond the control of Congress, the ITFA actually lapsed in gaining its extension because of all the terrorist threats that surrounded Washington after the September 11 tragedy. Finally, on October 16, 2001, the House of Representatives granted a two-year extension to the law. On November 15, 2001, the Senate approved the extension, and then on November 28, 2001, President Bush signed into law the Internet Tax Non-Discrimination Act. The new law extends the moratorium (which was originally enacted in 1998) on new, special, and discriminatory Internet taxes through November 1, 2003.

Central to the examination of these issues is the fact that the Internet is not constrained by geographical boundaries and by its very nature violates geographical boundaries that hinder other forms of commerce. The Commission analyzed the implications of personal privacy on the taxation of Internet purchases.

Some of the key issues, at least with certain states, concern their inability to collect sales tax revenue from Web businesses. Businesses collect sales tax only from customers in states in which they have physical presence. Many state officials are worried that as electronic commerce grows, local sales tax revenue will decline and basic services will be hurt.

The Advisory Commission on Electronic Commerce finished its work as of April 2000 and has been dissolved. Its report recommended to Congress that the Internet tax moratorium be extended for five more years, until 2006. In 2000, the U.S. House of Representatives approved the recommendation. Final approval of the extension was announced in June 2001. During this period, lawmakers will develop a simplified tax plan. The commission's report can be found at www.ecommercecommission.org.

For more information on e-commerce tax laws, go to www.ecommercetax.com.

Bit Tax

This new area of taxation has spawned the term *bit tax*, which means any tax on electronic commerce expressly imposed on or measured by the volume of digital information transmitted electronically or the volume of digital information per unit of time transmitted electronically, but it does not include taxes imposed on the provision of telecommunications services.

International Tax

The Internet Tax Freedom Act calls for a declaration that the Internet should be free of foreign tariffs, trade barriers, and other restrictions.

It describes the U.S. Congress's opinion that the president should seek bilateral, regional, and multilateral agreements to remove barriers to global electronic commerce through the World Trade Organization, the Organisation for Economic Co-Operation and Development, the Transatlantic Economic Partnership, the Asia-Pacific Economic Cooperation forum, the Free Trade Area of the Americas, the North American Free Trade Agreement, and other appropriate venues.

Customs

A growing concern of e-commerce is the importance of *customs*. In many cases, Web shoppers can now purchase products from anyone and have the products shipped directly to them. The traditional process of importing and exporting goods has been largely regulated by customs services. These services help ensure legal compliance and protect goods entering and leaving a country.

Intentional illegal importing and exporting will always occur, and an entire book could be written on that subject. Instead, we will explore unintentional illegal activity.

Many regulations and restrictions for importing and exporting can be easily overlooked in the e-commerce business. An e-commerce site could be offering goods that may have restrictions on exporting from the state of origin or restrictions at the state of entry. This discussion will not include obviously illegal items.

For example, an e-commerce site that sells technical books is required to document and charge additional taxes when shipping to Canada. If the e-commerce retailer is not aware of these restrictions, legal difficulties could result.

A software company that sells an application with high encryption capabilities could also be violating import/export and customs laws.

WARNING The United States has in place export laws that make it illegal to distribute strong encryption software to international consumers or friends. The stronger forms of encryption in the United States use long keys that are practically indecipherable, and these export laws are in place to prevent international use of them. Messages that are indecipherable could be used by persons who mean to do harm to the U.S.

The following sites contain information about various aspects of importing and exporting for different countries:

- Imex Exchange at `www.imex.com`

- Federation of International Trade associations at `www.fita.org`

- Asia-Pacific Economic Cooperation at `www.apecsec.org.sg`

- World Customs Organization at `www.wcoomd.org`

- United States Customs at `www.customs.ustreas.gov`

- World Trade Venue at `www.wtvusa.com`

Tariffs

For shipping goods across international borders, each state and country has its own set of taxes called *tariffs*. Tariffs can be very difficult to determine. Online services are available to help international marketers know and understand them.

In Exercise 21.4, you have an opportunity to visit the WorldTariff.com website, a subscription-based service, and research a sample tariff code. This exercise will introduce you to two new terms. The first is Harmonized System numbers (HS numbers), which are an international standard for referencing products. The next is Most Favored Nation (MFN), which means that countries have joined together and agreed on a common tax amount, adjusted for the exchange rate for products when trading with each other. (Neither term is imperative for the exam.)

EXERCISE 21.4

Visiting the WorldTariff.com Website

For this exercise, the actual values of the tariffs will be replaced with *X*s because you are using a guest account:

1. Enter `http://www.worldtariff.com` in the Address field in your browser and then click on Guest Login.

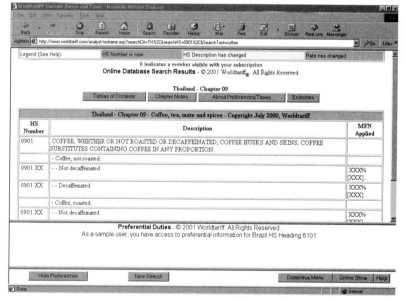

2. In the First Name field of the form, enter **ciw** (lowercase); then scroll down and click on the Submit Request button. You should not have to enter information in any other fields of the form.

3. Click on the Continue button.

4. From the main menu, click on Text Search.

5. From the Destinations menu, choose Singapore. In the Search Text field, type **coffee** and then click on Get HS Headings.

6. Choose heading 0901 and then click on Get Results.

7. Scroll down and examine the results. Notice that HS numbers and MFN numbers are available for some of the coffee types. To an exporter, these values are important for determining the tariff requirements.

Protecting a Brand

Once a brand has been established, others can unfairly capitalize on its success. It is estimated that e-commerce causes a loss of more than $20 billion each year. These losses come in the form of counterfeiting, unauthorized use of logos, domain name parodies, misinformation, rumors, and impostors. The loss is to legitimate companies because it is stolen by false advertising. For example, if you want to buy Nike sneakers and someone sells you Nikke sneakers, you've been cheated but so has the Nike.

Common places for misinformation and rumors are bulletin boards and chat rooms, where companies can be slandered with virtually complete anonymity and the reputations of reputable companies can be damaged. For example, during an 18-month period beginning in 1998, false and damaging information about Callaway Golf, which manufactures golf clubs, was begin posted to a Yahoo! message board. Through a series of legal maneuvers, the source was eventually tracked to a competitor, but as a result, Callaway's stock price fell more that 50 percent.

Some multinational companies have employees whose specific job description is to surf the Web and find those who are defacing or illegally using their brand. Other companies offer employees rewards if they report any infringement they encounter. For most companies, awareness of brand infringement comes from employees who report the incident because they are proud of their company and the brand they have helped to create.

Another possible solution is to outsource brand infringement issues. Here are the URLs for several companies offering assistance in this area:

- www.genuone.com

- www.ewatch.com

- www.cyveillance.com

Summary

The establishment of the Internet has created a sticky-wicket in regards to trademarks and copyrights, taxes, and even customs. While modern society progresses electronically, laws that have been on the books for years have not withstood the changes that the Internet and globalization require. Laws relating to copyright, intellectual property ownership, trademark, and patents that were never intended for modern-day Internet issues have had to be tweaked to fit modern needs on a variety of subjects. Various organizations have been established on behalf of intellectual property rights and trademark legislation, such as the Information Infrastructure Task Force (IITF). Even Internet taxation laws such as the Internet Tax Freedom Act (ITFA) have been passed to encourage consumers to purchase materials and services online and to protect businesses as they establish themselves in e-commerce.

Customs, in pre-Internet times, had been used to regulate the importing and exporting of goods. The purpose was to ensure legal compliance and protect goods entering and leaving a country. Now customs laws have become difficult to manage with the increasing ease and convenience of sending goods internationally through the mail.

As far as governments, individuals, and businesses have progressed in establishing a presence on the Internet, they must continue to examine laws and organizations to further legal protection in a globalized world.

Exam Essentials

Know the legal aspects of e-commerce.   Know the problems that arise from e-commerce in terms of intellectual property, security, taxation, and customs and the legal ramifications in place to control e-commerce dilemmas. Knowing your rights as well as the rights of other individuals and businesses will keep your organization out of hot water.

Understand Internet issues that may present legal challenges.   In electronic publishing of materials, you can get caught up in a whole new world of legal challenges that you never thought of before under standard commerce practices. Be able to recognize the issues that may present legal challenges, such as whether it's legal to send people certain materials found on the Internet and whether items that are perfectly legal to purchase in your country will be illegal in another country.

Know what the U.S. Lanham Act protects. Passed in 1964, the Lanham Act established significant U.S. trademark legislation and is still used in modern law to protect trademarks.

Know what trademarks are and know their importance. A trademark is any word, name, symbol, or device or any combination thereof adopted and used by a manufacturer or merchant to identify his goods and distinguish them from those manufactured or sold by others.

Know the laws involving ISP responsibilities and the distribution of copyrighted materials. The Online Copyright Infringement Liability Limitation Act, the No Electronic Theft (NET) Act, the Digital Millennium Copyright Act (DMCA), and the Children's Online Privacy Protection Act were each established to protect copyright holders as well as businesses and individuals. You should know each legislation and the circumstances behind each.

Understand how legal issues such as jurisdiction, copyright and patents apply to software. Because the Internet is a global entity, issues such as jurisdiction, copyright, and patents play essential roles in Internet law, and each can be threatened by individuals and organizations willing to take advantage of the Internet's broad reach. You need to understand the terminology involved in distinguishing what is a copyrighted form of material and what is patent protected and you need to know how jurisdiction plays a part in prosecuting offenders.

Know what constitutes intellectual property and how to protect it. The two major forms of intellectual property are industrial and copyright. Know the differences between the two and what laws are currently in place to protect these properties.

Understand the current taxation issues facing Internet commerce. In the United States, the Internet Taxation Freedom Act (ITFA) currently prevents states from taxing e-commerce sales. The ITFA is calling for all countries to form the same view of e-commerce, which would eliminate foreign tariffs, trade barriers, and other restrictions.

Key Terms

Before you take the exam, be certain you are familiar with the following terms:

bit tax	industrial property
Children's Online Privacy Protection Act (COPPA)	intellectual property
copyright	Internet Tax Freedom Act (ITFA)
cracker	No Electronic Theft (NET) Act
customs	Online Copyright Infringement Liability Limitation Act
Digital Millennium Copyright Act (DMCA)	patent
domain name	tariffs
Electronic publishing (EP)	U.S. Lanham Act
hacker	

Review Questions

1. Jordan is giving visitors to his website access to download pirated software in exchange for money or different programs. What law is Jordan breaking?

    A. No Electronic Theft Act (NET)

    B. Internet Tax Freedom Act (ITFA)

    C. Treaty of Versailles

    D. Pirate Law

2. Which of the following regulates the importing and exporting of goods?

    A. Tariffs

    B. Lanham Act

    C. Customs

    D. Taxes

3. Electronic publishing, or EP, refers to what?

    A. Digital technology

    B. Publishing documents, music, videos games, and movies over an electronic medium

    C. Publishing documents only over an electronic medium

    D. Publishing music and movies only over an electronic medium

4. Which of the following protects algorithms and techniques in software?

    A. Copyright law.

    B. Trademark law.

    C. Patent law.

    D. They are not currently protected.

5. What was created to allow U.S. copyright laws to conform to World Intellectual Property Organization (WIPO) treaties for international copyright standards?

   A. No Electronic Theft (NET) Act

   B. Lanham Act

   C. Digital Millennium Copyright Act (DMCA)

   D. The Online Copyright Infringement Liability Limitation Act

6. Jenny owns a large flower shop named Flowers 'R' US™. She discovers that another flower distributor is using her name. Jenny can stop the illegal use of her company's name because it's considered _____ .

   A. Intellectual property

   B. Electronic publishing

   C. Copyrighted material

   D. DMCA

7. Which of the following is not protected by copyright laws?

   A. Musical works

   B. Literary works

   C. Audiovisual works

   D. Inventions

8. The U.S. Lanham Act defines the scope of what?

   A. Internet standards

   B. A trademark

   C. Copyright laws

   D. Literary works

9. What are the two branches of intellectual property?

   A. Trademark and literary works

   B. Industrial property and inventions

   C. Industrial property and copyrighted material

   D. Copyrighted material and literary works

10. Joshua owns a drug company that sells over-the-counter drugs on the Internet. What should Joshua do before selling these products in other countries?

    A. Create a well-designed website.

    B. Check tariffs of each country.

    C. Check U.S. customs laws.

    D. Check the customs laws of each country he plans to sell to.

11. In creating an e-commerce website, you would like to use a number of pictures from different websites, some of which are from other countries. Which of the following would influence your decision to get permission before using these images?

    A. DMCA

    B. Berne Treaty

    C. Lanham Act

    D. No Electronic Theft (NET) Act

12. Which of the following laws protects website content?

    A. Patent laws

    B. Trademark laws

    C. Copyright laws

    D. Online Copyright Infringement Liability Limitation Act

13. Garrison sells products online worldwide. He has checked with customs in the countries to which he sells to make sure it's legal to sell his merchandise. Which of the following is another aspect of selling overseas that Garrison should be concerned about?

   A. Online catalog

   B. Screen flow

   C. Supporting many payment methods

   D. Tariffs

14. Scottie is creating a website and wants it to look great. He takes pictures and Flash images off of other sites and puts them on his. Which of the following violation is occurring?

   A. Patent violation

   B. Copyright violation

   C. Jaywalking violation

   D. Preregistering domains

15. What, in law, is a document that is issued by a government and confers some special right or privilege?

   A. Patent

   B. Trademark

   C. Invention

   D. Certificate

16. Tracy wants to use images of works created by a historical painter on his website. He is concerned about copyright laws, though, and wants to be sure it's legal to use these paintings. How long in general do copyrights usually last?

   A. For the owner's lifetime plus 50 years

   B. Forever

   C. 50 years

   D. 100 years

17. What do trademark laws protect against?

    A. The unauthorized use of any words, phrases, or symbols that identify a company or its products

    B. The unauthorized use of symbols that identify a company

    C. The illegal copying of literary works

    D. Copying an idea or invention with permission to do so

18. Audiovisual works are protected because they are considered
_____ .

    A. Industrial property

    B. Copyrighted material

    C. Trademarks

    D. Literary works

19. What is the term used to describe a person who breaks into websites and/or servers for malicious purposes?

    A. Cracker

    B. Administrator

    C. Hacker

    D. Slacker

20. Under international laws, where must a patent be secured?

    A. In every country in which the patent holder intends to do business

    B. In the country in which the patent holder lives

    C. In the country in which the patented item was invented

    D. In the United States

Answers to Review Questions

1. **A.** The No Electronic Theft Act (NET) amends U.S. copyright law so that "financial gain" includes the receipt of anything of value, including other copyrighted works. The ITFA is a valid law that governs the taxing of goods sold over the Internet. The Treaty of Versailles is a very important historical treaty, but it does not apply to Internet law. There is no such thing as Pirate Law.

2. **C.** Customs regulates the importing and exporting of goods sold both traditionally and through e-commerce. Regulating customs is becoming increasingly difficult with the increase in e-commerce.

3. **B.** Electronic publishing is the publishing of documents over an electronic medium such as the Internet with the use of computers rather than traditional print mechanisms. It includes music, movies, and video games as well as more traditional types of documents.

4. **C.** Patent law covers inventions, including algorithms and techniques in software products. Copyright and trademark laws have their place in legal protection but they don't involve algorithms and techniques in software products.

5. **C.** The Digital Millennium Copyright Act brings the U.S. copyright laws in harmony with (WIPO) treaties. It has four main parts: Anti-Circumvention Provision, Protect Copyright Management Information (CMI), Service Provider Liability, and Webcasting.

6. **A.** Intellectual property is defined as items such as music, written materials, and trademarks that are protected by copyright, trademark, and patent laws. The name of Jenny's company is a trademark and therefore is protected because trademarks are recognized as intellectual property.

7. **D.** Copyright law covers literary works, musical works, artistic works, photography, and audiovisual works. Patent law protects inventions.

8. **B.** The Lanham Act defines the scope of a trademark, the process by which a federal registration can be obtained from the Patent and Trademark Office for a trademark, and penalties for trademark infringement.

9. C.   Industrial property and copyrighted material make up the two branches of intellectual property. Industrial property covers industrial designs, inventions, and trademarks and service marks. Copyrighted material covers literary, musical, artistic, photographic, and audiovisual works.

10. D.   You should make sure products you plan to sell in foreign countries are legal in the countries you plan to sell them in, especially products such as over-the-counter drugs. To do this, you need to check each country's customs laws, which regulate importing and exporting.

11. B.   The Berne treaty involves international intellectual management laws. The other acts have their own purpose. The DMCA (Digital Millennium Copyright Act) brings the U.S. copyright laws in harmony with WIPO treaties. The Lanham Act is used for trademark protection. The NET Act amends U.S. copyright law so that "financial gain" includes the receipt of anything of value, including other copyrighted works.

12. C.   Website content is protected by copyright laws, which make it illegal to copy or use material without the owner's permission. Patent laws protect inventions; trademark laws protect symbols or words that represent a company and its products, and the Online Copyright Infringement Liability Limitation Act protects ISPs from being held accountable for the actions of their subscribers.

13. D.   Tariffs are the taxes levied by individual governments for goods being imported or exported from their countries. Of all the options, this is the most important because the products are sold worldwide

14. B.   Copyrighted material includes photographic images that are used without the authorization of the copyright owner. In this case, the images were created by another individual and have been placed on the website without permission from their creator.

15. A.   A patent is a document issued by a government to confer a special right or privilege. In the U.S., the term is restricted to patents for inventions granted under federal statute. The patent gives the inventor the exclusive right to use a certain process to make, use, or sell a specific device or product for a specified time. A trademark is a word, phrase, or symbol that identifies a company. An invention is what a patent pertains to, and a certificate is a signed document given by a third-party company to an online business to identify them to their clients.

16. A. In general, copyright laws protect a work for the lifetime of the creator plus 50 years. Most likely, the copyright of the historical painter's works have expired, allowing Tracy to legally use the images on his site.

17. A. Trademark laws protect against the unauthorized use of any words, phrases, or symbols that identify a company or its products. Trademarks are protected as industrial property, one of the two branches of intellectual property. The illegal copying of literary works is protected because it's copyrighted material. Any misconduct involving inventions is protected against because of industrial property laws.

18. B. Audiovisual works are protected because they are considered to be copyrighted material, one of the two branches of intellectual property. The other branch of intellectual property is industrial property.

19. A. A cracker is a person who breaks into websites and/or servers for malicious purposes. Crackers use their knowledge to do damage or perform illegal acts. Crackers are maliciously seeking to do harm. Hackers are a milder group. They are interested in obtaining knowledge. They use their knowledge of computers to obtain information without doing damage. An administrator is the proper owner and manager of a network or site.

20. A. Under international laws, in order for a patent to be recognized, it must be secured in every country in which the patent holder intends to do business. Patent laws have been enacted in most countries; the most important applicable international treaty is the International Convention for the Protection of Industrial Property.

Chapter
22

Web Marketing Goals

THE CIW EXAM OBJECTIVE GROUP COVERED IN THIS CHAPTER:

✓ Define the role of marketing in e-commerce site development, including but not limited to: market identification, pricing, promotion.

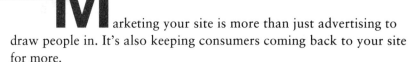

Marketing your site is more than just advertising to draw people in. It's also keeping consumers coming back to your site for more.

Without marketing, even the best websites can go unnoticed. In traditional commerce, a big factor in sales is location. Location is everything at times. Put a pizza place that makes average pizza in the middle of a mall and watch profits soar. The Web, however, is a bit of an even playing field because location is not a factor. To stand out and increase your profits, then, you need to ensure that you can market the site.

If you're designing an e-commerce site for customers, you should be able to offer basic advice, which is what this chapter provides. We'll discuss the benefits of marketing and give you some examples of who is doing it right. We'll also take a look at some goals and strategies and talk about different kinds of markets and product pricing in addition to product availability and demographics.

Marketing Overview

Products have been brought to the marketplace for hundreds of years in almost every society. The implementation of plans and ideas about how to offer a product or service is what characterizes marketing.

Businesses of all sizes need marketing strategies to be successful. Naturally, some marketing strategies require more extensive planning and study before they can be successfully launched.

Web marketing is still in its infancy, and marketing agencies and promotional campaigns are in high gear to determine how to effectively use the Web for marketing.

Web Marketing Benefits

During the time you spend using the Internet, you are probably exposed to several advertisements. Whether or not these advertisements are targeted at you depends on the marketing strategy of the company placing them.

We have all heard statistics that we are directly or indirectly exposed to thousands of advertisements each day. But what makes Web advertising different?

Personal Selection

When people are exposed to a radio or television advertisement, they are generally *passive recipients* of the message. Web advertising can become more personal because the recipient can make a selection of the content they might like to view. For example, when visiting a website, one might notice an ad about a low-interest credit card; it is entirely the user's choice whether to find out more by clicking on the link. The user may not even notice the ad.

The benefit to the advertiser is that if the user does click on the ad and visit the advertiser's website, they can be considered a qualified prospective customer because just by clicking on the ad, they showed interest in the product or service. Their interest is then stimulated by the information they immediately get at the advertiser's website. It would be difficult to apply that scenario to radio or television because you cannot provide information at the click of a button.

Certainly, radio and television are giving the Web general day-to-day exposure. Most commercials on radio and television display or announce a business's Web address. However, radio and television lack immediacy, the capability to immediately stimulate customer interest.

Imagine hearing an advertisement on your car radio with a corresponding URL to visit for more information. That message will not be fully effective until the you can access the Internet. By that time, you may have forgotten the whole ad or it may not seem as important. On the other hand, if you saw that same ad on the Internet, you could respond immediately.

Interactivity

Again, radio and television marketing offer very little interaction between the audience and the medium. Radio advertising requires listening and developing a mental picture; television advertising presents the image to the audience. Other than those factors, the audience's experience is limited.

With Web marketing, users experience interaction on a much higher level. They can be exposed to the same elements television exposes them to, but they have more control over where or how they continue the experience. Another important element is that the user controls the speed of the experience.

Some websites are considered static in design, meaning that they deliver only text content and images. Others can be media-rich, delivering audio and video and giving the user a chance to interact with the website or other visitors. Companies are working on new plug-ins that allow you to zoom in on a product, move it from side to side, and view it from different angles to see all sides of it. These give users a better feel for the product, which helps them to feel more comfortable with the purchase, as in traditional commerce.

For example, on Volkswagen's website, you can check out the new Volkswagen Beetle through a QuickTime viewer (`www.vw.com/newbeetle/360cam-1.htm`).

Integration

An important aspect of marketing on the Web is keeping customers interested in your products or services by keeping them interested in your site, and one of the best ways to do that is to have a functional site that offers continuous product support. This support can include such things as troubleshooting, upgrades, downloads, or commonly asked questions and answers. In Chapter 24, "Site Usability and Customer Relationship Management," we will further discuss the issues of product and customer support.

Unlike Web-based businesses, businesses that use television and radio to market their products don't offer the opportunity to provide continuous support once the product is sold. But Web-based businesses have a variety of support tools at their disposal, such as online communities and e-mail updates.

Online Communities

To build a loyal following for a Web business, you must build value and include information that will keep customers coming back for more. One of the techniques used is building *online communities*. These are services that allow customers to interact with or gather information from other customers or people with similar interests or viewpoints. These services can be online chat features, bulletin boards, or mail list servers. With radio and television, the only community created might be a discussion to see if others had seen or heard the ad and their opinions of it. Such discussions are mostly for entertainment or shock value and not necessarily a true form of community.

Directed or Opt-In E-Mail

Many sites offer to send visitors or customers periodic e-mail messages (called newsletters) containing specific information that they have requested. Such information may concern specials, news, or events.

Opt-in e-mail allows people to indicate their personal interest in certain types of information and to give permission for a business to send them that information via e-mail. This provides a comfortable solution for buyers and gives them a choice instead of making them feel badgered by a lot of unwanted mail.

Further Benefits of Web Marketing

In a million years did you ever think you would be using a computer to order books, get grocery deals, search for cars...? In a short period of time the Internet has ushered in this new wave of purchasing choices and convenience is a major factor. Consider some further benefits of Web marketing.

One-to-One Service

Some sites allow users to customize what they view, thereby allowing them to filter the content they want and do not want. When they return to the site, they have a customized view, eliminating the need to reenter personal information or view content they've chosen not to view. This benefits the buyer, but it also benefits the business. On Amazon.com, return visitors who have purchased books are greeted with a customized view and a welcome message. In addition, if the user had purchased, for example, books on computer-related topics, the page will include a list of other books about the same topics. A feature like this benefits the site owner as well as the user because it could lead to increased purchasing.

Online Purchasing

Enabling the user to immediately purchase a product or service is the most powerful tool marketers can offer. The less time consumers have to wait after deciding to buy, the more likely they are to complete the purchase.

Immediacy is an important component in marketing. If consumers see something they want, the selling business should want to give it to them as quickly as possible. The longer the wait, the more time customers have to shop around or change their minds.

Global Reach

When the largest radio or television ad campaign is placed, it does not have the reach that even the simplest web page can have. Enabling businesses with an unlimited and largely unrestricted resource to compete on a global scale is empowering. Until recently, global exposure was just a dream to most businesses, but now it is almost taken for granted.

These elements have created a new marketer/consumer experience. As Web marketing exists today, marketers are still learning how to be consistently effective, and many organizations are attempting to fine-tune Web marketing to get the best results.

Who Is Doing It Right?

What businesses are doing a good job of Web marketing? Trying to narrow it down is difficult, but we'll take look at several. One of the reasons this question is so difficult is that actual figures may not be conclusive or even available.

The next few examples are profiles of Web businesses that are marketing successfully. We'll look at how they designed their sites and see how they take advantage of the previously mentioned benefits of Web marketing. The following selections cover both business-to-business and business-to-consumer e-commerce pursuits.

Dell

Dell Computer Corporation is a fast-growing computer systems company that sells worldwide.

Dell's online store opened in July 1996. Visitors can review the Dell product line, customize their own systems, and get price quotes; order systems online; and track orders from manufacturing through shipping. Additionally, Dell offers detailed online customer support and gives business customers personalized information about their organization's approved configurations and pricing. You can visit the Dell home page at www.dell.com.

Dell's business model focuses on creating a direct connection with the customer. This approach allows the company to price very competitively because of the direct sale. Dell offers low prices but still provides fully customizable computers and tailored customer service. Dell's operations run on a custom front end that integrates into an Oracle database on the back end.

Much of this online business is based on Internet marketing. Dell leverages the benefits of Internet marketing in the following ways:

Personal selection   Dell has an extensive online and offline advertising campaign targeting people who are interested in purchasing computers. Dell advertisements in online magazines offer hyperlinks to the company's site. The company knows that the people who see the site have chosen to visit and are interested in computers. Once someone clicks on a Dell ad, they are taken directly to the Dell website for further research, customizing, and online purchasing.

Interactivity   The website is highly interactive, allowing potential customers to search for a computer to fit their needs, customize it online, obtain a price quote, and buy the computer.

Integration   Dell's marketing presence includes links from targeted banner advertisements and press coverage. The site offers customers numerous prepurchase information options and exposes them to advertising for additional items. A form for requesting a catalog or e-mail newsletter is also available.

One-to-one service   Besides the extensive customization options, Dell's online Premier pages present personalized pages detailing the customer's product configurations and pricing, order and inventory tracking, and account representative contact information. (Premier Dell.com is at `http://premier.dell.com/premier/`.) Seventy-six percent of order status transactions occur online.

Online purchasing   Purchasing is supported by product information and customization options.

Global reach   The Dell site is translated and customized for various countries and languages.

Cisco

Although it is not a household name as Dell is, Cisco Systems is a major supplier of networking products. Cisco's networking and computing products allow people to access or transfer information between computer systems. You can visit Cisco's home page by going to www.cisco.com.

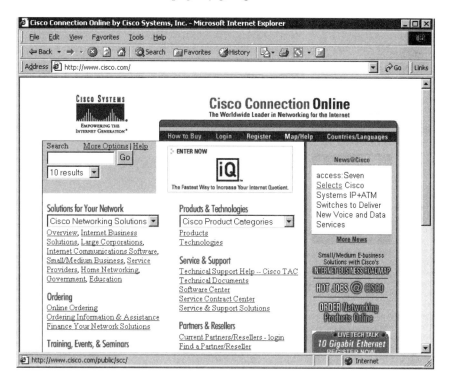

Cisco is one of the largest Internet commerce sites. It produces routers, switches, and hubs that connect the various parts of the Internet. With such an assured market niche, Cisco will undoubtedly continue to be very successful.

Because of the nature of its products, Cisco's online business can be characterized as business-to-business. Much of this online business relies on the benefits of Web marketing:

Personal selection   Cisco allows the site visitor to select from many types of networking products. It also categorizes these products, allowing users to easily identify which would best suit their needs.

Interactivity   The website offers online material and educational information so visitors can make sound choices.

Integration   Cisco's website includes links from targeted banner advertisements and press coverage. A form for requesting a catalog or e-mail newsletter is also available.

One-to-one service The site offers configuration tools to help buyers determine which components will be required.

Online purchasing Cisco offers different purchasing options. Products can be ordered directly from Cisco or from an authorized partner or distributor. This option gives buyers more control over selection and pricing.

Global reach The Cisco site is translated and customized for various countries and languages, reaching users in approximately 115 countries.

Amazon

Amazon.com claims to have the "Earth's biggest selection," offering millions of books, software, videos, and CDs at discount prices. The company has been in business since July 1995 and is growing fast. The company's managers are focusing on the long term and building brand recognition in hopes of future profits and customer loyalty. You can visit Amazon's home page by going to www.amazon.com.

Amazon.com's existence depends entirely on the Internet, and the company is changing both Internet commerce and publishing industry standards. It has regularly been recognized as one of the top 10 visited sites, as a leading online shopping site, and as the largest bookseller in the United States, online or offline.

Its major marketing leads come from extensive use of targeted banner and button advertisements, public relations, and the Amazon.com Associates Program, an online franchise program. A large percentage of the company's orders come from returning customers.

Amazon.com has created a successful business based on Internet marketing. This company takes advantage of all the benefits of Internet advertising:

Personal selection   Amazon.com has an extensive targeted advertising campaign and a rigorous public relations push, ensuring that anyone who might be interested hears about the company. Therefore, those who click an Amazon.com advertisement are interested and have a high potential to become customers.

Interactivity   The website is highly interactive, offering the user several ways to find the right product, listen to music samples, watch video clips, and read reviews.

Integration   Banner advertisements placed on other sites link to the website, which has almost no external links (because Amazon wants to keep you within its site). Direct e-mail is integrated into the book search, and during the purchasing process, the company requests the user's permission to periodically send information.

One-to-one service   Cookies and customer accounts are used to identify repeat visitors. When customers return to the site from the computer at which they made an earlier purchase, they get a list of recommended books based on their purchasing histories.

Online purchasing   Amazon.com publishes book cover copy and book reviews and has a patented 1-Click payment technology for repeat visitors.

Global reach   The company offers primarily U.S.-published books worldwide and is expanding into the United Kingdom and Germany through strategic purchases.

Now that you have seen these marketing elements at work, you should have a better idea of how Web marketing has more depth and greater potential than traditional advertising.

Marketing Goals

Defining what you want your business to achieve is how goals are created. Before any significant steps can be taken on a project, certain areas and ideas must be carefully considered. Goals that coincide with the company's direction must be established.

Although many questions can help start the process, a common initial question can be, What is the business trying to accomplish?

There are several possible answers:

- We want to improve customer service and satisfaction.

- We want to gain access to different markets.

- We want to sell new products.

- We want to automate our business process.

Although it is a very basic question, the answer an owner chooses is significant and is the root of larger questions to be answered later. If the real objective is identified early, the next steps will be easier to define.

Next, we will examine each of the four answers we've listed to see how they relate to the goals.

Improve Customer Service

The primary goal of any business is clear: increase profits. But how does a company stand out as different and, by extension, a better choice for customers? E-commerce not only increases profits by providing a global platform for a business' product, it also allows for tools that enhance customer service. That increase in service is a quality that boosts both initial and repeat business.

Consider, for example, Federal Express. The company decided to turn to the Internet, but not to ship more packages, although the decision to turn to the Internet may have incidentally increased business. Instead, FedEx decided to invest in Internet technology to better automate processes and to better serve customers. This automation and customer service improvement saved the company thousands of dollars monthly on customer service.

FedEx ships millions of packages every day. The two parties to every delivery are the sender and the recipient. Thus, FedEx could receive millions of calls to the company's toll-free number from people who want to check the status of their deliveries, and the cost of these calls could potentially be prohibitive to FedEx. However, with a tracking number and a visit to FedEx.com, customers can now obtain that information online. Customers and other e-commerce retailers can also get PC-based and server-based software to perform the same functions and more advanced package monitoring.

In Exercise 22.1, you can check out firsthand the customer service provisions that Federal Express has implemented for their customers.

EXERCISE 22.1

Looking at Federal Express on the Web

To see the benefits enjoyed by customers because of the use of web technology by this worldwide distributor, follow these steps:

1. Enter `http://www.fedex.com` in your browser's Address or Location field to go to the FedEx website.

2. If required, choose the appropriate country.

3. Click on the Track link on the top margin (or you can use the home page tracking section).

4. In the Airbill Number field, enter the following FedEx tracking number: **420369675123**. Then click on the Track It button to view the results. Notice the detail of the information, which can be printed for record-keeping purposes or sent via e-mail to the appropriate parties. (If the given air bill number does not produce results, use any tracking number to which you have access.)

5. Click on the e-Business Tools link toward the top of the page.

6. Scroll down to look at the other services that FedEx offers to support e-commerce. Some of the software you see can be used by a company to integrate its system with the FedEx delivery system. Its customers could then track packages through its website.

Access Different Markets

If the goal is to gain access into markets that were previously inaccessible, the focus changes. Do you want to be an international marketer? Ten years ago, this would have been a daunting task, even for large businesses. After all, contacts or partners in foreign countries had to be established, and then a strategy of distributing goods or services had to be planned. Payments, conversion rates, letters of agreement, and letters of credit all had to be discussed and formalized. And after such preparation, the market could still prove to be inactive and unresponsive.

The process of "going international" can appear easy. Offer a product, establish a Web presence, promote the site, take credit card orders, and ship the product. In some cases, the task can be that easy, but such cases are rare. However, the Web has made it faster, cheaper, and easier to gain access to different markets.

Accessing different markets does not guarantee that an e-commerce business will succeed. As with traditional market penetration, all the factors need to be examined. Once they have been evaluated, however, it will be easier to actually access different markets using the Web than by using traditional methods.

Sell New Products

It's exciting for a company to have new products that, if exposed properly to the market, would produce revenue. Bringing a new product to market with traditional means can be very costly. As a result, many products never make it to market because the risk seems too high when compared to the return on investment.

E-commerce has opened up an entirely new model for delivering new products to the market. For now, we will assume that the product does qualify as suitable for online sale. That is important itself. The risk that a company faces now to introduce a product online is much lower.

Promotion of the product can take many forms and budget sizes. We are not referring to the enormous ad campaigns that many of the dot-com companies are conducting. With a well-placed, methodical, relatively inexpensive marketing campaign, the product can find its market niche and be a success.

Automate a Business Process

The more processes that can be moved away from manual labor or processing, the more efficient the business will become. Once again, that blanket statement does not fit all models.

If someone were to approach Rolls-Royce Motor Cars to sell the idea of automation, you can be confident that the idea would encounter serious resistance. Conversely, Dell Computer relies heavily on the automation of its website ordering and customer service processes.

For many businesses, automation of certain processes is part of a natural evolution and a by-product of staying competitive in the market. One key reason for using automation is that it will allow a business to stay competitive with other businesses that have embraced (or are in the process of embracing) the technology. When processes have been automated, the interchange with other automated systems becomes possible.

Online Marketing Strategies

Setting your goals helps to shape your ideas. The next step is implementing them, and that is when marketing strategies need to be considered; they help move the project to reality.

Strategies are small, incremental steps taken toward a goal. Think of marketing as a pyramid-type object (Figure 22.1). At the top are the goals. The next level includes the strategies, and below the strategies are the tactics.

FIGURE 22.1   Marketing pyramid

Tactics are the building blocks of strategies. Strategies are the building blocks of goals. All work together to create an effective marketing campaign. For example, if the goal is to enter new markets, the strategy would be to target new customers. The tactic would be to advertise to specific customers who would use the product or service.

Online marketing strategies can include many focus areas:

- Website design
- Online promotion campaigns

- Targeted marketing programs
- Search engine placement methods

Website Design

The era of quickly designed HTML pages has evolved into one of more sophisticated websites. A multitude of considerations about site design will not be discussed in this portion of the book. However, because site design is part of a marketing strategy, we recommend you consider the earlier chapters.

Site owners should understand the reasons behind website design: the goal is not necessarily aesthetics, but rather functionality. There need to be goals for the site itself, and they should be supported by design strategies, which should be in turn supported by tactics.

Online Promotion Campaigns

To develop product awareness, a promotion campaign should be implemented. To target those already using the Internet, one way can be an online promotion to direct traffic to the site. Like site design, online promotion has some tested elements that should be followed for the most effective results.

Targeted Marketing Programs

This category does overlap the online promotion category a bit, but it goes into more detail. Online promotion is about how the audience sees the message. A targeted marketing program determines which audience should see the message and why.

For example, an online promotion should include banner ad placement on other websites. But which websites are chosen and why depends on the target market. If ads to promote a new home cleaning product are placed on a website that focuses on sports and sporting events, they are probably not as well targeted as they would be if they are placed on a site that focuses on home improvement topics.

Search Engine Placement Methods

If customers do not see the ads or hear about your business from another source, the only way they will find you is through search results. The goal is to ensure that the site will place in the top 10 results returned. Unfortunately, there is no way to guarantee such placement.

Each search engine has its own method of cataloging websites, ranking them, and returning results. In addition to persistence and following proper procedures during submissions, you can increase your chances of getting top-10 results by use the services many companies now offer.

One useful resource for learning how to best place and list a site with search engines can be found at Search Engine Watch.com (`http://searchenginewatch.com`). Search Engine Watch.com continually monitors the techniques and changes that the major search engines employ, allowing submitters to achieve optimum placement. They also offer a periodic e-mail update to which users can subscribe for the latest updates.

Drivers and Barriers to Growth

For businesses trying to enter new markets, factors that encourage growth are called *drivers*, and those that limit growth are called *barriers*. Being able to identify these factors and determine their effects can make the difference between profits or losses.

Following are some of the drivers for entering e-commerce:

Access   A larger customer base can increase profit potential.

Around-the-clock service   Time zones are no longer a hindrance to business.

Electronic Data Interchange   Electronic data interchange (EDI) allows businesses to exchange and use electronic data internally and with vendors, suppliers, and customers.

Increased bandwidth   More options are becoming available for high-speed Internet connections so media-rich content can be delivered more consistently.

Technology that is user friendly   Easy-to-use technology is allowing more businesses to enter e-commerce.

Cost   Options to implement e-commerce are available at little or no cost.

Ease of access   Internet access is becoming more common and an everyday necessity.

Critical mass The present state of the Internet indicates that pursuing e-commerce makes economic sense now.

Physical locations Businesses no longer need physical stores to be successful.

Diversification of offerings Companies can expand on new and existing products and services.

Centralization An online business need not be geographically dispersed. In some cases, however, cost benefits may result from such disbursement.

There are also many barriers that can keep companies from entering into e-commerce:

Fragmented data and data format Data is capable of being inter-changed (that is, data from one application can be pulled into another application, if the data is in a standardized format). The data format has not yet been standardized, although many businesses are turning to Extensible Markup Language (XML) to describe data in such a way that it can be manipulated by a variety of dissimilar applications.

Large segmentation Defining the target market is more difficult because the audience is so much larger.

Rapid change The models that work today on the Internet may not per-form well or may become obsolete in the future.

Increased competition Easier market entry has also increased the number of businesses vying for customer attention.

Physical locations Physical store locations, in which customers can touch the products before they buy, give customers a feeling of security because they can return to the location if problems occur.

Saturation Product or service uniqueness is becoming more difficult to attain.

Cost Large-scale projects can require sizable up-front investments.

Restrictions Although few laws and restrictions exist so far, regulation will probably increase.

Distribution Some products sold online can be very difficult to ship.

Hard Goods vs. Soft Goods

Some businesses offer software, music, news, or advice, which are referred to as *soft goods*, or digital goods. That term means that the product or service can be distributed via an electronic method, such as the Internet. The selling company can immediately distribute its products for free or for a charge. Soft goods offer immediate gratification because the user can quickly download or view the product or service.

Hard goods are items such as computer hardware, clothes, or books. Even though the goods can be purchased online, more traditional delivery methods are used: the U.S. mail, delivery services such as FedEx and UPS, and so on.

Whether the product is in the hard goods or soft goods category can affect its success in online sales. Most of the leading e-commerce sites offer hard goods, such as computers, networking equipment, and telecommunications devices. A few sell books and music.

Are companies that sell hard goods more successful than those that sell soft goods? The answer depends more on the product itself than on whether it is sold online. Consider perishables; they are hard goods, but they are not sold successfully online. What about soft goods? Services such as online project management are not very successful either.

There are several other considerations that affect product success:

Complexity   Is physical interaction required to order or set up the product or service? Complex products are difficult to market online.

Information intensive   Does the product require intensive prepurchase information gathering? These products are more easily marketed online.

Contact   Is the product or service best suited to physical contact? In other words, would a person want to touch the item before purchase to ensure it is exactly what they are looking for. If so, it will be more difficult to market online.

Product Pricing

A very expensive or very inexpensive item might not sell well on the Internet. Buyers generally want to see very expensive items to check quality, and the cost in shipping and time delays for an inexpensive item might make it less appealing. Both types of products could still be marketed online, however. Both Toyota (expensive products) and Coca-Cola (inexpensive products) have strong online marketing campaigns driving traffic to their retail channels.

Moderately priced items are more easily sold online. Also, products requiring frequent price or offering changes may be an excellent choice for online marketing because changing pricing or product descriptions in a database or web catalog is relatively easy. On the other hand, changing prices in printed catalogs can be expensive.

Global vs. Niche: Mass vs. Micro Markets

A product's market can be categorized in one of two ways. The first is a *global market* (or mass market), in which need is not constrained by geography and a large number of potential customers exists. For example, computer hardware is not specific to any geographic location; thus, it has a global or mass appeal and is a good product for online marketing.

The other type of market is a *niche market* (or micro market); a niche market product appeals to or is needed by a smaller number of customers. Niche market products might be advertised globally, but the ads target a select audience. For example, the market for mobile dog grooming services is not constrained significantly by geography (as, for example, surfing would be) because dogs are all over the world, but the number of potential customers is much smaller than the number of potential customers for, let's say, a product for humans. As a result, niche markets tend to be more difficult to reach online.

To take the analogy further, a company that installs the golden arches signs for McDonald's and services only the town of Springfield is most definitely serving a niche market. The company would probably be wasting its time with an e-commerce campaign. If that company is the sole source for this particular service in Springfield and works only in Springfield, there is little need to promote beyond the bounds of the community.

That leads to another reason for a Web presence though. Modern businesses may feel the need to hold a Web presence, not for sales purposes, but simply to show how "hip" they are in the modern world. It's a marketing technique in itself for a company to be able to say, "Check us out on the Web!" even if the full benefit of the Web is never realized.

Product Distribution and Availability

Product distribution depends largely on the distinction between hard goods and soft goods. Hard goods must be shipped, whereas soft goods may be shipped but are typically delivered online. The methods used for hard goods distribution will probably be determined by the cost and the importance of the delivery.

Product availability is another important consideration. If the product has other local distributors or retailers, it will be more difficult to sell online.

For example, a business that wants to sell cellular and wireless phones online will face extensive competition from other online companies and those with physical stores. For online marketers, such competition is one of the most difficult barriers to overcome. When a company has a physical location, a customer can walk into the store, touch and examine the product, and then buy. In this type of transaction, the customer has easy access to the product and a place to return it if needed.

The question then becomes this: Why would the customer choose to buy a cellular or wireless phone online? Perhaps the online marketer can offer the phone for a lower price. What about shipping charges? The cost of shipping can eliminate the discount advantage of shopping online. What about a return policy? If the customer has to return the phone, they may be required to pay the shipping and may not be able to use the phone in the interim. On the other hand, if the phone is purchased at a retail store, the customer can return it for immediate repair or replacement. Online marketers face serious challenges with issues of this type.

The problems discussed here may seem less like distribution and availability issues and more like product choice marketing issues, but the two areas are tightly interwoven and the boundaries are less distinct than they are with traditional marketing. Customer service is a major selling point that will help online businesses compete with traditional retailers.

Important Product Availability and Distribution Questions

Ease of shipment is another important consideration for online sellers of hard goods. Is the product large, small, perishable, or fragile? The legality of the product in various jurisdictions must also be considered, as must customs laws in various countries (discussed in greater detail in Chapter 21, "Law and the Internet").

So here is a list of important questions for a real-world design scenario:

- Are you selling hard goods or soft goods?

- Is the product available locally to the customer?

- Will the cost of shipping outweigh the benefits of online purchasing?

- Who will be responsible for the cost of return shipping of unsatisfactory products?

- Does the product ship easily?

- Is the product governed by laws or regulations for shipping and customs?

You may want to make a list of questions like these as you see them throughout the book and combine them into a real-world form that you can use to handle actual business scenarios.

With the answers to these questions in hand, you can now consider some other things that affect Web marketing.

Demographics

*D*emographics is the study of groups based on common characteristics. Good marketers base their decisions largely on demographic studies. Demographic studies of various groups, called populations, have been conducted for many years so marketers can learn how to best target prospective customers. The following are some of the most common demographic characteristics studied:

- Age

- Gender

- Race

- Income

- Location

- Education

When marketers understand the details of these characteristics, they can generalize about the group. They can then target a certain market segment and predict responses somewhat successfully based on experience.

When marketers have this type of information, they can best devise their campaigns to meet the target audience's needs and requirements. The needs of a teenage audience, for example, will differ from the needs of an audience of senior citizens.

In Exercise 22.2, you will consider demographic information.

EXERCISE 22.2

Exploring Demographics

Follow these steps to explore some demographics on blue collar occupations:

1. Enter `http://cyberatlas.internet.com/big_picture/` in your browser's Address or Location field. On the left side of the page, under Big Picture, click on the Demographics link.

2. Scroll down to the bottom of the page and click on the Demographic Archives link.

3. Scroll down and click on the link for the article entitled "Blue Collar Occupations Moving Online," dated 4/12/2001.

4. Take a moment to review the article and examine the demographic makeup it reports. Remember that these statistics are from only one source. Highly accurate demographics are available, but they usually have an associated access fee.

5. The following link provides a Yahoo! listing of other statistics and demographics: `http://dir.yahoo.com/computers_and_internet/internet/statistics_and_demographics/surveys/`.

Psychographics

*P*sychographics is defined as a science that can help anticipate the specific positive, negative, or neutral psychological impact of words, symbols, shapes, textures, colors, fonts, and even scale on consumer target market groups. These insights can offer a significant creative advantage to developers of corporate identities, promotional tools, and advertising campaigns.

Though lifestyles can be measured several ways, the most popular method is to understand people's perceptions of the following topics:

Activities   What people do with their time, including work, hobbies, vacation, and entertainment

Interests   What is important to people, such as family, home, community, and achievements

Opinions   The positions people hold on a variety of topics, including themselves, social issues, economics, politics, and culture

This information can be combined with demographics so marketers can develop a detailed focus on their target market.

Additional Guidance

Along with demographics and psychographics, there are other ways to focus your marketing in the intended directions. For example, you can use focus groups, surveys, and audience data:

Focus Groups   Another tool marketers have to evaluate product and service-marketing concepts is to pose them to a *focus group* for market testing. Focus groups can consist of employees in the marketing organization or you can use companies that supply them. One company providing this service is i.think inc. (`www.ithinkinc.com`).

Surveys   Surveys also help connect the marketer with the audience. Survey development is a special art and must be performed carefully to result in valid data. A company called Questionmark.com (`www.questionmark.com`) offers solutions for surveys.

Audience Data   Audience data is a combination of demographics, psychographics, and other survey tools that determines exactly *who is* actually receiving the message, whereas demographics alone determines *who should* see the message.

Summary

Each business benefits tremendously from the marketing strategy it establishes for itself. Web marketing strategies are no less important for e-commerce businesses than they are for traditional businesses. In fact, they are likely more important because of the numerous choices that consumers have both online and in standard brick-and-mortar establishments. The trick to marketing online lies in creating a strong Web presence and anticipating the needs of potential customers.

Tools such as online promotion campaigns, strong, well-thought out web designs, targeted marketing programs, and specific search engine placement can help carry e-businesses over the hump from Web startup to global dynamo. Looking at the successful Web presence of businesses such as Cisco, Amazon, and Dell, you can see how personal selection, interactivity, and integration play a vital role in grabbing a consumer's attention. Of course, several billions of dollars worth of marketing budgets certainly helps.

Businesses attempting a new Web presence need to consider such concepts as improving customer service and satisfaction, gaining access into new markets, selling new products, and automating the business process.

Of course, there are drivers and barriers associated with entering e-commerce. The drivers include increased access, around-the-clock service, EDI, increased bandwidth, easy-to-use technology, cost, easy access, the economic sense involved, the fact that there is no longer a need for physical stores, expansion of product offering, and global supply with business centralization still a possibility. The barriers include fragmented data and data format issues, large audience diversification, rapid changes, increase in competition, the lack of a physical presence that provides security for customers, more restrictions legally, and shipping needs.

By researching demographics and psychographics, along with using surveys and focus groups, businesses can make sure their marketing is directed correctly.

Exam Essentials

Understand e-commerce marketing goals. Know the common initial goals of an e-commerce business and how to determine which ones are relevant for your company. Sometimes a company needs to focus its marketing on automation of the selling process, and sometimes (as in the case with Federal Express) it needs to provide greater support for its customers. The end result should be that the business is profitable, either by encouraging repeat business, gaining a reputation for quality service, or even reducing costs through the use of e-commerce marketing.

Know the drivers and barriers to growth.   For businesses trying to enter new markets, factors that encourage growth are called drivers, and those that limit growth are called barriers. Being able to identify these factors and determine their effects can make the difference between profits or losses.

Understand the advantages and disadvantages of hard goods and soft goods.   Software, music news, or advice are referred to as soft goods. Soft goods can be distributed electronically, which eliminates the need for shipping resources. Items like computer hardware, clothes, and books are considered hard goods. Businesses that sell hard goods must consider delivery methods.

Understand product pricing ranges and price changes.   A very expensive or very inexpensive item might not sell well on the Internet because buyers generally want to see very expensive items to check quality, and the cost in shipping and time delays for an inexpensive item might make it less appealing.

Understand global versus niche product appeal.   A global market includes all people, everywhere, with the same needs. An example of a global market item would be computer hardware, which all people want in all countries. A niche market might be served globally, but the target is a select audience. For example, Irish flags may be sold globally, but they are basically a niche market item because only a small number of consumers (people who, most likely, are Irish) would be interested in the product.

Understand demographics and psychographics.   Demographics is the study of groups based on common characteristics. Psychographics is a science that can help anticipate the specific impact of certain words, symbols, and shapes on a consumer target market group.

Key Terms

Before you take the exam, be certain you are familiar with the following terms:

barriers	niche market
demographics	online communities
drivers	opt-in e-mail
focus group	passive recipients
global market	psychographics
hard goods	soft goods
immediacy	

Review Questions

1. Kayla is purchasing a pair of jeans over the Internet. What type of goods is she purchasing?

   A. Soft goods

   B. Hard goods

   C. Retail goods

   D. Clothing goods

2. What is the difference between a global market and a niche market?

   A. A global market is a narrow market; a niche market is more universal.

   B. A global market is one in which customers in all countries understand and appreciate the product.

   C. A niche market is one in which product offerings should be very upscale and expensive.

   D. A global market is not hindered by geography, whereas a niche market contains a narrowly selected group of people.

3. To dispense new information regarding a product or new products coming out, which of the following would be a solution that would allow people to choose whether they want further information from the company?

   A. Spamming

   B. Traditional mail

   C. Opt-in e-mail

   D. Website updates page

4. How do customer demographics help online marketers?

   A. By providing information about low-cost shipping options

   B. By providing detailed information about the customer base

   C. By providing detailed information about vendors and suppliers

   D. By categorizing information about customs requirements

5. In what way can electronic data interchange (EDI) help an online business grow?

  A. By allowing businesses to exchange data electronically with customers and other businesses

  B. By eliminating the need for business to operate in physical locations

  C. By offering e-commerce software packages at little or no cost

  D. By offering improved hardware with increased bandwidth and faster access

6. Bob sells high-end, expensive vacuum cleaners. Which of the following marketing strategies might Bob want to focus his attention toward in order to drive people to his site?

  A. Website design

  B. Online promotion campaigns

  C. Targeted marketing programs

  D. Search engine placement

7. Kenny's paintball factory has a Web presence that currently provides information only. Kenny would like to include an e-commerce store-front primarily because he would like to save money internally on the order-taking staff and the troubleshooting staff. Which of the following Web marketing goals is Kenny looking to accomplish?

  A. Improve customer service and satisfaction

  B. Access to different markets

  C. Sell new products

  D. Automate the business process

8. What marketing component should be considered of primary importance in online purchasing?

  A. Immediacy

  B. Shipping

  C. Payment methods

  D. Support

9. What is the chief difference between hard goods and soft goods for online sale?

    A. Sales tax is always charged on the sale of hard goods.

    B. Soft goods may be delivered to the customer electronically.

    C. Only hard goods may be marketed and sold online.

    D. Soft goods are always more successful in online sales.

10. How can online promotion function as a marketing strategy?

    A. By attracting non-Internet users to the online business

    B. By providing targeted marketing to selected customers

    C. By placing appropriate data with several search engines

    D. By directing a message to people who already use the Internet

11. Jack owns a company that sells golf equipment. What kind of market does Jack sell to?

    A. Global market

    B. Niche market

    C. Worldwide market

    D. Growing market

12. A computer game, which is purchased online and then received by the buyer via downloading it, is an example of what type of goods?

    A. Hard goods

    B. Game software

    C. Electronic goods

    D. Soft goods

13. What is one benefit of advertising on the Internet as opposed to using more traditional methods like radio or television?

A. Interactivity

B. More selective market

C. Security

D. No cost

14. It is more important to do which of the following before taking significant steps on a marketing project?

   A. Set up a payment gateway

   B. Set marketing goals

   C. Design an online catalog

   D. Include a shopping cart

15. Which of the following is a barrier to business growth when dealing with e-commerce?

   A. Rapid change

   B. Around-the-clock service

   C. Ease of access

   D. Centralization

16. How could a business that sells either very expensive or very inexpensive items use Internet marketing to draw customers to its website?

   A. By promising interstate customers that they need not pay sales tax

   B. By promising customers that the merchandise is of high quality

   C. By using a promotional site to drive traffic to its retail store

   D. By never changing its prices for any goods sold online

17. Which of the following is a driver to business sales when dealing with e-commerce?

    A. Increased competition

    B. Around-the-clock service

    C. Cost

    D. Distribution

18. Of the following, which is the most important aspect of site design?

    A. Looks

    B. Colors

    C. Page outline

    D. Functionality

19. What is one difference between targeted marketing programs and online promotion?

    A. With targeted marketing programs, you decide how audiences see the message.

    B. With targeted marketing programs, you determine which audience should see the message and why.

    C. With online promotion, you determine which audience should see the message and why.

    D. Online promotion involves e-mail marketing.

20. What is the benefit of building an online community around your e-commerce website?

    A. You can then sell products at a cheaper rate.

    B. You can provide efficient continuous product support.

    C. You can build a loyal following for your Web business.

    D. You can allow customers to customize what they want to view.

Answers to Review Questions

1. **B.** Hard goods are goods that have to be physically shipped, which is the case with a pair of jeans. Soft goods would include electronically dispensable goods. Retail and clothing might be somewhat reasonable conclusions, but only the terms *hard goods* and *soft goods* are used to refer to categories of goods on the Internet.

2. **D.** A global market is not hindered by geography, but a niche market contains a narrowly selected group of people. A niche market could still be a global market, but only a selected number of people are going to appreciate the product being marketed.

3. **C.** Opt-in e-mail give people a chance to indicate their personal interest in certain types of information and to give permission for a business to send them that information via e-mail. By using this solution, you can avoid sending the customer a lot of unwanted mail. Spamming is just the opposite in terms of showing concern for people's right to choose whether or not to receive e-mail. A website updates page is a valid solution, but it's not the best solution.

4. **B.** Demographics (or the study of groups based on common characteristics) provide detailed information about the customer base. This can be quite helpful in marketing a product because the studies can show how best to target a customer.

5. **A.** Electronic data interchange (EDI) allows businesses to exchange and use electronic data internally and with vendors, suppliers, and customers. Eliminating the need for business to operate in physical locations and increasing bandwidth are all good drivers for e-commerce growth, but they do not define EDI.

6. **D.** Although all of these methods might be considered effective, if a person were to purchase a vacuum online, they would most likely search for one through a search engine. The website design itself is going to mean little if people don't go to the site, and so again the search engine placement would be needed to drive customers to the site. Online promotional campaigns and targeted marketing are great ideas, but a vacuum (especially a high-end, expensive one) is not a daily purchase that will be driven by banner ads and advertising.

7. D. Automating the business process will save the company money or allow the company to move jobs over from one area of the company to another.

8. A. If consumers see something they want, the selling business should want to give it to them as quickly as possible. The longer the wait, the more time customers have to shop around or change their minds. The other options are important to consider, but online purchasing revolves around immediacy.

9. B. Soft goods can usually be delivered electronically. Hard goods need to be shipped through traditional methods. Both hard and soft goods can be marketed and sold online. It's difficult to say which is sold more successfully, but the top-selling sites sell hard goods.

10. D. To develop product awareness, a promotion campaign should be implemented. An online promotion to direct traffic to the site can be used to target those who already use the Internet. The other options describe different marketing approaches that work but are not considered online promotion campaigns according to the definition.

11. B. Jack sells to a niche market. A market that includes a subsection of the population is considered a niche market. A global market, which includes a majority of the population, would not be the kind of market for golf equipment.

12. D. There are two types of goods that can be sold through e-commerce, one of which is soft goods. Soft goods include items that can be shipped electronically to the buyer. The second form of goods in e-commerce is hard goods; these include items that need to be physically shipped to the recipient.

13. A. The interactivity involved in Internet advertising and purchasing is a key benefit of using the Internet instead of radio or television. The user has more control over where or how (including how fast) they continue the experience. Internet advertising is not free, and the need to ensure security wouldn't be considered a benefit. The market is wider, not more selective.

14. B. Establishing marketing goals is one of the first steps necessary for your e-commerce site to take form. Setting up a payment gateway, designing an online catalog, and including a shopping cart are tasks that you would perform based upon the goals you establish.

15. A. Rapid change is a barrier to business growth in e-commerce because you never know what new technology is going to replace your current e-commerce solution. E-commerce is changing daily, and businesses that utilize e-commerce technology will have to move with the technological changes, which will cost both time and money.

16. C. Very expensive or very inexpensive items might not sell well on the Internet. People generally want to see expensive items before purchasing them and the cost of shipping inexpensive items makes buying them online less appealing. Even so, a Web presence can benefit a company by driving traffic to its retail stores.

17. B. Around-the-clock service is a benefit, or driver, for e-commerce. Time zones are no longer a hindrance to business. Consumers can browse your website and make purchases at any time of the day, without any extra effort on your part, something that would be difficult and extremely expensive with traditional methods of commerce.

18. D. Functionality is an important part of site design. If your site doesn't work properly, consumers will not likely return.

19. B. When you use a targeted marketing program, you decide *which* audiences see the message. An online promotion involves *how* the audience sees the message. For example, an online promotion would include banner ad placement on other websites, but which websites are chosen and why depends on the targeted market.

20. C. Building an online community is one way to develop a loyal following for your e-commerce website. You must build value and include information that will keep your customers coming back for more.

Chapter

23

Online Product Promotion

THE CIW EXAM OBJECTIVE GROUPS COVERED IN THIS CHAPTER:

- ✓ Define the role of marketing in e-commerce site development, including but not limited to: promotion.
- ✓ Design an e-commerce site using web development software.

Basic marketing dogma is that if customers do not know about a product, they cannot buy it. That makes sense and explains why so many toy commercials are pushed into our homes in December. Product awareness results from promotion. Promotion means making others aware of something, someone, or someplace.

Some promotions are driven by marketing campaigns, and others might be driven by public opinion or demand. Promotions can be positive or negative, but the primary focus is to build awareness. There is no limit to the types of promotion and the methods used, but our primary focus in this chapter is online product promotion.

Within this chapter, we will examine several online promotions, including banner ads, banner exchange, referrer sites, search engine placement, and different types of e-mail (spam, targeted, and opt-in). Some should be familiar, and others may not be. We will also consider which characteristics make these promotions successful (and, in some cases, unsuccessful).

Remember that our discussion of promotions is meant to focus on the vehicle, not the message. The message is marketing; the vehicle is *promotion*. For example, a radio promotion is *how* people get the message; it is the vehicle. The marketing campaign decides *what* message listeners get from radio exposure.

Site Categories

In terms of promotion, there are two categories of sites: publisher sites and marketer sites. A *publisher site* is one whose primary focus is selling ad space as a means of revenue. Those who buy the advertising space on these sites are *marketers*.

Some publisher sites can be characterized as *revenue-supported* portals. Yahoo!, for example, is a portal. A *portal* is a website that many people visit and use to explore and participate in activities on the Internet. On Yahoo!, advertisers pay for space to place their ads. In return, by offering content and services, Yahoo! attracts users, who see and click on the ads. Yahoo! provides services such as a search engine, mail, news, stock quotes, and auctions. Internet users return to Yahoo! because of these features, which is why it is considered a portal, and a pretty good one at that. Most of these services are free, so the only way Yahoo! can generate revenue is to charge marketers money to place their advertising on the Yahoo! website. This structure makes Yahoo! a revenue-supported portal.

Publisher sites that contain heavy advertising and little content will not draw as many visitors; they may reap short-term profits, but their long-term viability will suffer. A publisher site must contain space for the marketer's message, but that message will probably not constitute the bulk of a site: The ratio of content to advertising tends to be higher than on a marketing site, which is the second category.

The second category is a *marketer site*, which differs from a publisher's site in that the primary focus is selling products or services for revenue. Once a customer arrives at a website to purchase something (perhaps as a result of clicking a banner ad), the destination site has received a *clickthrough*. That means a user saw a banner ad on another site that interested them and clicked it to go to the site offering the product or service.

Although the original site may have been a publisher (revenue-supported) site that drew the user in, the site that the user goes to after clicking on the link is a marketer site. The goal of a marketer site is to sell something. Therefore, a user will see very few banner ads for other products at other websites because the marketer site does not want to drive the customer away.

For example, if you went to McDonald's, you could order a Big Mac. But if the menu carried an ad directing you to Burger King for a Whopper, that ad would affect the number of Big Macs sold. This is the same philosophy that marketers use for visitors to their sites. They want to sell something, not send the customer elsewhere to make a purchase.

A marketer has a strong interest in keeping the visitor at the site as long as possible because the longer the visitor stays, the more chances the marketer has to convey the message. For this reason, many Web marketers advise against providing many (or even any) links away from the site. The marketer might, however, provide links to other sites that offer complementary products or services. For example, a site that offers sporting equipment may provide a link to a site that sells tickets to sporting events. One complements the other and neither causes the other to lose sales.

Publisher sites, however, usually rely on a multitude of shorter marketing messages created by different companies. These messages can be communicated in a brief visit, and their effectiveness is often measured in terms of how many users leave the publisher's site to access the advertiser's site. Publishers, then, have a much lower stake in keeping users at their sites; repeat visits are usually more important to them than long visits.

Because publishers can rely on repeat visits, they can use a value model that is not advisable for marketers. Publishers can provide directory and search engine sites, whose value consists chiefly in providing links away from the site. These are among the most successful advertising sites online: In November, 2001, according to *PC Meter*, 4 of the top 10 sites for homes and offices include publisher sites that offer search engine capabilities and directory information.

Banner Ads

Banner advertising is one of the most common forms of online promotion. Banner ads are the type of online advertising that you'll see the most. They have been used for many years, so their effectiveness has been tested over time. Banner ads address some sort of marketing objective, whether it be to promote a purchase or to initiate a registration.

Some will say that banner ads are not effective, but they are still the number-one form of promotion on the Web according to statistical data. The average response rate to banner ads on the Web is between 0.5 and 1.0 percent, which is comparable to other forms of media response rates. In fact, some studies show that Web banner ads have higher awareness rates than television ads. This rate is partially due to Web users' active participation in the medium, whereas television is a passively received medium. When banner ads are responded to, conversion rates are approximately 60 percent within the first 30 minutes.

Banner ads seem to be effective for up to four exposures per user. The user response to ads increases for each exposure up to four, after which it begins to drop. So leaving the same ad up for too long can reduce effectiveness beyond a point.

Banner ads do seem to increase site traffic and lead to sales, but they do not appear to increase brand awareness. *Brand awareness* is created on the product's or service's website through extensive use of a logo and/or slogan. Studies indicate that the best branding technique is to have the business' logo on every page of the site.

Banner Vocabulary

You need to be familiar with some terms as they relate to banner ads. These terms identify different aspects of banner ad use:

Ad clicks   The number of times users click a banner ad.

Banner   An ad (on a web page) that links to the advertiser's site.

CASIE   The Coalition for Advertising Supported Information and Entertainment; it was founded in May 1994 by the Association of National Advertisers (ANA) and the American Association of Advertising Agencies (AAAA) to guide the development of interactive advertising and marketing.

Clickthrough Rate   The percentage of ad views that resulted in a user clicking on the banner ad (a clickthrough is a user clicking on a banner ad to "click through" to the advertiser's site). The clickthrough rate indicates how many visitors out of each 100 click on the ad.

CPC   The *cost-per-click (CPC)*, an Internet marketing formula used to price ad banners. Advertisers will pay Internet publishers based on the number of clicks a specific ad banner receives. Cost generally ranges from $0.10 to $0.20 per click.

CPM   The *cost per thousand (CPM)* for a particular ad. A website that charges $10,000 per banner and guarantees 500,000 impressions has a CPM of $20 ($10,000 divided by 500).

Hit   Each instance of a web server sending a file to a browser. Hits are recorded in the server log file. Hits are generated for every element of the requested page, including graphics, text, and objects. If a user views a page containing four graphics, five hits will be recorded in the server log: one for the page itself and one for each of the four graphics. Webmasters use hits to measure server workload. Hits are a poor guide to visitor traffic measurement because they represent element requests rather than the actual number of visitors.

Impressions The number of times an ad banner is downloaded and presumably seen by visitors. *Impressions* correspond to net impressions from traditional media. Browser caching of images affects the accuracy of impressions.

Log file A file that tracks actions that have occurred. Web servers maintain log files listing every request made to the server. With log analysis tools, site managers can determine where visitors are coming from, how often they return, and how they navigate through a site (including how long they stayed). Using cookies allows even more details to be tracked.

Page views The number of times a user requests a page containing a particular ad.

Unique users The number of different users who visit a site within a specific time period.

Visits A sequence of requests made by one user at one site. Any user activity within a rolling 30-minute time frame is considered one visit.

Understanding these terms will assist you in your endeavors to become CIW Master Design certified, and they are necessary terms for everyday web design in relation to e-commerce.

Effective Banner Ads

Some steps that have been shown to increase the clickthrough rate can be applied to banner ad creation. Studies indicate that the highest clickthrough rate occurs between the third and fourth impressions by a given user.

Here are some additional thoughts on using banner ads effectively:

Questions Questions initiate user action and entice site visitors to click on the banner. Questions can include phrases such as "Do you...?" or "Have you...?" or "Are you looking...?" Questions may also contain the words *free*, *quick*, or *try*, as in "Would you like a free...?"

Calls to action A phrase can tell the user to take action. The most common call to action on banner ads is "Click Here." Others include "Go," "Find," "Last Chance," and "Help."

Refreshed banners A banner ad will "burn out" and clickthrough rates will fall as users repeatedly see the same ad. Changing the banner periodically helps increase clickthrough. Yahoo! claims that burnout occurs in two weeks.

Minimal file size   Most users' chief complaint about the Web is speed. If users must wait for the banner to download, they may become distracted, frustrated, or bored. As with all web design, download speed must be a key consideration. Making the banner ad file as small as possible will help shorten download time.

Animation   Web marketers once believed that animated banner ads received a higher clickthrough rate than static ads. This model is changing and more ads are static. One of the other drawbacks of animated banners is larger file size, resulting in longer downloads.

No false claims   Do not claim something on the banner that is not really what users will experience or learn if they do click through. Such claims only frustrate users, who will probably click the Back button and not stay at the site.

Visual quality   The banner should be visually attractive and have a high-quality look. Poorly designed banners have lower clickthrough. Color combinations work better than black and white or gray and white.

Obvious hyperlinks   It's sometimes helpful to apply a blue border around the image to make the banner appear as an obvious link. Also, it is becoming common to have a link labeled "Click Here" in plain text under the ad.

Standard sizing   Standard banner ad sizes should be used. Most publisher sites will require that the banner comply with these standard sizes before they will display it. Examples of these sizes are presented in the next section.

Banner Sizes

The Interactive Advertising Bureau (IAB) has developed standard banner ad sizes (`www.iab.net`). Examples of the standard sizes are seen in Figures 23.1 through 23.8. As mentioned earlier, websites selling advertising space will require that advertisers provide a banner based on these sizes because these sizes typically correspond to their rate schedules.

FIGURE 23.1   468×60 pixels (full banner)

FIGURE 23.2 392×72 pixels (full banner with vertical navigation bar)

FIGURE 23.3 234×60 pixels (half banner)

FIGURE 23.4 120×240 pixels (vertical banner)

FIGURE 23.5 125×125 pixels (square button)

FIGURE 23.6 120×90 pixels (button 1)

FIGURE 23.7 120×60 pixels (button 2)

FIGURE 23.8 88×31 pixels (micro button)

Recently, the IAB produced some new voluntary guidelines for seven new Interactive Marketing Unit (IMU) ad formats. These new formats have been added to the recommended formats already in place. The Ad Unit Task Force meets biannually and will determine the effectiveness of these new formats.

The Keys to Banner Ad Usage

Banner ads can be quite effective if used properly. Finding banner ad space and knowing how to position the ads on that space are important, as are establishing banner exchanges and referrer programs and watching the ads' performance.

Finding Banner Ad Space

Choosing a website on which to advertise can have a significant effect on the campaign. One of the benefits advertisers have when using banner ads is the ability to precisely target their markets.

If an ad were to be placed randomly on a website such as Yahoo!, it would not be considered a targeted placement. Yahoo! would offer extremely high visibility, but it does not target a specific market. The Yahoo! website is a portal, so a variety of people use it.

Placing a banner ad on a site that is addressed more specifically to a particular market can result in better clickthrough. Placing a banner for a new golf club on Yahoo! would give it high visibility but not necessarily a high clickthrough. However, if the ad were placed on Golf.com, the same number of impressions would probably have a higher clickthrough rate.

Choosing a site on which to advertise is an important decision. Due to the complex nature of ad placement, many companies are turning to advertising representatives to place banner ads on the Web. These advertising representatives can save the advertiser considerable time and effort by knowing where to place ads most effectively, which is referred to as *targeted placement*. They can also find other Web businesses that are willing to place ads on your site. They make money by taking a percentage of the revenue paid by the advertiser.

Many business and publisher websites have a rate card, which is used as the basic guide to determine how much the banner ad placement will cost. By visiting a Web publisher site and looking for the link to "advertise," you should be able to locate the rate card and determine approximately how much the placement will cost. Exercise 23.1 gives you a chance to visit a site to investigate its ad rates.

EXERCISE 23.1

Determining Ad Rates at Individual Sites

In this exercise, you'll learn how to investigate different portal site fees. To do so, follow these steps:

1. Choose a portal site of your choice. This site can be a search engine or any commonly used site that sells ad space. If you cannot select one, try www.northernlight.com or www.yahoo.com.

2. Look for the link that leads to advertising information at the bottom of the home page.

3. Select that link and then consider the variety of information provided on advertising. For example, what is the cost-per-thousand (CPM) for random placement? Usually, the cheapest placement is referred to as "run-of-the-site" or something similar. This type of placement means your ad will appear randomly. More expensive rates will have more targeting characteristics based on searches for keywords or categories.

Banner Ad Positioning

After choosing the best site on which to place the ad, the next important consideration is the ad's position on the page. Many believe that to achieve the highest clickthrough rate, the banner should be at the top of the page.

Web pages load into the browser from top to bottom; therefore, if the ad is at the top, the user sees it first and will notice it more often. Depending on download speed, that banner ad may be the only thing users see while they are waiting. Obviously, this exposure is a benefit. However, some studies have indicated that another position receives a higher clickthrough.

Advertising professionals debate about why this position seems to have a higher rate. Look at Figure 23.9 to see the position in question. Then see if you can determine why that position might have a higher clickthrough rate than other positions.

FIGURE 23.9 Possible banner ad placement area

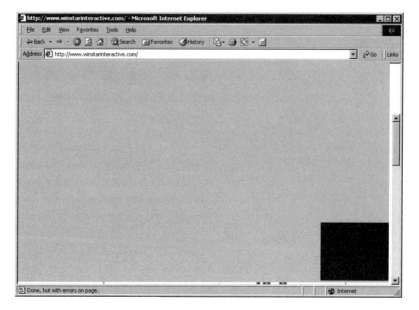

If you said this position has a higher clickthrough because the user is more likely to accidentally click the ad, you may be right. If the user wants to scroll down, they will need to position the mouse in the lower-right corner of the browser and click. If the mouse is not over that very small area, the user might miss the navigation arrow, thereby clicking the banner ad instead.

Others claim that in the English language we read from top to bottom, left to right, leaving the banner ad the most recent item seen before the user scrolls. However, other studies assert that Web users do not actually read; they scan. If they scan from left to right, however, the argument might still have some merit.

This position might have a higher clickthrough, but still might not generate higher sales. Of the number of visitors who do accidentally click through and go to the site, most are probably not interested in the product or service.

Other common placements are on the left margin and at the bottom. So, these are not definitive scientific findings, just some good ideas based upon experiences.

Banner Exchange

Exchanging ad banners with other websites is one of the ways marketers can help reduce advertising costs and drive business in two directions.

For example, a Web-based business that offers online travel packages might want to engage in a banner ad program to help promote its site yet keep costs down. A cost-effective move would be to find a site that offers corresponding but not competing services. A good choice might be to exchange banner ads with a site that offers luggage. If the owners of these sites agreed to exchange banners, they would be promoting each other's sites and remaining in a targeted market.

Using targeted markets is highly effective, but it can be time-consuming to find them. Another useful method is to join a banner exchange program.

In a banner exchange, a site owner agrees to display banner ads on their site to earn credits each time the banner is viewed. As these credits accumulate, they can be used to "pay for" displaying the banner ad on other sites. In effect, the more people who come to the site, the more banners are viewed, resulting in more points earned and more free placements in exchange. Visit a banner exchange program in the Exercise 23.2.

EXERCISE 23.2

Visiting a Banner Exchange Program

LinkBuddies is a banner exchange program that you can consider as an option for link placement. Follow these steps to visit the site:

1. Enter `http://www.linkbuddies.com` in your browser's Address or Location field and press Enter.

2. Scroll down the page to the Discover More About section.

3. Select the "How the free ad exchange works" link to learn more about this feature.

4. Go back to the home page and select the link labeled "The different ad sizes available."

5. Scroll down and examine the information listed. As a member, you would have access to the network's reporting and statistics capabilities, along with ad placement services.

Here are some other popular exchange networks you can check out:

- Hitexchange at www.hitexchange.net

- Link Hut at www.linkhut.com

Referrer Programs

Referrer sites or programs operate differently from banner exchange programs mainly because they direct traffic in one direction. In such an arrangement, one site pays another site for traffic sent to the first site.

Consider the following example: Company A sells snowboards. Company A is willing to pay other company's commissions. Company A might pay commissions for new visitors or for only new visitors who make purchases, a structure called performance-based advertising. In some cases, Company A might pay for new traffic or pay a higher commission if the new visitor makes a purchase.

Company B sells snowboarding vacations. Company B agrees to place a banner on its site directing visitors to Company A's website. Company B will be paid only for results. If no visitors click through from Company B's website, Company B does not earn a commission. Logs must be kept so that any commission due will be paid. Logs can be kept in different ways, depending on the agreement. Common methods of tracking include cookies, special URLs, special account names, and page redirections.

If the visitor's browser supports cookies, where the user came from and other important information can easily be detected. Third-party server logging software can also provide vital statistics. Special URLs that redirect users provide only a rough estimate of clickthroughs but are often used. A special URL that contains an ID and follows the user through the site provides more information than a simple redirection.

Commonly utilized referral programs are offered by the following sites:

- Amazon at www.amazon.com

- Barnes and Noble at www.bn.com

- CDnow at www.cdnow.com

- Reel.com at www.reel.com

Banner Ad Performance

Once a banner ad campaign has begun, an evaluation of its performance is required to determine its effectiveness. Depending on the size of the campaign, the data can become an information overload nightmare. To effectively manage the performance review, several companies provide software that can streamline the load and provide a clear picture of success or failure. Following are a few companies offering such services and their products' names:

- Paramark.com offers PILOT (Paramark's Interactive Learning and Optimization Technology)

- Doubleclick.com offers DART

- Engage.com offers AdManager and AdBureau

Traditional banner ads sometimes lack visual interest, but Bluestreak.com (`www.bluestreak.com`) has provided an alternative. Bluestreak creates interactive banners that allow the viewer to interact with the ad before being linked to the destination. Many banners are on display in the website's gallery.

Advertising Representatives

Trying to locate a website on which your advertising will be effective can be a time-consuming and difficult task. Advertising representatives can help with decisions and placement choices and usually can achieve greater success. Representatives and their organizations have well-established networks and statistical data that can help the marketer plan and execute a successful ad campaign.

In Exercise 23.3, you can visit Winstar Interactive Media, an ad rep site that will assist in placing banner ads at strategic sites.

EXERCISE 23.3

Visiting an Advertising Representative Website

To see how one advertising representative website works, follow these steps:

1. Enter `http://www.winstarinteractive.com/index.html` in your browser's Address or Location field.

EXERCISE 23.3 *(continued)*

2. Click on the Rate Card link to view the rates.

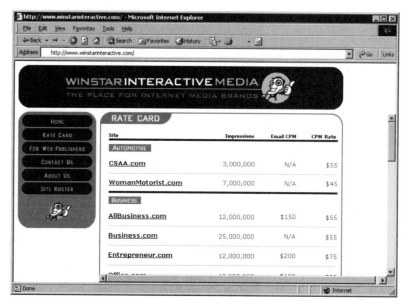

3. Click on the Site Roster link for a more detailed listing of sites.

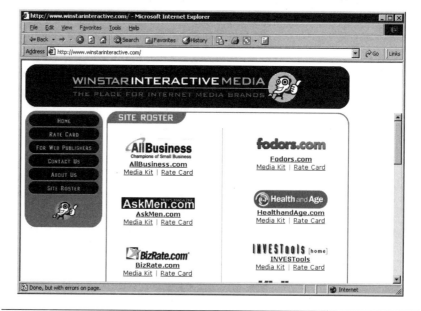

Tracking

When developing a site and attempting to draw people to it, you might reasonably ask yourself some of the following questions: Did the user stay at the site? Did they request information or make a purchase? How long did the user stay? Where did they come from? Knowing the answers to these questions helps marketers understand if the banner ad is effective (or if it is as effective as they had hoped) and how users are responding.

The only way that banner ad effectiveness can be understood is to track the process. Tracking has many components, and all must be examined to determine true effectiveness. For example, knowing just the total number of impressions a banner has is inconclusive..The number of impressions plus the number of clickthroughs is more conclusive. Knowing what users did once they reached the site offers even more conclusive information.

Trackers can identify the number and percentage of visitors, the type of operating system, the browser type, and the user's domain. They can also determine traffic by the hour, day, week, and month. Many services offer tracking for free if you place their logo on your site. Some also offer a service for a nominal fee so that you do not need to post the logo on your site.

To use these tools, all you will need to do is add some HTML coding (provided by the tracker) to the pages of the site you want to track. The tracking data is then followed and stored on the tracking service's servers for you to review and use to generate reports. Remember that trackers are not as powerful as log analysis tools that use the actual server logs to examine traffic. In Exercise 23.4, you can examine a tracking service.

EXERCISE 23.4

Examining Tracking Service Data

To examine a tracking service to learn how it can help generate more conclusive ad and user data, follow these steps:

1. Enter `http://www.mycomputer.com` in your browser's Address or Location field and press Enter.

2. Select the Small Business image hyperlink.

3. Select More Info under the SuperStats tool. Then select Demo on the left side of the page. Click on the SuperStats Premium button under Online Live Demos.

EXERCISE 23.4 *(continued)*

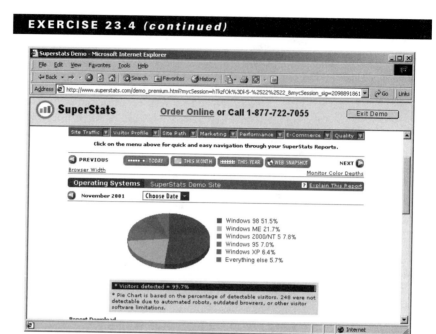

4. Under Visitor Profile Reports, select Operating Systems.

5. Scroll down to view the report.

EXERCISE 23.4 *(continued)*

6. Click the browser's Back button and choose one of the other types of reports from the list.

Using these different types of reports, you can track the effectiveness of banner ad placements by identifying the sites from which visitors were referred. Examine the other reports to learn how usage can be tracked. Many of these services exist; here are two other popular ones:

- Extreme Tracking at `www.extreme-dm.com` (free service)
- Dynamic Logic at `www.dynamiclogic.com` (paid service)

Customer Incentives

In general, customers' online buying habits differ from their practices in shopping at "brick-and-mortar" businesses. One thing that remains consistent, however, is the fact that customers expect to get the maximum value for their money.

By offering *incentives*, Web businesses give customers a reason to do business with them and to return in the future. Incentives can be in the form of discounts, credits, or free items. To provide incentives, a business needs to tell prospective customers about them and motivate the customers to visit the website.

Becoming an affiliate or partner with a well-known customer incentive program is often a reliable method for generating sales. Some sites offer to market and provide coupons to customers. These coupons are sent via permission or opt-in e-mail, discussed later in this chapter, or in some cases by the less-preferred direct e-mail marketing. Other incentives allow customers to earn credits or rewards that can be redeemed later for merchandise or services.

Whatever the incentive, it must be something the customer believes is valuable. The following sites help provide customer incentives:

e-centives.com   Provides digital coupons tailored to the shopper's interests.

Clickrewards.com   Provides customers with a way to earn ClickMiles, which work the same as frequent flyer miles and can be redeemed in the same way.

Search Engines

A search engine is a database system designed to index URLs, Usenet groups, FTP sites, and image files. The typical search engine contains a special application called a *spider*, or *crawler*. The purpose is to map selected Web content and return URLs to which users can link when they search for a topic. When the search engine visits a new site, it will attempt to categorize the site based on its content. Fortunately, most search engine spiders look for special HTML tags that help them in the cataloging process. When a user performs a search, links to websites relating to the topic will be returned based on their relevance to the search topic. The important thing to understand about the spider is that it performs an automated process.

A *directory* is basically a manual-entry database system. Website owners who want to be listed on a directory should notify the directory's management about their sites. They will usually need to provide a URL, a title, and a short summary of the website.

The main distinction between search engines and directories is how they get their information. Search engines catalog entries automatically, whereas directories do it manually.

Registering a site with all the major search engines and directories can be overwhelming because so many exist. The most effective registration is usually from a service or software package that automates the process. A number of online services request information one time and then automatically submit it to hundreds of search engines and directories simultaneously.

The following list includes several online services that help the search engine submission process. Keep in mind that these services are not free; companies can make an entire business out of search engine placement:

- bCentral Submit It! at www.submitit.com

- SiteAnnounce.com at www.siteannounce.com

Software is also available to help automate the process:

- Promotion Expert at www.search-engine-submit.com

- SitePromoter at www.sitepromoter.com

- WebPositionGold at www.webpositiongold.com

- AddWeb at www.cyberspacehq.com

If you choose to perform your own manual submission, you need to manually visit each search engine and go though the process several times.

The time and effort involved makes that choice less appealing than using an automated service or a software package. Nevertheless, if you choose to perform manual submission, some sites can help simplify the process by providing links to each of the search engine submission pages, which will save some time:

- The search engine guide at `www.searchengineguide.org`

- URL submission at `www.tiac.net/users/seeker /searchenginesub.html`

<META> Tags

Most likely you've already read the section "<META> Tags and Search Engines" in Chapter 9. In this section, we'll review the concepts of <META> tags for emphasis. *<META> tags* are placed within your web pages in the HTML coding that users don't generally see. Search engines look for them to place your site in the query results from a user's search. Using banner ads to advertise your site is great for drawing in visitors, but people sometimes use a search engine to look for a product, and the search engine can help lead new visitors to your site.

The term *search engine* is used loosely in the Web community to include both search engines and directories. The distinction between the two is that a search engine uses an automated process to discover new web pages. The program that handles this search, sometimes called a *robot* or a *spider*, crawls around the Web following hyperlinks and indexing the content that it finds. Therefore, eventually a search engine will find your page, assuming that a link to your site exists somewhere on the Web.

Because you cannot determine how long it will be before a search engine "finds" your site, you should consider submitting your site to the search engines. Submitting your site speeds the process and increases your chances for higher placement in search results. This may give website designers some control over placement. Consider listings in the phone book. Have you ever noticed how many company names begin with the letter *A*? Business owners want their companies to appear first. This is also the goal of e-commerce businesses, to be first in the search results from search engines.

Some search engines will search for values specified by the CONTENT attribute on pages that use the <META> tag NAME attribute value of `"keywords"`, as shown in the following example:

```
<META NAME="keywords"
CONTENT="keywordA, keywordB, keywordC">
```

Directories differ slightly from search engines in that they find sites based on manual submission only. If you don't manually submit a site, it will never be listed in query results. Where directories benefit users is that they do a better job of classifying content so that search results are more likely to contain a match for a query.

Which Search Engine or Directory?

How many search engines exist? Certainly hundreds, if not thousands. Does this mean that you must submit your site to each of them? You could if you wanted to. However, in spite of the great number of users on the Web, only the top 22 search engines are used by the majority of Web users. They are listed here in alphabetical order:

AlltheWeb	HotBot	Netscape
AltaVista	Infoseek	Northern Light
AOL NetFind	Inktomi	OpenDirectory
Ask Jeeves	Iwon	RealNames
Direct Hit	LookSmart	Snap
Excite	Lycos	WebCrawler
Go2Net	Microsoft	Yahoo!
Google		

Ensuring that your site is registered with these search engines and directories will cover more than 90 percent of the searches conducted on the Web. However, your site's ranking is an entirely different matter.

Keyword Development and Placement

These guidelines were included in Chapter 9, but they're worth repeating because keywords contribute greatly to your site's ranking by search engines and directories:

- Choose keywords that are relevant to your site and do not use misleading words.

- If possible, choose a domain name that includes your keywords.

- Do not use HTML framesets; most search engines have difficulty ranking sites that use them.

- When possible, use keywords when naming your HTML files (for example, `cellular1.htm`, `cellular2.htm`, and so forth).

- Test your chosen keywords on some popular search engines to see what results are returned. Then visit the sites mentioned and look at the text and source code to see other keywords that were used.

- Check to see if the keywords you have selected are among commonly misspelled words. Commonly misspelled words can be used in the <META> tags to help users find your site, but do not misspell words on your pages.

- Avoid using keywords that search engines do not index, such as *to*, *the*, *and*, *or*, *of*, and so forth.

- Use both singular and plural spellings of keywords, as well as other variations (for example, *phones*, *phone*, *telephone*, and so forth).

- Use abbreviations (if appropriate) as well as both uppercase and lowercase spellings.

- Use the HTML <TITLE> tag to include a brief 7-to-12-word description of your site, using as many as three of your keywords. Many search engines use the title as the site description, so make it appealing. The length should not exceed 70 characters. Do not use all uppercase letters. Avoid using your company name (unless it is highly recognizable) because this practice wastes space that could be used for keywords.

- Create a logical descriptive summary paragraph using as many keywords as possible. Place it in the first section of the body of the document, within the first 200 characters. Remember that users will read this description, so it must make sense. Also, include the keywords in other areas of the document, including the last sentence.

- Use the `ALT` attribute of the <IMG> tag to include keywords.

- Avoid using graphics exclusively on your home page. Search engines read text, not graphics.

- Do not try to mask a field of repeated keywords with background color.

- Do not place a banner ad at the top of your home page. Using the ALT attribute and hyperlink this way describes keywords other than your own.

E-Mail Marketing

The abundance of e-mail addresses makes it very tempting to use e-mail as a mass marketing tool. Several different categories of e-mail marketing have different connotations and perceptions.

Spam E-Mail

Spam is unsolicited e-mail. It is the Internet equivalent of bulk junk mail. Lists of e-mail addresses are gathered from discussion and news groups or purchased from companies that specialize in creating distribution lists. Proper network etiquette forbids the use of spam. It is considered a nuisance, very much like unsolicited phone marketing calls or door-to-door sales. Newsgroups can be flooded with irrelevant or inappropriate messages; this technique is also called spamming.

Because of its negative connotation, clearly a company or business that wants respect in the marketplace will not use spam. Most spam marketers are just trying to move products or services and are not considered to have merit as legitimate businesses. "Get rich quick" and "lose weight fast" are common themes for spam marketing.

It may be tempting to send out tens of thousands of unsolicited e-mail messages to get exposure and drive people to your website, but the negative implications can outweigh the results. Large Internet service providers often block domains that engage in spamming.

Targeted E-Mail

Targeted e-mail is spam that has been slightly tailored for a particular customer base. Usually, targeted e-mail uses specific e-mail addresses that have been qualified. Thus, a company that creates an e-mail list has categorized the addresses on it. For example, someone may compile a list of e-mail addresses of people interested in health food and vitamins from a magazine or store that has that data. The e-mail company compiles a list and then sells it to marketers who want to reach those people.

Again, this type of marketing is not seen as legitimate and should be avoided by businesses that want to maintain a solid reputation.

Opt-In E-Mail

Opt-in e-mail is the only legitimate form of e-mail marketing. With this method, recipients have agreed to receive the information and have given the business permission to send it to them.

This choice is usually made when a user signs up for a service and is asked if they would like to receive news and updates. Because the user has given permission, they have already visited the website. Therefore, opt-in e-mail is not a primary marketing method but rather a follow-up or continued form of marketing. Businesses that engage in opt-in e-mail must also use discretion when sending messages and should not treat the user's permission as an invitation to send an unlimited number of messages.

Opt-in e-mail is not a license to distribute a user's e-mail address to other agencies for their marketing purposes. This is completely contrary to the purpose of "opt-in" choice.

Online Catalogs

Once you get someone to your site and you've promoted it well, part of the key to getting them to stay is providing a clear, easy-to-use, functional online catalog.

An *online catalog* is similar to a paper-based catalog; it includes all the products, codes, and prices. It can also include product images, product descriptions, and attributes such as size or color. To develop the catalog, you can follow any existing model, whether electronic or paper-based, assuming the business is not a startup.

At this stage, design concepts are fused with applications to form a total e-commerce environment. When designing the catalog, think in terms of real-world usage. How would your customers approach the site? How would they search for items? What approach makes the most sense in grouping and departmentalizing the items?

Creating a catalog that looks good is important, but it is far more important to make it effective.

Catalog Components

The term *catalog*, used here generically, implies a series of products grouped together that a customer can browse. The standard catalog can usually be separated into divisions or departments, then into products and items, then into sizes, shapes, and colors, with specific pictures or descriptions of each product or service.

Once a customer has located a product or service to buy, the next step is to add the product to what is typically called a shopping cart. The *shopping cart* is the component of an e-commerce site that helps users keep track of the items they plan to buy. It resembles a physical shopping cart because it follows customers around the site, allowing them to continue adding items until they are finished shopping and ready to buy.

The next step of the online catalog experience is the user's completion of a transaction, thus finalizing the sale. This part of the site is not directly related to the catalog, but it will sometimes be included if a software package is purchased or used in conjunction with an online catalog service.

Some software packages provide complete online catalogs, shopping carts, and transaction tools. These packages rely on open standards as well as proprietary coding. Some solutions require installation on the web server that is hosting the site, and others are hosted as outsourced methods.

An example of an outsourced method would be a *purchase button*, which is a generic term for a button used to pass information and conduct a transaction on another server, typically for ease of implementation and increased security. Many businesses and developers cannot afford the costs and time to develop a complete transaction system to accept credit cards online. The merchant provides the catalog, but when the customer is ready to add something to the cart or to purchase a product, they are directed to a server that provides the transaction and security capabilities.

Depending on the service, users may not even know that they have been connected to another server to perform the transaction because the look and feel of the website on that server have been customized to match those of the original site. When the user completes the transaction or wants to continue shopping, he or she is returned to the original website, while the shopping cart and purchase information remain on the secure transaction server.

Building an Internet Catalog

A company's catalog is probably the most widely seen part of its Web content. Launching an online catalog involves more than converting an existing print catalog into HTML text with scanned images. The guidelines for attracting customers to Web storefronts are different. An online catalog must offer more than a traditional catalog: lower prices, more information, better searching capabilities, or easier ways to find products. A well-designed online catalog can also help a company expand into new markets inexpensively or cross-sell products.

Identify Business Objectives

Identifying the business objectives is imperative to establishing the focus of the online catalog: Is the catalog meant to attract new business? Is the catalog meant to service existing customers quickly? Provide additional information? The more clearly the objectives are defined, the more effective the catalog will be.

The two highest startup costs involve how much of the content is already in digital format and the number of photos the catalog will include. A catalog with a website and full ordering capabilities could be available for a modest price. However, adding more features to the catalog will increase the cost.

Here are a few good catalog-building suggestions:

- *Build online catalogs slowly.* Many commercial products are available for starting an online catalog. iCat (`www.icat.com`) produces software that allows a commerce-enabled website to be designed for less than $20,000. This package includes catalog description and ordering capabilities. The online catalog can be as simple as a textual listing of goods and services, or as complex as a hyperlinked web of goods and services in which ordering and inventory control work together.

- *Categorize data properly.* An online catalog's design must be carefully planned. It must be easier to read than a traditional catalog because it can leverage the Web infrastructure. The best-designed catalogs accommodate users with 14.4Kbps or 28.8Kbps modems (always gear your site toward your weakest link in terms of bandwidth); thus it is important to allow customers to access graphics as needed. The data in the catalog must also be categorized properly, perhaps with search engines and indexes.

- *Provide special pricing.* To interest customers in the online catalog (at least initially), consider offering special prices on goods and services ordered through the catalog. Remember, the catalog lowers distribution costs and allows the merchant to access markets previously difficult to target; thus, as an online merchant, you should consider passing some of these savings on to the customer.

Microsoft's Commerce Server 2000 is an excellent product for building catalogs for your e-commerce site. The procedure is quite simple: select to the Catalogs option and create one. The format is in place already and you can easily customize it to suit your needs, including adding your products and their corresponding definitions. You won't need to know the details of this type of software for the exam, but they are good to know in the real world.

Summary

One of the greatest challenges a website designer and e-business manager faces is the question of how to drive visitors to a website. Fortunately, the Web seems to have evolved with simple solutions to marketing a site. By utilizing such elements as banner ads, banner exchanges, referrer sites, search engine placement, and opt-in e-mail, e-businesses have a leg up in gaining access to potential visitors. Some websites have attempted to provide an Internet portal for visitors by enticing them with incentives, Web coupons, credits, and even free products.

Helping visitors find the products they need or want is an essential part of maintaining a successful Web business. Online catalogs can offer fast and efficient search engines for visitors to find what they are after. Online catalogs should be user friendly and easily integrated into an existing inventory database.

The saying goes, "If you build it, they will come," but the logic is much more complicated in Web business. As much as a website is available to users all over the world, finding the right method to catch a Web surfer's attention and drive them to a specific site will always be a challenge. By getting creative with marketing and advertising tools, e-commerce designers can hope to see more traffic, and certainly more than they would just waiting for visitors to arrive. The saying in this case should be, "If you build it, advertise it well and actually have something good to sell at a reasonable price; then they will come, and possibly again and again."

Exam Essentials

Understand the most common methods of online promotions.   The most common types of online promotions are banner ads, banner exchanges, referrer sites, search engine placement, spam e-mail, targeted e-mail, and opt-in e-mail. You should know the nuances of each method and understand when each should be used.

Understand the difference between a publisher site and a marketer site. A publisher site is one whose primary focus is selling ad space as a means of revenue. On the other hand, marketer site is one whose primary focus is selling products or services for revenue.

Understand clickthrough and clickthrough rates, CPC, and CPM.   A clickthrough occurs when a user clicks on a banner ad and is taken to the advertiser's site. The clickthrough rate is the percentage of ad views that results in a user clicking the banner ad; it is based on how many visitors out of each 100 click on the ad. CPC is the cost-per-click, an Internet marketing formula used to price ad banners. Advertisers pay Internet publishers based on the number of clicks a specific banner ad receives. CPM is the cost per thousand for a particular ad.

Know the various sizes and types of banner ad placement mechanisms. Banner sizes can vary and the desired size of the banner can determine the cost for placement on other sites. Placement mechanisms include exchanging ad banners with other websites (this is one of the ways marketers can help reduce advertising costs and drive business in two directions) and referrer sites or programs (direct traffic in one direction and, in such an arrangement, one site pays another site for traffic sent to the first site).

Know the various ways to enhance a site's search engine placement. Be able to explain the concept of spiders or crawlers and the use of <META> tags. In addition, know the methods involved in registering your site with various search engines.

Know your e-mail marketing choices, especially opt-in. Be able to explain the differences between spam (unsolicited junk e-mail), targeted e-mail (spam that has been slightly tailored for a particular customer base), and opt-in e-mail (the only solicited form of e-mail marketing).

Understand the needs of an online catalog. Online catalogs are different than real catalogs because they have to hold viewers' attention in different ways; in some cases, without immediate pictures. Creating a catalog includes entering all the products, codes, and prices. Other catalog entries can include product images, product descriptions, and attributes such as size or color.

Key Terms

Before you take the exam, be certain you are familiar with the following terms:

<META> tags	opt-in e-mail
brand awareness	portal
clickthrough	promotion
cost per thousand (CPM)	publisher site
cost-per-click (CPC)	purchase button
crawler	revenue-supported
directory	shopping cart
impressions	spam
incentives	spider
marketer site	targeted e-mail
marketers	targeted placement
online catalog	trackers

Review Questions

1. Thai owns a company that sells snowboarding equipment. To bring in more site traffic and revenue, he decides to exchange banners with another online company. What kind of website should Thai exchange with?

   A. A website selling snowboarding equipment

   B. A website selling hot tubs

   C. A website selling photo albums

   D. A website selling ski lift tickets and snowboarding vacations

2. Karl is looking into forms of advertisement to raise product awareness for his new company and website. He hires Megan, a marketing consultant, who informs him of acceptable practices of e-mail advertisement. What kind of e-mail marketing would Megan encourage Karl to conduct?

   A. Opt-in e-mail

   B. Spam e-mail

   C. Targeted e-mail

   D. Referrer e-mail

3. What is the difference between a banner exchange and a referrer program?

   A. In a banner exchange, both sites advertise for each other; a referrer program is a one-way deal.

   B. A banner exchange is a one-way deal, and in referrer programs, both sites advertise for each other.

   C. A referrer program involves e-mail advertisement and the banner exchange is for banner ads.

   D. There is no difference.

4. Lamar needs to get his site on directories and search engines alike. He also needs to move his site up in the list of websites returned when a search is performed. What is the best course of action for him to take to accomplish this?

   A. Do nothing; search engines and directories will automatically find his site.

   B. Register his site on the directories but do nothing for the search engines because they will automatically find and list the site.

   C. Register his site on both search engines and directories

   D. Use <META> tags on his site to ensure that his site is found and categorized properly.

5. To find out the effectiveness of a banner ad, what should you do?

   A. Divide hits by the number of files on your site

   B. Use <META> tags

   C. Check the total number of impressions

   D. Use tracking tools to track the process

6. What is the main purpose of a website categorized as a publisher site?

   A. To sell products and goods for revenue

   B. To sell ad space for revenue

   C. To provide information only

   D. None of the above

7. To achieve the highest clickthrough rate, where should a banner be placed?

   A. To the left of the page.

   B. In the bottom corner.

   C. In the top header.

   D. There are common placements and theories as to why they are effective, but there are no definitive scientific findings.

8. Which of the following options describes an outsourcing method you would use when you want to establish a shopping cart for your online catalog but you want another company to handle the transaction side?

   A. Contract transaction placement

   B. A purchase button

   C. A shopping cart companion

   D. Compliance toolkit

9. Julie visits a site that includes links to many other different types of sites, like Yahoo! What is this type of site called?

   A. A mall site

   B. A workgroup

   C. A portal

   D. A commerce water fountain

10. What does having a well-designed online catalog accomplish for a successful e-commerce site?

    A. It lets the consumers know more about the product.

    B. It makes desired products easier to find.

    C. It allows a customer to choose products and continue to find more before buying via a shopping cart.

    D. All of the above.

11. James is an administrator for a large computer manufacturer. His boss requests information on the company's banner ads. He specifically wants to know how many times they have been effective in getting users who view them to click the ad to find out more. What should James examine to see these numbers?

    A. Clickthrough rate

    B. Hits

    C. Screen flow

    D. CPM

12. In e-commerce, what is a shopping cart?

    A. A catalog description of various products

    B. The component that helps users track items to buy

    C. A complete transaction system including purchase buttons

    D. An online product search capability

13. What feature can be used on an online catalog to allow consumers to select items for purchase and continue to browse for more products to buy?

    A. Shopping basket

    B. Shopping cart

    C. Payment gateway

    D. Wallet

14. Of the following statements about <META> tags, which is most accurate?

    A. <META> tags are required for an e-commerce site.

    B. <META> tags help identify a site to individual users.

    C. <META> tags allow customers to enter billing and shipping information.

    D. <META> tags help a search engine properly index a site.

15. Jenny is reviewing the hit count for her website's pages after the first month of being online. She notices that her home page has excessively more hits than any other page on her site. What is the most probable cause of such a drastic difference?

    A. There is a large number of separate files on the page.

    B. There has been a mistake in her logging.

    C. The name of Jenny's site is similar to another popular site.

    D. Jenny has enabled the use of cookies.

16. Which of the following measurements corresponds to a standard size for a banner ad?

   A. 100×100

   B. 400×90

   C. 468×60

   D. 243×50

17. Wayne is creating his online catalog. He wants it to be as descriptive about his products as possible because he is making a complete transition to e-commerce and will no longer have a physical store. Which of the following should Wayne include in his catalog to accomplish his goal?

   A. Incorporate a shopping cart into his catalog

   B. Include graphic depictions of his products

   C. Provide a site map for easier navigation

   D. Employ cross-selling to entice customers into more purchases

18. What is the main purpose of a marketer website?

   A. To sell products or services for revenue

   B. To sell ad space for revenue

   C. To provide a third-party website that acts as an arbitrator for banner exchange programs

   D. To provide a nonprofit website

19. An advertising representative can help with what feature of promoting your e-commerce company?

   A. The type and size of banner you use

   B. The sites on which to place your banner ads

   C. The form of online advertising other than banner ads you use

   D. Offline advertisement

20. Why should a banner ad have the smallest possible file size?

    A. To prevent image distortion

    B. To encourage greater spending

    C. So it does not slow down a website's load time

    D. To slow down a website's load time so the ad is viewed for a longer time

Answers to Review Questions

1. D. Thai would want to exchange with a website that sells his own rather than ones that would compete with his items. Because he is selling snowboarding equipment, there is a good chance that people buying ski lift tickets and snowboarding vacations would need equipment from Thai.

2. A. Opt-in e-mail is really the strongest form of e-mail marketing because you've solicited permission from the recipient ahead of time. This is quite different from spam e-mail, which is unsolicited and the equivalent to junk mail and is never an acceptable form of advertisement. Any company wanting to keep a respectable reputation would not partake in spam e-mail.

3. A. A banner exchange is for two companies that sell complimentary products and can use each other's websites to boost traffic. On the other hand, a referrer program is a one-way transaction in which a company pays another to post an ad on its website, sending traffic one way.

4. C. For a website to be indexed on a directory, it must be registered. A search engine will automatically find websites, but there is no way to know how long this process will take and where the site will be ranked. So to ensure that both directories and search engines know of Lamar's website, he should register with both; that will also ensure that his site will be at the top of the list of sites returned in a search.

5. D. The only way to know if a banner ad is effective is to track the process. Trackers can identify the number and percentage of visitors, the type of operating system, the browser type, and the user's domain. There are some that offer the service for free in exchange for their logo being placed on your site. Others charge a nominal fee.

6. B. A publisher site focuses on selling ad space as a means for revenue. Another category is a marketer site, for which the main source of revenue is from selling products or services.

7. D. Many people have their own idea on where the banner should be placed. Some think it should go in the bottom corner because visitors might accidentally click it. Others think it should go in the header or the left portion of the page as a sort of directory of banners. But these are all just theories based on experience, not scientific findings. Consider the design of the page to determine if the banner is in the correct placement for your site.

8. B. *Purchase button* is a generic term for a button that users select to complete their purchase. It connects the user's transaction to an alternate server for processing. This method of purchasing (using a transaction service) is an easier, more secure, and more affordable solution for many smaller businesses than implementing their own transaction services would be.

9. C. A portal, such as Yahoo!, is a website that includes links to other sites. It gives people an easy way to explore and participate in activities on the Internet.

10. D. A well-designed online catalog should accomplish each of these tasks. Consumers will be happy with their buying experience when they can find products easily and get a good description of what they are buying.

11. A. The clickthrough rate is the percentage of ad views that resulted in a user clicking the ad. A hit is when a web server sends a file to a browser. Screen flow describes navigation through a website. CPM is the cost per thousand for a particular ad.

12. B. A shopping cart tracks users' purchases until they are ready to "check out." It keeps a full listing of what users would like to purchase and then gives them the ability to see the list, make revisions to it, choose a shipping method, and then proceed to checkout.

13. B. A shopping cart allows potential customers to select items for purchase and then continue to browse for more before making the actual purchase. *Shopping basket* is a not a term associated with online catalogs. A payment gateway is the component that processes credit-card payment. A wallet, in e-commerce, involves payment with digital cash.

14. D. <META> tags are useful for an e-commerce website because, by giving a description of the site, they help search engines place the sites. They do make websites more available to users, but the normal user will not see the <META> tags or their results unless they use a search engine. <META> tags are not required to conduct e-commerce.

15. A. Each file downloaded counts as a hit. If a particular page, in this case the home page, is made up of many small files, its hit count will be much higher than a page with only a few files. The amount of visitors is determined by the hit count divided by the number of files used to make up a page. If the name of Jenny's site is similar to another popular site, this could cause an increase in hits but that is not the most likely cause.

16. C. A banner ad is an image with a hyperlink that points to an advertised site. The Interactive Advertising Bureau (IAB) has developed eight standard sizes for banner ads: 468×60, 392×72, 234×60, 120×240, 125×125, 120×90, 120×60, and 88×31.

17. B. The best action Wayne can take is to include graphic depictions of his products for his customers. Letting customers see what they are considering purchasing is important to the customer and therefore to a sale. Each of the other options are features Wayne should consider adding to his catalog, but are not the best choice when only selecting one.

18. A. A marketer site sells products or services for revenue. This type of site has a strong interest in keeping the consumer at the site as long as possible because the longer the visitor stays, the more chances the marketer has to convey the message.

19. B. Advertising representatives can help with decisions and placement choices and usually can achieve greater success. These organizations have well-established networks and statistical data that can help the marketer plan and execute a successful ad campaign. The type and size of banner ads are generally decided by the site owner but could be a recommendation of the representative.

20. C. A banner ad should have the smallest possible file size to allow the web page it is located on to load quickly. A website that has a slow load time will frustrate users and turn away business. It could also cause websites that host your banner ad to remove it.

Chapter

24

Site Usability and Customer Relationship Management (CRM)

THE CIW EXAM OBJECTIVE GROUPS COVERED IN THIS CHAPTER:

✓ Define website usability and its significance, and identify ways it can be analyzed and improved.

✓ Define the role of customer service in e-commerce operations.

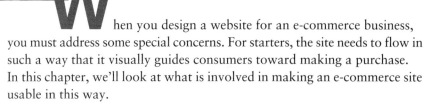

When you design a website for an e-commerce business, you must address some special concerns. For starters, the site needs to flow in such a way that it visually guides consumers toward making a purchase. In this chapter, we'll look at what is involved in making an e-commerce site usable in this way.

Customer support is also a concern. The extent to which you provide support may determine the comfort level of a buyer. If they feel that they get assistance (much as they might get at a regular store), they'll make a purchase and return to make more purchases. You can enable e-commerce support (e-service) in several ways, and we'll look at those in this chapter.

E-commerce websites require a bit more than the average information-only site. There may be a need for a knowledge base, an FAQ page, a shopping cart, co-browsing technology, transaction support, and so on. These are all part of site usability and Customer Relationship Management (CRM) and are covered in this chapter.

An Overview of Usability Issues

A poorly designed website that uses the latest technology will not be as successful as a site that is better designed but does not use the latest technology. The effectiveness of a website is referred to as its *usability*, which is a measure of how successfully users can interact with the site. If their visits to the site are trouble-free, efficient, and intuitive, they consider the usability of the site effective. Effective usability results in an increase in customer purchases, better customer retention, and brand loyalty, which improves business productivity and reduces services costs.

The goals for the effective usability of an e-commerce site correspond to a user's progression through the site and can be stated as follows:

1. Users visit the site.

2. Users search for and find a product or a service.

3. Users acquire information about products and services.

4. Users purchase a product or a service.

Let's look at each of these as they relate to usability.

Users Visit the Site

Without the visit, usability doesn't matter. A visitor's arrival at your site can result from marketing, promotion, a search, or random chance, although it usually results from product or site promotion.

For information on marketing your site, see Chapter 23.

Users Search For and Find a Product or a Service

The site does not need a built-in search engine in order for visitors to search for and find a product or a service. Visitors can easily find what they are looking for if the site design is effective and includes simple hyperlinks.

For example, you're looking for a special part for the sunroof of your new Volkswagen Passat, and you visit www.everyautopartmade.com. This site sells parts for every new and used vehicle you can think of. The site doesn't have a search engine, but it is easy to navigate with hyperlinks. Here's how you find the part:

1. On the home page are links to Import and Domestic. All vehicle makes are listed under Import, so you click Volkswagen.

2. All models are listed under Volkswagen, so you click Passat.

3. All production years are listed under Passat, so you click 1999.

4. Equipment similar to that on a detailed dealer invoice is listed under 1999, so you click Sunroof.

5. Under Sunroof, you find a diagram that identifies the part ID for the item you want to purchase.

Navigating to this item took five clicks. A successful website is easy to use, and visitors can comfortably find what they want on it. A search engine isn't always necessary.

Search engines help considerably, and your site should include one if possible. However, a visitor should not have to rely on the search engine to find items. No two search engines work in exactly the same way, and visitors are not likely to catch on to the searching nuances intuitively.

Users Acquire Information about Products and Services

The web is an ideal environment for getting information about products and services. In particular, products and services that require considerable pre-purchase research are ideal for online marketing.

When a user does navigate to a point that requires more detail, the supply of information should be abundant. Understanding how users navigate will help the site designer arrange the information effectively.

Most surveys conclude that users do not read web pages; they merely scan them. Thus, providing too much information on high-level pages may hinder the user. Building depth into a site allows the navigation to be relatively free of unrelated information until the topic becomes specific. For example, if the information about the sunroof had been placed on the main Volkswagen page, it would have been too early and irrelevant. Proper placement is critical.

Users Purchase a Product or a Service

The ultimate goal is to convert a shopper into a buyer. In actuality, the buying process may start when the visitor searches for the item.

Most e-commerce software packages let you create catalogs and shopping carts, as discussed in Chapter 23. When a user searches the catalog, they are preparing to buy, so how the product is identified in the catalog is important.

Ideally, when the user finds the product or service, they should not have to go far to make the purchase. Most sites employ a shopping cart to which the user can add the item and then check out or continue shopping. Although the shopping cart is an expected component of an e-commerce site that sells multiple items, not all sites need shopping carts. For example, if a site collects a single fee for an annual service, a shopping cart is unnecessary; only a way to make the payment is required.

You can increase the usefulness of a shopping cart by displaying its contents continuously. In this way, the customer can see what is in the cart at all times, rather than having to click a button to display a list of the items in the cart. Most out-of-the-box shopping cart software does not offer this option; so additional programming may be required.

Some e-commerce software allows little customization, whereas other software allows the developer almost unlimited customization. In general, the less control the developer has over the software, the easier it is to implement. Software packages that allow high-level customization require that developers have the advanced skills needed to create and modify code.

Click Patterns

You can discover the most-traveled path of a website by analyzing your server logs for click patterns. A click pattern is the path that a user takes while navigating a website. Click patterns are of two types: *random* and *controlled*.

Random-click patterns allow users to go where they want. You can analyze random-click patterns to determine the strengths and weaknesses of your site. Use the server logs to find out which links users most often clicked on the home page, where they went after that, and whether they made a purchase. You can also use the server logs to find out how much time they spent in transit and whether there is any consistency to the paths they take through your site.

Identifying these patterns can point to areas of your site that need improvement. For example, you might want to remove pages that aren't being viewed, or you might want to update or better define the links to these pages. If a particular page contains important information, but users do not seem to find it, you probably need to improve navigation.

The *controlled-click pattern* is a path that is defined by requirements at a site. For example, an e-commerce site that requires first-time customers to register before making a purchase is using a controlled-click pattern. The customer can locate items and add them to a shopping cart, but before actually buying the items, the customer must register. This registration is the controlled part of the navigation as it relates to the purchase. Until the user decides to purchase, they could have been anywhere within the site, but at the point of purchase, the user is directed into the controlled environment.

The controlled-click pattern is modified for returning visitors. They can shop at random, and when it comes time to purchase, they need not register. The pattern for returning users can begin when they log in, or it can begin when they are ready to check out by asking whether they are new or returning customers.

Screen Flow

Screen flow, or the way in which the content of a site is displayed, is as important as the information itself. Presentation has to be compatible with users and their habits. As mentioned earlier, users typically don't read a web page; they scan it. Certain *screen flow* techniques can enhance scanning, thereby reducing frustration during navigation.

Keep in mind that less is more when it comes to web design. Thus, a web page with too much content will not be as effective as one with less content. When users visit a page, their eyes first focus on the screen as a whole. They then start to look for keywords and hyperlinks. Keeping content organized and clutter-free helps users find what they want.

Most major newspapers are excellent examples of how to organize large amounts of information. The front page usually has a lead story along with some accompanying photos. The front page might also carry several small or local-interest stories. Along the left side you often see a summary of the section that gives readers a headline and a sentence or two about each story. Readers don't have to find and read the story; they can check the summary, and then if they want to read more, they simply turn to the page (hyperlink) for the full story.

Usability Analysis

Always test your site for usability before final release. No matter how sound the development team's strategy was for deploying the site, you will find problems that were either overlooked or not exposed. The testing can be a formal, scheduled process, in which users are asked to participate, or it can be much like a beta release of software, in which users test the product and report problems.

Guidelines for Testing

Here are some guidelines that you can follow to ensure that testing procedures are accurate.

- Be sure that the site is almost ready for release before you test. Otherwise, the test will not be valid because many elements change in production. In effect, you won't be testing the real site.

- If you are following a formal process, give the testers actual tasks that would be expected of real users. Give them written assignments, and ask them to take notes.

- Be sure that you test group includes users who have various skill levels.

- Do not interfere during the testing. It may be uncomfortable to watch someone have difficulty performing a task, but interference will contaminate the results.

Guidelines for Evaluating the Testing

When your testing is complete, you must evaluate the results and implement appropriate changes to your site. It is highly unlikely that no flaws will be uncovered. You must pool and analyze all the results. Some issues, usually those that are most reported, will be clear and understandable. Determine how they affect the intended outcome and how they can be improved.

Usually, you will not be able to fix every problem that is identified, not because you want to leave the site incomplete, but because each user has predefined ideas of how the site should work. Some individual users' goals may conflict with the site's objectives. To properly evaluate your test results, follow these steps:

1. Look at all reports, and focus on commonly reported issues.

2. Address commonly reported issues first.

3. Address secondary issues if time permits and if they will help meet the site's goals.

4. If you make significant changes to your site, consider a follow-up usability test.

Customer Relationships

Online customer service, also known as *e-service*, is the one aspect of e-commerce that can set it apart from other business in customers' minds. With all the options that consumers have, many people will no longer tolerate poor service, because they know they can take their business elsewhere. Good customer service is not something a consumer hopes for any longer; they now expect and demand it.

The Internet is a buyers' market, and poor service will be the downfall of any e-commerce business. Customers know what they want and how they want it, and they believe that "the customer is always right."

To compete on the Internet, e-commerce owners need to understand that to attract and keep customers, they must offer much more than the sale of products or services. One advantage of the Internet is that it can greatly enhance customer service for both e-businesses and those with physical stores. In fact, some think that the Internet's long-term purpose will be customer service, because it offers businesses and customers many ways to do something better or faster, to provide more options, and to create relationships continually.

E-Service

E-service is rapidly changing relationships for business-to-business and business-to-consumer firms. An increase in service features used to mean that a business had to increase costs, thereby reducing profits. Still, even with increased services, consumers often were not served effectively.

E-service allows both the business and the consumer to save time and money. The business incurs added expense to develop and deploy a system, but such an expenditure is expected with any business improvement. However, once the system is operational, the cost of providing consumer support starts to decline. At the same time, the quality of the customer service begins to improve. Earlier, in Chapter 22, I discussed FedEx and how it uses a website for customer service and support, resulting in cost savings and improved service.

E-service is not only expected now, it also makes good business sense. Today a consumer can switch vendors with the click of a mouse. Businesses that do not develop strategies to offer consistent customer service will undoubtedly suffer. Consumers who are connected to the business after the initial transaction will probably be motivated to return.

E-service allows business owners to learn about their customers through information exchange. This exchange creates working relationships and allows the business to better understand the consumer, thereby providing personalized service.

Traditional consumer service usually referred to the salesperson's treatment of the customer in the store. As times changed and customer expectations of service began to rise, service standards began to increase correspondingly. Products and services began to carry guarantees and warranties to convince consumers that problems would be addressed.

As the emphasis on customer service and support grew, a new service concept called *personalization* began to evolve. Now the Internet economy has heightened the requirement for and the ability to further customize and improve consumer services. Customer service can include any assistance or technical support given before, during, and after a transaction.

The methods used to facilitate e-service vary. In the following sections, we'll look at some popular methods and point out their advantages and disadvantages.

Synchronous E-Service

Synchronous e-service allows the customer to communicate in real time with the merchant. It has the advantage of being highly personal and immediate, but it may require a learning curve, additional hardware or software, or higher-than-average bandwidth. It may also not be compatible with the customer's system.

Chat Services

Chat can be a useful tool that allows immediate and specific information to be exchanged in real time. With chat, the customer can read and type questions and answers with the customer services representative in real time. Chat can use software that supports Internet Relay Chat (IRC) or a third-party software package. It may have its own chat client, sometimes using Java or ActiveX. Some chat clients are application-based, but web-based applications that use a Java applet are also available.

The following companies, among others, offer this technology:

- Live Assistance at `http://www.liveassistant.com`

- Live Person at `http://www.liveperson.com`

- Interchange Chat at `http://www.primus.com`

Audio and Voice Connection Services

Audio and voice connections over the Internet are still developing but are emerging as popular forms of consumer support and contact. The main limitation is bandwidth. For several years, products have been available to enable live voice communication over the Internet through a technology known as telephony. More typically, the telephone is used as part of a synchronous e-service solution.

Telephone

Some online businesses allow customers to communicate with customer service via a standard telephone. Third-party technology allows the customer to click a hyperlink, enter their phone number, and then click a button to initiate a call to the merchant's customer service center. The advantage is that the consumer does not have to pay for the call. When the customer initiates the call by clicking the button, a central-calling hub places two calls, one to the customer and another to the merchant. The hub then puts them on the line together. Because the call technically came to the customer, they are not billed; the merchant pays for the call. This type of service is symmetric in that there are two parties involved, the user and the service support person.

A disadvantage to this type of customer service is that the customer needs simultaneous Internet connection and telephone access. For office users, this is usually not an issue, but many home users do not have a second phone line or a broadband connection.

Companies offering this type of service include the following:

- LivePerson at `www.liveperson.com`

- GlobalPhone Corporation at `www.webcallback.com`

- NetCall Telecom at `www.netcall.com`

Telephony

This technology transmits voice over the Internet. Although *telephony* has existed for a long time, its growth has been limited because of the poor voice quality that resulted from low-bandwidth connections and inadequate sound cards. More users now connect with higher bandwidth and better sound cards, so telephony is becoming more popular. Many companies now use the Internet for interoffice telecommunications to reduce costs.

The basic principles of telephony are similar to those of a modem. The analog signal, your voice, is digitized and sent over the Internet using TCP/IP (Transmission Control Protocol/Internet Protocol). On the other end, depending on the setup, the signal is either converted back to analog or left digital, depending on the recipient's output device.

Telephony for the e-commerce site plays the same role as the telephone when connected to the merchant's customer service center. The user can click a button and establish a toll-free connection via the Internet. The drawback to using telephony as a means of synchronous e-service is that the customer needs a sound card and a microphone. Another important ingredient is a high-bandwidth connection, to prevent user frustration from poor voice quality.

The following companies, among others, offer this type of service:

- EGain at `www.egain.com`

- Net2Phone at `www.net2phone.com`

- ITXC at `www.itxc.com`

- InterCall at `www.intercall.com`

Co-browsing

Co-browsing allows a customer assistance center to control a customer's browser during a live session. A recent statistic indicates that more than

60 percent of shopping transactions are incomplete because customers do not know what to do or have questions they cannot get answered. Co-browsing can help solve such problems by walking the customer through the purchasing process. Several vendors offer co-browsing tools. One that is gaining wide use is a product by Webline, which was acquired by Cisco Systems in December 1999. It offers a co-browsing applet that can work behind firewalls, greatly increasing its compatibility and universal use. The customer downloads an applet that then communicates with the customer service representative and enables co-browsing.

Asynchronous E-Service

*A*synchronous e-service is the most popular method because it is the easiest (ahem…cheapest) to implement. Asynchronous implies that steps in the process do not occur at the same time. For example, a telephone call is a synchronous session. Talking on two-way radios is an asynchronous session. Each person has to wait for the other to finish before beginning to speak. E-mail is also an asynchronous session, because someone sends an e-mail message and then someone responds.

E-mail

E-mail is the most widespread, though not the most effective, form of asynchronous service; it allows the customer to send a question or comment to the merchant and, with luck, receive a reply. Sample customer service e-mail addresses are: information@companyname.com or service@companyname .com. Each of these indicates a basic type of request for service. Providing a customer service link on your site is a useful and timesaving feature. A customer can click the link to launch a pre-addressed e-mail inquiry.

The drawback to e-mail customer service is that it is not effective for urgent matters. The amount of e-mail can be overwhelming, depending on the traffic at the site. Responding to these messages can be time-consuming and ineffective if it is not done promptly. E-mail messages vary widely, from short requests to long letters of explanation, thus making them more difficult to process.

Studies show that many customer e-mail inquiries are not answered efficiently, with response times ranging from several days to several weeks. The result is frustrated and lost customers. Some companies that receive a large amount of e-mail outsource the processing of inquiries and orders to firms that specialize in processing e-mail inquiries.

Web Forms

Asking a question via a web form is similar to e-mail support. The slight difference might be that questions via a web form are more likely to be entered into a database. This method allows for easier distribution of the inquiries when consumer service centers are geographically dispersed. Additionally, web forms can require the customer to provide necessary information and details. This structure allows for a more formalized and standard method of addressing each inquiry.

Self-Service in E-Commerce

Self-service is often faster than asynchronous service and sometimes faster than synchronous service, because the customer finds their own answers. Sometimes speaking to a customer service representative or sending an e-mail message is the best choice, but when it is not, self-service can be a viable alternative. In addition, not all customers want direct, personal contact and prefer to find answers for themselves. The faster a consumer can get the answer, the more likely they are to remain and conduct business. In this section, we'll look at the various types of self-service that are appropriate for an e-commerce site.

Client Accounts and Profiles

The speed, ease, and depth with which consumers can access their own accounts and personal profiles makes consumer self-service an attractive option. Accounts and profiles can be anything from stock portfolios and trading accounts to business-to-business account balances and inventory notifications. The essence of such service is that the consumer receives personalized assistance, even if they don't talk to anyone.

Frequently Asked Questions

Frequently asked questions (FAQ) ranks high as a form of customer self-service. A listing of frequently asked questions can reduce the number of phone calls and e-mail messages dramatically and immediately. An *FAQ* is the most cost-effective form of customer service. Once the question and answer are posted on the website, the merchant is relieved of the need for another form of correspondence. An example of an FAQ page is shown in Figure 24.1.

FIGURE 24.1 The Sybex FAQ page

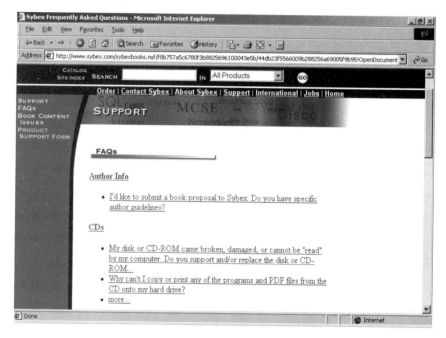

Knowledge Database

A *knowledge database* is similar to an FAQ but more customized. The customer selects from a list of products or categories defined by the merchant, and then the FAQ is searched based on the customer's selection. A list of questions relating to the topic is displayed for the customer to examine. These databases can store and retrieve any number of FAQs, allowing the most appropriate topics to be displayed. The difference between a knowledge database and an FAQ is that the consumer does not have to read each question to find their answer. In effect, the database narrows the selection to the relevant questions.

HTML-Based Help

HTML-based help is a relatively new form of customer assistance because older browsers have difficulty supporting the technology. Now, with Dynamic HTML, a robust interface that can be launched in the customer's browser has the same look and feel of help that comes with many software applications. Some of these agents are entirely HTML, and others use Java for cross-platform performance.

EXERCISE 24.1

Examining HTML Help from ehelp.com

In this exercise, you will visit a vendor whose software builds HTML help. You will also view a sample. This service may look like software application help, but it is actually rendered in the browser, which is the only client application required.

1. Open your web browser, and in the Address bar enter **http://www .ehelp.com/products/robohelp/demos/quicktours.asp**.

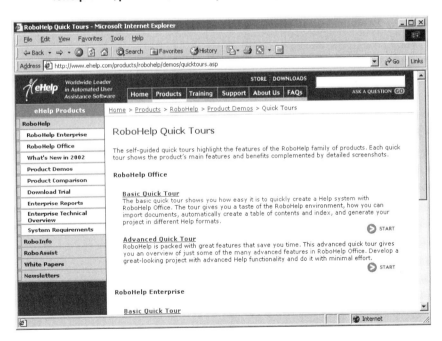

EXERCISE 24.1 *(continued)*

2. Under the RoboHelp Enterprise heading, select Basic Quick Tour.

3. Select some of the options and notice that working with RoboHelp is similar to using Help in Windows or an application.

Online Communities

Online communities allow customers to develop relationships with one another. Communities are considered a value-added service and do not directly relate to customer transactions. Communities can be bulletin boards, message boards, and chats in which consumers can exchange ideas.

The following companies offer this technology:

- Webb at www.webb.net

- Multex at www.buzzpower.com

Surveys

Surveys are an additional way to retrieve customer data that will help gauge how customers perceive the level of customer service your site offers. Getting customers to complete surveys is difficult, which means that surveys should not be your only form of feedback. One way to encourage customers to complete surveys is to offer them an *incentive* such as a free item, service, or download if they participate.

A survey is only as effective as the questions it asks. As you develop a survey, do the necessary research to ensure that you are asking the appropriate questions and that the answers you receive will give you the information you want.

The following companies offer survey development software:

- CustomerSat at www.customersat.com

- Inquisite at www.inquisite.com

Customer Feedback

Feedback must be easy for customers to provide, and you must respond to it effectively. Allowing customers to provide immediate feedback can have both pros and cons, but will improve long-term customer satisfaction. Some customers need to provide feedback so that they can convey their praise or frustration. You must determine, case by case, whether such feedback is accurate and meets the company's goals.

Customers can provide feedback by e-mail, web forms, or phone calls. Be sure to provide easy access to one of these methods. At least one company, PlanetFeedback, specializes in outsourcing feedback. For information, visit `www.planetfeedback.com`.

An E-Service Action Plan

Developing an effective e-service plan is not the job of the information systems department alone; the marketing and communications departments must also participate. Providing the highest level of e-service requires times and experience. Developing a plan involves the following:

Identify the customer   Identifying the customer correctly is a basic marketing principle. The principle has not changed in the world of e-commerce, but some methods of identifying the customer have.

Examine current web traffic patterns   Using web server analysis tools, identify patterns that indicate visitors' online habits. Patterns identify what the customer wants or needs, thus allowing closer identification of the typical consumer.

Use suppliers when appropriate   If your e-commerce site relies on suppliers for its products or services, those suppliers can sometimes help identify ways to improve customer service. They should be motivated to do so, because their success is at least partly tied to the success of your web-based business.

Use existing information   Existing businesses that already have information about their clients have an advantage over newer businesses. Use this information as you implement your website.

Analyze potential tools   Analyzing support tools is the most difficult and time-consuming part of the process. Weigh all factors to determine which systems are the most reliable, intuitive, efficient, and cost-effective. Your company will not benefit from opening its web-based business with inefficient tools; wait until you can identify the proper tools. A poorly implemented system can drive away customers, who may not return even after an upgrade.

Determining the need for synchronous and asynchronous support is key in choosing tools and applications. Also, remember that some tools require additional staff. For example, if you choose to support live chat, someone must be available to staff the chat around the clock.

Create a close relationship with the customer   E-commerce sites can create a virtual one-on-one relationship with customers. When consumers believe they are individually important to the business, relationships can be fostered. These relationships make consumers feel valued and create a loyalty to the merchant. E-commerce businesses must focus beyond the first sale, because repeat business is much more cost-effective.

Gather information for future planning   After you implement your website, you can gather and analyze information in a much more stream-lined manner. Use this information and the tools you choose to support your customers.

Remove the fear of online purchasing   Customer fear is still a limitation for e-commerce. Although fear may not seem like a consumer-service issue, it does play a part in the customer's confidence and trust. Establishing visible relationships with other established e-commerce businesses is a generally trusted and respected technique. One e-commerce company working alone can do little to change the fear of online purchasing, but ignoring consumer concerns is worse.

Ensure privacy   Information exchange is making privacy more difficult. As part of online purchasing fears, customers are concerned about the importance and security of their information. For a business to gain the confidence of the consumer, it must be forthcoming and clear about its privacy policy. This is typically a written statement that the consumer can read on your website. Obviously, you must rigidly enforce your privacy policy.

Provide transaction incentives   Incentives provide a twofold benefit: they help the consumer and they help the merchant. Incentives can take the form of discounts, free items, special services, and so forth. They can also give customers a reason to return, building loyalty and repeat business.

Conduct service metrics *Metrics* is an approach to measuring website performance by looking at the total consumer experience, including speed, availability, and consistency of performance. A consumer benefits from a site that consistently performs well. Long upload and download times or intermittent availability can cause customers to lose confidence in the business and become frustrated. A metrics study combines reports and surveys that evaluate performance to analyze the site's overall activity. Some e-commerce companies turn to third-party resources that can be either software or services.

Customer Relationship Management

*C*RM is different from customer service; it deals with the management of customers from a business process viewpoint rather than that of the direct customer. A business that uses CRM is concerned with how it manages its customer information service and how to better serve those customers based on that information. This service helps tighten the relationships with customers and can improve customer retention. Several elements of CRM relate to the entire customer experience and use data to drive service and revenues.

Establishing New Customers

Establishing new customers is usually a major goal of most businesses, traditional or e-commerce. To attract new customers, the business must understand what the customer wants and must create a need to be filled. You can evaluate and refine information obtained about existing customers to help attract a continual flow of new customers.

Improving Value to Existing Customers

Once a customer relationship is established, you must maximize resources to gain maximum value. Adding customer value does not mean that services must be free; however, customers do expect and appreciate extras. For example, a customer does not expect to pay an additional charge to be notified of new products or services. They may, however, pay for a membership that provides additional savings when making purchases, similar to membership-style retailers. Value additions can help reinforce and build on customer expectations and create brand loyalty among competing business.

Generating Repeat Business

The cost of developing a new customer is much higher than the cost of retaining a customer. Businesses must try to reduce this expenditure by serving their existing customers through repeat business. Failure to do so can directly affect profits and may even contribute to the failure of the business.

Customer retention should be the goal of any business. Developing new customers is a daunting task on its own, but converting a new customer into a repeat customer is even more difficult. The total customer experience will be the deciding factor in whether that customer will return. Therefore, developing repeat customers is not a final step in the customer transaction, but is part of every step along the way. A customer may be willing to purchase from a site, but if the product takes too long for delivery or is damaged during transit, repeat business is in jeopardy.

Data Mining

Data mining is a relatively new term in the customer service sector. It refers to the use of customer data to improve CRM. Marketing and sales departments are using data mining as a value-added resource to improve customer satisfaction.

Some data mining uses include defining customer needs and cross-selling or up-selling based on the statistical data from like-minded customers. Being able to predict what customers will be interested in or how they will react to a set of circumstances allows marketing teams to better predict the target audience. Data mining tries to increase the number of qualified prospects for a target, thus increasing the number of qualified responses, in hopes of improving the return on investment.

CRM Initiatives

A CRM initiative may encounter some roadblocks. CRM applications require more data than customer service representatives may be used to or willing to implement. As a result, unless those who will be implementing and using the system agree, customer service representatives may resist using it. Such resistance can diminish the reasons for implementing the CRM. Another difficulty is the ability to validate the return on investment, which may cause a CRM to fall short in budget allocation.

Summary

A website must be designed with common browsing characteristics in mind. By analyzing user habits and patterns, an e-commerce designer can anticipate a visitor's next move through a website and even force a visitor to click in certain areas so that they are one step closer to making a purchase. Using specific screen-flow techniques, a web designer can enhance user scanning, thus reducing the frustration users sometimes feel when navigating a site.

Anticipating customer support needs is also an integral part of an e-commerce designer's responsibilities, including the implementation of synchronous and asynchronous services. In this chapter, you saw examples of these services and learned how they can add value to the services you offer. You also reviewed a customer service (e-service) action plan to help evaluate and implement an effective model. In addition, you learned about CRM and its components and how you can use them effectively to address customer needs.

Exam Essentials

Understand usability and its importance. Usability is measured in terms of how effectively users interact with a site. If a site is not considered usable or not as usable as another site, users will choose where they are the most comfortable. One of the important ways to make a site usable is to include a method for users to locate specific resources, either through a site search engine or through an easy-to-use navigational hyperlink design. Usability is an incredibly important feature because it results in an increase in customer purchases, better customer retention, and brand loyalty, which improves business productivity and reduces services costs.

Understand click patterns. Developers can analyze the server logs to determine click patterns, which indicate the way users navigate through sites and help site designers to see the most-traveled path within a website. If it's obvious that users move through your pages along a specific trail or pattern, you can use those patterns as clues for future development. Know the difference between random-click patterns and controlled-click patterns and know the appropriate uses for both types.

Understand the concept of screen flow.   Screen flow is the way that content is displayed on a site. Screen flow is a presentation concept that takes into consideration users' habits. When users visit a page, their eyes first focus on the screen as a whole. They then start to look for keywords and hyperlinks (especially those that are of interest to them). Keeping content organized and clutter-free helps users find what they want and allows for a smoother screen flow.

Know how to test a website and analyze its usability.   Testing your site is best done when the site is near completion, in the final stages of development. Testing at this stage lets you more easily determine the true weaknesses of the site. Once you get reports from your testing, analyze them to determine and fix the most commonly reported problems first, and then fix other problems if time permits.

Understand e-services.   E-services are online customer service solutions that typically take one of three formats: synchronous, asynchronous, and self-service.

Know the difference between synchronous and asynchronous e-services. A synchronous e-service allows the customer to communicate in real time with the merchant. Examples include chat, Internet audio and voice services, and co-browsing. Asynchronous services are the more commonly used method and involve a request for assistance and an eventual reply. Examples of asynchronous service include e-mail and web forms.

Understand Customer Relationship Management (CRM).   CRM goes beyond customer service in that it deals with managing customers from a business process viewpoint rather than that of the direct customer. A business that uses CRM is concerned with how it manages its customer information service and how to better serve those customers based on that information. This service helps tighten the relationships with customers and can improve customer retention.

Know the methods involved in CRM.   Because CRM is a business-oriented structure, a key consideration is the need to establish new customers, a major goal of most businesses. Another important consideration is improving value to existing customers and trying to generate repeat business.

Key Terms

Before you take the exam, be certain you are familiar with the following terms:

asynchronous	knowledge database
chat	metrics
co-browsing	random-click pattern
controlled-click pattern	screen flow
Customer Relationship Management (CRM)	self-service
data mining	synchronous
e-service	telephony
FAQ	usability
incentive	

Review Questions

1. A business defines a customer's needs and provides cross-selling or up-selling based on statistical data. What is this method of using customer data called?

   A. Screen flow

   B. Data mining

   C. Co-browsing

   D. Guessing

2. Sebastian is handling the Nissan e-service site for both asynchronous and synchronous support. Which of the following is not considered part of asynchronous or synchronous support?

   A. Chat

   B. Telephony

   C. E-mail

   D. FAQ

3. Online communities help to accomplish which of the following for an e-commerce site?

   A. They allow customers to develop relationships with one another for the purpose of exchanging ideas about the product.

   B. They help customers become acquainted with one another for personal connections.

   C. They help customers share viewpoints on philosophical issues.

   D. They provide ways to sell more goods by allowing for portals.

4. True or False. For a an e-commerce site to be designed properly with usability in mind, you must have a searchable site.

   A. True

   B. False

5. Which technology transmits voice over the Internet?

A. Co-browsing

B. Anonymous usage

C. Secure Sockets Layers

D. Telephony

6. Quinn is developing a site that require users to complete a form before they can search for what they want. What kind of pattern has Quinn developed for his site?

A. A random-click pattern

B. A hybrid-click pattern

C. A controlled-click pattern

D. A directional-click pattern

7. Which of the three forms of e-service is the most welcome and comfortable for customers?

A. Synchronous

B. Asynchronous

C. Self-service

D. Isochronous

8. Wayne has developed a complex site for e-commerce, attempting to include all the standard design features to promote purchases and return clientele. When should he test his website?

A. After the site goes live on the Internet

B. Early on in the development stage

C. During the development process

D. After development is complete and the site is ready to go live

9. Chris is noticing that users at his site are following specific links. What is he analyzing?

   A. Click patterns

   B. E-service

   C. Shopping cart usage

   D. Hits per page

10. Chrissie is attempting to purchase jeans from a well-known company that has a store in the mall. The problem is that the jeans she wants are no longer sold in the store; they are only sold online. She doesn't have any luck finding them online though. How can the e-service department best help her while she makes her online purchase?

   A. Through e-mail

   B. Through co-browsing

   C. Through a knowledge base

   D. Through a web form

11. Which of the following is an example of symmetric service and support?

   A. Telephone call

   B. E-mail

   C. Message board

   D. FAQ page

12. Steve is the administrator for an e-commerce site of a company that sells household appliances. He has configured the online catalog to be as easy as possible to use. Even so, it seems consumers are having a hard time finding what they want. To solve this problem, what should Steve add to the site?

   A. An FAQ page

   B. A search engine

   C. A site map

   D. Support numbers on each page

13. Jonathan has created an e-commerce site, and he administers the site himself. Orders came in regularly at first, but have now begun to slow. He decides to use a database to track users on his site. After some time, he notices that most customers do not revisit his site. What is the best course of action for Jonathan to take?

   A. Add more advertisements

   B. Add an FAQ page

   C. Simplify navigation

   D. Implement security

14. Bill's car-accessories company has grown into a large auto-parts chain. He has an e-commerce website, and sales are going extremely well. On his site, he lists a support number and has implemented co-browsing as one of his many service features. Bill also has an FAQ page that has grown large. Now he wants to set it up in such a way that customers can easily and quickly find questions pertaining to specific products. What does he need to create?

   A. A knowledge database

   B. E-mail support

   C. 128-bit encryption

   D. Cookies for client computers

15. Michelle is having trouble with a company's website. She is trying to order a bracelet but cannot find where to register. After looking at several pages, she locates a call button. What will happen when Michelle clicks this button?

   A. She will set up a co-browsing session with a service representative.

   B. She will receive a list of phone numbers that she can call for answers about the ordering process.

   C. She will need to provide her phone number, and a call will be initiated to her and the merchant's service center via a third party.

   D. She will now be in a controlled-click environment where she will be guided in how to place her order.

16. When speaking about an e-commerce site, what word or phrase describes ease of navigation?

   A. Bandwidth

   B. Click-through ratio

   C. Usability

   D. Screen flow

17. True or False. All e-commerce sites require a shopping cart.

   A. True

   B. False

18. Which of the following statements is not true?

   A. Less is more when it comes to web design.

   B. When users visit a page, their eyes begin to focus first on the screen as a whole.

   C. Try to put as much on one page as possible, regardless of how cluttered the page looks.

   D. Most major newspapers provide an excellent example of how to organize large amounts of information.

19. Which of the following allows for a robust interface that can be launched in the customer's browser and has the same look and feel of help that comes with many software applications?

   A. Dynamic HTML

   B. HTTP

   C. TCP/IP

   D. Flash

20. Which of the following is an approach to measuring website performance by looking at the total consumer experience, including speed, availability, and consistency of performance?

   A. Benchmarking

   B. Demographics

   C. Bionics

   D. Metrics

Answers to Review Questions

1. **B.** Data mining is a relatively new term in the customer service sector. It involves using customer data to improve CRM. Marketing and sales departments are using data mining as a means of improving customer satisfaction. Guessing may also be involved, but that is not a real methodology. Screen flow and co-browsing are real terms, but they don't apply here.

2. **D.** An FAQ page is self-service and is, therefore, not part of asynchronous or synchronous e-support. Chat and telephony are considered synchronous; e-mail is considered asynchronous.

3. **A.** Online communities are good for both support (among consumers) and a feeling of belonging. Options B and C could certainly be the goal of an online community, just not necessarily an e-commerce online community. Portals are good for newly formed, low-budget business promotion, but they have no connection with online communities.

4. **B.** If a site is designed properly with hyperlinks, information is considered usable without a search engine. Search engines are a great feature but should not be the only way to retrieve information.

5. **D.** Telephony has existed for a long time, but its growth has been limited because of poor voice quality. With advancements in technology, telephony is becoming a more popular way to communicate.

6. **C.** When you require a customer to complete a form, you control click patterns. Random-click patterns allow users to go where they choose. A hybrid pattern may be in effect here, because after users complete the form, they might be allowed to randomly click, but that isn't specifically detailed within the question. A directional-click pattern is a fictional term.

7. **A.** Usually a customer who wants support needs immediate, personalized attention. Synchronous e-service gives them an opportunity to deal directly with another person who can help them.

8. **D.** Test your site when it is complete and before it goes live on the Internet. You then have an opportunity to fix problems that will occur on the real site.

9. **A.** Click patterns tell Chris which portions of his site appeal to users more than other portions. Using this information can help him design the site properly.

10. B. Co-browsing allows a customer assistance center to control the customer's browser during a live session. This is the best option because, although the other options might work, co-browsing allows the support person to direct Chrissie right to what she wants, much like an in-house sales floor support team.

11. A. A telephone call is an example of symmetric service and support. Symmetric means that it must be a two-way procedure between the user and service personnel.

12. B. The best way to help consumers find what they want is to add a search engine. Although an FAQ page will help, it will not necessarily help consumers to find individual products. A site map might be helpful to some potential buyers, but it will not have the same impact as a search engine. Listing support numbers on each page will not be effective because in addition to clogging support lines, it doesn't answer consumer questions.

13. C. Most customers are not revisiting Jonathan's site because their first experience there was not a good one. If a site is easy to use and navigate, customers will return. Although adding an FAQ page might help users find an answer to a problem, it doesn't ensure them of a trouble-free stay. Adding advertisements can have the opposite effect, causing the site to load slower and thus driving customers away. Security is not an issue in this scenario.

14. A. A knowledge database allows customers to review only relevant questions for individual products. Using e-mail for support wouldn't get answers to customers faster, and neither encryption nor cookies have any effect on a knowledge database.

15. C. A call button provides e-service by a telephone. Third-party software allows a customer to click a hyperlink, type their telephone number, and click a button to initiate a call to the merchant's service center. When the customer initiates the call by clicking the call button, a central hub places two calls, one to the customer and one to the merchant. The two lines are then put together, and support is provided. Co-browsing is an e-service in which the service personnel take control of the customer's browser to walk them through processes. Controlled-click is not an example of e-service; rather it is a type of environment on a website.

16. D.   Screen flow deals with how easy it is to use a site. Bandwidth has to do with Internet connection speed. Click-through ratio is the number of times an ad has been viewed that then led to a click.

17. B.   Not all sites need shopping carts. For example, if a site collects a single fee for an annual service, a shopping cart is unnecessary; only a way to make the payment is required.

18. C.   It's really better not to clutter a page. Many people will not be interested in viewing everything, so the information needs to be structured properly.

19. A.   Dynamic HTML (DHTML) allows for a newer form of web-based help. Older browsers have difficulty with DHTML, but most users are currently using browsers that support it.

20. D.   A metrics study combines reports and surveys that evaluate performance to analyze the site's overall activity. Some e-commerce companies turn to third-party resources that can be either software or services.

Chapter 25

Business-to-Business Frameworks

THE CIW EXAM OBJECTIVE GROUP COVERED IN THIS CHAPTER:

✓ Define standards and initiatives that support supplier transactions using e-commerce, including but not limited to: EDI, OBI.

I n Chapter 20 we looked at two models of electronic commerce:

Business-to-Consumer (B2C)   The business-to-consumer model is driven by many variables. Issues such as inventory, shipping, and suppliers depend on the type of product or service being supplied. The business-to-consumer model is less complex than its business-to-business counterpart.

Business-to-Business (B2B)   The business-to-business model is largely driven by redundant, high-volume transactions conducted between two companies. Suppliers of commodity goods and services want standard, low-cost, cost-effective methods to sell to corporate customers.

To start, maintain, or support business-to-business (B2B) applications, you must understand the existing infrastructure and the integration issues. B2B e-commerce includes every aspect of business that can be merged with or integrated into an automated or electronic process. The business-to-business commerce model is more complex than its business-to-consumer counterpart. Much of this complexity results from the additional needs of business commerce: Most businesses buying commodity items in bulk expect discounts, and most sellers of such items expect payment within certain time-frames. A business-to-business transaction might also require stricter delivery and processing guidelines.

For e-commerce to occur, data and information must be exchanged. In this chapter, we'll look first at some exchange protocols such as electronic data interchange (EDI), Extensible Markup Language (XML), and Secure/ Multipurpose Internet Mail Extensions (S/MIME). Then we will briefly examine various methods for hosting and staging these exchanges, including Open Buying on the Internet (OBI), B2B marketplaces, vertical and horizontal marketing, supply chain and procurement management, inventory and distribution control, portals, chat, translation, and other technologies.

Electronic Data Interchange (EDI)

For electronic commerce to succeed, we need a standard way to transfer information between computer networks and companies. *Electronic data interchange (EDI)* is a messaging protocol meant to ensure that data sent between normally incompatible computers retains its integrity and is formatted consistently. This protocol is popular with financial institutions and large businesses that need to communicate large volumes of detailed, repetitive information over company networks.

EDI allows the inter-organizational exchange of documents in standardized electronic form directly between participating computers. It can be considered an electronic replacement for paper-based transaction infrastructure, including purchase orders, invoices, bills of material, and material releases.

EDI is designed to standardize electronic commerce throughout organizations. To that extent, its goals are as follows:

- To enable easy and inexpensive communication of structured information throughout the lifetime of an electronic transaction

- To reduce the amount of data capture and the number of transcriptions, in hopes of improving processes because of fewer errors, reduced time spent handling errors, and fewer delays due to incorrect or unformatted data

- To ensure faster handling of transactions to increase cash flow

Until recently, EDI's overall place in the market was limited to large corporations. Electronic commerce is helping EDI enjoy more widespread use, because agreeing on a standardized document exchange is key to expanding electronic commerce. In the past few years, EDI has found a niche in certain industries, including automotive, retail, chemical, electronics, electrical, petroleum, metals, paper, and office products. However, its widespread use has been hampered partly because there are so many standardized document formats; each industry uses its own flavor of EDI. Not only must the document formats match, but the data representation within the document must also match precisely.

Another limitation affecting widespread use has been the cost associated with EDI. Small and medium-sized companies once considered EDI too costly to implement, but that perception seems to be changing as EDI matures and becomes a standard for e-commerce. Two organizations that exchange EDI transmissions are known as *trading partners*. These trading partners must agree on a standard format. Unfortunately, this format is seldom acceptable for other trading partners, resulting in multiple formats and interoperability issues.

The relatively recent electronic commerce push has done more to standardize EDI than any initiative over the past two decades. Today, EDI messages are encoded in a standard data format governed by the American National Standards Institute (ANSI) and other specifications.

Companies and industries that do one or more of the following are strong candidates for conversion to EDI:

- Handle many repetitive standard transactions

- Operate on a tight margin

- Face strong competition that requires significant productivity improvements

- Operate in a time-sensitive environment

- Have received requests from partners to convert to EDI

An EDI message contains a string of data elements, each of which represents a singular item, such as a price, a product model number, and so forth, separated by delimiters. The entire string is called a *data segment*. One or more data segments framed by a header and trailer form a *transaction set*, which is the EDI unit of transmission, equivalent to a message. A transaction set often consists of what would usually be contained in a typical business document or form. EDI messages can also be encrypted and decrypted.

EDI defines communication on the basis of transactions, which perform specific tasks in the business commerce cycle. Knowing that the transaction includes the following components allows for standardization: a header containing data common to an entire transaction; a detail section that contains line-item data; and a summary section for data containing the totals, taxes levied, and other information. The transaction is then sent to the corresponding party for processing.

Figure 25.1 shows an EDI transaction between a buying organization and a selling organization. The buying organization processes its orders through a purchasing application to create application files. These files go through an

EDI system to create an EDI-standardized file. This file contains one or more records in the EDI format described previously. The EDI standard files are then sent through an EDI network, which may be the Internet, a virtual private network (VPN), a secure network between two sites using Internet technology such as the transport layer, or a value-added network (VAN), to the selling organization. When the transaction arrives at the selling organization, it is filtered through an EDI translator to create the application files that the order-processing program expects. The order-processing program fulfills the order and ships the product to the buyer.

FIGURE 25.1 An EDI transaction

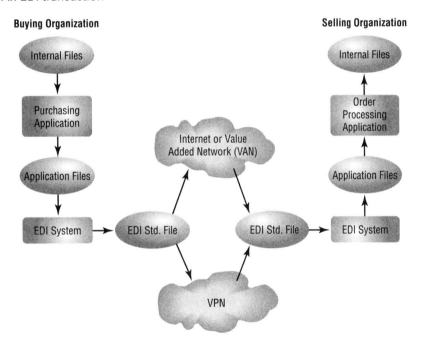

The following is a sample EDI message. Each line has its own designation and contains information in an agreed-upon format for two or more trading partners. As you can see, some of the information is easily understandable, such as the address and the type of product, whereas other information can be understood only by EDI applications. EDI messages are often formatted as plain text files with each field on a separate line. The first characters in each line contain a code that identifies the field, and the actual content follows.

```
ISA~00~            ~00~             ~ZZ~YOUR COMM-ID
  ~14~SLKP COMM-ID   ~000227~1053~U~00401~000000012~0~P~>
GS~IN~YOUR COMM-ID~SLKP COMM-ID~20000227~1053~3~X~004010
ST~810~0001
BIG~19991118~001001~19990926~11441~~~DR
N1~RE~REMIT COMPANY, INC~92~002377703
N3~P.O. BOX 111
N4~ANYTOWN~NC~27106
N1~ST~SARA LEE FOOTWEAR
N3~SHIPPING STREET
N4~OUR TOWN~PA~17855
N1~BT~SARA LEE FOOTWEAR~92~10
N3~470 W. HANES MILL RD
N4~WINSTON SALEM~NC~27105
ITD~05~3~~~~~60
DTM~011~19991118
IT1~0001~1470~YD~2~~BP~BUYERPART
PID~F~~~~Square Rubber Hose
TDS~294000
ISS~1470~YD
CTT~1~1470
SE~19~0001
GE~1~3
IEA~1~000000012
```

EXERCISE 25.1

Researching EDI Standards

In this exercise, you will visit the home page of the Data Interchange Standards Association (DISA), which is the organization that promotes EDI, to consider some additional materials on EDI standards.

1. In your web browser, enter **http://www.disa.org** to go to the DISA home page.

2. Click the About DISA link at the top left and read the organization's mission.

EXERCISE 25.1 *(continued)*

3. Click the Back button to return to the home page.

4. Under Affiliates, click Accredited Standards Committee (ASC) X12.

5. Click the About X12 link, and select the menu link for What is ASC X12.

6. Read the information provided.

7. From the navigation menu on the left, click the X12 Members link to view a listing of companies and organizations that support X12.

Internet EDI

EDI will enjoy long-term use in business-to-business transactions, because it already has a 20-year head start over other technologies. You should expect several major shifts in its use, however. The traditional model for EDI was to use a dedicated connection or a VAN to transport the EDI message, both of which were expensive. However, the Internet will probably replace the private networks in most cases, thereby opening the use of EDI for small to medium-sized businesses.

A twofold benefit is anticipated. First, for established EDI users, new trading partners will have access to EDI. Until now, the cost of doing business with non-EDI vendors was about 25 times higher. Second, small to medium-sized businesses will be able to compete for business with organizations that had previously been out of reach. In the past, some large organizations conducted business only with other organizations that used EDI, leading to a stifling of competition.

Products that allow for EDI transactions range from server- or PC-based applications to web applications. Some provide more features than others, resulting in varying costs. Most of the products also have varying ranges of usefulness, based on the number of transactions they are designed to support. Many levels exist, depending on the requirements of the business.

Some of the leading products are the following:

- ADX Exchange (`www.adx.com`)

- GE Global Exchange Services (`www.geis.com`)

- Peregrine (`www.peregrine.com`)

EXERCISE 25.2

Previewing Advanced Data Exchange

In this exercise, you will preview a simulated EDI transaction using a PC-based EDI application interface. You will learn how small to medium-sized businesses can become involved in EDI transactions and become trading partners without expensive startup and operation costs.

1. In your web browser, enter **http://www.adx.com** to go to the Advanced Data Exchange home page. Click Enter to continue.

2. Move the mouse cursor over the Services link, and select the Mid-Size & Small Enterprise Services link.

3. Click the ADX Network link.

4. Scroll down to view a partial list of EDI trading partners that the ADX Exchange supports.

EDI and Security

One of the less-attractive features of delivering EDI over the Internet is security. In a traditional EDI environment, most communication is accomplished via e-mail messages properly formatted through a secure line, such as frame relay or a leased line. On the Internet, the security risk increases.

With no built-in privacy measures, an Internet e-mail message is similar to a postcard. Anyone who handles the postcard can read the message. With a secure e-mail facility, the message is similar to a letter in a sealed and registered envelope: Only the intended recipient can receive the letter and read its contents.

In July 1995, a group of leading networking and messaging vendors, in conjunction with cryptography developer RSA Data Security, endorsed a specification that allows encrypted messages to be exchanged between various e-mail applications. The specification, called *Secure/Multipurpose Internet Mail Extension (S/MIME)*, allows vendors to independently develop interoperable RSA-based security for their e-mail platforms. Thus, an S/MIME message composed and encrypted on one vendor's platform can be decoded and read on another's.

S/MIME is based on the Multipurpose Internet Mail Extension (MIME) protocol. MIME is a standard that provides a general structure for the content of Internet e-mail messages and allows extensions for new applications such as security. The security services are authentication (using digital signatures) and privacy (using encryption). S/MIME assumes that both senders and receivers of secure e-mail messages have public/private key pairs.

Because encrypting large messages with a public key is computationally expensive, S/MIME uses a concept called *enveloping*. The bulk message is composed using a session key and a symmetric cipher, and public-key encryption is used to transfer the session key securely to the intended recipient. S/MIME recommends three symmetric encryption algorithms: DES (Data Encryption Standard), Triple DES, and RC2. The adjustable key size of the RC2 algorithm makes it especially useful for applications intended for export outside the United States. RSA encryption (Rivest-Shamir-Adleman encryption) is the required public-key algorithm.

XML and EDI

Most experts agree that EDI will remain widely used while it evolves into a mix of traditional methods combined with newer technology. One area generating considerable momentum is the *Extensible Markup Language (XML)* with EDI. XML is a meta-language derived from its predecessor, Standard Generalized Markup Language (SGML), which allows the description of documents and the data they contain. The XML/EDI combination will allow much more flexibility than EDI offers on its own. An additional benefit of XML is that it is both human- and machine-readable, whereas EDI is only machine-readable.

For the near future, XML and EDI will co-exist in many businesses that currently use EDI. These businesses have large investments in EDI applications that integrate with many of their back-office applications, including inventory and accounting systems. Simply discontinuing the use of EDI and adopting XML does not make good business sense. The likely evolution for these businesses is a hybrid implementation, with XML as a transport vehicle to transmit and receive EDI messages among themselves. XML can describe the same data that is in the EDI messages and then translate or map back into EDI when it reaches the EDI applications, thus allowing participants to reach more trading partners and their supply chains. This approach will allow small to mid-sized businesses that do not have an EDI infrastructure to download the XML data directly into their business systems, eliminating the need for EDI applications. When the non-EDI business sends an XML message to an EDI trading partner, the message can be translated into its own native EDI format.

The following two examples show a sample EDI message and then that message converted to XML. These examples are hypothetical and are meant to provide a visual understanding of important structural differences between general EDI and XML data formats. They should not be considered a valid or accurate conversion of the EDI or XML messages.

EDI Message:

```
ISA~00~          ~00~          ~ZZ~YOUR COMM-ID
  ~14~SLKP COMM-ID   ~000227~1053~U~00401~000000012~0~P~>
GS~IN~YOUR COMM-ID~SLKP COMM-ID~20000227~1053~3~X~004010
ST~810~0001
BIG~19991118~001001~19990926~11441~~~DR
N1~RE~BIG COMPANY, INC~92~002377703
N3~P.O. BOX 111
N4~ANYTOWN~NC~27106
N1~ST~SARA LEE FOOTWEAR
N3~SHIPPING STREET
N4~OUR TOWN~PA~17855
N1~BT~SARA LEE FOOTWEAR~92~10
N3~470 W. HANES MILL RD
N4~WINSTON SALEM~NC~27105
ITD~05~3~~~~~60
DTM~011~19991118
IT1~0001~1470~YD~2~~BP~BUYERPART
PID~F~~~~Oakley Big Smoke
TDS~294000
ISS~1470~YD
CTT~1~1970
SE~13~0001
GE~1~3
IEA~1~000000012
```

EDI Message described using XML:

```
<PURCHASEORDER>
    <poID>000271053</poID>
    <VENDORINFO>
        <VENDORADDRESS>P.O. Box 111</VENDORADDRESS>
```

```
            <VENDORID>BIG Company 20000227</VENDORID>
        </VENDORINFO>
        <PAYMENTTERMS>Net 60</PAYMENTTERMS>
        <PRODUCTS>
        <PRODUCTINFO>
            <PRODUCTNAME>Sara Lee Footware</PRODUCTNAME>
            <PRODUCTDESC>Walking shoes</PRODUCTDESC>
            <PRODUCTID>92</PRODUCTID>
            <PRODUCTSIZE>10</PRODUCTSIZE>
        </PRODUCTINFO>
        <PRODUCTINFO>
            <PRODUCTNAME>Oakley Big Smoke</PRODUCTNAME>
            <PRODUCTDESC>Casual Sandals</PRODUCTDESC>
            <PRODUCTID>1970</PRODUCTID>
            <PRODUCTSIZE>13</PRODUCTSIZE>
        </PRODUCTINFO>
        </PRODUCTS>
        </PURCHASEORDER>
```

As you can see, the XML version of the data is easy to understand and provides structure to the information. By using XML, businesses and business data will become more easily interchangeable.

You can learn more about this topic at the following websites:

- XMLSolutions (`www.vitria.com`)

- Biztalk (`www.biztalk.org`)

- World Wide Web Consortium (`www.w3.org`)

Open Buying on the Internet (OBI)

*O*pen Buying on the Internet (OBI) is an Internet e-commerce specification based on open technologies. OBI was developed to target high-volume, low-cost transactions.

High-volume, low-cost transactions account for almost 80 percent of most companies' purchasing activities, according to some estimates.

OBI has several corporate sponsors, including American Express, Visa, Netscape, Microsoft, and Dell. OBI is used by these companies and has begun to emerge as a viable method for B2B transactions. Because OBI is based on open technologies, it does not have the incompatibility problems commonly associated with EDI. OBI supports the open technologies described in Table 25.1.

TABLE 25.1   Open Technologies—OBI support

Technology	Purpose
HTTP and W3C HTML	Content display
X12 850 EDI Standards	Order request
HTTP 1.0	Order transmission
SSL	Transmission security
SSL	Cryptography
X.509 version 3	Public-key certificates

OBI works well for purchasing non-production items such as office supplies, cleaning products, and computer equipment. Such purchases are expensive with traditional methods. Once an OBI system is in place, the cost of processing falls dramatically. OBI allows any approved person in an organization to buy needed products or services.

Following are four components of an OBI transaction.

- Requisitioner, the person or software that initiates the transaction to purchase

- Buying organization, the company that represents the requisitioner and has an OBI server

- Selling organization, the company that is offering the product or service for sale and has an OBI server

- Payment authority, the organization that acts as a neutral third party to settle the financial component of the transaction

OBI Transactions

An OBI transaction undergoes a four-step process of validation and authorization to ensure that the purchase is authentic and approved. This process reduces the possibility of fraud and unauthorized purchases.

Step 1   The requisitioner needs to order, for example, office supplies. That person accesses the selling organization's online catalog, which can be hosted on the selling company's OBI server or the buying company's OBI server. The online catalog will list prices specific to the buying organization. For example, a buying organization with a higher volume will probably receive lower prices than other buying organizations with lower volume. This customized catalog eliminates the need for continual price negotiations and adjustments for each buyer. The requisitioner adds the needed products to the shopping cart and places the order with the selling organization's OBI server.

Step 2   The selling organization's OBI server automatically returns the order to the buying organization's OBI server for approval. Such approval involves properly identifying the requisitioning individual and ascertaining their spending authority. The approval process can be automatic or can require management intervention.

Step 3   After approval from the buying organization, the transaction is returned to the selling organization's OBI server for fulfillment.

Step 4   A payment authority, such as a bank or the lender's OBI server, handles the billing and money transfer.

OBI Interaction

OBI can work with EDI and XML due to the standards set for it. In addition, companies are creating OBI-based products for businesses to work with. OBI has an additional advantage over EDI because OBI orders are formatted in ANSI EDI X12 850. Companies that use this format have already invested heavily in EDI and can make their current systems OBI-compliant. Like EDI, XML also has a future role in OBI to create flexibility and help formalize business processes.

The following companies offer OBI products:

Epic Systems   OBI Toolkit, at `www.epic-systems.com`

Allaire   ColdFusion, at `www.macromedia.com`

To learn more about the OBI standards, visit the Open Buying on the Internet standards organization at www.openbuy.org.

Business-to-Business Marketplaces, Portals, and Hubs

Rather than investing in an e-commerce infrastructure, some businesses are using B2B websites that create networks focused on bringing buyers and suppliers together. Most of these networks have their own e-commerce packages and policies and provide the purchasing support many organizations need.

A *portal* is a central site that targets specific users, customers, organizations, or markets. Some portals offer direct affiliations with pre-established suppliers. Others use the auction format for acquisitions. In either case, the use of these networks allows companies to enter the e-commerce arena quickly. They offer customers the ability to browse many catalogs from different vendors on the same website. Vendors can then use that site to check and fulfill orders. One of the benefits of a portal is that all the vendors implement the same payment systems online. Offline, however, each vendor must manually convert or batch the online data into its own proprietary system.

Portals are a short-term way for a business to conduct e-commerce, but portals are not a suitable long-term solution because they cannot completely automate a B2B transaction from supplier to customer. The following are some of examples of portals:

- www.freemarkets.com, an online auction for buyers of industrial parts, raw materials, commodities, and services

- www.supplyworks.com, provides goods and services

- www.eb2b.com, fosters trading relationships

- www.works.com, provides computer accessories, office supplies, furniture, break room items and janitorial products

- www.newview.com, a materials supply network

- `www.facilitypro.com`, provides facilities maintenance, repair, and operation (MRO)

- `www.globalfoodexchange.com`, provides food industry services.

- `www.dovebid.com`, surplus business equipment purchase and sale

- `www.freetradezone.com`, inventory and pricing of electronic components

- `www.liquidation.com`, surplus business equipment purchase and sale.

- `www.4officesupplies.com`, office supplies sale

- `www.covisint.com`, the Ford Motor Company B2B exchange

E-Business

E-business encompasses all forms of business conducted electronically, including e-commerce. Thus, e-commerce itself is a subset of e-business. When discussing e-commerce, one is typically referring to the electronic selling and purchasing of products or services between a seller and a buyer. E-business extends beyond e-commerce to tie the elements of e-commerce into an automated system.

E-business applications are much more complex to develop and integrate than e-commerce applications because they involve more variables. A typical e-business transaction can be as follows: The supplier of brake assemblies has an e-business application that integrates with an automobile manufacturer's supply inventory and production forecasts. Based on agreed-upon inventory and production forecasts, the brake assembly supplier has the authority to ship more brake assemblies to the automobile manufacturer. The brake assembly supplier's e-business application analyzes its current inventory of assemblies ready to ship and raw materials in inventory to produce new ones. It then calculates whether inventory is high enough to meet the automobile manufacturer's forecasts. If supplies are low, the brake assembly supplier's e-business application places an order to the supplier of brake pad materials requesting more inventory. The brake pad supplier's e-business application accepts the order, processes the order. and ensures that the products are shipped when requested. The brake assembly supplier receives the shipment, notifies the brake pad supplier that the shipment arrived, and transfers funds to the supplier. The transaction is now complete.

Ideally, in a true e-business environment, this entire transaction takes place without the need for human initiation and requires limited, if any, human intervention. Additionally, this model can exist throughout the entire supply chain. This series of tasks is large and complex, presenting a major challenge to e-business. How does a supplier integrate its e-business applications with those of its suppliers and its vendors? The answer can be found in standards under development that still need to be refined and accepted.

Technology giants such as IBM, Sun, Oracle, Ariba, Microsoft, and CommerceOne are working toward the technologies that will eventually evolve as standards used in all industries. One of the most promising technologies in this arena is XML.

Universal Description, Discovery, and Integration (UDDI) is an e-business industry initiative to help create platform-independent, open frameworks to allow companies to discover services and business rules that other businesses use and help them integrate their services using the Internet. It is a one-stop location to find out what types of technology specific organizations and companies are implementing. To learn more, visit www.uddi.org.

Supply Chain

A *supply chain* is the channel used to get the raw materials needed to build a product from all sub-part manufacturers to the final assembly of a product and then to the end user. Supply chains are responsible for producing, delivering, and transporting raw materials and meeting customer demands.

A good example is the automobile manufacturer. Large automobile manufacturers rely heavily on suppliers and other manufacturers to provide them with parts that will eventually be assembled into an automobile. One supplier supplies a drive train, another supplies a brake assembly, and yet another supplies the tires. All these suppliers must work together to create the final product. If one supplier cannot fulfill its requirements, the entire process of automobile production is affected.

The supply chain requires effective management for success. If the supplier that produces the brake assemblies cannot obtain brake pads from its suppliers, the entire supply chain for the automobile can be halted. If the tire manufacturer cannot acquire the raw material to produce tires, it becomes a weak link in the supply chain.

In traditional industries such as automotive, these supply chains have had years to develop and mature to a state of high reliability. Mature companies have alternative plans to cope with breakdowns, which might include excess inventory or backup suppliers. Even with alternative plans in place, production or delivery delays can occur.

With new industries, especially with e-commerce, these supply chains have had to grow rapidly, and as a result, many breakdowns have jeopardized the final delivery or assembly of products. You hear many stories about rapid expansion in e-commerce that left companies unable to deliver because of ineffective supply chain management. One of the most common reasons is that suppliers themselves are new to the industry and e-commerce and are thereby unable to fill demands. Over-promising and under-delivering have been the results. In some cases, entire businesses that could have been successful have failed under the pressures of the supply chain.

Some product supply chains are easier to manage than others. Products that do not change frequently allow the supply chain to follow patterns. Products that change rapidly or frequently keep the supply chain in motion by reacting to circumstances.

For example, if the brake-assembly manufacturer has too much inventory, it can run into cash flow or warehousing problems. If it runs short on inventory, it may not have time to replenish supplies to meet the demands of the automobile manufacturer. Manufactures and suppliers must walk a fine line. To achieve successful supply chain fulfillment, companies should carefully investigate their suppliers and systems, to identify any potential performance shortfalls.

By automating some parts of e-commerce, businesses can help relieve some of the unknown pressures in the supply chain process. Major manufacturers are developing marketplaces for their suppliers. These marketplaces are a one-stop location that provides services, including inventory status, forecasts, and procurement. Their goal is to allow suppliers to know more about one another and to integrate their businesses. This approach produces a stronger supply chain by reducing fulfillment time and operating expenditures. If a supplier knows when inventories are running low, it can take steps to deliver products to the right place at the right time, reducing fluctuation in the chain.

EDI used to control supply chain management; now, high-tech firms must rely more heavily on the Internet and supply chain management software.

The following companies offer supply chain management software:

- SAP (www.sap.com)

- I2 (www.i2.com)

- Ariba (www.ariba.com)

Procurement

*P*rocurement is the process that companies use to buy items from suppliers. In the past, procurement relied heavily on paper and manual processes. For example, if an employee needed a new laptop, they would complete a form or request approval for a purchase order. The employee would then find sources for the laptop based on approved criteria. Once a selection was made, the product was ordered. An invoice was delivered to the employee or the accounts payable department, which then used additional manual processes to complete the transaction and settlement with the supplier. During the process, tracking the status typically required the employee to make calls and follow up with e-mail messages.

Radical changes have fueled the growth of automated procurement, also known as *e-procurement*. E-procurement is one of the main concepts behind B2B transactions. Packages that automate the entire procurement process and allow for substantial cost and time savings are available.

With e-procurement, a transaction can be completed in a controlled and consistent way. For example, to order a laptop, the employee visits an intranet application to place the order. Via a logon, the employee can view approved items in a custom catalog. The approval chain process is controlled, and notifications are sent to all involved organizations, such as management, purchasing, accounts payable, and the supplier. Electronic transactions are generated, including the specified order, order receipts, order status, and electronic settlements.

Examples of enterprise-wide procurement products include the following:

- mySAP Supplier Relationship Management (SRM) (www.sap.com /solutions/e-procurement)

- iPlanet BuyerXpert (www.iplanet.com/products/iplanet_ buyerxpert/home_buyerxpert.html)

A *vertical marketing system* (VMS) unites multiple manufacturers in the same industry to coordinate and streamline distribution channels and the supply chain. The three basic types of vertical marketing systems each create a different control and management structure.

- In an *administered vertical marketing system*, the flow of products from producer to end-user is controlled by the power and size of one member of the channel system rather than by common ownership or contractual ties. For example, one dominant manufacturer or distributor might own or control the VMS. Channel users pay service fees to this company when they use the VMS to buy or sell products.

- In a *contractual vertical marketing system*, independent firms at different levels of distribution are tied together by contract to achieve economies of scale and greater sales impact. The VMS can be developed and run by a consortium of several firms. This model allows greater industry participation in VMS management and can reduce competitive and regulatory conflicts in comparison with an administered VMS.

- In a *corporate vertical marketing system*, product flow is controlled by common ownership of the different levels of the system. VMS users must join an organization or consortium that develops and manages the corporate VMS as an industry-based shared resource.

A *horizontal marketing system* is a venture between two or more companies that do not compete, but complement each other. These companies can join together in production, distribution, or marketing to achieve their individual goals and pursue new opportunities. The goal is to achieve a higher level of success together than they would alone. For example, a company that manufactures luggage might join a horizontal marketing system with another company that offers a fabric sealant and stain guard. Both products complement each other; combined, they offer the customer more value.

Inventory, Shipping, and Order-Tracking Data

E-business reduces the amount of human interaction needed to complete a transaction. But unless the e-business application extends beyond the transaction, it will not reach its full potential. Servicing customers online means that the online service must replicate traditional methods as much as possible.

An issue that troubles many online customers is the inability to determine available inventory or the status of their transaction. With traditional methods, the customer had some sort of confirmation, perhaps by speaking to a customer service representative. The online model does not inherently offer that convenience. In traditional methods, a customer can call a customer service representative to find out about inventory status or whether an order has been shipped. In an effort to control costs, many online businesses provide little telephone support.

Moving these common inquiries online helps bridge the gap between online businesses and their customers. Many online businesses lack the resources to handle the influx of calls from customers worldwide. A simple solution is to give customers online access to inventory, order information, and shipping status. Such information reduces customer frustration and increases the possibility of repeat business.

Inventory

Inventory is the quantity of product held between the time the merchant produces or acquires that product and the time it is shipped to a customer. The amount of inventory depends on the time needed to produce or acquire the product, the cost of the product, and the demand for the product.

Many online businesses have found that the traditional models of inventory control have changed. The biggest factor driving this change is demand. With worldwide accessibility, a new online company can learn that orders placed will far outnumber the standard quantities of inventory that were acceptable in the traditional business model.

Additionally, the rate at which the orders arrive can also be overwhelming. Thus, an inventory that may be adequate at the beginning of the business day can easily be depleted by the day's end.

Typically, inventory information is stored in a database. You can usually access this information by a dynamic query to the database when a customer requests the catalog page listing the item.

The type of schema that the database uses to store inventory information depends on the relation and design of the system. The information about the quantity in stock can be a form of a business rule for the company and can indicate many things. For example, business A sells an item on its website. When a user accesses the site to purchase the item, the web page indicates that 100 items are in stock. However, when an employee in the purchasing department checks the database, it shows an inventory of only 25, which tells the employee to place a purchase order for more products to replenish the inventory. This scenario might be considered a business rule that, along with other checks and balances, helps ensure the smooth and timely flow of products in and out of inventory.

Order Tracking

Allowing customers to check the status of their shipments with a confirmation number first emerged as a differentiating feature of customer service. Order tracking is now a customer requirement in many markets. Customers should be told the status of their shipments so they will know where their orders are and whether they were fulfilled. This notification will reduce the number of customer calls, thereby saving time and money for both the customer and the merchant. Order tracking can also be provided on an website, allowing customers 24/7 access to delivery data.

Like the inventory information, the shipping information is also stored in a database. The order ID for any order is usually used to track the status. The level of information and confirmation you choose to offer customers depends on your information security needs.

Whatever database is used, the technique will be similar. You must develop a naming or a numbering convention to determine status. For example, you can use a zero if the order processing has not begun. You can use a 1 if the order has been packed, but not shipped. You can use a 2 if the order has been packed and shipped. You can use a 3 if the product is on back order. Whatever convention you use, it must be clearly identified and able to hold the information that your customers need.

Freight and Shipping

Selecting the proper freight hauler is critical to reducing costs. Successful shipping companies offer prompt pickup and delivery services, along with electronic information about routing and tracking.

Information technology has led to substantial improvements in the shipping process. It begins at the time of pickup when a bill of lading (BOL) is entered into a handheld scanning apparatus. The electronic information is often sent via radio frequency to the shipping hub, which begins to route and track the package.

Large shipping companies allow online tracking of packages via a standard web browser. Some can integrate into existing e-business software, allowing the sender (merchant) and the receiver (customer) to view real-time shipping data on the merchant's website, without involving the shipping company.

Shipping goods, especially across international borders, is a multifaceted task. The size and quantity of the goods and the shipping time expected will determine if land, air, or maritime methods should be used.

Following is a list of freight and shipping brokers, each offering different options and services:

- Airborne Express (www.airborne.com)
- Federal Express (www.fedex.com)
- FreightQuote.com (www.freightquote.com)
- Traffic Management (www.trafficmgmt.com)
- United Parcel Service (www.ups.com)

Language Translation and Localization

Localization is the process of translating material into a specific language or culture. Most multinational companies have been addressing this issue for years, but as more cultures have web access, more businesses must begin to consider the ramifications of multilanguage options. Currently the most popular language on the Web is English, but the balance is beginning to shift. By providing content in multiple languages, a business can grow with evolving markets.

When content is localized, more than just the national language is considered. Many details, such as geographic location and climate, cultural practices, currency, observed holidays, and gender distinctions or preferences, are also included. For example, certain words or phrases can be used in one region of a country, but not in another region of the same country. Even though both regions speak the same language, they observe region-specific dialects.

If precise translation and localization is the goal, translation specialists should be included in the process. Following are some companies that provide such services.

- Bowne Global Solutions (www.bowneglobal.com)
- GlobalSight (www.globalsight.com)
- LanguageWorks (www.languageworks.com)

- Translate Central (www.translatecentral.com)

- translate.IT (www.translate-it.de)

- Welocalize (www.welocalize.com)

Translation in a simple form can be achieved through language translation programs. These tools are mediocre at best, however, and you should use them with caution. Machine translation can be highly inaccurate, because software may not understand idioms, national or regional differences, and other linguistic variations.

Some services take content as a string and then produce output in the desired language. Others translate the content on the fly, delivering the translated content to the web browser. When using these types of translation tools, remember that only content that is in text format such as ASCII is updated. Text inside graphics cannot be updated, because the translation tools do not recognize them as words. Systran (www.systransoft.com) offers translation services and software. Alta Vista (world.altavista.com) offers an online translation engine that uses Systran software.

Interoffice Productivity and Cost-Reduction Tools

Many companies are turning to the Internet to improve communication and reduce costs. Besides the basic cost of access, the Internet is free. And because most companies already have access, using the Internet for additional services is cost-effective and can increase productivity.

E-mail has transformed the way workers communicate with co-workers, clients, and customers. However, aside from e-mail, the use of Internet technology to communicate is still in its infancy. Many categories of services are supported via Internet technology; some require little or no investment, and others are costly to implement. Using these tools can reduce costs, even if an initial investment is required.

Telecommuting

Office requirements have changed as networking has improved. One change is that more people can work from remote locations. E-mail was the first influence in telecommuting, allowing messages to be sent wherever workers were located. Next, Internet and intranet applications created more flexibility, giving remote employees access to company networks. With these changes, going to the office is no longer a daily requirement for many employees. These and other technologies allow employees to have both a business office and a home-office, allowing greater flexibility.

Telephony

Telephony is the technology by which telephone calls that would normally be routed via standard telecommunications means are instead sent over the Internet. The average mid-size company spends a high monthly sum on telecommunications, thus making telephony an attractive option. With high-bandwidth connections, voice degradation is unnoticeable.

For practical solutions, you can install special servers inside a firewall that route calls outside the company to the public phone system or to a remote office. For example, if a company has three main locations, in California, Arizona, and Texas, it can dramatically reduce telecommunications costs by routing interoffice calls over the Internet. Each location needs to make an initial investment in hardware, but the return on investment is achieved in a relatively short time, even if call volume increases. Telephony vendors include the following:

- RightVoice.net (www.rightvoice.net)
- ITXC (www.itxc.com)

Web Conferencing

Web conferencing is becoming more popular as the average desktop computer continues to improve in computing power and bandwidth. Accessories such as sound cards and microphones have also bolstered web conferencing.

Web conferencing can be conducted on many levels, depending on the meeting requirements. In its most basic form, web conferencing can be a slide presentation that is posted to a website where visitors view the presentation at their convenience. E-mail can also be a component with this format. One web-conferencing product, HelpSlides, is sold by www.helpslides.com.

Windows Messenger (messenger.microsoft.com) supports text, audio, video, and white-boarding features for conferencing.

For more interaction, people can join a conference call and follow a web-based or PowerPoint-style presentation that is hosted by someone who narrates the slides. A conferencing service provides a high level of interaction and control over the presentation. Most services require only a recent version browser such as Internet Explorer 5. Conference attendees can log on to a presentation, each having preferences based on those set by the moderator.

Most services allow the presenter to control the attendees' browser windows; navigate them to selected websites; and use whiteboards, chat, and polling or survey features. Additionally, sound can be added by traditional telephone conferencing or over the Internet with the use of a sound card and speakers. All these services combine to create a fully interactive meeting session that can include anyone around the world within a moments notice. Conferencing service vendors include:

- WebEx (www.webex.com)
- RainDance (www.raindance.com)
- Mshow.com (www.mshow.com)
- Genesys Conferencing (www.genesys.com)
- iMeet (www.imeet.com)

Scheduling

Coordinating schedules is often difficult, especially in offices that require frequent travel or allow flexible hours and telecommuting. Many scheduling products are available. Some are application based, and others are web-based. Some of the common features of scheduling software include postings for meetings and available conference room times, office hours, vacation, sick time, and travel locations. Some online-scheduling applications allow customers to schedule their own appointments with service companies.

You can find scheduling software at the following sites:

- www.xtime.com
- www.ecal.com
- www.webevent.com
- www.schedulesource.com

Video Monitoring

Video monitoring through digital cameras can replace expensive closed-circuit monitors. Many cameras require only a PC and Internet connectivity to deliver live full-motion video on the web. Of course, video quality depends on the bandwidth.

Instant Messaging (IM)

Instant-messaging clients allow participants to quickly exchange text messages. IM is a popular Internet service, allowing users from around the world to chat in real time. Employees in some organizations often use IM clients for text messaging fellow colleagues in a team, workgroup or department. Because most client applications indicate if the participants are currently online and available, some employees user IM software to keep track of their fellow workers' activities and availability in real-time. Some IM software also includes audio, video, and white-boarding capabilities that are useful for business conferencing.

Instant messaging is offered through the following sites:

- AOL Instant Messenger (`www.aim.com`)

- ICQ (`www.icq.com`)

- Windows Messenger (`messenger.microsoft.com`)

- Yahoo! Messenger (`messenger.yahoo.com`)

Voice Recognition and Voice Portals

Voice recognition software advancements have created a new service industry around mobile phone users. Using a phone, a person can receive information by giving voice commands to a voice recognition software application.

For example, business travelers can get directions to a destination or check airline schedules or stock quotes from their mobile phones, without needing an Internet-capable phone. Some services, such as Tellme, offer free public access to information; others offer tailored information. For example, Charles Schwab has its own voice recognition system to service its clients and is open to account holders only. The following companies offer voice recognition:

- BeVOCAL (`www.bevocal.com`)

- Tellme Networks (`www.tellme.com`)

- Yahoo! By Phone (`phone.yahoo.com`)

Summary

Two distinct models are used in e-commerce structure: business-to-business (B2B) and business-to-consumer (B2C). The B2C model is simplistic in structure, whereas the B2B e-commerce model includes every aspect of business that can be merged with or integrated into an automated or electronic process.

For e-commerce to occur, data and information must be exchanged. In addition to data exchange, for B2B e-commerce, business processes and rules must occur electronically. The most common form of data exchange is Electronic Data Interchange (EDI). EDI is a messaging protocol meant to ensure that data sent between normally incompatible computers retains its integrity and is formatted consistently. This standard is popular with financial institutions and large businesses that need to communicate large volumes of detailed, repetitive information over company networks. Extensible Markup Language (XML) complements EDI by providing a meta-language for structuring machine readable data.

Secure/Multipurpose Internet Mail Extension (S/MIME) is a specification that allows encrypted messages to be exchanged among various e-mail applications. S/MIME uses a concept called enveloping. The bulk message is composed using a session key and a symmetric cipher, and public-key encryption is used to transfer the session key securely to the intended recipient.

Open Buying on the Internet (OBI) provides a specification to assist in the purchasing of products between businesses, and it was developed to target high-volume, low-cost transactions such as the buying and selling of office supplies, cleaning products, and computer equipment. OBI is geared mainly toward the B2B model.

In working out e-commerce B2B structuring, two terms come into play: vertical marketing and horizontal marketing. Vertical marketing unites multiple manufacturers in the same industry to coordinate and streamline distribution channels and the supply chain. Horizontal marketing is a venture between two or more companies, which do not compete, but instead complement each other.

With your merchant structure in place, the next set of concerns in e-business relate to keeping track of inventory, shipping, and orders. Inventory is more a concern to the merchant, who should be aware of what they have (or have received in) through a database. Shipping allows those products to get to your consumers. Order tracking really provides a greater convenience and comfort to the buyer because they often want to know where the goods are in transit.

Business can truly use the Internet for more than the selling side of their business. Many categories of services are supported via Internet technology; some require little or no investment, while others are costly to implement. Using these tools can reduce costs, even if an initial investment is required.

Exam Essentials

Know the difference between business-to-business and business-to-consumer e-commerce. Business-to-consumer (B2C) e-commerce takes place when an individual purchases something from a company. Business-to-business (B2B) e-commerce has to do with a transaction between two or more entities.

Know the key protocols used in business-to-business e-commerce transactions. Business-to-business transactions use technologies, or technologies in development, such as EDI, S/MIME, XML/EDI, and OBI.

Know how to explain supply chain, procurement, and telephony. The supply chain is the channel used to get raw materials needed to build a product from all sub-part manufacturers to the final assembly of a product. Procurement is the process that companies use to buy items from suppliers. Telephony is the technology in which telephone calls that are normally be routed via standard telecommunications means are instead sent over the Internet.

Know the goals of EDI. The three goals of EDI are to enable easy and inexpensive communication of structured information, to reduce the amount of data capture and number of transcriptions, and to ensure faster handling of transactions to increase cash flow.

Know what kind of companies can benefit from EDI. Businesses that do the following are candidates for EDI: handle many repetitive standard transactions; operate on a very tight margin; face strong competition, requiring significant productivity improvements; operate in a time-sensitive environment; and have received requests from partner companies to convert to EDI.

Know the components of OBI.   OBI was developed to target high-volume, low-cost transactions. The components of OBI include the requisitioner, the buying organization, the selling organization, and the payment authority. OBI allows any approved person in an organization to buy needed products or services.

Know what a portal is.   A portal is a central site that targets specific users, customers, organizations, or markets. Portals are a short-term way for a business to conduct e-commerce, but portals are not a suitable long-term solution because they cannot completely automate a B2B transaction from supplier to customer.

Key Terms

Before you take the exam, be certain you are familiar with the following terms:

e-business	portal
Electronic Data Interchange (EDI)	procurement
enveloping	Secure Multipurpose Internet Mail Extension (S/MIME)
Extensible Markup Language (XML)	supply chain
horizontal marketing system	telephony
localization	trading partners
Open Buying on the Internet (OBI)	vertical marketing system

Review Questions

1. What is a simple definition of Electronic Data Interchange (EDI)?

    A. An Internet e-commerce specification based on open technologies

    B. An open protocol that defines trading protocol options

    C. A business-to-business network focused on bringing buyers and sellers together

    D. The inter-organizational exchange of information in standardized electronic format

2. Shannon owns a company that sells computers online. She decides to join with another company that sells printers and scanners in a marketing venture. Which type of marketing system is this?

    A. Vertical

    B. Horizontal

    C. Supply chain

    D. Complimenting

3. The Encore Corporation is discussing a conversion to EDI. Of the following characteristics, which would make the Encore Corporation lean in favor of EDI?

    A. Encore is a small company.

    B. Encore deals mostly with the public.

    C. Encore operates on a tight margin.

    D. Most of Encore's transactions are high-priced, low-volume sales.

4. Worldwide Inc. is concerned about the security of sensitive information that is being delivered via e-mail. What technology should they employ to secure their e-mail from interception and/or tampering?

    A. EDI.

    B. OBI.

    C. S/MIME.

    D. XML.

5. Which of the following is a benefit of XML over EDI?

   A. XML is human readable.

   B. XML is only machine-readable.

   C. XML has been in use for a longer period of time.

   D. XML has no benefits over EDI.

6. Micah is in charge of keeping the inventory for Auto Parts Elite at appropriate numbers. He is authorized by the company to make purchases when needed to keep the inventory suitable for business. Seeing that a certain part is no longer in stock, he begins an order from the manufacturer. In the OBI model, what component has Micah become?

   A. Buying organization

   B. A requisitioner

   C. Selling organization

   D. Payment authority

7. What is the hierarchical relationship between suppliers and manufacturers that feed the channel in which raw materials are manufactured and assembled into the final product known as?

   A. EDI

   B. Virtual enterprise

   C. Supply chain

   D. B2C e-commerce

8. In what area has the Internet had an effect in improving Electronic Data Interchange (EDI)?

   A. Security

   B. Cost

   C. Reliability

   D. Service and support

9. Kevin has implemented an automated process that his company will use to purchase items from its suppliers. What is this type of process called?

   A. OBI

   B. Procurement

   C. Supply chain

   D. E-procurement

10. Open Buying on the Internet (OBI), an Internet e-commerce specification based on open technologies, was created to handle what type of transactions?

    A. Low-volume, high-cost

    B. Large transactions

    C. High-volume, low-cost

    D. Small transactions

11. In the OBI model, which component is an organization that acts as a third party to settle the financial process of the transaction?

    A. Payment authority

    B. ACH

    C. Payment gateway

    D. Requisitioner

12. Jose wants to give customers more tools to use on his e-commerce site in hopes of encouraging repeat business. One of the features he adds is order tracking through the carrier he uses. What element of a successful e-commerce business did Jose revise?

    A. Service and support

    B. Fulfillment

    C. Order-process

    D. Repeat business

13. A company that sells hand-made pocket books keeps a stock of their product in a warehouse, in order to quickly fulfill orders. What is the term to describe this company's stock?

   A. Order stock

   B. Inventory

   C. Soft goods

   D. Merchant goods

14. Which of the following best describes the type of transactions in B2B commerce?

   A. Low-volume, high-cost

   B. Redundant, high-volume

   C. Large purchases

   D. Non-complex transactions

15. Which type of marketing system unites multiple manufacturers within the same industry to coordinate and streamline distribution channels and supply chains?

   A. Horizontal marketing system

   B. Industry marketing system

   C. Supply chain marketing system

   D. Vertical marketing system

Answers to Review Questions

1. D. EDI is an inter-organizational exchange of information in standardized electronic format. The other definitions are important and correlate to EDI in certain ways, but only the last option is the correct answer.

2. B. A *horizontal marketing system* is a venture between two or more companies that do not compete, but instead complement each other. These companies can join together in production, distribution, or marketing to achieve their individual goals and pursue new opportunities. A *vertical marketing system* unites multiple manufacturers in the same industry to coordinate and streamline distribution channels and the supply chain.

3. C. A company that does any of the following might want to convert to EDI: handles many repetitive standard transactions; operates on a tight margin; faces strong competition, requiring significant productivity improvements; operates in a time-sensitive environment; has received requests from partner companies to convert to EDI.

4. C. S/MIME is a specification that allows vendors to develop interoperable RSA-based security for their e-mail platforms. Thus, an S/MIME message composed and encrypted on one vendor's platform can be decoded and read on another's. S/MIME uses a concept called enveloping for encrypting large e-mail messages.

5. A. Because XML is human readable, it has an immense advantage over EDI. If necessary, XML can be interpreted by a worker. Even with this benefit, however, XML is not expected to push EDI out of the market. Instead, a combination of the two is a more likely scenario.

6. B. In the OBI model, the requisitioner is the person or software that initiates the transaction to purchase. The actions Micah takes put him in that role. The three other components of OBI are the buying organization, the selling organization, and the payment authority.

7. C. A supply chain is the channel that gets raw materials needed to build a product from all sub-part manufacturers to the final assembly of a product and then to the end user. Supply chains are responsible for raw materials production and delivery, transportation, and meeting customer demands.

8. B.   The use of the Internet with EDI has made the process more cost-effective. The Internet provides a cheaper route instead of using the expensive delivery methods of a dedicated connection or a value-added network to transport the EDI message.

9. D.   Procurement is the process that companies use to buy items from suppliers. E-procurement is a primary concept in B2B transactions. Total packages that automate the procurement process and allow for substantial cost and time savings are available.

10. C.   OBI was developed to target high-volume, low-cost transactions, mainly business-to-business transactions. A low-volume, high-cost is most likely a business-to-consumer transaction.

11. A.   A payment authority is an organization that acts as a neutral third party to settle the financial component of the transaction. It is one of four OBI components, the other three being the requisitioner, the buying organization, and the selling organization. The other terms have there own meanings separate from the OBI model.

12. B.   Supplying an order tracking number is part of the fulfillment process in a successful business. This gives customers the ability to see the progress of their merchandise as it is being shipped to them. Fulfillment refers to ways in which a merchant satisfies its customer's requests for goods. Other elements of a successful e-commerce business are the order process, payment processing, service and support, and generating demand, security, and community.

13. B.   An inventory is stockpiled goods kept by a company and is either made or acquired to fulfill orders. Soft goods are products that can be sent to buyers electronically, for example, by downloading or e-mailing.

14. B.   B2B transactions are made up of mostly redundant, high-volume transactions. B2B commerce is much more complex than B2C commerce. The B2B model is largely driven by redundant, high-volume transactions conducted between two companies.

15. D.   A vertical marketing system unites multiple manufacturers within the same industry to coordinate and streamline distribution channels and supply chains. The three basic types of vertical marketing systems each create a different hierarchy. The horizontal marketing system is a venture between two or more companies that do not compete but complement each other. Industry marketing and supply chain marketing are fictitious.

Chapter

26

Electronic Commerce Site Creation Packages— Outsourcing

THE CIW EXAM OBJECTIVE GROUP COVERED IN THIS CHAPTER:

✓ Develop and host an e-commerce site using outsourcing and instant storefront services.

Throughout this book, we have discussed various models and methods for designing and developing effective e-commerce websites. In this chapter, we will review two available methods for quickly developing and implementing an e-commerce presence on the Web.

At the heart of each method is outsourcing, which allows merchants to develop their own sites while hosting them on someone else's web servers. Merchants can set fixed prices for their products. By letting the web host handle certain design, administrative, distribution, fulfillment, and maintenance duties, the merchant can concentrate on their company's pricing and marketing strategies. We will discuss the application service provider (ASP) model, which is a key element of e-commerce outsourcing.

The first method, auctions, provides a simple way to advertise and sell specific items. This format, made popular by eBay, is used by thousands of individuals and businesses every day to sell merchandise without the expense of site development and hosting. Auction users can benefit by the bidding structure of the auction, which can hold down prices to what the most interested buyers will pay.

The second method is the instant storefront. Merchants use online tools within a website or offline software design tools to create a complete e-commerce site. The instant storefront approach gives merchants the flexibility of hosting an e-commerce site on their own or on another company's web servers.

Outsourcing

We will begin our discussion of electronic commerce site creation with *outsourcing*. A business can transfer some daily responsibilities or tasks to another company that specializes in performing these services.

For example, many companies hire contract maintenance firms to clean and maintain their buildings and facilities. Some companies use a payroll service that issues and tracks compensation to the company's employees. These are examples of outsourced services.

A crucial and attractive component of outsourcing is the delegation of responsibility to the firm that is actually providing the outsourced services. Successful outsourcing firms can provide consistent quality of service while efficiently managing overhead and human resources. The outsourcing firm takes on the responsibility of hiring and firing the workers who provide the services. Some large clients transfer employees and assets to the outsourcing firm, divesting themselves of much of the responsibility of managing these resources on a daily basis. Outsourcing can help a company focus on strategy and tactics rather than implementation and administration.

By reducing costs, the outsourcing firm can lower its fees to client companies. However, an outsourcing firm must strike an acceptable balance between low costs and service quality. Clients often insist on measurable goals in service contracts. In fact, outsourcing firms often compete with each other based upon service quality and consistency.

Outsourcing is an important part of information systems management. Because information technology changes at a fast pace, some companies have decided to let outsourcing firms manage the technology, as well as the employees who implement the technology.

For example, large companies routinely outsource their data backup responsibilities to outside forms that specialize in secure off-site storage of corporate data. Remote storage can increase the security of corporate data in case a corporate facility is damaged or destroyed. The Iron Mountain Group is one company that provides these services. The company offers storage in secure vaults buried deep underground, hence the company's name.

You can also outsource various functions that are part of e-commerce. For a small business, it may not be practical to operate a web server or maintain a redundant Internet connection. Some businesses may host their own servers but need design and programming assistance. Others may need assistance with inventory management, collections, sales tax calculation, or other tasks.

The rapid acceptance of e-commerce has spurred the development and offering of a wide variety of outsourced e-commerce services and solutions. E-commerce design and administration is often outsourced to companies that specialize in this work.

A popular model for this kind of outsourcing is the *application service provider (ASP)*. A web hosting service becomes an ASP by offering the use of server-based applications to customers. The ASP can host existing third-party applications, but some ASPs try to differentiate themselves by developing and hosting their own applications. Sometimes a flat monthly fee is offered, but transaction fees may also apply depending upon the services required.

Do not confuse the term *application service provider* with *Active Server Pages*! The abbreviation for *application service provider* is ASP, so the plural would be *ASPs*, which is the abbreviation for *Active Server Pages*. Active Server Pages emerged in 1996 when Microsoft launched this web development technology. The term *application service provider* was first popularized by Netscape founder Marc Andreesen in 1998 when he launched a startup provider called LoudCloud. You can sometimes determine the appropriate meaning for the acronym ASP from the context. In discussions of outsourcing, application hosting, leasing, and other related terms, we are usually referring to application service providers. In discussions of programming, especially VBScript or JavaScript, ODBC databases, and Microsoft Internet Information Server (IIS), we are referring to Active Server Pages.

Online Auctions

When most people think of electronic commerce, they think of a site on the Internet from which consumers can purchase products. Amazon.com is one of the first such sites that comes to mind. Yet one of the most popular e-commerce sites is eBay (www.ebay.com), one of the first online auction services.

An Internet auction is similar to a traditional auction. Sellers enter into a contract with an auction company to accept bids for a particular item or service. The auction company lists the item in the catalog, runs the actual auction proceedings, collects funds from the winning bidders, and collects an auction fee from the seller in return. The seller receives the remaining proceeds from their auction.

The major *auction sites* are actually high-volume application service providers that specialize in auction hosting. Merchants use a website for listing items and receiving bids, which are managed through the site's own server-based applications. Where a traditional auction house collects an inventory of items for sale, an Internet auction may not have an item inventory. The items remain with the sellers, who must negotiate with the buyer for shipping arrangements and the collection of payments.

There are a variety of different rules for auctions, including the traditional method in which the highest bid wins the item. A reserve price auction works in a similar fashion but allows the seller to set a minimum acceptable bid. If the bidders do not match or exceed this reserve price, the seller may choose not to sell the item. There is also the Dutch auction, in which the seller lists a specific quantity of the item. Bidders may then list the quantity of items they wish to purchase, along with their desired unit price. The first individuals with the highest per-unit bids will receive their desired quantity of items.

Auction sites actually play a large role in e-commerce. By using a community auction site, an individual can conduct e-commerce without the need for an in-house, outsourced, online, or offline e-commerce package. Auctions also represent a convenient entry point for novice buyers and merchants, who can become comfortable with the rules and practices of e-commerce by learning the auction format.

eBay was originally started in 1995 as an auction site for collectible items. The timing of the site's release, coming during a wave of North American consumer interest in the Internet, helped drive the site's rapid expansion into a wide range of items across many countries. eBay also added high-value items, such as real estate, automobiles and art, during 1998 and 1999 as investor enthusiasm for the Internet economy continued. Charity auctions are also listed on eBay; a seller lists an item and donates the bid proceeds to a specific nonprofit organization.

The eBay site allows users to quickly browse auction listings without any registration procedure. To bid on or post an item, the user must register and obtain an eBay username and password.

eBay has expanded its application services to include payment receipt and verification. Merchants can use eBay's payment services to receive payments from buyers after an auction had ended. eBay has made its in-house payment service very convenient for buyers to use, but some established merchants continue to use less-expensive third-party payment services such as PayPal (`www.paypal.com`).

Vertical Auction Sites

Some topics and markets attract only a few businesses and consumers. A vertical auction site adapts auction technology to a specific market niche.

Just like the major online auctions, vertical auction sites are application service providers. Vertical auction sites differentiate themselves from larger auction sites through the development of special features tailored to the auction participants. For example, a coin collector's site may include the extensive coin pricing and grading information that coin collectors rely on to efficiently describe specific items.

Of course, a vertical auction site must attract enough audience and sales volume to cover its overhead expenses. Vertical auction sites sometimes cross-promote each other to increase their exposure. For example, a site that specializes in Chevrolet automobile parts might agree to swap ad banners and links with a site that auctions Pontiac equipment.

Because of budgetary constraints, most vertical auction sites do not have an extensive feature set in their auctions. Some auction sites use auction server software written by third-party companies.

Auction Management Software

Many businesses that depend on high-volume auction sales use auction listing and management software packages to help automate the process of posting and monitoring auctions. Because auction sites require the seller to hold inventory, some sellers may need inventory management software to effectively manage their business. Auctions are listed online, so this software must be able to interact with auction sites, especially when posting auctions and monitoring bids. Auction management software should also perform other activities online, including responding to queries on shipping rate information online.

We have listed several of this software packages, including brief descriptions of their capabilities:

- Timber Creek Auction Trakker (`www.auctiontrakker.com`) provides auction management for multiple eBay user identities and also automates invoicing and shipping.

- BlackMagik Software (`www.blackmagik.com`) offers a suite of auction management tools, including eLister, Auction Monitor, and eNotifier.

- FairMarket (`www.fairmarket.com`) offers MarketSelect, a software package that can integrate auction posting and management functions with payment authorization and inventory management systems.

- Microsoft bCentral Commerce Manager (`www.bcentral.com`) combines a browser-based interface with FrontPage 2002, allowing users to list items on eBay. bCentral is an application service provider that focuses on small businesses, and offers a range of Microsoft technologies and server-based applications.

 Because bCentral uses Active Server Pages extensively to create some server-based tools that it offers as an application service provider, you can begin to see the possible confusion that the abbreviation ASPs might cause.

Instant Storefront Overview

Numerous site creation packages are available, but not all are appropriate for every size or style of business. For small businesses, novice entrepreneurs, or those offering a small range of goods or services, an online instant storefront package may be the most appropriate e-commerce site creation/administration option. Online storefront packages can be divided into two subcategories: independent storefronts and portal storefronts. The type of site you can create with the interactive site creation method Yahoo! offers is one example of the portal or community-type storefront.

We can define an *instant storefront* as an e-commerce site created without using extensive programming or HTML coding. The instant storefront approach allows inexperienced users and developers to create their own sites, usually using predesigned templates, scripts, objects, images, and other features. This method can reduce development time, but as we will discuss, it may also offer few customization options.

Instant storefronts generally use a web hosting service that maps the domain name to a virtual or dedicated web server operated by the hosting service. As you might guess, another advantage of instant storefronts is that important IT functions such as network administration, security, maintenance, and backup can be outsourced to the web hosting service. Again, this can limit the level of customization that the customer can perform, especially at the server level.

Security can be a major concern because the customer's perceptions of the merchant's reputation may be affected by the presence or lack or adequate security measures. For example, forms that collect credit card information but do not use SSL may cause concern among some shoppers.

Any instant storefront offers a range of features that may include some or all of the following categories:

- Customization options, including the ability to use *HTML*, ASPs, Java, or other scripting and dynamic web page features.

- Security options, including SSL transactions, password protection, database security, and scripting security.

- Ease of client-side software use, including simplicity in setting up and creating the website. An online storefront typically uses a web browser as its client, whereas offline storefronts use other software.

- Server and client software installation requirements, including hardware considerations, as well as any constraints imposed by web hosting capabilities.

There are two methods for creating instant storefronts: online and offline.

Online Instant Storefront

The online instant storefront package requires only a Web browser to develop the site. All online instant storefronts follow the application service provider model. Yahoo! and other site servers allow the small business owner, for example, to create an e-commerce site that the site server administers at a fixed monthly cost. The cost varies and depends on the selected plan.

The creation of the site is an interactive process taking little time, effort, or expertise on the owner's part. On many online storefronts, changes to the site take effect immediately, without an additional publication step.

Online instant storefronts are generally easier to use and manage than offline storefronts, but they tend to offer fewer customization options. For example, an online instant storefront may offer a small number of graphics, banners, and site styles that a developer can use. If the site does not offer support for server-side scripting, then the developer cannot create server-side scripts.

Online storefronts are also limited by the security technology used on the site's server. For example, if the server is not configured to support Secure Sockets Layer (SSL), the site cannot offer SSL. The developer outsources the site's security measures to the site administrators.

Because online instant storefronts use the web browser as the primary client, the web browser itself becomes a constraint on the developer. Site operators can deal with this issue by offering ActiveX or Java client-side controls to add features within the browser. However, the developer must be willing to use these controls.

The site's infrastructure is essentially a black box as far as the administrator is concerned. In a *black box* model, the inner workings of the site are hidden from general view. Only the site's administrators and designers know how the site actually works. For some e-commerce developers, this is actually a benefit of outsourcing in the online instant storefront model.

Miva Merchant (`www.miva.com/products/merchant/`) is a browser-based online instant storefront service that is marketed to web hosting services. These services can install a companion product called Miva Empresa on their servers and offer Miva Merchant as an optional feature to web hosting clients. Because Miva Merchant can be enabled as a site feature, it automatically allows merchants to offer e-commerce under their own domain name.

Portal Storefronts

Once known as cybermalls, large Internet *portals* now create a new source of revenue and offer the entry-level e-commerce business an inexpensive introduction to the marketplace.

One feature that may not appeal to some business owners is that customized, fully qualified domain names cannot be readily used. A merchant would have an address such as `http://store.yahoo.com/~abcStore`. It is, of course, possible to register a domain name and post an index page that uses an HTTP redirect to send visitors to the portal storefront.

Portal storefronts are also loaded with links back to the portal itself. Portals introduced storefronts to make their sites "sticky" by keeping customers at the site for longer periods of time. The portal links in the storefront make it possible for the buyer to surf back to the portal and search competing portal storefronts for better prices on other products. The mall aspect of portals is evident here.

There are many web design firms that specialize in portal storefront design. Some portals certify or approve web designers that have demonstrated their skill in designing storefronts for merchant customers. This is another example of how portal storefronts allow merchants to outsource e-commerce design activities.

The following are examples of portal storefronts:

Yahoo! Stores   Yahoo! is one of the busiest independent sites on the Internet. Yahoo! offers merchants high visibility, along with Yahoo!'s brand recognition. Yahoo! Stores (`stores.yahoo.com`) offers merchants a selling opportunity on the Yahoo! site. The store owner names the store and creates categories for later use as store sections warehousing various products. During the setup process, the merchant continually sees the catalog as it will appear to customers.

Although setup and maintenance are easy, the charges for medium to large businesses can accumulate quickly. Yahoo! charges several monthly fees, including an insertion fee for each item listed on the site and transaction fees. Yahoo! also collects a small percentage of each sale, which is called revenue sharing. Yahoo! can also provide merchant accounts for credit card processing, which incur additional setup and transaction fees. Transactions are followed with electronic confirmation as well as calculation of shipping charges and taxes.

Yahoo! Stores include many brand-name merchants who use this as an outsourcing opportunity for providing an easily managed e-commerce solution.

Amazon zShops   Amazon's zShops (`www.zshops.com`) are similar to other portal offerings, except that Amazon is primarily an e-business itself. zShops can leverage Amazon's existing hardware, software, and customer base to offer goods to Amazon customers. Like Yahoo! Stores, Amazon has also targeted brand-name retailers who desire an outsourced e-commerce offering with strong brand-name recognition. Amazon also charges monthly and transactional fees.

iWon Stores   This offering (`iwonstores.com`) differs from other online instant storefronts in that it doesn't allow merchants to list their own products. Instead, the merchant selects existing lines of brand-name products that are offered in iWon's store catalog. The merchant can also choose a store and server name, such as `geek.iwonstores.com`. The merchant receives a small commission of each sale that is completed in their store.

JUMBOMALL   JUMBOMALL (`www.jumbomall.com`) offers different services for various levels of e-commerce businesses. At its most complex level, JUMBOMALL offers a wide array of outsourcing features, leaving only the responsibilities of warehousing and shipping to the e-commerce business.

The setup and basic customization of a JUMBOMALL e-commerce store is done with wizards. The e-commerce business enters inventory information, edits situation-specific responses, finalizes the HTML code for the Website, and adds tax and shipping calculations. At the higher levels, the business adds shopping cart capabilities, personalizes the look of the cart, and creates secure settings for checkout.

Offline Instant Storefronts

In this section, we'll examine the benefits and drawbacks of offline packages. These packages are usually organized around a suite of software tools that the e-commerce designer uses to create and maintain an e-commerce site. Choosing between the numerous e-commerce site creation packages, which includes considering the variables involved in choosing between them and customizing your choice for a variety of purposes, can pose an overwhelming challenge.

It is possible for a merchant to create and implement their own offline instant storefront software. However, it may not make economic sense for any but the largest companies to do so. Often, commercially available software can perform most, if not all, of what a merchant requires. Some commercial software can implement features that help attract and keep buyers.

Offline products also allow for additional customization of the site, including its user interface, graphical look, and differentiating features. It is important for e-commerce businesses to generate demand and build community to enhance the business-consumer relationship so that customers will return. The relative ease of creating an e-commerce site requires merchants to offer customers compelling reasons to return to their site rather than a competitor's. For example, the ability to offer customized discounts based on advertisement codes, past purchases and other factors can help differentiate a merchant from a close competitor. Maintaining a list of customer interests can also help a merchant identify sales trends. Commercial software often uses additional databases to help store and manage these kinds of information.

Of course, with an offline product, any changes to the site will actually be made available to web users when the site is published to the web server. It is when the site is published that the changes are reflected in the site online.

To aid the selection process, you can easily generalize by placing the outsourcing products in three categories:

- Entry-level products that provide ease of implementation and administration, though they reduce the business owner's control over the site. With some packages, the merchant must use a web hosting service.

- Mid-level products that require a more substantial capital outlay, as well as more time and effort for implementation; these give the owner more control. As with entry-level packages, some mid-level offline storefronts require the merchant to use a web hosting service.

- High-level products that sometimes require a large capital outlay but can give all administrative power to the business owner, at least after implementation. Some high-level products sometimes require the merchant to provide their own web hosting. Others offer an option to lease the software through a web host that acts as an application service provider.

Entry-Level Offline Storefront Products

Entry-level products are designed for ease of use and are aimed at business and e-commerce developers who have little e-commerce experience. These packages are similar to online instant storefronts in that they can be used to quickly implement a site that has few customization options.

These products allow developers to host on their own servers or to choose web hosting services. If the developer uses a web hosting service, they are actually outsourcing site administration and security. As a result, the developer faces limits that are similar to the limits of the online instant storefront in terms of software support and scripting capabilities. However, this may be a better choice than hosting the site in-house, especially if the developer or the merchant has limited experience with web server administration and security.

In both of the following examples, the customer purchases the software for use on their own systems. Thus, we are not dealing with the application service provider model.

WebCatalog Smith Micro's WebCatalog Builder (www.smithmicro.com) is an offline storefront development tool designed for entry-level operations. WebCatalog allows larger companies to create more advanced websites. The WebCatalog site creation wizard facilitates price changing and report generation, as well as shipping and tax calculation. Developers can choose from approximately 250 site templates included with the product.

StoreFront   LaGarde Software's StoreFront (`www.storefront.com`) software is actually a series of add-ins for Microsoft FrontPage and Macromedia DreamWeaver. StoreFront leverages the user interface and features of these packages to provide site administration and to give the designer the opportunity to customize the site's overall appearance. StoreFront adds e-commerce features such as catalog administration, shipping cost calculation, and inventory management.

Mid-Level Offline Storefront Products

The mid-level offline instant storefront package offers the experienced e-commerce marketer, the established business owner, or the more developed business additional levels of customization and administration. These packages represent a more expensive option for e-commerce storefront creation and administration than the entry-level option.

Again, mid-level products are not always an ASP solution because the merchant is purchasing a license to the design software and running it on their own clients. With some mid-level packages, the merchant is also hosting their own site on their own server. This requires more capital outlay than an ASP solution but bypasses the ongoing hosting and transaction fees that might be charged by an ASP. The mid-level option is represented by MerchandiZer and ShopZone.

Mid-level products can also offer merchants the ability to create discount and promotional programs that offer price breaks and benefits to repeat buyers. These programs can sometimes be implemented through add-on modules to the storefront. This is another example of the higher level of customization that a medium-level product may have when compared to an entry-level product.

MerchandiZer   The MerchandiZer (`www.merchandizer.com`) setup combines a web infrastructure with design and development software. Developers can host their site on their own server or choose a web hosting company that supports MerchandiZer. This approach is more complex than other independent storefront solutions. That feature may attract the e-commerce business owner who wants more control over storefront administration.

Setup is accomplished with a wizard that includes catalog configuration. Design is a separate process, allowing the importation of the business's own HTML pages. Using Microsoft Access, you can import an existing product database into MerchandiZer. MerchandiZer does allow automatic processing of discount pricing based on discount clubs. It also automatically calculates sales taxes and shipping rates by customer locale and sends confirmation via e-mail to the customer. Customers may pay for their store purchases through several available methods, including credit card, debit card, check, and purchase order.

ShopZone   ShopZone (`www.automatedshops.com`) is a mid-level storefront package that combines offline development with online web hosting.

As an offline product, ShopZone provides site creation and site maintenance capabilities. It can handle relatively complex transaction and payment processing scenarios such as multiple-state company transactions. More advanced processes such as discount strategies may require mastery of web scripting.

The ShopZone development software runs on the Windows operating system. ShopZone sites are hosted by AutomatedShops using Linux as the server operating system. Developers can register and use a customized domain name for their store. ShopZone acts as an application service provider.

Store administration is fairly basic, allowing review and optional e-mail notification of incoming orders. Export of order information is limited to QuickBooks or command-delimited file formats. ShopZone supports transaction security and smoothness, including SSL security if supported by the Web host.

High-Level Offline Storefront Packages

The high-level offline instant storefront offers the well-established mid-sized to large business a sophisticated software package for site creation, implementation, and administration. This type of package offers the business owner the most control over the administration of the site, but it is the most expensive to purchase and administer. Some examples of offline storefront options are InternetCommerce and WebCatalog.

InternetCommerce.com   The InternetCommerce.com Enterprise Server (`www.internetcommerce.com`) software allows business owners to quickly develop an Internet storefront with no special expertise.

The Enterprise Server is compatible with Microsoft Windows NT and 2000 Server and includes strong encryption capabilities. Administrative features of the Commerce Suite include inventory management and Internet ordering, as well as order tracking and the capability to manage operations remotely. Companies can also choose to lease the enterprise server from a web hosting service, using an application service provider model.

WebCatalog   WebCatalog (`www.smithmicro.com`) is an advanced development environment for e-commerce development. We have classified it as an offline instant storefront tool, but the developer must use a web browser as the development client. Users may upload image and HTML files from the browser onto their own Microsoft or Apache web server. WebCatalog also allows developers to link existing ODBC databases to the site or to create new databases for accounting, shipping, and inventory.

WebCatalog is classified as a high-level offline tool because it requires skilled developers and administrators who are willing to learn the software and choose appropriate server technologies. Merchants who use WebCatalog can avoid ASP fees if they are willing to host the site themselves.

Summary

E-commerce site creation relies on the outsourcing of important IS functions to companies that are skilled in website hosting. Some of these web hosts act as application service providers (ASPs) who charge fees or rents for server-based e-commerce applications.

Auctions represent an entry point for aspiring online merchants who want to try selling a product at little expense. Online auctions act as an ASP, managing bids and buyers for the merchant. The merchant handles inventory. The merchant can also use an Application Service Provider to handle the payment process. Volume sellers can use auction management software to help manage multiple auctions, billing and inventory.

The next level of e-commerce site creation is the instant storefront solution. With an online instant storefront, the merchant can use a Web browser and sometimes a Web host to create a storefront. With this type of solution, the site server administers the site at a fixed monthly cost. It can take little time, effort, or expertise on the owner's part to create the site. An online instant storefront is one that allows merchants to make changes to their site from anywhere.

Additional online options that are available to merchants include the use of portal storefronts. Portals provide an easy entry into the world of e-commerce for merchants. They offer an inexpensive introduction to the marketplace. Another choice is a community auction site, through which an individual can conduct electronic commerce without the need for an in-house, outsourced, online, or offline e-commerce package.

An offline solution provides a way to make changes internally. Companies create their own in-house solution, but this may make sense for only the largest companies.

Offline storefront products can be categorized based upon the skill required to use and implement them effectively. Entry-level products provide ease of implementation and administration, though they reduce the business owner's control over the site. Mid-level products require a more substantial capital outlay, as well as more time and effort for implementation; these give the owner more control. High-level products sometimes require a large capital outlay but give all administrative power to the business owner, at least after implementation.

Exam Essentials

Know what outsourcing is   Outsourcing is a business model that allows companies to obtain services and skill sets from other companies.

Know what an application service provider is   An application service provider is a web host that charges its merchant customers fees for using server-based applications.

Know what an auction site is   An auction site allows companies to conduct e-commerce business online without the need for an in-house, outsourced, online, or offline e-commerce package. An example of one such site is FairMarket. Hosting and customization allow the businesses owner to retain control of user registration, listing information, pricing, and other elements of auctions, including user interface.

Know what an online instant storefront is and its advantages and disadvantages   An online instant storefront is the entry-level online package that uses an web browser as the merchant's client application.

The merchant outsources most of the e-commerce functions to a portals or large Web merchants and concentrates of product selection and pricing.

Know the advantages of an entry-level offline instant storefront package
The entry-level offline instant storefront package allows a merchant to design their own site using inexpensive software. Often the merchant must use a web hosting service. Although the merchant can choose a specific domain name, they may face other limits that are similar to the limits of the online instant storefront, including limited customization, administration, and security.

Know the advantages of a mid-level offline instant storefront package
The mid-level online or offline instant storefront package offers the experienced e-commerce marketer, the established business owner, or the more developed business a more thoroughly customized, more personally administered, and more expensive option for e-commerce storefront creation and administration than the entry-level option. A mid-level solution requires more capital outlay.

Know the features of a high-level offline instant storefront solution
The high-level instant storefront offers the well-established, mid-sized to large business a sophisticated software package for site creation, implementation, and administration. This type of package offers the business owner the most control over the administration of their site, but it is the most expensive to purchase and administer.

Key Terms

Before you take the exam, be certain you are familiar with the following terms:

application service provider (ASP)	instant storefront
auction sites	outsourcing
black box	portals
HTML	

Review Questions

1. What is an advantage of using a portal storefront?

   A. It's an inexpensive way to do business online.

   B. A business can always have its own fully qualified domain name.

   C. It allows the most control of all the storefront options.

   D. It allows for a higher level of customization than the other storefront options.

2. What is one advantage of using an offline instant storefront instead of a portal storefront?

   A. Startup costs are always higher for an online instant storefront.

   B. If the business offers a unique product, a search will list the business adjacent to its competitors.

   C. The online business can be referenced by a fully qualified domain name.

   D. Online instant storefronts always offer complete flexibility in website design.

3. Which of the following should be a primary consideration when evaluating an online instant storefront offering?

   A. Timely order processing

   B. Effective order tracking

   C. Encryption and other security issues

   D. Encouragement of future business

4. What customization features, available with mid and high-level offline instant storefront packages, can help build community and generate demand?

    A. Product descriptions

    B. Customer discounts and customer-interest databases

    C. Product catalogs

    D. A search engine

5. Who is the most suitable possible user of a mid-level storefront package?

    A. An experienced e-commerce marketer

    B. A novice online business owner

    C. A newly developing business

    D. A beginning website designer

6. What characteristic of a mid-level storefront differs from those in most entry-level packages?

    A. Less personal administration

    B. Higher cost

    C. Less customization

    D. Less control by the business owner

7. At what point are changes in a site's design or configuration reflected in the actual site?

    A. When the owner or designer initiates the changes

    B. When the site is published to a web server

    C. When the first sales transaction occurs

    D. When a new customer visits the site

8. What features does a typical high-level e-commerce package offer?

    A. Little control over site administration and a relatively high cost

    B. Complete control over site administration at a relatively low cost

    C. Entry-level software that provides no control over site administration

    D. The most control over site administration but also the highest cost

9. What is a possible disadvantage of using a high-level e-commerce package?

    A. The relatively high startup and operating cost

    B. The lack of options for configuring the site

    C. The lack of inventory management capabilities

    D. The lack of any security features for online transactions

10. Mike owns a small company that sells baseball and other sports equipment. He is looking into options for an e-commerce site to improve sales. What type of solution would be best for Mike's company?

    A. A high-level e-commerce package

    B. A mid-level storefront package

    C. An offline storefront

    D. A portal or community storefront

11. Which of the following is the best example of outsourcing?

    A. A company uses a web hosting service to host an e-commerce site.

    B. An organization hires a network administrator.

    C. A company buys a server computer for its network.

    D. A company buys an operating system from Microsoft.

12. Carmen owns a small company that is fairly new. She would like to have an e-commerce website but she is not experienced with site creation. Another difficulty for Carmen is that she travels frequently and the type of business she owns would require her to make regular updates and price changes while on the road. What kind of solution would best fit Carmen's circumstances?

    A. An online instant storefront

    B. An in-house solution

    C. A mid-level offline instant storefront

    D. A high-level offline instant storefront

13. What is a main benefit of an offline storefront over online storefronts?

    A. Cheaper price

    B. Ability to back up website files automatically

    C. Brand recognition

    D. Independent domain addresses

14. What fulfillment and order processing steps should an effective e-commerce package allow the online merchant to follow?

    A. Publishing customer information to the Web

    B. Processing only credit card payments immediately

    C. Building community by publishing customers' e-mail addresses

    D. Offering security for customer information

15. Which of the following best describes an application service provider?

    A. A company that installs and maintains applications.

    B. A company hires employees for other companies.

    C. A company that hosts server-based web applications and charges other companies a fee for their use.

    D. A company that writes Active Server Pages applications.

16. Why is it important to generate demand and build community by using customization features available with any storefront package?

    A. To give the consumer a new look

    B. To market a company's website and products

    C. To enhance business-customer relationship

    D. To provide synchronous service

17. What does the most basic entry-level online package require of the business owner?

    A. T1 connection speed or greater

    B. Web browser

    C. Online catalog

    D. Experience with administering an e-commerce website.

18. Auction sites allow merchants to do all but which one of the following choices?

    A. List individual or multiple items for sale

    B. Take bids on items

    C. Manage inventory

    D. Collect payments

19. A company that requires minimal control at the lowest cost should use which model of offline instant storefront?

    A. Any of the three levels

    B. Low-level

    C. Medium-level

    D. High-level

20. A vertical auction site is different from a regular auction site in which one of the following ways?

    A. Vertical auction sites cannot show product images; regular auction sites can.

    B. Vertical auctions allow users to manage inventory; regular auction sites do not.

    C. Vertical auctions typically specialize in a specific product, service, or geographic area.

    D. Vertical auction sites can accept any form of payment; regular auction sites must use third-party payment methods.

Answers to Review Questions

1. A. Portal can give entry-level e-commerce businesses an inexpensive way to do business online. However, this type of online storefront sacrifices customization options.

2. C. By using an independent online instant storefront instead of a portal or community storefront, a company can have its own fully qualified domain name. Offline storefronts tend to have higher startup costs than online storefronts, most often hardware and software. Offline storefronts usually offer greater customization options than online storefronts.

3. C. Encryption and security issues should play a key role in the selection of an online storefront because they are features that are controlled by the site provider and that can also affect the reputation of the site. The merchant should choose features that provide additional value and security for the site while remaining within budget. An offline instant storefront may add these features by default.

4. B. Customer discounts and customer-interest databases can be generated and used for targeted marketing. Product descriptions should be standard offerings regardless of the storefront method. Product catalogs are a more elaborate way of storing descriptions and associated information in a database. A search engine is also an essential tool if an e-commerce site offers more than a few items.

5. A. Because a mid-level storefront package allows for more customization and control over an e-commerce site, it is better suited for an e-commerce marketer who has prior experience in managing an e-commerce site.

6. B. A mid-level storefront package costs more than entry-level packages. It contains more features and great options for customization by the business owner.

7. B. Changes to an offline application won't take place until the site is published to a web server. At that time, changes will be reflected in the actual site online.

8. D. A high-level e-commerce package offers the most control over site administration to the site owner, but because of features like this, it is the highest priced.

9. A. Because a high-level e-commerce package offers greater control over site administration, it is a more costly product. This can be a disadvantage, especially for small businesses and beginning companies.

10. D. For a small, entry-level e-commerce business, a portal or community storefront provides an inexpensive way to do business online.

11. A. Outsourcing occurs when an organization allows daily responsibilities or tasks to be handled by another company that specializes in performing these services. Purchasing a product or hiring an employee does not qualify as outsourcing.

12. A. An online instant storefront is the best choice for inexperienced users. It will allow her to make changes to her website from anywhere with an Internet connection. The other options require an experienced administrator and the cost would be prohibitive for a small company.

13. B. Offline storefronts automatically back up the site data because the files are stored offline and uploaded to the web server. The owner has full control of the website and when changes are made. With online solutions, depending on the host, a change may take time to be reflected on the website. Offline storefronts, however, are usually more expensive, so cheaper price is not a benefit. Brand recognition is a benefit of portals, especially well-known ones like Yahoo! and iWon that also offer online storefronts. Independent domain names can also be used with some online storefront solutions, so it's not the main benefit.

14. D. An effective e-commerce package would allow the online merchant to offer security (such as encryption) for customer information, which would provide a reasonable level of protection and comfort to customers in their purchases.

15. C. An ASP offers the use of server-based applications to customers for a fee. The ASP can host existing third-party applications, but some ASPs try to differentiate themselves by developing and hosting their own applications. Sometimes a flat monthly fee is offered, but transaction fees may also apply depending upon the services required.

16. C. It is important for e-commerce businesses to generate demand and build community to enhance the business-consumer relationship so that customers will return. Customization allows, for example, the creation of customer-interest databases, which can in turn provide targeted marketing.

17. B.   An entry-level online instant storefront requires only a web browser. Entry-level products are typically designed for inexperienced users and developers.

18. C.   An auction site allows the owner to control many features, set prices, and manage an online catalog. Amazon, eBay, and Yahoo! offers their own payment collection options and support third-party payment methods. Auction sites do not help a merchant manage inventory. Separate online and offline systems are offered that include inventory management.

19. B.   A company that requires a low level of control should use a low-level storefront, which offers a standard set of customization options and features at a relatively low cost. A high-level offline storefront offers the business owner a high-level of control and should be used by experienced e-commerce administrators. It is also much more expensive than its entry-level counterpart.

20. C.   Vertical auction sites resemble regular auction sites in most respects, but vertical sites differentiate themselves through product/service offerings or geographic scope.

Chapter

27

Electronic Commerce Site Creation/ Development Software

THE CIW EXAM OBJECTIVE GROUPS COVERED IN THIS CHAPTER:

- ✓ Configure web server software for an e-commerce site
- ✓ Manage inventory and fulfillment for an e-commerce site

nce your site is created, you need to choose a server on which to host it. In Chapter 26, "Electronic Commerce Site Creation Packages-Outsourcing," one option we looked into was outsourcing the entire process, in which case you delegate both the site creation and the server hosting issues. If you decide to keep the project under internal control, however, there are important issues to bear in mind when choosing a web server. One consideration is the type of web server software that will be best suited for your needs, and then you'll need to decide which operating system you should use to support that software. Knowing your options will enable you to make choices, or make recommendations as a design expert, for the site to function well.

To illustrate the basic configuration options of web server software, we use Microsoft Internet Information Server (IIS). Microsoft plays an important role in the computer industry; no one can deny its presence in almost every aspect of the PC environment. Its growth in the server environment has spawned further application development in the electronic commerce field. Although seemingly vendor specific, in some ways analyzing Microsoft's implementation of certain web development software will, in addition to showing you one vendor's approach, effectively provide you with the concepts necessary to use site creation and development software.

Web Server Overview

You probably understand the nature of a web server. The following list includes brief descriptions of the elements of web servers used in the discussions throughout this chapter:

- A web server commonly serves HTML and several image formats (GIF, JPEG, and PNG). It can also deliver program files of almost any type, including Java, ActiveX, streaming video and audio, PDF, DOC, TXT, and so forth. The Web server's ability to present files depends on the proper files' placement in the proper directories.

Although a browser is designed to work primarily with HTML and certain image formats, it will generally render additional document types. Depending upon how many plug-ins a browser has, it could render any text or image format. A *plug-in* is a program that integrates seamlessly within your browser and handles specific file types that the browser would not be able to handle alone.

- A web server uses the *Hypertext Transfer Protocol (HTTP)*. This protocol enables the web server to receive requests and transmit replies, usually in the form of the documents described in the preceding list item. E-commerce sites use many aspects of HTTP, including its capability to use cookies, operate seamlessly with other servers, and work with databases.

- Generally, a web server runs as a daemon process on Unix machines or as a service on Windows NT/2000 machines. By default, the server process binds to TCP port 80 and listens for incoming requests from clients such as web browsers. If you configure a web server for Secure Sockets Layer (SSL) communication, the port is 443. A *port* is similar to a channel in that various protocols use ports to key in on specific communication lines, much in the same way we know what channel we want for specific television shows.

- You can extend the features of a web server through additional programs and servers. The programs are called *Common Gateway Interface (CGI)* scripts. You can also use proprietary products, such as Allaire ColdFusion or Microsoft Active Server Pages (ASPs). Many server types exist. For example, you can use RealServer (`www.real.com`) to provide streaming video and audio from your site. Microsoft SQL Server, Oracle 8i, and IBM DB2, for example, are databases for your web server to work with.

- Web servers often deploy both client-side and server-side scripting. Client-side scripting includes the use of JavaScript and VBScript. If you embed these scripting languages into an HTML page, you are engaging in client-side scripting. Server-side scripting is the use of scripting languages to create programs that run on the web server itself.

Apache Web Servers

Apache Web Server is a tested, well-accepted solution. As of this writing, more than half of all websites deliver their information with this server. Originally designed to support Unix, Apache now supports Linux, Novell NetWare 6, Windows NT, and Windows 2000 as well. You do lose some of the security capabilities with Apache if you are running it on a Windows box because Unix systems have a stronger security subsystem. All versions of Apache are available free of charge as *open source* code, which is free source code offered to the development community at large to develop a better product (the code for Netscape Communicator and Linux is also offered as open source code).

Apache Web Server includes no formal support system (such as a customer support desk) because it has been developed by a not-for-profit, membership-based group called the Apache Software Foundation (`www.apache.org`). However, you can obtain configuration and support information from many sources by entering the keyword "Apache" in a search engine.

A downloadable version is available at the Apache HTTP Server Project site (`httpd.apache.org`). Apache Web Server is not packaged with additional Internet services. You must obtain other server programs for news, FTP, and so forth.

Lotus Domino Series

The Lotus Domino series includes all the most-used servers, including certificate, HTTP, SMTP, and FTP. One of the strengths of the Domino server series is its ability to serve applications over intranets and the Internet. Additionally, the Domino series is adept at connecting with databases; Domino products also support Java servlets as a preferred database connection method.

Because the Domino series is offered by Lotus, an IBM-owned company, institutional support is available, as is a large knowledge base.

An additional consideration is that Domino supports several operating systems, including AS/400, S/390, OS/2, Windows NT/2000, Sun Solaris, AIX, and HP-UX. For more information, consult the Lotus Domino home page (`www.lotus.com/home.nsf/welcome/domino`).

Sun-Netscape Alliance Servers (iPlanet)

Two of the more established server vendors, Netscape and Sun Microsystems, formed an alliance called iPlanet. This alliance provides services similar to those of its competitors. Because these companies have helped define the Web, many of the alliance's servers are the most tested, and the alliance also provides fee-based support. Additionally, alliance products support many platforms, including AS/400, S/390, OS/2, Windows NT/2000, Sun Solaris, AIX, and HP-UX.

The Sun-Netscape Alliance includes servers with server-side JavaScript interpreters, which allow you to use JavaScript to connect to databases and implement other server-side scripting applications. For more information, consult the iPlanet site (`www.iplanet.com`).

Internet Information Server (IIS) 5

Internet Information Server (IIS) is a popular choice among Windows NT/2000 users. IIS is tightly integrated into the workings of the Windows NT/2000 operating system. In fact, IIS runs only on the Windows NT/2000 platform. In spite of this possible limitation, tight integration with the operating system provides at least two advantages:

- IIS takes advantage of the Windows NT/2000 security structure. This structure simplifies site administration because it uses the same account database as the server upon which it is running.

- IIS has a familiar interface. An administrator who understands Windows NT/2000 Server can easily understand how IIS works. An administrator, therefore, can install and maintain the server more easily.

Microsoft IIS Considerations

Once you've chosen a site name, determined the precise nature of your product, and considered some of the front-end and back-end issues involved in selling your product, you can take the first step in creating an e-commerce site. If you've decided to host your site yourself instead of outsourcing, the first step is to choose and install your web server. Microsoft Internet Information Server (IIS) is suitable for most e-commerce needs. It has a large development base and strong industry support, and it supports all standard web file formats. We'll introduce you to some of its features and use it to illustrate some basic administrative principles present with a static website.

Certificates and SSL Support

IIS 5 was designed to communicate securely. It allows you to use certificates obtained from a *certificate authority (CA)*, such as VeriSign, to conduct transactions with a reasonable amount of confidence. IIS also allows you to generate and manage your own certificates.

IIS allows you to use encryption of up to 128 bits for SSL services.

Active Server Pages (ASP)

Microsoft *Active Server Pages (ASPs)* technology allows you to create pages through client-side scripting. You can use a scripting language such as VBScript or JavaScript to enable e-commerce. You can combine HTML, scripts, and reusable Java and/or ActiveX server components.

Active Server Pages is a direct competitor to Netscape server-side JavaScript, Macromedia Cold Fusion MX, and PHP 4.1.

FTP Support

IIS has built-in *File Transfer Protocol (FTP)*. FTP is a protocol for transferring files over the Internet. The FTP utility is a command-line utility, although many graphical programs are available for download (oftentimes for free) on the Internet.

By default, the FTP service is configured to start automatically when the IIS system starts, and users can upload and download files located in the `inetpub\ftproot` directory. From a security standpoint, remember not to store sensitive files in the `ftproot` directory. The following possible security threats exist:

- Most site administrators allow anonymous access to the FTP server.

- Most FTP servers transmit passwords using very low encryption, and sometimes even in clear text. Therefore, a hacker could gain access to your FTP site with a protocol analyzer.

Integration Simplicity

Because IIS is a Microsoft product, it is designed to integrate well with other Microsoft products. For example, IIS works well with Microsoft SQL Server (Microsoft's database application) and with Microsoft Exchange

Server (Microsoft's e-mail application). In an attempt to become an e-commerce leader, Microsoft has also developed Commerce Server, which can help you to create a Web-based business in a short time, specifically enhancing catalog creation.

Virtual Directories and Virtual Servers

IIS allows you to map URLs to different physical locations on your hard drive. These are called virtual directories, and IIS allows you to create them easily. Virtual servers are similar to virtual directories, allowing you to run several websites on the same NT/2000 system.

Additional IIS features

The following is a short list of IIS features:

- Content management and site analysis
- Support for multiple websites with one web server
- Automated management support
- ASPs script debugging
- Built-in site search engine
- Limited remote administration capabilities

Preparation/Installation of IIS 5

The actual installation of IIS is accomplished by installing Windows 2000 Server. IIS 5 will automatically install with your Server installation. Following the default installation, you can install additional components to make your web server more functional:

- Certificate Server
- Transaction Server
- Index Server

Several things happen in the background during the IIS installation. As an e-commerce specialist, you should be aware of them.

Default User Account

We mentioned earlier that IIS is closely integrated with the rest of the Windows 2000 operating system. During the installation, IIS creates a default user account for anonymous logins. This account is important to note because any web user who connects to your server is considered to have logged on to the system. Those connections can be logged (*audited* is the proper word) and they help you determine how many connections have been made to the site. Statistics that you gather will be vital in making your e-commerce business work well.

You may have thought that when you visit a website, you don't provide any logon connections and the server doesn't care who you are. On the contrary, it is impossible to view any materials on a Windows 2000 server without some form of verification/authentication to let you in.

Figure 27.1 illustrates the anonymous login account, which is found in Computer Management.

FIGURE 27.1 The IUSR account under Windows 2000

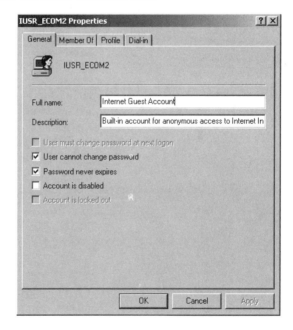

The default name for the anonymous account is IUSR_*computername*. If you delete or disable this account, one of two things might happen: users will be unable to access your website without proper authentication, or they will not be able to access the site at all. If you want to enhance security for your web pages, you can establish a request for a "real" logon. Then visitors would be required to enter a username and password that would also reside on the server as an authentication account.

Microsoft Management Console

The Microsoft Management Console (MMC) provides a framework for network administration programs for IIS and, optionally, other servers or services. It is designed to make administering IIS more simple. The MMC console hosts programs (called snap-ins) that administrators can use to manage their networks. MMC provides a common framework in which the snap-ins can run, helping administrators manage their network products within a single integrated interface. Figure 27.2 shows the default MMC interface for IIS. You can customize this interface to suit your needs.

FIGURE 27.2   The IIS Microsoft Management Console (MMC)

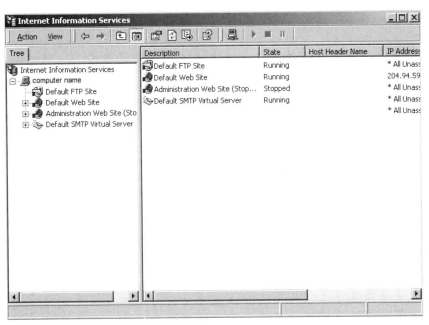

IIS also allows you to administer the server using a browser, such as Microsoft Internet Explorer or Netscape Communicator. However, your administrative abilities are somewhat limited if you choose this option.

Accessing IIS Settings

You can view and customize IIS settings by highlighting a server shown in the MMC and then right-clicking it. Alternatively, you can use the Properties button in the MMC main toolbar. Figure 27.3 shows the initial default settings for IIS.

FIGURE 27.3   The IIS Default Website Properties dialog box

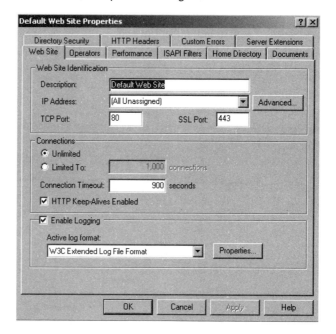

As you can see, IIS organizes its configuration settings into specific categories. You can access these categories by clicking each of the tabs: Documents, Directory Security, HTTP Headers, Custom Errors, Web Site, Operators, Performance, ISAPI Filters, Server Extensions, and Home Directory. It's not completely necessary for you, as an e-commerce design engineer, to know each and every setting for the web server. In the following sections, we'll discuss the most important settings and tabs.

The Web Site Tab

The Web Site tab (shown in Figure 27.3) contains the following important options:

Description   This isn't the site's web name (like www.*whatever*.com), although it could be. The description is used to make it easier to find the site when trying to administer it.

IP Address   This could be left as it is by default if there is only one site and one IP address, but if you are looking to really use your IIS server, you'll want to choose the IP address that goes with your site for the Domain Name System (DNS) to work properly.

TCP Port   The default is 80—here you can change it to something else.

The Connections section contains the following options:

Connections   The default is Unlimited, but you could limit the number of connections if you have bandwidth or memory issues. The default limitation is 1,000, but you can place it where you want. If this begins to seriously hinder the site's availability, you may consider adding more memory or a better bandwidth connection.

Connection Timeout   Sometimes a person will connect to a site and walk away. That connection is maintained on the server as being alive for the number of seconds placed here. The default is 900 seconds, but you can raise or lower it based upon your needs. If you want to improve performance, you usually lower this number to force out unused connections, but if you have low-bandwidth connections, leave it alone or some users may not be able to connect.

The Documents Tab

The Documents tab, shown in Figure 27.4, allows you to point the server toward a default document. The initial default document for IIS is default.htm. However, you can add a new name if you prefer. In the case of multiple default page names, IIS searches for the one listed first and then goes down the list.

FIGURE 27.4 The Documents tab

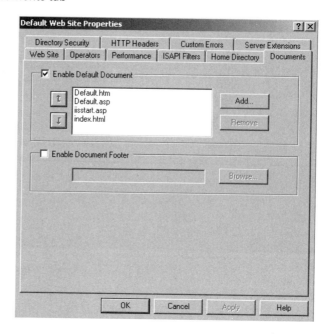

Therefore, if a directory (i.e., a folder) has a default.htm page, it will be chosen first, even if this directory contains default.asp or index.htm. If another folder contains only index.html, IIS would present that document first after searching for default.htm, default.asp, and index.htm.

The Home Directory Tab

The Home Directory tab is quite important because it enables you to identify the default documents you will use. Figure 27.5 shows how you can link a local directory to a particular server. By default, as shown, the directory is located on the local computer, at the \inetpub\wwwroot portion of folders. You can change this location to point toward other folders on the server. You might also choose to point your server to a folder on a different server altogether through a UNC path (\\servername\sharename). You might even point off to another site through a URL like http://www .whatever.com.

FIGURE 27.5   The Home Directory tab

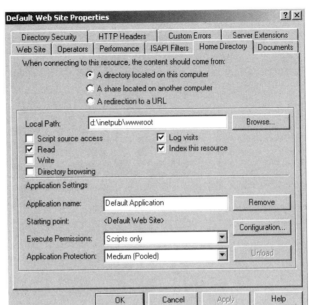

Note that you can set the permissions from this tab. Finally, notice that you can use IIS to provide content from an entirely different server.

The Directory Security Tab

Because security is always important in e-commerce, you should note the features in the Directory Security tab, shown in Figure 27.6. By default, IIS allows anonymous access. You can use this tab to limit access and to enable password protection.

SSL connections are obligatory in an e-commerce site. You can use the Secure Communications section to access to the Web Server Certificate Wizard. And finally, you can limit or grant access to your site based upon IP addresses.

If a certificate is not installed, the View and Edit options under Secure Communications on the Directory Security tab will not be available.

FIGURE 27.6 The Directory Security tab

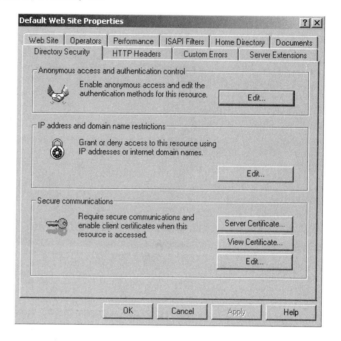

The Performance Tab

To improve the performance of a site, use the Performance tab, shown in Figure 27.7. You can tune (adjust) your site's performance based on the number of hits you expect each day. You have no way of knowing for sure how many you will get, but you'll notice in the figure that your options are pretty broad. These options will tell the web server how much memory to allocate for this particular site. Keep in mind that you can have multiple sites located on the same server and the server needs to know how to allocate resources for each one.

Bandwidth throttling is another important feature. This prevents all bandwidth resources from being used for one connection. For example, if you have a 56Kbps connection to your server and a user connects over the Internet to the server with a DSL connection, the server will have little to no bandwidth left for other connections. With bandwidth throttling, you can control the amount of bandwidth the users can take. This is usually a good feature for web servers that have limited bandwidth coming into their site. It can be eaten up quickly if it isn't throttled down on the server's end.

FIGURE 27.7 Performance tab

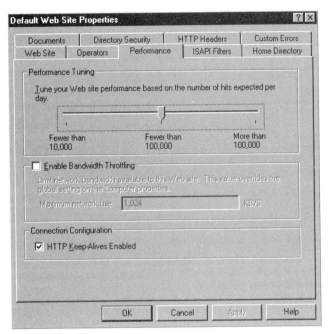

Additional Tabs

Table 27.1 summarizes the purpose of each of the remaining tabs in the Default Website Properties dialog box.

TABLE 27.1 IIS Website Properties Configuration Categories

Tab	Purpose
Operators	Specify who can administer the site.
ISAPI Filters	Identify ISAPI programs you can use as alternatives to CGI. Once programmed, ISAPI filters respond to user events. You can also set their priorities from this tab.

T A B L E 2 7 . 1 IIS Website Properties Configuration Categories *(continued)*

Tab	Purpose
HTTP Headers	Customize the headers sent from the web server to a browser. For example, you can define content expiration settings, use the MIME map setting to identify new file types that the server can present, use the HTTP header to send a rating concerning the site's textual and visual content, and customize the HTTP header that will be sent to the browser.
Custom Errors	Customize the HTML pages that report the errors sent when IIS cannot respond to a client or server request. Although the W3C and IETF strictly define the reasons for error messages, you can, for example, format a page to automatically return a lost user to the home page.
Server Extensions	Set the publishing controls for a website that uses FrontPage Server Extensions. FrontPage Server Extensions allow website authors to use advanced functionality within their sites without excessive workload on both the author or the administrator.

Aliases and Virtual Directories

Earlier we mentioned that IIS allows you to map URLs to different physical locations, called virtual directories, on your hard drive. You can also use virtual servers to run several websites on the same NT/2000 system. This section includes a more in-depth discussion of how they work.

As part of their configuration options, most web servers allow flexible mapping of URL pathnames to local filenames. This kind of mapping creates what are called virtual directories, also sometimes called aliases.

One of the advantages of flexible mapping is that it gives you the ability to serve files that do not reside immediately within the web server root directory. Many web servers require that all files be located directly beneath the web server root. However, a virtual directory allows you to include any local file or folder into the web server directory structure regardless of the location of that file or folder. This enables you to have multiple locations for your actual information, but those viewing that information are unaware that it's in multiple locations. Now, instead of having to locate all files and folders beneath the web server root, an administrator can arrange files on disk at their discretion. This allows for a simplified organizational structure.

For example, suppose you want your web server to present a collection of documents called `doc1.html` and `doc2.html`. However, they are located in the `systemroot\home\sales\docs` directory. Your web server's root directory is `systemroot\inetpub\wwwroot`.

You want to make this folder accessible to users under the URL `http://www.anycompany.com/sales/doc1.html`. To allow this access, you must configure the server to map the URL path `/sales/doc1.html` to the local file path `\home\sales\docs\` instead of to `\inetpub\wwwroot\docs\sales\`.

To understand virtual directories, you must first understand the difference between how an operating system (such as Windows) accesses a file and how a web server (such as IIS or Lotus Domino Go Webserver) presents a file. Windows NT refers to files using backward slashes, as in `\winnt\inetpub\wwwroot\html\docs`. IIS, on the other hand, presents files on the Web as `/html/docs`.

Virtual Servers

Most enterprise-grade web servers allow you to create multiple virtual web servers on the same machine. You can bind multiple IP addresses to the same network interface card (NIC) or place multiple NICs into the computer. You can even run multiple sites using the same IP address, as long as you use a different TCP port for each server. For example, your first server would use port 80, the default. Alternative port numbers include 8080 and 1080.

If you decide to use a different port number, make sure you don't choose a number from 0 to 1023. These "well-known" port numbers are reserved for other programs.

Keep in mind that anyone who wants to access a web server running on a port other than 80 or 443 (the HTTP SSL port) will have to specify the port. For example, if you were to access www.mycompany.com on port 8080, you would enter the following into your browser: http://www.mycompany.com:8080. Web browsers always default to port 80, so the port indication is necessary.

Quite honestly, port numbers are rarely changed. Adding another card or IP address is usually a better way to handle virtual servers, although using different port numbers is a good way to enhance security. A person who doesn't know the port being used would never be able to access it, even if they knew the name of the site.

Virtual Servers and DNS

If you use multiple IP addresses, you can register each with a DNS server, allowing multiple companies or departments to use one system running multiple web servers. Many sites that you have accessed on the Internet are served from only one of many virtual servers residing on a Unix or NT system.

Originally, IIS was designed to support multiple web server scenarios, ranging from simple websites on a corporate intranet to large ISP web farms. A *web farm* is service provider that serves multiple websites. Web farms cohost (i.e., they provide hard drive space on their computers for your site), or they co-locate (i.e., they provide a connection for a computer that you maintain).

Web farm is a term that has also been used to describe a company's internal collection of web servers that are handling large loads of incoming connections. Services like Network Load Balancing (NLB) are used to cluster the farm for fault tolerance and performance improvements.

With IIS, all web servers are considered virtual; even if you are running only one web server, IIS treats it as the primary virtual server.

Default Documents and Directory Browsing

When a server receives a request for a URL that refers to a directory rather than to a specified document, the server may operate in one of the following ways, depending on how it is configured:

- It may return a default document present in that directory; the *default document* is the first document a web server refers to when it receives a nonspecific request.

- It may generate an error and refuse the request. (Common errors are the 404: Object (or File) Not Found and the 403: Access Forbidden.)

- It may return a formatted directory listing to the browser. In most cases, the server constructs an HTML document, which associates an HTML link with each file. By clicking the corresponding link, the user may obtain the listed file.

Default Document

The first option listed is the most common. You can configure any web server—whether it is IIS, Lotus Domino Go Webserver, or Apache Web Server—to automatically refer to a default document if the user does not specify a document. For example, a request for the URL `http://www.anycompany.com/` usually returns the default document, or "home page," from the server resource root directory on the machine `www.anycompany.com`. You can name your default document anything you want, as long as you configure the server to recognize this name. Common default document names include `index.htm`, `index.html`, `default.htm`, `welcome.html`, and so forth. IIS uses `default.htm`, although you can change this name at any time, as you saw earlier in the chapter.

Error Messages

Error messages occur for many reasons. For example, the folder or site might not allow anonymous access or might require SSL. An error message could also be due to server error or because the server is too busy processing other user requests.

Directory Browsing

Directory browsing makes the server operate in much the same way an FTP server operates. As you develop your e-commerce business, you should not enable directory browsing because it could reveal confidential or sensitive files. For example, someone could access CGI scripts and other executables, allowing possible misuse of these files.

In ISS you can enable or disable directory browsing on the Home Directory tab of the IIS Default Website Properties dialog box (refer back to Figure 27.5).

Site Development Software Considerations

When your site is up and running, you need to consider your development software. Choosing the development software for your e-commerce site is an extremely important decision. Elements involved in the product choice include ease of use, cost, support software, hardware, and development learning curves.

Installation of support software is vital in the successful development of an e-commerce site. Although Microsoft software is mentioned frequently within this section, your focus should be on the concept of multiple software applications working together to create the e-commerce site.

Whether you choose Novell, Oracle, Netscape, Microsoft, or any other software vendor, you will probably become familiar with several major common components to assist you in the total site development. These components will include a web server (already discussed), a database application, and a web development tool.

Choosing Your Website Development Software

The decision of which web development tool to use must be evaluated based on your organization's business requirements. Your choice must match, as closely as possible, the needs of your e-commerce objectives. You should weigh issues of cost, control, customization, and security. For example, Microsoft Commerce Server 2000 relies on Windows 2000 as the operating system coupled with Microsoft SQL Server for database support. In many respects, this can be considered a proprietary solution, but it can still allow considerable flexibility. Software products offered by CommerceOne and IBM include a suite of applications that include the same features and use different database systems, again allowing flexibility.

Databases

A *database* is a formally arranged set of persistent information stored by a computer program. It is organized to provide easy access to the data so it can be updated and managed efficiently. *Formally arranged* means that the information is structured in some particular way. *Persistent information* means that the data remains intact after the program that accessed the information has ended. Most database systems offer the ability to manage the data as well as access it.

Several different types of databases have been used over the years. Many older databases were defined in a hierarchical manner or were structured as networks of information, but the most popular type of database today is the relational database, which consists of formally defined tables containing data that relates to other tables in the database.

File-Based Databases

One of the primary purposes of computers is information storage. From mainframes to desktop computers, many different types of data storage systems have been devised. File-based data storage systems were probably the earliest attempt at computerizing the traditional manual filing system. They were also the most common type of data storage system before today's database systems. They were created to address the need for more efficient data access. A file-based system is one in which a collection of application programs interact with data held in various files, performing such services as report creation. These types of systems are often referred to as *flat-file databases* (which are files containing records that have no structured interrelationship). A flat-file database is a file in which data is collected in lines of text; each value is separated by a tab character or a comma, and each row is represented by a new line. This type of flat file may also be referred to as a comma-separated values (CSV) file. These systems generally used a decentralized approach: each department in an organization would be responsible for managing its own data.

These systems inevitably cause problems, including repetition of data, separation of data, incompatibility of files, data dependence, and inflexibility of the application programs that access the data. You might be able to visualize it a little better with a simple illustration. Imagine that two people each has their own small CSV flat-file database that holds people's names, addresses, and phone numbers. Here is flat-file database one:

Name	Address	Phone
Tom Duggan	15 Central Ave.	555-8989

Here is database two:

Full Name	#	Addr.
Tom Duggan	555-8989	15 Central Ave.

You can see from the two examples that flat-file databases are simple and easy to use, but it's difficult to ensure consistency of headings and structure.

The Evolution of Databases

Databases emerged from the need for a more efficient method for storing and manipulating data. As previously discussed, the file-based approach was a substantial improvement over manual filing systems, but it still needed improvement.

In a database, a single repository of logically related data replaces the files that once held the data in many different places. Instead of many files with a great deal of repeated data, the data is integrated with minimal replication. The data is normally contained in two-dimensional tables.

What is important is that a database also contains a description of the data. This description is referred to as the system catalog. Some databases use the term *data dictionary* (or *metadata*, which is data about data).

Relational Databases and Database Management Systems (DBMSs)

A *relational database* is a body of data organized as a set of formally defined tables. Data can be accessed or reassembled from the database in many different ways without the database tables having to be reorganized. The tables can (and usually do) contain data that relates to data held in other tables within the same database.

As databases have evolved, so has the software that stores and manages the data. This software is referred to as a *database management system* (DBMS). A DBMS is software that supports the creation and management of databases and provides controlled access while still allowing users to define, create, and maintain databases. Many DBMSs are available for use on different platforms. Though each DBMS has unique features, most usually provide a well-defined set of features, such as the following:

- The DBMS can support a specific language (a query language) to facilitate the manipulation of the data. The actual language for relational DBMSs is the *Structured Query Language (SQL)*. Database designers can define databases using a data definition language (DDL), a subset of SQL. The DDL permits the database designer to specify the data types held in the database as well as constraints on the data.

- The DBMS allows users to retrieve, insert, update, and delete data in the database using a DML.

- The DBMS typically provides a security system, an integrity system for preserving the consistency of the data, a concurrency control system for shared access to the database, a recovery system for restoring the database to a previous state in case of hardware or software failure, and a system catalog (or data dictionary) for describing the data in the database.

- The DBMS provides a view mechanism, which allows the database administrator (DBA) to create views particular to each set of database users. A view is a subset of the data in the database. Views are useful when users do not need to see or access all the data in the database.

The preceding list is general and is not intended to describe all DBMSs. Some DBMSs may provide more functionality; others may provide less. For example, a DBMS for a desktop computer may not provide concurrency control and may have limited security and integrity mechanisms. A DBMS intended for large, multiuser systems would definitely provide the functionality listed earlier and usually more. With the important role that the database plays in today's corporate and business communities, the DBMS must be completely reliable and provide availability of data even if the hardware or software should fail.

A database is one of the main requirements for an e-commerce site, so the business can store and deliver the online catalog. The type of database largely relies on the type of applications being used to access the database. Some applications have specific requirements beyond the standard ODBC-compliant database. *Open Database Connectivity (ODBC)* is the standard by which communications with a database are translated into the native language of the used database.

Database Language

The purpose of a database is to store information for retrieval. A standard language has been specifically designed to work with databases. Structured Query Language (SQL, pronounced "sequel"), which is an ANSI and ISO standard, is the language most commonly used. With SQL, a programmer can structure queries, updates, and inserts into databases. Most databases have proprietary languages to use internally, and SQL is the common language among them.

Oracle8i Database

Oracle8i, developed by Oracle, provides database applications for networked environments and data warehousing. The following list includes some of its features:

- Ease of use. Its installation procedures are simple and its database is preconfigured and pretuned.

- Multithreaded architecture. It uses multithreaded architecture and offers multitasking and I/O capabilities.

- Platform independence. It can run on the Linux, NetWare, and NT/2000 platforms.

- Support for high-end Online Transaction Processing (OLTP) and decision-support systems.

SQL Server Database

SQL Server is the Microsoft relational database application for storing, retrieving, and warehousing data. Its features include the following:

- Ease of installation and use

- A set of administrative and development tools that help you install, deploy, manage, and use SQL Server on several sites

- Scalability

- A multiplatform database engine

- Data warehousing

- Tools for extracting and analyzing summary data for Online Analytical Processing (OLAP), and for visually designing databases and analyzing data using English-based questions

- System integration with other server software

- Integration with e-mail, the Internet, and Windows

Development Tools

Although we have focused on the Microsoft development tools, many other applications exist. Some may provide additional features that are more suitable for a particular company's business requirements. A few of these products will be introduced in the following sections.

ColdFusion Studio

ColdFusion Studio allows you to build applications ranging from e-commerce to business automation. Building applications does not require coding in a traditional programming language, but instead using a server-side processing language called ColdFusion Markup Language (CFML). CFML looks similar to HTML, but you need some knowledge of programming operations to understand the language well. ColdFusion and Homesite are similar, providing specialized tabs and drop-down menus during development. You can learn more at `www.macromedia.com`.

IBM WebSphere

IBM's WebSphere Commerce Suite allows businesses to develop complex storefronts and online catalogs sufficient for most e-commerce operations.

These features are implemented though editing tools that allow customization. Commerce Suite runs on several operating systems, including Windows NT/2000 and Solaris. Commerce Suite works only with IBM's DB2 database or Oracle's Oracle8 and Oracle8i. Detailed information is available at www.ibm.com.

iPlanet

iPlanet provides a number of software applications for buying, selling, and billing solutions. Depending on the business requirements, one or more of the applications can be combined to provide a total solution. For more information, go to www.iplanet.com.

Commerce Server 2000

Commerce Server 2000 is Microsoft's latest package to create e-commerce-enabled Web applications. This version can support enterprise-level business architecture for most e-commerce requirements.

Commerce Server 2000 is managed through three main interfaces—BizDesk, Commerce Server Manager, and Pipeline Editor—which allow application customization to support a single site and local database architecture for multiple distributed database architectures.

With BizDesk, you can creating online catalogs, manage user accounts, analyze applications, and manage campaigns and profiles. With Commerce Server Manager, you can administer multiple site resources and properties. And with Pipeline Editor, you can define business processes and sequencing requirements.

Solution Sites

Additional components that can be used with Commerce Server are Solution Sites. These are preconfigured and defined e-commerce sites that help create a quick start for your e-commerce site. The Solution Sites can be downloaded separately from the Microsoft site and unpacked to create a site foundation. The three current types of solutions sites are as follows:

Blank Provides an empty shell for development; requires extensive coding and development.

Retail   Provides a shell of an online catalog for a business-to-consumer site; requires minimal coding.

Supplier   Provides a shell to support a business-to-business application; requires some coding and Microsoft Active Directory.

Summary

Choosing your web server is the first step in implementing a back-end solution. Web servers serve HTML and several image formats (GIF, JPEG, and PNG) and deliver program files of almost any type (Java, ActiveX, streaming video and audio, PDF, DOC, TXT, and so forth). Web servers use the Hypertext Transfer Protocol (HTTP), which enables the web server to receive requests and transmit replies, usually in the form of the documents.

There are different types of web server software available, including Apache (an open source application) and Microsoft's Internet Information Server. Learning the administration options available for one application will help you understand others.

In addition to your web server, a database server is necessary to maintain your catalog of products and keep track of inventory. There are different types of database management system (DBMS) software available, including Oracle8 and Microsoft SQL Server, to provide the database support for your e-commerce site. Most usually provide a well-defined set of features.

The database server needs to be tied in to your online catalog. One package you can use to create online catalogs is Microsoft's Commerce Server 2000. It supports enterprise-level business architecture for most e-commerce requirements.

Your decisions for web server, database, and catalog creation will be based partially upon cost, partially on ease of use for administration, and partially on your existing platform choices. Logically, if you have a predominantly Microsoft shop, then you will most likely be comfortable with Microsoft products. If cost is a factor, then open source options are a better choice.

Exam Essentials

Know your web software options and how to make choices based upon the design scenario.   There are several options for site creation/development software. For example, if a company already uses Microsoft products, Microsoft IIS would be a good choice for web server software. In addition, know what open source software is and when it's appropriate to use it.

Understand the features and capabilities of IIS.   The exam is vendor neutral, but you can gain a lot of insight into all web server software by knowing the basic features of IIS. You should be able to transfer that knowledge to configuring other types of software, such as Apache Web Server.

Understand the difference between virtual servers and virtual directories. Virtual servers allow you to run several websites on the same system. From a web hosting standpoint, this saves money on additional hardware and software needs and it makes administration a lot easier because multiple web sites are located on one system. Virtual directories allow information for a website to be pulled from many different locations within your network. This means that the web pages people see do not need to be located directly on the web server; they can be located on another system if need be.

Understand the concept of binding multiple IP addresses to a single network interface card (NIC).   Each website should have its own IP address. DNS servers help your users to get to a site through the IP address. By binding multiple IP addresses to a single NIC, you make it easier to have multiple sites on the same server. Another approach for greater performance is to add more NIC cards and give them different addresses.

Know which development software to recommend and the different kinds of databases.   Be familiar with the different types of software—such as Microsoft SQL Server, Oracle 8i, and IBM DB2—for database support. Understand the difference between a flat-file database and a relational database.

Key Terms

Before you take the exam, be certain you are familiar with the following terms:

Active Server Pages (ASPs)	metadata
Certificate Authority (CA)	Open Database Connectivity (ODBC)
Common Gateway Interface (CGI)	open source
database	plug-in
database management system	port
default document	relational database
File Transfer Protocol (FTP)	Structured Query Language (SQL)
flat-file databases	web farm
Hypertext Transfer Protocol (HTTP)	

Review Questions

1. Which of the following protocols does a web server typically use for serving information?

   A. HTML

   B. HTTP

   C. POP

   D. SMTP

2. Joel is connecting to a site through an SSL connection to purchase books online. What port number is an SSL connection made through?

   A. 80

   B. 21

   C. 443

   D. 8080

3. Which of the following is a collection of data organized as a set of formally described tables?

   A. A flat-file database

   B. A shopping cart

   C. A DBA

   D. A relational database

4. What technology is typically used to extend a web server's features?

   A. The Hypertext Transfer Protocol (HTTP)

   B. A daemon process or a service

   C. CGI scripts, ColdFusion, or Active Server Pages

   D. HTM and several image formats

5. When considering security in selecting web server software, what encryption level might you typically find for SSL services?

   A. 128 bits

   B. 40 bits

   C. 64 bits

   D. 56 bits

6. Bill needs to change the default page for a website from `default.htm` to `home.htm`. Each type of web server handles this differently, but Bill's company is using IIS v5 to host its pages. What tab would Bill use to make this change?

   A. Web Site tab

   B. Documents tab

   C. Performance tab

   D. Home Directory tab

7. Tom hops from one website to another searching for a pair of new sunglasses. He hits one site where he is asked for a username and password. What has changed?

   A. The site is missing a home page.

   B. His browser has been infected with a virus.

   C. He can't access this page with the anonymous account.

   D. Bandwidth throttling is in place.

8. Which of the following options best defines *open source code*.

   A. Free source code offered to the development community at large to develop a better product

   B. A channel for connecting to a web server

   C. Files containing records that have no structured interrelationship

   D. Data about data

9. You have a website development team that is working on the ultimate website for your company. The host for your site is a server named WebServer and the website files are located on a server named Bilbo on a share named Shire. Which of the following would be your URL?

    A. www.bilbo.com/shire

    B. \\bilbo\shire

    C. WebServer/Bilbo/Shire

    D. \\Shire

10. Tim is a network administrator who is using Microsoft's IIS 5 to host web pages on his internal network. He wants to prevent users from seeing the directory structure of his pages. He has the server directed to show the home page to users who connect to the site, but he notices that users are still able to view the directory structure and all files within his web site's folder. To prevent this from happening, what feature should Tim disable within the IIS Default Website Properties dialog box?

    A. Bandwidth throttling

    B. Directory browsing

    C. Connection timeout

    D. Default document

11. Superior Enterprises (a fairly new upstart company with limited funding) is developing an e-commerce plan. The development team is thinking about developing their own database management system to manage inventory and fulfillment. In making their determinations as to what type of system to implement and the work involved in such a project, to whom should they turn?

    A. Software vendor marketing teams.

    B. A database administrator

    C. The webmaster

    D. The network administrator

12. The part of a database that describes the data is called

_____ .

  A. The DBA

  B. SQL

  C. The system catalog

  D. Relational

13. Which of the following is not a feature of Microsoft SQL Server?

  A. Ease of installation

  B. Scalability

  C. Data warehousing

  D. Creation of an online catalog

14. Which of the following operating system platforms can Oracle 8i not run on?

  A. DOS

  B. Linux

  C. NetWare

  D. NT/2000

15. Which of the following options is a language used to create professional, high-performance corporate databases?

  A. RPC

  B. SQL

  C. HTML

  D. Word Basic

16. Which of the following options is a form of client-side scripting? (Choose all that apply.)

A. C+ Script

B. XML Script

C. JavaScript

D. VBScript

17. What is the default connection time-out for Microsoft Internet Information Server?

A. 400 seconds

B. 550 seconds

C. 900 seconds

D. 60 seconds

18. Which of the following is obligatory for an e-commerce site?

A. An online catalog

B. SQL Server

C. SSL

D. IIS 5

19. In the IIS Website Properties dialog box, what is the HTTP Headers tab used for?

A. To determine who can administer the site

B. To customize the headers sent from the web server to a browser

C. To identify ISAPI programs you can use as alternatives to CGI

D. To configure IIS to send a basic error message when it cannot respond to a client or server request.

20. Which of the following is a common web page error?

A. 303

B. 404

C. 666

D. 191

Answers to Review Questions

1. B.   Hypertext Transfer Protocol (HTTP) is used to transfer HTML-based web pages to users over TCP/IP connections. POP stands for Post Office Protocol, which is used to receive e-mail. SMTP stands for Simple Mail Transfer, which is used for sending e-mail.

2. C.   Port 443 is generally used for SSL connections. Port 80 is for HTTP connections, and port 21 is for FTP. You can use port 8080 for more secure connections by designating it yourself.

3. D.   A relational database is a collection of data organized into tables. The tables can interact with one another, making it possible to query a relational database. A flat-file database has no structured interrelationship. A shopping cart is for e-commerce purchases. A DBA is a database administrator.

4. C.   You can extend the features of a web server through additional programs called CGI scripts. You can also use proprietary products, such as Macromedia ColdFusion or Microsoft Active Server Pages (ASPs).

5. A.   IIS allows you to use encryption of up to 128 bits for SSL services. This is considered strong encryption.

6. B.   You can change the home page for a website on the Documents tab in the IIS Default Website Properties dialog box. The other tabs are important and necessary but have no functionality in terms of the home page.

7. C.   The anonymous account is good on most sites, but for additional security, you can require a username and password to protect users from seeing pages they shouldn't see.

8. A.   Open source code is code that is offered for free to the development community. The source code for many applications (for example, Apache Web Server and Linux) is open source code.

9. B.   A UNC path that correctly links to a server and shared folder is `\\computername\sharename`, so the correct URL is `\\bilbo\shire`.

10. B.   Directory browsing makes the server operate in much the same way as an FTP server. As you develop your e-commerce business, you should not enable directory browsing because it could reveal confidential or sensitive files.

11. **B.** A database administrator would have the most amount of information regarding the best solution for the company. Software vendors would only pitch their solution. The webmaster and the network administrator may (or may not) know enough information about database needs.

12. **C.** The correct answer is system catalog, although some databases may use the terms *data dictionary* or *metadata*. DBA stands for database administrator. SQL stands for Structured Query Language. *Relational* is a term used to describe a type of database.

13. **D.** You can't use SQL Server to create an online catalog. Microsoft (along with other vendors) provides additional software for catalog creation and management. Microsoft's version is called Commerce Server 2000.

14. **A.** Oracle 8i provides database applications for networked environments and data warehousing. It can run on Linux, NetWare, and NT/2000 operating system platforms.

15. **B.** The correct answer is SQL, which is the actual language for relational DBMSs. A remote procedure call (RPC) allows servers of different types to communicate across a dedicated network, accessing files, services, and information. HTML is used to create web pages. Word Basic was an early programming language for Microsoft Word, but it hasn't been used in any versions after Word 6.

16. **C, D.** Web servers often deploy both client-side and server-side scripting. Client-side scripting includes the use of JavaScript and VBScript. If you embed these scripting languages into an HTML page, you are engaging in client-side scripting. Server-side scripting is the use of scripting languages to create programs that run on the web server itself. C+ and XML are programming languages.

17. **C.** The default is 900 seconds, but you can raise or lower it based upon your needs. If you want to improve performance, you usually lower this number to force out unused connections, but if you have low-bandwidth connections, you should leave it as it is or some users may not be able to connect.

18. **C.** SSL connections are obligatory in an e-commerce site. An online catalog is great, but it's not obligatory. SQL and IIS are Microsoft products and, although easy to work with, are not necessary for your e-commerce environment.

19. B.   You can use the HTTP Headers tab to customize the headers sent from the web server to a browser. You can also use the tab to define content expiration settings, identify new file types that the server can present, send a rating concerning the site's textual and visual content, and customize the HTTP header that will be sent to the browser.

20. B.   404: Object (or File) Not Found is a common website error, as is 403: Access Forbidden.

Chapter

28

Configuring and Using Payment Gateways

THE CIW EXAM OBJECTIVE GROUP COVERED IN THIS CHAPTER:

- ✓ Accept payments through an e-commerce site, including but not limited to: setup and processing of electronic payment services.

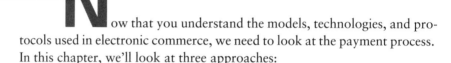

ow that you understand the models, technologies, and protocols used in electronic commerce, we need to look at the payment process. In this chapter, we'll look at three approaches:

- Credit-card processing, which requires the use of merchant banks and authorization systems

- Digital cash, which is an ad-hoc payment system based on electronically stored currency

- Online check processing, a popular alternative that supports customers who have bank accounts but cannot or do not want to use "plastic" money

We'll then look at the Automated Clearing House (ACH) network, which provides batch processing of financial transactions for merchants and banks. And, finally, we'll look at some myths about electronic commerce security. The implementation of SSL provides a level of security for transmitting payment information between the web client and the merchant, but the technical requirements of this process are sometimes lost on users and professionals alike.

Preparing for Online Transactions

Preparing for online transactions involves three main tasks:

Prepare the server and the e-commerce site   Preparing your host or web server, along with programming or configuring your web pages, is essential. Your web pages must be able to handle requests and integrate with the database for each transaction.

Set up an online merchant account   You need an *online merchant account* to process the payment transaction online. An online merchant account identifies your business to a payment authorization service and provides various methods for handling payments. Online merchant accounts typically include both a merchant ID (MID) and a terminal ID (TID).

Install payment software   A growing number of payment software products are available today from vendors such as CyberCash and VeriSign. The software your organization chooses should allow online validation of credit-card or payment information, including network access, to properly communicate with your bank.

Credit-Card Processing

Credit cards are a convenient payment method for many Internet users in North America. Many banks also process debit-card transactions for their customers. When you implement an online payment transaction process for credit cards, several options are available for payment software. After you acquire the merchant account information from your financial institution, you are ready to install the payment software. Table 28.1 lists some vendors that provide payment software.

TABLE 28.1   Vendors of Payment Software

Vendor	URL
BCE Emergis	www.bceemergis.com
ClearCommerce	www.clearcommerce.com
CyberCash	www.cybercash.com
CyberSource	www.cybersource.com
DataCash	www.datacash.com
EPX	www.epx.com

TABLE 28.1 Vendors of Payment Software *(continued)*

Vendor	URL
VeriFone	www.verifone.com
iBill	www.ibill.com
Paymentplus	www.paymentplus.com
SurePay	www.surepay.com
Trintech	www.trintech.com
VeriSign	www.verisign.com

Some of the vendors listed in Table 28.1 provide downloadable testing versions of their software. Each package usually provides detailed instructions on installing and configuring the software. Some provide tools and utilities to help with implementation and management.

As you evaluate and test your online transaction payment software, be sure that Internet access is available to the payment gateway. A *payment gateway* is the connection between an online catalog and a merchant bank. The payment gateway for these payment solutions is usually one of the company sites.

You can practice using a payment gateway by going to the VeriSign payment products website at www.verisign.com/products/payment.html. From this page you can select the Try option associated with a VeriSign payment product that you would like to use. Additional documentation on this site describes the various features of these products.

You should understand that VeriSign is not a credit card company. VeriSign provides only the vehicle (payment gateway) to connect to the financial institutions. The financial institutions transfer the funds.

Most payment gateway applications allow a merchant to process manual transactions. This step requires the merchant to manually enter all the relevant information for the transaction, such as the credit-card number and expiration date, along with the charge amount and billing address. This process is very time-consuming and is effective only for a small number of transactions. The most typical manual transaction for most merchants is a return or a credit to a customer account.

The process used to move the transaction onto the settlement stage is called *batching*. In this process, all the transactions are collected, verified, and submitted for settlement. VeriSign conducts an automatic batching process every evening at 9:00 P.M. local time. The advantage of automatic batching is that the merchant need not manually batch the transactions daily, which can be a time-consuming process depending on the number of transactions. The disadvantage of automatic batching is that errors can occur and unwanted transactions can be processed.

Because a transaction is not immediately processed at the time of purchase, it is considered a *delayed-capture transaction*. The transaction is not complete until it has been batched. Therefore, in the case of VeriSign, a transaction that occurs at 9:00 A.M. will not be completed until 9:00 P.M. During the delay, the transaction awaits processing. Even though the transaction is not formally charged to the account holder, an authorization is placed on the account to reserve the funds. With delayed captures, the merchant has time to review the transaction and make any necessary changes.

When a company sells internationally, various monetary issues arise. International currency transactions can be handled by one of several packages.

If you plan to accept international currencies, the merchant account that is created with a financial institution must be able to process multiple currencies. Along with the merchant account, the online transaction payment software must be able to translate the customer's currency into the merchant's preferred currency. Each vendor will provide detailed information about how to install and configure its payment software.

EXERCISE 28.1

Viewing International Currency Options

In this exercise, you'll look at some options available through the DataCash online transaction payment software.

1. In the Address bar of your web browser, enter **http://www.datacash .com/currency/all.html**.

EXERCISE 28.1 *(continued)*

2. Scroll down the list to see which currencies are trading, as shown in the following graphic:

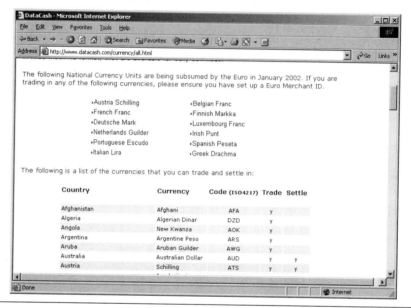

Digital Cash

$\mathbf{S}$o far, we have focused on credit-card payment options. That model seems to work best for most organizations, but electronic money (or *digital cash*) can be a viable option. It is used on many sites.

The primary reason for infrequent use of electronic money is the requirement that everyone use the same package. A handful of vendors are currently providing digital money components, but each is incompatible with the others. All require that the consumer preload the software before making a purchase. These problems have prevented widespread use of this technique.

Despite the problems, some benefits are associated with using digital cash. The first is the lack of back-end processing. Unlike in the credit-card model, transactions using digital cash are completed immediately. The second significant benefit is that digital cash transactions are free. This combination makes the digital cash option attractive to companies that process high-volume, low-dollar transactions. Many credit-card companies require minimum charge amounts. Using digital cash, companies can process certain types of transactions that would not otherwise be possible.

Another benefit of using digital cash is customer anonymity. Credit-card transactions always involve a mechanism for tracing the transaction, and identification must be presented to prevent fraud. Properly implemented, digital cash does not leave any trails that could be traced.

To use digital cash, a consumer needs a *wallet*, a program so-named because it mimics the functionality of a physical wallet; that is, it holds the digital cash. Both consumers and merchants need wallets of the same type.

In addition to the wallet, the merchant needs a *point-of-sale module*, which integrates with the website, the merchant's wallet, and the bank's financial network. This point-of-sale module acts much like the payment gateway in credit-card models. It is responsible for several merchant activities, and it initiates the funds transfer between the consumer's wallet and the merchant's wallet. It also validates and logs activity and provides reporting and administrative functions. It is usually integrated with the merchant's website through CGI scripts or similar website extensions.

To implement the point-of-sale module, the merchant must register with the digital cash component supplier so that the merchant's systems can be configured to respond and store information appropriately. Once the point-of-sale module is integrated, the merchant can accept digital cash payments. The consumer must load their wallets with money before they can spend it. During this process, the currency is converted to digital cash. Once the buyer with a loaded wallet indicates a willingness to purchase something from the merchant's site, the digital cash is transferred from the consumer to the merchant. Merchants can transfer funds from their wallets to their regular bank accounts.

Online Check Processing

*O*nline check processing is becoming more popular because more than twice as many people use checking accounts as use credit cards. With online check processing, users enter the ABA routing number and the bank account number from the bottom of their checks instead of credit-card numbers. The credit-card process and the online check process are similar in that payment transactions are still required and financial institutions must still conduct them. On average, online check processing is slower than credit-card processing, and there is a better chance of incomplete transactions due to insufficient funds.

Two basic models exist for processing checks online. In one model, users enter their checking information in a form, including the routing numbers. The online check-processing service then prints a hard copy of that information in the form of a check. That hard-copy check is then deposited by traditional means to the bank, and the normal check-processing sequence begins.

In the other model, the same information is gathered, but it is retained in electronic form, and the processing is completed via Electronic Funds Transfer (EFT).

EXERCISE 28.2

Processing Checks Online

In this exercise, you will visit an online check-processing provider that uses the EFT method.

1. In the Address bar of your web browser, enter **http://www .telecheck.com/** to open the TeleCheck home page. Click the Services option at the top of the page to go to http://www .telecheck.com/products/products.html.

2. On the left side of the page, scroll down and click the TeleCheck Internet Check Acceptance link, which should take you to http: //www.telecheck.com/products/checkmain.html. Read the information provided on the page.

3. Scroll down and click the Take a Virtual Tour link in the right margin, under the heading "Want to Know More?" Follow the directions to see a simple demonstration of how a check is accepted over the Internet with TeleCheck. Basically, the customer enters the information contained at the bottom of their personal check and some identifying information into a form during the checkout phase.

Another online check service is Electracash (www.electracash.com).

The Automated Clearing House (ACH) Network

The *Automated Clearing House (ACH) Network* is a nationwide batch-oriented EFT system governed in the United States by the National Automated Clearing House Association (NACHA) operating rules. These rules provide for the inter-bank clearing of electronic payments for participating financial institutions. An ACH is a central clearing facility through which financial institutions transmit or receive ACH entries. Various organizations including Visa, the Federal Reserve, the American Clearing House Association, and the Electronic Payments Network, act as ACH operators. The electronic network transfers and clears funds between banking institutions for merchants and customers. Figure 28.1 shows how the ACH process works.

FIGURE 28.1 The ACH process

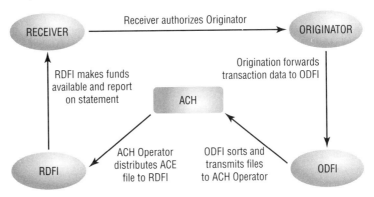

The following parties participate in an ACH transaction:

Originator Any party such as an individual, organization, corporation, or other entity that initiates entries into the ACH Network.

Originating Depository Financial Institution (ODFI) A participating financial institution that originates ACH entries at the request of and by agreement with its customers and merchants. Each ODFI must abide by the *NACHA Operating Rules and Guidelines*.

Receiving Depository Financial Institution (RDFI)   Any financial institution that is qualified to receive ACH entries and agrees to abide by the *NACHA Operating Rules and Guidelines*.

Receiver   An individual, a corporation, or other organization that has authorized an originator to initiate a credit or debit entry to a transaction account held at an RDFI.

The ACH network does not have direct contact with public customers or merchants. It is the mediator between financial institutions during the transfer of funds.

The following steps are involved in an ACH payment:

1. A merchant establishes a merchant account to accept credit-card payments or EFT payments.

2. The merchant collects the credit-card or banking information and then sends the information in batch format to the institution providing the merchant account (typically, the merchant's bank).

3. The merchant's bank uses the ACH network to clear the funds from the credit-card issuer's bank or the customer's bank (checking account) on behalf of the merchant.

4. The transaction is complete.

ACH does not process in real-time and usually needs 24 hours to complete a transaction. ACH should not be confused with real-time credit card authorization, which verifies only card validity and available funds.

An ACH network is involved in almost every financial transaction except wire transfers. Each country has its own form of ACH; and that country's laws and regulations govern its own form. In 2000, nearly 6.9 billion U.S. ACH transactions were processed, with a total value of more than $20.3 trillion.

Alternative Payment Methods

Over the past several years, several alternative Internet payment methods have emerged. Some of these services follow a traditional model that uses existing networks of payment offices and centers. These allow

customers to go to a local office, such as Western Union (`www.westernunion`
`.com`) or 7-Eleven Stores (`www.7-11.com`) and make a cash payment. Some
services allow customers to make payments directly to companies, and others
convert payments to a debit card that can be used for online purchases.

Others, such as PayPal (`www.paypal.com`), Yahoo! PayDirect (`http:`
`//paydirect.yahoo.com`), and eBay Payments (`www.billpoint.com`),
allow direct person-to-person payment. As mentioned in Chapter 26, these
methods have proven popular with auction sellers and bidders and are also
used by small online merchants.

Another alternative form of payment allows a person to send a credit
to another person (typically a gift) that equates to actual cash to be used
by the recipient at participating websites. Two services that attempted
to offer this payment type in North America were Flooz (`www.flooz.com`)
and Beenz (`www.beenz.com`). Both sites filed for bankruptcy protection
in 2001, citing their high overhead and poor market penetration as contributing factors.

Electronic Commerce Security Myths

The media have done much to raise the level of concern regarding electronic commerce security. Although their critical evaluation of security is
healthy, they have unfortunately most often focused on points that are not
the true problems and targets of attackers.

The first objective for any e-commerce site is to assure clients or customers that their personal information, although necessary for the transaction,
is private and safe in transmission across the Internet. Some of the media
coverage, whether accurate or not, has made it difficult to provide this level
of comfort. Let's look at some of those wrong beliefs so that we can focus on
the true risks.

**Myth #1: Crackers can copy any credit-card information transmitted
across the Internet.**   Like most myths, this one is partly true. Any information transmitted on any network can be obtained through the use of
programs called *packet sniffers*. For such copying to succeed, however,
the packet sniffer must be installed on the same physical wire and must
be listening while the information is transmitted. Because of the volume
of traffic transmitted across the backbone of the Internet, gathering all

information is a practical impossibility. Specialized sniffers look only for credit-card numbers, but again, the practicality of their being widely successful is still so minimal that the risk is incredibly small. In reality, why would an attacker try to gather a few account numbers using this technique when sites all over the Internet have easily accessible databases containing thousands of account numbers? However, if a risk (even a small one) can be eliminated, it should be. The easiest way to thwart packet sniffing is through the use of encryption.

Keep in mind that while people are afraid of giving out their numbers over the Internet, they readily give the physical card to every service station attendant, waiter/waitress, grocery store clerk, mall employee, and so on, assuming that only people on the Internet are dishonest, certainly nowhere else.

Myth #2: The encryption used on the Internet can be easily broken. The truth of this statement depends on how one defines the word "easily." Although the encryption in protocols such as Secure Sockets Layer (SSL) can be broken, the effort involved so far exceeds the benefit that it makes the attempt ludicrous. SSL is a stateful protocol that protects transmitted information with a key whose maximum size is 1024 bits. In actual practice, keys between 56 and 128 bits are used. SSL uses port 443 to exchange data.

Recently, a group known as distributed.net used more than 10,000 computers linked via the Internet to crack a key using the same type of encryption. The task required 38 days using a program that worked on the crack in the background. Alternatively, Ron Rivest of RSA estimates that for approximately $1,000,000, a specialized computer could be designed and created that could crack this type of encryption in less than a week. Neither of these solutions is practical. This effort would have to be expended for every session. The gain is not remotely worth the cost.

Myth #3: All that is needed to protect a website is to install a digital certificate and use SSL. This misconception is common. SSL is an encrypted transport protocol. It protects only the data in transit, but it does nothing to secure the server itself. Too many sites fall prey to this myth when they discover their databases have been compromised. Worse yet, most probably never realize their databases have been breached.

Myth #4: Securing a site is impossible. Although complete security cannot be achieved, you can achieve a level of security high enough that the effort involved to penetrate it exceeds the gain of doing so. Indeed, this principle is the essence of successful Internet security. If the required effort to penetrate the site costs more than the gain that results from doing so, perpetrators will seek easier targets.

Summary

As an e-commerce site designer, you first need to decide on a method of payment, and then you need a payment gateway. A payment gateway is the connection between the online catalog and a merchant bank. For an electronic transfer to be completed, information must be traded between merchant banks. A growing number of payment software products are available today, such as CyberCash and VeriSign. The software your organization chooses should allow online validation of credit-card or payment information, including network access, to properly communicate with your bank.

In addition to credit, you can use digital cash. Digital cash doesn't require the overhead needed in the credit-card model. It doesn't use back-end processing, the cash transactions require no cost on the merchant's side, and true anonymity is possible for the purchaser, although using digital cash does require that the buyer and the seller use the same software to process the transaction. Digital cash is useful for companies that conduct high-volume, low-dollar transactions.

In online check processing, users enter the routing and account numbers from the bottom of their checks instead of credit-card numbers. On average, online check processing is slower than credit-card processing, and there is a greater chance of incomplete transactions due to insufficient funds.

Concerns regarding the transfer of funds between banking institutions led to the development of the Automated Clearing House (ACH). This electronic network transfers and clears funds between banking institutions for merchants and customers. The ACH network does not have direct contact with public customers or merchants. It is the mediator between financial institutions during the transfer of funds.

Exam Essentials

Understand the advantages and disadvantages of online credit-card transactions.   Credit-card transactions work best for most consumers who want to make a purchase over the Internet. The transaction requires a payment gateway, which is the connection between the online catalog and a merchant bank. For an electronic transfer to be completed, information must be traded between merchant banks. Not all transactions require online processing; a manual format uses SSL and the manual handling of the account numbers. The disadvantages associated with online credit-card transactions include the fear that people have about transmitting credit-card information over the Internet and that some buyers don't have a credit card. Nevertheless, credit-card transactions are the most-used payment method on the Internet.

Understand how digital cash transactions work.   Several advantages are associated with using digital cash. The first is the lack of back-end processing. Unlike in the credit-card model, transactions using digital cash are completed immediately. The second advantage is that cash transactions are free for the merchant. This combination makes the digital cash option attractive for companies that process high-volume, low-dollar transactions. Many credit-card companies require minimum charge amounts. Using digital cash, companies can process certain types of transactions that would not otherwise be possible. Another advantage of using digital cash is customer anonymity. Credit-card transactions always involve a mechanism for tracing the transaction, and identification must be presented to prevent fraud. Properly implemented, digital cash does not leave any trails that can be traced. The disadvantage of digital cash is that the buyer and seller need to use the same software package ("wallet" software). Several options are currently in use, and that complicates the situation.

Understand the advantages and disadvantages of online checks.   Online checks are becoming more popular because more than twice as many people use checking accounts than use credit cards. With online check processing, users enter the routing and account numbers from the bottom of their checks instead of credit-card numbers. The credit-card process and the online-check process are similar in that payment transactions are still required and financial institutions must still conduct them. The disadvantage associated with online check processing is that, on average, it is slower than credit-card processing, and there is a greater chance of incomplete transactions due to insufficient funds.

Understand the Automated Clearing House procedures.   The Automated Clearing House (ACH) Network is a nationwide batch-oriented EFT system governed in the United States by the National Automated Clearing House Association (NACHA) operating rules. These rules provide for the interbank clearing of electronic payments for participating financial institutions. The American Clearing House Association, Federal Reserve, Electronic Payments Network and Visa act as ACH operators, or central clearing facilities through which financial institutions transmit or receive ACH entries. The electronic network transfers and clears funds between banking institutions for merchants and customers. The following parties participate in an ACH transaction: Originator, Originating Depository Financial Institution (ODFI), Receiving Depository Financial Institution (RDFI), and Receiver.

Key Terms

Before you take the exam, be certain you are familiar with the following terms:

Automated Clearing House (ACH)	payment gateway
batching	point-of-sale module
digital cash	sniffers
online check processing	wallet
online merchant account	

Review Questions

1. Which of the following defines a wallet in e-commerce?

    A. The leather square item that fits in your pocket

    B. A program that allows funds to transfer through online checks

    C. A program that works with digital cash

    D. A method of adding security to your site

2. Which of the following online payment methods appeals to the masses?

    A. Credit card

    B. Online check

    C. Digital cash

    D. Western Union

3. Which of the following is an individual, a corporation, or an organization that initiates entries into the ACH Network?

    A. The Originator

    B. The Originating Depository Financial Institution (ODFI)

    C. The Receiving Depository Financial Institution (RDFI)

    D. The Receiver

4. Which of the following statements about Secure Sockets Layer (SSL) transmissions is the least correct?

    A. A third party can decrypt SSL transmissions with relative ease.

    B. SSL transmission employs a stateful connection.

    C. SSL is a common method for encrypting web browser communications.

    D. The maximum encryption length allowed in SSL 3 is 1024 bits.

5. Which of the following organizations must agree to abide by the *NACHA Operating Rules and Guidelines* when sending an ACH transaction?

   A. The originator

   B. The originating depository financial institution (ODFI)

   C. The receiving depository financial institution (RDFI)

   D. The receiver

6. Gary is worried about a cracker getting his credit-card information off the Internet when he makes online purchases. Which of the following technologies is used to do this?

   A. Secure Socket Layer (SSL) encryption

   B. Automated Clearing House (ACH)

   C. Online check processing.

   D. Packet sniffers

7. Why might an online merchant elect to gather information online but not conduct real-time transactions?

   A. Because this method eliminates the need to charge state sales tax and shipping charges

   B. Because this method eliminates the need to interface a point-of-sale component on the web page

   C. Because it is more profitable to wait for customers to place orders on the telephone and pay by check

   D. Because the Internet is inherently insecure and telephone transactions are much safer

8. What is batching?

   A. A process in which all transactions are collected, verified, and submitted for settlement

   B. The final step in the ACH process

   C. A way of maintaining security with SSL

   D. Data about data

9. Which protocol is commonly used to provide a more secure environment?

    A. Transmission Control Protocol (TCP)

    B. Hypertext Transfer Protocol (HTTP)

    C. Secure Socket Layers (SSL)

    D. Internet Protocol (IP)

10. In considering the advantages and disadvantages associated with the various types of online transactions, which of the following is a good reason to use digital cash? (Choose two.)

    A. The ability to trace the customer

    B. The high cost of cash transactions

    C. The need to use the same form of digital cash software package

    D. Lack of back-end processing

11. Which payment method takes the longest to complete a business transaction, including transfer of funds?

    A. Credit card

    B. Online check

    C. Digital cash

    D. E-mail

12. Which of the following is an example of EFT?

    A. Buying an item at a local store with hard cash

    B. Using your debit card to make a purchase

    C. Making a credit card purchase online

    D. Paying a bill online with a check

13. Joseph is creating his e-commerce site and is now developing his payment process. He plans to accept as many payment methods as possible, including credit card transactions. What does he need in order to accept credit cards for purchases?

   A. Shopping cart

   B. Online catalog

   C. Knowledge database

   D. Merchant account

14. Which of the following is a network that transfers and clears funds between banking institutions for merchants and customers?

   A. Shopping cart

   B. ACH

   C. Payment gateway

   D. Checkstand

15. Tony has found a CD online he would like to purchase. He goes through a registration process and is now ready to order the item. When buying this CD, he uses the most popular payment method in use on the Internet. Which method does Tony use?

   A. Digital cash

   B. Check

   C. Credit card

   D. COD

16. Which of the following is the connection between an online catalog and a merchant bank?

   A. ATM

   B. Payment gateway

   C. ACH

   D. Credit card issuer

17. Which of the following numbers must be supplied by a user, along with an account number, when using online check processing?

A. The bank's telephone number

B. Social Security number

C. Routing number

D. Check number

18. Which of the following companies has the strongest reputation for Internet security and e-commerce transactions?

A. Microsoft

B. Oracle

C. New Horizons

D. VeriSign

19. Which of the following ports is commonly used for SSL connections?

A. 80

B. 21

C. 443

D. 110

20. Which of the following ports is used (commonly) on SSL connections?

A. 80

B. 21

C. 443

D. 110

Answers to Review Questions

1. **C.**   A wallet handles digital cash and makes it easy to transfer funds from the wallet of the customer to the wallet of the business, but only as long as the form of digital currency matches.

2. **B.**   More than twice as many people have a checking account than have a credit card; so the possibility of appealing to the masses is greater with online checks. The next most convenient method of payment is credit cards.

3. **A.**   There are four participating facets to the ACH network, and the Originator initiates the entries into the ACH network.

4. **A.**   Option A represents a common myth regarding SSL encryption. Although the encryption in protocols such as Secure Sockets Layer (SSL) can be broken, the effort involved so far exceeds the benefit that it makes the attempt ludicrous.

5. **B, C.**   There are four participating facets to the ACH network. The RDFI is the financial institution qualified to receive ACH entries, and the ODFI enters or sends transactions into the ACH network.

6. **D.**   Any information transmitted on any network can be obtained through the use of programs called packet sniffers. For such copying to succeed, however, the packet sniffer must be installed on the same physical wire and must be listening while the information is transmitted. It would be too much work for a cracker to even bother with the process.

7. **B.**   One approach to online transactions involves the use of SSL to transmit sensitive data back and forth between the buyer and the business. The information is encrypted, and the transaction takes place, but the process is handled manually from this point. Obviously this is not the fastest way to collect your money, but it does eliminate the point-of-sale part of the configuration.

8. **A.**   The advantage of automatic batching is that the merchant need not manually batch the transactions daily, which can be a time-consuming process depending on the number of transactions. The disadvantage associated with automatic batching is that errors can occur and unwanted transactions can be processed.

9. C. Secure Socket Layers allows for greater security through encryption. It's not infallible, but it is relatively strong and deters data theft. The real problem is with the servers themselves. SSL is good for securing data in transit, but does nothing to secure the server.

10. D. Several advantages are associated with using digital cash. Three of the more popular being no back-end processing, anonymity for the customer, and low-cost transactions. However, the biggest deterrent is the need for the merchant and the consumer to use the same form of digital cash software.

11. B. Online check processing takes the longest to complete, including the transfer of funds, because of the back-end processing. Digital cash is the fastest but is the most difficult to implement. The credit card is the most widespread payment method used on the Internet.

12. B. Electronic Funds Transfer (EFT) is the preauthorized transfer of funds from one bank account to another. Examples of EFT are using a debit card, an automated teller machine (ATM) card, or point-of-sale credit transaction. The Automated Clearing House (ACH) uses EFT.

13. D. Joseph need a merchant account. This account is provided by the merchant's bank, and before issuing it, the bank does a thorough credit check to ensure of the stability of the company. An online catalog is an important part of an e-commerce site but is not required for a sale to take place. Neither is a shopping cart or a knowledge database.

14. B. The ACH, Automated Clearing House, is a network that transfers and clears funds between banking institutions for merchants and customers. A checkstand allows customers to enter billing and shipping information for an order as well as calculate the total of items in a shopping cart and add taxes and shipping costs. A shopping cart allows customers to select items for purchase but still continue to look for more before paying. A payment gateway is an online component that processes credit-card transfers to validate account numbers and commence transfers of funds.

15. C. The credit card is the most widely used payment method on the Internet. Of the three methods, digital cash is the fastest in transaction time but the most difficult to implement because both the buyer and seller must use the same type of cash. An online check transaction takes the longest to complete since it requires the most back-end processing.

16. B.   A payment gateway is the connection that introduces the transaction details into the credit-card payment system.

17. C.   The user must supply the routing number that is printed on the check. This number is assigned by the ABA as a unique identifier for the account holder's bank. A check number may be assigned by the user or the online check processor. The user generally must include their own telephone number, but not the bank's telephone number.

18. D.   VeriSign (www.verisign.com) is a well-known company that provides all sorts of helpful information and services relating to Internet security and e-commerce transactions. It provides certificate services and stands in as a third-party certificate authority.

19. C.   Port 443 is the SSL port that is commonly used. Port 80 is for HTTP web transactions. Port 21 is for FTP transactions. Port 110 is for POP3 receiving e-mail connections.

20. C.   Port 443 is the SSL port that is commonly used. Port 80 is for HTTP web transactions. Port 21 is for FTP transactions. Port 110 is for POP3 receiving e-mail connections.

Chapter

29

Transaction Security

THE CIW EXAM OBJECTIVE GROUP COVERED IN THIS CHAPTER:

- ✓ Identify various types of security available for e-commerce, including but not limited to: encryption, certificates, SET, SSL.

A solid comprehension of the security infrastructure will help you understand the details of electronic commerce. The proper use of encryption, certificates, and other techniques can help provide adequate security for your site, its data, and your customers. Such knowledge will help you select the appropriate technologies for particular situations. The payment systems described in other chapters rely on different mechanisms to establish identity and intent of all the parties involved in an electronic transaction.

Underlying all the mechanisms are cryptographic techniques. *Cryptography* protects against a variety of attacks on the communications between two parties. This chapter introduces the essential cryptographic techniques necessary to understand how electronic payment systems function. We'll look at various encryption methods, including asymmetric and symmetric techniques. We'll also look at the application of cryptographic techniques to infrastructures, such as S/MIME, Secure Sockets Layer (SSL), and Secure Electronic Transactions (SET), and at the certificate issuance process.

The Goals of Security

In the last chapter, we looked at some myths related to the security of e-commerce and the Internet. Although no site is completely invulnerable, you can take steps to secure your e-commerce environment. Essentially, security serves the following goals:

Authentication and identification   Identification helps ensure that someone is who they claim to be. Particularly in an e-commerce transaction, parties need to trust that others are actually who they say they are. You implement authentication using digital signatures, and we'll look at digital signatures in detail later in this chapter.

Access control   *Access control* governs the resources that a user or a service can access on the system or network. It protects against the unauthorized use of accessible resources. Only users with valid IDs and passwords have access to system resources. However, access control goes beyond passwords. For example, on an FTP server, access controls specify when the services can be accessed and by whom (by user or host name).

Data confidentiality   Data confidentiality concerns how secure the data remains. For example, the data confidentiality required for a report transmitted on the Internet is high when the report contains a corporation's about-to-be-released quarterly earnings. Conversely, when the report contains information such as previous quarterly earnings (which are probably public knowledge), the data confidentiality requirement is relatively low. Data confidentiality is provided by encryption (and decryption).

Data integrity   Data integrity ensures that information has not been modified en route to its destination. The Internet is a *packet-switched network*. Thus, a packet stops at various routers on its way to the destination. What is to prevent a malicious router vendor or a malicious cracker from eavesdropping on the network and capturing and altering a packet? An electronic payment system should ensure data integrity and discard the data (or notify appropriate personnel) if it detects that integrity has been breached. Data integrity is provided by a message digest or hashing.

Non-repudiation   Properties of *non-repudiation* are important to prevent merchants or customers from denying that they agreed to a sale or a purchase. For example, if a customer walks into a retail store and purchases a television set, the store issues a receipt. That receipt means that the store cannot repudiate the purchase because the receipt proves the purchase occurred. Thus, if the television set malfunctions within a prescribed time limit, the customer can return the damaged goods to the store for an exchange or a refund. Establishing similar forms of non-repudiation is important for electronic commerce. Non-repudiation is also implemented with a digital signature.

Encryption and Decryption

In cryptography (the science of encrypting and decrypting plaintext messages), a message that humans can read is in plaintext or cleartext. The process of disguising a message to make it unreadable by humans is called *encryption*, and the resulting message is called *ciphertext*. The reverse process, called decryption, takes an encrypted (or ciphertext) message and restores it to the original plaintext. Figure 29.1 demonstrates this process.

FIGURE 29.1 The process of encryption and decryption

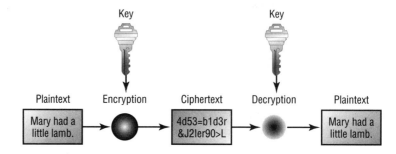

You use a cryptographic algorithm called a *cipher* to encrypt and decrypt plaintext messages. A cipher is a mathematic function. Most of today's encryption algorithms use a key, whose value affects the encryption and decryption functions. Without the key, decrypting a ciphertext message is difficult (although not impossible). As you might expect, most attacks on cryptographic systems focus on finding the key.

Encryption Strength

A commonly discussed, but frequently misunderstood aspect of cryptography is the strength of encryption. What constitutes strong encryption, which is protected by U.S. export laws? What level of encryption is required for various security needs? How do you determine the effective strength of different types of encryption?

Encryption strength is based on three primary factors:

- The strength of the algorithm, which includes the inability to mathematically reverse the information with any less effort than trying all possible key combinations. For our purposes, we rely on industry-standard algorithms that have been tested and tried over time by cryptography experts. View any new or proprietary formula with significant distrust until it has been verified commercially.

- The secrecy of the key. No algorithm can protect you from compromised keys. Thus, the degree of confidentiality that stays with the data depends directly on how secret the keys remain.

- The length of the key. In terms of encryption and decryption formula application, the key length is determined in bits. Adding a bit to the length of the key does not increase its possibilities by two, but rather doubles them. In simple terms, the number of possible combinations of bits that can make up a key of any given length can be expressed as $2n$; n is the length of the key.

Thus, a formula with a 40-bit key length is expressed as 2^{40}, or 1,099,511,627,776 possible keys.

Working against this encryption is the speed of today's computers. Although the number of possible keys is indeed large, specialized computers can now try that many combinations of keys in less than a day. In 1993, Michael Wiener designed a computer specifically for breaking DES (Data Encryption Standard), an algorithm that uses a 56-bit key. In doing so, he discovered that the cost of design was very linear.

Let's look at an analogy. Placing something valuable in a safe place can be difficult. You must first find a spot that no one can access. Then, you must lock the valuable away. For example, most people put their money in a bank for safekeeping. The bank has a vault with a combination lock on the front. It also has locks on the front door and, in most cases, an alarm system too.

The combination on the front of the vault is similar to the key length in bits. If you add another number to the combination, it increases the possible combination count dramatically, not just by one. Therefore, the longer your key bit, the more possible combinations and the more difficult it is to break into the system.

Types of Encryption

Three types of encryption standards are available today. The main differences among them have to do with how they use keys. In general, keys with more bits provide stronger encryption than those with fewer bits. However, no matter how many bits a key contains, it can always be broken with enough time and computing power. The key you choose should be directly proportional to the data to be protected: the more confidential the data, the higher the number of bits in the key.

Symmetric Encryption

In *symmetric encryption*, both parties in the communication must possess a single secret key, as shown in Figure 29.2.

FIGURE 29.2 Symmetric encryption

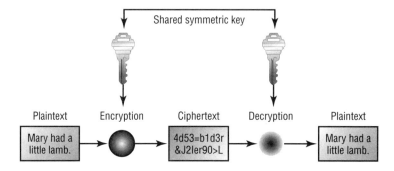

For symmetric encryption to work, however, a secure channel must exist between the two parties so that they can transfer the shared key. You can establish a secure channel quickly, using standards that in themselves provide a basic level of security. Symmetric-key encryption is also easier to implement than other methods, given the default features included in web server software to support the efficient creation and exchange of the single key with a client. Symmetric-key encryption is widely used because it balances speed and security. The following algorithms use symmetric-key encryption:

Data Encryption Standard (DES)   The most widely used algorithm for symmetric encryption, DES uses a 56-bit key. The algorithm has 19 distinct stages, each working on the result produced by its predecessor.

The 56-bit key DES has been cracked several times with the brute-force attack method.

Triple DES   More secure than DES, *Triple DES* uses two 56-bit keys. It may be an appealing successor to DES because it requires no new algorithms or hardware other than that required by conventional DES.

International Data Encryption Algorithm (IDEA)   Like DES, IDEA is a block cipher, using symmetric-key encryption. It uses a 128-bit key to operate on 64-bit plaintext blocks in 8 iterations.

IDEA's key length is 128 bits, more than twice as long as that of DES. Breaking it by brute force takes a very long time. IDEA appears to be significantly more secure than DES.

Blowfish   Developed by the well-known cryptographer Bruce Schneier, Blowfish has a variable key length, with a 448-bit maximum.

Rivest Cipher 1 (RC2)   RC2 is a 64-bit block cipher with a variable key length, and was developed by Ron Rivest, another well-known cryptographer (the R in RSA).

Rivest Cipher 4 (RC4)   This algorithm also uses a variable key length, but does not divide the plaintext into blocks. Instead, it operates on the stream represented by the plaintext.

In September 1994, code to implement RC4 was posted to a network newsgroup. This knowledge was used in late 1995 to mount a successful brute-force attack against a single ciphertext message encrypted with 40-bit RC4.

Rivest Cipher 5 (RC5)   This algorithm is a totally parameterized system. Items that can be changed include the block size, the key length, and the number of rounds. The basic algorithm is a block cipher, but stream versions are also available.

Skipjack   Originated by the National Security Agency (NSA), this algorithm uses an 80-bit key that is encrypted within the message using a process called *enfolding*. Skipjack supports a minimum key space of 225 to the 2000th power, a number comparable to the number of atoms in the universe.

Asymmetric Encryption

Asymmetric encryption, or *public encryption* as it is more commonly called, allows previously unacquainted parties to conduct a transaction. For example, it allows a customer to buy goods or services from an e-commerce merchant with whom they have no previously business relationship. It was first proposed in 1976 by Whitfield Diffie and Martin Hellman. In public-key cryptography, each person or entity (such as a web server) gets two pairs of keys: a private (or secret) key and a public key. The public key is published and widely disseminated, and the private key is kept secret. The need for exchanging secret keys is eliminated because all communication involves only the need to send the public key in a public manner. Asymmetric encryption involves both the public and private keys. No secret key is ever shared or exchanged.

Users can register their public keys on many public-key servers available on the Internet. Alternatively, users can send the public key to correspondents via e-mail.

To understand how public-key cryptosystems work, let's look at two users, Alicia and Bob. Both have a public/private key pair. When Alicia wants to send an encrypted message to Bob, she looks up Bob's public key in a public directory or obtains it by some other means, uses it to encrypt the message, and sends the message to Bob. Bob uses his private key to decrypt the message and read it in plaintext. Anyone who has access to Bob's public key can send him an encrypted message, but no one other than Bob, not even the individual who encrypted the message, can decrypt it. Figure 29.3 demonstrates this process.

FIGURE 29.3 Asymmetric encryption

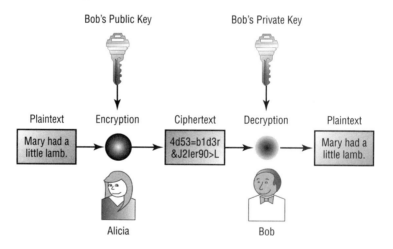

Asymmetric or public-key cryptosystems have the following general properties:

- Applying the algorithm with the encryption key on a plaintext message produces ciphertext. Applying the algorithm with the decryption key on the ciphertext produces the original plaintext message.

- Both public and private keys are easy to compute mathematically, but not easy to guess.

- By publicly revealing their public key, the user does not disclose an easy way to compute the corresponding private key.

The advantages of asymmetric-key encryption are obvious: no secure channel is required to transmit the public key; and the algorithms and encryption strength are secure. The disadvantage is that asymmetric-key encryption algorithms can be slow. A typical software implementation of a symmetric-key algorithm (such as DES) is about 100 times faster than an asymmetric-key algorithm. One algorithm that uses asymmetric key encryption is *RSA*.

RSA is the de facto standard for public-key cryptosystems. It is named after its inventors, Ronald Rivest, Avi Shamir, and Leonard Adleman, who developed it in 1978 while working at the Massachusetts Institute of Technology (MIT). Its security is based on factoring very large prime numbers. The size of the key used in RSA is completely variable, but for normal use, a key size of 512 bits is typical. In applications for which key compromise would have serious consequences or for which the security must remain valid for many years, 1024-bit and 2048-bit keys are used.

One-Way Encryption

The notion of *one-way encryption* is central to cryptography. A one-way encryption is relatively easy to compute in one direction, but difficult to compute in the other direction. Historically, these functions have been used primarily for storing items such as passwords on NT and Unix systems or personal identification numbers on ATM cards.

Message Digests

A *message digest* is a specific application of a one-way function. In many business applications, users are not concerned about eavesdroppers, but worry about the contents of their messages being altered in transit. One way to provide message integrity is through a message digest. This involves applying a digest or hash algorithm to the (long) message to produce a (short) message digest. This message digest is unique to the message from which it was produced; changing even a single bit in the message changes about half the bits in the message digest. The message digest is stored in the message itself and sent to the recipient. When the recipient gets the message, the same hash algorithm is applied. If the message has not been altered in transit, the message digest is the same.

A good hash function has two properties. First, it is difficult to invert; that is, the message cannot be derived from a message digest (hence, the one-way function property). Second, a good hash function is resistant to collisions, which means that the probability of finding two messages with the same hash is extremely low.

The following are two well-known hash functions:

MD5 *MD5* is one in the series (including MD2 and MD4) of message digest algorithms developed by Ronald Rivest. It involves appending a length field to a message and padding it to a multiple of 512-bit blocks. Each of these 512-bit blocks is fed through a 4-round process to result in a 128-bit message digest.

Secure Hash Algorithm (SHA) *SHA* is a function that was developed by the National Institute of Standards and Technology (NIST) and is based heavily on Ronald Rivest's MD series of algorithms. The message is first padded with MD5 and then fed through four rounds, which are more complex than the rounds used in MD5. The resulting message digest is 160 bits in length.

Authentication and Identification

Authentication is the process by which the receiver of a digital message can be confident of the sender's identity. Revisiting our two friends, Bob and Alicia, if Bob receives a message that appears to come from Alicia, he may want to verify that it actually came from Alicia and not from someone else. Bob wants to prove the sender's authenticity. One way to achieve this proof is as follows:

1. Alicia encrypts the message to Bob using Bob's public key (Pub_B).

2. Alicia then encrypts the resulting ciphertext with her secret key (Pri_A) and sends it to Bob.

3. Bob gets the message and first uses Alicia's public key (Pub_A) to decrypt it. Because Alicia's Pri_A was used to encrypt the message, only Alicia's Pub_A can be used to decrypt it. A decryption failure would prove that Alicia did not send the message.

4. Bob uses his secret key, Pri_B, to decrypt the message that was originally encrypted using his public key Pub_B in Step 1.

This process is called the *digital signature* process. Steps 1 through 4 show how you can use public-key systems to encrypt a message with the recipient's public key for confidentiality or to encrypt a message with the sender's secret key for message authentication. Both involve applying the public-key algorithm to the entire message. The public-key algorithms used today are computationally intensive; with large messages, they may be too expensive or too slow for the application. However, other solutions, including SSL acceleration hardware, are available for message encryption, authentication, and confidentiality.

The Payment and Purchase Order Process

To understand transaction security, you need to know all the participants in an electronic transaction, the role of each participant, and how participants link to other participants in the transaction. The participants and processes in the payment and purchase order process are as follows:

Customer   Also called the buyer, account holder, or cardholder, this entity is interested in initiating an electronic transaction to buy a product or service.

Merchant   Also referred to as the Web storefront owner, the merchant sells products or services using the electronic commerce infrastructure.

Processing network   This intermediary facilitates the transfer of financial data between Web storefronts and banks.

Card/check-issuing bank   This is the bank that issued the customer's credit card or checking account.

Merchant's bank   This bank holds the merchant's account.

Trusted third party   The trusted third party is an entity, usually a certifying authority, that verifies the merchant's identity to the customer and vice versa. A third party can correspond to a particular account type (Visa, MasterCard, and so forth) or can act as a clearinghouse for many account types.

Digital Certificates

A *digital certificate* is a standard file format for storing a user's or server's public key and related identification. The certificate provides a standard way to store and exchange public keys. With current technology, a key pair cannot be forged. That is, the private key cannot be extrapolated from a public key and used to impersonate someone using digital certificates.

However, the holder of a certificate still may not be who they claim to be. Anyone can generate a key pair claiming to be anyone. If you want to pose as the CEO of your company and intercept and read their e-mail, you might generate a key pair claiming to be Joe CEO and distribute the public key. How would others know that the key they have really belongs to the right person? Certificate authorities provide this information.

Certificate authorities (CA) are to the digital world what notaries public are to the physical world—trusted third parties. A certificate authority's job is to verify the identity of an individual before endorsing a certificate. This endorsement occurs when the certificate authority cryptographically signs the contents of a certificate file with its private key. Anyone can then verify the signature using the certificate authority's public key. The result is that if you trust the certificate authority, you can trust that the certificate holder is who they claim to be.

Public-key cryptography is based on the idea that an individual generates a key pair, keeps one component secret, and publishes the other component. Other users on the network must be able to retrieve this public key, associate it with an identity of some sort, and use it to communicate securely with, or authenticate messages from, the user claiming that identity.

If a cracker can convince a user that a fraudulent public key is associated with a valid identity, the cracker can easily masquerade as that identity's owner. The simplicity of this attack demonstrates that public-key cryptography works only when users can associate a public key with an identity in a trusted fashion.

One way to form a trusted association between a key and an identity is to enlist the services of a trusted third party. This party is an individual or an organization that all system users can trust, such as a government organization or a banking institution. The trusted third party guarantees that a user is indeed who they claim to be. It does so by constructing a message, referred to as a certificate, that contains a number of fields, the most important of which are a user identity and the associated public key, as shown in Figure 29.4. The trusted third party signs this certificate using its private key and thereby guarantees that the public key is associated with the named user.

FIGURE 29.4 Typical certificate fields

Subject (Identity of user)	Public Key	Vaiidity Period	Issuer (Identity of third party)	Other fields	Signature of third party

The certificate is used when the message recipient wants access to the sender's public key. The recipient can consult an online directory service to obtain this information, or the sender can append their certificate to the message.

Certificate Types

Four types of certificates are currently used:

- The *certificate authority certificate* is used by organizations such as VeriSign to sign other certificates.

- The *server certificate* is used on web servers to identify the web server and the company running it and to allow for encrypted SSL sessions between the server and browsers. Server certificates are also necessary for a server to participate in SET (Secure Electronic Transactions).

- The *personal certificate* allows individuals to be strongly authenticated and to engage in S/MIME, SSL, and SET.

- The *software publisher certificate* is used by software authors to sign and identify their released code so that the author can be identified and the integrity of the code verified.

Certifying Authorities

Trusted third parties that issue certificates are called certifying (or certificate) authorities (CAs). CAs are organized into a hierarchy to make them easier to manage. The root of the hierarchy is a CA that issues certificates to other CAs, which, in turn, certifies the users of the systems. Each system user need only hold the public key of the root CA. When sending a message, users include a copy of all certificates in the path between themselves and the root.

For example, Alicia has been certified by CA1, and Bob has been certified by CA2. The two CAs use a common root CA that has issued certificates for both CA1 and CA2. All system users have the root CA's public key. When Alicia sends a message to Bob, she includes her own certificate, signed by CA1, and CA1's certificate signed by the root CA. When Bob receives this message, he uses the PK_{Root} to verify PK_{CA1}, PK_{CA1} to verify PK_{Alicia}, and PK_{Alicia} to authenticate the message. This action is called traversing the trust chain of certificates; a similar process can be used in the reverse direction.

When the certification hierarchy is extensive, including all certificates with each message can result in a substantial overhead. This can be alleviated if all users keep a copy of the certificates they receive. Instead of including the certificate in the message, the sender includes a message digest of the certificate in its place. The recipient compares this message digest with a digest for each certificate of which they have a copy; if a match cannot be found, the receiver asks the sender to forward a copy.

If a user's private key becomes compromised or if the certificate expires (because the user did not pay the monthly dues), the certificate associated with the public key is revoked. To completely trust the authenticity of the message, users must contact the CA for each certificate in the trust chain to ensure that none have been revoked.

The X.509v3 Standard

All four types of certificates use the X.509v3 standard, which established the format and contents of the physical certificate file. X.509v3 is an ITU (International Telecommunication Union) standard issued as a corollary to the X.500 messaging standard. Table 29.1 summarizes the elements of certificates as set forth in the X.509v3 standard.

You don't need to memorize the X.509v3 standards for the exam.

TABLE 29.1 Certificate Elements in the X.509v3 Standard

Field	Description
Version	The version number of the certificate; currently it can be 1, 2 or 3.
Serial number	A unique serial number for the certificate file.
Signature algorithm ID	Indicates which message digest algorithm was used to sign the certificate file so that it can be verified using the same message digest.

TABLE 29.1 Certificate Elements in the X.509v3 Standard *(continued)*

Field	Description
Issuer name	The company name of the certificate issuer, most often VeriSign for public certificates.
Validity period	The start and end dates for which the certificate file is valid. This range is usually one year from issuance. Once a certificate expires, it has no value.
Subject (user) name	Contains the holder's ID, usually the individual's name or the company's name for a server certificate.
Subject public key information	Contains the holder's actual public key, usually 1024 bits in length.
Issuer-unique identifier (v2 and v3)	Contains a unique number identifying the issuer, most often VeriSign's unique ID.
Subject-unique identifier (v2 and v3)	Similar to the issuer identifier but unique to every certificate holder.
Extensions (v3)	Can contain whatever the generating authority wants. This non-standard field can contain additional information such as date of birth.
Signature	A cryptographic signature of the contents of all previous fields. When certificate files are viewed in Windows, this field is most often referred to as the fingerprint.

Revocation

VeriSign and other CAs maintain revocation lists, which identify certificates that were revoked after their release. Most protocols that support certificates allow real-time verification of the certificates. This process involves sending the certificate information electronically to the CA, which checks the certificate against the revocation list. The advantage of this step is the definite verification of certificate validity. The disadvantage is that the verification takes a few seconds, which can be an unacceptable delay on busy electronic commerce servers. Consider real-time verification carefully on a site-by-site basis.

A certificate can be revoked if the private key is compromised, if the wrong certificate is issued, if the individual or service to whom the certificate was issued is no longer valid, or, in the worst case, if the CA is compromised. All these problems are serious and invalidate the certificate.

 VeriSign is the most widely accepted CA on the Internet and can be found at www.verisign.com.

The Secure Sockets Layer (SSL) Protocol

The first step in setting up your electronic commerce site for online transactions is to make it secure. The SSL protocol, developed by Netscape Communications and submitted to the IETF (Internet Engineering Task Force) as a standard, is a security protocol that provides privacy over the network. It allows client/server applications (such as a database on a server that is accessed by a client) to communicate in a way that prohibits data transmission from being altered or disclosed. SSL provides both encryption and authentication. It operates at the Transport layer to provide a stateful connection between server and client, usually through TCP. The intent is that if the transport is secure, all data flowing over that transport is secure. Thus, if two hosts are communicating using SSL-secured TCP transport, all traffic between them (Web, FTP, or Telnet traffic) is secure. SSL provides channel security (privacy and authentication) through encryption and provides reliability through a message integrity check (secure hash functions).

SSL uses a three-part process:

- Information is encrypted to prevent unauthorized disclosures.

- Information is authenticated to ensure that it is being sent and received by the correct parties.

- Message integrity prevents the information from being altered during interchanges between the source and destination.

Figure 29.5 shows a typical exchange between an SSL server and an SSL client, which involves the following steps:

1. The client sends a request to connect to a secure server.

2. The server sends its pre-signed certificate to the client. This and the first step are collectively known as the *handshake*.

3. The client checks to see if the certificate was issued by a trusted CA. If so, it proceeds to the next step; otherwise, it can cancel the connection or proceed without authentication.

4. The CA validates (and authenticates) the server to the client.

5. The client tells the server which ciphers (types of encryption keys) it supports.

6. The server consults its own cipher list and chooses the strongest cipher it has in common with the client. It informs the client of this cipher.

7. Using that cipher, the client generates a session key (a symmetric encryption key used only for this transaction), encrypts the session key using the server's public key, and sends it to the server.

The client has now authenticated the server, a session key has been exchanged, and the peers can communicate.

FIGURE 29.5 An SSL transaction

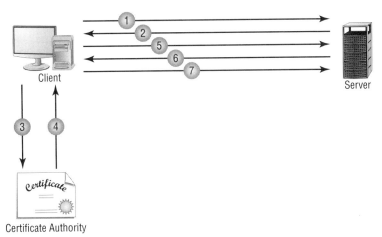

Notice that the server has not authenticated the client in these steps. By default, in SSL, a client *always* authenticates the server, and the server can *optionally* authenticate the client. This arrangement is mainly for the benefit of clients who do not have public keys to participate in SSL.

SSL is a good solution for securing the transport for Internet communications. Once deployed as part of browsers, it is transparent to users and easy to use.

Obtaining Certificates

For certificates to perform at the maximum level of security, a trusted third party must issue them. As mentioned earlier, the largest issuer of digital certificates is VeriSign. In December 1999, VeriSign acquired Thawte of South Africa, which was the second-largest issuer of digital certificates, thus ensuring VeriSign's dominance of the digital certificate market.

Ideally, to achieve maximum credibility, an e-commerce business should install one of these trusted third-party digital certificates on its server. When customers arrive at a site that has a certificate, they are told that they are about to enter a secure connection. This process is done though the exchange of the server's digital certificate.

Each web browser is installed and configured with a list of trusted CAs. This list allows the acceptance of digital certificates issued by one of the trusted CAs. If a business chooses to create its own digital certificate, that certificate is not considered a trusted third-party-issued certificate. Additional warnings remind users that they are entering a secure connection but that the certificate issuer is not a trusted third party. This arrangement might deter customers from continuing the transaction.

If your browser checks a certificate and does not recognize it, you will receive the message shown in Figure 29.6.

FIGURE 29.6 The security alert for a foreign certificate

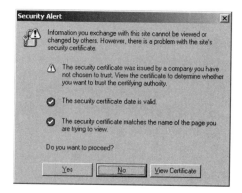

A valid VeriSign certificate can currently cost from $300 to $1,500, depending on the level of deployment. For practice purposes, you can obtain a test certificate through VeriSign that will work with your browser. Because of its popularity, VeriSign is already trusted by your browser.

Installing the Certificates

Once certificate requests have been processed, you must install them on the web server that created the request. This requirement is related to the key pair creation. When a certificate request is generated, two keys are created. One is a public key, which is the request file you saved and submitted. The other is a private key, which is automatically stored in a secure location and is not accessible to anyone other than the administrator of the server that created the request.

After the certificate is created and installed, you must implement it. For the secure SSL connection needed to transmit personal or confidential information, you must establish a connection to HTTPS port 443. This port is the well-known port for SSL. The standard HTTP port is 80, which does not support SSL.

To connect to this port, you simply designate which directories or files are to use the certificate and then link to those files using HTTPS. For example, to link to the page `addform.asp`, you use `https://<computer name>/addform.asp`. Notice that the only difference is the use of `https://` instead of `http://` in the URL.

The Limitations of Certificates

When deciding how to use certificates, remember their limitations as well as their capabilities. Certificates provide critical support for verifying servers, but this support requires that designers and users make certain assumptions that may not always be true:

Identification, not proof Certificates significantly assist in authentication but do not provide absolute proof. The possibility always exists that the files were stolen from a user's hard drive or that the pass phrase was broken. The pass phrase assigned when a certificate is created is actually used as a symmetric key for encrypting the private key on the physical hard drive. Choosing a good password significantly increases the private key's protection level. If the key is physically copied, it is still useless without the corresponding key to decrypt and use it. On the other hand, loss of this key also compromises your own ability to use the certificate, so this information should be well protected.

Too many John Does Recall from examining the certificate contents that only the name is stored. The CA's verification process attempts to ascertain that someone claiming to be John Doe is indeed John Doe. This step does not guarantee that it is the correct John Doe for your system. In this case, the subject-unique identifier could be used, but the identifier must be known in advance for comparison.

Not enough information Certificates are not the solution if you want to establish an electronic commerce site for a specialized user group. For example, your site provides services only for red-haired women and allows entrance only to red-haired women. Nowhere is information such as sex or hair color stored. The extensions field can be used for this type of information, but realistically it cannot be used publicly because the information must be included ahead of time in the certificate and CAs do not currently include that type of information. Modifying a certificate after the fact is not possible because doing so would render the signature invalid, thereby invalidating the entire certificate.

No selective disclosure What if you want to reveal only certain fields of the certificate and not the entire contents? Currently, such limited disclosure is not possible. All contents of the certificate are sent to the other end, and any information contained therein can be seen.

Easy data aggregation Because of unique identifier fields, certificates can easily be used for data aggregation to a previously unattainable degree. Most organizations currently use such information as Social Security numbers or e-mail addresses to track users' usage and spending habits for market data. This method is not particularly reliable because lying about this information is easy. Also, miscommunication exists because errors can occur in data entry. These problems all contribute to unreliable data aggregation. With the advent of digital certificates, the ability to achieve privacy-invading levels of information increases. The unique identifiers, combined with the fact that all information is sent electronically and cryptographically secured, means that misinformation and user errors can also be eliminated.

Certificate lending   Without a certificate, you need supply only your password if a co-worker must retrieve your e-mail for you. If certificates are used for identification, however, this legitimate activity is no longer feasible. Much of the intention of certificates is to allow only the actual user to access the data. Portable technologies such as smart cards and similar physical storage methods are being used to store certificates, but their usage is not standardized or widespread.

The industry is currently addressing all these problems, but you need to be aware of them because they do present barriers to implementation.

Payment and Security Requirements

In any transaction, the buyer and seller must trust each other. Electronic transactions require a higher assurance of trustworthiness because the parties have no physical contact. To complete electronic transactions with trust and to ensure that the payment information is not compromised, you need to ensure the following:

- Confidentiality of payment information
- Integrity of payment information transmitted over public networks
- Verification that the account holder is using a legitimate account
- Verification that a merchant can accept that particular account
- Interoperability between software and network providers

To achieve these goals, a system called Secure Electronic Transactions (SET) was created. It is currently being used widely in Europe, but less so in the United States.

Secure Electronic Transactions (SET)

The 1995 launch by the alliance of MasterCard, Netscape Communications, IBM, and others of the Secure Electronic Payment Protocol (SEPP) occurred a few days after the launch by a Visa and Microsoft consortium of a different network payment specification called Secure Transaction Technology (STT). This timing led to an unfortunate situation in which the two major credit card companies were each backing a different electronic payment protocol. Ultimately, good sense prevailed, and in January 1996 the two protocols were merged into a unified system called *Secure Electronic Transactions (SET)*. Currently, SET is expected to become the de facto payment standard on the Internet. This plan was further strengthened when American Express, another credit-card company with a global presence, endorsed SET.

In a conventional credit-card transaction, a cardholder forwards details to the merchant, who then contacts their acquirer to obtain clearance for the payment. The acquirer can obtain this authorization from the institution that issued the card via a financial network operated by the card association. These private networks have existed for some time and have their own proprietary protocols operating on dedicated links with appropriate security measures. Thus, an infrastructure of links and transaction-processing computer hardware already exists to electronically authorize credit card payments. SET assumes the existence of such a facility and specifies only the subset of dialogs between the customer and the merchant and between the merchant and an entity known as the payment gateway.

Figure 29.7 shows an overview of the SET payment process. The cardholder initiates payment with a designated merchant using SET. The merchant uses SET to have the payment authorized. The entity involved in authorizing the payment is called a payment gateway and can be operated by an acquirer, or it can be a shared facility operated by a group of acquirers. The payment gateway acts as a front end to the existing financial network; through it, the card issuer can be contacted to explicitly authorize every transaction.

FIGURE 29.7 The phases of credit-card payment addressed by SET standards

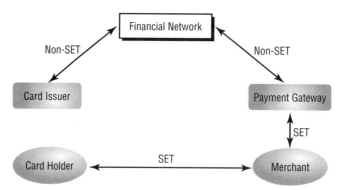

SET is not intended to be a general-purpose payment protocol and is restricted to applications in which parties will take on the role of buyer, merchant, or acquirer. It does not address transfer of funds between individuals, and it relies on the existing credit-card infrastructure for payment. Cardholders will see SET transactions on their credit-card statements along with conventional transactions. The acquirer will see this as an extension of their current relationship with merchant customers.

Each of the parties that participates in a SET payment is required to authenticate themselves at some point in the payment process. SET uses *both* the public-key and symmetric encryption techniques discussed in previous sections. It uses the concept of enveloping for faster encryption and decryption. DES is used as the symmetric algorithm, RSA as the asymmetric algorithm, and MD5 for signing the message. SET is also designed to allow more complex transactions such as returning goods and obtaining a credit or reversing an authorization for an amount when goods cannot be shipped. The current version of SET, 1.0, has been successfully used in the United States, Japan, and Denmark. Figure 29.8 shows a typical transaction using SET that involves the following steps:

1. The cardholder indicates to the merchant that they want to make a credit card purchase.

2. The merchant sends the buyer an invoice, a merchant certificate, and a merchant bank's certificate, which are encrypted with the CA's private key.

3. The cardholder uses the CA's public key to decrypt the information.

4. The cardholder generates order information and sends it to the merchant (encrypted with the merchant's public key).

5. The merchant generates an authorization request and sends it to the merchant bank (encrypted with the bank's public key).

6. The merchant's bank sends a request for payment authorization through the acquirer (or through traditional bank card channels).

7. The acquirer sends a settlement response to the merchant's bank after receiving a response from the cardholder's bank.

8. After the cardholder's bank authorizes payment, the merchant's bank sends a response to the merchant (encrypted using merchant's public key). This response includes a transaction identifier. The transaction is complete.

FIGURE 29.8 A SET transaction

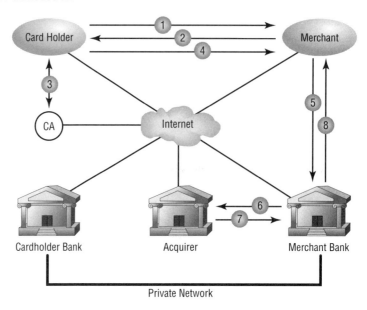

The Confidentiality of Payment Information

The issue here is securing the integrity of the payment information as it travels from the buyer to the seller. This transmission might contain credit card and other account numbers. Without adequate security measures, payment information can be picked up by crackers at routers, communication lines, or host levels.

The technology to achieve the needed security is encryption and has existed for decades. I discussed the two types of encryption methods, symmetric-key cryptography and asymmetric-key cryptography, earlier in this chapter. To ensure maximum security, asymmetric cryptography is used. Symmetric-key cryptography is usually avoided because it requires merchants to administer and distribute secret keys to all their customers over a secure channel. Creating a key pair using asymmetric cryptography and publishing the public key is easier. This method also allows customers to submit secure payment information by simply downloading and using the merchant's public key.

The Integrity of Payment Information

The problem here is to ensure that the information from the customer to the merchant arrives without modification. Such modification can occur, for example, if a network eavesdropper captures packets going from a valid customer to a merchant and replaces the customer's address with their own, thus obtaining goods that were paid for by the unsuspecting customer.

To eliminate this potential for error or fraud, hashing is used, along with digital signatures. The main problem with hash algorithms is that they are public information; therefore, anyone can alter the data and recalculate a new, "correct" hash value. To prevent this problem, the hash value is encrypted using the sender's private key, which the receiver uses to decrypt the hash value. This encryption of the hash value is called a digital signature.

Merchant Authentication

So far, this discussion has assumed that fraud occurs only on the customer's end of the transaction. However, an unscrupulous individual can pose as a merchant to gather account information for future criminal use. To counter this threat, the third-party process described earlier is used. For a merchant to be valid, their public key must be issued by a third party under its own digital signature. Customers subsequently decrypt the merchant's public key using the third party's public key. The same requirements identified earlier must be met for this process to work.

The Interoperability of Hardware and Software

For any customer to do business with any merchant, security and process standards must support all hardware and software platforms. Interoperability is achieved by ensuring that both merchants and customers use a particular set of publicly announced algorithms and processes in electronic commerce. Standards such as DES and SET are important for establishing a process and a security infrastructure.

Summary

The three types of encryption are symmetric, asymmetric, and one-way. Symmetric encryption uses a single key, and asymmetric encryption uses a public and a private key to enhance security. Two of the more popular forms of symmetric encryption are DES and TripleDES. RSA is the de facto standard for asymmetric encryption. A one-way function is relatively easy to compute in one direction, but difficult to compute in the other direction. Historically, these functions have been primarily used to store items such as passwords on NT and Unix systems or personal identification numbers on ATM cards.

Additional security concerns for transactions go beyond simple eavesdropping and reach into the realm of message altering. You can use message digests (or hash algorithms) such as MD5 or SHA to ensure the integrity of the message.

Digital certificates provide a standard file format for storing a user's or a server's public key and related identification. To further ensure that the certificate is secure, third parties called certificate authorities (CAs) issue digital certificates and revoke them when necessary.

Secure Socket Layers (SSL) is a protocol that provides privacy over the network. It allows client/server applications to communicate in a way that prohibits data transmission from being altered or disclosed. SSL provides both encryption and authentication.

SET is expected to become the de facto standard of payment method on the Internet between the merchants, the buyers, and the credit-card companies. When SET is used, the merchant itself never has to know the credit-card numbers being sent from the buyer, which provide a benefit for e-commerce that doesn't exist in traditional transactions.

Exam Essentials

Know the symmetric, asymmetric, and one-way encryption schemes. Symmetric encryption is sometimes called secret-key, shared-key, private-key, or session-key encryption. In symmetric encryption, both parties must possess a single secret key, but a secure channel must exist between the two parties so that they can transfer the shared key. DES is the most widely used algorithm for symmetric encryption. It uses a 56-bit key. Triple DES (the next in line as the standard) is more secure than DES because it uses two 56-bit keys.

Asymmetric encryption (sometimes called public-key encryption) involves each person or entity (such as a web server) using two pairs of keys: a private (or secret) key and a public key. The public key is published and widely disseminated, and the private key is kept secret. The need for exchanging secret keys is eliminated because all communication involves only the need to send the public key in a public manner. Asymmetric encryption involves both the public key and the private key. No secret key is ever shared or exchanged. RSA is the primary standard for public key cryptography.

One-way cryptography is relatively easy to compute in one direction, but difficult to compute in the other direction. Historically, these functions have been primarily used to store items such as passwords on NT and Unix systems or personal identification numbers on ATM cards.

Understand message digests, hashing, and digital signatures.   A message digest is a specific application of a one-way function. A message digest applies a digest or hash algorithm (in a hashing process) to the (long) message to produce a (short) message digest. This message digest is unique to the message from which it was produced; changing even a single bit in the message changes about half the bits in the message digest. The message digest is stored in the message itself and sent to the recipient. When the recipient gets the message, the same hash algorithm is applied. If the message has not been altered in transit, the message digest is the same. A good hash function has two properties: (1) it is difficult to invert, (2) it is resistant to collisions. MD5 and SHA are two of the more well-known hash algorithms.

A digital signature allows the receiver of a message to ensure that the message came from the person it appears to have come from. This method involves using public-key systems that encrypt a message with the recipient's public key for confidentiality or that encrypt a message with the sender's secret key for message authentication.

Know the four types of digital certificates.   A certificate authority certificate is used by organizations such as VeriSign to sign other certificates. A server certificate is used on web servers to identify the web server and the company running it and to allow for encrypted SSL sessions between the server and browsers. Server certificates are also necessary for a server to participate in SET. A personal certificate allows individuals to be strongly authenticated and to engage in S/MIME, SSL, and SET. A software publisher certificate is used by software authors to sign and identify their released code so that the author can be identified and the integrity of the code verified.

Understand Secure Sockets Layer (SSL).   SSL uses a three-part process. First, information is encrypted to prevent unauthorized disclosures. Second, the information is authenticated to ensure that it is being sent and received by the correct parties. Third, SSL provides message integrity to prevent the information from being altered during interchanges between the source and the destination. SSL involves seven steps that you should know for the exam.

Know how to implement Secure Electronic Transactions (SET).   In the SET payment process, the cardholder initiates payment with a designated merchant. The merchant uses SET to have the payment authorized. The entity involved in authorizing the payment is called a payment gateway and can be operated by an acquirer, or it can be a shared facility operated by a group of acquirers. The payment gateway acts as a front end to the existing financial network; through it, the card issuer can be contacted to explicitly authorize every transaction.

SET uses *both* the public-key and symmetric encryption techniques. It uses the concept of enveloping for faster encryption and decryption. DES is used as the symmetric algorithm, RSA as the asymmetric algorithm, and MD5 for signing the message. SET is also designed to allow more complex transactions such as returning goods and obtaining a credit or reversing an authorization for an amount when goods cannot be shipped.

Key Terms

Before you take the exam, be certain you are familiar with the following terms:

access control	cryptography
asymmetric encryption	Data Encryption Standard (DES)
certificate authority (CA)	digital certificate
certificate authority certificate	digital signature
cipher	encryption
ciphertext	handshake

MD5

message digest

non-repudiation

one-way encryption

packet-switched network

personal certificate

public encryption

RSA encryption

Secure Electronic Transactions (SET)

Secure Hash Algorithm (SHA)

server certificate

software publisher certificate

symmetric encryption

Triple DES

Review Questions

1. Which of the following contributes the least to encryption strength?

    A. Algorithm strength

    B. The secrecy of the key

    C. The certificate authority

    D. The length of the key

2. What algorithm is the most widely used for symmetric encryption?

    A. MD5

    B. DES

    C. TripleDES

    D. SHA

3. What is asymmetric encryption?

    A. A type of encryption that requires both participants to have a single secret key

    B. A type of encryption that requires each participant to have a public key and a private key

    C. A type of encryption that is easy to compute in one direction but difficult to compute in the other direction

    D. A message digest involving a digest or a hash algorithm that produces a short unique message

4. In an SSL connection, the client contacts the server and asks for authentication. What is this process known as?

    A. The payment gateway

    B. Cipher

    C. SET

    D. A handshake

5. What is one-way encryption?

   A. A type of encryption that requires both participants to have a single secret key

   B. A type of encryption that requires each participant to have a public key and a private key

   C. A type of encryption that is easy to compute in one direction but difficult to compute in the other direction

   D. A message digest involving a digest or hash algorithm that produces a short unique message

6. When you encrypt a message, it is changed from cleartext to what?

   A. Mush

   B. A digest

   C. Hashing

   D. Ciphertext

7. What is one of the advantages of asymmetric encryption over symmetric encryption?

   A. A secure connection is not needed.

   B. It's much faster than symmetric encryption.

   C. A single key is used, rather than a public and a private key.

   D. Only one-way encryption is necessary.

8. Bob wants to send Tim an e-mail message and provide Tim with proof that it is from him. What can Bob use, thanks to public key processes?

   A. SSL

   B. SET

   C. Digital certificate

   D. Digital signature

9. Which one of the following methods does SET utilize?

   A. Symmetric encryption

   B. Enfolded encryption

   C. One-way encryption

   D. Digital signatures

10. Which one of the following is an encryption type?

    A. SHA

    B. RSA

    C. RC5

    D. MD5

11. The action taken by a company to prevent hacking messages in transit is called what?

    A. Security

    B. Cryptographic method

    C. SSL

    D. No Electronic Theft Act

12. Which security protocol provides channel security through encryption, provides reliability through a message integrity check; and uses a three-part process including seven steps?

    A. SET

    B. S/MIME

    C. Digital signature

    D. SSL

13. What type of encryption does not require both parties involved in an interchange to share an individual key?

A. Asymmetric encryption

B. Symmetric encryption

C. Strong encryption

D. One-way encryption

14. Roger is concerned about messages being altered in transit. He has considered a few types of encryption involving public and private keys but is unfamiliar with them. Roger wants to look into the use of a message digest. Which of the following is a one-way function that will give Roger peace of mind?

    A. Asymmetric

    B. Symmetric

    C. Secure Hash Algorithm (SHA)

    D. International Data Encryption Algorithm (IDEA)

15. From the viewpoint of Internet consumers, what is considered the most important aspect of e-commerce transactions?

    A. Security

    B. Screen flow

    C. Transaction time

    D. Price

16. Giro is ordering a painting online. He types in his name and other pertinent information along with his credit-card number. To prevent an unscrupulous person from posing as a merchant, the e-commerce site Giro is purchasing this painting from is set up so that in order for a merchant to be valid, its public key must be issued by a third party under its own digital signature. What type of standard has this site implemented?

    A. SSL

    B. Payment gateway

    C. SET

    D. VPN

17. S/MIME is a form of security used mainly with e-mail. S/MIME encrypts messages by using what method?

    A. Tunneling

    B. SSL

    C. Enveloping

    D. Cryptography

18. George is responsible for choosing an encryption type for his employer's e-commerce site. He is reviewing a technology in which the company's e-commerce server would share a common key with each customer. What type of encryption method is this?

    A. Asymmetric

    B. Public key

    C. One-way

    D. Symmetric

19. Which of the following is true concerning Secure Sockets Layer (SSL)?

    A. The client always authenticates the server.

    B. SSL is required for e-commerce.

    C. SSL is the strongest type of encryption.

    D. The client must have public keys to communicate with the server.

20. For what and by whom is a packet sniffer most commonly used?

    A. Authorities scanning for illegal activity online

    B. Administrators looking for harmful viruses in packets being sent through the network

    C. Hackers looking to intercept credit card information

    D. Search engines looking for new websites to index

Answers to Review Questions

1. C. Encryption strength is based on is the algorithm strength, the secrecy of the key, and the length of the key. The certificate authority acts as a registrant and issuer for the certificate, but must use a standard method to generate the certificate.

2. B. Data Encryption Standard (DES), which uses a 56-bit key, is the most widely used symmetric encryption method. TripleDES is fast becoming the new standard, however, because of its additional strength. MD5 and SHA are popular hash functions.

3. B. Asymmetric encryption requires each participant to have a public key and a private key. The other options define other types of encryption and hashing.

4. D. The first couple of steps in an SSL transaction involve the "handshake," which is needed for an SSL transaction to continue.

5. C. A one-way function is relatively easy to compute in one direction, but difficult to compute in the other direction. Historically, these functions have been primarily used to store items such as passwords on NT and Unix systems or personal identification numbers on ATM cards.

6. D. When a message is encrypted, regardless of the method used, it becomes known as ciphertext. You can decrypt the message using legitimate or illegitimate methods, but the decryption is definitely not cleartext.

7. A. Secure connections are not needed because a public and a private key are used. One of the negative aspects of asymmetric encryption is that it is slower (not faster) than symmetric. It is a two-way process, not a one-way process.

8. D. Digital signatures allow for messages to be encrypted using public and private keys to ensure that a message received is from the supposed sender.

9. A. SET uses *both* the public-key (asymmetric) and symmetric encryption techniques. It uses the concept of enveloping for faster encryption and decryption. DES is used as the symmetric algorithm, RSA as the asymmetric algorithm, and MD5 for signing the message. Skipjack uses enfolding to embed the encryption key directly within the message.

10. B.   RSA is the de facto standard for asymmetric encryption, and DES is the current standard for symmetric encryption. SHA and MD5 are hash algorithms.

11. B.   Cryptography is the science of encrypting and decrypting plaintext messages. It protects against a variety of attacks on the communications between two parties. Methods such as S/MIME, SSL, and SET are commonly used. Options C and D are incorrect because SSL is a form of cryptography, and the No Electronic Theft Act (NET) is an amendment to U.S. copyright law to include anything of value as monetary gain.

12. D.   Secure Sockets Layer (SSL) is a protocol that provides privacy over the network. SSL is a good solution for securing the transport for Internet communications. Once deployed as part of browsers, it is transparent to users and easy to use. Options A, B, and C are incorrect. Secure Electronic Transactions (SET) is expected to become the main payment standard for the Internet. S/MIME is mainly used as security for e-mail message. And a digital signature is most commonly used to authenticate users' messages.

13. A.   Asymmetric encryption, or public encryption, allows previously unacquainted parties to conduct a transaction. This is a benefit over symmetric encryption, which requires two parties to share a key prior to any communication. Another benefit to asymmetric encryption is that the connection doesn't have to be secured, as in symmetric.

14. C.   SHA is a one-way function that doesn't require either of the parties involved to have an encryption key, although for added security, keys can be used along with SHA. SHA ensures that a message was not altered en route by using an algorithm or digest, which is applied to the message to create a short code known as the message digest. If the message is changed before reaching the intended recipient, the message digest is noticeably changed. When the message is received, the same algorithm is applied, and the resulting message digest is compared to the first. If the message hasn't been distorted, both are identical.

15. A.   Most Internet users view security (or privacy) as the most important concern when participating in e-commerce. These users are usually sending credit card numbers or other sensitive information across the Internet and want to be sure of their privacy.

16. C. The site is using Secure Electronic Transactions (SET), which is a protocol that specifies the subset of dialogs between the customer and the merchant and between the merchant and the payment gateway.

17. C. S/MIME uses enveloping to encrypt e-mail messages, because encrypting large messages with a public key is computationally expensive. The bulk message is composed using a session key and a symmetric cipher, and public-key encryption is used to transfer the session key securely to the intended recipient. Tunneling does not have to do with e-mail security, and Secure Socket Layer (SSL) is a security protocol. Cryptography is the method and implementation of security to prevent attacks, which is in this case S/MIME.

18. D. George is looking into symmetric encryption. With symmetric encryption, both parties share single copies of the encryption key and exchange this key back and forth through a secure channel. One limitation of symmetric encryption is that if this secure channel is available, there might not be a need for a key. Asymmetric encryption, or public encryption, allows previously unacquainted parties to conduct a transaction.

19. A. When SSL is used, the client computer always authenticates the server. First, the client makes a request to establish a connection with a secure server, and then the server sends its pre-signed certificate from a CA for verification by the client. After the certificate is recognized, the client returns a list of keys it supports, and the server chooses the strongest one that it supports. In this way, clients that don't have public keys can communicate.

20. C. Hackers commonly use packet sniffers to intercept sensitive information, such as credit-card numbers. After these numbers are stolen, they can be used for illegitimate purchases or sold to others. Network administrators can also use packet sniffers for security or patrolling purposes, but this isn't the most common use.

Chapter 30

Website Management and Performance Testing

THE CIW EXAM OBJECTIVE GROUP COVERED IN THIS CHAPTER:

✓ Analyze and improve the performance of an e-commerce site using a transactional system model.

In choosing your transactional system to support your e-commerce site, you should already be aware of the caveats involved. You learned the advantages and disadvantages of the three methods of payments within a transactional system in Chapter 28, "Using and Configuring Payment Gateways," and in Chapter 29, "Transaction Security," you learned the security issues and solutions involved with e-commerce. You've spent a good portion of time learning too how to spruce up your site and design one that is appealing to the eyes and holds to a comfortable screen flow.

However, even the most attractive, most secure, and best-planned electronic commerce website will not run itself. Once the site is operational (and truly running as a transactional system with monetary exchanges taking place), its performance must be monitored so that you can continue to fine-tune and modify it to deliver the best possible results. In this chapter, we'll examine some of the computer components of a site and learn how they affect its performance. Next, we'll review different tools you can use to determine some characteristics of the site. Once the performance data is collected, you can evaluate it and determine how to make the necessary modifications.

Site Management

The party responsible for the site content and integrity (usually the information technology department or a person with the title of *webmaster*) has three primary tasks. The first is maintaining the site and its contents, including updating the web pages, maintaining the database, and checking for broken links. If potential customers are browsing your site and encountering outdated information and broken links, they may be concerned about your company's security and professionalism. Proper site maintenance is important to maintaining a professional image.

The second task is maintaining the security of the site. This task is especially critical. Simply planning a secure site is not enough. The security must be continually evaluated and tested. As new security threats are discovered, a site must be updated to resist them. E-commerce sites are very attractive targets to hackers/crackers due to the potential financial gain and notoriety that may be obtained from a successful break-in.

The third primary task is monitoring the performance of the site. If customers close their browsers or move elsewhere because they are frustrated waiting for the web server to respond, a sales opportunity has been lost. The first part of this book covered site design, and Chapter 29 covered security issues; this chapter will focus on evaluating, measuring, and optimizing site performance.

You must first understand what the critical performance areas are, how to measure performance in those areas, and what options you have to increase performance. The overriding performance criterion is to control the responsiveness of the website. This responsiveness is measured by how long it takes users to see results in their browsers.

Basics of Website Performance

To understand the factors affecting website performance, you should know about queues and bottlenecks. A *queue* is a sequence of requests for services from one or more servers. The requests arrive one at a time and are processed after the requests that arrived earlier are processed. A queue grows as more service requests arrive and shrinks as the requests are processed. The rate at which requests arrive and the time the server needs to handle each request varies with each request and cannot be predicted; however, they can be monitored, which will indicate a common pattern of performance. If the server handles requests at least as fast as new ones arrive, the queue will remain relatively small. However, if requests arrive faster than the server can process them, the queue will grow.

In a web server, the primary input queue is where all incoming HTTP requests are processed. Factors affecting how well the primary queue is processed include how well the network device driver manages its queue of received packets. This factor, in turn, is affected by how well the operating system manages its queue of processes waiting for CPU time. The performance of these queues is directly affected by the amount of available memory and disk resources and by how well the queues for these resources are managed.

When the requests on these resources are small, or widely spaced, the resources needed to handle the request are available on demand. As the number of requests increases, waiting will begin for various resources. If the system is working efficiently, the waiting periods will be short and of relatively uniform duration. Beyond this point, as the rate of incoming requests exceeds the rate at which the system can service them, queuing will begin. If the requests continue to enter the queue until the queue has no more space, a *bottleneck* will result. At this point, other parts of the system will run more slowly to block new requests.

Running a successful web server involves working effectively with reports to manage web server performance. By measuring performance, you can immediately tune your server. By analyzing the reports generated by the server, you can adjust the content it provides. Attending to server performance and reports will result in a more responsive, content-relative service for your visitors.

Logging Information

By checking system and service logs, you can determine a system's ability to meet demands. Logs can also inform you about security issues.

Almost all services provide logging. You can use your logs for a number of purposes:

Server efficiency   Log files from the Windows 2000 Event Viewer or from the Unix/Linux /var/log/ messages file can inform you of failed services or services that are experiencing problems.

Usage rate   Logs can help you determine the amount of work a server is handling.

Revenue generation   Your business may be able to sell information derived from your logs for statistical analysis.

Security   Logs can help you determine possible security problems. For example, a failed logon attempt may be the sign of an intruder trying to break into your system.

Setting Priorities

For a system administrator, checking logs will be an essential task. Because your resources are limited, you will have to set priorities according to the following criteria (your security policy should determine how often you check server logs):

Mission-critical information   Determine the most important servers and services for your particular business, such as e-mail and e-commerce web service, and check those logs daily.

Service type   Check web, e-mail, and database server logs often because these servers handle large loads of traffic. Also, hackers frequently target these services.

Server location   Many organizations place their web servers outside the firewall. A *firewall* is a security barrier that controls the flow of information between the Internet and private networks. It prevents outsiders from accessing an enterprise's internal network, which accesses the Internet indirectly through a proxy server. If a server resides outside your company's firewall, consider viewing its logs for failed logons and other problems more frequently than you view logs for servers behind the firewall.

Recent installations   After you upgrade a system, check for problems that occur later.

Evaluating Log Files

As you check log files, evaluate the following:

Peak usage rates   Evaluating peak rates can help you determine how to adjust system performance and, if necessary, obtain a more powerful server.

Error messages   Errors reported by the server or one of its services may be evidence of an overburdened server, a faulty executable file, or an unstable operating system.

Failed logon attempts   Although failed logon attempts can signal an attempted break-in, they can also be evidence that users need to be trained to be more careful when logging in; for example, they should be more careful about remembering their passwords and about pressing the correct keys.

Logging and System Performance

Logging has a direct effect on system performance. The more events you log, the harder your system will have to work. You should log only selected events for your server.

One key point to keep in mind is that if you have logging enabled on your server and then want to check the performance levels of the processor, memory, and disk usage, you will have a contradiction in results. The system may appear to be taxed, when in reality, the logging is causing the added strain. Now, if logging is taking place during a specified time period, this is not a problem. If you plan to keep logging on for the server and the server is taxed, you should consider strengthening your resources for the server, whether that involves a faster processor, more memory, or other upgrades.

Commercial Log File Analysis Software

There are a number of commercial web server log file analysis software packages available:

- AccessWatch (www.accesswatch.com)
- WebReporter (www.imagossoftware.com)
- Accrue Insight (www.accrue.com)
- WebTrends (www.webtrends.com)

HTTP Server Log Files

Probably the most important source of information about the stream of HTTP requests and responses is the server log files. They record the time of each HTTP transaction along with the number of bytes transferred. Analysis of these files provides a complete picture of each transaction handled by the server.

One major advantage of HTTP server logs is that you can analyze them offline. More intrusive performance analysis tools complicate the performance question because the tools themselves use system resources. This problem will not occur if the logs are analyzed on a computer other than the server.

Because so many different types of web servers exist, it is difficult to write a log analysis program tailored to every server's log file. Instead, almost all servers produce access log files in a standardized form called National Center for Supercomputing Applications (NCSA) Common Log File (CLF) format. The access log, the error log, the referrer log, and the agent log are consistently created through log analysis and warrant some consideration.

Access Log

The access log contains information about URL fetches. Included in this log file is the following:

- The IP address of the client accessing the server
- The time of day the connection occurred
- The name of the URL (e.g., `/index.html`)
- The HTTP request

Error Log

The error log file is used to record any errors that occur, including these:

- Server startup and shutdown
- Malformed URLs
- Erroneous CGI scripts

Referrer Log

Whenever you browse from Page A to Page B by clicking a hyperlink, Page A is said to "refer" Page B. An HTML page can also refer images, other HTML documents, and any other file the page needs to render completely. A referrer log can show the number of files one page requires to render in a browser.

Agent Log

The agent log file records the version of any user agent (client software used to browse a website). All agents send a special header that identifies them. If you configure the agent log properly, the web server can record this information. The log file in Figure 30.1 shows that this particular website was visited by end users using Netscape Navigator 4.7 and Microsoft Internet Explorer 5, respectively. It is an example of a log that was generated by IIS.

FIGURE 30.1   An IIS log file opened in WordPad

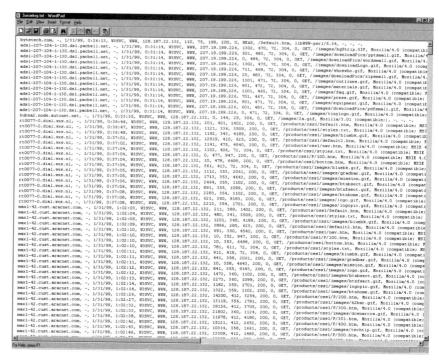

When viewing a file of this type, you could scroll through and (with time) find the peak usage times for the server, the number of server errors, and even the most often used browser. This would help you monitor performance. But as you can see by looking at Figure 30.1, it would take a long time. Third-party software analysis products could prove to be more helpful. Figure 30.2 shows an example of a WebTrends report.

You can see how much easier it is to view and find the data in this type of report. You can easily navigate to examine the various pieces of information, including the pages visited the most.

FIGURE 30.2 WebTrends default report

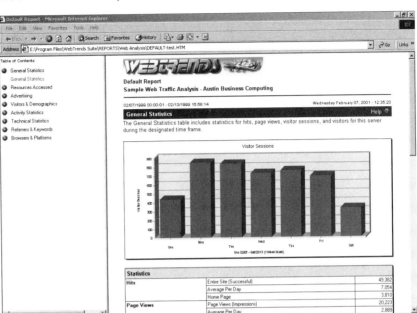

Performance Testing

Selecting the appropriate web server software for your company will have significant effects on your site's performance. The web server may not have been chosen with performance in mind but instead for other reasons, such as employees with expertise in particular products, existing use of a particular platform in a company environment, or specific capabilities offered by certain server software.

The only conclusive way to measure performance is to actually test the working site. Before selecting a particular server, test several packages from different manufacturers. Many programs will enable you to evaluate a site's performance by simulating heavy use.

To get the most accurate benchmarks for a web server, use several different types of testing software. Often, running two different benchmarking utilities will yield different results for each type of server software. The more utilities that can be used to test the performance of the software, the more accurate the overall results will be.

Notice the example provided in Figure 30.3. Five tests are completed using Webserver Stress Tool. The start time and frequency are displayed horizontally in milliseconds. The time each response took is displayed vertically in milliseconds. What you are looking for are trends in the time required for responses. Notice that the response time increased on the third and fourth tests but decreased on the fifth test. (Real-world results may vary). Ideally, the server should continue to handle the load as requests increase.

FIGURE 30.3 Webserver Stress Tool performance test

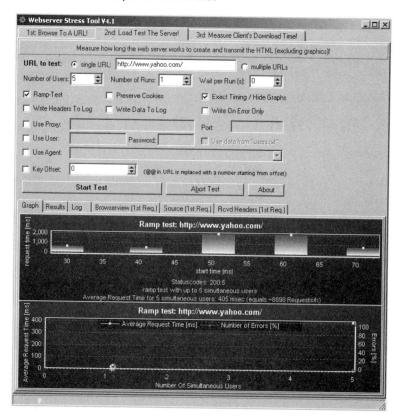

A test with five users cannot be considered a valid test, but at some point, the server will be pushed to its capacity and server errors will result. Notice too in the figure that there are additional tabs above the graphs that will provide more information about the performance tests.

System Performance Monitoring

Performance Monitor is included with Windows 2000 and is the primary tool for determining server bottlenecks and problems on that system. This tool monitors objects that belong to the server, including Server Work Queues, Active Server Pages, Processor, TCP, Server, Logical Disk, Web Service, and FTP Service. Each object has subelements that can be tracked as well. You track subelements by adding specific object counters. For example, the Web Service object uses the CGI Requests/sec counter, which allows you to determine how many times your server processes a particular CGI script. You add counters to Performance Monitor's graphical interface. Once added, the counter tracks the usage of the corresponding object.

You can also use simple TCP/IP utilities such as Netstat to determine the number of connections that exist on a system. Although Netstat only informs you about the time and number of connections, it can provide a quick glimpse into the factors affecting server performance at a given moment.

In Exercise 30.1, you'll use Windows 2000 Performance Monitor.

EXERCISE 30.1

Using Windows 2000 Performance Monitor

This exercise will work only on systems running Windows 2000 (or NT 4). To use Performance Monitor, follow these steps:

1. Log on as administrator.

2. From the Start menu, select Programs ➤ Administrative Tools ➤ Performance. Select System Monitor.

3. Right-click in the graph area, and choose Add Counters.

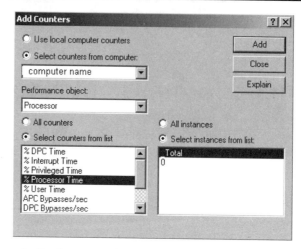

4. From the Performance Object drop-down menu, select Processor.

5. From the counters list, select interrupts/sec and % Processor Time.

6. Click Add.

7. From the Performance Object drop-down menu, select Process.

8. Select % Processor Time from the counters list.

9. Click Add.

10. From the Performance Object drop-down menu, select System.

11. Select Processor Queue Length from the counters list.

12. Click Add.

13. Click Close.

The monitor displays graphs for each performance object. (Your graph will vary from the one shown here.)

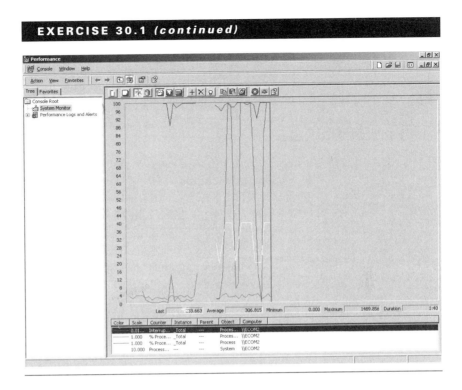

You may be wondering how monitoring your system will be helpful to your web server. By running Performance Monitor, you will be able to clearly see the affect people connecting to your server is having on your system's resources. This is but one way that performance tools can be helpful in determining the needs of your site and server.

Analyzing Server Performance

When you analyze the performance of a particular service, you must also analyze the operating system on which the service runs. For a particular service to function properly, the underlying operating system must operate at peak efficiency.

You can use several methods and tools to measure server performance. Here are the three main resources for measuring the stream of server requests and responses:

- Server and service log files

- Protocol analyzers (i.e., packet sniffers)

- System performance tools

You have already learned about reviewing logs. Following is a short discussion of the two additional methods for analyzing server performance.

Packet Sniffers

Packet sniffers capture packets as they cross the network. Examples of packet sniffers include tcpdump (for all flavors of Unix), Network Monitor (Windows NT/2000), and Sniffer Basic by Network Associates. A packet sniffer operates by placing a host's NIC into *promiscuous mode*; in promiscuous mode, the NIC can capture packets from the network.

You can capture packets for a particular host or port. For a web server, for example, you can monitor port 80 to collect statistics on failed and successful connections. You should note that packet sniffers can produce sizable amounts of data that might place a load on the packet-capturing host.

Interpreting Data

Interpreting the data is a subjective task because all sources provide reports in different formats and values. In general, in graphical reports, graphs with small peaks or changes indicate better performance because fewer resources are being used to process the request. A queue of more than two processes for a sustained period of time indicates that your CPU may need an upgrade.

It is important to understand that the system you may be using at home is, most likely, far less powerful than a standard web server. Primarily, you would need more RAM, more powerful input/output devices, and greater processor speed than what you are using. Tests conducted on a high-performance system would return acceptable values.

Correcting Bottlenecks

Three methods of correcting bottlenecks exist:

- Speed up the component (or components) causing the bottleneck by replacing it with an upgraded version.

- Replicate the component (or components) causing the bottleneck by distributing the demand for a service across multiple servers. For example, you may want to use a cluster server, which is a specialized server used to distribute processor load across several different systems.

- Increase the capacity of the queues in the system to tolerate more requests before turning away new ones.

A system can tolerate only one bottleneck at a time, produced by its slowest component. Speeding up one component may reveal another that is not as slow but still slower than it should be.

Hardware Concerns

Improving your hardware will always improve Internet server performance. Here are ways you can improve performance:

- Increase RAM.

- Improve the quality of the NIC.

- Upgrade the TCP/IP stack.

- Upgrade to a faster CPU.

- Upgrade to a motherboard with a faster system bus.

Web Server Memory

The most important factor when considering web servers is the amount of RAM. Once a server runs out of dedicated RAM, it can obtain it through other sources, such as by caching the hard drive, for example. Caching the hard drive is often referred to as *swapping*.

Swapping diminishes the server's capability to serve requests. A slow web server can cause many problems; primarily, a slow response time can cause users to repeatedly attempt to reload pages. These attempts place further demands on the server, causing a chain reaction that could lead to further slowing and even system overload.

Web Applications and Session State

You can adjust the amount of time a web application will keep a connection alive. Microsoft IIS refers to this as "enabling session state." If you want to adjust this setting, you can do so from the Home Directory tab in the Properties dialog box for your web server. Once you have defined a web application, click the Configure button and select the App Options tab. You can enable or disable session state there. Other products, at various levels of sophistication, are available:

- Webload (www.radview.com)

- Paessler Webserver Stress Tool (www.paessler.com)

- NetPoint (www.mindcraft.com)

Summary

Site maintenance is an integral part of any e-commerce structure. Hardware degradation or changing Web conditions affect performance over time. For example, a link from your site that used to work just fine may no longer work, or perhaps a new security hole is found to affect websites and you need to prevent it from damaging yours.

Your site's performance can be evaluated through a number of different utilities. You initially use these tools (like Microsoft's Performance Monitor) on your web server in its early, "healthy" state. This gives you a baseline that you can then compare your performance issues against. Additional software can be used to place stresses on your site to create a simulation of server load.

Checking system and service logs allows you to determine a system's ability to meet demands. Logs can also inform you about security issues, which are ever present as you maintain and monitor your site. Eventually, you make decisions as webmaster (the administrator of the website) that will improve hardware, software, configuration, and security for your web server's continued benefit.

Exam Essentials

Know the issues and tools used to run your e-commerce website.
When monitoring your site's performance, you must first understand
what the critical performance areas are, how their performance is
measured, and what options you have to increase performance in those
areas. Your primary goal is to control the responsiveness of the website.
Some of the tools at your disposal include built-in logs for your system
and for specific services, logging evaluation software that you can evaluate and purchase, built-in performance monitoring tools, packet sniffers,
network analyzers, and system analyzers.

Identify the need for server monitoring and optimization. To understand the factors affecting website performance, you should know about
queues and bottlenecks. A queue is a sequence of requests for services
from one or more servers. If the requests continue to enter the queue until
the queue has no more space, a bottleneck will result. Knowing the problem areas can help you to work against them and optimize performance
for your web server.

Identify site strengths and weaknesses. Considering the various tools
available, you want to be able to search out problems or potential problems
on both your network and your individual system. Look for hardware
bottlenecks (CPU weakness, hard disk speed, or memory issues) on the
web server that might slow your system down. Consider areas of your network that might hinder the e-commerce process from flowing smoothly
for users trying to access the site you've created.

Key Terms

Before you take the exam, be certain you are familiar with the following terms:

bottleneck	queue
firewall	swapping
packet sniffers	webmaster
Performance Monitor	

Review Questions

1. What is a queue and bottleneck?

   A. A queue is an area in which requests are stored, and a bottleneck occurs when all pending requests are handled.

   B. A queue and bottleneck provide website security.

   C. A queue is a sequence of requests for services, and a bottleneck occurs when the queue grows so large the requests cannot be handled in a timely manner.

   D. A queue and bottleneck are features of the e-commerce fulfillment process.

2. What is a log measuring when it lists the amount of work being handled by a server?

   A. Security

   B. Usage rate

   C. Server efficiency

   D. Revenue generation

3. Which of the following is an important source of information about the stream of HTTP requests and responses?

   A. Server logs

   B. HTTP transaction logs

   C. Pricing logs

   D. Efficiency logs

4. The access log contains information about URL fetches. Which of the following is not included in the log? (Choose all that apply.)

   A. The IP address of the client

   B. The time of day the connection occurred

   C. The hard disk size of the server

   D. The client's operating system

5. Troy is concerned about making purchases online because he has heard about a protocol analyzer that can be used by hackers to intercept data. What tool is Troy worried hackers will use to find out user-sensitive information?

   A. IP intercepts

   B. Packet sniffers

   C. System tools

   D. Cybersquating

6. Windows 2000 provides what tool for monitoring objects that belong to the server?

   A. Knowledge databases

   B. System Monitor

   C. Performance Monitor

   D. Server Checkup

7. A _____ is a security barrier that prevents outsiders from accessing a company's internal network.

   A. Proxy server

   B. Firewall

   C. Commerce server

   D. Internet Information Server

8. What kind of an effect does logging have on system performance?

   A. The more events you log, the harder your system has to work.

   B. Logging has no effect on system performance.

   C. Logging improves system performance.

   D. The less events you log, the harder your system has to work.

9. Which of the following is one of the three ways to correct a bottleneck?

   A. Change the protocol used on the web server.

   B. Restart the queue.

   C. Remove the component.

   D. Replicate the component.

10. Which of the following hardware upgrades will not improve your Internet system performance?

   A. Increasing RAM

   B. Upgrading the CPU

   C. Improve the quality of the NIC

   D. Upgrading the sound card

11. The person that is responsible for the integrity and content of a website is usually called the _____ .

   A. Webwizard

   B. Webmaster

   C. Webinar

   D. Webster

12. Which of the following is a good security tip for a web server that is placed outside of your firewall?

   A. Provide manual administrative surveillance on the server.

   B. Increase the amount of RAM the server uses.

   C. Check the logs more frequently for failed logon attempts and other problems.

   D. Deny all incoming ports on the server, especially port 80.

13. In what way can logs generate revenue for your company?

    A. Your logs can be sold to companies that are seeking information on certain types of statistics.

    B. You can sell your logs to training schools for scholastic purposes.

    C. You can sell your logs back to the software manufacturer for rebates.

    D. Profit cannot be generated in any way for the sale of log material.

14. A failed logon attempt may be evidence that someone has attempted to break in to your server. What is another possible reason for a failed logon attempt?

    A. Faulty network cabling

    B. Improper auditing configuration

    C. Administrative error

    D. Users not logging on properly

15. What is one of the major advantages of HTTP server logs?

    A. They are self analyzing.

    B. They can be analyzed offline.

    C. They show the need for more hardware resources.

    D. They ignore transactions that occur on the web server.

16. Which of the following HTTP logs will help you determine if a CGI script is executing?

    A. Access log

    B. Agent log

    C. Error log

    D. Referrer log

17. When you are using Performance Monitor, which of the following do you need to choose to monitor your processor?

    A. Counters

    B. Instances

    C. Performance objects

    D. Hardware

18. Which of the following is the most important factor in your web server?

    A. RAM

    B. Processor

    C. NIC

    D. Faster motherboard system bus

19. The duration of a web connection is called _____ .

    A. Bottleneck

    B. Queue

    C. Baseline

    D. Session state

20. When memory exchanges information with the hard drive, what is this called?

    A. Trading

    B. Crossfire

    C. Thrashing

    D. Swapping

Answers to Review Questions

1. C.   A queue is a sequence of requests for services from one or more servers. If the requests build up in the queue, a bottleneck will result. At this point, other parts of the system will run more slowly, much in the same way a traffic bottleneck occurs.

2. B.   When a log lists how much work a server is handling, it is measuring usage rate.

3. A.   Probably the most important source of information about the stream of HTTP requests and responses is the server log files. These logs keep track of the time of each HTTP transaction. In addition to the time, they record the number of bytes transferred. Administrators can analyze these log files for performance monitoring.

4. A, B.   An access log contains information about URL fetches including the client's IP address and the time of day the connection is made. Access logs also contain the name of the URL and the HTTP request.

5. B.   Information transmitted on any network can be obtained through the use of programs called packet sniffers. For the process to be a success, however, the packet sniffer must be installed on the same physical wire and must be listening while the information is transmitted. This procedure would be too much work for any hacker to even attempt.

6. C.   Performance Monitor is included with Windows 2000 and is the primary tool for determining server bottlenecks and problems on that system. This tool monitors objects that belong to the server, including Server Work Queues, Active Server Pages, Processor, TCP, Server, Logical Disk, Web Service, and FTP Service.

7. B.   A firewall is a security barrier that prevents outsiders from accessing a company's internal network, which accesses the Internet indirectly through a proxy server. A commerce server facilitates the creation and deployment of an online catalog. IIS is a web server.

8. A.   Logging has a direct effect on system performance. The more events you log, the harder your system will have to work. For this reason, you should only log selected events to prevent overburdening your server with excess monitoring requests.

9. D. Replicating the component causing the bottleneck by distributing the demand for a service across multiple servers is one of the three ways to correct a bottleneck. You can also speed up the component by replacing it with an upgraded version and increase the capacity of the queues in the system to tolerate more requests before turning away new ones.

10. D. Although the other changes will have an effect for the better, some drastically, upgrading your sound card will not improve system performance.

11. B. The person responsible for the site is usually called the webmaster, or simply the administrator of the site. The webmaster is responsible for the usability, screen flow, maintenance, and security of a site.

12. C. Many organizations place their web servers on the outside of their firewall. This allows outsiders to see the company's website but allows those on the inside of the firewall to be protected. But this server becomes an unprotected target, so it would be good to check its logs more often. Manual surveillance is too personnel intensive. Increased RAM doesn't improve security (although it may improve performance). Deny port 80 and you've taken your web server offline to users, so that is a poor choice.

13. A. Logs can be sold for statistical analysis as long as you have a willing buyer and substantial log information has been generated. The other options are not true generators of profit.

14. D. Failed logon attempts can also be evidence that users need more training on their systems. Users are, at times, forgetful and may not log on properly because they cannot recall their passwords. Or they may accidentally press the wrong keys on the keyboard. More training will solve some (although not all) of these problems.

15. B. HTTP server logs can be analyzed offline, which means you don't use any system resources to analyze the logs themselves, which often-times taints the results. The other options are not advantages. For example, HTTP logs do not self analyze and they do not ignore transactions; rather, they collect transaction information.

16. C. The error log file will record any errors that occur, including server startup and shutdown, malformed URLs, and erroneous CGI scripts. The other logs mentioned as options perform other tasks in HTTP logging.

17. C. Once you've selected the computer you wish to monitor, you need to select a performance object, such as processor, memory, system, or disk. Then you would choose the counter and the instance.

18. A. The most important factor when considering web servers is the amount of RAM. The other resources listed are important too, but none is the most important factor for a web server.

19. D. The session state allows a connection to continue for a specified period of time. You can change the session state to a higher or lower time allotment, or you can enable and disable the session state altogether. *Bottleneck*, *queue*, and *baseline* are other performance terms.

20. D. Exchanging data between the memory and the hard drive is called swapping. Excessive levels of page swapping can indicate that there is not enough physical memory in the system.

Appendix A

HTML Quick Reference

able A.1 lists commonly used tags that are worthwhile for you to know. However, some are nonstandard as of HTML 4.01.

TABLE A.1 HTML Elements

HTML Element	Description
<HTML>...</HTML>	Identifies document type as HTML
<HEAD>...</HEAD>	Encloses document header
<TITLE>...</TITLE>	Specifies document title
<!-- -- >	Specifies comments (not displayed in browser)
<BODY>...</BODY>	Encloses body of HTML document
<H1>...</H1>	Creates level-one heading
<H2>...</H2>	Creates level-two heading
<H3>...</H3>	Creates level-three heading
<H4>...</H4>	Creates level-four heading
<H5>...</H5>	Creates level-five heading
<H6>...</H6>	Creates level-six heading
 	Creates line break without white space

TABLE A.1 HTML Elements *(continued)*

HTML Element	Description
<P>	Creates line break with white space
<PRE>...</PRE>	Creates preformatted text while preserving spacing
<BLOCK>...</BLOCK>	Indents text; useful for quotes and citations
<B>...</B>	Creates boldface text
<I>...</I>	Creates italic text
<STRIKE>...</STRIKE>	Strikes text (draws a line through the text)
<LI>	Creates list element used in ordered and unordered lists
<UL>...</UL>	Creates unordered (bulleted) lists
<OL>...</OL>	Creates ordered (numbered) lists
<HR>	Creates horizontally ruled lines on a Web page
<IMG SRC="file">	Inserts image in documents
<A>...</A>	Creates hypertext links; anchor tag used with HREF and NAME
<FORM>...</FORM>	Creates an HTML form
<INPUT>...</INPUT>	Defines input fields used in forms
<TABLE>...</TABLE>	Creates an HTML table
<CAPTION>...</CAPTION>	Creates a table caption

TABLE A.1   HTML Elements *(continued)*

HTML Element	Description
<ADDRESS>...</ADDRESS>	Creates document footer (such as author's e-mail address or URL)
<DIR>...</DIR>	Creates directory list; used for lists with items that have short names
<MENU>...</MENU>	Creates menu list for presenting menus
<CITE>...</CITE >	Specifies citation style; used for citing other works or titles
<EM>...</EM>	Creates an emphasis when pronounced by a text-to-speech application; typically represented in a graphical browser as italic
<STRONG>...</STRONG>	Creates strong emphasis when pronounced by a text-to-speech application; typically represented in a graphical browser as bold text
<SAMPLE>...</SAMPLE>	Creates sample style; used for examples
<TT>...</TT>	Creates typewriter text style using monospaced font
<KBD>...</KBD>	Creates keyboard style to indicate text to be typed into a keyboard
<IFRAME SRC="URL></IFRAME>	Creates a floating frame

Advanced Table Features

Table A.2 lists attributes and values that can be used in an advanced table with the <TABLE> tag. These attributes and values can be seen only in Microsoft Internet Explorer 3 or later.

TABLE A.2 Advanced Table Attributes and Values

Attribute	Description	Values
FRAME=	Applies to the border around the table	hsides, vsides, lhs, rhs, none
RULES=	Applies to the row and column of each cell	cols, rows, none
ALIGN=	Applies to the alignment of text around a table	left, right

Appendix

B

The HTML 4.01 Recommendation

In this appendix, we'll discuss the new elements and attributes added in the HTML 4.01 Recommendation (www.w3.org/TR/html401). We'll also discuss how to avoid deprecated elements and attributes and provide a list of obsolete elements. In creating the HTML 4.01 Recommendation, the World Wide Web Consortium (W3C) sought to make HTML as functional as possible. HTML's mission is to be a language that defines the content and structure of web pages. The following quote is from section 2.2.1 of "Introduction to HTLM" (www.w3.org/TR/REC-html401/intro/intro.html):

> HTML has been developed with the vision that all manner of devices should be able to use information on the Web: PCs with graphics displays of varying resolution and color depths, cellular telephones, hand held devices, devices for speech output and input, computers with high or low bandwidth, and so on.

HTML 4.01 adds new elements designed to further define and organize the content and information within Web pages. With the 4.01 Recommendation, HTML allows developers to cleverly present graphics and content and to take as much control over their pages as possible. From this perspective, it becomes clear why the visually useful elements relating to frames were so long in gaining acceptance. How does one render a frame for use with a cellular telephone or for audio output and input?

The HTML 4.01 Recommendation, accepted by W3C at the end of 1999, focuses especially upon elements that allow pages presented on the World Wide Web to become more accessible and intuitive.

HTML 4.01 and Cascading Style Sheets

Despite the regular use of elements to format text on an HTML page, HTML elements were designed to define content and structure, not merely the visual appearance of text. With the acceptance of Cascading Style Sheets (CSS1 and part of CSS2), website developers should move instructions regarding the visual appearance of text, images, and other elements to external style sheets, the STYLE header section in a page, or the STYLE attribute within a tag.

Pages designed this way will not only be more accessible to everyone, they will also last longer as technologies continue to emerge and evolve in relation to the language. Because developing a high-quality web page takes so long, designers should take full advantage of any specification that allows a web page to remain compatible with new technologies and developments.

The use of the proper HTML element can also greatly facilitate user agent tools, such as spelling or grammar checkers, by specifying that certain text is a verbatim quote or an acronym or that it belongs to another language.

New Tags in HTML 4.01

A number of new tags have been added to HTML 4.01:

<ABBR>	<FRAMESET>	<OPTGROUP>
<ACRONYM>	<IFRAME>	<PARAM>
<BDO>	<INS>	<SPAN>
<BUTTON>	<LABEL>	<TBODY>
<COLGROUP>	<LEGEND>	<TFOOT>
<DEL>	<NOFRAMES>	<THEAD>
<FIELDSET>	<NOSCRIPT>	<Q>
<FRAME>	<OBJECT>	

Each of these tags will be discussed in this section. Some should already be familiar to you, such as <IFRAME>, <FRAMESET>, and <TBODY>. Some, such as <Q>, are so new that they are not yet supported by any of the major rendering agents.

<FRAME>, <FRAMESET>, <IFRAME>, and <NOFRAMES>

HTML 4.01 now formally includes standards for creating frames. These elements define separate regions within a single page, each of which can contain a separate document.

<THEAD>, <TBODY>, <TFOOT>, and <COLGROUP>

The <THEAD>, <TBODY>, and <TFOOT> tags allow you to define row groups. If you use the <TFOOT> tag, it must precede the <TBODY> tag. This sequence allows the user agent (e.g., a web browser) to display the start and end of the table while the usually bulky <BODY> section downloads incrementally. If you use <THEAD>, <TBODY>, or <TFOOT> as specified, you need not supply a closing tag for them.

You can use the WIDTH attribute of the <COLGROUP> tag to specify a finite width for a group of columns. This technique allows for the incremental rendering of tables, thereby increasing accessibility. Additionally, the <COLGROUP> tag has a SPAN attribute that defines the number of columns in the group.

For example, if a table has 10 columns, the last three of which need to be 15 pixels wide, you could write the code as follows:

```
<COLGROUP SPAN="3" WIDTH="15">
```

Contrast this with the following code, which renders the same result:

```
<COL WIDTH="15">
<COL WIDTH="15">
<COL WIDTH="15">
```

<ABBR> and <ACRONYM>

The <ABBR> tag is used to define abbreviations, and <ACRONYM> defines the use of acronyms. These particular tags allow translation engines and search engines to readily interpret and report web page content. Because HTML describes content and not form, it should be no surprise that browsers do not render these tags.

Consider how much simpler it would be to present a page in a different language if the translation engine did not need to determine whether some text was meant to be a word, an abbreviation, or an acronym. You can avoid such problems by enclosing acronyms and abbreviations in the container tags of <ACRONYM> and <ABBR>, respectively.

<Q> and <BDO>

Quotations should be enclosed between <Q> and </Q> tags. According to the W3C, users should not put quotation marks at the beginning or ending of <Q> sections; the web browser should provide the appropriate quotation marks.

The <Q> element has two useful attributes: LANG and DIR. LANG controls the language in which the quotation should appear, and DIR governs the direction of the text. Some languages, such as English, are read from left to right. Others, such as Hebrew, are read from right to left. DIR uses the value "ltr" for "left to right" and the value "rtl" for "right to left." The following example demonstrates how you could include a Hebrew quotation in text:

```
<Q LANG="He" DIR="rtl">...Hebrew quotation...</Q>
```

Most browsers provide algorithms to calculate the direction in which the text will appear. Should you need to reverse a native direction, use the BDO element for a bidirectional override of the algorithm. In such cases, the DIR attribute is mandatory and can take the values of "ltr" or "rtl" as described.

The *LANG* Attribute

The LANG attribute allows you to specify the language in use and takes a language code value. Table B.1 lists codes for some common languages.

TABLE B.1   LANG Attribute Values

Language Indicated	Value
French	FR
German	DE
Italian	IT
Dutch	NL
Greek	EL
Spanish	ES
Portuguese	PT
Arabic	AR
Hebrew	HE

TABLE B.1   LANG Attribute Values *(continued)*

Language Indicated	Value
Russian	RU
Chinese	ZH
Japanese	JA
Hindi	HI
Urdu	UR
Sanskrit	SA

<DEL> and <INS>

The <DEL> and <INS> tags identify text that has been deleted from a previous version or inserted into a new version. This information is especially important for legal documents in which revision tracking is essential.

These two elements take two attributes: CITE and DATETIME. CITE specifies the reason for a deletion or insertion. DATETIME specifies the date and time the change was made.

This is how you would see the code written:

```
<DEL>This text has been deleted from the original.</DEL>
    This text is still in the original. <INS>This text has
    been added to the original.</INS>
```

This is how the code would render on the browser's screen:

~~This text has been deleted from the original.~~ This text is still in the original. <u>This text has been added to the original.</u>

<LABEL>, <FIELDSET>, <LEGEND>, <OPTGROUP>, and <BUTTON>

Each of these new tags relates to forms and the custom elements they can provide.

<LABEL>

<LABEL> identifies a form field. There are two ways to use the <LABEL> tag. Either the form field element must reside within the opening and closing <LABEL> tags, or you must use the FOR attribute, where the value matches the ID value of the field being labeled. The following examples demonstrate these two methods for using <LABEL>; here is the first method:

```
<LABEL>Vendor Name: <INPUT TYPE="text"></LABEL>
```

Here is the second:

```
<LABEL FOR="vendor">Vendor Name: </LABEL>
<INPUT TYPE="text" ID="vendor">
```

<FIELDSET>

<FIELDSET> allows you to group fields together. Field grouping can affect the tabbing order between fields. The following code shows how a few fields might be grouped together using the <FIELDSET> tag:

```
<FIELDSET>
<INPUT TYPE="checkbox" VALUE="swimming"> Swimming<BR>
<INPUT TYPE="checkbox" VALUE="tennis"> Tennis<BR>
<INPUT TYPE="checkbox" VALUE="archery"> Archery<BR>
</FIELDSET>
```

<LEGEND>

<LEGEND> works with <FIELDSET>, allowing you to provide a label for the group of fields in the field set. The following code shows how to use <LEGEND> in conjunction with <FIELDSET>:

```
<FIELDSET>
<LEGEND>Favorite Sport Activities</LEGEND>
<INPUT TYPE="checkbox" VALUE="swimming"> Swimming<BR>
<INPUT TYPE="checkbox" VALUE="tennis"> Tennis<BR>
<INPUT TYPE="checkbox" VALUE="archery"> Archery<BR>
</FIELDSET> <BR><BR>
<FIELDSET>
<LEGEND>Required Foods</LEGEND>
<INPUT TYPE="checkbox" VALUE="pizza"> Pizza<BR>
<INPUT TYPE="checkbox" VALUE="won tons"> Won Tons<BR>
<INPUT TYPE="checkbox" VALUE="salmon"> Salmon<BR>
</FIELDSET>
```

Figure B.1 shows the preceding code as it will render in an HTML 4.01–compatible browser.

FIGURE B.1 <FIELDSET> using the <LEGEND> tag

<OPTGROUP>

<OPTGROUP> allows you to group <OPTION> tags together within a <SELECT> tag. In long lists, this capability gives users with visual disabilities a way to hop more quickly through the list. For visually rendered pages, these option groupings may ultimately be displayed as a series of cascading menu choices. The following code shows a common application of <OPTGROUP>:

```
<SELECT NAME="Courses">
<OPTGROUP LABEL="End User">
<OPTION VALUE="12IE">Internet Explorer
<OPTION VALUE="4BA3">Netscape Navigator
</OPTGROUP>
<OPTGROUP LABEL="Developer">
<OPTION VALUE="23L4">Introduction to JavaScript
<OPTION VALUE="156L">Advanced VBScript
</OPTGROUP>
<OPTGROUP LABEL="Engineer">
<OPTION VALUE="I83S">Using NT 4.0
<OPTION VALUE="J34N">Apache Web Server
</OPTGROUP>
<OPTION>
```

<BUTTON>

The <BUTTON> tag allows you to create buttons containing both images and text, as shown in Figure B.2.

FIGURE B.2   Image within <BUTTON> tag

The source code for this button might resemble the following:

```
<BUTTON>
<P STYLE="text-align: center">
<B>UNIX Tip</B><BR>
<BR>
<IMG SRC="unix.gif">
</P>
</BUTTON>
```

<OBJECT> and <PARAM>

One of the most important tags, <OBJECT> is used to include video clips, images, applets, and ActiveX controls. You can even use it to include another HTML document within an HTML page.

HTML developers should especially note that the W3C has deprecated the <APPLET> tag in favor of <OBJECT>.

Normally, a user agent should render the object immediately. If the object is not available, the browser should render any internal object contents. On occasion, you may want to declare and make an object available but not render it immediately. See the following code samples for different ways to include data as an object in an HTML document. For the complete explanation, refer to the HTML 4.01 Recommendation section on objects (www.w3 .org/TR/REC-html40/struct/objects.html).

To obtain a copy of the entire HTML 4.01 Recommendation, go to www.w3 .org/MarkUp/#html4.

<PARAM> is used in the context of <OBJECT> or <APPLET> to specify additional internal properties of the object.

Following are several examples that show how to use the <OBJECT> tag to include scripts, active content, images, and other objects important to Internet and intranet developers.

This example shows how to use the <OBJECT> tag to include a reference to a server-side script in an HTML page:

```
<OBJECT classid="http://www.server.com/pythonscript.py">
You would have seen an applet written in the Python
    language here.
</OBJECT>
```

This code will insert a Java applet in an HTML page:

```
<OBJECT
codetype="application/java"
classid="java:nextad.class"
codebase="http://www.anywhere.com/java/applets/">
Ad-changing applet here.
</OBJECT>
```

In this code, an ActiveX object is being added to a page:

```
<OBJECT classid="clsid:
663C8FEF-1EF9-11CF-A3DB-080036F12502"
data="http://www.acme.com/ole/clock.stm">
Your browser cannot display this ActiveX component.
</OBJECT>
```

This code inserts an image file into an HTML page:

```
<OBJECT data="building.png" type="image/png">
This is a photo of our facilities.
</OBJECT>
```

To insert a video file, you would use code like this:

```
<OBJECT data="grandop.mpeg"
type="application/mpeg">
Video of our grand opening.
</OBJECT>
```

A document would be embedded like this:

```
<OBJECT data="included.html">
```

```
Warning: included.html not found.
</OBJECT>
```

This example shows how to include standby content in a web page:

```
<OBJECT classid="http://www.anywhere.com/specialap"
standby="Loading Animation...">
<PARAM name="Init_Pic"
value="images/start.gif"
valuetype="ref">
</OBJECT>
```

To include alternate content, you would use code similar to this example:

```
<OBJECT data="dragon.png" type="image/png">
<OBJECT data="dragon.gif" type="image/gif">
Picture of a dragon.
</OBJECT>
</OBJECT>
```

<NOSCRIPT>

Some web browsers do not support client-side scripting languages. This includes the early versions of Microsoft Internet Explorer and Netscape Navigator.

To accommodate these legacy browsers, website designers should always use the <NOSCRIPT> tag. In many ways, <NOSCRIPT> is similar to the <NOFRAMES> tag because it provides alternative text when a user agent cannot run the intended code.

Following is an example of how to include the <NOSCRIPT> tag after a script:

```
<SCRIPT type="text/javascript">
... JavaScript here ...
</SCRIPT>
<NOSCRIPT>
<P>
Your browser does not render scripts. Please e-mail us
    your address so we can send you some information that
    you missed here.
</NOSCRIPT>
```

\<SPAN\>

\<SPAN\> denotes an inline element. Any formatting attributes associated with the inline element defined by the \<SPAN\> and \</SPAN\> tags must be included by means of the STYLE or CLASS attribute.

The following is an example of text defined and formatted by using the \<SPAN\> tag:

```
This book, written by <SPAN class="Author">Emily
    Wills</SPAN>, describes....
```

New Attributes in HTML 4.01

HTML 4.01 added several new attributes. The following five apply to nearly every HTML element:

- ID
- DIR
- STYLE
- TITLE
- LANG

A number of event attributes now apply to a broad range of elements:

onBlur	onKeypress	onMouseover
onClick	onKeyup	onMouseup
onChange	onLoad	onReset
onDblclick	onMousedown	onSubmit
onFocus	onMousemove	onUnload
onKeydown	onMouseout	

Finally, several new attributes can be used in conjunction with forms and tables. These attributes will be discussed later in this appendix:

- ACCESSKEY
- DISABLED
- SUMMARY

- READONLY

- TABINDEX

Document-wide Attributes

You learned about DIR and LANG in the discussion about <Q> and <BDO>. Other attributes enable you to modify the appearance of elements within a document. ID and TITLE are extremely useful element, and you should become familiar with them. They can be used in conjunction with any document-level element.

ID

The ID attribute is a unique identifier for any document element. It serves as both a bookmark for an internal link and an object reference for use with styles and scripts.

TITLE

The TITLE element allows you to add a pop-up label that appears whenever a user passes the cursor over the text:

```
<B TITLE="Pretty cool, eh?">Move your mouse over this text
    and pause the mouse. Do you see the label?</B>
```

Whenever a user pauses the mouse cursor over this text, the message "Pretty cool, eh?" will appear, as shown in Figure B.3.

FIGURE B.3   TITLE value appearing in Internet Explorer

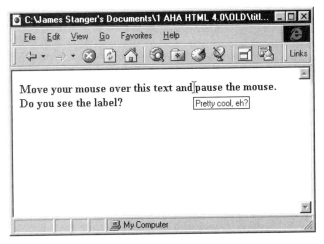

Remember not to confuse TITLE with the ONMOUSEOVER event. Also, even though this attribute is included in the HTML 4.01 Recommendation, only Internet Explorer 4 and later versions supports it as of this writing.

Event Attributes

Some event attributes have been added to those from HTML 3.2. They are shown in Table B.2.

TABLE B.2 Objects and Event Attributes

Event Attribute	Object(s)	Event Description
onAbort	Image	User aborts loading the page.
onBlur	Password, Text, Select, Window	User leaves the object.
onChange	Text	User changes the object.
onClick	Area, Button, Checkbox, Link, Radio, Reset, Submit	User clicks on the object.
onError	Window	Script encounters an error.
onFocus	Password, Text, Textarea, Window	User makes an object active.
onKeydown	Password, Text, Textarea	User depresses a key.
onKeypress	Password, Text, Textarea	User presses or holds down a key.
onKeyup	Password, Text, Textarea	User releases a key.
onLoad	Window	Object loaded in window.
onMousedown	Button, Checkbox, Link, Radio, Reset, Submit	User depresses a mouse button.

TABLE B.2   Objects and Event Attributes *(continued)*

Event Attribute	Object(s)	Event Description
onMouseout	Area, Link	Cursor moves off an object.
onMouseover	Area, Link	Cursor moves over an object.
onMouseup	Button, Checkbox, Link, Radio, Reset, Submit	User releases a mouse button.
onReset	Form	User resets a form.
onResize	Window	User or script resizes a window or frame.
onSelect	Password, Text, Textarea	User selects the contents of an object.
onSubmit	Form	User submits a form.
onUnload	Window	User leaves the window.

Form and Table Attributes

The HTML 4.01 Recommendation includes several attributes directly related to the presentation of forms and tables, greatly extending your ability to define them. These attributes include ACCESSKEY, DISABLED, READONLY, SUMMARY, and TABINDEX.

ACCESSKEY

In most applications, when a form is presented, the user is offered two methods for accessing any field: clicking the mouse on the field or using the hot key assigned to that option. For example, in Windows menus and dialog boxes, one letter is usually underlined in each option to indicate that it is the access key for that option. When you press Alt and the underlined letter, the option is selected.

In Macintosh systems, a combination of the Cmd key and the indicated letter will invoke menu and dialog boxes.

Figure B.4 shows an HTML form with the access keys defined.

FIGURE B.4 ACCESSKEY attribute used in a form

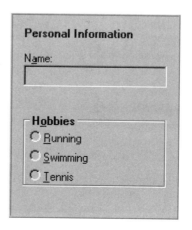

 The HTML 4.01 Recommendation says the user agent should provide some rendering of the access key. Internet Explorer does not yet support this feature, so the underlining of the access key letter has been performed here manually.

ACCESSKEY provides a trigger key whether or not any visual representation of that key exists. The code that created this form is as follows:

```
<FORM STYLE="font-family: 'MS Sans Serif'. Arial,
     Helvetica, 'Sans Serif"; font-size: 9pt">
<B>Personal Information</B><BR>
<BR>
<LABEL>
N<U>a</U>me:<BR>
<INPUT TYPE="text" ACCESSKEY="a" SIZE="20"></LABEL>
<BR><BR>
<FIELDSET>
<LEGEND ACCESSKEY="o"><B>H<U>o</U>bbies</B></LEGEND>
<INPUT TYPE="radio" NAME="hobbies"
     ACCESSKEY="r"><U>R</U>unning<BR>
```

```
<INPUT TYPE="radio" NAME="hobbies"
    ACCESSKEY="s"><U>S</U>wimming<BR>
<INPUT TYPE="radio" NAME="hobbies"
    ACCESSKEY="t"><U>T</U>ennis<BR></FIELDSET>
</FORM>
</TD></TR>
</TABLE>
```

The following code would produce a Submit button labeled as "Send" that is tied to the Alt+S keystroke. This would make the button emulate the behavior of Microsoft Outlook and Outlook Express, which link the Alt+S keystroke to the Send command that is available in the Edit Message window:

```
<INPUT TYPE=SUBMIT ACCESSKEY="s" VALUE="Send">
```

DISABLED

DISABLED is a Boolean attribute used with form controls. If included, the value of the form control is not submitted. Additionally, disabled controls cannot receive focus.

READONLY

READONLY is a Boolean attribute used with form controls. You cannot change the text of a field when the READONLY attribute is present.

SUMMARY

SUMMARY is an attribute of the <TABLE> tag. Developers should include summary information about the table's purpose and contents to help those using text-to-speech interfaces.

The following code demonstrates the use of the SUMMARY attribute in a table:

```
<TABLE SUMMARY="This table provides summary information
    on sales figures from 1997.">
. . . Table contents here . . .
</TABLE>
```

TABINDEX

The TABINDEX attribute allows you to specify the order in which fields will receive focus if the user presses Tab to move from field to field. For example,

Figure B.5 shows how a user's cursor would move to a field other than the one expected. If you were to press Tab, the cursor would follow the numerical order shown in the image rather than the visually sequential tabbing order.

FIGURE B.5 TABINDEX attribute

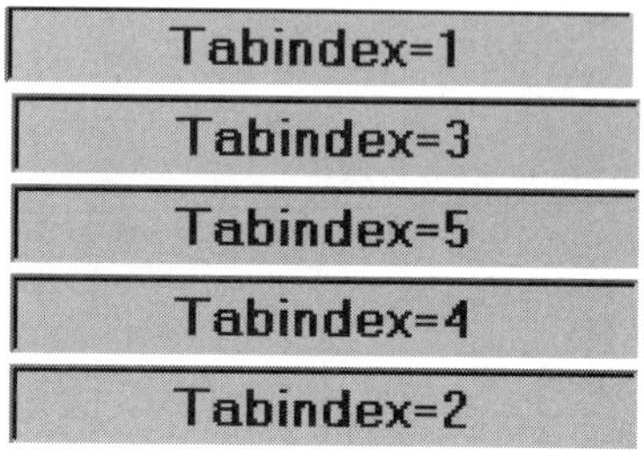

Deprecated Elements

As HTML evolves, the elements accepted in one version are not necessarily accepted in the next version. Although elements have been added to HTML in level 4.01, other elements have been marked as "deprecated." Deprecated elements are elements for which a newer, better technology is now in place. According to the W3C, "a deprecated element or attribute is one that has been outdated by newer constructs. . . . Deprecated elements may become obsolete in future versions of HTML."

The W3C discourages the use of deprecated elements, although it recommends that browsers continue to support them for a limited time so that Web pages will be backward compatible with older browsers.

These elements are deprecated in HTML 4.01:

<APPLET> In place of the Java-specific <APPLET> tag, the W3C recommends that developers and vendors use <OBJECT>. In fact, the <OBJECT> tag applies not only to Java applets, but also to any language attribute. See the discussion about <OBJECT> and <PARAM> earlier in this appendix.

<BASEFONT> <BASEFONT> specifies the default font size for a page. The default font should now be set with the <STYLE> tag. The following code demonstrates the recommended way to set a new default font for the page:

```
<STYLE>
BODY {font-size: 11pt}
</STYLE>
```

<CENTER> Long a favorite of web developers, the <CENTER> tag has been deprecated in favor of the STYLE attribute's "text-align" value. The following code demonstrates the recommended method for centering a simple heading on a page:

```
<H3 STYLE="text-align: center">Business Proposal</H3>
```

<DIR> and <MENU> <DIR> and <MENU> serve a purpose similar to that of <UL> in terms of rendering or content definition. The W3C recommends you use <UL> in place of <DIR> and <MENU>.

<ISINDEX> <ISINDEX> is a text-box tag that looks and functions as an <INPUT> text box. The W3C recommends using the <INPUT> tag instead of the <ISINDEX> tag.

<S>, <STRIKE>, and <U> The W3C has deprecated text-formatting elements in favor of the line-through and underline values of the text-decoration style attribute.

Deprecated Attributes

The W3C has deprecated not only HTML tags, but many of the HTML attributes as well. The following quote from section 2.3.5 of "Introduction to HTLM" (www.w3.org/TR/REC-html40/intro/intro.html) should motivate you to master style sheets:

> HTML 3.2 included a number of attributes and elements offering control over alignment, font size, and text color. Authors also exploited tables and images as a means for laying out pages. The relatively long time it takes for users to upgrade their browsers means that these features will continue to be used for some time. However, since style sheets offer more powerful presentation mechanisms, the World Wide Web Consortium will eventually phase out many of HTML's presentation elements and attributes.

The following commonly used attributes are no longer recommended by the W3C:

- ALIGN (relative to all tags except <COL>, <COLGROUP>, <TBODY>, <TD>, <TFOOT>, <TH>, <THEAD>, and <TR>)
- ALINK
- BACKGROUND
- BGCOLOR
- BORDER (relative to <IMG> and <OBJECT> but not to <TABLE>)
- CLEAR
- COLOR
- FACE
- HEIGHT (relative to <APPLET>, <TH>, and <TD>)
- HSPACE
- LINK
- SIZE (relative to <BASEFONT>, <FONT>, and <HR>)
- TEXT
- TYPE (relative to <UL>, <OL> and <LI>)
- VLINK
- VSPACE
- WIDTH (relative to <TH>, <TD>, <HR> and <APPLET>)

Table B.3 will help you map the deprecated attribute to the appropriate replacement style attribute.

TABLE B.3 Deprecated Attributes

Deprecated Attribute	Replacement Style Attribute
ALIGN (relative to all elements except <COL>, <COLGROUP>, <TBODY>, <TD>, <TFOOT>, <TH>, <THEAD>, and <TR>)	Use the text align style attribute.

TABLE B.3 Deprecated Attributes *(continued)*

Deprecated Attribute	Replacement Style Attribute
ALINK, LINK, VLINK	These attributes refer to the display color of, respectively, the active link, an unvisited link, and a visited link.
BACKGROUND	Use the BACKGROUND-IMAGE style attribute.
BGCOLOR	Use the BACKGROUND-COLOR style attribute.
BORDER (relative to tables)	Use the BORDER style attribute. It differs from the values given to the BORDER attribute of the <TABLE> tag.
CLEAR	Use the CLEAR style attribute.
COLOR (relative to the <FONT> tag)	Use the COLOR style attribute.
FACE (relative to the <FONT> element)	Use the FONT-FAMILY style attribute.
HSPACE	Use any combination of the following to affect the horizontal white space around an element: "margin-left", "margin-right", "padding-left", or "padding-right".
VSPACE	Use any combination of the following to affect the vertical white space around an element: "margin-top", "margin-bottom", "padding-top", or "padding-bottom".
SIZE, HEIGHT, WIDTH	Use the FONT-SIZE style attribute, the height style attribute, or the width style attribute to affect the visual size of the element.
TEXT	Define the BODY or P elements with the COLOR style attribute.
TYPE (used with lists)	Use the LIST-STYLE-TYPE style attribute.

Obsolete Elements

The following tags are now considered obsolete and should not be used in any HTML pages:

- <LISTING>
- <PLAINTEXT>
- <XMP>

Conclusion

Most vendors who create languages simply add to the language to cope with demands for new features. HTML, however, does not follow this model. With each new version, the W3C adds new elements and attributes; it also removes, or deprecates, those tags that limit the functionality and future of HTML. Remember that as an HTML developer, you must consider not only what works now, but what worked in the past and what may or may not work in the future.

To learn more about the differences between HTML 3.2 and HTML 4.0, see www.w3.org/TR/html401/appendix/changes.html#h-A.3.

Appendix

C

Electronic Commerce
Planning Checklist

Planning is an integral part of any successful venture. This short checklist will help guide you in your e-commerce planning phase.

The following questions are important to your overall planning goals for your e-commerce business:

- What advantages will your company gain from becoming accessible on the Web?

- How will the website support and enhance your company's strategy and operations?

- How will your company fund and support the website?

- What disadvantages might your company encounter from becoming accessible on the Web?

- How will you overcome those disadvantages?

These question involve your target market.

- Who makes up your e-commerce target market? How many of these potential targets are ready and willing to use your e-commerce site?

- Where is the market located? What kinds of web access does this target market have?

- Which business model is most suitable for your company: the business-to-business model or the business-to-consumer model?

- How does your electronic business compare with your traditional business?

The following questions should be considered before you can set up your website:

- Have you secured and registered a domain name for your online business?
- What hardware do you plan to use?
- What software do you plan to use?
- What type of communication service do you plan to use?

Here are some questions related to advertising and promotion:

- How will you generate demand for your products and services?
- Will you offer banner ad space?
- Will you offer referrer bonuses?
- Will you offer contest-based promotions?

Here are some questions to keep in mind for customer service and support:

- What payment options will you offer: check, credit card, electronic funds?
- How and will you support your website's customers (and who will fill that role)?
- How and when will you process orders?
- How and when will you fulfill orders?
- How and when will you process payments?

These questions should be considered with regard to maintenance and support:

- Who will support and maintain your e-commerce website?
- Will you offer a telephone number for customers who have trouble accessing your site? Who will pay for the call? When and how will the telephone line be staffed?
- Will you offer an e-mail address for customer service? Who will monitor this address and when?

The following questions involve security for your website:

- What type of security will you use on your e-commerce website?

- How will your e-commerce business provide secure shopping for customers?

- How will you convince customers that your site is secure?

- Will your e-commerce business use Secure Sockets Layer (SSL) to encrypt transmissions between the web server and browser?

- Have you obtained a digital certificate for your e-commerce business?

- Will your e-commerce business use electronic data interchange (EDI) standards?

- Will your e-commerce business follow the Open Buying on the Internet (OBI) standards?

- Will your e-commerce business support the Open Trading Protocol (OTP) standard?

- Will your e-commerce business use Secure Electronic Transactions (SET)?

Consider these questions about legal issues:

- Does your domain name support any current or potential trade or service marks?

- Does your domain name infringe on other trade or service marks?

- What legal issues will your electronic commerce business encounter? Do they include copyright, trademark, or patent concerns?

- What privacy and confidentiality concerns will exist for your e-commerce business?

- What jurisdictional issues will affect your business? Is it legal for you to sell and/or distribute your products and/or services to your customers?

The following questions relate to globalization:

- Do you need to establish your website in several languages? If so, how will you localize and maintain the sites, and how will the customers of these localized sites be supported?

- Will you accept payment in credit cards issued outside your home country?
- Will you support more than one currency as a payment method?
- How will you handle customs duties?
- How will you handle local and national taxes, such as Value Added Tax?
- Will you offer import and export assistance?

Glossary

A

access control   One of the goals of providing security for a Web-based business. Protects against the unauthorized use of accessible resources.

Active Server Pages (ASPs)   A technology developed by Microsoft that uses the server to run scripts and then passes the output back to the browser.

additive colors   Colors that create white when mixed together.

animated GIF   A compilation of still images that is set into motion at a designated sequence, speed, and repetition.

anti-aliasing   A process that makes text appear smoother by blurring the lines between text and background.

application service provider (ASP)   A web hosting service that offers the use of server-based applications to customers. The ASP can host existing third-party applications, but some try to differentiate themselves by developing and hosting their own applications. Sometimes a flat monthly fee is offered, but transaction fees may also apply depending upon the services required.

applets   Small applications that do not run outside of a browser; they adhere to a set of conventions that enables them to run within a Java-compatible browser. Applets are embedded in HTML pages for web viewing.

asymmetric encryption   Sometimes called public-key encryption; allows previously unacquainted parties to conduct a transaction through the use of two pairs of keys: a private (or secret) key and a public key.

asynchronous   Term used to describe a process in which steps do not occur at the same time.

asynchronous e-service   The most commonly used method of customer service, because it is easier and less expensive to implement than the synchronous customer service. Examples include e-mail or web forms, in which the merchant does not offer an immediate response to the customer's request.

auction site   A form of e-commerce site that allows companies to conduct e-commerce business online without the need for an in-house, outsourced, online, or offline e-commerce package.

Automated Clearing House (ACH)   A nationwide batch-oriented Electronic Funds Transfer (EFT) system governed in the United States by the National Automated Clearing House Association (NACHA) operating rules.

B

B2B   Business-to-business. An e-commerce model that involves one business purchasing goods from another business.

B2C   Business-to-consumer. An e-commerce model that involves a consumer purchasing goods from an online business.

bandwidth   The amount of data that can be transmitted in a fixed amount of time.

bandwidth throttling   A general name for any method that prevents all bandwidth from going toward one connection, thus not having enough bandwidth for other connections.

banner ads   Clickable advertisements found on frequently visited websites.

barriers   Factors that limit the growth of a business, such as rapid change and increased competition.

batching   In credit-card processing, collecting, verifying, and submitting all transactions for settlement.

bitmap   Graphics that are composed of individual values for each color displayed.

bit tax   Tax on electronic commerce expressly imposed on or measured by the volume of digital information transmitted electronically or the volume of digital information per unit of time transmitted electronically; does not include taxes imposed on the provision of telecommunications services.

black box   A type of online instant storefront. The inner workings of the site are hidden from general view. Only the site's administrators and designers know how the site actually works. For some e-commerce developers, this is actually a benefit of outsourcing in the online instant storefront model.

bottleneck   A condition that results when a resource's capacity has been overwhelmed.

bottom-up approach   An approach to website design in which the look, feel, and functionality of a website emerge as the various user scenarios are developed from the user's point of view.

brand awareness   One of the goals of promoting and advertising a product or service. On a website, brand awareness is created through extensive use of a logo and/or slogan.

bread crumbs   Symbols such as arrows or lines that indicate the navigational path that the user took to arrive at the current location.

broadcast medium   Medium such as print, radio, and television in which information is broadcast to a passive audience.

C

Cascading Style Sheets (CSS)   Multiple and overlapping style definitions that control the appearance of HTML elements.

cash model   E-commerce payment model that uses digital cash that allows for anonymity of the buyer, fast transactions and lower cost of business. The negative side is that both buyer and seller need to use the same software or payment service for digital cash.

certificate authorities   Trusted third parties. They are to the digital world what notaries public are to the physical world.

certificate authority certificate   Certificate used by organizations such as VeriSign to sign other certificates.

chat   Service that allows immediate and specific information to be exchanged in real time. Used for e-commerce, the customer can read and type questions and answers with the customer services representative in real time.

check model   E-commerce payment model; users enter the transit numbers from the bottom of their checks instead of credit card numbers. Payment transactions are still required and financial institutions must still conduct them.

Children's Online Privacy Protection Act (COPPA)   A U.S. law passed by the Congress in 2001 requiring websites to implement privacy measures that prevent the collection of personal information about children 13 and younger without a parent's verifiable permission. The law also requires website operators to block access by anyone 17 or younger to materials deemed "harmful to minors" by requiring all users to provide a credit card or personal ID number.

cipher   A cryptographic algorithm used to encrypt and decrypt plaintext messages. A cipher is a mathematical function.

ciphertext   The output of an encryption process. For example, a plaintext message that has been encrypted is said to be in ciphertext and therefore unreadable without decryption.

clickthrough   The percentage of ad viewings that results in a user clicking an ad.

client-pull   Term used to describe what happens when files are downloaded sequentially with numerous exchanges between the user's computer and the server at the request of the client. HTTP works in this manner.

co-browsing   Allows a customer assistance center to control the customer's browser during a live session. Once a consumer has been assigned an operator through automatic callback or click-to-dial, the operator can assist the consumer by sharing the web page being viewed.

Common Gateway Interface (CGI)   A protocol that can be used to communicate between HTML forms and an application. CGI permits Macintosh, PC, and Unix computers to post data to or retrieve data from an HTTP server through a web browser.

concatenation   Linking two or more units of information, such as strings or files, to form one unit.

controlled-click pattern   Method for directing the user in a specific pattern or path within the site. An example of this would be the use of a form that must be filled out before allowing a person to move further within the site.

cookie   Small text file stored on the client's computer and retrieved by the server that sent it. Includes information to help maintain state and track user activities. Cookies can reside only in memory or may be placed on a hard drive in the form of a text file.

copyright   Legal protection of literary, musical, artistic, photographic, and audiovisual works. Copyright protection generally means that certain uses of the work are lawful only with the authorization of the copyright owner.

cost per thousand (CPM)   Term used to describe how Web advertising space is sold. A $10,000 banner ad that guarantees 500,000 impressions has a CPM of $20 ($10,000 divided by 500).

cost-per-click (CPC)   Internet marketing formula used to price ad banners. Advertisers will pay Internet publishers based on the number of clicks a specific ad banner receives. Cost generally ranges from $0.10 to $0.20 per click.

cracker   A user who breaks into sites for malicious and/or illegal purposes.

credit model   E-commerce payment model. Credit card transactions work best for most consumers. The transaction requires a payment gateway, which is the connection between the online catalog and a merchant bank.

crawler   A special application in a typical search engine. Its purpose is to map selected Web content and return URLs to which users can link when they search for a topic. Same as a spider.

cryptography   The science of encrypting and decrypting plaintext messages.

Customer Relationship Management (CRM)   The management of customers from a business process viewpoint rather than that of the direct customer. A business that uses CRM is concerned with how it manages its customer information service and how to better serve those customers based on that information.

customs   Duties paid on goods entering or leaving a country. Used to regulate or control the importing and exporting of goods to ensure legal compliance.

D

database   A formally arranged set of persistent information stored by a computer program. It is a collection of data organized to provide efficient management of as well as easy access to the data.

database management systems (DBMSs)   Application that supports the creation and management of databases and allows users to define, create, and maintain them. Many DBMSs are available for use on varying platforms.

Data Encryption Standard (DES)   The most widely used algorithm for symmetric encryption. It uses a 56-bit key. The algorithm has 19 distinct stages, each working on the result produced by its predecessor.

data mining   The use of customer data to improve CRM. Marketing and sales departments are using data mining as a value-added resource to improve customer satisfaction.

Data Source Name (DSN)   In ODBC, a unique name or identifier associated with a specific database or data file. The DSN may include the physical location of the database, its filename, the associated database driver, and security information required for database access. ODBC uses the name to connect, extract, and update information to databases.

default document   The first document a Web server refers to when it receives a nonspecific request.

demographics   The study of groups based on common characteristics.

deprecated tags   Tags that have been replaced by other HTML elements.

digital cash   Electronically stored currency, or electronic money.

digital certificate   Standard file formats for storing a user's or server's public key and related identification. The certificate provides a standard way of storing and exchanging public keys.

Digital Millennium Copyright Act (DMCA)   Act that was created to allow U.S. copyright laws to conform to World Intellectual Property Organization (WIPO) treaties for international copyright standards. The act has four main parts: Anti-Circumvention Provision, Protect Copyright Management Information (CMI), Service Provider Liability, and Webcasting.

digital signature   A method that allows the receiver of a message to ensure that the message came from the person it appears to have come from. The method involves using public-key systems that can be used to encrypt a message with the recipient's public key for confidentiality or to encrypt a message with the sender's secret key for message authentication.

digital subscriber line (DSL) A high-speed data and Internet connection that utilizes standard copper phone lines and is capable of speeds up to 1.5Mbps.

directory A tool used to find websites; only find sites based on manual submissions. If you do not manually submit your site to the directory, the directory will never know of or index your site and therefore never list it in search results.

distributed database A database that includes multiple files that can be housed at different locations on the enterprise.

dithering Process by which the browser approximates a color to the closest browser-safe color it supports.

Document Object Model (DOM) Model that enables programmers to create document structure, navigate it, and add or change content. Manipulated by script and often used with forms.

domain name A company's logical address or source identifier on the Internet.

download time The amount time of it takes for a file to get from the server to the client.

Download Copying data from a server to a client.

drivers In this context, factors that encourage a business's growth, such as access, around-the-clock service, and technology that is user friendly.

dynamic Constantly changing.

Dynamic HTML (DHTML) A set of interrelated scripting, markup, and programming technologies that allows the website author to create pages that are more interactive than pages created with just HTML. DHTML is made possible through the use of scripting languages such as JavaScript and VBScript, the Document Object Model (DOM), and the HTML 4 and CSS1 specifications.

E

e-business Term that encompasses all forms of business conducted electronically, including e-commerce.

e-commerce   An integration of communication transport, data management, and security capabilities that allows organizations to exchange information about the sale of goods and services.

editors   Tools that help website designers create web pages and the technology that supports them.

electronic data interchange (EDI)   A messaging protocol meant to ensure that data sent between normally incompatible computers retains its integrity and is formatted consistently. It is the inter-organizational exchange of documents in standardized electronic form directly between participating computers. It can be considered an electronic replacement of paper-based transaction infrastructure, which includes purchase orders, invoices, and bills of material and material releases.

electronic publishing   The use of computers rather than traditional print mechanisms to distribute information.

embed   The process of making a file part of a website. When a file is embedded in an HTML document, the user doesn't have the choice of accessing it.

embedded style   A style defined for a single web page by placing style information within the <STYLE> tag, located in the <HEAD> section of the HTML document.

encryption   The process of disguising a message to make it unreadable by humans.

enveloping   Technique with which a message is composed using a session key and a symmetric cipher and public-key encryption is used to transfer the session key securely to the intended recipient.

e-service   Online customer service, or e-commerce.

event   In an HTML document, anything that occurs during the life of the HTML page in the browser.

event-driven model   Common programming model in which an event occurs whenever an element on a web page is clicked. The Web, for example, is based on an event-driven model.

Extensible Markup Language (XML)   A metalanguage derived from its predecessor, Standard Generalized Markup Language (SGML). XML may be used to define formats for machine-readable data. These formats may be specific to an application, industry, or other area of interest.

extensions   Proprietary features browsers such as Internet Explorer and Netscape create to "extend" the existing HTML standard. They may or may not be included in the next HTML standard.

extranet   A TCP/IP network designed to provide secure access to selected external business users, often expediting the exchange of products, services, and key business information. Extranet users may include customers, vendors, suppliers, resellers, and other parties who may benefit from such a resource.

F

fields   A column in a database.

File Transfer Protocol (FTP)   An Internet protocol used to transfer files between computers; allows file transfer without corruption or alteration.

firewall   A security barrier that controls the flow of information between the Internet and private networks. It prevents outsiders from accessing an enterprise's internal network, which accesses the Internet indirectly through a proxy server.

flat-file database   Database containing records that have no structured interrelationship. In a flat-file database, data is collected in lines of text; each value is separated by a tab character or a comma, and each row is represented by a new line.

focus group   Marketing tool used to evaluate product and service-marketing concepts. Focus groups can consist of employees in the marketing organization or you can use companies that supply them.

frame   A scrollable region in which pages can be displayed; a single element of a frameset. Each frame contains its own URL.

frameset   A web page that defines a set of frames in which other Web pages are displayed.

frequently asked question list (FAQ)   Frequently asked question lists (FAQs) rank high as a form of customer service. A listing of frequently asked questions can reduce the number of support calls dramatically and immediately.

G

global market   Market in which need is not constrained by geography, therefore a large number of potential customers exists.

graphic interlacing   The progressive rendering of images in the browser.

graphical user interface (GUI)   Interface that provides graphical navigation with menus and screen icons, whether they use Windows, Macintosh, Unix, or some combination thereof. Users click on buttons to execute command sequences, enter values into text boxes, and choose options from menu lists.

H

hacker   A user who attempts access to computers, web sites, programs, and other information resources to obtain knowledge. They use their knowledge of computers to obtain information without doing damage.

handshake   Process in an SSL transaction; the client sends a request to connect to a secure server and the server sends its presigned certificate to the client.

hard goods   Items such as computer hardware, clothes, or books. Even though the goods can be purchased online, more traditional delivery methods are used: the U.S. mail, delivery services such as FedEx and UPS, and so on.

hashing   A one-way encryption method that is difficult to invert and should be resistant to collisions, which means that the probability of finding two messages with the same hash would be extremely low.

horizontal marketing system   A venture between two or more companies that do not compete, but instead compliment each other. These companies can join together in production, distribution, or marketing in order to achieve their individual goals and pursue new marketing opportunities.

HTML text editor   Software that assists website developers in writing HTML with the use of tag completion tools and validators. They require knowledge of HTML in order to use.

Hypertext Markup Language (HTML)   The standard authoring language used to develop web pages.

hyperlinks   Within a text file, embedded instructions that link it to a separate file.

hypermedia   An extension of hypertext. It includes images, video, audio, animation, and other multimedia data types, which can be incorporated into HTML documents.

hypertext   An information resource composed of separate documents, files, or other electronic media that are linked together in a nonlinear fashion.

hypertext database   Stores information as objects. This format is useful for storing different types of information, such as text, images, and multi-media (video or sound files). All data within this database is treated as objects; the data type is irrelevant.

Hypertext Transfer Protocol (HTTP)   The primary protocol that enables a web server to receive file requests and transmit replies, usually in the form of the requested documents, including HTML documents and several image formats (GIF, JPEG, and PNG) and binary files of almost any type, including Java, ActiveX, streaming video and audio, PDF, DOC, TXT, and so forth.

Hypertext Transfer Protocol (HTTP) server   Also known as a web server. It serves HTML documents over the Internet, intranets, extranets, local area networks (LANs), and wide area networks (WANs).

I

image editing program   Software used to perform such tasks as modifying photographs, creating buttons and banners, optimizing images, and creating special effects with images and text.

imported style   A style that has been accessed from another web site or network resource and applied to a web page or site by using the `@import` method.

immediacy   An important component in marketing. If consumers see something they want, the selling business needs to give it to them as quickly as possible. The longer the wait, the more time customers have to shop around or change their minds.

Impressions   The number of times an ad banner is downloaded and presumably seen by visitors.

incentive   Discounts, credits, free items, and other financial inducements offered to customers. By offering incentives, Web businesses give customers a reason to do business with them and to return in the future.

industrial property   A type of intellectual property. Includes inventions, trademarks, and industrial designs.

inheritance   The principle of passing on style definitions from parent elements to other elements.

in-house   As it relates to e-commerce, a solution for an e-commerce website. A Web business must buy or develop and integrate an electronic commerce software package, a service platform, redundant Internet connections, secure payment processing network connections, and round-the-clock maintenance. Generally speaking, this approach is reserved for large businesses that have the staff and financial resources to support this effort.

inline style   A style attribute added directly within HTML tags.

instant storefront   An e-commerce site created without using extensive programming or HTML coding. The instant storefront approach allows inexperienced users and developers to create their own sites, usually using predesigned templates, scripts, objects, images, and other features.

Integrated Services Digital Network (ISDN)   A high-speed data connection that uses standard copper phone lines and is capable of speeds up to 128Kbps.

intellectual property   Products such as written materials, musical compositions, and trademarks that are protected by copyright, trademark, or patent law.

inter-company commerce   Business conducted between two different companies.

Internet Architecture Board (IAB)   Standards organization that provides leadership for technical management and direction of Internet; defines rules and standards for Internet operation.

Internet Corporation for Assigned Names and Numbers (ICANN)   A non-profit organization located in the United States that allocates IP address ranges, assigns protocol parameters, manages the domain name system and its root servers. Oversees the accreditation of domain name registrars.

Internet Engineering Task Force (IETF)   Organization that addresses short-term technical Internet issues; makes recommendations to the IAB for standards approval.

Internet Research Task Force (IRTF)   Organization whose members research and develop new technologies, Internet protocols, and the future of the Internet (long-term issues). Consists of small research groups.

Internet Society (ISOC)   Organization that heads groups responsible for Internet infrastructure standards.

Internet Tax Freedom Act (ITFA)   United States legislation that initially placed a three-year moratorium, due to expire October 2001, on various local and federal sales taxes and user fees on Internet access and e-commerce so the U.S. Congress would have time to review the issues before making recommendations. On October 16, 2001, the House of Representatives granted a two-year extension to the law. On November 15, 2001, the Senate approved the extension, and then on November 28, 2001, President Bush signed into law the Internet Tax Non-Discrimination Act. The new law extends the moratorium (which was originally enacted in 1998) on new, special, and discriminatory Internet taxes through November 1, 2003.

Internet TV   A technology by which users can connect to the Internet through a cable modem box, using their television set as a display device and a specially designed keyboard for navigation and text entry.

intranet   A proprietary enterprise network that uses TCP/IP and other Internet protocols to send, deliver, store, and provide access to content.

inventory   Stockpiled goods kept by a company either made or acquired to fulfill orders.

K

knowledge database   Similar to a FAQ but more customized. The customer chooses from a list of products or categories defined by the merchant and then the FAQs are searched based on the customer's selection. A list of questions relating to the topic is displayed for the customer to examine.

L

linear   Term used to describe a model in which readers read one line to the next, one page to the next. The print medium is a linear medium.

linked style   A style defined by using a single style sheet that controls the appearance of multiple web pages.

load event   Command that executes when a page loads.

localization   The process of translating material into a specific language or culture.

lossless   Image format in which no information is lost as an image is compressed.

lossy   Image format in which colors are dropped from the image color palette as the compression of an image is increased, resulting in image degradation.

lowest common denominator   A list of minimum hardware and software requirements that users of an information system are expected to have. This list may include display resolution, input devices, connection speed, language settings, operating system, and other factors.

M

marketers   Those who buy the advertising space on publisher and marketer sites.

marketer site   A site whose primary focus is selling products or services for revenue.

MD5   One in the series (including MD2 and MD4) of message digest algorithms developed by Ron Rivest.

message digest   Specific application of a one-way function. This involves applying a digest or hash algorithm to the (long) message to produce a (short) message digest.

metadata   Data about data. It is data that embraces and describes a larger body of data.

metaphor   A figure of speech in which one object or experience is described by using another to suggest a likeness. The most common metaphors used by websites are brochures, prospectuses, and catalogs—all tools of the print medium. Some sites use the familiar metaphor of television.

<META> tag   A multipurpose tag placed within web pages in the HTML header so that users cannot see the information on the actual web page. The <META> tag can carry several different kinds of information, including keywords, author, and creator application. Search engines often examine <META> tag values to rank a site in the query results from a user's search.

method   An action performed by an object.

metrics   An approach to measuring website performance by looking at the total consumer experience, including speed, availability, and consistency of performance. A metrics study combines reports and surveys that evaluate performance to analyze the site's overall activity. Some e-commerce companies turn to third-party resources that can be either software or services.

Microsoft Management Console (MMC)   A software application that provides a consistent user interface for network administration programs within the Windows 2000, XP and .NET operating systems. MMC is designed to make administering IIS more simple. The MMC console hosts programs called snap-ins that administrators can use to manage their networks.

mindmapping   Process that allows you to structure ideas on paper in the order your brain follows rather than the linear order normally used when forming ideas.

N

niche market   Market consisting of a select or small number of customers. A niche market product appeals to or is needed by a smaller number of customers. Niche markets might also be served globally, but they audience is select.

No Electronic Theft (NET) Act   Act that amends U.S. copyright law so that "financial gain" includes the receipt of anything of value, including other copyrighted works.

nonlinear   Term used to describe a model in which users can link (hyperlink) to different areas within a site or to websites outside of a site; a user decides where to go and does not have to follow the strict organization set forth.

non-repudiation   A method of validating the parties in a financial transaction so that no one can rescind the transaction once it has been processed. Important to prevent merchants or customers from denying that they agreed to a sale or purchase.

O

object   A programming function that models the characteristics of abstract or real objects; they are often grouped with similar objects into classes.

object-based   Term used to describe a language that depends on a collection of built-in objects for functionality. JavaScript is an object-based language.

object-oriented   Term used to describe a program that is handled as a collection of individual objects that perform different functions and not as a sequence of statements that performs a specific task.

offline storefront   An e-commerce website solution that typically requires installing software on the business's computing infrastructure. The owner builds and maintains the online business inside the application. When the site is ready, it is then uploaded to the hosting web server to be accessed by the public. Any changes are made offline using the software and uploaded when ready.

one-to-one medium   A medium that enables the user to decide what information to access and when to access it, creating the capability for one-to-one relationships.

one-way encryption   A type of encryption that is relatively easy to compute in one direction but very difficult to compute in the other direction. Historically, these functions have been primarily used for storing items such as passwords on NT and Unix systems or personal identification numbers on ATM cards.

online catalog   A portion of a website that includes all the products, codes, and prices. Other catalog entries can include product images, product descriptions, and attributes such as size or color.

online check processing   Method of collecting payments for goods or services sold online. With online check processing, users enter the ABA routing number and the bank account number from the bottom of their checks instead of credit-card numbers. The credit-card process and the online check process are similar in that payment transactions are still required and financial institutions must still conduct them.

online communities   Services that allow customers to interact with or gather information from other customers or people with similar interests or viewpoints. These services can be online chat features, bulletin boards, or mail list servers.

Online Copyright Infringement Liability Limitation Act   Act that amends U.S. copyright law to exempt an online provider, such as an ISP, from liability for direct infringement based on the intermediate storage and transmission of material over the provider's network.

online merchant account   Account needed to process a payment online for credit card transactions. Online merchant accounts typically include both a merchant ID (MID) and a terminal ID (TID).

online storefront   An e-commerce solution in which the entire electronic commerce package is on the service provider's infrastructure. The business accesses it with a web browser. Most appropriate e-commerce site-creation/administration option for small businesses, novice entrepreneurs, or those offering a small range of goods or services.

Open Buying on the Internet (OBI)   An Internet e-commerce specification based on open technologies. OBI was developed to target high-volume, low-cost transactions.

Open Database Connectivity (ODBC)   A popular standard by which communications with a database are translated into the native format of the used database.

open source   Term used to describe free source code provided to the development community at large to develop a better product; includes source code for Apache Web server, Netscape Communicator and Linux.

Open Trading Protocol (OTP)   An open protocol that defines trading protocol options, and tells the consumer how the transaction will occur and which payment options are available.

opt-in e-mail   A Web marketing tool that allows people to indicate their personal interest in certain types of information and give permission for a business to send that information to their e-mail address.

outsourcing   The act of transferring some daily responsibilities or tasks from one company to another company that specializes in performing these services.

P

packet sniffer   Program that capture packets as they cross the network. Examples of packet sniffers include tcpdump (for all flavors of Unix), Network Monitor (Windows NT/2000), and Sniffer Basic by Network Associates.

packet-switched network   A network in which a packet stops at various routers on its way to its destination. The Internet is a packet-switched network.

passive recipients   Potential customers who are exposed to a radio or television advertisement.

patent   A document issued by a government conferring some special right or privilege. In the United States, the term is restricted to patents for inventions granted under federal statute.

payment gateway The connection between an online catalog and a merchant bank. For an electronic transfer to be completed, information must be traded between merchant banks. Before this trade can occur, the transaction must be introduced to the system via a payment gateway.

Performance Monitor Included with Windows 2000, the primary tool for determining server bottlenecks and problems on that system.

personal certificate Certificate that allows individuals to be strongly authenticated and to engage in S/MIME, SSL, and SET.

pixel Short for "picture element." The smallest element that can display on a screen. The screen uses pixels to display text or graphics; each pixel can display only one color at a time.

plug-in A program installed as part of the browser to extend its basic functionality. Allows different file formats to be viewed as part of a standard HTML document.

point-of-sale module One of the components necessary for collecting digital cash as payment for goods or services online. Integrates with the website, the merchant's wallet, and the bank's financial network. It is responsible for several merchant activities, and it initiates the funds transfer between the consumer's wallet and the merchant's wallet. It also validates and logs activity and provides reporting and administrative functions.

port A logical connection point. Clients access servers using a consensual specified port, depending on the service. Port numbers range from 1 to 65535. Ports 1 through 1023 are reserved for use by certain privileged services.

portal A website that many people visit and use to explore and participate in activities on the Internet.

positional awareness An understanding of where any parent, peer, or child pages are relative to the current location in a website.

primary navigation elements Navigation elements that are accessible from most locations within the site.

procedural model Common programming model in which the user is expected to interact with the program in a fairly sequential manner.

procurement   The process that companies use to buy items from suppliers.

promotion   In marketing, making others aware of something, someone, or someplace.

property   A characteristic, such as color, width, or height, that the programmer stipulates in the creation of the object.

psychographics   A science that can help anticipate the specific positive, negative, or neutral psychological impact of words, symbols, shapes, textures, colors, fonts, or even scale on consumer target market groups.

public encryption   Allows previously unacquainted parties to conduct a transaction. For example, it allows a customer to buy goods or services from an e-commerce merchant with whom they have no previously business relationship.

publisher site   A site whose primary focus is selling ad space as a means of revenue.

purchase button   A generic term for a button used to pass information and conduct a transaction on another server, typically for ease of implementation and increased security.

Q

query   Question from a user to a database table. The query returns a value, which provides information stored in the database.

queue   A sequence of requests for services to one or more servers.

R

random-click pattern   Web site design in which users are allowed to move through the site using a variety of methods, including menus, hyperlinks, and other interface elements.

RealOne   Streaming audio and video player made by RealNetworks.

record   Within a database table, a collection of fields that represents a single unit of collected data .

relational database   Body of data organized as a set of formally defined tables. Data can be accessed or reassembled from the database in many different ways without the database tables having to be reorganized. The tables can (and usually do) contain data that relates to data held in other tables within the same database.

requisitioner   The person or software that initiates the transaction to purchase in an OBI transaction.

Requests for Comments (RFCs)   Requests to collect information on all types of Internet-related issues and give Internet users the opportunity to provide input concerning emerging standards. RFCs are referenced by ID numbers and cover most topics relating to Internet standards and organizations. Currently, more than 2,200 RFCs exist. RFCs are received and posted by the IAB.

revenue-supported   Term used to describe websites that offer free content to users and make money by selling advertising space.

rollovers   Buttons, images, or other designated areas of the web page that trigger actions when an event such as the user passing the mouse cursor over them occurs. Rollovers are commonly used as navigation elements.

RSA encryption   The de facto standard for public-key cryptosystems. Named after its inventors, Ronald Rivest, Avi Shamir, and Leonard Adleman, who developed it in 1978 while working at the Massachusetts Institute of Technology (MIT). Its security is based on factoring very large prime numbers. The size of the key used in RSA is completely variable, but for normal use, a key size of 512 bits is typical. In applications for which key compromise would have serious consequences or for which the security must remain valid for many years, 1024-bit and 2048-bit keys are used.

S

sans-serif font   Fonts that do not have serifs, the small decorative strokes added to the ends of a letter's main strokes.

schema   The structure of a database system; often depicts the structure graphically. The schema defines tables and fields and the relationships between them.

screen flow   The way in which a web page is laid out to enhance users' experience when they scan the page.

search engine   Tool that uses an automated process to discover new web pages.

secondary navigation elements   Navigation elements that allow the user to navigate within a specific location, such as within a web page.

Secure Electronic Transactions (SET)   Payment standard on the Internet. In a conventional credit card transaction, an infrastructure of links and transaction processing computer hardware already exists to electronically authorize credit card payments. SET assumes the existence of such a facility and specifies only the subset of dialogs between the customer and merchant and between the merchant and an entity known as the payment gateway.

Secure Hash Algorithm (SHA)   A function that was developed by the National Institute of Standards and Technology (NIST) and is based heavily on Ron Rivest's MD series of algorithms.

Secure/Multipurpose Internet Mail Extensions (S/MIME)   A cryptographic method for e-mail. S/MIME uses a concept called enveloping. The bulk message is composed using a session key and a symmetric cipher, and public-key encryption is used to transfer the session key securely to the intended recipient. The security services offered are authentication (using digital signatures) and privacy (using encryption). S/MIME assumes that both senders and receivers of secure e-mail messages have public/private key pairs.

Secure Sockets Layer (SSL)   An encryption protocol used to protect data transmitted between a client browser and a server.

self-service   Type of customer service support in which the customer finds their own answers. Can include accounts the customer can access, FAQs, and knowledge databases.

serif font   A font that has serifs, the small decorative strokes added to the ends of a letter's main strokes.

server certificate Certificate used on web servers to identify the web server and the company running it and to allow for encrypted SSL sessions between the server and browsers. Server certificates are also necessary for a server to participate in SET (Secure Electronic Transactions).

server-push A file transfer method in which a server initiates the transfer of files or data to a client computer, sometimes according to a predetermined schedule.

shopping cart A component of an e-commerce site that keeps track of the items customers want to buy, allowing them to continue browsing for products before having to make a purchase.

site map A graphical representation of a website's hierarchy.

slicing The process of dividing images into several smaller images.

sniffer Software that captures packets in transit as they cross a network. It operates by placing a host's NIC into "promiscuous mode," from which it can capture packets from the network wire.

soft goods Products or services such as software, music, news, or advice; also referred to as digital goods. The product or service can be distributed via an electronic method, such as the Internet. The selling company can immediately distribute its products for free or for a charge.

software publisher certificate Certificate used by software authors to sign and identify their released code so that the author can be identified and the integrity of the code verified.

spam Unsolicited e-mail. It is the Internet equivalent of bulk junk mail.

spider A special application in a search engine whose purpose is to map selected Web content and return URLs to which users can link when they search for a topic. Same as a crawler.

Standard Generalized Markup Language (SGML) A format for the consistent encoding of electronic documents. SGML has been used as the basis for other file formats, notably HTML.

statement A single line of code to be executed in a script or program.

static Unchanging. For example, a static table will not change as content changes and as browser window size changes.

streaming   Term used to describe a continuous flow of data, usually sound or image files, that creates a seamless delivery into a browser.

Structured Query Language (SQL)   The actual language for relational DBMSs. With SQL, a programmer can structure queries, updates, and inserts into databases. Most databases have proprietary languages to use internally, and SQL is the common language among them.

style guide   A standards document or manual that establishes a set of conventions or rules for performing common tasks.

style sheet   A predefined HTML document structure that includes heading fonts, text layout commands, graphic object placement, and other design guidelines.

subtractive color   Colors that create black when mixed together.

supply chain   The channel used to get the raw materials needed to build a product from all sub-part manufacturers to the final assembly of a product and then to the end user. Supply chains are responsible for producing, delivering, and transporting raw materials and meeting customer demands.

swapping   Term often used to refer to caching the hard drive.

symmetric encryption   Sometimes called secret-key, shared-key, private-key, or session-key encryption. Both parties to the communication must possess a single secret key.

synchronous   Term used to describe a process in which events or steps occur at the same time.

synchronous service   Model that allows the customer to communicate in real time with the merchant. It has the added benefit of being highly personal and immediate. Examples include online chat and the telephone.

T

T1   A high-speed (1.5Mbps) connection to the Internet using dial-up leased lines.

T3 A high-speed digital carrier capable of 44.74 Mbps; usually used by major ISPs and other large organizations.

<TABLE> tag The first required tag in constructing your table. A table is contained within the opening and closing <TABLE> tags.

tags Special pieces of code, enclosed in angle brackets, that tell the HTML interpreter how to process or display text.

targeted e-mail Bulk e-mail sent to target consumers; the electronic equivalent of targeted junk mail.

targeted placement The technique of placing ads where they'll be most effectively. Sometimes performed by advertising representatives, who make money by taking a percentage of the revenue paid by the advertiser.

tariffs A set of taxes levied by individual states and countries.

<TD> tag The tag that defines a cell within a row.

telephony Technology that enables live voice communication over the Internet. The analog signal, your voice, is digitized and sent over the Internet using TCP/IP (Transmission Control Protocol/Internet Protocol). On the other end, depending on the setup, the signal is either converted back to analog or left digital, depending on the recipient's output device.

three-click rule The concept that users should not have to click more than three times once inside a site to find the information they seek, depending on the website's purpose.

<TR> tag The second tag that is required when constructing a table. It is used to define the rows of a table.

trackers Tools used to identify the number and percentage of visitors, the type of operating system, the browser type, and the user's domain. They can also determine traffic by the hour, day, week, and month.

trademark Any word, name, symbol, or device or any combination thereof adopted and used by a manufacturer or merchant to identify their goods and distinguish them from those manufactured or sold by others.

trading partners Organizations that exchange EDI transmissions.

traditional database   Database that stores and organizes information in fields, records and files.

transparent GIFs   Images of varying sizes that have a transparent background, so that the background of the web page appears through the image. They are invisible to the user.

Triple DES   Encryption algorithm that is more secure than DES because it uses two 56-bit keys. It may be a successor to DES and is appealing because it requires no new algorithms or hardware besides the conventional DES.

U

Uniform Resource Locator (URL)   A text string that supplies an Internet or intranet address and the protocol by which that site can be accessed.

usability   Indicates, to a degree, a measure of effectiveness that users have when visiting a site. If a site is not considered "usable," or perhaps not as usable as another site, users will not stay.

U.S. Lanham Act   A 1964 law that was an important early step toward U.S. trademark legislation.

V

vector   Graphics file type that stores the information about the image in mathematical instructions that are interpreted to display the image.

vertical marketing system   Marketing system that unites multiple manufacturers in the same industry to coordinate and streamline distribution channels and the supply chain.

virtual private network   A method for creating a secure encrypted data stream between two computers, allowing transmission through firewalls. Frequently used to give authorized external users access to a secure internal network.

vision statement   The fundamental framework that defines the scope and intent of a website.

W

wallet   A program so-named because it mimics the functionality of a physical wallet; that is, it holds the electronic cash. Both consumers and merchants need wallets of the same type.

Web Accessibility Initiative (WAI)   Initiative created by the W3C to ensure that core technologies used on the Web, such as HTML, CSS, XML and DOM, are equally accessible to users with physical, visual, hearing, and cognitive disabilities. The WAI works with worldwide organizations in five main areas: technology, guidelines, tools, education and outreach, and research and development.

web-based animation   Technology used for high-end multimedia websites and presentations. It adds interactivity to websites while conserving bandwidth by using vector-based images to create animation.

web farm   A service provider that serves multiple websites. Web farms cohost (i.e., they provide hard drive space on their computer for your site), or they co-locate (i.e., they provide a connection for a computer that you maintain).

webmaster   The person responsible for the administration of a web site.

white space   Area with no text or images on a page. Can be used in web page layout to reduce page element clutter and separate elements on the page.

Windows Media Player   Video player produced by Microsoft.

World Wide Web Consortium (W3C)   An international industry consortium founded in 1994 to develop common standards for the World Wide Web.

WYSIWYG (What You See Is What You Get)   A display format in which the file being edited appears on the screen just as it will appear to the end user.

WYSIWYG editor   Software that allows the beginning website developer to start designing web pages without having mastered HTML. These applications require little technical knowledge of website design and the coding that creates web pages.

X

X.509v3 A framework for the provision of authentication services under a central directory. X.509 describes simple authentication with a password and strong authentication with certificates.

XHTML Recommendation from the W3C that combines HTML and XML to create a transition from HTML to XML while still providing current browsers with backward compatibility.

Index

Note to the Reader: Page numbers in **bold** indicate the principle discussion of a topic or the definition of a term. Page numbers in *italic* indicate illustrations.

B

C

J

N

O

R

RAM, web server, **845–846**

random-click patterns, **641, 911**

RC (Rivest Cipher) algorithms, **799**

RDFI (Receiving Depository Financial Institution), **778**

READONLY attribute, **879**

RealNetworks RealOne player, 99, **911**

records, database, *395*, **395–396, 912**

referral services, banner ad, **610**

referrer logs, **837**

Relational Database Management Systems (RDBMSs), **397**

relational databases, **752, 912**

relationship, targeting links by, *206–207, 206–207*

relative sizing in framesets, 198

remote administration of HTTP servers, 414

Requests for Comments (RFCs), **434, 912**

revenue-supported portals, **598–599, 912**

RGB (additive) colors
  browser-safe colors, 24–25
  defined, **20, 892**
  values, 21–22, 23

RIAA v. Napster copyright case, **531–532**

Rifkin, Adam, 343

rights. *See* legal issues

Rivest Cipher (RC2, RC4, RC5) algorithms, **799**

Rivest, Ron, 780, 799, 801, 802, 906, 912, 913

robots, **617**

"robots" values, **235**

rollovers, **96–97, 299–300, 912**

rows, database, *395*, **395–396**

rows, frameset, **198–199,** *199,* **201–202**

RPG (Report Program Generator), **398**

RSA (Rivest, Shamir, Adleman) algorithm, **801**

S

<S> tag, **881**

S/MIME (Secure/Multipurpose Internet Mail Extension), **676–677, 913**

sans-serif fonts, *28, 28*

Scalable Vector Graphics (SVG), *78, 78*

scheduling software, **693**

schema, database, **395–396,** *396,* **913**

Schneier, Bruce, 799

screen flow, **642, 913**

screen resolutions, *17–19,* **17, 70,** *See also* monitor displays

<SCRIPT> tag, **282–283**

scripting languages, *See also* JavaScript; languages
  client-side scripting, 733
  in DHTML, 318–320
  ECMA Script and, 282
  JScript, 282
  versus programming languages, 277, 279
  server-side scripting, 733
  VBScript, 281

scrolling, users and, **17**

search engines, *See also* HTML metadata; promotion
  defined, **616, 913**
  "description" values and, 232, 234–235
  versus directories, 235–236, 616, 617, 618
  keyword guidelines, 618–620
  "keywords" values and, 231–234, *231*
  listed, 618
  <META> tag and, 617–618
  overview of, 232–233, 640
  placement ranking, *576–577,* 617, 618–620
  preventing site access by, 235
  relevance ranking in, 236
  "robots" values and, 235

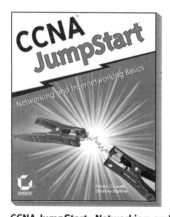

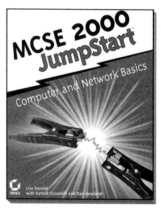

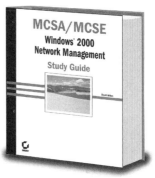

TELL US WHAT YOU THINK!

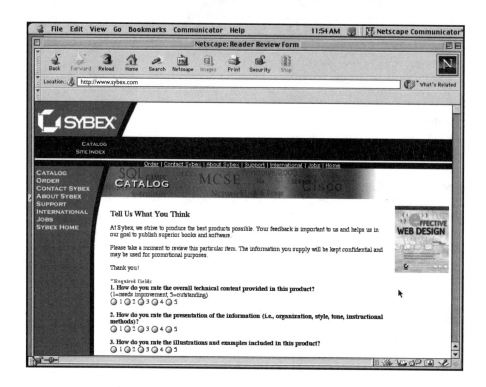

Your feedback is critical to our efforts to provide you with the best books and software on the market. Tell us what you think about the products you've purchased. It's simple:

1. Visit the Sybex website
2. Go to the product page
3. Click on **Submit a Review**
4. Fill out the questionnaire and comments
5. Click **Submit**

With your feedback, we can continue to publish the highest quality computer books and software products that today's busy IT professionals deserve.

www.sybex.com

SYBEX Inc. • 1151 Marina Village Parkway, Alameda, CA 94501 • 510-523-8233